Recent Studies in Early Christianity

A Collection of Scholarly Essays

Series Editor

Everett Ferguson

A GARLAND SERIES

Series Contents

Christianity in Relation to Jews, Greeks, and Romans

Edited with an introduction by

Everett Ferguson

GARLAND PUBLISHING, INC.
A MEMBER OF THE TAYLOR & FRANCIS GROUP
New York & London
1999

Library of Congress Cataloging-in-Publication Data

Christianity in relation to Jews, Greeks, and Romans / edited, with
  introductions by Everett Ferguson.
      p.   cm. — (Recent studies in early Christianity ; 2)
      Includes bibliographical references.
      ISBN 0-8153-3069-3 (alk. paper)
      1. Christianity and other religions—Greek. 2. Christianity and
  other religions—Roman. 3. Judaism—Relations—Christianity.
  4. Christianity and other religions—Judaism. 5. Theology,
  Doctrinal—History—Early church, ca. 30–600. 6. Church history—
  Primitive and early church, ca. 30–600. I. Ferguson, Everett,
  1933–   . II. Series.
  BR128.G8C48 1999
  261.2—dc21   99-24676
                                                       CIP

Printed on acid-free, 250-year-life paper
Manufactured in the United States of America

Contents

Series Introduction

Garland published in 1993 *Studies in Early Christianity: A Collection of Scholarly Essays*, an eighteen-volume set of classic articles on the early history of Christianity. The present set of six volumes, *Recent Studies in Early Christianity*, continues that first series by selecting articles written during the last decade. The chronological scope is the same, the first six centuries of the common era. The arrangement once more is topical but with a conflation and realignment of topics to fit the smaller number of volumes. The present series of essays will serve as an important supplement for those who possess the first series. For those without the first series, it will introduce key areas of research and debate on the early history of Christianity.

The growing academic interest in Christianity during its early centuries, as noted in the series introduction to *Studies in Early Christianity*, has greatly accelerated. There has been a proliferation of studies during the last decade on the subject of Christianity in late antiquity. The very popularity of the designation "late antiquity" says something about the current intellectual climate in which these studies arise: a shift from a primary emphasis on Christianity itself to the larger cultural setting of which it was a part, a shift from doctrinal studies to the church as a social institution, and a shift from concern for orthodoxy to the popular religious attitudes and expressions.

The increased study of this period finds expression in more doctoral students, record membership in professional organizations, like the North American Patristics Society and the Association internationale d'études patristiques, and large attendance at the International Conferences on Patristic Studies in Oxford (August 16-21, 1999, marks the thirteenth of these meetings that occur every four years), in addition to participation in specialized conferences on Origen, Gregory of Nyssa, Augustine, and others. Expanded literary productivity is evidenced by new journals (*The Journal of Early Christian Studies*, edited by Elizabeth Clark and Everett Ferguson, a continuation of *The Second Century*; *Zeitschrift für Antikes Christentum/Journal of Ancient Christianity*, edited by H.C. Brennecke and C. Markschies), new reference works (*The Encyclopedia of Early Christianity* [New York: Garland], edited by Everett Ferguson, first edition in 1990, second and greatly expanded edition in 1997, paperback edition 1998; *The Encyclopedia of the Early Church* [New York: Oxford University Press, 1992], English translation of *Dizionario Patristico e di Antichità Cristiane*, edited by Angelo Di Berardino), and substantial scholarly monographs in the field.

In some ways the selection of articles for six volumes on a decade of scholarship is more difficult than eighteen volumes on a century: We do not have the perspective of time to judge what is of enduring worth. Although some of these pieces will no doubt become classics, the guiding principle in selection has been to point to areas that are drawing the greatest attention. Some subjects have become virtually independent subdisciplines in the study of religion in late antiquity. This is notably true of Gnosticism, although the very term is under attack as a proper category.

The six volumes of this collection of scholarly essays take up the following broad topics: (1) the social setting of the early church, with attention to such matters as women, family, friendship, funerary practices, education, and slavery; (2) the political, cultural, and religious setting of early Christianity in relation to Romans, Greeks, and Jews; (3) the internal development of the church as it recognized its canon of scriptures, interpreted those scriptures, defined its confession of faith, and articulated standards of conduct; (4) the diversity — geographical, doctrinal, disciplinary — that counterbalanced the efforts to achieve a unified orthodoxy; (5) the many expressions of devotion and spirituality that both nourished and manifested faith; and (6) the varied ways in which early Christians wrestled with the limitations of historical existence and human language yet voiced their hopes for another and better world.

These topics represent the emphases in the modern study of early Christianity: social history and the application of the social sciences to the understanding of the historical texts, women's concerns and gender issues, Christians' relations with their Jewish and pagan neighbors, variety in early Christianity (especially fueled by the Nag Hammadi texts but not exclusively so), types of asceticism, literary forms and criticism, and Christianity's relationship to late antiquity and the transition to the medieval world. Some themes long present in the study of early Christianity continue to gain attention: the creedal definition of the faith, the causes and effects of persecution, different approaches to the interpretation of the Bible, forms of worship and spirituality, Christian morality, and the Christian hope.

One person's judgment and one small set of essays cannot do full justice to the rich flowering of studies in the field of early Christianity. We can only point to the areas of emphasis and call attention to some significant studies. These studies will lead teachers and students into the larger field and, we hope, spark their interest in pursuing some of these questions and related matters more extensively, thereby enlarging the number of researchers in a field not only intellectually challenging but also spiritually significant.

Volume Introduction

The specific aspects of the social setting of Christianity in the early centuries of the common era (examined in Vol. I) lead into consideration of the religious, philosophical, and political setting of early Christianity. These overlapping factors in the environment of early Christianity involve contacts respectively, but not exclusively, with Jews, Greeks, and Romans.

Contacts between Christians and Jews were sometimes positive. A learned and influential Christian thinker was Origen, and two views of his relations with Jews (by Paul Blowers and John McGuckin) are presented for consideration here. Christians and Jews are usually thought to have come to a parting of the ways by the end of the second revolt by Judean Jews against Rome in 135. Recent study is emphasizing contacts, and these not always negative, much later.[1]

The positive side of relations with Jews and the continuing influence of Jews on developing Christianity is further shown by Jewish elements in Christian faith and worship, especially evident in Syriac Christianity.[2] On the other hand, the Christian appropriation of the Jewish scriptures and supercessionist theology, which found expression in art (Margaret Miles) and architecture as well as literature, could have negative consequences, as too often proved to be the case in the fourth and subsequent centuries.

Much of the discussion of Jews and Judaism in early Christian literature is more of a literary construct than reflective of actual contact with Jews. Much that seems negative was a matter not so much of "anti-Judaism" as a matter of Christian self-definition. There was built into Christianity a dialectic that must keep the Jewish Bible as a legitimation of Christian claims (as a religion developing from an ancient heritage and having divine authority from the fulfillment of prophecy) but that must reject the Jewish interpretation of that Bible.[3] Paula Fredriksen argues that Augustine's positive assessment of the Jewish place in history belongs in this context. Augustine was not affirming Jews per se but was defending the justice of the God of Israel against charges made by the Manichees, dualists who rejected the Old Testament.

Some aspects of Christian thought usually considered to derive from the Greek philosophical context of early Christianity may in fact also come from Judaism. It has long been recognized that Christian apologetic literature drew arguments and claims from earlier Jewish precedents. The Christian identification of Christ with the Logos (already in the prologue to the Gospel of John) drew on both Greek and Jewish antecedents. The general view, however, has been to trace Christian speculation about the Logos primarily to Greek philosophical sources, especially Stoicism and Middle Platonism. In an important article, Mark Edwards argues for the affinities of the Christian understanding of the Logos with Jewish views of the word of God.

The contacts of Christian faith with Greek philosophy produced the considerable apologetic enterprise of early Christianity. Many Christian writers known for other things were also apologists, such as Eusebius, who is better known as a historian but who would have thought of himself more as an apologist.[4] This apologetic endeavor required the refinement of certain Christian beliefs. For instance, the biblical view of creation ran counter to much Greek philosophical thought, but aspects of the Platonic tradition offered points of contact.[5] Clement of Alexandria, as one of his foremost modern interpreters, Eric Osborn,[6] shows in a significant article on "Arguments for Faith in Clement of Alexandria," used Greek philosophical views of faith to argue for scriptural faith and for scripture's God. His was one of the great defenses of faith in Christian history and also a subtle and profound reworking of philosophical problems.

The Platonic tradition, especially Neoplatonism, was the main philosophical context for Christian theology, but Stoicism and other schools of thought made their contributions too. Heine demonstrates an instance of this in the use of Stoic logic in the service of exegesis and theology by Origen in his commentary on the Gospel of John.

The interplay of faith and philosophy resulted in both borrowing and differentiation by Christian thinkers, even by those like Arius and Athanasius who are remembered more as theologians than as philosophers (Wiles). Outstanding among the Christian philosophical theologians were Gregory of Nyssa in the Greek East and Augustine in the Latin West. Mosshammer has made a number of significant contributions to the clarification of Gregory of Nyssa's rich appropriation of the church's Hellenistic heritage but radical reinterpretation of parts of it in the interests of a new Christian world view.[7] In the article included in this collection he approaches the encounter between Hellenism and Christianity by examining Gregory's use of one Neoplatonic idea, that of non-being, to inform the Christian understanding of sin and salvation. In a similar way, Enrico Peroli has demonstrated that Gregory of Nyssa's doctrine of the soul was taken from Neoplatonism but used in a quite non-Platonic way to argue for the resurrection of the body.[8] Among the many facets of Augustine's influence, concern with his philosophical work has always been prominent (Teske). John Cavadini interprets Augustine's great treatise on the Trinity as a polemic against Neoplatonism.

More frequent than contact with pagan philosophy was the contact of Christians with popular Greek and Roman religious thought, represented in the selections in this volume by one of the contributions of a leading student of Christianity in late antiquity, Robert Markus. There has come a clearer recognition of the presence of elements of popular religion in the belief systems of those who accepted Christianity and a demonstration of the extent to which pagan religious practices persisted well beyond the official triumph of the church.[9]

Christianity's relations to Rome involved conflict from an early date. Although the number of the martyrs was not large, the experience of martyrdom defined early

Christian identity, spirituality, and view of the State. Martyrdom may be studied with reference to individual martyrs[10] (including women martyrs noted below), the martyr literature that was produced,[11] the function of this literature,[12] martyrdom's place in the thought of individual church leaders,[13] as a political act (Ferguson—in the words of Henry Chadwick, "When was it ever anything else?"), or its theology (Farkasfalvy).

Martyrdom was an equal opportunity experience, so women attained a fame and individuality as martyrs not accorded to them in other ways. Women were more likely to be remembered by name in the earliest centuries because of martyrdom than for any other reason. Stuart Hall reminds us of the prominence of "Women among the Early Martyrs."[14] Not only does martyrdom by women offer a contact with Volume I, but, since martyrdom led to the cult of the martyrs, it was important for Christian devotion and spirituality and so connects with Volume V (McGuckin).

The major turn in the church's relations with Rome came with the conversion of Constantine, who was celebrated by Eusebius, sometimes too readily identified as a "court theologian," according to Hollerich. The building policy of Constantine is the chief surviving monument to his support of Christianity. The major modern student of early Christian architecture, Richard Krautheimer, offers his mature assessment of "The Ecclesiastical Building Policy of Constantine." Constantine's buildings in Jerusalem were inspired in part by the ideology of a Christian Jerusalem.[15] His policies impinged on Christianity in another direct way in his promotion of church unity (Drake). Constantine continues to be a fascination to historians,[16] but other members of the imperial family come in for study also.[17]

Notes

[1] Wolfram Kinzig, "'Non-Separation': Closeness and Co-operation Between Jews and Christians in the Fourth Century," *Vigiliae Christianae* 45 (1991):27–53.

[2] G. Rouwhorst, "Jewish Liturgical Traditions in Early Syriac Christianity," *Vigiliae Christianae* 51 (1997):72–93.

[3] Robert Louis Wilken, "Something Greater Than the Temple," in William Farmer, ed., *Anti-Judaism and the Gospels* (Harrisburg: Trinity Press International, 1999).

[4] Eugene V. Gallagher, "Eusebius the Apologist: The Evidence of the *Preparation* and the *Proof*," *Studia Patristica* 26 (1993):251–60.

[5] N. Jospeh Torchia, "Theories of Creation in the Second Century Apologists and Their Middle Platonic Background," *Studia Patristica* 26 (1993):192–99.

[6] Osborn has consistently related early Christian thought in its similarities and its differences to Greek philosophy, as in "The Christian God and the Platonic One," *Studia Patristica* 20 (1989):110–31.

[7] E. g., Alden A. Mosshammer, "Gregory of Nyssa and Christian Hellenism," *Studia Patristica* 32 (1997):170–95.

[8] Enrico Peroli, "Gregory of Nyssa and the Neoplatonic Doctrine of the Soul," *Vigiliae Christianae* 51 (1997):117–39.

[9] E. g., A. Dihle, "Astrology in the Doctrine of Bardesanes," *Studia Patristica* 20 (1989):160–68.

[10] E. g., Peter Brock, "Why did St. Maximilian Refuse to Serve in the Roman Army?" *Journal of Ecclesiastical History* 45 (1994):195–209.

[11] An important treatment is Ekkehard Mühlenberg, "The Martyr's Death and its Literary Presentation," *Studia Patristica* 29 (1997):85–93.

[12] Maureen Tilley, "Scripture as an Element of Social Control: Two Martyr Stories of Christian North Africa," *Harvard Theological Review* 83 (1990):383–97.

[13] Annewies van den Hoek, "Clement of Alexandria on Martyrdom," *Studia Patristica* 26 (1993):324–41.

[14] Although women were at a disadvantage under the law, in punishment they had an equality with men — Chris Jones, "Woman, Death, and the Law during the Christian Persecutions," *Studies in Church History* 30 (1993):27–34.

[15] E.D. Hunt, "Constantine and Jerusalem," *Journal of Ecclesiastical History* 48 (1997):405–24.

[16] H.A. Drake, "Policy and Belief in Constantine's 'Oration to the Saints,'" *Studia Patristica* 19 (1989): 43–51; Charles Odahl, "God and Constantine: Divine Sanction for Imperial Rule in the First Christian Emperor's Early Letters and Art," *Catholic Historical Review* 81 (1995):327–52; Linda Jones Hall, "Cicero's *instinctu divino* and Constantine's *instinctu divinitatis*: The Evidence of the Arch of Constantine for the Senatorial View of the 'Vision' of Constantine," *Journal of Early Christian Studies* 6 (1998):647–71.

[17] Mark D. Smith, "Eusebius and the Religion of Constantius I," *Studia Patristica* 29 (1997):133–40; J.W. Drijvers, "Helena Augusta: Exemplary Christian Empress," *Studia Patristica* 24 (1993):85–90.

Christianity in Relation to Jews, Greeks, and Romans

ORIGEN, THE RABBIS, AND THE BIBLE: TOWARD A PICTURE OF JUDAISM AND CHRISTIANITY IN THIRD-CENTURY CAESAREA

Paul M. Blowers
University of Notre Dame

A series of excellent recent monographs have helped to illuminate Origen's relation to the Judaism of his time. In the most exhaustive study to date, Nicholas de Lange has exposed abundant, if sometimes episodic, evidence of Origen's contacts with Jewish institutions and traditions.[1] Other studies have enhanced our knowledge of the social and religious history of third-century Palestine, the period of Origen's tenure in Caesarea.[2] I wish in this brief paper to stand back for a moment and observe the broader historical

---

[1] Cf. N. R. M. de Lange, *Origen and the Jews: Studies in Jewish-Christian Relations in Third-Century Palestine*, Cambridge Oriental Publications 25 (Cambridge, 1976); also H. Bietenhard, *Caesarea, Origenes und die Juden* (Stuttgart, 1974); G. Sgherri, *Chiesa e Sinagoga nelle opere di Origene*, Studia patristica mediolanensia 13 (Milan, 1982).

[2] Cf. L. Levine, *Caesarea under Roman Rule*, Studies in Judaism in Late Antiquity 7 (Leiden, 1975), especially chaps. 4-7; R. Kimelman, *Rabbi Yohanan of Tiberias: Aspects of the Social and Religious History of Third-Century Palestine* (diss., Yale University, 1977); M. Goodman, *State and Society in Roman Galilee, A. D. 132-212* (Totowa, N. J., 1983).

spectrum of Origen's connection with Judaism. How "typical" is his confrontation with the Jews of the patterns of Jewish-Christian relations we see emerging in the second, third, and fourth centuries? Conversely, how can these larger patterns help to fill in our picture of the encounter between Origen and the Jews in Caesarea?

Research on Origen's contacts with Judaism has proceeded in the shadow of a larger debate on the actual extent of Judaism's impact on the emerging Church in late antiquity. Numerous scholars have followed Marcel Simon's basic position that Judaism continued to be a vital force, rivaling the Church in Palestine and the cities of the Diaspora well beyond the disastrous Bar Kochba Revolt of 132-135 C. E.[3] Only recently, however, David Rokeah has revived Adolf Harnack's original thesis that Jewish proselytism disappeared altogether after Bar Kochba. The Jews accordingly became passive "middlemen" in the prevailing conflict between Christianity and paganism,[4] and Christian polemic *adversus Judaeos* degenerated merely into edifying propaganda for the Church.[5] Rokeah cites Origen's *Contra Celsum*, with its theoretical defense of Judaism, and reticence to censure the

---

[3]Cf. M. Simon, *Verus Israel: Étude sur les relations entre chrétiens et juifs dans l'empire romain (135-425)*, 2nd. ed. (Paris, 1964); more recently, *int. al.* R. L. Wilken, *John Chrysostom and the Jews: Rhetoric and Reality in the Late Fourth Century*, The Transformation of the Classical Heritage 4 (Berkeley, 1983); H. Drijvers, "Jews and Christians at Edessa," *Journal of Jewish Studies* 36 (1985): 88-102. See also Y. Baer, "Israel, the Christian Church, and the Roman Empire from the Time of Septimius Severus to the Edict of Toleration of A. D. 313," *Scripta hierosolymitana* 7 (1961): 79-149.

[4]Cf. D. Rokeah, *Jews, Pagans and Christians in Conflict*, Studia Post-Biblica 33 (Jerusalem and Leiden, 1982), pp. 47ff, 78.

[5]Ibid., pp. 47, 65-76.

Jews, as evidence that the Synagogue no longer hindered the Church's designs on the pagan world.[6]

Were the Jews in fact only harmless bystanders lurking in the background of Origen's ministry in Caesarea? Scattered evidence from his Caesarean writings, including the *Contra Celsum*, point to a more dynamic pattern of Christian-Jewish relations in third-century Palestine. Common interests and frontiers engendered a tacit competition which occasionally gave way to open strife. I will examine here three interrelated fronts of this contention: (1) Origen's personal contacts with the rabbis; (2) the wider missionary conflict between Church and Synagogue in Palestine; and (3) Origen's exegetical-homiletic disputations with the rabbis.

I.

Origen's allusions to his private *magister hebraeus*, and to other Jewish Christians and Jews who assisted him in his biblical scholarship, are, along with his testimony to various contemporary Jewish traditions and institutions, well-documented elsewhere and need not be covered here.[7] The turning-point in Origen's relation with Judaism was his relocation in Caesarea around 233, at a time when Caesarean and Galilean rabbinism was just beginning to reach the zenith of its power. He founded his school within only a few years of the academy of R. Hoshaya in Caesarea, which helped to train some of the greatest halakhists in third-century Palestine: R.

---

[6]Ibid., pp. 69-71.

[7]Cf. G. Bardy, "Les traditions juives dans l'œuvre d'Origène," *RB* 34 (1925): 221-223; de Lange, *Origen and the Jews*, pp. 15-37. See also S. Krauss, "The Jews in the Works of the Church Fathers," *JQR* 5 (1983): 139ff (on Origen).

Yohanan of Tiberias, R. Eliezar b. Pedat, and Resh Laqish.[8] Origen may
have come across one or more of this elite group in his discussions with
"men whom the Jews allege to be sages" (οἱ λεγόμενοι παρὰ Ἰουδαίοις
σόφοι).[9]

Rabbinic sources confirm that Tannaitic and early Amoraic rabbis in
Palestine bore certain traits of late antique popular philosophers, a fact which
Morton Smith has noted of first-century Pharisees.[10] Origen himself used
Josephus' description of the Pharisees as philosophers to characterize the
rabbis of his own time: they are "the pre-eminent rank (τάξις) and school
(αἵρεσις) in Judaism, professing a well-balanced lifestyle and precision in
interpreting the law and prophets"; though "brash and ostentatious", they
"separate themselves from the entire Jewish nation, as surpassing in their
wisdom (φρόνησις) and way of life (βίος). . ."[11] Origen had heard of
certain esoteric practices within rabbinic academies.[12] He had probably

---

[8]Cf. Levine, *Caesarea*, p. 88.

[9]*C. Cels.* 1.45, GCS 1.95.3f; ibid. 1.55, GCS 1.106.3f; ibid. 1.56,
GCS 1.107.27f; ibid. 2.31, GCS 1.159.1f. (GCS references include volume
number in the Origenes Werke, page, and where appropriate, lines.
Translations of primary texts are my own unless otherwise noted).

[10]Cf. M. Smith, "Palestinian Judaism in the First Century," repr.
in *Essays in Graeco-Roman and Related Talmudic Literature* (New York,
1977), pp. 195-196.

[11]*Comm. in Joann.*, frag. 34, GCS 4.510.2-8. Cf. Josephus, *Bell.*
2.162-166; *Ant.* 18.11-17.

[12]Cf. *Comm. in Cant.* Prol., GCS 8.62.22-30, where Origen
specifically mentions how certain texts of scripture, the so-called
δευτερώσεις, were withheld from immature students, who were to be
initiated in these writings only by the sages.

5

observed first-hand the school of R. Hoshaya in Caesarea, which was more than a sedentary institution, having distinct ascetic features.[13]

The rabbis are known in some cases to have exploited this philosophical repute. Not only did Greek ethical and philosophical idioms influence moral discourse within certain Tannaitic circles,[14] but some rabbis actively sought a larger hearing for their teachings. Writes Martin Goodman, "As Greek philosophers were expected to teach practical ethics as physicians of souls rather than impractical theorisers, so the rabbis meted out moral advice in the midrash they delivered to the wider public on Sabbaths."[15] They also engaged pagans and Christians in public debates.

The rabbinic literature unfortunately never affords details of the rabbis' encounters with various *minim* (heretics), but it does report certain instances where the rabbis confuted Christian "philosophs" (philosophers) and other *epiqursim* ("Epicureans") who distorted scripture or questioned Israel's election. These derisive labels, far from suggesting an anti-philosophical attitude on the part of the rabbis, were aimed at branding the opponents petty sophists in comparison with the erudite sages.[16] R. Gamaliel II (early second century) reportedly confronted a "philosopher",

---

[13]Indeed, its precursors included the "open-air" academies in Palestine, teaching groups meeting in everything from marketplaces to vineyards, "touring" academies like that of R. Gamaliel (Tosefta *Pesahim* 2.16), and the like. See the discussion of M. Goodman, *State and Society*, pp. 76ff; also the study of S. Krauss, "Outdoor Teaching in Talmudic Times," *Journal of Jewish Studies* 1 (1948-49): 82-84.

[14]Cf. J. Goldin, "A Philosophical Session in a Tannaite Academy," *Traditio* 21 (1965): 1-21.

[15]*State and Society*, p. 74.

[16]Cf. Goldin, "A Philosophical Session," p. 20-21.

probably a gentile Christian, perhaps a trained orator,[17] who cited Yahweh's "withdrawal" in Hosea 5:6 in order to dispute Israel's election.[18] R. Yohanan, Origen's contemporary from Tiberias, warned against gentile as well as Jewish "Epicureans" who wreaked havoc on the Torah.[19] Another celebrated pericope[20] records how R. Hoshaya, Origen's major Jewish counterpart in Caesarea, answered a "philosopher's" query about circumcision. If circumcision was so precious, why did God create Adam uncircumcised? R. Hoshaya responded that all of God's hexaemeral creations needed perfecting, and circumcision was conducive to man's perfection. Wilhelm Bacher, the great rabbinics scholar, surmised a century ago that this philosopher was Origen himself contending with R. Hoshaya.[21] Yet this particular derogation of circumcision is found earlier in Justin,[22] and was probably a stock argument in Christian polemic against Jewish observances.

It is little surprise, then, that Origen too should boast to Celsus of his victories in debate with the sages, often pitting his knowledge of their teachings against Celsus' Jewish persona.[23] Some of his confrontations

---

[17]This is T. Herford's view in *Christianity in Talmud and Midrash* (London, 1903; repr. ed., New York, 1975), p. 148.

[18]*Midrash Ps.* 10.8; cf. B. Yebamot 102b. See also *Genesis Rabbah* 1.9; B. *Shabbat* 116a. References to the Babylonian Talmud are cited under "B" and specific tractate; those to the Talmud of the Land of Israel under "J" and specific tractate).

[19]B. *Sanhedrin* 38b.

[20]Genesis Rabbah 11.6.

[21]W. Bacher, "The Church Father, Origen, and Rabbi Hoshaya," *JQR* 3 (1891): 357-360.

[22]Cf. *Dial. c. Trypho* 19, PG 6.516C.

[23]Cf. *int. al. C. Cels.* 2.31, GCS 1.159.1-5.

with the rabbis were probably informal discussions in private,[24] but others were public debates or symposia before an audience, focusing on interpretations of scripture, the miracles of Jesus and Moses, and the like.[25] Lee Levine notes that Caesarea, like other Graeco-Roman cities, had a meeting-place for religious controversies where the Bible, New Testament, and other Jewish and Christian texts were deposited for easy reference.[26] Such debates no doubt played an important role in securing the popular appeal and intellectual integrity of Judaism and Christianity in late antiquity.

Origen respected the skills of his rabbinic opponents enough to be concerned that Christians might shame themselves in these public disputes.[27] Perhaps he composed the Hexapla in part for the purpose of controverting the sages on the text of scripture.[28] At any rate, he leaves little doubt that the Jewish scholars were a force to be reckoned with if Christianity was successfully to appropriate the Hebrew Bible. We may reasonably assume that Origen himself was no weakling in debate. His inquiries into the Hebrew language may well have scandalized the rabbis in view of the Caesarean Jewish laity's ostensible ignorance of Hebrew;[29]

---

[24]Cf. *Ep. ad Afr.* 6, PG 11.61B.

[25]Notably, *C. Cels.* 1.45, GCS 1.95.3-5.

[26]*Caesarea*, pp. 82-83.

[27]*Ep. ad Afr.* 5, PG 11.60B-61A.

[28]So argues S. P. Brock, "Origen's Aims as a Textual Critic of the Old Testament," *StPatr* 10 (TU 107; Berlin, 1970), pp. 215-218.

[29]The Shema was recited in Greek in at least one of Caesarea's synagogues because the congregants did not read Hebrew (cf. J. *Sota* 1.21b). On the extensive use of Greek among Jews in hellenized towns like Caesarea, see S. Lieberman, *Greek in Jewish Palestine*, 2nd. ed. (New York, 1965), pp. 37-59. Notably, Lieberman suggests (pp. 2, 39) that the rabbis in towns like

moreover, his ability to cite biblical texts at will, and his knowledge of certain Jewish haggadic traditions, would very well have impressed Jewish and non-Jewish audiences alike. Perhaps Origen, among others, inspired R. Yohanan's poignant remark that "a gentile who studies the Torah deserves capital punishment."[30]

II.

Religious debates over shared scriptures were only the outward sign of an implicit competition, and broader coincidence of interests, between the Church and the Synagogue in the second and third centuries. Marcel Simon argues that if Judaism had not been proselytizing in this period, this conflict would have been merely "un lutte toute théorique, livresque et stérile controverse autour des textes sacrés"; if proselytizing, Judaism would constitute "un rival véritable et dangereux" to Christianity.[31] Simon has of course vigorously argued for the latter, insisting that early Hadrianic bans on circumcising gentiles never extinguished the Jewish mission. He contends that rabbinic dicta favorable to proselytism presume its reality, and that epigraphical allusions, patristic references, and Constantinian counter-measures adequately attest its persistence well into the fourth century.[32]

Caesarea preached in Aramaic but illustrated passages in Greek for the sake of the townspeople. Yet Levine (*Caesarea*, p. 198, n. 124) rightly argues that Aramaic preaching would be hard to imagine in Caesarea, where, not only was the Shema recited in Greek, but the speaker frequenly addressed gentiles as well as Jews.

[30]B. *Sanhedrin* 58b.

[31]*Verus Israel*, p. 315.

[32]Ibid., pp. 323-351.

David Rokeah denies Simon's conclusions, and cites, among other things, select negative comments of the rabbis about proselytizing.[33] In reality, the rabbis' statements vary greatly in this period, indicating a constant alternation between the desire for expansion and disillusionment with unfaithful converts.[34]

For our purposes, it is especially significant that in third-century Galilee, R. Yohanan and other leading sages sought stricter regulation of ritual entry requirements (i.e., circumcision and baptism),[35] but still encouraged Jewish missionary activities.[36] Origen himself complained of Judaizing Christians being lured to the synagogue by Jewish missionaries,[37] and portrayed the success of Christian proselytism precisely in terms of the spiritual Israel usurping the carnal.[38] Caesarean Jews were probably incited

---

[33]*Jews, Christians and Pagans in Conflict*, pp. 42-43.

[34]See the relevant texts gathered by B. Bamberger, *Proselytism in the Talmudic Period*, rev. ed. (New York, 1968), pp. 149-173.

[35]B. *Yebamot* 46a.

[36]Cf. *int. al.* R. Yohanan in B. *Nedarim* 32a. See also M. Avi-Yonah, *The Jews under Roman and Byzantine Rule* (New York, 1976), p. 82, who observes that all of R. Yohanan's outstanding pupils endorsed proselytism. Independent testimony of Jewish proselytism specifically in Caesarea is offered in a funerary inscription mentioning a particular convert to Judaism: Μεμοριον της προσσυλητου [προσηλυτου] Αστη και Παρηγοριου Ευχαριστουσα, as recorded by B. Lifshitz in his "Inscriptions greques de Césarée en Palestine (Caesarea Palaestinae)," *RB* 68 (1961): 115-116 (no. 2).

[37]*Hom. in Matt.* 16, GCS 11.29-31.

[38]Cf. *Hom. in Luc.* 5, GCS 9.87.24-88.3: *Nunc autem populi credentium accedunt ad finem Jesu, et angeli, quibus creditae fuerant ecclesiae, roborati praesentia Salvatoris multos adducunt proselytos, ut congregentur in omni orbe conventicula christianorum. Quapropter consurgentes laudemus Dominum et fiamus pro carnali Israhel spiritualis Israhel.*

by competition with Christian missionaries for the same pool of potential converts.[39]

The competition for proselytes gave rise to an ideological exchange as well. Classic arguments *adversus Judaeos* were probably leveled in just this context, the destruction of the Temple and dispersion of the Jews being seen as divine punishment for the execution of Jesus.[40] Origen mentioned a Jewish response to such allegations from a debate with the sages over the Servant Songs in Isaiah: Israel's chastisement and subsequent diaspora were a providential means for her to make proselytes of the nations.[41] This very rationale was espoused by R. Eliezar b. Pedat, a Galilean contemporary of Origen, and seconded by R. Yohanan.[42] The rabbis took the offense too at times. R. Yohanan was probably reacting to Christian notions of original sin when he insisted that the gentiles ("idolaters") were contaminated only by not having participated in the lawgiving at Sinai,[43] for which he apparently prescribed proselytism as the solution.[44] Confronted by Christian attempts to spiritualize the Law, the rabbis asserted the eternal and universally binding

---

[39]On this mass of potential proselytes, cf. *Hom. in Jesu Nave* 9.9, GCS 7.354-355.

[40]Cf. int. al. *C. Cels.* 2.8, GCS 1.134-135; ibid. 4.22, GCS 1.291-292. See also Sgherri, *Chiesa e Sinagoga,* pp. 78-132; Kimelman, *Rabbi Yohanan,* pp. 266-271.

[41]*C. Cels.* 1.55, GCS 1.106.5-8.

[42]B. *Pesahim* 87b.

[43]B. *Shabbat* 145b-146a; =B. *Yebamot* 103b. See also the discussion of this passage in Kimelman, *Rabbi Yohanan,* pp. 255-256.

[44]See above, note 34.

validity of the *mitzvot*.[45] A missionary universalism thrived on both sides: if Christianity was a moral leaven and "army of piety" quietly undergirding the imperial order,[46] Judaism was a stabilizing "hedge to the world".[47]

The actual missionary success of the Church and the Synagogue of course depended on various factors. Judaism enjoyed the greater antiquity and an ancient moral code that accorded well with the pagan κοιναί ἔννοιαι. Certain of its customs were venerable and inspiring, and Origen knew this when he complained of Judaizing Christians who persisted in hand-washing before meals,[48] attending synagogue,[49] and observing Passover.[50] Yet Origen was also well aware that these rituals could be a stumbling block to pagans.[51] Christianity could in turn appeal to the simplicity of faith in Jesus and the universal need for moral regeneration.[52] Origen maintained in his *Commentary on Romans* that Israel believed only after observing Yahweh's miracles, but Abraham (the prototype of believers) had the truly

---

[45]Cf. J. *Aboda Zara* 2.1.40c, cited by Levine, *Caesarea*, p. 84 and 209, n. 251.

[46]Cf. *C. Cels.* 8.73-74, GCS 2.290-291; also ibid. 3.50-61 *passim*.

[47]R. Yohanan in *Exodus Rabbah* 2.5.

[48]*Comm. in Matt.* 11.8, GCS 10.47.5-15.

[49]*Hom. in Lev.* 5.8, GCS 6.349.4; *Sel. in Exod.* 12.46, PG 12.285; *Hom. in Jer.* 12.13, GCS 6.100.

[50]*Hom. in Jer.* 12.13, GCS 6.99-100. On the appeal of Jewish traditions and customs to Judaizing Christians in an analogous context in fourth-century Antioch, see Wilken, *John Chrysostom and the Jews*, pp. 66-94.

[51]Cf. *Comm. in Rom.* 2.11, PG 14.897A: *Ridicula etiam ipsis gentibus fiunt.*

[52]*C. Cels.* 1.9-11, GCS 1.61-64.

virtuous faith which demanded no such wonders.[53] Yet Resh Laqish similarly lauded gentile proselytes to Judaism as dearer to God than Israel at Sinai, because they had not witnessed the miraculous signs on the mountain, but were converted through spontaneous piety.[54]

Perhaps, however, the singularly most important instrument in luring proselytes both to Judaism and to Christianity continued to be their shared treasure: scripture, the Hebrew Bible in Greek recensions.[55] A number of second-century rabbinic allusions suggest that gentiles contemplating conversion to Judaism busied themselves with reading scripture, and expressed their reservations to Jewish friends whose answers were often determinative.[56] *Sifre Deuteronomy* tells of a "philosopher" who was martyred for protesting the burning of the Torah scroll (presumably during the Bar Kochba war).[57] Though sophisticated pagans sometimes derided scripture as crude or distasteful,[58] Origen still recorded in the third

---

[53]*Comm. in Rom.*, frag. 6.1 (ed. J. Scherer, Cairo, 1957), pp. 182, 184.

[54]*Tanhuma B. and N. Lek Leka* 6, selected and quoted by Bamberger, *Proselytism*, p. 155.

[55]On the use of Greek recensions for Jewish proselytism, see Simon, *Verus Israel*, pp. 348-351. On the importance of scripture in general in the early Christian mission, see W. H. C. Frend, "The Missions of the Early Church 180-700 A. D., " in *Miscellanea Historiae Ecclesiasticae* 3 (Louvain, 1970), pp. 4-5.

[56]See the relevant evidence adduced and assessed by I. Heinemann, "The Attitude of the Ancient World toward Judaism," *Review of Religion* 4 (1940): 387-388.

[57]*Sifre Deut.* 307.4.

[58]Cf. e. g. Arnobius, *Adv. gentes* 1.58, CSEL 4.39.8ff; and Celsus in *C. Cels.* 6.49-65 (against the Mosaic cosmogony); ibid. 7.1-26 (against the OT prophecies).

century that the Church converted souls principally "through readings of the Bible and explanation of the readings" ($\delta\iota$ ' $\dot{\alpha}\nu\alpha\gamma\nu\omega\sigma\mu\dot{\alpha}\tau\omega\nu$ $\kappa\alpha\grave{\iota}$ $\delta\iota\dot{\alpha}$ $\tau\hat{\omega}\nu$ $\epsilon\iota\varsigma$ $\tau\dot{\alpha}$ $\dot{\alpha}\nu\alpha\gamma\nu\dot{\omega}\sigma\mu\alpha\tau\alpha$ $\delta\iota\eta\gamma\dot{\eta}\sigma\epsilon\omega\varsigma$).[59] Isaak Heinemann has reasonably concluded that converts both to Judaism and to Christianity "were won less through dogmas and rites than through Scripture, to which other religions in antiquity, both official and mystery, had nothing comparable to oppose."[60]

Jews and Christians, nevertheless, were not the only ones using scripture for proselytism. Gnostic and Marcionite sects in Palestine also sought adherents, and exploited the popularity and availability of the Bible. Already in the second century, the so-called "two powers" heretics had begun to show their heads in Palestine, raising exegetical questions about the unity of the Godhead, theodicy, and the like. Caesarean and Galilean rabbis championed the cause of biblical orthodoxy, propounding rules of monotheistic exegesis for sensitive passages like Genesis 1:26-27.[61] Marcionism was a common enemy of Christianity and Judaism, attacked by Origen in his homilies,[62] by R. Yohanan,[63] and later in the third century by R. Abbahu of Caesarea.[64] Alan Segal's observation about the rabbis'

---

[59]C. Cels. 3.50, GCS 1.246.17-19.

[60]"The Attitude of the Ancient World," p. 388.

[61]Cf. R. Yohanan in B. Sanhedrin 38b.

[62]Cf. int al. Hom. in Luc. 16, GCS 9.108; Hom. in Num. 7.1, GCS 7.38. On one occasion, Origen actually borrowed from a Jewish midrash to refute an exegesis of Apelles concerning the dimensions of Noah's ark (Hom. in Gen. 2.2, GCS 6.28f).

[63]Cf. Exodus Rabbah 13.3; and Kimelman, Rabbi Yohanan, pp. 179-182.

[64]See S. Lachs, "Rabbi Abbahu and the Minim," JQR 60 (1969): 209ff.

dilemma with these sects could also apply to Origen's: "Although the answers to the heretics were worked out by the academies, the questions must have been raised in relation to Bible-reading and by groups who were interested in hearing the Jewish Bible expounded."[65]

III.

This wider missionary struggle between the Church and the Synagogue in Palestine, in which scripture doubtless played a crucial role, intensified their rival claims to the Bible and its legitimate interpretation.[66] Christian-Jewish confrontations in this period were therefore more than trivial or bookish disputes over the scriptures; they were genuine struggles for credibility. Newly ordained and burdened in Caesarea with the responsibilities of a preacher, Origen took Jewish exegesis to task in his commentaries and homilies. Despite his deeper appreciation for the rabbinic hermeneutics, he perpetuated the "myth of Jewish literalism",[67] as de Lange has called it, because it continued to be an effective rhetorical *reductio ad absurdum* with which to oppose Judaism.

---

[65]*Two Powers in Heaven: Early Rabbinic Reports about Christianity and Gnosticism,* Studies in Judaism in Late Antiquity 25 (Leiden, 1977), p. 154.

[66]On the centrality of biblical intepretation in Christian-Jewish exchanges throughout late antiquity, see the recent studies of M. Simon, "Le Bible dans les premières controverses entre juifs et chrétiens," in *Le monde grec ancien et la Bible,* ed. Claude Mondésert, Bible de tout les temps 1 (Paris, 1984), pp. 107-125; also J. Maier, *Jüdische Auseindersetzung mit dem Christentum in der Antike,* Erträge der Forschung 177 (Darmstadt, 1982).

[67]Cf. *De princ.* 4.3.2, GCS 5.326; *C. Cels.* 2.4-6, GCS 1.130-132; and de Lange, *Origen and the Jews,* pp. 82-83.

Origen persistently refused, for example, to admit any rationale at all for the literal interpretation of the ceremonial laws. He was aware of current Jewish *halakhah* which sought to revise Sabbath regulations so as to make them more practicable in extenuating circumstances. He refuted such qualifications as endlessly bothersome: the wearing of one kind of sandal a burden, another not, *ad infinitem*.[68] With similar bluntness he argued that the impossibility of Jews making their paschal offerings in the Temple (Deuteronomy 16:6f) after its destruction was adequate grounds for discontinuing all such rituals.[69] Though many Jews admirably studied the Torah from infancy to old age,[70] their literalist teachings were nothing but "myths and rubbish" (μύθοι καὶ λῆροι)[71] without the higher (Christian) interpretation of the Law.

Origen likewise warned against the Jews' literalism in interpreting the prophets: "The prophets also do not limit the meaning of their sayings to the obvious history and to the text and letter of the law."[72] Yet in one of his debates with the rabbis, the sages themselves interpreted Isaiah's Servant

---

[68]*De princ.* 4.3.2, GCS 5.326.

[69]*Comm. in Rom.* 2.13, PG 14.906ff. For a fuller discussion of such arguments, see de Lange, *Origen and the Jews*, pp. 89-102; Bietenhard, *Caesarea, Origenes und die Juden*, pp. 48-52.

[70]*Comm. in Rom.* 2.14, PG 14.915C: *Videmus plurimos Judaeorum ab infantia usque ad senectutem semper discentes.*

[71]*C. Cels.* 2.5, GCS 1.132.12. On Jewish "fables" (μύθοι), see also *Hom. in Gen.* 6.3, GCS 6.69ff; *Hom. in Exod.* 5.1, GCS 6.184; *Hom. in Lev.* 3.3, GCS 6.306.

[72]*C. Cels.* 2.6, GCS 1.132.25-27. The translation here is H. Chadwick's from his magisterial *Origen: Contra Celsum* (Cambridge, 1953; rev. ed., 1965), p. 71.

16

Songs allegorically, rendering the Servant as the whole people of Israel.[73] Origen's response was predictable: their allegory simply did not fit. Rather than confuting an allegorical interpretation as such, he resorted merely to an *ad hominem* argument: "Why is this man said to have been led to death because of the iniquities of the people of God, if he is not different from the people of God?"[74] Rhetorically speaking, the rabbis failed to take the prophecy "literally" enough. The rabbis could, of course, respond in kind. Origen mentioned a Jewish response to another prophecy used by Christians as a pivotal Christological *testimonium*: Zechariah 9:9-10. Granted Jesus' entry into Jerusalem "on an ass", when did he ever "cut off" the "chariot from Ephraim", the "war horse from Jerusalem", or the "battle bow"? Why indeed did he have to ride into Jerusalem at all, when the journey was so short?[75]

One other aspect of these ongoing exegetical disputations in third-century Palestine has only recently been examined closely: Origen's exchanges with rabbis over the Song of Songs. The Song had been elevated by the sages to a kind of "nationalist ode on the chosenness of Israel",[76] and its interpretation had become a veritable battleground for Jewish and Christian claims to divine election. Here there was an initial consensus on the *peshat* (plain sense) of the text: for the rabbis, the allegorical interpretation of the Song was the only possible *peshat*,[77] a love song

---

[73]Ibid. 1.55, GCS 1.106.

[74]Ibid. GCS 1.106.23-24, trans. Chadwick, p. 51.

[75]*Comm. in Joann.* 10.27, GCS 4.199ff, cited by de Lange, *Origen and the Jews*, p. 100.

[76]S. Baron, *A Social and Political History of the Jews*, vol. 2, 2nd ed. (New York, 1952), p. 145.

[77]Y. Muffs, "Joy and Love as Metaphorical Expressions of Willingness and Spontaneity in Cuneiform, Ancient Hebrew, and Related

between God and Israel; for Origen it was an allegory of Christ's marriage to his Church.

Building on Ephraim Urbach's earlier work, Reuven Kimelman has demonstrated a thoroughgoing cross-fertilization in Origen's exegetical disputations with R. Yohanan.[78] In Song 1:2, for example, R. Yohanan found that the mystical "kiss" of God was destined for Israel at Sinai,[79] and to obviate the potential anthropomorphism, he introduced into his exegesis an angelic mediator who kissed the Holy One.[80] Origen countered by claiming that the "kiss" was Christ's and intended for the Church; he downplayed the meditorial role of an angel, asserting that angels merely brought down the Law to the Church (cf. Galatians 3:19).[81] Origen's equations of Bridegroom=Christ and Bride=Church, which denigrated the idea of the kiss being a mediation of the Torah, in turn triggered R. Yohanan's attempt to show that God gave the commandments directly at Sinai,[82] with

---

Literatures," in *Christianity, Judaism and Other Graeco-Roman Cults* 3, Studies in Judaism in Late Antiquity 11 (Leiden, 1975), p. 21; cited by R. Kimelman, *Rabbi Yohanan*, p. 239, n. 1. Origen himself, of course, was aware of the esoteric esteem in which the rabbis held the Song as a source-book for allegorical and mystical speculation (cf. *Comm. in Cant.* Prol., GCS 8.62.22-30).

[78]Cf. E. E. Urbach, "The Homiletical Interpretations of the Sages and the Expositions of Origen on Canticles, and the Jewish-Christian Disputation," Scripta hierosolymitana 22 (1971): 247-275; R. Kimelman, "Rabbi Yohanan and Origen on the Song of Songs: A Third-Century Jewish-Christian Disputation," *HTR* 73 (1980): 567-595 (=ch. 6 of Kimelman's dissertation, *Rabbi Yohanan*, cited above, note 2 and *passim*).

[79]Cf. Urbach, "The Homiletical Interpretations," p. 254.

[80]*Song of Songs Rabbah* 1.2.2.

[81]*Comm. in Cant.* 1, GCS 8.90.

[82]*Pesikta Rabbati* 21.5, quoted by Kimelman, "Rabbi Yohanan and Origen," pp. 575-576.

Moses playing the role of an arranger of the rendezvous between Yahweh and Israel.[83] Other examples notwithstanding,[84] this exchange will suffice to show that in the debate over the Song, Origen refuted the rabbis precisely by attempting to best their allegories. He in no way underestimated the profundity or the appeal of the rabbis' homilies. In fact, in his sermons on Ezekiel, as David Halperin has discovered, Origen actually exploited the colorful Sinai and ascension imagery of Galilean rabbis' Pentecost homilies in order to embellish his own preaching.[85]

The dispute over the Song of Songs clearly shows that Origen was capable of entering into extensive and sophisticated exegetical controversies with the rabbis. The upshot was nonetheless the same. His aim was not to attack any certain mode of Jewish exegesis, but to undermine the entire Jewish claim to the authoritative interpretation of the Bible. In his disputes with the rabbis, there was no shared, highly articulated language about the method of rendering texts. Such debates thrived on rhetorical strategies and *ad hoc* arguments. For the same reasons, therefore, that he dismissed the literal interpretation of Jewish laws, Origen rejected the rabbis' allegorical exegeses or tried to outstrip them. In so doing, he testified to the skill of the

---

[83]*Song of Songs Rabbah* 1.2.3.

[84]Kimelman ("Rabbi Yohanan and Origen," pp. 574-595) finds no less than five "topics" of this ongoing disputation on Song 1:1-6: a covenant mediated by Moses vs. one negotiated by him; the NT vs. the Oral Torah as "superseding" scripture; Christ vs. Abraham; the heavenly vs. the earthly Jerusalem; and Israel being repudiated vs. Israel being disciplined.

[85]See David Halperin, "Origen, Ezekiel's Merkabah, and the Ascension of Moses," *Church History* 50 (1981): 261-275.

rabbinic preachers who, like himself, addressed the concrete needs of a religious community.[86]

IV.

Because Origen's allusions to his contacts with rabbinic Judaism are fairly scattered and episodic, we are hard-pressed to fill in the gaps in his picture of the Christian-Jewish encounter in third-century Caesarea. The rabbis he debated publicly and in his preaching--not to mention those Jews who assisted him privately[87]--are elusive figures never clearly identified by Origen. By comparing Origen's evidence with parallel rabbinic traditions, and with analogous developments in Christian-Jewish relations throughout this period, his confrontation with Judaism begins to take shape. We see Judaism not only as a resource in Origen's scholarly background, but as a vibrant rival community in the foreground of his commentaires and homilies composed in Caesarea.

Indeed, the Jews in Origen's purview did not stand idly by in Christianity's ongoing engagement with the pagan world. Inspired by a strong rabbinate of scholars and preachers with their own missionary vision, the Jews of Caesarea, as in the Diaspora cities, were very much in the thick of current religious controversies. As Han Drijvers emphasizes in a recent study of their relations in Edessa, Jews, Christians, and pagans did not live in some idyllic isolation in the setting of an ancient town, where most of life was lived in public and privacy was almost unheard of. Their mutual

---

[86] As Levine notes (*Caesarea*, p. 102), the Caesarean rabbis in particular were distinguished by their heavy involvement in preaching and the practical affairs of synagogue life.

[87] See above, note 7.

ideological conflicts arose within the context of daily experience, where, in the ancient world, religious behavior was precisely a matter of public conduct informed by the standards of a tradition.[88]

Origen's own interaction with the rabbis followed, in some respects, the pattern of disputes of popular philosophers in late antiquity. In private, of course, their relations could be rather peaceable, even convivial, Origen researching those Jewish traditions which would enrich his own scholarship, and at times openly admitting his curiosity--a remarkable, albeit naïve curiosity[89]--about rabbinic hermeneutics. Theologically, too, he could extol the ancient and venerable "Jewish" sages and prophets for their relative proximity to the spiritual truth,[90] and assess the positive place of Judaism in the unfolding history of salvation, in a way unprecedented amid strong the Christian antipathy toward Judaism in his time. Such is the aspect of Origen's relationship with Judaism which is atypical in its ancient context, and which brings the admiration of modern critics anxious to find in him a model for sholarly interchange between Christians and Jews today.[91]

---

[88]See Drijvers, "Jews and Christians in Edessa," p. 89.

[89]One is reminded here of the passage in *Sel. in Ps.* (PG 12.1080B-C) in which Origen concurs with "the Hebrew" that the whole of scripture mysteriously resembles a single house with a number of locked rooms. By each room is a key, but not the one fitting that room, such that the exegete's task is to match keys with rooms and thereby gain access to the Bible innermost secrets. Origen admired the rabbis' sense of the mystical depth of scripture, and sometimes borrowed isolated pieces of haggadah, but he did not venture, beyond his means, into the labyrinth of rabbinic hermeneutics.

[90]Cf., in particular, *C. Cels.* 7.7ff, and the study of P. Gorday in this volume, "Moses and Jesus in contra Celsum 7.1-25: Ethics, History and Jewish Christian Eirenics in Origen's Theology."

[91]I am thinking here principally of de Lange, in the Afterword to his *Origen and the Jews*, p. 135.

Yet, from most indications, Origen's scholarly and theological interest in Judaism did not betray itself openly in his public dispositon toward the Jews. Here Origen's debates with the rabbis over the Bible presented less a scholarly exchange of ideas than a platform for mutual disclaimers.   Origen's anti-Jewish maneuvers in his homilies and commentaries reflect just this same inflexibility. There was no question here of negotiation in these "philosophers'" debates. The rabbis' exegetical arguments had to be dismissed *in toto* because Judaism continued to be a viable threat to the Christian mission, a live option for those seeking to be faithful to the tradition of the Bible. In this adamant public posture toward Judaism, Origen remained indeed quite typical of the patterns of Christian-Jewish relations in late antiquity.

ORIGEN ON THE JEWS

by JOHN A. McGUCKIN

THIS present study is a note added to what has already become an extensive bibliography concerning Origen's doctrinal relation to Judaism in general, and the extent and significance of his awareness of Jewish exegetical procedures in particular. Among that list[1] of previous studies on the theme, special reference ought to be made to the seminal work *Origen and the Jews*,[2] by Professor Nicholas de Lange, which demonstrated Origen's knowledge of rabbinic traditions in his exegeses. This present study will offer, firstly, a general contextual discussion of the question of Origen's dependence on Jewish tradition, and, secondly, a small test-case analysis of his attitude to the Jewish question from observing his New Testament exegesis of those passages directly concerning the issue. From the latter some interesting biases will emerge that throw some light on his personal attitudes.

The personality and work of Origen of Alexandria (though it may be more to the point to call him Origen of Caesarea Maritima) is a

---

[1] The full bibliographical details for most of the relevant studies can be found chronologically listed in H. Crouzel, *Bibliographie critique d'Origene*, suppl. 1 – *Instrumenta Patristica* VIIIa (Steenbrugis, 1982). Here I will list the relevant works to 1982 with reference to that index, by author and year, with some of the pertinent articles that have appeared since that date: 1898, Ginzberg; 1925, Murawski; 1927, Ginzberg; 1928, Marmorstein; 1929, Ginzberg; 1941, Bieder; 1956, Baer; 1961, Taylor; 1968, Kötting; 1968, Roncaglia; 1968, Simon-Benoit; 1969, Judant; 1970, Philippou; 1970, Roncaglia; 1971, Hruby; 1971, Urbach; 1971, de Lange; 1974, Bietenhard; 1975, Levine; 1975, de Lange; 1976, de Lange; 1976, Sgherri; 1977, Wasserstein; 1979, Judant. There is also a bibliography appended to N. de Lange, *Origen and the Jews* (Cambridge, 1976), pp. 209–15: for other relevant studies listed in that source see entries for Bardy, Daniélou, Daube, Hanson, Krauss, Lachs, Liebermann, Loewe, and Wilde. A short relevant bibliography and discussion of the texts can also be found in E. A. Clarke, *Ascetic Piety and Women's Faith* (New York, 1986), pp. 391–2. Other recent and relevant works mentioned in or relevant to this present study include D. J. Halperin, 'Origen, Ezekiel's Merkabah, and the Ascension of Moses', *Church History*, 50 (1981), pp. 261–75; R. Kimelman, 'Rabbi Yohanan and Origen on the Song of Songs', *HThR*, 73 (1980), pp. 567–95; J. A. McGuckin, 'Origen on the Glory of God', *Studia Patristica*, 21 (Louvain, 1989), pp. 316–24, and 'Caesarea as Origen knew it', in *Origeniana Quinta* (forthcoming, Louvain, 1992); Roger Brooks, 'Straw Dogs and Scholarly Ecumenism: the Appropriate Jewish Background for the Study of Origen', in C. Kannengiesser and W. L. Petersen, eds, *Origen of Alexandria* (Notre Dame, Indiana, 1988), pp. 63–95; Paul Blowers, 'Origen, the Rabbis, and the Bible', in ibid., pp. 96–116; D. Rokeah, *Jews, Pagans, and Christians in Conflict* – *Studia Post-Biblica*, 33 (Jerusalem and Leiden, 1982); S. Krauss, 'The Jews in the works of the Church Fathers', *JQR*, 5 (1983), pp. 139ff. (on Origen).

[2] De Lange, *Origen and the Jews*.

---

particularly fine lens through which to observe a critical period in developing Jewish and Christian self-definitions, when the old apologetics caused by immediate strifes and local frictions in the context of the Diaspora urban communities, throughout the first and second centuries, were giving way to new revisions for a different political and religious climate. The traumatic destruction of central and sacred institutions of Judaism by the Romans, in the latter half of the first century, provided conditions for the rise of a rabbinic Judaism that was much more conscious of its international status as a religious tradition focused on scholarly exegesis of the biblical text, and which was to develop its socio-ethical and theological norms (its Halachah and Haggadah) on that basis.

Alexandria, Rome, Caesarea, Tiberias, and Babylon became important points in the Jewish network of trade and scholarly connections that wrapped the Empire and extended beyond it.[3] In the time (c.230) that Origen took refuge permanently in Caesarea—to escape from the difficulties being caused by his bishop Demetrios in Alexandria—Caesarea, once a notoriously pagan and secular city in all Jewish eyes, was being accepted back into the concept of Eretz Israel, to the extent that a great rabbinical tradition was already beginning to establish itself there, one that would flourish from CE 230 to 260. The most famous name associated with the city in less happy days is the martyred Rabbi Akiba, who lies buried in the unexcavated vaults to the south of the present city ruins, but in Origen's day Rabbi Hoshaya and Rabbi Abbahu are perhaps the most important figures, along with Rabbi Yohanan (later of Tiberias) and Resh Laqish. The 'Rabbis of Caesarea' are mentioned no less than 140 times in the Palestinian Talmud, and there is evidence to suggest that they enjoyed notable legal privileges, to the extent of holding high and important status in the Caesarean judiciary, something for which there is no Christian parallel at this period.[4]

The growing fame of the Jewish academies at Caesarea was possibly one of the main reasons why the scholarly Bishop Alexander of Jerusalem and the Metropolitan, Theoctistus of Caesarea, were so keen to attract Origen to their provincial capital. On his permanent arrival, after a preliminary lecture tour which greatly annoyed his Alexandrian bishop, Origen was ordained as a Caesarean presbyter and given the task of

---

[3] See H. Drijvers, 'Jews and Christians at Edessa', *JJS*, 36 (1985), pp. 88–102; Y. Baer, 'Israel, the Christian Church, and the Roman Empire from the time of Septimius Severus to the Edict of Toleration of A.D. 313', *Scripta Hieroslymita*, 7 (1961), pp. 79–149; H. Bietenhard, *Caesarea, Origenes und die Juden* (Stuttgart, 1974); L. Levine, *Caesarea under Roman Rule* (Leiden, 1975).

[4] Levine, *Caesarea under Roman Rule*, pp. 86–106.

expounding the Scriptures in the two weekday liturgical services. These expositions formed the basis of his extensive published commentaries on the Old Testament books. Bishop Alexander[5] was engaged in establishing the Church's library at Jerusalem, and it seems likely, from Origen's subsequent travels to Athens and around Palestine, from which tours he procured manuscripts, that a similar office was allotted to Origen in Caesarea. The emergence in the next generation of a library that was the glory of the Christian world was a testimony to his success.[6] Knauber[7] has suggested that the establishment of a Christian academy was part of the Caesarean Christian community's conscious attempt to create a missionary outreach among the middle-class civic dignitaries that formed such a large proportion of Caesarea's third-century population. There was also, undoubtedly, a desire to establish an international reputation for the school—something that became a reality even in Origen's lifetime, as we can deduce from the correspondence of Porphyry, and certainly continued into the fourth century, when the footsteps of such luminaries as Gregory Nazianzen, Basil, Didymus, Pamphilus, Eusebius, and Jerome can all be traced in the Caesarean arcades heading for the Christian library.

The valedictory *Thanksgiving Oration*[8] of Theodore (perhaps Gregory Thaumaturgos), one of Origen's pupils at Caesarea, gives an indication of just this type of imperial official's child, entrusted for his philosophical and rhetorical education to Origen and his school; and from that oration we gain an idea of just how wide Origen's curriculum was, covering secular sciences, literature, philosophy, and theology. There is no corresponding indication that the rabbinic schools ever entertained any such desires to extend their curriculum or their clientele so widely, and in terms of the necessity of Jewish birth or conversion, Semitic linguistic constraints, and the strict focus on biblical interpretation and Jewish law, the rabbinic academies surely could not be expected to employ the same strategy as Origen's school. The range and quality of education offered would suggest that Origen's academy was deliberately designed to be

---

[5] Bishop Alexander was a fellow student of Origen at Alexandria, and a personal friend. He died in the Decian persecution, at Caesarea, which also sentenced Origen to suffer torture (cf. Eusebius, *Historia ecclesiastica*, GCS, 9: 6.39.2).

[6] For further details see McGuckin, 'Caesarea Maritima as Origen knew it'.

[7] A. Knauber, 'Das Anliegen der Schule des Origenes zu Caesarea', *Münchener Theologische Zeitschrift*, 19 (1968), pp. 182–203. See also H. Crouzel, 'L'École d'Origène à Césarée', *Bulletin de littérature ecclésiastique*, 71 (1970), pp. 15–27.

[8] St Gregory Thaumaturgus, *The Oration and Panegyric Addressed to Origen*, tr. S. D. F. Salmond — *Ante Nicene Christian Library*, 20 (Edinburgh, 1871).

poised between the pagan and Jewish institutions, and, in deliberate contradistinction, attempting to offer the best aspects of both its rivals, while reserving higher Christian studies to a much more restricted circle of hearers—just as had been Origen's earlier practice in Alexandria.

This suggested context of Origen's work is an important factor to keep in mind when discussing the question of his specific dependencies, or his polemical attacks, on Jewish religious traditions. In other words, with Origen, we are not simply dealing with a religious or doctrinally motivated apologetic, but a different cultural and missionary vision is also at work.

Two other aspects of the relation between Origen and the Jews that ought to be kept firmly in mind can be characterized as the local and the universal contexts of how the two respective communities related in third-century Caesarea. In terms of local factors, Origen's homilies give several indications that there was a slight blurring of the line at a popular level between Church and Synagogue practices of worship.[9] Origen complains of Christian women who dress up attractively on Friday evenings. This is not just another patristic tirade against cosmetics, but one of several indications that Christian members of the congregation observed several aspects of the Jewish law, to the great annoyance of the clergy. Origen reminds the women that far from dressing up to celebrate (the Sabbath eve meal), they are expected in terms of their own tradition to be fasting for the Friday commemoration of the Lord's Passion. So, at the local level, we can envisage two ascendant communities who were both cautiously watching their neighbour and rival lest they push ahead, and yet were not averse to pushing ahead themselves if they ever got the chance. Each community was possessed of certain advantages and disadvantages in this matter of the expansion of their intellectual and social fortunes. In terms of the universal context of Jewish–Christian relationships in the third century, we might say that it was a question of the same thing writ larger. Origen is typical of this jostling for position throughout the final century before the Constantinian revolution cast such a decisive lot, but although he is a formidable anti-Jewish polemicist, Judaism and Christianity at that period were not in a position where the one could or did oppress the other, and that made a great difference. Both communities lived energetically by their religious traditions in a world

---

[9] Origen, *Homily on Jeremiah, 12.13*, PG 13, col. 395; see also *Commentariorum in Evangelium secundum Matthaeum* 15, PG 13, col. 1621. For a fuller discussion see Levine, *Caesarea under Roman Rule*, chs 5 and 7.

that was dominated by pagans, who were felt by both to be ultimately untrustworthy, religiously as well as politically.

De Lange's book has admirably set out the extent of Origen's awareness of Jewish exegetical opinions at an important time, when the Mishnah was being laid down. We can observe from the outset that Origen's attitude is not uniform throughout his work. In the *Contra Celsum*, for example, he takes the learned pagan Celsus to task, accusing him of being misinformed in his arguments against Jewish doctrine and practice. It is clear that Origen offsets Celsus's Hellenistic Jewish paradigm with his own knowledge of a rabbinic style of Judaism that was much less universalist in outlook. It is interesting, for example, to see Origen denying that Logos Christology could ever be part of the Jewish religious construct,[10] despite his knowledge of Philo. Where Celsus ridicules the Jewish tradition, however, Origen is not ready to follow him. This is largely because he is defending his own ground on his own terms. Celsus's overall position was that Christianity was a corrupt deviation of a corrupt original system. Origen, in composing his reply to this argument, in a missionary work that has its face set from the outset towards a pagan audience, defends the Jewish tradition as an inspired route of sacred revelation. He has not forgotten Christianity's grounding in the Jewish tradition, but he never follows the line that Christianity 'developed' its religious system from that of Judaism. He uses the argument of the historical relation rather to offset one of Celsus's most sustained attacks on Christian religion—its barbarous novelty. The radical discontinuities, new beginnings, corrections, and patterns of fulfilment that mark Origen's understanding of the theological relationship between Christianity and Judaism do not allow such a historically linear developmental model to stand; and neither does his radically a-historical hermeneutical method.

On the other hand, in his works that were aimed directly at a Christian readership, especially his scriptural commentaries, he engages in a more robust apologetic against Judaism. The range and extent of Origen's knowledge of Jewish exegetical traditions seems to have been mediated to him through a few closely related channels. He speaks of his 'Magister Hebraeus', a shadowy figure, whom opinion largely recognizes as a Christian,[11] and one could be fairly certain that among Origen's several

[10] Cf. de Lange, *Origen and the Jews*, pp. 63–73, for a detailed discussion of the relevant passages in the *Contra Celsum*.

[11] Origen, Epistle to Africanus, 6–8, tr. in *Ante-Nicene Christian Library*, 10 (Edinburgh, 1869),

professional assistants and scribes in the Caesarean church he had the services of other Jewish Christians, who occasionally drew his attention to various interesting and relevant points. There is also evidence of direct personal contact in the form of face-to-face disputations with rabbis.[12] The Caesarean halls, not least the well-appointed Odeon near his own school, might also be envisaged as places where more formal lectures and disputations could have taken place. Kimelman[13] has demonstrated a protracted literary exchange between Rabbi Yohanan and Origen on the interpretation of the Song of Songs, but it was an exchange where Origen largely rejected the allegorical interpretations of the rabbis out of hand, bettering them with his own, which he regarded as truly Logos-inspired.

The awareness of Origen's dependence on rabbinic traditions was given an immense boost by the careful analysis of de Lange, and shortly afterwards by Bietenhard,[14] and the number of known parallels greatly increased. Indeed, more instances have since emerged, as in the article by Halperin,[15] which demonstrates Origen's use of an esoteric tradition on the *Merkabah* taken from Caesarean rabbinic homilies on Pentecost.

The initial and very positive assessment of the significance of those rabbinic dependencies for Origen's overall scheme as a biblical theologian was largely provided by de Lange's own conclusion to his study, which suggested: 'Origen's reliance on the living Jewish tradition is one of the most distinctive features and serves to mark him out from all earlier and contemporary Greek fathers. It is no exaggeration to say that there is not a single aspect of his biblical writings that is not touched by it to a greater or lesser degree.'[16] This high claim quickly entered the Origenian canon when Henri Crouzel, without further analysis, adopted it in substance, shifting the limelight in the process from the rabbinic tradition itself back on to Origen: 'The most important influences are clearly Hebraic and Hellenic ... But there are also the rabbinic exegeses which had already influenced the New Testament through Paul, and which were to affect

---

pp. 376–7. Cf. G. Bardy, 'Les Traditions juives dans l'œuvre d'Origene', *RBen*, 34 (1925), pp. 221–3; de Lange, *Origen and the Jews*, pp. 15–37; Levine, *Caesarea under Roman Rule*, p. 205, nn. 209–12.

[12] For references see de Lange, *Origen and the Jews*, pp. 15–47, 1123–31; Levine, *Caesarea under Roman Rule*, pp. 79–80, 205.

[13] R. Kimelman, 'Rabbi Yohanan of Tiberias: aspects of the social and religious history of third century Palestine' (Yale University dissertation, 1977).

[14] See works cited in nn. 2–3, above.

[15] D. J. Halperin, 'Origen, Ezekiel's Merkabah, and the Ascension of Moses', *Church History*, 50 (1981), pp. 261–75.

[16] De Lange, *Origen and the Jews*, p. 134.

Origen too, who shows a very advanced knowledge of them acquired from friends among the rabbis.'[17] Such is the way of our scholarly trade that the subtle and carefully chosen shades of a work such as that by de Lange, when summarized in a few pages of what the author himself describes as initial tentative conclusions, can suddenly re-emerge as great washes of colour when these pages alone travel on in an independent afterlife. The crude, schematized divisions, of Hellenistic, Hebraic, Qumranic, Apocryphal, Rabbinic, and New Testamental, with which Crouzel operates, are not merely non-sustainable as hermeneutic categories for the whole three centuries of nascent Christianity, but in fact they entirely beg the two great questions in hand, which are, firstly, what significance one ought to attribute to any single type of literary borrowing by one of the great polymathic synthesists of the age; and, secondly, how does one begin to separate out a specially distinct kind of 'rabbinic' hermeneutic from the standard use of allegorical analysis common to all the period's interpreters? Moreover, how Origen was transformed into a 'friend of the Rabbis' on available evidence remains a mystery.

Subsequent Origen studies, however, have begun to question the positive nature of that earlier assessment more and more. The elegant monograph by Karen Torjesen[18] demonstrated the great extent to which Origen searched for a systematic literary schema in his commentaries, in a conscious attempt to create a scientific hermeneutic (whatever may be our opinions on the subjectivity of his method). The massive importance Origen gave to the direct inspiration of the Logos led him to set the Logos's own dispensation in the Christ-event as the normative key for the interpretation of all God's salvific revelation, past, present, and future, and to attribute to the Logos's own transfigured saints of the covenant, particularly the Apostles, the God-given power of illuminating the more obscure revelation of the Hebrew Scriptures, which a few chosen saints in the ancient generations, the prophets inspired by the Logos, had sketched out in figures that could only be clarified retrospectively. Such a system is facing in a radically different direction from that of Rabbinism. This is the root of Origen's frequent dismissal of Jewish exegesis in general apologetic terms as 'following only the literal level'. What stands out from his method is its great freedom from any anxiety to follow only linear

---

[17] H. Crouzel, *Origen*, Eng. tr. (Edinburgh, 1989), p. 78.
[18] K. J. Torjesen, *Hermeneutical Procedure and Theological Method in Origen's Exegesis* (Berlin and New York, 1986).

historical process in its unfolding of what he defines as transcendent biblical meaning. Such a systematic orientation is not, *prima facie*, good grounds for allowing us to suppose Origen considered Jewish exegesis of the Hebrew Scriptures to be any more 'normative' or necessarily endowed with any greater historical authenticity than subsequent Christian efforts; in fact, for him, far from it. His presuppositions, therefore, reverse the fundamental belief in linear, historically conditioned, development that characterizes most contemporary scholarly work, and again one ought to be careful to keep this fact in mind when considering the weight and significance of his borrowings. These differences in systematic orientation are precisely the reason Origen himself gives for apparently very negative Christian–Jewish relations in his own experience:

> The Jews are not antagonistic to the gentiles ... but against the Christians they are filled with an insatiable hatred, although we have abandoned idolatry and given ourselves over to God. They are irritated with us; they hate us as though we were a foolish people, and they come saying that they are wise because the first divine oracles were given to them.[19]

Origen's work on the Hexapla suggests that his Hebrew was very limited indeed. He relies heavily on Aquila's version to give him the sense of the Hebrew text, and when he does quote the Hebrew itself it is usually only in the form of a learned allusion, designed to impress his Gentile audience with his general erudition. The very lack of systematic pattern in Origen's use of rabbinic exegeses is indicative.

Four years ago a test study which I conducted on Origen's attitude to the theme of the Shekinah theology, a distinctive and characteristic aspect of the Tannaitic school,[20] demonstrated that his entire awareness of this theme, one that he himself developed considerably, came to him from Paul alone. Other, more recent studies, by Brooks[21] and Blowers,[22] have similarly tended to suggest that although Origen undoubtedly has an awareness of rabbinic traditions, the significance of those dependencies must be questioned.

Brooks's work, analogously to Torjesen's, approaches the question from a desire to establish the overall direction of Origen's systematic

---

[19] *Homily 1 on Psalm 36*, PG 7, col. 1321: cited Bardy, 'Les Traditions juives', p. 227.
[20] Cf. McGuckin, 'Origen on the Glory of God', pp. 316–24.
[21] Brooks, 'Straw Dogs and Scholarly Ecumenism', pp. 63–95.
[22] Blowers, 'Origen, the Rabbis, and the Bible', pp. 96–116.

concern, a systematic, needless to say, which was dominated by the biblical text, just as much as was that of the rabbis. Brooks makes a particular study of passages from Leviticus treated by both Origen and the Mishnah, but finds no points of connection. He therefore concludes negatively:

> The Jewish background and culture available to Origen throughout his life seems to have been remarkably superficial. Certainly Origen had some familiarity with a few scraps of Jewish exegesis . . . yet on the whole Origen simply had no understanding of the rabbinic movement gaining prominence around him.[23]

Blowers, working from a more comprehensive perspective, arrives at a similarly cautious and negative conclusion:

> From most indications, Origen's scholarly and theological interest in Judaism did not betray itself openly in his public disposition towards the Jews. Here Origen's debates with the rabbis over the bible presented less a scholarly exchange of ideas than a platform for mutual disclaimers. Origen's anti-Jewish maneuvers [*sic*] in his homilies and commentaries reflect just this same inflexibility. There was no question here of negotiation in these 'philosophers'' debates. The rabbis' exegetical arguments had to be dismissed *in toto* because Judaism continued to be a viable threat to the Christian mission, a live option for those seeking to be faithful to the tradition of the bible. In this adamant public posture towards Judaism, Origen remained indeed quite typical of the patterns of Christian–Jewish relations in late antiquity.[24]

This more negative assessment of the significance of the influence of Jewish theology on Origen is borne out by another small piece of evidence which seems hitherto to have received no mention. In trying to ascribe the extent of indebtedness, most previous works have attempted to locate the context of Origen in terms of Hellenistic rhetorical practice, the local church–synagogue friction over feast-day observance and the like, or the overarching theological divergences between Christianity and Judaism based on the perennial issues of Christology, Election, Law, and

---

[23] Brooks, 'Straw Dogs and Scholarly Ecumenism', p. 94. He goes on to say (p. 95): 'In an attempt to lay the foundations for modern rapprochement between Jews and Christians, scholars have rendered far too positive an evaluation of Origen's relationship to, and reliance upon, Rabbinism.'

[24] Blowers, 'Origen, the Rabbis and the Bible', p. 116.

Covenant. One picture that formerly emerged from such a synthesis, and still to an extent underlying the image in Blowers's conclusion, though not that of Brooks, was of an Origen who was personally interested in Jewish scholarship, but who presented a more official face, as Christian presbyter in Caesarea, as both a theological and a practical critic of the rival system. The massive extent, however, to which the overall shape of his Jewish apologetic is indebted to Paul might suggest more the image of someone who is more concerned with progressing along in a relatively enclosed system than working by any form of converging dialogue. And it may well be the case that the significance of the points of convergence there are between Origen and the rabbinic interpreters are really provided, by his day, more from the shared Hellenistic hermeneutical method and the partially shared sacred text than from any real ecumenical connection. Such was the conclusion that emerged from an earlier study on Origen's use of the concept of God's Shekinah,[25] and this too is the conclusion suggested by the final exegetical test-case I would like to offer to conclude this paper.

Origen has a phenomenal and encyclopaedic knowledge of the biblical text. He cross-references passages throughout the Scriptures and frequently interprets one text by means of the same or a similar key term that occurs elsewhere. In an age without concordances he demonstrates time and time again how well he knew his sources. In addition, he knew his Pauline literature with the intimate acquaintance of the liturgist and one who had written formal commentaries on most of the Pauline letters. This being so, it is surely indicative, for a revealing indication of how Origen regarded Christianity and Judaism, to look to his overall systematic employment of the primary New Testament materials concerning that theme, and, given Origen's atomistic method, we can best proceed by isolating the textual instances.

This is quite easily accomplished, for there is a very limited number of New Testament texts which engage in a specific apologetic on the relation of Christianity to Judaism, where the two communities start to be more and more understood as different religious entities, moving further away in mutual distinctness. Both sociologically and theologically this systematic separation was not something that happened all over the Hellenistic world at the same time or at a similar pace, but the process is already clearly visible in Acts and the Pauline writings.

There are only eleven texts in Acts that have reference to such an

---

[25] Cf. McGuckin, 'Origen on the Glory of God'.

explicit Jewish–Christian apologetic;[26] to which we can add five more in Hebrews,[27] and, of course, considerable sections, rather than atomistic texts, in the Pauline writings that focus on the issue, particularly Romans, Galatians, and parts of II Corinthians and Colossians. Many of those texts provide the raw building-materials for centuries of subsequent Christian apologetic against Judaism—themes such as the following of the letter that kills, the stubborn refusal to repent, and so forth. It is not our concern here to look at Origen's employment of those themes, but rather to look at the way he chooses to highlight some texts and relegate others from that relatively small body of primary New Testament materials.[28]

Most of the eleven Acts passages gain only a few mentions in Origen's work, running to approximately three citations throughout the *opera*, but two receive a relatively extraordinary amount of attention, being cited ten times each; and of the eleven there are only two which are entirely neglected. What is of significance, however, is that these two passages which he avoids altogether are the only two texts from the whole Acts apologetic in which the privileges of the Jews and their priority in the story of salvation are freely admitted, indeed, positively emphasized.[29] Moreover, the two texts from the eleven, which he chooses to amplify heavily, are the two most negative from that whole list.[30] Both these negative texts seem to have been highly relevant to Origen's own local context, but the stress he puts on them seems to indicate a sense of failed personal contact more than anything else. It is interesting to see how, by what can only be a highly personal combination of amplification and suppression, he has chosen to sharpen the Jewish polemic significantly.

The evidence from Origen's use of Hebrews needs more careful use, since his surviving commentary on Hebrews is now so fragmentary. Nevertheless, Hebrews offers five texts relevant to the Jewish apologetic.[31] Four of them appear to have little or no interest for Origen,[32] but one of them he applies no less than sixty-nine times—so frequently, in fact, that it is clearly a favourite quotation and an abiding theme for him. This text—'Since the Law has no more than a reflection of these realities, and

---

[26] Acts 2. 29; 2. 34; 2. 23; 2. 38; 3. 25; 7. 35; 7. 42; 7. 51–2; 13. 17; 13. 46; 28. 26–8.

[27] Hebrews 3. 3; 7. 12; 7. 18 (none of these three texts is cited in the extant works of Origen); 10. 1 (69 citations by Origen); 12. 24 (1 citation by Origen).

[28] The Origen citation-instances are listed in *Biblia Patristica*, 3, Centre d'Analyse et de Documentation Patristiques (Paris, 1980).

[29] Acts 3. 26; 13. 17.

[30] Acts 7. 51–2; 13. 46.

[31] See n. 26, above.

[32] Hebrews 3. 3; 7. 12; 7. 18 (entirely neglected); and 12. 24 (only 1 citation).

no finished picture of them, it is quite incapable of bringing worshippers to perfection' (Hebrews 10. 1)—once more demonstrates his favourite conception of a Judaism interpreted through a Platonizing hermeneutic.

Origen's use of the numerous Pauline passages dealing with the stature and place of Judaism demonstrates quite decisively that the policy apparent in the treatment of Acts was not accidental. Ten Pauline texts can be isolated which are of interest for our case. These can be further subdivided into two groups. The first group amounts to a total of six Pauline texts[33] where the Apostle, for all his attacks on the Jewish system, speaks with laudatory affection, as we find also in Acts, emphasizing the privileges of Judaism and its priority in the story of salvation—a priority which he argues has not been forgotten by God, despite a new dispensation. These six texts are quite remarkable in tone and demonstrate a genuine personal feeling on the part of the theologian whom Origen regarded as the great example and leader of all those who had been initiated by God's Logos. Origen, however, though he comments heavily on almost every Pauline verse, quite clearly censors all but one of these laudatory texts, and the one exception he makes[34] is the palest and most non-committal of them all, which refers to the Jews as the people to whom the message was sent. This text receives a high average attention, that is, twenty-three citations restricted to his Commentaries on Romans and Matthew alone. But Paul's doctrine of the priority of Israel has quite clearly and deliberately been overlaid.

This interesting bias of his censorship of the laudatory texts is further borne out by looking at which other Pauline texts, of those specifically dealing with the issue of Judaism, Origen most relies on. The picture that emerges reproduces what we saw in his treatment of Acts. There are four such Pauline passages which Origen uses with a high average level of frequency (some 30 to 40 citations each throughout his *opera*). These are Romans 2. 5, on the refusal of the Jews to repent (26 citations); II Corinthians 3. 13–15, on how the Jewish understanding of Scripture is hindered by a veil over their minds (30 citations); Romans 2. 20, on how real circumcision is a matter of the heart not the flesh (32 citations); and Colossians 2. 16–18, on how the observance of festivals is now outmoded and irrelevant (38 citations). Once again all these apologetic concerns fit exactly the third-century Caesarean context, particularly the last, which also evidences Origen's most abundant use. Origen has clearly been ready

---

[33] Romans 1. 17; 3. 2; 9. 3; 10. 1; 12. 15; 12. 28.
[34] Romans 3. 2.

to alter the tenor of St Paul himself, his master theologian, to firm up the apologetic at those instances the Apostle might be seen to have given too much away because of his love and respect for Judaism.

The conclusion that seems to arise from this is that Origen's personal attitude, as well as his professional theological approach to Judaism, might not be in reality as positive as has sometimes been suggested; and that his undoubted knowledge and use of rabbinical exegetical traditions may largely have come to him sporadically and without system, implying that the significance of such dependencies must be questioned. Indeed, the personal reshaping by Origen of the Pauline Jewish apologetic suggests someone whose dialogue with the Jewish tradition in Caesarea had been neither successful nor particularly happy. Perhaps, if it really was Origen who was behind Rabbi Yohanan's testy remark,[35] 'A gentile who studies the Torah deserves capital punishment',[36] then the unhappiness might well have been mutual.

University of Leeds

[35] See Blowers, 'Origen, the Rabbis and the Bible', p. 103.
[36] Mishnah, B. Sanhedrin, 58b.

Excaecati Occulta Justitia Dei: Augustine on Jews and Judaism

PAULA FREDRIKSEN

Seen in the perspective of the *contra Iudaeos* tradition, Augustine emerges as
an idiosyncratic and innovative thinker whose tone when speaking of Jews and
Judaism is exceptionally mild and whose estimate of the Jewish role in history is
surprisingly positive. This essay argues that Augustine's relatively ironic "theology of Judaism" is the measure of his affirmation, against the Manichees, not of
Jews per se, but of the God of Israel. This affirmation drove him ultimately to
affirm, as with divine acceptance of Saul (*ad Simplicianum*) so with divine rejection of carnal Israel (*c. Faustum*), that God is just, though his justice is in
principle hidden, *occultissima*. Against Blumenkranz, the essay concludes that
theological encounters with Manichees, and not social encounters with Jews,
stimulated Augustine's peculiar teaching.

Augustine's vision of the Jews as a living witness to Christian truth was
both original[1] and, compared with his attitude toward pagans and non-
Catholic Christians, uncharacteristically tolerant. Unlike these two other
groups, contemporary Jews, Augustine argued, had a continuing positive

This essay draws on a larger work in progress on Augustine's thought during the
390s. I thank Professors Ora Limor, David Satran and Guy Stroumsa, for providing me
with my first opportunity to present these ideas at a session of the XIIIth World Congress
of Jewish Studies in Jerusalem; and Jeremy Cohen, for inviting me to participate in a
seminar on Christian perspectives on Jews and Judaism held at the Herzog August
Bibliothek in 1993. An earlier version of this essay will appear in the forthcoming
volume from that seminar: *From Witness to Witchcraft: Jews and Judaism in Medieval
Christian Thought*, ed. J. Cohen (Wolfenbüttel: Wolfenbüttler Mittelalterichen-Studien).
Research upon which this essay draws was subvened by the National Endowment for
the Humanities, the Lady Davis Fellowship Trust of the Hebrew University, and by
Boston University: I am most grateful.
    1. Bernhard Blumenkranz, *Die Judenpredigt Augustins* (Paris: Études augusti-
niennes, 1973; orig. pub. 1946), 211. This has proved to be the foundational study of
Augustine's teaching on Jews and Judaism; see also, idem, "Augustin et les juifs: Augustin et le judaïsme," *RA* 1 (1958): 225–41.

Journal of Early Christian Studies 3:3, 299–324 © 1995 The Johns Hopkins University Press

role to play in the story of redemption. Dispersed throughout the earth since the Roman destruction of rebel Jerusalem, their hostile community witlessly preserved the original prophecies to Christ, and thereby testified to Christian truth:

> The Jews who killed him and who refused to believe in him . . . were dispersed all over the world . . . and thus by the evidence of their own Scriptures they bear witness for us that we have not fabricated the prophecies about Christ. . . . It follows that when the Jews do not believe in our Scriptures, their own Scriptures are fulfilled in them, while they read them with blind eyes. . . . It is in order to give this testimony which, in spite of themselves, they supply for our benefit by their possession and preservation of those books, that they themselves are dispersed among all nations, wherever the Christian Church spreads. . . . Hence the prophecy in the Book of Psalms: " . . . Do not slay them, lest at some time they forget your Law; scatter them by your might."[2]

But Augustine's position on contemporary Jews, with its attendant argument for an immunity from religious coercion enjoyed by virtually no other community in post-Theodosian antiquity,[3] had been preceded by an equally novel, and surprisingly positive, evaluation of the Jewish past— both the distant past of the Scriptures, and the more recent past of the transitional generation of Paul, the other apostles, and Jesus himself. These views emerge together with—I will argue in consequence of—the understanding of divine justice and human freedom that Augustine comes to as he learns to read the Bible, and especially the letters of Paul, in new ways in the decade following his conversion.

I propose, then, to account for Augustine's teaching on Jews and Judaism by anchoring it in the biblical hermeneutic that he develops during the 390s. I will trace the evolution of this hermeneutic along a trajectory of his anti-Manichean writings, beginning with the c. *Fortunatum* (392), passing through his early commentaries on Paul (394/5), his radical reassessment of the Pauline dynamics of grace and faith in the *ad Simplicianum* (396) and its autobiographical companion-piece, the *Confessions* (397), and

---

2. Ps 59.10f. in *civ.* 18.46 (CCSL 48.644–45); trans. Henry Bettenson, *The City of God* (Penguin: Harmonsworth, 1972), 828. This argument, with Psalm 59 as prooftext, appears also in *psal.* 58.1.18–2.7 (CCSL 39.743–51); *fid.* 6.9 (CCSL 46.16); and *iud.* 7.9 (PL 42.57).

3. For this legislation, the excellent source compendium by A. Linder, *The Jews in Roman Imperial Legislation* (Detroit: Wayne State Press, 1987); for analysis of its social intent, M. R. Salzman, "The Evidence for the Conversion of the Roman Empire to Christianity in Book 16 of the *Theodosian Code*," *Historia* XLII/3 (1993): 362–78. See, too, the earlier essays by P. Brown, "St. Augustine's Attitude toward Religious Coercion," 260–78; and "Religious Coercion in the Later Roman Empire: The Case of North Africa," 301–331, in *Religion and Society in the Age of Saint Augustine* (New York: Harper & Row, 1972).

ending with his massive refutation of Latin Manichaeism, the *c. Faustum* (398). Finally, I shall close not on a historical point but a historiographical one, suggesting ways in which the work of the great student of Augustine's anti-Jewish polemic, Bernhard Blumenkranz, might be reconsidered.

I

The church that Augustine joined in 387, in Milan, was not the church he joined in 391, when he was inducted into the clergy at Hippo Regius. Milanese Catholicism in the 380s had flourished in the light of Greek philosophical learning.[4] It was here that Augustine encountered the books of the Platonists—Plotinus and Porphyry, in translation—and heard the sermons of Ambrose, who incorporated the Alexandrian allegories of Philo and Origen into his own preaching. The perspective of paideia had finally provided Augustine with a coherent theodicy in answer to Manichaean dualism and moral determinism. God did not create evil, since evil was nothing, an absence rather than a substance, the *privatio boni*. Man sinned not because an evil soul compelled him, but because of a defective movement of his own free will: sin was a choice.[5] In the months following his conversion and, later, baptism, Augustine deployed these arguments to refute the Manichaean explanation of evil, criticizing their philosophical inconsistency (*de ordine*; *de duabus animabus*; *de libero arbitrio* I), their ethics (*de moribus Manichaeorum*), and finally, through philosophical allegory, their reading of Scripture (*de Genesi c. Manichaeos*).

His new arsenal did him little good, however, once he returned home, and became publicly involved in the life of the church. The traditions, temperament, and circumstances of North African Christian culture distinguished it in telling ways from its Italian cousin. Catholics and Donatists alike saw in their respective communities the "church of the martyrs," which they celebrated through public readings of *acta martyrorum* and community-wide *laetitiae*, feasts held over the holy tombs;[6] and both communities

---

4. On the Neoplatonic renaissance of Milan in this period, see esp. the two classic studies by P. Courcelle, *Late Latin Writers and their Greek Sources* (Cambridge: Harvard University Press, 1969) and *Recherches sur les Confessions de Saint Augustin* (Paris: Études augustiniennes, 2ème édition, 1968), esp. 157–67, for a reconstruction of Augustine's reading in the time surrounding his conversion.

5. Cf. Augustine's retrospective description of this moment, *conf.* 5.14.24 the effect of Ambrose's sermons (James J. O'Donnell, *Augustine: Confessions* [Oxford: Clarendon Press, 1992] 1.57); 7.3.4–5 Manichaean theodicy (O'Donnell, 1.74–75); 7.9.13 the *libri platonicorum* (O'Donnell, 1.80).

6. On the African churches' temperamental liaison with the earlier heroic age, A.-G. Hamman, *La vie quotidienne en Afrique du Nord au temps du S. Augustin* (Paris, 1979),

affirmed ancient Christian hopes for the approaching End of Days, with the attendant belief in the fleshly *prima resurrectio* and bodily thousand-year reign of the saints with Christ on earth.[7] African Catholics, Donatists and even Manichees, further, shared a conservative orientation toward biblical texts, preferring regional and traditional Latin renderings and fundamentalist interpretations.[8] The international intellectual culture of Italian Catholicism in its hellenizing mood was of little local consequence.

Augustine discovered this the hard way: in public. In 392, one year after his forced entry into the clergy at Hippo, he was approached by a mixed delegation of Catholics and Donatists. "Distressed by the plague of Manichaeism [which] had taken hold both of citizens and visitors in great numbers," this group requested that he debate a local Manichaean priest, Fortunatus, whom they held responsible for the sect's successes. Augustine

---

318; R. A. Markus, *Saeculum: History and Society in the Theology of S. Augustine* (Cambridge: Cambridge University Press, 1970), 106–109; older and exhaustively documented, P. Monceaux, *Histoire littéraire de l'Afrique chrétienne* (Brussels: Culture et Civilisation, 1966; orig. pub. 1901), 1.28–96. On the cult of the dead, particularly the feasting and drinking associated with it, F. van der Meer, *Augustine the Bishop* (New York: Sheed and Ward, 1961), 471–526; Peter Brown, *Augustine of Hippo* (Berkeley: University of California Press, 1967), 207, 299; idem, *The Cult of the Saints* (Chicago: Chicago University Press, 1981) for the Western churches generally; V. Saxer, *Morts, martyrs, reliques en Afrique chrétienne aux premiers siècles* (Théologie historique, 55. Paris, 1980); W. H. C. Frend, *The Donatist Church* (Oxford: Clarendon Press, 1952), 114, 174; idem, "The North African Cult of the Martyrs," *Jahrbuch für Antike und Christentum* 9 (1982): 154–67.

7. A specifically African chronographical tradition, represented by Julius Africanus in the third century, Lactantius in the fourth, and Augustine's colleague, the bishop Hilarianus in the fifth, all targeted the year C.E. 500 as the 6000th year since the creation of the world, hence the expected time of Christ's Parousia: Julius Africanus, *Chronica* (fragments), in *Reliquae sacrae*, vol. 2, ed. M. J. Routh (Oxford: Clarendon Press, 1846), 238–309; Lactantius, *Divinae Institutiones* 7.24–25 (CSEL 19.658–65); Hilarianus, *de cursu temporum*, in *Chronica minora*, vol. 1, ed. C. Frick (Leipzig, 1892), 155–72. On this chronographical tradition generally, R. Landes, "Lest the Millennium be Fulfilled: Apocalyptic Expectations and the Pattern of Western Chronography," *The Use and Abuse of Eschatology in the Middle Ages*, ed. W. Verbeke, D. Verhelst, and A. Welkenhuysen (Leuven, 1988), 141–208; in the African context in particular, P. Fredriksen, "Apocalypse and Redemption in Early Christianity," *VC* 45 (1991): 151–83, esp. 158ff. and notes 33–38 on the *laetitiae* as the popular expression of this belief.

8. On this aspect of African biblical culture, Brown, *Augustine*, 42f., 136. For the Manichaean use of Scripture, F. Decret, *Aspects du Manichéisme dans l'Afrique romaine* (Paris: Études augustiniennes, 1970), 123–49 (OT) and 151–82 (NT); on local allegiance to Old African translations of the NT, Monceaux, *Histoire littéraire*, 1.136; *retract.* I.21(20).3 (CSEL 36.100), on the variety of African readings. African Catholics, evidently, would have preferred not to switch to Jerome: Aug., *ep.* 71.3.5 (CSEL 34.253) on the near-riot that broke out at a service when the presiding bishop introduced Jerome's translation of Jonah.

consented, and on the 28th and 29th of August, before a "large and interested crowd" of all creeds, he and Fortunatus, a former colleague from his Manichee days in Carthage, met to debate the nature of evil.[9] Practically the entire debate turned upon the interpretation of certain New Testament texts. Fortunatus urged that only a separate and independent malevolent force sufficiently protected God from implication in the problem of evil; that a true physical embodiment of God's son would be both unreasonable and unscriptural; that moral evil is best understood as a battle between contrary natures. Augustine responded continually with the assertion that only *his* God was the consistently philosophical (i.e., impassable) one, and that only the uncoerced movement of a single will sufficiently accounted for sin, since if sin were not voluntary, God would not be just in punishing sinners. Augustine made his case through argument and philosophical tautology;[10] Fortunatus, interestingly, through a near-continuous appeal to Scripture: the Gospels of John (*Fort.* 3) and Matthew (14), and especially the letters of Paul.[11]

Not until the second day of the debate, buffeted by a sudden fusillade from Fortunatus of Matthean and Pauline texts urging the existence of non-moral evil—"for, apart from our bodies, evil things dwell in the whole world" (21)—did Augustine change his tack. He again invoked human will, but this time nuanced the concept by tying the will's operation into two earlier moments: Adam's sin, and the preceding sins of the individual agent. Adam's sin affected all subsequent humanity, and the individual's sin, through the creation of habit, affects all subsequent action.

---

9. Possidius, *vita S. Augustini* 6 (PL 32.38). The topic of the debate is nowhere spelled out, but it seems to have focused on the origin of evil and the respective virtues of Catholic and Manichaean theodicies, *Fort.* 19 (CSEL 25/1.96–97); cf. *Retr.* 1.16(15) (CSEL 36.82–83).

10. E.g.: "God gave man's rational soul free will. For merit is possible only if we do good voluntarily, not neccessarily," *Fort.* 15, to which Fortunatus responds by quoting Eph 2.1–18, Rom 11.1 and Rom 1.1–4 (*Fort.* 16, 17; CSEL 25/1.91–95). All English citations of the *c. Fortunatum* are taken from the translation by A. H. Newman, *Nicene and Post-Nicene Fathers,* First Series, Vol. 4 (Grand Rapids: Wm. B. Eerdmans, no date; orig. pub. 1887), 113–124.

11. Phil in *Fort.* 3; Eph in 17. Fortunatus inadvertently brought the first day of the debate to a close when he concluded his citations with 1 Cor 15.53: "caro et sanguis regnum dei non possidebunt, neque corruptio incorruptelam possidebit." The crowd at this point vociferously intervened, and then broke into various small discussions (19: I think that they objected strongly to Fortunatus' adducing 1 Cor 15.53 against the possibility of both Incarnation and fleshly resurrection; see above, n. 7). When they reconvened the following day, and took up the question why man sins, Fortunatus effortlessly adduced more Scriptural support for his position: Mt 15.13 and 3.10; Rom 8.7; Gal 5.17; Rom 7.23–25; Gal 5.14 (*Fort.* 21; CSEL 25/1.102–103).

I say that there was the free exercise of the will in that man who was first formed. . . . But after he freely sinned, we who descend from his stock were plunged into necessity. . . . For today in our actions, before we are implicated by any habit, we have free choice. . . . But when by that liberty we have done something [evil] . . . and the pleasure of that deed has taken hold on the mind, the mind by its own habit is so implicated that it cannot afterwards conquer what it has fashioned for itself.[12]

By so linking moral choice both to Adam's fall and to the individual's psychological/moral development, Augustine had, de facto, reduced the free operation of the will: these historical events—one distant, one proximate—necessarily impinged. But Augustine was still committed to his fundamental principle: to be justly punishable, sin had to be utterly voluntary, just as did virtue, if it were meritorious. And if "Adam" and "habit" implied that human agents, though culpable, functioned with diminished capacity, then the origins of their condition had to be compatible with the justice of God, the source of their condition. Thus, in the wake of his encounter with Fortunatus, Augustine turned first to Genesis,[13] then again to Paul's letters, to construct an historical and Scriptural understanding of sin and salvation against the Manichees that would neither "seem to condemn the Law [and thus the God who gave it] nor take away man's free will."[14]

To this end, explicitly in his comments of 394, the *Expositio Propositionum ex Epistola ad Romanos*, and implicitly in the other Pauline writings that followed, Augustine worked out a four-stage scheme of history:

12. "Liberum voluntatis arbitrium in illo homine fuisse dico, qui primus formatus est. . . . Postquam autem ipse libera voluntate peccavit, nos in neccessitatem praecipitati sumus, qui ab eius stirpe descendimus. . . . Hodie namque in nostris actionibus antequam consuetudine aliqua implicemur, liberum habemus arbitrium faciendi aliquid, vel non faciendi. . . . Cum autem ista libertate fecerimus aliquid, et facti ipsius tenuerit animam perniciosa dulcendo et voluptas, eadem ipsa sua consuetudine sic implicatur, ut postea vincere non possit, quod sibi ipsa peccando fabricata est," *Fort.* 22 (CSEL 25/1.103–104). NP–NF, 121.

This is an argument for diminished capacity, brought on by the freely willed acts of the individual agent; it is *not* an argument for involuntary sin. Cf. M. Alflatt's two essays, "The Development of the Idea of Involuntary Sin in St. Augustine," *REAug* 20 (1974): 113–34, and "The Responsibility for Involuntary Sin in St. Augustine," *RA* 10 (1975): 170–86; and R. J. O'Connell's recent critique, " 'Involuntary Sin' in the *de libero arbitrio*," *REAug* 37 (1991): 23–36; see also the analysis of this moment in Augustine's theological development in James Wetzel, *Augustine and the Limits of Virtue* (Cambridge: Cambridge University Press, 1992), 86–98.

13. His first, and failed, attempt at a non-allegorical reading of Genesis against the Manichees appeared in 393, the *de Genesi ad litteram imperfectus liber*.

14. *Propp.* 13–18.1. Latin text and English translation in Paula Fredriksen Landes, *Augustine on Romans: Propositions from the Epistle to the Romans; Unfinished Commentary on the Epistle to the Romans* (Chico: Scholars Press, 1982), 5.

ante legem, sub lege, sub gratia, and *in pace*.[15] Earlier, Augustine had divided history into six periods, corresponding to the six days of creation, and the six ages of an individual's life.[16] In that scheme, the six periods corresponded to successive stages in God's dealings with humanity and, specifically, Israel: the first five related to Old Testament times; the sixth, to the period of the New; the seventh would begin with the Second Coming and the millennial rest of the saints. His four-stage model likewise periodized history from humanity before Israel to the second coming of Christ. But these periods also recapitulated the stages of spiritual development for the individual believer. They thus placed at dead center the crucial transition, the moment of conversion, the movement between Stage 2 and 3:

> *Ante legem*, we pursue fleshly concupiscence; *sub lege*, we are pulled by it; *sub gratia*, we neither pursue nor are pulled by it; *in pace* there is no concupiscence of the flesh. . . . Thus [under grace] we still have desires, but, by not obeying them, we do not allow sin to reign in us (Rom 6.12). These desires arise from the mortality of the flesh, which we bear from the first sin of the first man, whence we are born fleshly (*carnaliter*). They thus will not cease save at the resurrection of the body. . . . Then there will be perfect peace, when we are established in the fourth stage.[17]

Scriptural history and the individual's experience coincide at their shared extremes: birth in Adam, eschatological transformation in Christ. Augustine thus expanded on the one biblical theme that he had sounded against Fortunatus: the price for Adam's sin paid by all humanity in the moral and physical lability of flesh (*Fort.* 22). But his new schema also united salvation history into a single, telescoped development: the Law of the Old Testament *is the same* as the Law of Christ; the Christian who serves the Law of sin is in *the same moral position* as the Jew (*Propp.* 52). God's work of redemption is thus continuous from the foundation of

15. *Propp.* 13–18.2 (Landes ed., 4); cf. qu. 66–68 of *quaest.*, which I would date after the works on the epistles (CCSL 44A.150–83); *ad Simplicianum* I.1 treats the first and second stages, before and under the law; I.2, the moment of transition, when man passes *sub lege* to *sub gratia*. For a detailed consideration of the argument of these treatises, Paula Fredriksen, "Beyond the Body/Soul Dichotomy: Augustine on Paul against the Manichees and the Pelagians," *RA* 23 (1988): 87–114, esp. 89–93.

16. *Gen. Man.* I.23.35–24.42 (PL 34.190–93); cf. *ver. rel.* 26.49 (CCSL 32.218–19); qu. 58.2 (CCSL 44A.99–101). Augustine never abandons the seven-stage scheme, though he interprets it variously. It reappears shortly after these commentaries, in *Faust.* 12.8 (CSEL 25/1.336); and structures the finale of the huge *City of God*, 22.30 (CSEL 48.862–66). On this earlier period, the fundamental essay by F. E. Cranz, "The Development of Augustine's Ideas on Society before the Donatist Controversy," *HTR* 47 (1954): 255–316; on such schemes and their place in Christian theology, A. Luneau, *Histoire du Salut chez les Pères de l'Église: La Doctrine des âges du monde* (Paris, 1964).

17. *Propp.* 13–18.2 and 10 (Landes ed., 5, 7).

Israel—indeed, from Creation itself—through the coming of Christ and the establishment of his church. This is a radical and original response to the Manichaean critique and repudiation of the Old Testament.

How, then, the transition from law to grace? "One must take care," cautions Augustine, "lest he think that these words deny our free will, for it is not so."[18] The key, he insists, lies precisely in man's will. Insufficient to prevent sin, man's will can at least prompt him, *sub lege*, to turn in faith to Christ and implore his aid (44.3). Receiving grace through faith, man then moves *sub gratia*. The motor of this movement is the will.[19]

But is man really so free? What about God's choice of Jacob over Esau, "which moves some people to think that the Apostle Paul has done away with the freedom of the will" (60.2; cf. Rom 9.11–13)? What about Pharaoh: how free was he after God hardened his heart (Rom 9:17)? In response, Augustine adduces a line from Matthew's gospel: "Many are called, but few are chosen" (Mt 22.14; *Propp.* 55.1–2). God justly distinguishes between those he calls and those he chooses by his inerrant foreknowledge. God foreknows the movements of the human heart; he foresees who will respond freely with *bona voluntas* to his *vocatio*. The reward to the man of good will is to be called so that he receives faith as a gift.

Thus God chose Jacob, whom he foreknew would respond to his call, which Esau would spurn. So too Pharaoh, whose heart God justly hardened as punishment for foreknown infidelity (55.2–5). God is just; he is neither arbitrary nor ineluctable; he distinguishes between those whom he calls and those whom he chooses justly, on the basis of merit, the merit of faith freely willed. *Non opera sed fides inchoat meritum* (62.9).

I review Augustine's position in such detail because it erodes so entirely over the course of the next eighteen months. Between the composition of the *Propositiones* and the completion of qu. 1 of his response to Simplicianus, Augustine returned repeatedly to Paul's letters, to the episodes in Genesis they evoked—Adam's sin, the choice of Jacob over Esau, the hardening of Pharaoh—and to the points of principle of a Catholic theodicy vis-à-vis Manichaean dualism. These issues remain paramount, his

---

18. *Propp.* 44.1 (Landes ed., 17).

19. "Quod autem ait: *Non enim quod volo, hoc ago, sed quod odi, illud facio. Si autem quod nolo, hoc facio, consentio legi, quoniam bona est,* satis quidem lex ab omni criminatione defenditur, sed cavendum ne quis arbitretur his verbis auferri nobis liberum voluntatis arbitrium, quod non ita est. Nunc enim homo describitur sub lege positus ante gratiam. Tunc enim peccatis vincitur, dum viribus suis iuste vivere conatur sine adiutorio liberantis gratiae dei. In libero autem arbitrio habet, ut credat liberatori et accipiat gratiam, ut iam illo, qui eam donat, liberante et adiuvante non peccet atque ita desinat esse sub lege, sed cum lege vel in lege implens eam caritate dei, quod timore non poterat," *Propp.* 44.1–3 (Landes ed., 16).

commitment to the uncoerced nature of sin as unambiguous as ever. Yet in 396, Augustine executed a dazzling exegetical *volte-face*: man's will itself, he then argued—not just the will to fulfill the Law, but the good will with which man might choose to greet God's call—is from God. The initiative of conversion lies entirely outside the individual:

> For the good will does not precede the calling, but the calling precedes the good will. The fact that we have a good will is rightly attributed to God who calls us. . . . So the sentence, "It is not him who wills nor him who runs but God who has mercy" cannot be taken simply to mean that we cannot attain what we wish without the aid of God; but rather that, without his calling, *we cannot even will.*[20]

Restat ergo voluntates eliguntur. Election, Augustine concludes, is *entirely unmerited.* He makes this case in the *ad Simplicianum* especially by focusing on the solidarity of the race in Adam. Since Eden, all humanity is part of the *massa damnata*, literally the "lump of perdition": damnation is all anybody deserves. From this *massa* God mysteriously, and in complete freedom, chooses whomever he wishes: the initiative is solely and totally his.[21]

The torturous intricacy of Augustine's reasoning in the *ad Simplicianum*, the startling novelty of its conclusion, and its significance as a turning point in his understanding of Paul, are well known to students of Augustine's thought. But this treatise also marks the beginning of a new hermeneutical and theological trajectory—how to read the Bible and what it means—that leads to his teaching on Jews and Judaism. This becomes clearer if we attend to two aspects of the treatise's concluding argument: Augustine's views on divine justice and the radical nature of divine freedom, on the one hand; and his presentation of human freedom at the conversion of Saul, on the other.

How are humans to understand God's justice? In 394, in his unfinished commentary on Romans begun shortly after the *Propositiones*, Augustine had argued that divine justice transcended human precisely because God's mercy was incomparably greater. For this reason, man should never despair of gaining God's pardon, since God pardons much more readily and fully than do men. On the basis of this understanding, Augustine had

---

20. "Et enim quia non praecedit voluntas bona vocationem, sed vocatio bonam voluntatem, propterea vocanti Deo recte tribuitur quod bene volumus, nobis vero tribui non potest quod vocamur. Non igitur ideo dictum putandum est, *Non volentis neque currentis, sed miserentis est Dei*, quia nisi eius adiutorio non possumus adipisci quod volumus, sed ideo potius quia nisi eius vocatione non volumus," *Simpl.* 1.2.12 (CCSL 44.37); transl. John H. S. Burleigh, *Augustine: Earlier Writings* (Philadelphia: Westminister Press, 1953), 395.

21. Fredriksen, "Body/Soul," 96, for discussion of the *massa* and the way it transmutes in the Pauline works that cluster in the mid-390s.

defined the "sin against the Holy Spirit which can never be forgiven" as despair (cf. Mt 12.31–32). If one despairs of divine forgiveness, he has no motivation for repentance; if he does not repent, he cannot reform, and so he continues to sin. To be driven by this hopeless despair, then, to so profoundly misunderstand the nature of divine mercy, hence justice, "is to resist the grace and peace of God."[22]

If arguments can have opposites, then Augustine in 396, concluding his response to Simplicianus, had reversed his position entirely. Divine justice, such a brief time earlier seen as incomparable to human justice on account of God's great mercy, Augustine now held to be incomprehensible in its very operation. God is not required to be merciful; all humankind has been justly condemned, and all are bound, justly, into the Adamic equalizer of the species, the *massa damnata*. That God chooses to remit punishment to anyone at all is a great mystery. There must be some principle of differentiation, since God does make choices. But, Augustine concluded, again citing Paul, the reasons for his choices are unfathomable in principle: "Inscrutable are his judgments, and his ways past finding out" (Rom 11.33, at 1.2.16). Augustine, in short, abandoned any thought of God as an exemplar of justice. Piety demands that man—on precious little evidence—believe that God judges by some standard of equity; but that standard of equity, hidden from human understanding, is *occultissima*.[23]

---

22. "Quid aliud restat nisi ut peccatum in spiritum sanctum, quod neque in hoc saeculo neque in futuro dimitti dominus dicit, nullum intelligatur nisi perseverantia in nequitia et in malignitate cum desperatione indulgentiae dei? Hoc est enim gratiae illius et paci resistere. . . ." *Epistolae ad Romanos Inchoata Expositio* 22.3–4, also 7; cf. 14.1, and the concluding passage of this treatise in 23.13 regarding those who "continue in their sins with despairing and impious stubbornness" (Landes ed., 86, 70, 89).

23. Augustine again quotes Paul, criticizing those who cannot bear this seeming arbitrariness—O homo tu quis es (Rom 9.20)—and then concludes this passage: "Sic enim respondet Deo, cum ei displicet quod de peccatoribus conqueritur Deus, quasi quemquam Deus peccare cogat, cum ipse neminem peccare cogat, sed tantummodo quibusdam peccantibus misericordiam justificationis suae non largiatur, et ob hoc dicatur obdurare peccantes quosdam, quia non eorum miseretur, non quia impellit ut peccent. Eorum autem non miseretur, quibis misericordiam non esse praebendam, *aequitate occultissima et ab humanis sensibus remotissima judicat*," 1.2.16 (CCSL 44.42). Cf. his comment on precisely this verse, regarding God's hardening of Pharaoh, in qu. 68.4 of *quaest.*, written between the commentaries and *Simpl.*: "Prorsus cuius vult miseretur, et quem vult obdurat; sed haec voluntas Dei injusta esse non potest. Venit enim de *occultissimis meritis*; quia et ipsi peccatores cum propter generale peccatum unam massam fecerint, non tamen nulla est inter illos diversitas" (CCSL 44A.179–80).

This same defense of God's inscrutability in the face of the challenge of evil, by allusion to Paul's metaphor of the pot challenging the potter in Romans 9, had also occurred in the course of Augustine's debate in 392; but there it had been invoked by Fortunatus (*Fort.* 26; CSEL 25/1.109).

The way that Augustine illustrates his point about divine inscrutability—God's radical moral freedom (from the human point of view) to choose whom he will—is the second interesting aspect of this treatise's finale. Augustine turns, again, to Paul. But for the first time Paul provides something other than the occasion for exegesis: he stands as a concrete historical example[24] of the way that God, in his freedom, works:

> What did Saul will but to attack, seize, bind and slay Christians? What a fierce, savage, blind will was that! Yet he was thrown prostrate by one word from on high, and a vision came to him whereby his mind and will were turned from their fierceness and set on the right way towards faith so that, suddenly, from a marvelous persecutor of the Gospel a more marvelous preacher was made. What then shall we say? . . . "Is there unrighteousness with God? God forbid!"[25]

Paul's personal history could not be accommodated to Augustine's earlier construal of the movement *sub lege* to *sub gratia*, which in the *Propositiones* he had argued turned upon God's foreknowledge of the individual's *bona voluntas*. Saul had had no preceding good will: a ruthless and unconflicted persecutor—indeed, a murderer—he had liked his work. Presumably, on the basis of prior record, Saul would have declined God's call if he could have.[26] Yet God, irresistibly, chose him anyway. Perhaps it did not seem fair, but there it was. Who was man to answer back to God?

The exegetical tour de force of *ad Simplicianum* qu. I ends abruptly on this moment of conversion, Saul into Paul, constructed not exegetically (as in the Romans commentaries of 394/5) but historically. And this ending, in turn, serves as a condensed paradigm for the narrative argument of the work that immediately followed, and followed from, it: the story of the "historical" Augustine as presented in the *Confessions* (397).[27] The *Con-*

24. References to Paul's conversion as depicted in Acts suddenly appear and cluster in the works of the 390s. See the *mémoire de licence* of Guy LeRoy, "Ac. 9 dans la prédication de Saint Augustin," Institut d'études théologiques, section fracophone (Bruxelles, 1986), esp. the charts on 17–21; also L.C. Ferrari, "Saint Augustine on the Road to Damascus," *Aug. Stud.* 13 (1982): 151–70, esp. 156–68.

25. *Simpl.* 1.2.22 (CCSL 44.55); Burleigh, 406.

26. Cf. *Inch. Exp.* 9.3: illi . . . qui vocantem deum non spreverunt (Landes ed., 62). By implication, some *could* choose to spurn God's call; see also qu. 68,4–5. Augustine later does not hesitate to speak of Paul as having been coerced, *serm.* 24.7; de *correctione donatistarum* (*ep.* 185) 6.21 (where Christ, not God, does the forcing).

27. The opening passage of the *Confessions* concludes with an allusion to Paul, 1.1.1: "Invocat te, domine, fides mea, quam dedisti mihi, quam inspirasti mihi per humanitatem filii tui, per ministerium *praedicatoris tui*"; cf. 10.23.34, where Paul is "homo tuus verum *praedicans*" (O'Donnell ed., 1.3, 133); *Simpl.* 1.2.22, "repente ex evangelii mirabili persecutore mirabilior *praedicator* effectus est" (CCSL 44.55). Cf. Wetzel's

fessions is the most idiosyncratic, original and creative of Augustine's anti-Manichaean polemics;[28] and it represents the substantiation of his new understanding of Paul, of grace, sin, and will, by his applying the theological argument of the *Simpl.* to the data of his own past.[29]

If the *Confessions* can be seen as a symphony in three movements—autobiographical (Books 1–9), epistemological (10, on knowledge, time, memory, and the Church), and exegetical (11–13 are an allegorical reading of the first thirty-one verses of Genesis)—the human experience of opacity threads like a minor-key theme throughout the whole. Its expression in Augustine's depiction of his own past, the narrative of 1–9, is the most accessible and in many ways the most poignant.[30] The inscrutable God of the *ad Simplicianum,* who gave grace to the unrepentant Saul and who hated Esau when Esau was still in the womb, is the God who had eluded Augustine throughout the latter's searches for him, the God who failed to respond clearly even once Augustine was intellectually and morally convinced of the truth of the Catholic Church.[31] And Augustine's experience of God's opacity within his own history is terrifyingly duplicated in his experience of himself, and thus of everyone: because of the great sin that marks the beginning of history,[32] man can neither know nor control himself. The spirit wars against the flesh, habit disorders love, compulsion governs desire, the will itself is divided. Consequently, as Augustine illustrates by examples from his own past, man fails to understand

---

close analysis of Augustine's parallel arguments between Paul's history and his own, *Augustine and Virtue,* 169–73.

28. See O'Donnell's remarks, *Augustine, Confessions,* 1.xlix and n. 97; also Wetzel, *Augustine and Virtue,* 138–60.

29. For the position that this retrospect created these data, Ferrari, "Augustine on the Road . . . ," 168–70; more conservatively, I have concluded that Augustine's new perspective on Paul led him to revise (in the literal sense: to see again) his own experience "Paul and Augustine: Conversion Narratives, Orthodox Traditions, and the Retrospective Self," *JTS* 37 (1986): 3–34, esp. 21 and 24; also Wetzel, *Augustine and Virtue,* 191–97.

30. Though the theme marks the whole. Book 10 poses the problem of how we know what we (think we) know, working from sense-knowledge to purely intellectual knowledge, and emotional knowledge as memory; 11–13, the difficulty of knowing God for time-bound human consciousness, and the ways the Church allays this. On these complex closing books, O'Donnell, *Confessions,* 1.xl.

31. Augustine is intellectually ready for Catholicism by Book 7; the problem of evil, and of appreciating Scripture, had been resolved. See O'Donnell's remarks, *Confessions,* xxxvii–xli.

32. Evoked immediately in the opening lines of Book 1: "et laudare te vult homo, aliqua portio creaturae tuae, et homo circumferens *mortalitatem suam,* circumferens *testimonium peccati* et testimonium quia superbis resistis," (O'Donnell ed., 3).

both his interior life and his exterior experience. The self, like God, is hidden from the self.[33]

In the five years between his debate with Fortunatus and the appearance of the *Confessions*, Augustine had repeatedly tried to construct a reading of Paul against the dualism, moral determinism, and Scriptural criticism of the Manichees. Against their dualism, Augustine had always insisted on one God, the God of both Old Testament and New; but now, post-396, this God's ways, to time-bound humans, were unknowable in principle, opaque. Against their moral determinism, he continued to insist that sin, to be justly punishable, could only be voluntary. But human will, in his new view, was so divided and its motivations so obscure that it was utterly, radically dependent on grace. His arguments are superior to those of the Manichees, but this victory has a Pyrrhic quality. His response to Manichaean readings of the Bible, however, is haunted by no such *tristesse*.

Augustine had begun his assault on the Manichaean understanding of the Old Testament back in 389, while still in Italy, with a philosophically allegorical interpretation of the first two chapters of Genesis, *de Genesi contra Manichaeos*. Evidently dissatisfied with this line of approach, he later began, and soon abandoned, a more historical reading, the *de Genesi ad litteram imperfectus liber* (c. 393). Two events in the 390s then conspired to set Augustine along a new path: the Origenist controversy, which cast a pale of suspicion over the use of philosophical allegory as a technique of Scriptural exegesis, exploded in the Latin West;[34] and Augustine read Tyconius.[35]

33. On this opacity of God and of personal experience, Fredriksen "Apocalypse and Redemption," 164–66.

34. The Origenist controversy in the West formally begins in 398, with Rufinus' translation in Rome of the *Peri Archon*. Rufinus translated his commentary on Romans in 404, and continued with the project of putting Origen into Latin until his death in 410. On the convulsions in fourth/fifth century Latin theology occasioned by this controversy, see the rich study by Elizabeth A. Clark, *The Origenist Controversy: The Social Construction of an Early Christian Debate* (Princeton: Princeton University Press, 1993), 194–244.

These dates put the full outbreak of the controversy a little late for our period. Enough of Augustine's argument in the later sections of *de libero arbitrio* (completed in 395), however, speaks against Origen's in the *Peri Archon* to allow me to suspect that rumors of Origen's (now unacceptable) positions were circulating well prior to Rufinus' translations. Cf. *lib.* 3.23.68 and *PA* 1.8.1, on the sufferings of infants; *lib.* 3.5.16 against psychic transformation into lower bodies and *PA* 1.7.4; *lib.* 3.20.56–21.59 on theories of the soul's origins and *PA* 1. praef. 4.

35. Our surest date for Augustine's reading of Tyconius comes in his enthusiastic review of the *liber regularum* in *ep.* 41, to Aurelius of Carthage, written in 396. I have argued, on the basis of correspondences between Tyconius' argument on Paul in *lib. reg.*

The encounter with Tyconius was decisive.[36] In his handbook on Scriptural exegesis, the *liber regularum*, Tyconius had laid out rules for finding one's way through "the immense forest of prophecy" that depended on the use of typology. Typology is allegory: It says that Datum A prefigures or finds its meaning in Datum B. But it is allegory with a difference: it historicizes what is figured. The "future" and spiritually realized meaning of an interpreted event neither denies nor eviscerates the historical givenness of that event.[37] Further, Tyconius emphasized the continuity of biblical salvation history, disowning any sharp rupture between Old Dispensation and New. The Law *is* the Bible, and thus the Law encompasses God's promises; the Law speaks both to the period of Israel and to the age of the Church. Both Law and promise obtain at all times, and the Law works in the predestined to arouse faith.[38] Finally, focusing especially on Paul,[39] Tyconius interpreted the history of salvation as a process as much interior as linear. The subtle and mysterious interplay of grace, free will and divine foreknowledge, he argued, are constant across nations, times, and individuals; whether for Jacob or the generation in Babylon, for Paul or the contemporary believer, they remain the same.[40]

The constancy of the way that God works in history, the religious validity of the Law, the historical integrity of events in the biblical past—these

---

3 and Augustine's in *Propp.*, that we can date Tyconius' influence to 394, the year Augustine writes his Pauline commentaries: see Fredriksen, "Apocalypse and Redemption," 163 and n. 54. Cited here is F. C. Burkitt's text, edited in 1894, as reproduced in the edition and translation by William S. Babcock, *Tyconius: The Book of Rules* (Atlanta: Scholars Press, 1989).

36. The classic study is A. Pincherle, *La formazione teologica di Sant'Agostino* (Rome: Edizioni Italiane, 1947), 175ff.; see also W. S. Babcock, "Augustine's Interpretation of Romans (A.D. 394–96)," *Aug. Stud.* 10 (1979): 55–74; my earlier essays "Body/Soul Dichotomy," 99–101, and "Apocalypse and Redemption," 157–64.

37. On Tyconian typology, "Apocalypse and Redemption," 158–60.

38. Thus, in a dazzling conflation of Genesis, Galatians and Romans, Tyconius characterizes the man who loves God as one who serves the Law not out of fear but love, like Isaac, the son of the free woman, "qui non accepit servitutis in timorem sed adoptionem filiorum clamantem Abba, pater'" *lib. reg.* 3 (Babcock ed., 44). Cf. Augustine's equally dazzingly conflation of Genesis (the creation of lights in the firmament) and Acts (the creation of the Church at Pentecost): "ecce enim tamquam deo dicente, 'fiant luminaria in firmamento caeli', factus est subito de caelo sonus, quasi ferretur flatus vehemens, et visae sunt linguae divisae quasi ignis, qui et insedit super unumquemque illorum, et facta sunt luminaria in firmamento caeli verbum vitae habentia," *conf.* 13.19.25 (O'Donnell ed., 193).

39. Esp. in Book 3, *de promissis et lege*.

40. In Book 3, Tyconius continuously weaves together verses from the Pauline epistles and from the Old Testament, arguing that Israel's faith was always continuous with the gospel: "Lex inquam fidei erat demonstratrix. . . . Iusti enim Israhel ex fide in eandem fidem vocati sunt." See Babcock's remarks, *Tyconius*, 29 n. 1.

are the core convictions, articulated exegetically, that Augustine discovered in and took over from Tyconius. They turned him toward sacred history, the record of saving events in the Biblical past as the place where divine activity would be most clearly perceived. They contoured the way that Augustine grappled with his increasing sense of God's moral unknowableness, both with respect to the divine choices narrated in Romans 9, and with his retrospective assessment of the ways that God had acted in his own past, and especially in his own conversion.[41] Finally, they compelled his construction of a biblical hermeneutic against the Manichees that is marked by an historical simplicity and an historical realism. We see this most clearly in the huge work of anti-Manichaean polemic that followed the *Confessions*, the *contra Faustum*; and it is there as well that we can see the ways that Augustine's historicizing hermeneutic affected his understanding of Jews and Judaism.

II

"Contra Faustum manichaeum blasphemantem legem et prophetas et eorum Deum et incarnationem Christi; scripturas autem novi testamenti quibus convincitur falsatas esse dicentem, scripsi grande opus."[42] Since the *c. Faustum* is a work of Scriptural reclamation, references to Jews lie scattered throughout its thirty-three books. Of particular concern to us are Books 12 and 13, on the prophets. We can best appreciate their argument, and the consequences of Augustine's historical understanding of Scripture for his teaching on Jews and Judaism, if we view these books, briefly, from the perspective of two earlier writings likewise directed against Christian dualists: Justin Martyr's *Dialogue with Trypho* (c. 150) and Tertullian's *adversus Marcionem* (207).

Justin in his dialogue had championed an allegorical understanding of the Septuagint directed against the views of his Jewish interlocutor, Trypho; but in the immediate ideological background of his presentation stood his Christian competition, Marcion and Valentinus.[43] These men, complained Justin, denied that God the Father of Jesus had anything to do with God the Creator in Genesis, whom they identified and repudiated as

---

41. Which is to say, through the generation of historical narrative, whether of Saul's conversion (derived largely from Acts 9) or of his own; Fredriksen, "Paul and Augustine: Conversion Narratives," 23ff.

42. *Retr.* 2.7.1 (CCSL 57.95).

43. Invoked obliquely as the dialogue gets underway in ch. 11; specifically repudiated in ch. 35. The Greek text with facing French translation is available in G. Archambault, *Justin, Dialogue avec Tryphon*, 2 vols. (Paris, 1909).

the God of the Jews. Tertullian argued directly against Marcion; and in Book III of his treatise, excoriating the docetic Christology that cohered with the dualist position, he leaned heavily on Justin's work.[44]

Both authors strained to rehabilitate the Jewish Scriptures in the face of the dualist critique while reclaiming them interpretively for their own church. To this end, they relied on the twin tools of polemic and allegory. Thus, argued Justin (and, following him, Tertullian), the Jews had always understood their Scriptures literally, which is to say, carnally; attending to God's instruction, they had supposed that he wanted his commandments literally fulfilled. Not so. The true import of the Law was always exclusively allegorical, hence spiritual, but the Jews had never realized this. True circumcision is of the heart's foreskin (*Trypho* 18, and frequently); the true sabbath is the Sabbath in Christ (12). The Law was actually given because of Jewish hardness of heart (18, 21, 22, 27, and frequently). In fact, the God who appears throughout the Jewish Scriptures cannot have been the High God, God the Father: that would be unphilosophical.[45] Rather, the God who appeared to Abraham at Mamre and Jacob at Jabbok was the *heteros theos*, the pre-incarnate Christ; and the Jews, failing to grasp his true identity, consequently misunderstood their own Scriptures (56–62; 126–27)—"rather, not yours, but ours" (29). Thus, since Jews denied that the Christ has come, they share their poison with dualist heretics, whose docetic Christology amount to the same thing (*adv. Marc.* 3.8).

Augustine's opponent, Faustus, was the fourth-century avatar of these second-century dualists; and on many points of doctrine—docetic Christology, repudiation of Jewish Scriptures, divorce of God the Father of Jesus from the lower material realm—Marcion and the Manichees agreed. But Justin and Tertullian, in refuting these points, had placed the Old Testament in an ironic double context. In their view, the Law, embraced by the Jews as a blessing, had actually been intended as a curse. Literal obedience

44. I have used the edition by E. Evans, *Tertullian, Adversus Marcionem*, 2 vols. (Oxford, 1972); see esp. his useful introductions, both on Marcion, and on Tertullian's use of sources, 1.ix–xx.

45. It was a principle of Platonic (and later platonizing) philosophy that the High God was absolutely impassive, perfect, and without change: indeed, these aspects are essentially synonymous. According to Justin, God is "that which always maintains the same nature, and in the same manner, and is the cause of all other things," *Trypho* 3. Two centuries later, the pagan Sallustius opined similarly: "All God is good, free from passion, free from change," *On the Gods and the World* 1. This definition of God, which commanded the intellectual allegiance of the well educated in antiquity whether pagan, Jewish, or Christian, sat poorly astride the active deity depicted in the narratives of the Septuagint (cf. Philo's *de opificio mundi*, where intermediaries, whether angels or the Logos, do a lot of the work). Justin's pre-incarnate Christ protects God the Father from too direct an involvment with time, hence change.

to God's commands was the last thing that God had wanted, and the last thing Jews would have done had they truly understood the Law. Israel was not, and never had been, the Jews, but whether before or after Christ's incarnation had always been the Church. Thus these theologians refuted their opponents' docetic Christology; but in so doing, they created a docetic history.

Such an ironic double context, Augustine felt, undermined the authority of Scripture, and so played into Manichee hands. Thus when Jerome, in his commentary on Galatians, suggested that Paul's falling-out with Peter over the issue of judaizing (Gal 2) had actually been a pretense enacted for the edification of their audience, Augustine insisted that the text must be read literally, as the accurate report of a true disagreement.[46] So too with the text of the Jewish Scriptures: they could fortify Christian faith and yet still be read—indeed, must be read—in a straightforward, literal way.

We see the fruit of such a reading in the *c. Faustum*. The Jews, like the Manichees, may read the Law with "a veil drawn over their hearts" (2 Cor 3.15); but the Law itself, Augustine urged, had been intended and received as a good thing—otherwise, how could Paul have praised Israel for having it?[47] The Jews had been right to practice the Law "literally": the fault lay not with their observance, but with their failure to realize when the things the Law pointed forward to had been realized in Christ (12.9). They are like Cain who, once asked his brother's whereabouts, pled ignorance: "And what answer can the Jews give even today, when we ask them with the voice of God—that is, sacred Scripture—about Christ, except that they do not know the christ that we speak of?" What might have been the opportunity for an ugly charge of deicide instead becomes an elaborate ecclesial metaphor:

> Then God says to Cain, "What have you done? The voice of your brother's blood cries from the ground." So the voice of God in the Holy Scriptures accuses the Jews. For the blood of Christ has a loud voice on the earth, when the responsive Amen of those who believe in Him comes from all the nations. This is the voice of Christ's blood, because the clear voice of the faithful redeemed by His blood is the voice of the blood itself.[48]

---

46. See on this point his *Sermo super verbis Apostoli ad Galatas*, preached in 397, and recently edited by François Dolbeau in *Revue Bénédictine* 102 (1992): 52–63; see too Dolbeau's remarks, and his review of the controversy with Jerome, 45–49. "[Augustin] ne modifia nullement ses positions, de peur de laisser une porte ouverte aux critiques scriptuaires des Manichéens," 48 (cf. Augustine's especially clear statement to this effect, *ep.* 82.6). While earlier in their correspondence, Jerome and Augustine differed on the implications of lying (*epp.* 28, 40), their final salvos (*epp.* 75 and 82) are much concerned with the theological status of Jewish Law and custom.

47. *Faust.* 12.3–4; Rom 9.4.

48. " 'Dicit Deus Cain: Quid fecisti? Vox sanguinis fratris tui clamat ad me de terra.'

Augustine proceeds to find typological resonances between figures or events in the Jewish Scriptures and in the life of Christ and the teachings of his Church. Thus Noah saved his family by water and wood, as Christ did also (baptism and crucifixion). The dimensions of the ark, through a Christian gematria, conform to precise aspects of doctrine (12.14). The variety of animals saved from the flood recalls the variety of nations saved in the Church (12.15). The waters came seven days after Noah entered the ark; Christians hope for salvation in the seventh day, the sabbath rest of the saints. Abraham left his country and kindred; so Christ, going out from his Jewish patrimony, extended his power among the Gentiles. Isaac carried the wood for his sacrifice, Christ for his. Christ recalls the angel at Jabbok, the stone under Jacob's head; the evangelists, the angels ascending and descending the ladder (12.26). The parallels go on and on.

Augustine, through this typological reading, clearly savored the Christian significance of these biblical episodes; but he likewise insisted upon their historical and social reality. Thus he taunted Faustus: "Everyone must be impressed. . . . For although God is the God of all nations, even the Gentiles acknowledge him to be in a peculiar sense the God of Israel" (12.24). The salvation wrought by God is continuous between the two dispensations: "The same law that was given by Moses became grace and truth in Jesus Christ" (22.6). Christ's bride is the Church, but his mother is the Synagogue (12.8). Fleshly circumcision typologically embodied nothing less than the resurrection of Christ, and thus the redemption of all who believe (19.9).[49]

This same historical realism, and a sure pastoral sense, marks as well Augustine's discussion of the Torah-observant first generation of Christians: they were brought to change their hereditary customs only by degrees. Some, like Timothy, even chose to conform fully to the ancient practices: no reason he should not (*non prohiberentur*, 19.17). This Jewish-Christian generation understood that these ordinances had pointed forward to and found their fulfillment in Christ. Forcing observance on Gentiles not brought up in these customs would have been confusing and counterproductive, and Paul rightly reprimanded Peter on precisely this point. But this unique Jewish generation, the font of the Church, was right

---

Sic arguit in scripturis sanctis vox divina Iudaeos. Habet enim magnam vocem Christi sanguis in terra, cum eo accepto ab omnibus gentibus respondetur, Amen. Haec est clara vox sanguinis, quam sanguinis, ipse exprimit ex ore fidelium eodem sanguine redemptorum," 12.10 (CSEL 25/1.339). All English translations are based on the version by Richard Stothert, *Nicene and Post-Nicene Fathers*, First Series, 4.155–345.

49. Cf. Justin, *Trypho* 16–17, where circumcision functions as a way to identify and so victimize Jews in order to punish them for deicide.

to cease the *actio prophetica* (as Augustine strikingly characterized Torah-observance) only gradually once the prophecy, through Christ's coming, had been fulfilled, "lest by compulsory abandonment it should seem to be condemned rather than closed" (19.17).[50]

Thus, in Augustine's perspective, Jewish practice and tradition had a certain religious and historical integrity of their own. Biblical Jews, and even the Jews of the apostolic generation, had been right to observe the ordinances of the good Law given by God to Israel through Moses at Sinai. But Augustine's Jewish contemporaries continued to cling to these practices long after their purpose, through Christ, had been fulfilled, and thus as a community they denied and defied not only the universal Church, but divine intention. What of them?

Precisely because of the integrity of their religious identity, argued Augustine, contemporary Jews performed a unique, and uniquely important, service of witness for the Church. They are a *scriniaria*, a "desk for Christians, bearing the Law and the Prophets, testifying to the doctrine of the Church" by disclosing in the letter what Christians honor in the sacrament.[51] So replete with Christian referents are the Jewish Scriptures that believers might fear an outside sceptic would suspect that Christians made these writings up *ex eventu*, were it not for the Jews who, like servants, carry these books for the church: "From the Jewish manuscripts we prove that these things were not written by us to suit the event, but were long ago published and preserved as prophecies in the Jewish nation" (13.10).

> It is a great confirmation of our faith that such important testimony is borne by enemies. The believing Gentiles cannot suppose these testimonies to Christ to be recent forgeries; for they find them in books held sacred for so many ages by those who crucified Christ, still venerated by those who daily blaspheme Him. . . . The unbelief of the Jews has been made of signal benefit to

---

50. "Sed posteaquam in unum Apostoli congregati, etiam consilio suo censuerunt Gentes ad huiusmodi opera Legis non esse cogendas; displicuit quibusdam ex circumcisione Christianis, non valentibus mente discernere, illos solos ab huiusmodi observationibus non fuisse prohibendos, quos fides quae revelata est his iam imbutos invenerat; ut in eis iam consummaretur ipsa actio prophetica, quos ante adimpletionem prophetiae iam tenuerat, ne si et ab ipsis removeretur, improbata potius quam terminata videretur. . . . Prima atque populus Dei, antequam Christus veniret Legem Prophetasque adimplere, illa omnia quae hunc promittebant observare iubebatur: liber in eis qui haec quo pertinerent intelligebant," 19.17 (CSEL 25/1.515f.). Cf. his later statement, made in 405 to Jerome, that the first generation of Jewish converts to Christianity felt bound to observe the Law "propter commendandam scilicet auctoritatem divinam et sacramentorum illorum propheticam sanctitatem," *ep.* 82.9.

51. "Quid est enim aliud hodieque gens ipsa nisi quaedam scriniaria Christianorum, baiulans Legem et Prophetas ad testimonium assertionis Ecclesiae, ut nos honoremus per sacramentum quod nuntiat illa per litteram?" 12.23 (CSEL 25/1.351).

us, so that those who do not receive these truths in their heart for their own good nonetheless carry in their hands, for our benefit, the writings in which these truths are contained. And the unbelief of the Jews increases rather than lessens the authority of these books, for this blindness is itself foretold. They testify to the truth by their not understanding it.[52]

In consequence of their blindness to Christian truth, contemporary Jews, scattered and bereft of their commonwealth, live in constant anxiety, subjected to the immensely more numerous Christians; terrified, like Cain, of bodily death. But as God marked Cain for his protection, so through the Law has he marked the Jews. Indeed, God himself protects them from murder, vowing seven-fold vengeance on would-be fratricides (12.12). Nor may any monarch coerce conversion, that is, "kill" Jews by forcing them to cease living as Jews: again, like Cain, they stand under the protection of God (12.13). Thus until the end of time, "the continued preservation of the Jews will be a proof to believing Christians of the subjection merited by those who, in the pride of their kingdom, put the Lord to death" (12.12).

But the very clarity of the Scriptural prophecies of Jewish unbelief, and their unambiguous confirmation, raised once again the constellation of questions that had dogged Augustine during his earlier reading of Romans and in his examination of his own life. If the sin of unbelief is mandated by heaven (as in the case of Esau, Pharaoh, or anyone languishing *sub lege*), how is God just in punishing the sinner? If prophesied through the spokesmen of God, who has inerrant foreknowledge, is sin nonetheless fully voluntary? If not voluntary, can it still be "sin"? If God is just, how can he condemn those to whom he has chosen not to give grace? If he had offered grace, could the sinner possibly have refused?

Augustine's answers to these questions, as we have seen, had shifted dramatically between the Romans commentaries of 394 and his answer to Simplicianus in 396. In 394, the sinner had the freedom to resist God's offer of grace: this resistance had informed Augustine's definition of de-

---

52. "Eo ipso nimirum fortius atque firmius, quod ex manibus inimicorum tanta de Christo testimonia proferuntur; in quibus ideo Gentes quae credunt, nihil de illo ad tempus possunt putare confictum, quia in eis libris inveniunt Christum, quibus a tot saeculis serviunt qui crucifixerunt Christum, et quos in tanto apice auctoritatis habent qui quotidie blasphemant Christum. . . . Magnum aliquid actum est in usum nostrum de infidelitate Iudaeorum, ut iidem ipsi qui haec propter se non haberent in cordibus, propter nos haberent in codicibus. Nec inde auctoritas illis libris minuitur, quod a Judaeis non intelliguntur; imo et augetur: nam et ipsa eorum caecitas ibi praedicta est. Unde magis non intelligendo veritatem perhibent testimonium veritati: quia cum eos libros non intelligunt, a quibus non intellecturi praedicti sunt, etiam hinc eos veraces ostendunt," 16.21 (CSEL 25/1.463); NP-NF, 227.

spair.[53] But by 396, grace was not only unmerited, it was also utterly irresistible: "voluntati eius nullus resistit."[54] Hence his depiction of Saul "thrown prostrate," wrenched involuntarily into a new life *sub gratia*, chosen through some divine standard of justice that remained, by human measure, *inscrutibilia*.

Where in the *c. Faustum* Augustine considers the Jews, both ways of conceiving these issues appear. In 12.11, developing the theme of Cain the fratricide as a type of the Jews who killed Christ and who continue to resist the embrace of the Church, the pre-396 language of uncompromised volition creeps in. Jews are "the people who *would* not (*nolentis*) be under grace, but under the Law." Their lack of faith, within this discourse, seems the result of choice.

But in *c. Faustum* 13.11, considering Jewish freedom of choice in the perspective of prophecy, the question of God's justice again arose, since someone might object "that it was not the fault of the Jews if God blinded them so that they did not know Christ."[55] In defense of divine justice, Augustine again invoked divine inscrutability. Jewish blindness, Augustine grants, is a punishment, but not for the sin of killing Christ: evidently (this is my inference, not his argument) in fulfilling that prophetic script, and in so doing bringing salvation to the Gentiles, the Jews had committed a discrete sin. Their continuing blindness, however, was the penalty for some other sin. But what? God knows, says Augustine. We can with security only affirm his justice: "ex *aliis occultis peccatis Deo cognitis* venire iustam poenam huius caecitatis. . . . et [Jeremias] ostendit *occulti eorum meriti* fuisse ut non cognoscerent."[56] Jews too, then, like the rest of the unredeemed *massa damnata*,[57] languish *sub lege*. Whether God chooses to

---

53. See above, pp. 306–7.

54. *Simpl.* 1.2.17; cf. Rom 9.19. See J. M. Rist's discussion of will and grace in *Augustine: Ancient Thought Baptised* (Cambridge: Cambridge University Press, 1994), 130–35. I am puzzled by Rist's assertion that Augustine "does not say that grace is irresistible, but that it is 'effective' in that it provides the will with 'most effective strength,'" 133; cf. 134 and n. 110, that, according to Augustine, no one can be compelled to will: Saul was.

55. "Quod si diceret, Quid ergo peccaverunt Judaei, si Deus illos excaecavit ne agnoscerent Christum?" (CSEL 25/1.390).

56. CSEL 25/1.390–91. Cf. *Psal.* 68.26, where the Jews' blindness is God's *occulta vindicta* for their sin of malice; also *fid.* 6.9: "Nam eos non intellecturos ab eisdem prophetis ante praedictam est: quod ut certa oportebat impleri, et *occulto iustoque iudicio Dei* meritis eorum poenam debitam reddi. . . . Tamen propter ceteros, quos *occultioribus causis* fuerat deserturus, per prophetam tanta ante praedixit. . . ."

57. So too *Simpl.* 2.19, commenting on Rom 9.24, "*Quos et vocavit nos*, inquit, *non solum ex Iudaeis sed etiam ex Gentibus*; id est, vasa misericordiae quae praeparavit in gloriam. Non enim omnes Iudaeos, sed ex Iudaeis: nec omnes omino homines Gentium,

leave them or to bring some *sub gratia*, he does so, for them as for anyone, for inscrutable reasons, but justly.

III

Augustine's teaching on Jews as a protected witness people, a defining theme of his discussion in the *City of God*, was already in place by 398, in the course of his refutation of Faustus the Manichee. It was one aspect of a more general resolution to the hermeneutical, political and polemical problems that marked his development as a theologian in the decade of the 390s. The years intervening between these two works were marked by other controversies—with the Donatists, with the Pelagians, and with millenarian enthusiasts both within Africa and without. Yet the positions he first formulated against the Manichees, and the sources he drew on to formulate these positions—Tyconius, Paul, Genesis; his conviction that an historical reading of Scripture (which resulted ultimately in another mature masterpiece, *de Genesi ad litteram*) was essential to Christian faith[58]—remained fundamental to all his later work.

Augustine's position on the continuing religious importance of the Jewish people, eventually sanctioned by his invocation of Ps 59:12 ("Slay them not, lest my people forget") ultimately served to safeguard later generations for centuries in medieval Christian Europe. Seldom has a biblical hermeneutic had such an immediate and perduring social effect. This is all the more striking, I think, given the absence of a social stimulus to the formulation of this hermeneutic. Put simply: it is his reading of the Bible in the course of his struggles against the Manichees, and not encounters with real Jews, that led Augustine to formulate his teaching.[59]

To claim this, of course, is to part company with Bernhard Blumenkranz. In his classic study of Augustine's anti-Jewish polemic, *Die Juden-*

---

sed ex Gentibus. Una est enim ex Adam massa peccatorum et impiorum, in qua et Iudaei et Gentes remota gratia Dei ad unam pertinent conspersionem."

58. For Augustine's new emphasis on the historical dimension of Christian theology and, thus, biblical interpretation, see Rist, *Augustine*, 121–29.

59. Jeremy Cohen argues similarly that the correct context for understanding Augustine's position on Jews and Judaism is "Augustine's method of interpretation—his interpretation of history as well as his interpretation of Scripture," in "Anti-Jewish Discourse and its Function in Medieval Christian Literature," unpublished paper for the 1992 New Chaucer Society Meeting, MS p. 6. However, he locates this historicizing hermeneutic specifically after Augustine's anti-Manichaean phase, in works written between 412–430. I thank Prof. Cohen for sharing his paper with me.

predigt Augustins (1946), and again in his later, more discursive reprise of this theme, "Augustin et les Juifs: Augustin et le judaïsme" (1958), Blumenkranz situated Augustine in a social context where the Jewish presence imposed, where Jews competed with the Church for both pagan and even Christian converts, and where Augustine in turn himself sought to persuade Jews to join the Church.[60]

Against these points, I would simply repeat what I hope I have demonstrated: Augustine's remarks on Jews and Judaism arise primarily from his theological concerns, particularly against the Manichees. *That* is the encounter for which we have evidence in abundance: transcripts of debates, eyewitness accounts of controversies, the titles of Augustine's own treatises, his review of these works in the *Retractationes*. Real Jews, however—as opposed to "biblical" Jews (whether in the Old Testament or the New) or "hermeneutical" Jews[61] (the Jews as shorthand for a particular, non-Christological reading of the Old Testament)—whatever their actual numbers in the cities of Roman North Africa, are by comparison in short supply in Augustine's writings.[62]

Secondly, a supposed market competition between these two communities, Jewish and Catholic, cannot account for anti-Jewish polemic for the

60. The problematic Jewish presence, "Augustin," 226, 230; Jewish missionary efforts, 227; "missionary" counter-arguments, 233, 235–36; *Judenpredigt*, 110ff., 211.
61. Cohen's phrase, MS p. 28.
62. Most frequently cited on this question of population is P. Monceaux, "Les colonies juives dans l'Afrique romaine," *Revue des études juives* 44 (1902): 1–28. See too Blumenkranz, *Judenpredigt*, 59–68; H. Z. (J. W.) Hirschberg, *A History of the Jews in North Africa* (Leiden: E. J. Brill, 1974), 21–40, with the map of population distribution, 22; review and analysis of archaeological data by Yann LeBohec, "Inscriptions juives et judaïsantes de l'Afrique romaine," *Antiquités africaines* 17 (1981): 165–207, and "Juifs et judaïsants dans l'Afrique romaine: Remarques onomastiques," *Ant. afr.* 17 (1981): 209–229.

Ep. 8* reveals an epistolary encounter between Augustine and Licinius, a Jew who had been defrauded of land by a certain Victor, Augustine's episcopal colleague. Augustine instructs Victor to settle with Licinius lest the case go to the bishops' court; and he likewise suggests that Victor restore the peace of Licinus' family (Licinius and his mother had quarreled, which had given Victor his opportunity). For text and French translation, *Lettres 1 *-29 **, *Bibliothèque augustinienne* 46b (Paris: Desclée de Brouwer, 1987), 152–57; analysis, H. Castritius, "The Jews in North Africa at the Time of Augustine of Hippo," *Proceedings of the IXth World Congress of Jewish Studies*, Division B, Vol. 1 (Jerusalem, 1986), 31–37; idem, with generous annotation, " 'Seid weder den Juden noch den Heiden noch der Gemeinde Gottes ein Ärgernis' (1. Kor. 10,32): Zur sozialen und rechtlichen Stellung der Juden im spätrömischen Nordafrika," *Antisemitismus und jüdische Geschichte*, ed. R. Erb and M. Schmidt (Berlin: Wissenschaftlicher Autorenverlag, 1987), 47–67.

simple reason that we have little evidence for actual Jewish missions in antiquity generally. Jews in principle welcomed converts, but do not seem to have mounted missions to attract them.[63] By Augustine's period, further, such activities would have long been illegal.[64] Both Blumenkranz and his friend and contemporary Marcel Simon, author of another classic study of Jewish-Christian relations in antiquity, had pointed to such competitive encounters by way of explaining Christian hostility toward Judaism and Jews.[65] The actual evidence we have, though, is too slight to comfortably bear the weight of such an interpretation.

I note, too, that both men published their studies in the years immediately following World War II—1946 and 1948, respectively. To place Christian anti-Jewish invective in such a context is to rationalize it, to give it some sort of reasoned and reasonable explanation. I respect and sympathize with the impulse for wanting to do so, especially in the wake of the antisemitic horrors of World War II: if something can be rationally explained, then perhaps it can also be rationally addressed and even made right. Methodologically, however, the explanation offered by this kind of functionalism—an academic form, perhaps, of wistful thinking—too fre-

---

63. I review the literature and arguments for and against the possible existence of Jewish missions to gentiles in antiquity in "Judaism, the Circumcision of Gentiles, and Apocalyptic Hope," *JTS* 42 (1991): 532–64, esp. 535–48; now see Martin Goodman, *Mission and Conversion: Proselytizing in the Religious History of the Roman Empire* (Oxford, 1994).

64. On this legislation and its effects on conversion, Goodman, *Mission*, 134–35; Linder, *Jews in Roman Legislation*.

65. Simon, *Verus Israël: Étude sur les relations entre Chrétiens et Juifs dans l'empire Romain (135–425)* (Paris, 1946), 433f., concluding his study (and passim); cf. Blumenkranz, who sees a general situation with Jews competing for pagan souls as well as Christians' ("Augustin," *art. cit.*, 226ff.) The Jew from Uzalis, mentioned by Augustine in *City of God* 22.8.21, becomes a closet missionary for Blumenkranz ("Le problème se pose quand ces Juifs veulent attirer à leurs pratiques des fidèles chrétiens. Tel fut le cas de ce guérisseur d'Uzalis. . . . "p. 226), a "type du rabbin miraculeux" for Simon (p. 416).

This is one of the few times Augustine really does allude to a Christian's contact with an actual Jew, and it occurs during the catena of local miracle-stories that fills the middle chapters of his concluding book. Augustine's point is simply to emphasize the reality and efficacy of the manifest power of the saints who, through their (non-eschatological) thousand-year reign on earth, in the Church, by means of their relics, work healing miracles for those who have faith. Petronilla, in 22.8, went to a Jew for an amulet to wear *while* she went to a saint's monument for a cure: hers was a both/and, not an either/or approach. (She was divinely frustrated: the talisman mysteriously came undone.) Going to a Jew for a cure, however, hardly constitutes evidence of religious outreach or competitive contact, as both these later authors interpret this episode.

quently goes far beyond our ancient evidence, and the degree to which we can wring social data from it.[66] Finally, and briefly, I note that Blumenkranz based much of his reconstruction of Augustine's circumstances vis-à-vis Jewish contemporaries on his construal of the *Tractatus adversus Iudaeos*. In his view, the *Tractatus* served as prime evidence both of the challenge these Jews posed and also of the concern Augustine felt to convert them. But the *Tractatus* occupies a quite minor part in Augustine's rich corpus;[67] and as a sermon addressed to Christians, it would at best provide an oblique view of Augustine's supposed concern to convert Jews—a concern that would run completely counter to his clear statement in the *c. Faustum*: Jews are to remain Jews until the close of the age (12.12).

In his later essay, Blumenkranz comments on the degree to which, for Augustine, "la polémique antijuive est intimement liée à la polémique antihérétique."[68] I am struck by the degree to which the opposite is true. Augustine is no philo-Semite, and much of his anti-Jewish polemic is traditional and not particularly imaginative.[69] But it is precisely his *positive* statements on Judaism, and his insistence that Jews serve as authentic witnesses even *after* the coming of Christ and their own consequent condemnation, that so imaginatively and effectively undergird so much of his

66. I am indebted on this point to David Satran, whom I thank for sharing with me an MS of his essay, "Anti-Jewish Polemic in the *Peri Pascha* of Melito of Sardis: The Problem of Social Context." He notes: "The reconstruction of context is no simple matter, nor is it unburdened by larger questions of meaning and order. The presumption of a meaningful setting for anti-Jewish sentiments is, in no small measure, an assumption of their ultimate role and purpose in society. . . . [But] with what assurance or security do we impose a functionalist and rational purpose on all the many and varied expressions of anti-Judaism? Are we willing to dismiss the possibility that certain anti-Jewish phenomena may be irrational in an essential way and deeply disfunctional within their social context? . . . The argument from (and for) social context must itself be placed in the broader and determinative context of our own ignorance and uncertainty," MS 11, 14. This essay is forthcoming in *CONTRA IUDAEOS. Ancient and Medieval Polemics between Jews and Christians*, ed. O. Limor and G. G. Stroumsa (Tübingen: J. C. B. Mohr [Paul Siebeck], 1995).

67. It looms large for Blumenkranz in part because he looks at it from the perspective of earlier Latin *adversus Iudaeos* literature, composed by authors whose anti-Jewish polemic really did describe a significant aspect of their work, e.g., Tertullian, Commodian, and (though with a difference) Jerome, *Judenpredigt*, 9–11; 19–26; 45–47.

68. "Augustin," 237.

69. Blumenkranz, *Judenpredigt*, 62–68, reviews some of Augustine's more dismal remarks; cf. Augustine's endorsement of Jerome's view that any contemporary Christian who Judaizes, "sive ex Iudaeis sive ex Gentibus . . . eum in barathrum diaboli devolutum," *ep.* 82.18.

anti-heretical work. And, finally, it is in the course of his extended battle against those heretics *par excellence*, the Manichees, and thus of his protracted struggle to defend both divine justice and human freedom, that Augustine's argument, in its odd way, becomes as well a defense of Jews and Judaism.

Paula Fredriksen is the William Goodwin Aurelio Professor of the Appreciation of Scripture at Boston University

Santa Maria Maggiore's Fifth-Century Mosaics: Triumphal Christianity and the Jews

Margaret R. Miles
Harvard University

■ Introduction

The fifth-century mosaics of Santa Maria Maggiore in Rome represent the oldest surviving program of mosaic decoration in a Christian church.[1] Its political context includes the steady drain of political authority and power to the Eastern empire from the early fourth century forward, the proscription of paganism at the end of the fourth century, and the massively disruptive Sack of Rome by Alaric in 410 CE. In the vacuum of political power in the West, the papacy under Sixtus III made a strong claim for a new basis of Roman power—the religious primacy of the city of Peter and Paul under papal leadership.[2] The building and decoration of

---

[1]Suzanne Spain, "'The Promised Blessing': The Iconography of the Mosaics of Santa Maria Maggiore," *Art Bulletin* 61 (1979) 518.

[2]Richard Krautheimer writes ("The Architecture of Sixtus III: A Fifth-Century Renascence?" in Millard Meiss, ed., *Essays in Honor of Erwin Panofsky* [New York: New York University Press, 1961] 301), "The Empire in the West had collapsed. The emperor in Ravenna was a mere shadow. The Eastern emperor, powerful though he was, was distant and uninterested. The Roman aristocracy, pagan to the last, was gone as a political force."

HTR 86:2 (1993) 155–75

Santa Maria Maggiore played an important role in the consolidation and public announcement of papal power.

The first goal of this article is to reconstruct the social world of a work of art that appeared at a pivotal intersection of ecclesiastical and imperial power. The second goal, interwoven with the first, is to demonstrate the value of interdisciplinary methodology for making visible features of history that might not appear if the tools of a single discipline were used. I begin, then, with a work of art and proceed to investigate its role in a complex social, political, legal, and theological discourse.

In the later Roman Empire, effective power was *visible* power. In 313 CE, Christianity had emerged from persecuted sect to authorized and imperially funded religion almost overnight. Formerly without trace in the landscape of Roman cities, the building of Christian churches under Constantine altered the appearance of ancient cities. The fourth-century historian Eusebius, an admirer of Constantine, eulogized Constantine's church buildings because they made Christianity's dramatic change in status visible. Just as the incarnation of Christ had made God visible, Eusebius said, the triumph of Christianity was visible, incarnated in the magnificent new cathedrals that were springing up in the empire's major cities during the fourth century. These buildings witnessed silently to the power of the God who had given the victory at the Milvean Bridge to an outnumbered and outmanoeuvered Constantine. Describing the church at Tyre, Eusebius wrote, "The cathedral is a marvel of beauty, utterly breathtaking. . . . The evidence of our eyes makes instruction through the ears unnecessary."[3]

If the city of Rome was to be recognized as the spiritual center of Christianity under the pope's leadership, papal foundations needed to equal or overtake those of the fourth-century emperors. A sermon by Sixtus III's archdeacon, Leo—later Leo I—exults in the new vision of a Christian Rome. No longer to be seen as a major site of imperial power, the city of Peter and Paul "has become a priestly and royal city, the head of the world through this holy see of Peter. Wars, indeed, have made fewer conquests [for the city] than the Christian peace."[4]

It may seem odd, then, that in a Christian church, built and decorated by a pope, the entire length of the nave is covered with scenes from the Hebrew Bible. Why not miracle stories from the New Testament? Why not

---

[3]Eusebius *Hist. eccl.* 10.44.2; see my discussion of fourth-century Christian architecture and decoration, "The Evidence of Our Eyes: Fourth-Century Roman Churches," in Margaret R. Miles, *Image as Insight: Visual Understanding in Western Christianity and Secular Culture* (Boston: Beacon, 1985) 41–62.

[4]Leo I *Sermo* 82 (PL 54. 422–28); quoted in Krautheimer, "Architecture of Sixtus III," 302.

episodes from the lives of Christian martyrs and saints? Yet Jewish tradition and scriptures would not have received such prominence in an important Christian church had they not been crucial to the articulation of Christian—more specifically, papal—triumphalism. Power newly made visible demonstrated its authority not merely by magnificence, but also by effectively reinterpreting public life. It is neither accidental nor coincidental that Santa Maria Maggiore and its extensive mosaic program were commissioned and executed at the same time and in the same city in which the Jewish people were being dramatically and rapidly "repositioned" within the Roman Empire, marginalized and restricted in their activities.

The mosaic program at Santa Maria Maggiore did not *cause* the marginalization, oppression, and popular violence against Jews that was contemporary with its execution. Nor do social, political, and ecclesiastical events explain or account for the content or style of the mosiacs. Rather, both the artworks and the events are related in the public life of a city at a particular historical moment. Although the events and the works of art can be assumed to relate to one another, the nature of the relationship between the mosaics and the social and political realities can be reconstructed only through a careful examination of fifth-century Roman society.

■ Santa Maria Maggiore and its Legend

Although the legend associated with the building of Santa Maria Maggiore can be traced back no further than the thirteenth century, it is relished to this day by Roman tourist guides.[5] In 358 CE, in August—the hottest month in Rome—a Roman patrician named John and his wife,

> being childless and wishing to leave their wealth to the Virgin, were
> visited by her in their sleep and told to build a church in her honour
> in a spot that would be marked by snow. Approaching Pope Liberius
> to inform him of their intention, they were surprised to learn that he
> had had an identical dream.[6]

As predicted, snow appeared on the noble's property on the Esquiline Hill, and Pope Liberius built the basilica with the couple's money. The exact

---

[5]A fifteenth-century painting, Masaccio and Masolino's "Miracle of the Snow," depicts the legend of Santa Maria Maggiore's founding; see Allan Braham, "The Emperor Sigismund and the Santa Maria Maggiore Altarpiece," *The Burlington Magazine* 122 (1980) 106–12; Jill Dunkerton, Susan Foister, Dillian Gordon, Nicholas Penny, *Giotto to Dürer, Early Renaissance Painting in the National Gallery* (New Haven: Yale University Press, 1991) 252–54; Paul Joannides, "The Colonna Triptych by Masolino and Masaccio," *Arte Cristiana* 728 (1988) 339–46; Brandon Strehlke and Mark Tucker, "The Santa Maria Maggiore Altarpiece: New Observations," *Arte Cristiana* 719 (1987) 105–24.

[6]Spain, "'Promised Blessing,'" 518.

location of this first building has been lost; its replacement, the present Santa Maria Maggiore, was built by Pope Sixtus III (432–440) "who wished to single out for honour the Blessed Virgin, whom the Council of Ephesus (431 CE) had recently declared, in opposition to Nestorius, to be the Mother of God."[7]

Santa Maria Maggiore so closely resembles a second-century imperial basilica that it has sometimes been thought to have been adapted from a basilica for use as a Christian church. Its plan was based on Hellenistic principles stated by Vitruvius at the time of Augustus.[8] The exterior dates from much later times: the twelfth-century facade has been masked by an eighteenth-century reconstruction, and its campanile—the highest in Rome— was completed in the fourteenth century.

The interior of the church features a nave divided from the aisles by thirty-six marble and four granite columns (fig. 1). The columns were origi- nally unmatched, but an eighteenth-century architect, Ferdinando Fuga, "boldly transformed the existing heterogeneous collection of columns by paring down those that were too thick, shortening those that were too long, and providing them with identical Ionic capitals and bases."[9] The coffered ceiling of the nave is leafed with Peruvian gold, said to be the first gold brought back from America by Columbus and given to Pope Alexander VI by the Spanish rulers, Ferdinand and Isabella. Five lavishly decorated side chapels enhance the magnificence of the interior.

Upon entering the church, the eye is initially caught by the apse mo- saic, a coronation of the Virgin with angels, saints, the contemporary pope, Nicholas IV, and other ecclesiastical and political leaders. As one architec- tural historian has written,

> In the building designed for worship, the whole building is directed axially to the center of worship, the altar. . . . The whole decoration of the church interior. . . is arranged in such a way as to lead the eye towards the altar. . . . The same principle applies to pictorial decora- tion. The apogee is reached in the "culminating point" of the axis, in the vault of the apse.[10]

---

[7]Ibid.

[8]Roloff Beny and Peter Gunn, *The Churches of Rome* (New York: Simon & Schuster, 1981); the "height of the columns is 9 1/2 times their base diameter; spacing between col- umns is five times the diameter" (p. 61, see also p. 104).

[9]Ibid., 106.

[10]H. P. L'Orange and P. J. Nordhagen, *Mosaics* (trans. Ann E. Keep; London: Methuen, 1958) 18; see also Yvon Thébert, "Private Life and Domestic Architecture in Roman Africa," in Paul Veyne, ed., *A History of Private Life*, vol. 1: *From Pagan Rome to Byzantium* (trans. Arthur Goldhammer; Cambridge, MA: Harvard University Press, 1987) 339.

This principle is especially evident in Santa Maria Maggiore. The present apse mosaic dates from 1295 and is signed by Jacapo Torriti; it is purported, however, to be a reproduction of the original fifth-century mosaic.[11]

Santa Maria Maggiore's Fifth-Century Mosaics

The fifth-century mosaic program lines the walls of the nave and appears on the triumphal arch. Twenty-seven of the original forty-two panels remain, although some are damaged.[12] The nave mosaics, set above the Ionic columns and below the clerestory windows are rich and complex. Scenes from the Hebrew Bible feature moments of covenant and promise between God and the Hebrew people: God's promise to Abraham that his progeny would become a great nation and that they would inherit the land of Canaan, for example, and the promise of the Messiah. On the left wall facing the altar are scenes from the lives of Abraham, Isaac, and Jacob; on the right wall are scenes of Moses and Joshua (fig. 2). Many of the scenes are difficult or impossible to identify; they depict obscure stories from the Hebrew Bible featuring God's support and guidance of the Jewish people. Panels on the left wall narrate events in Genesis from the separation of Abraham and Lot to the offspring of Jacob (Genesis 13–34). As the eye passes along the nave and reaches the mosaics of the triumphal arch, Melchizedek, Isaac, Jacob, Moses, and Joshua all become types and foreshadowings of the Christ whose advent appears on the arch (fig. 3).[13]

The throne of God is depicted at the center of the triumphal arch, while on the left (top to bottom) there is the annunciation (to Joseph and to Mary), the betrothal of Mary and Joseph, the Epiphany, the Massacre of the Innocents, and the city of Jerusalem. The presentation in the temple, the

[11]Santa Maria Maggiore has been celebrated for having in this mosaic the earliest known representation of the imperialized Mary, Mary Queen of Heaven. Recently, however, Suzanne Spain has questioned this, showing that in the Latin West it was not until the late sixth century that Mary was placed in imperial garments and depicted ruling from a throne. The original apse mosaic was indeed dominated by the figure of Mary, Spain concludes, but a traditionally clothed Mary, "wearing a tunic of dark material, her head covered by a maphorion or shawl, her hair bound in a white cap. . . with youthful features, wearing red shoes." Like the thirteenth-century mosaic, the original Mary was shown seated on a throne, her child on her lap, surrounded by angels and martyrs, accompanied by Pope Sixtus. See Spain, "'Promised Blessing,'" 534.

[12]Half of the clerestory windows were boarded over sometime in the baroque period, reflecting the baroque preference for crepuscular lighting in churches. This adjustment of the lighting of the interior means, among other things, that the nave mosaics are now barely visible by natural light; with the full complement of clerestory windows, they were well lighted.

[13]Spain identifies (ibid., 524) the figures in this panel (see fig. 3) as David and Isaiah meeting the infant Christ.

flight into Egypt, the Magi before Herod, and the city of Bethlehem appear on the right side of the arch (top to bottom). The mosaics of the triumphal arch insistently connect the events from the Hebrew Bible that are pictured on the nave walls with those associated with the birth of Christ by including figures from the Hebrew Bible in events surrounding Christ's birth. Sarah and Abraham are present at the betrothal of Mary and Joseph (fig. 4),[14] and David and Isaiah greet the infant Christ; these figures act as witnesses to the fulfillment of the prophecies and promises made to the Hebrew people. On the triumphal arch, the long series of nave mosaics showing God's covenanted promises with the Jewish people culminates in and is superceded by Christ's incarnation.

■ The Mosaics' Theological Agenda

The fifth-century mosaic program of Santa Maria Maggiore has two theological agenda: (1) the glorification of the Virgin as *theotokos*, God-bearer,[15] and (2) a systematic and comprehensive articulation of the relationship of the Hebrew Bible and the Christian scriptures as one in which the Hebrew Bible foreshadows Christianity. These themes were featured in a sermon delivered by Pope Leo I (the former archdeacon of Sixtus III) soon after the completion of Santa Maria Maggiore. The incarnation, he said, was

> promised from the foundation of the world, and had always been prophesied by many intimations of facts and words: but how small a portion of mankind would these types and foreshadowed mysteries have saved had not the coming of Christ fulfilled these long and secret promises, and had not that which then benefitted but a few believers in the prospect, now benefitted myriads of the faithful in its accomplishment.

---

[14]On iconographical grounds, Spain identifies the figure holding the Christ Child as Sarah. In this scene, Mary and Joseph are betrothed, with an angel playing the part of the priest, and they see a vision of the child to be born to Mary. Abraham appears on the right (just outside the reproduction). Abraham and Sarah are present at the betrothal "as ancestors of Mary, Joseph, and Christ, as antetypes of Mary and Joseph, and as witnesses to the fulfillment of the promises made to them" (ibid., 535).

[15]Spain questions the relevance of the Council of Ephesus to the theological concerns of Santa Maria Maggiore's fifth-century mosaics: "In Rome, the decisions of the Council were inconsequential. . . . The christology and mariology of S. Maria Maggiore are orthodox, but it is doubtful that they are so in response to the acts of a distant council" (ibid., 534 n. 69). It is important to remember, however, that the Mediterranean provided an expeditious route for the circulation of ideas as well as commerce: twenty days' sailing was sufficient to traverse the Mediterranean from one end to the other. Also, Krautheimer has pointed out ("Architecture of Sixtus III," 296) that there is evidence of stylistic influence in architecture from Constantinople to Rome; if such influence can be demonstrated, theological influence is also probable.

Now no longer are we led to believe through signs and types, but being confirmed by the gospel story we worship that which we believe to have been done; the prophetic lore assisting our knowledge, so that we have no manner of doubt about that which we know to have been predicted by such sure oracles. For hence it is that the Lord says to Abraham: "In thy seed shall all nations be blessed"; hence David, in the spirit of prophecy sings, "The Lord swore truth to David and he shall not frustrate it"; hence the Lord again says through Isaiah: "behold a virgin shall conceive in her womb, and shall bear a son, and his name shall be called Immanuel, God with us."[16]

I shall consider separately the two themes that are connected in Pope Leo's sermon: (1) glorification of the Virgin and (2) supercessionist theology.

(1) The rebuilding of Santa Maria Maggiore began in 432 CE, only a year after an ecumenical council met at Ephesus to decide a matter of contemporary debate and schism. The building and decoration has been called "Sixtus III's ex-voto gift to the Virgin."[17] After an intense discussion, the Council of Ephesus had ruled that it was theologically accurate to call the Blessed Virgin Mary "*theotokos.*"[18] The central issue of the debate was Mary's role in the Incarnation. Was she to be thought of as a mere "vessel"[19] through which the incarnated Christ passed, as Nestorius said?[20] Or, was she to be seen as the mother whose flesh provided Christ's flesh and from whom he was born as all human babies are born? The Council decided for the latter interpretation. The "majority leader," Cyril of Alexandria, described what was at stake in the decision:

For if he had not been born as we according to the flesh, if he had not taken part like us of the same, he would not have freed the nature of humanity from the blame contracted in Adam, nor would he have driven away from our bodies the decay.[21]

(2) In the iconographical program of Santa Maria Maggiore, scenes from the Hebrew Bible receive their contextualization and interpretation as the

---

[16]Leo I *Sermo* 24.1; the translation is that of Charles Lett Feltoe, *Letters and Sermons of Leo the Great* (NPNF 2d ser.) 12. 134; see also Joanne Deane Sieger, "Visual Metaphor as Theology: Leo the Great's Sermons on the Incarnation and the Arch Mosaics at Santa Maria Maggiore," *Gesta* 26 (1987) 83–91.

[17]Krautheimer, "Architecture of Sixtus III," 295.

[18]Kenneth G. Holum, *Theodosian Empresses, Women and Imperial Domination in Late Antiquity* (Berkeley: University of California Press, 1986) chap. 5, 147–74.

[19]See Robert L. Ottley, *The Doctrine of the Incarnation* (London: Methuen, 1919) 391–400.

[20]Holum notes (*Theodosian Empresses,* 188) that the Nestorian "heresy" "appeared to contemporaries to be of Jewish origin."

[21]"Epistle of Cyril to Nestorius" (NPNF 2d ser.) 14. 203.

prologue to the Christian saga. Christians had of course used stories and scenes from the Hebrew Bible—especially those that featured God's miraculous deliverance—in the earliest Christian catacombs. Worship, liturgical ritual, and sacraments, as well as Christian scriptures and prayer, demonstrate Christians' systematic dependence on Jewish rites. Clearly Christians felt themselves to be in continuity with the Jewish people. It is, however, one thing to picture a community—even a worldwide community—as a shoot recently grafted onto an ancient and powerful trunk; it is another to think of the trunk itself as existing only to support and supply the new branch.

The catacomb paintings of Hebrew Bible stories—Daniel in the den of lions, Jonah and the great fish, Adam and Eve—were executed in times of potential or actual persecution. They witness to Christians' need for well-known and deeply interiorized images that reassured and comforted. In a society in which Christians were marginalized and powerless, such an appropriation of stories and images from the Hebrew Bible represents an entirely different impulse than that of the triumphal imagery of Santa Maria Maggiore. Moreover, in the catacomb images, there was seldom an attempt to reposition figures and events from the Hebrew Bible within a Christian narrative. Although both catacomb images and mosaics appropriate aspects of Jewish scriptures and history, different social conditions directed the selection of different topics, creating a vastly different representational communication. At Santa Maria Maggiore a powerful social, political, and religious institution reinterpreted Jewish history and the Jewish people as precursors, shadowy adumbrations, types, and signs of the fulfillment of God's promises in Christianity.

■ Augustine's Interpretation of Jewish Tradition

Forty years before the Santa Maria Maggiore mosaics were designed and executed, one of the most respected and influential theologians of the dominantly Christian West, Augustine, bishop of Hippo in North Africa, wrote a detailed exposition on the culmination of Jewish scriptures and tradition in Christianity. One of his sermons to his congregation contains a striking statement of his assessment of the relationship of Judaism to Christianity:

> The Jew carries the book from which the Christian takes his faith. They have become our librarians, like slaves who carry books behind their masters; the slaves gain no profit by their carrying, but the masters profit by their reading.[22]

---

[22] Augustine *Enarrationes in psalmos* 56.9.

Augustine's most detailed exposition of the role of Jewish tradition in relation to Christianity occurred in the context of his debate with North African Manichaeans. Those who identified themselves as Manichaean Christians did not accept the Hebrew Bible as authoritative for Christians. Thus, in his carefully recorded public debate with the Manichaean Faustus, Augustine reiterated story after story from the Hebrew scriptures in order to demonstrate that each was a foreshadowing of Christianity: "The New Testament lies hidden in the Old; the Old Testament becomes plain in the New."[23]

The basis of Faustus's rejection of the Hebrew Bible was that since Christians no longer "keep the precepts," they should not lay claim to the documents.[24] Faustus apparently respected the integrity of Jewish scripture and ritual practice. Augustine, however, saw a distinct advantage in reinterpreting Jewish practices and events as "shadows" of Christianity although dispensing with its ritual practices. For example, he cited Jewish circumcision of the flesh as the prefigurement of Christian circumcision of the heart:[25] "What was then a type is now revealed truth."[26]

Augustine identified a parallel—and pernicious—theological logic in Faustus's denial of Christ's incarnation, death, burial, and resurrection and in his rejection of the transformation of the "letter" of Judaism into the "spirit" of Christianity.[27] Unable to accept that matter can be transformed into spirit, Faustus, according to Augustine, simultaneously missed *both* the significance of the body in Christianity *and* the transformation of the literal practices of Judaism into the spiritual truth of Christianity. Augustine, by contrast, understood Judaism and Christianity to be in essential—not accidental—relationship to one another: just as in the resurrection of the body it is not that "one garment is to be laid aside and a better one taken instead," but "that *the same* body will be changed for the better"—that is, from material to spiritual—so Jewish tradition is *the same* tradition, transformed in Christianity.[28]

---

[23]Augustine *Contra adversarium legis et prophetarum* 1.7.35.

[24]Augustine quotes Faustus: "Christians have not adopted these observances, and no one keeps them; so that if we will not take the inheritance, we should surrender the documents" (Augustine *Faust.* 4.1); "I reject circumcision as disgusting; and if I mistake not, so do you. I reject the observance of Sabbaths as superfluous: I suppose you do the same. I reject sacrifice as idolatry, as doubtless you also do" (Augustine *Faust.* 6.1).

[25]Ibid., 6.3.

[26]Ibid., 6.9.

[27]Faustus denied, according to Augustine, "that Jesus was born of the seed of David. . . that he was made of a woman. . . he denies his death, burial, and resurrection. . . [and] he denies, too, that our mortal body will be raised again, changed into a spiritual body" (ibid., 11.3).

[28]Ibid.

Book twelve of Augustine's treatise against Faustus endeavors to demonstrate his claim that "the whole contents of [Jewish] scriptures are either directly or indirectly about Christ";[29] "the whole narrative of Genesis, *in the most minute details*, is a prophecy of Christ and the Church"[30] (my emphasis). For example, "as a wife was made for Adam from his side while he slept, the Church becomes the property of her dying Savior, by the sacrament of the blood which flowed from his side after his death."[31]

It would be tedious to enumerate the myriad examples Augustine cited as evidence of the intimate relationship of Jewish and Christian scripture and tradition; several will suffice. The story of Noah's ark leads Augustine to give a slightly different metaphor—yet with the same intent—as his depiction of the Jews as Christians' "librarians": "For what else is this nation [Jews] but a desk for the Christians, bearing the law and the prophets, and testifying to the doctrine of the church, so that we honor in the sacrament what they disclose in the letter?"[32] Noah's naked drunkenness prefigures the disclosure—"uncovering"—of "the mortality of Christ's flesh."[33] The blessing of Japheth, the promise to Abraham, the near sacrifice of Isaac, the stone placed under Jacob's head, Jacob's dream, Judith's murder of Holofernes,[34] and many other stories demonstrate that the Jewish scriptures "teem" with predictions of Christ's coming.[35] A similar repertoire of scenes appears in the nave mosaics at Santa Maria Maggiore.

Augustine acknowledged the "ingenuity" of his reinterpretation of Jewish tradition: "Will it be said that these things happened in the regular course of things, and that it is a mere fancy to make them typical of Christ?" he asks, in order to preempt such a question. He insists, "Whoever with a candid mind reads all these things that are contained in the Old Testament Scriptures, must feel constrained to acknowledge that they have a meaning"[36] and that this meaning must be "read in the clear light of Christ."[37]

In juxtaposing "Old" and New Testament accounts, Augustine used a strategy repeatedly employed in Christian sermons, prayers, and works of

---

[29]Ibid., 12.7.
[30]Ibid., 12.8.
[31]Ibid.
[32]Ibid., 12.23.
[33]Ibid.
[34]"What is that woman boldly piercing the temples of the enemy with a wooden nail, but the faith of the church casting down the kingdom of the devil by the cross of Christ?" (ibid., 12.2).
[35]Ibid., 12.25.
[36]Ibid., 12.37.
[37]Ibid., 12.42.

art. His debate with the Manichaeans, conducted at the beginning of the fifth century, however, represents a more systematic treatment of this theme and demonstrates it in more detail than earlier sermonic or artistic references. Moreover, although by the end of the fourth century his interpretation was conventional, it was reinforced, reiterated, and supported in fifth-century society in newly vivid and detailed ways. Augustine's attention to detail and precise correspondence was matched in the depiction of "the most minute details" of Jewish tradition as incorporated in the Christian story in the mosaics of Santa Maria Maggiore. Even the tiny size of the mosaic tesserae that make up the mosaics can be seen as a stylistic reflection of the thoroughness with which Jewish tradition and scriptures were, in this most public, accessible, and impressive way, located in relation to Christianity.

The two theological agenda of the mosaics of Santa Maria Maggiore each makes a powerful statement; their intersection represents an even more complex, subtle, and skillful communication. The new imperative of honoring the Virgin as the Mother of God created a potential embarrassment: if Christ received his specific humanity and particular flesh from his mother, Christ could not be thought of as racially neuter, but explicitly Jewish. Roman Jews in the mid-fifth century were, however, as we shall see in a moment, publicly labeled "beasts and madmen."[38] How could Jesus' irreducible Jewishness be rationalized in a society that increasingly ostracized Jews?

The answer lay in demonstrating visually—and therefore more powerfully, concretely, and accessibly—what Augustine had argued theologically, namely, that the incarnation of Christ simultaneously appropriated and canceled the independent existence of the Jewish people. Christ's flesh was the concrete medium in which his Jewishness was transmogrified into the church, the "Body of Christ."[39] The church had "inherited," in Christ, the physical and historical "substance"—the flesh—of Judaism. Henceforth, the Christian attitude toward the Jews would be disparaging. In Augustine's words,

> The Church admits and avows the Jewish people to be cursed, because after killing Christ they continue to till the ground of an earthly circumcision, an earthly Sabbath, an earthly passover, while the hidden strength or virtue of making known Christ, which this tilling contains, is not yielded to the Jews while they continue in impiety and unbelief, for it is revealed in the New Testament.[40]

---

[38]*Codex Theodosianus* 16.1.2.
[39]Augustine *Faust.* 11.7.
[40]Ibid., 12.11.

■ The Social World of Fifth-Century Roman Jews

Fifth-century Roman society, its laws, politics, social arrangements, and current events corroborate the picture of Jewish marginalization suggested by Christian mosaics and theology.[41] How did Santa Maria Maggiore's artistic agenda relate to contemporary Jews in the city in which their scripture, tradition, and ritual practices were being appropriated and reinterpreted by Christians? The Santa Maria Maggiore mosaics must ultimately be understood in the context of an imperial church that actively and effectively sought to eliminate other religious alternatives within the Roman Empire.

What was happening to Jews in the Roman Empire, and especially in Rome itself, at the time of the rebuilding and decoration of Santa Maria Maggiore? The situation can be grasped most readily by comparing it with Jews' earlier position in the Roman Empire. From the first century CE, Judaism had enjoyed the status of a *religio licita*, a privileged religion in the Roman Empire; such privilege was still in effect at the end of the fourth century. Because fourth-century legislation supports arguments on both sides, scholars disagree about the extent to which Judaism and the activities of Jews were curtailed after the Peace of the Church and throughout the fourth century.[42] Christian emperors seem to have been genuinely ambivalent about the status of Jews: their "policies toward Jews varied as to whether they thought of themselves principally as emperors or as Christians."[43] To the extent that they thought of themselves as emperors, they protected Jews; if they thought of themselves primarily as Christians, they

---

[41]Historians often seek to show how societies work; they therefore adopt the perspective of those for whom the society worked. This privileging of privilege accords well with extant historical evidence; the authors, lawmakers, artists, and other spokespersons who wrote descriptions and evaluations of their society were the beneficiaries of educational institutions, and their perspectives were authorized by their participation in dominant political, social, and legal institutions. Evidence of the perspectives and insights of those for whom a society did *not* work is more difficult both to find and to interpret. Yet the modes and victims of ostracization, marginalization, and oppression can reveal a great deal, not only about the costs and damages, but also about the successes of a society. The values, preoccupations, and loyalties of historical authors and artists that seem mysterious to twentieth-century historians can frequently be clarified by taking into account the exclusionary strategies upon which a triumphal society is built.

[42]See Marcel Simon's discussion in chapter four of *Verus Israel* (New York: Oxford University Press, 1986) 98–134, and Robert Wilken's somewhat different evaluation: "It seems that the status of the Jews in the empire was changing rapidly during this period [the fourth century], but, if so, these changes were probably not perceptible to the people living at that time" (see Wilken's *John Chrysostom and the Jews: Rhetoric and Reality in the Late Fourth Century* [Berkeley: University of California Press, 1983] 54).

[43]Simon, *Verus Israel*, 126.

frequently overlooked illegal and unjust actions against Jews and their property.

In the first decades of the fourth century, Constantine's legislation recognized and sometimes even reinforced the privileges of Jewish communities as long as Jews did not seek to attract Christians to Judaism. He exempted Jewish clergy from compulsory state service of all kinds and, in effect, "made possible a system of Jewish self-government that strengthened Jewish life and identity."[44] At the end of the fourth century, Theodosius—the emperor under whom Christianity became the official religion of the Roman Empire—still reminded anti-Semitic bishops such as Ambrose of Milan that Judaism, as an ancient and honorable religion, was protected by the state.[45] Moreover, public offices were open to Jews until the beginning of the fifth century.

Although Constantine's espousal of Christianity did not immediately lead to dramatic legal changes, Jews nevertheless gradually came to be regarded as second-class citizens, and Jewish privilege began to shrink. For example, Jews were not permitted to circumcize slaves, and marriage between Christians and Jews was prohibited both by ecclesiastical and by imperial law.[46] Moreover, Constantine's edicts already reflect the language of vitriolic sermons and anti-Jewish propaganda. Judaism was, for the first time, referred to as a "shameful" (*secta nefaria*) or "bestial" (*feralia*) sect, as contemptible and perverse (*turpes, perversi*).[47]

Increased imperial hostility toward all non-Christians is evidenced in Theodosius I's edict of February 380, by which Christianity was established as the official religion of the Roman Empire. Although this edict did not single Jews out for opprobrium or punishment, it clearly stipulated official attitudes of intolerance:

> We desire that all peoples who fall beneath the sway of our imperial clemency should profess the faith which we believe to have been communicated by the Apostle Peter to the Romans and maintained in its traditional form until the present day. . . . And we require that those who follow this rule of faith should embrace the name of Catholic Christians, adjuring all other madmen and ordering them to be designated as heretics. . . condemned as such, in the first instance, to suffer

[44]Wilken, *John Chrysostom*, 51.

[45]"Judaeorum sectam nulla lege prohibitam satis constat" ("no law prohibits the sect of the Jews") (*Codex Theodosianus* 16.8.9).

[46]Canons 17 and 78 of the Council of Elvira; *Codex Theodosianus* 3.7.3 and 9.67.5: "No Jew shall receive a Christian woman in marriage, nor shall a Christian man choose marriage to a Jewish woman."

[47]Joseph Jacobs, "Rome," *The Jewish Encyclopedia* 10 (1905) 446.

divine punishment, and therewith, the vengeance of that power which we, by celestial authority, have assumed.[48]

Universal enforcement of this edict was not immediately attempted, but outbreaks of popular violence against Jews indicate that official attitudes were reflected and reinforced by popular anti-Semitism.

Late fourth-century and early fifth-century emperors had, however, often insisted on the rebuilding, at Christian expense, of synagogues that had been destroyed by Christian mobs.[49] This measure was effectively challenged and criticized by Bishop Ambrose of Milan.[50] In the 380s, a Christian mob burned a Jewish synagogue in Rome; the Emperor Maximus ordered it rebuilt at the expense of the state, but he was overthrown and killed by Theodosius I before this was done.[51]

Theodosius's laws relating to Jews continued to demonstrate the ambivalence of earlier fourth-century Christian emperors. He wavered between laws inhibiting and laws protecting Jews. In addition to already existing laws forbidding Jews to proselytize and protecting Jewish converts to Christianity, Jewish parents were forbidden to disinherit children who became Christians. The Theodosian Code also prohibited the building of new synagogues and stipulated that "Christians could escape punishment for violence against synagogues simply by converting them into Christian churches and returning any treasures which had been confiscated."[52] Many details could be added to supplement this picture of gradual but systematic suppression and curtailment of the activities of the large Jewish population in late fourth-century Rome.[53]

---

[48]*Codex Theodosianus* 26.1.2; compare Constantine's Edict of Toleration which has a very different tone. In the edict of 313 CE, Constantine proclaimed himself "unwilling to constrain others [religiously] by the fear of punishment"; see Eusebius *Vita Const.* 2.56.

[49]Imperial attempts to discourage the razing of synagogues can be documented as late as the reign of the Ostrogoth Theodoric.

[50]Ambrose *Epistulae* 40.23.

[51]A progressive weakening of the state's protection of synagogues can be traced in early fifth-century laws. Laws of 397, 412, and 418 restate protection of existing synagogues, but "what had been a crime that must be remitted to the imperial tribunal now became a matter for the jurisdiction of local authorities" (Simon, *Verus Israel*, 228). Three laws published in 423 no longer mention restitution; they merely required those responsible for the destruction of a synagogue to return cult objects or to pay for them and to provide land for their rebuilding—at the expense of the Jewish community. Another law of 423 forbade Jews to build new synagogues (except when an existing synagogue had been destroyed) or to repair or improve already existing synagogues.

[52]E. D. Hunt, "St. Stephen in Minorca, An Episode in Jewish-Christian Relations in the Early 5th Century AD," *JTS* 33.(1982) 118.

[53]Simon (*Verus Israel*, 127–32) details these laws.

Contradictory laws continued to be promulgated between 398 and 404, but anti-Jewish policy began to dominate in 404 when Honorius declared "Jews and Samaritans" unfit for military service. In 415, Theodosius II issued the first edict that forbade the construction of new synagogues and even suggested that synagogues "in desert places" could be destroyed, "if it can be accomplished without riots." This edict apparently acted as "an invitation to fanatics to go about their work of intimidation and destruction."[54] Furthermore, by August 425, all Jews and pagans were expelled from imperial service. This meant that henceforth Jews could not practice law in imperial courts and thus marks another significant increment in Jewish marginalization from positions of public authority. In sum, by the early fifth century, it was clear that Jews were rapidly losing many of their traditional privileges as they were marginalized from public life, their growth circumscribed, and their authorities disempowered.

The so-called *Novella* of 31 January 438—published as Santa Maria Maggiore was being completed—amounted to a total prohibition on Jews' holding public office of any kind. It also forbade any act of Jewish proselytism under pain of death. In this legislation, Theodosius II declared himself the protector of true religion against "Jews, Samaritans, pagans, and heretics":

> Among the other duties which our love of the common weal indicates to us in an every vigilant consideration, we perceive the search for the true religion as the imperial majesty's foremost care. If we could maintain its cult, we shall open the way of prosperity to human endeavor. . . . The blindly senseless Jews, Samaritans, pagans, and other kinds of monstrous heretics dare to question that Christianity is the true religion. If we endeavor to recall them to sanity. . . by a healing law, they themselves shall bear responsibility for its severity, they who do not leave room for mercy by their obstinate crime of an obdurate front. For this reason we decree in this law—that shall stand forever—that no Jew. . . shall accede to honors and dignities, to none of them shall be opened an administration with public obedience.[55]

Official attitudes toward Jews, incendiary language, and discriminatory legislation were supplemented by popular violence against Jews and their property. Anti-Jewish riots occurred in 388 in Callinicum on the Euphrates. Similar events, instigated by the local bishop, occurred in Minorca in 415. In Alexandria, Bishop Cyril led attacks on synagogues, expelled Jews from the city, and turned synagogues into churches. Edessa, Dertona, and Constantinople recorded similar anti-Jewish activities. By the second de-

---

[54]*Codex Theodosianus* 16.8.22; Holum, *Theodosian Empresses*, 98.
[55]*Codex Theodosianus* 16.1.2.

cade of the fifth century, "official utterances were increasingly coming to reflect and acknowledge the anti-Jewish violence which was taking place locally around the empire."[56] A law of 420 cautioned Jews against provoking Christian attacks, revealing an official attitude of blaming the victim. Synagogues continued to be destroyed by Christian mobs. Even when emperors attempted to protect Jews, anti-Jewish riots were often instigated by bishops in apparently deliberate attempts to create acrimony between Jews and Christians.[57] This pattern of episcopal denunciation of Jews is attested in many locations within the Roman Empire. In Antioch, for example, John Chrysostom preached notoriously vitriolic sermons against Judaism, depicting the synagogue as the "haunt of vices of every description."[58]

Christian leaders, moreover, began to assimilate Jews into a growing pool of "heretics." As a category of intolerable dissidence was constructed, dissident groups lost their particularity in Christian eyes and were conflated with one another. Name calling—perennially indifferent to particularity and difference—identified Jews with heretics and heretics with Jews. Nestorius, the opponent of "*theotokos*" at the Council of Ephesus, was called—apparently without further reason than his unpopular views—"Nestorius the Jew."[59]

■ Conclusion

At approximately the same time that the mosaic program of Santa Maria Maggiore was designed and executed, Sozomen, the church historian, reported that in the Eastern empire, the relics of the Hebrew prophets Habakkuk, Micah, and Zechariah were revealed as a sign of God's favor to the Christian rulers, Theodosius I and Valentinian, during whose reigns they were found.[60] These purported discoveries were considered material evidence validating a by-now stabilized method of dealing with the Jewish foundation of Christianity: the bones of the prophets gave concreteness to the claim that Judaism had existed only as a preparation for Christianity

---

[56]In one of these riots, the Platonic philosopher Hypatia was murdered by a Christian mob; see Hunt, "St. Stephen in Minorca," 118.

[57]Ibid., 115.

[58]Chrysostom compared the synagogue to the theater and a brothel, calling it a "den of robbers," a "lair of wild beasts," and a "place of idolatry"; *Adversus Judaeos* 1.3 (PG 48. 847); quoted in Hunt, "St. Stephen in Minorca," 115.

[59]Holum, *Theodosian Empresses*, 168 n. 111; also 188.

[60]Sozomen *Historia ecclesiastica* 9.16–17: "It seems as if God openly manifested his favor towards the present emperor, not only by disposing of warlike affairs in an unexpected way, but also by revealing the sacred bodies of many persons who were of old most distinguished for piety" (trans. in NPNF 2d ser., 2. 427).

and that it was decisively superceded, eviscerated, and fulfilled by the incarnation of Christ.

This chauvinistic interpretation would perhaps never have achieved its long-term effects if it had not been amply and *visibly* supported in popularly accessible forms. As we have seen, a thorough, complete, and detailed appropriation of Jewish scripture and tradition effectively reinforced this interpretation. A Christian population heard in sermons and liturgies and saw in mosaics their own roots traced from the creation of the world, through the history of the Jewish people's relationship with their God, to the birth, life, death, and resurrection of Jesus. They saw it first at Santa Maria Maggiore in Rome.

The traditional status of Jews within the Roman Empire as members of an ancient and honorable religion was challenged and overturned in the first half of the fifth century. It is safe to conjecture that none of the theological, artistic, and legal Christian revisions of Jewish privilege would have worked in isolation as powerfully and effectively as they did in concert. Together, they reflected and reinforced a massive social marginalization of Judaism as well as Jewish people.

A composite Christian portrait of "the Jew" was gradually constructed. Ironically, it was composed largely by pasting together prophetic denunciations of the Jewish people from their own scriptures. The Hebrew Bible "provided the Christians with a repertoire of offensive and damaging epithets with which they invariably accompanied every mention of the Jews": Jews were regularly characterized as "uncircumcized and stiff-necked people."[61]

Historians of art and religion often explain representations of Judaism within Christianity by tracing them back to the earliest Christian liturgies, sermons, literature, and images. This historical genetic fallacy, however, will not adequately explain the specific power of such representations in the particular dominantly Christian societies that gave them credence and acted upon them. In the first half of the fifth century, as I have argued, the power of these ideas and images can be reconstructed only in relation to a triumphal Church and in the context of the multiple fronts on which Jews were losing social ground.

Even though Christians appropriated Jewish images throughout the history of Christianity, one cannot assume that the selection and meaning of images were prompted by similar religious needs in different times and places. In changing societies, similar images and ideas occupy different positions, respond to different situations, and are interpreted according to

---

[61]Simon, *Verus Israel*, 215.

different associations, attitudes, and values.[62] Images from the Hebrew Bible apparently provided comfort for Christians in the times of persecution; figures and events from Jewish tradition carried very different religious and social meaning when represented in the context of a triumphal church. The mosaics at Santa Maria Maggiore represent an important moment in the public representation of supercessionist theology. In fifth-century Roman society, these powerful visualizations of the triumph of Christianity contributed to an attitude toward Judaism and the Jewish people that would persist—acted out variously by different Christian societies—to our own time.

[62]Michel Foucault wrote (*The Archeology of Knowledge* [San Francisco: Harper Torchbooks, 1972] 176), "Even if a statement is composed of the same words, bears exactly the same meaning, and preserves the same syntactic identity, it does not constitute the same statement if it is spoken by someone in the course of a conversation, or printed in a novel; if it was written one day centuries ago, and if it now reappears in an oral formulation. A statement must have a substance, a support, a place, and a date. And when these requisites change, it too changes identity."

Fig. 1: Nave toward apse, Santa Maria Maggiore, Rome.

Fig. 2: Abraham and the three angelic visitors. Nave mosaic,
Santa Maria Maggiore, Rome.

Fig. 3: The meeting of David and Isaiah with Christ. Triumphal arch,
Santa Maria Maggiore, Rome.

Fig. 4: Sarah and the Christ Child at the Betrothal and Vision of Mary and
Joseph. Triumphal arch, Santa Maria Maggiore, Rome.

Justin's Logos and the Word of God

M. J. EDWARDS

Scholarship has generally attempted to show that the notion of the Logos in Justin's Apologies is largely indebted to Stoic or Platonic philosophy. If, however, we trace its roots in the Biblical tradition, we shall find that these may be adequate to explain it. Such an explanation avoids the difficulties inherent in its rivals and makes the thought of the Apologies continuous with that of Justin's contemporaries and his Dialogue with Trypho.

It seems that for many scholars Justin Martyr was two people. One produced, in his *Dialogue with Trypho*, a vast and eloquent compilation of those texts in the Greek Old Testament which can be made to prefigure Christ. Though this work engaged him in controversy with the Jews, this Justin was pre-eminently a Biblical theologian, and Nygren can subsume him with the "*nomos*-type" in Early Christian ethics, which has at least the virtue that it is not the "*eros*-type.[1]" The other Justin wrote the two *Apologies*, where, in order to woo the Greeks through their philosophy, he sometimes keeps his Bible at his back.[2] The proofs of his acquaintance with the schools are found in the opening of the *Dialogue with Trypho*, in the obvious erudition of the *Apologies*, and above all in his doctrine of the

1. A. Nygren, *Agape and Eros*, part 2, vol. 1, trans. P. S. Watson (London: SPCK, 1938), 49–72. A recent book devoted to Justin's exegetic practice is W. A. Shotwell, *The Biblical Exegesis of Justin* Martyr (London: SPCK, 1965). A. Grillmeier, *Christ in Christian Tradition*, vol. 1 (London: Mowbrays, 1975), 90, observes that the notion of Christ as Nomos is carried over to the *Apologies*, though he does not attempt the consistent reading of the term *Logos* offered here.
2. In my article, "On the Platonic Schooling of Justin Martyr," *JTS* 42 (1991): 17–34, I attempt to identify the Platonic models that guided Justin in his construction of a theology. I am here concerned with what was only cursorily treated there, namely the antecedents of the term *Logos*, and shall refer to other treatments of this subject in the course of the present paper.

Journal of Early Christian Studies 3:3, 261–280 © 1995 The Johns Hopkins University Press.

Logos, which is widely held to have been deducible only from Greek sources, though some would name the Platonists where others commend the Stoics.

While there can be no doubt that Justin tempers his exposition to his audience, and that his early studies put him abreast of at least one school of pagan thought, it is seldom necessary, or even possible, for a thinker of such magnitude to cut his mind in half. The search for pagan elements in his concept of the Logos has all but blinded us to the numerous occurrences of the same term in his *Dialogue with Trypho*, whose important contribution to the problem of Christian thought is thus severely underrated. I shall argue here that even the *Apologies* cannot be elucidated from the pagan schools alone, and that the womb of his Logos-doctrine was the *Dialogue*, where the term is used to confer on Christ the powers that were already attributed in Jewish literature to the spoken and written utterance of God.

I

Jewish tradition from the earliest period had revered the Word of God. "You shall not add to the word that I have given you" (Deuteronomy 4.2), says the legislator, and, though the Septuagint has *rhema* here, it calls the ten commandments the *deka logoi* at Exodus 34.28. Up to Hellenistic times this legislative Word had been repeated and embellished by the prophets, whose succession was once thought to be unending. Sometimes God himself is represented as the speaker, proclaiming that his *rhema* will not return to him empty, but bear fruit in his creation (Isaiah 55.11); only a fool would doubt the efficacity of the logos by which "the heavens were made" (Psalm 33.6).[3]

It thus required no Hooker or Aquinas to discover that the Law which moves the elements is the source and sum of moral ordinances. A striking note of the Biblical tradition is, however, that in the present age these are not inscribed on hearts at birth,[4] but are imparted and renewed by the

---

3. I follow G. Kittel's *Theological Wordbook*, vol. 4, trans. G. Bromiley (New York, 1967), 69–136 in taking as one the usual Hebrew terms for "word" and their usual equivalents in the Septuagint. The practice of the Septuagint itself is not uniform, the words *logos* and *rhema* are related to different tenses of the same verb, and we have no reason to think that Justin's acquaintance with Hellenistic Judaism was confined to the written Bible. The most relevant passages in Kittel are 94–8 on the prophetic word, 98–9 on the Word as Law, 99–100 on the Word of creation.

4. Though this is of course the hope of prophecy: see Jeremiah 31.31–4 and II Corinthians 3.3. A referee points out the use of prophetic passages to illustrate the role of

daily hearing of a text. The Book, not moral reasoning, is the cause of those repentances which follow the exposure of Israel's corporate dereliction.[5] The very Psalm which tells us that the heavens declare the glory of God (19.1ff), that day and night extol him in succession, that the voices of the sun and moon are heard in every nation,[6] does not imply that these suffice to make his creatures righteous; they manifest in visible, though silent, form the power that underwrites the spoken Law:

> The Law of the Lord is without blemish, converting souls; the witness of the Lord is faithful making wise the simple. The judgments of the Lord, being righteous, rejoice the heart, the commandment of the Lord shines far, enlightening the eyes (Psalm 19.7–9 Septuagint).

When prophets failed, the written Word assumed an inexhaustible dominion. Rabbis of the early Christian era fixed the limits of the Torah, yet subjected it to such ingenious rules of exegesis that they were never at a loss to reach the heights of metaphysics or the extremes of casuistry.[7] This written text was the all-sufficient symbol of the word that God had spoken, and the latter, as the one sure intermediary between the ailing people and their hidden King, acquired the characteristics of a superhuman being. The Memra has a place above the angels as that agent of the Deity who sustains the course of nature and personifies the Law.[8]

How common or how orthodox these speculations were in the second century we cannot decide; we do, however, find that personality is bestowed upon the Word in a Jewish author who lived earlier than Justin and was known by name at least to younger Christians of his age. Philo's Logos, jointly formed by the study of Greek philosophy and of the Torah, was at once the written text, an eternal notion in the mind of the Creator and the organ of his work in time and space.[9] Under this last aspect, it receives such epithets as Son, King, Priest and Only-begotten; in short, it becomes a person, though perhaps not a different person from the Speaker. The influence of Philo (or his milieu) on the development of early Christian

---

Christ as the heart of the covenantal Law at *Dial.* 93, and also the implied equation of Law with the prophetic word at Isaiah 1.10, 8.16 and 30.9–10.

5. See esp. I Esdras [Ezra] 8 and IV Kings [II Kings] 22–3 in the Septuagint.

6. On the original and subsequent interpretation of this phrase, see N. Frye, *The Great Code* (London: Routledge and Kegan Paul, 1982), 24.

7. See now H. L. Strack and G. Stemberger, *Talmud and Midrash* (Edinburgh: T. and T. Clark, 1993).

8. On the testimonies to the Memra and the difficulties of using it, see G. F. Moore, "Intermediaries in Jewish Tradition," *HTR* 15 (1922): 41–61. On Wisdom, Paul and Torah, see W. D. Davies, *Paul and Rabbinic Judaism* (London: SPCK, 1948), 147–176.

9. On Philo, see H. A. Wolfson, *Philo* (Cambridge, Mass.: Harvard University Press, 1947), 177–246.

doctrine must have been profound, though its initial conduits are obscure.[10]

If it be thought tendentious to reckon Philo as a Jew, it would be even more tendentious to enroll him in the calendar of philosophy under the constellation of Middle Platonism. There was never a school of Middle Platonism, as there were schools of Neoplatonism; the term is a convenient designation for those philosophers who wrote before Plotinus and exhibit an important debt to Plato. These authors, for the most part, would appear to have been unknown to one another,[11] and no thought that occurs in one should be treated as the property of all. All the admitted Platonists whose work survives in quantity were born after Philo's death, and, even where they coincide with him in thought or language, we cannot deduce immediately that they point to Philo's model. It is possible that Philo's own conjectures found their way into the schools of Apamea or Alexandria;[12] it is probable that Hellenic and Hebraic minds were never so estranged by their respective tongues as some are wont to argue;[13] in cases like the present, where he has both Biblical precedent and orthodox Jewish comment to support him, we should not call Philo a Platonist (or even a Pythagorean),[14] but take him at his own word as a pious intellectual, who expressed in Greek the spirit of a Jew.

If Justin drew on Philo, then, it was as a representative of current Judaism.[15] Certainly known to him, since it occurs in the Book of Proverbs, is the portrayal of divine Wisdom, or Sophia, as a female being, capable of utterance, who sits by God at the moment of creation (Proverbs 8.22ff). In the Wisdom of Solomon, the metaphor is prolonged into an allegory, in which Sophia herself accepts the functions of creation and of government, and differs from God, if anywhere, in being the agent only of his most

10. See H. A. Wolfson, *Philosophy of the Church Fathers*, vol. I (Cambridge, Mass.: Harvard University Press, 1956), 200–359; D. T. Runia, *Philo in Early Christian Literature* (Assen: Van Gorcum, 1993), esp. 132–156 on Clement. On the relevance of Philo to Justin, see Runia, *Philo*, 97–105 (showing that most scholars have postulated a common environment, if not dependence); R. Holte, "Spermatikos Logos," *Studia Theologica* 12 (1958): 123–128 and 147–8.

11. For recent discussion, see H. Ziebrinski, *Heilige Geist und Weltseele* (Tubingen: Mohr, 1994), 22–43.

12. See J. Whittaker, "Moses Atticizing," *Phoenix* 21 (1967): 196–201 for a defence of this (possible, though not proven) view.

13. See, e.g., J. Barr, *Biblical Words for Time*, Studies in Biblical Theology 33 (London: SCM Press, 1962), attacking the theories of Cullmann, Robinson and Marsh.

14. See D. A. Runia, *Philo*, 136, citing Clement, *Stromateis* I.72.4, II.100.3.

15. See on this question D. A. Runia, *Philo*, 99–104, reviewing O. Skarsaune, *The Proof from Prophecy*, Novum Testamentum Supplement LVI (Leiden: E. J. Brill, 1987) and W. A. Shotwell, *Biblical Exegesis*, 93–113.

benevolent deeds towards humanity and Israel.[16] Her acts are thus recorded in the heavens and in history; she is as potent, as mysterious and as present as the Law. The latter, we are told in Deuteronomy (30.12–14), is not to be sought in heaven or overseas, but in the faith of the obedient; and Job, who knows that Wisdom too transcends the height and depth and has her only seat in God, is therefore all the more desirous to receive her in his heart (28.20–28).

The Word which rules the heavens and that which makes the written Law are thus the same, and yet there is no place for an intuitive discovery of God. There is not so much one spirit that joins man with his creator as a dual revelation; and the revelation of deity in the heavens is accessible only to those, who, like the Psalmist, know the Maker through his Law. Even at Wisdom 13.5, the one case where the handiwork of heaven is adduced as a revelation to the Gentiles, Wisdom herself is not the subject of this revelation, and her voice is audible only to the readers of the Word which she inspires.[17] This distinction in Jewish thought between immanent and mediated Wisdom could not fail to have a bearing on the theology of Justin, since he is among the first to equate this figure with the pre-existent and exalted Christ.

He was not the first, since Paul styles Christ the Wisdom of God at I Cor 1.18–25. Even in the "Hellenistic" Gospel of John, as has recently been argued by John Suggit, the conception of Christ as Logos is pervasive and indebted to the Jewish encomia of the Word of God.[18] While broaching the possibility that this had been personified already in Rabbinic teaching, Suggit finds it more illuminating to match the properties of Jesus in the Gospel with the functions of the Word in Psalm 119, the alphabetic *magnum opus* of its genre. In the Psalm, the Law or Word is called the bearer of truth, the Way, the source of life and the giver of light; all this is said of Jesus in the Gospel. Both Jesus and the Law enjoin the keeping of commandments, but in the new dispensation the Holy Spirit supersedes the Law as teacher, while Jesus must succeed it as the object of our love. As the Psalmist celebrates the permanence of the Law, so Christ extends the promise of eternity to all who abide in him.

---

16. See especially Wisdom 10–11, which may have helped to inspire the Gnostic contrast between Sophia and the Demiurge.

17. I rely here upon J. Barr, *Biblical Faith and Natural Theology* (Oxford: OUP, 1994), 66–7, though he does not look for the distinction that I am making.

18. J. Suggit, "John 17.17," *JTS* 35 (1984): 104–117. He compares Ps 119.142 with John 8.32; 119.9 with 14.4–6; 119.93 with 6.35; 119.105 with 1.4; 119.60 with 15.13; 119.97 with 21.15; 119.12 with 16.13; 119.89 with 15.4–11.

The titles *Nomos* and *Logos* are applied to Christ in a work of the second century, which has recently been proposed as a source or parallel for Justin.[19] The few surviving fragments of the *Preaching of Peter* show that it made no peace with Greek or Jew: Christ is Nomos as the author of a new covenant, and Logos as the power by which, according to the Psalm, God made the world.[20] As Rordorf (and Justin) note, the source for the combination of the titles is Isaiah 2.3 (Micah 4.2): "there shall come forth a law and word from Zion." *Arche* is another appellation of the Savior in this document; the usage, endorsed by Justin's pupil Tatian, will no doubt have been supported by some version or congener of the opening verse of John.[21]

The "Nomos-Logos" thesis attains its classic form in Melito of Sardis, a contemporary of Justin who was later to be (for some at least) a canon of orthodoxy.[22] In his *Homily on the Pascha*, he expounds the typological relation between the acts of God through Moses and his epiphany in Christ. The mystery which by the old dispensation was expressed through Law is now revealed more clearly in the Logos (9–10); the Law is old, the Word is new (19–20); the Law has been fulfilled because the Gospel has shone forth (236–7). As the last example shows, the Logos here is not so much the Word in Jesus as the word about him; yet it is treated in the metaphors that John applies to the incarnate Jesus, and Melito also says that whereas Christ, in so far as he judges, is the Law, his true name when he teaches is "the Word" (55–6).

We cannot prove that Justin was acquainted with rabbinic thought,[23] or even with the Fourth Gospel, but the Johannine terms for Christ were in his own vocabulary,[24] and he shared with John a desire to trace the thread

19. See W. Rordorf, "Christus als Nomos und Logos" in A.M. Ritter (ed.), *Kerygma und Logos* (Gottingen: Vandenhoeck and Ruprecht, 1979), 424–434.

20. See Rordorf, "Christus als Nomos," 426, citing Clement, *Strom.* VI.5.41.4–6.

21. See Rordorf, "Christus als Nomos," 427/9. E. F. Osborn, *Justin Martyr* (Tubingen: Mohr, 1973), shows that there are cogent grounds for thinking that Justin used a harmony of the Gospels.

22. See Rordorf, "Christus als Nomos," 431 for reference to Melito. On the theology, see S. G. Hall, *Melito of Sardis: On Pascha and Fragments*, xl–xli. The association with John is made by Suggit (n. 18), 115–117. Melito's Quartodeciman practice did not lead to any doubts of his doctrinal orthodoxy.

23. E. R. Goodenough, *The Theology of Justin Martyr* (Jena, 1923; reprinted Amsterdam: Philo Press, 1968) makes a case for the influence of Hellenistic Judaism. It is now not widely believed that his Trypho was the Rabbi Tarfon: see, e.g., N. Heydahl, "Tryphon und Tarphon," *Studia Theologica* 9.2 (1955): 77–88. For other discussions of Rabbinic influence, see W. A. Shotwell, *Biblical Exegesis*, 93–113, and E. F. Osborn, *Justin Martyr*, 107–110.

24. Not only Logos, but "vine" to judge by *Dial.* 110.4. The term *monogenes* is cited

from Judaism to Christianity. "Nomos into Logos" is the gist of Melito's homily, and will be our guiding principle in the following attempt to extract a single definition of the Logos from the whole of Justin's work.

II

No reader of an ancient book should overlook the prologue. When we detach this portion of the *Dialogue with Trypho*, as a frontispiece to the study of the *Apologies,* we have already failed in our task as commentators, having forestalled the possibility of learning from the text. This skirmish with the pagans at the outset gives a preliminary savor of that method which the author will apply with greater intricacy in the main part of the *Dialogue.* This consists of using a familiar term in unexpected company, to convey an intimation of truths too great to be expressed at one attempt.

In his opening chapter Justin notes that the founder of a school is called the "father of its *logos*" (2.2). This is one of the earliest occurrences of the latter term in the *Dialogue,* and even had it not been used elsewhere to denote the Father of the Trinity (35.6), the sacred connotation of the whole phrase could hardly fail to strike a Christian. Justin next describes his misadventures in philosophy, from which he was converted through discussion with an old man by the sea. Even at the beginning of this colloquy, however, he personifies the Logos in a style that is not Platonic "what greater work could there be than this, to show that the Logos rules all things, then conceiving it within and riding on it, to look down upon the errors of those below" (3.1)? His aim is not to reproduce the exact words of a scene that may in any case be fictitious,[25] but to adumbrate a more plausible account of his salvation, in which an inner logic lifts him from the intellect to the Logos, from his speculative desire for the unseen to faith in Christ as the infallible and present Word of God.

Elsewhere in this conversation, *logos* denotes the faculty of reason, or the use of it. Justin is required to give a "reason" (3.6) for his confidence that his own beliefs and acts are in accordance with "right reason" (*orthos logos*: 3.3); this is another phrase that will acquire a Christian force when it recurs (141.1). Justin's interlocutor exposes the variety of meanings in the word *logos* when he presses him for "arguments" (9.1–3) after finding

---

at *Dial.* 98.5 and 105.1, though it is not clear whether this shows knowledge of the Johannine usage.

25. See Edwards, "Platonic Schooling," 18–21 for discussion and bibliography. For full commentary on the prologue, see J. C. M. van Winden, *An Early Christian Philosopher: Justin Martyr's Dialogue with Trypho Chapters One to Nine*, Philosophia Patrum 1 (Leiden: E. J. Brill, 1971).

previous offerings void of "sense" (5.2). His irony thus annihilates the claim, endorsed by Trypho (1.3), that philosophy is distinguished by its possession of "the whole *logos*". The standard English rendering of the last word would be "argument" or "account," but we may note in anticipation that at 2 *apol.* 8.3 the "whole *logos*" is Christ.

Trypho is made to use the word *logos* rarely, and almost always to invite a further argument from Justin (48.1, 55.1, 57.3, 77.1, 94.4). The latter may reciprocate by asking for the *logos* or "interpretation" of a crucial passage, but in the great majority of instances the text itself is the object signified. Appeal is made in chapter after chapter to "the Word" alone (49.1, 60.4–5, 67.7 etc.), the Word of God (38.2 etc.), the "prophetic Word" (56.6, 77.2, 110.3, 128.4), the "Word that spoke" to or through Isaiah (87.2), Moses (56.13, 58.4, 62.1), David (68.5, 85.4), Solomon (62.4) or Zechariah (49.2). The Word that can so often be the subject of a verb is never far from being personified, and the idiom that makes a human being its instrument would seem more proper to an author, or his powers, than to the written medium. If we apply the Rabbinic (and Origenistic) principle that the meaning of a term in any context may be present in all the others,[26] we shall be required in Justin's case to unify the original, divine *communication* with its material *expression* in the Bible and the *sense* read into this by a discerning commentary.

The noun *Logos* had served Christians for over half a century[27] as a title of the Lord. Yet nothing in this period, save the prologue to the fourth Gospel, can compare with the *locus classicus* in Justin, which extols "the Word of Wisdom, God begotten of the Father" (61.3), and adorns him with the other appellations of his pre-existent glory. The keynote of the *Dialogue with Trypho* is that all the riddles in the Jewish Scriptures are resolved by the birth, the ministry, the death and the exaltation of this Person; as God and man he is both the author and the latent sense of what is written. Not by his dogmatic formulations (it was an age of scant resources), but by the frequency with which he confers two meanings on the same expression, Justin harps on the interpenetration of the Savior and his Word.

At 109.2 Justin quotes the prophecy of Micah (4.2) that a "Law and Word" (*nomos kai logos*) will issue forth from Zion for the vindication of Israel. For him, as for the prophet, this betokens the renewal of the Torah, but he presumes that, like himself, the Jews apply it to a personal redeemer. They do not know "who it is" that issues from the sanctuary, because they

26. See Strack and Stemberger, *Talmud and Midrash*, 22 for the Rabbinic principle.
27. See Grillmeier, *Christian Tradition*, 26–32 (on the New Testament) and 86–89 (on Ignatius).

do not acknowledge the dual advent of the saviour, first in passible humanity, then in the consummating power of "Law and Word." The insight that the Logos is the perfection of the Nomos is therefore not peculiar to Melito and John.

Another ambiguity has already occurred at 109.1: the nations are declared to have received from the Apostles and to have understood through them "the word proclaimed." Is this word (*logos kērukhtheis*) the word which constitutes the proclamation or the Word whom it proclaims? Passive forms of the verb *kerusso* are found throughout the *Dialogue*, the subject being occasionally an abstract proposition, but more often Christ himself under a title.[28] Here the equivocal syntax may be intended to convey what we have noted in the case of Jewish Wisdom: the logos is the vehicle of the Logos, the Word of God is known to us primarily through the word that speaks of him.

At 23.3 Justin undertakes to proclaim the "divine word" (*theios logos*), which he himself heard from "that man." Both the epithet *theios* and the allusion to the old man are unique outside the prologue, where the right rule (*orthos logos*) for discovering *to theion* is the matter in dispute. By this echo Justin means to intimate that his quest is now fulfilled, and we should thus expect the locution *theios logos* to refer, not to the Scripture, but to its omnipresent Subject. This conjecture is strengthened by the ascription of the title *theios logos* to Christ in both *Apologies* (1 *apol.* 33.9, 2 *apol.* 13.3), and all but proved by the course of Justin's argument in this section of the *Dialogue*, where his case is that the ceremonial law has been abolished by the renewal of God's covenant with Abraham in Christ.

In a text of great importance for the history of dogma (100.5), Mary is found superior to Eve because the one "conceived the *logos* of the serpent" to engender death and sin, while the other by "faith and joy" prepared her womb for the Son of God. While Justin cannot speak of any temporal conception of the Logos, he brings this title into play by contrast with the offspring of the serpent, thus explaining how the fruits of Mary's faith could avert the penalty of our sins against the legislative Word. After all, Christ's demiurgic power was clearly present in the Paradise which saw all creatures made "by the word of God" (84.1); and the Jews, when they "despised the Word of God" (102.2) did equal violence to the Scriptures and to the one of whom they tell.

Chapter 61 begins with a puzzling exclamation: "setting forth a *logos*, let us generate a *logos*, not by taking anything away so that the *logos* we set

28. For impersonal uses see *Dial.* 85.7 and 100.1; for personal uses *Dial.* 14.8, 34.2, 36.1, 71.2, 110.2; for both together *Dial.* 76.6.

forth will be diminished." These properties of the spoken word, as soon appears, are adduced to render credible the *genesis of* Christ, the "Word of Wisdom" (61.3), whose divinity entails no diminution in the substance of his Father. The intervening commentary observes that when a fire is lit from fire there is no subtraction from the stock; the prologue uses a variant of this Platonic metaphor to express the zeal that the old man has awakened in his soul.[29] So twice again the analogy is drawn, with Justin's customary obliqueness, between the word that bears the revelation and the Word whom it reveals. Perhaps the same complicity may be observed between the title "Word of Wisdom" and his later appeal to "what is said in Wisdom" (129.3), making "Wisdom" first an attribute of deity, then the title of a book.

In every case a polysemic symbol is created by two simultaneous drafts upon a well-stocked bank of meanings. No suspicion of heedless ambiguity or gratuitous complication will survive comparison with the Jewish precedents, which make the same expression, "Word of God," connote an agent and his instrument, the Book and its authority, the power of cosmic government and its manifest decree.

III

A summary of the uses of the term *logos* in the *Apologies* must be brief if it is to be uncontroversial. It signifies at times the human faculty of reason or its products, but, when combined with epithets like "divine" or "whole," will also stand for Christ. Identical with or closely related to him is the *logos spermatikos*, which is the source of revelation and is styled a part or image of the whole *logos*. This implants in us a seed or *sperma*, which enables us to think and live in accordance with the *logos*, and conveys a dim perception of "the whole *logos*," the incarnate Son of God. The theory is presented in epitome towards the end of the *Second Apology*[30]:

> For each, from part of the divine spermatic *logos* seeing that which was akin [or, partially seeing that which was akin to the divine spermatic *logos*], spoke well. But those who contradicted themselves in their cardinal doctrines are seen not to have possessed the infallible understanding and incontrovertible knowledge. What was said well by all was thus the property of us, the Christians, for we worship and love, after God, the Word from the unbegotten and

29. See Edwards, "Platonic Schooling," on the relation between *Dialogus* 8.1 and Numenius, Fr. 14 Des Places.
30. On the alternative translations in the first sentence, see Edwards, "Platonic Schooling," 33–4, commenting on R. Holte, "Logos Spermatikos," 147–148.

ineffable God, since for our sakes he became a man, so that, becoming a partaker of our sins, he might also perform the healing. For all the writers, through the sowing within them of the implanted word (*emphutos logos*), were able to see dimly what was the case [or, what existed]. For the seed of something and the image (*mimema*) given according to capacity are one thing, but that of which there is participation and imitation is another, [and these are possible] by reason of his grace (*2 apol.* 3–6).

Carl Andresen, in a famous study, traces back this doctrine to the Middle Platonism in which Justin, by his own account, was schooled.[31] The term *spermatikos logos* is not found in this tradition, but Antiochus and Cicero had acquainted the Old Academy with *semina virtutum*, "seeds of virtue," which are implanted in the soul by intermediaries of God in much the same way as the ideas have been impressed upon the matter of the world. Since Justin can be shown to have subscribed to this cosmology, he might also, Andresen says, have joined the Platonists in holding that a feeble intimation of divinity is at work in every soul. The Platonists, for their part, had derived their terms from Stoicism, but not without an important change of meaning; neither they nor Justin could embrace the Stoic opinion that the soul, being made of fire, is but a part of that intelligent material which informs and comprehends the universe.

In a still more famous article, Ragnar Holte observes that Andresen cannot supply the evidence for all the steps that are needed to effect the transformation, and he therefore attaches more weight to the absence of the phrase "*spermatikos logos*" in the vocabulary of Middle Platonism.[32] He also notes that those who seek Platonic antecedents have been puzzled to find an origin for the notion that the seed is consubstantial with the Logos who imparts it. Among such scholars, Cramer suggests a borrowing from Philo, with perverse contamination of Justin's text, while Pfättisch can give rather more of a hearing to the Stoics.[33] Andersen adduces many passages which affirm that moral insight comes by nature, though these do not entail that man is born with an intuition of the Gospel or of God.[34]

31. C. Andresen, "Justin und die mittlere Platonismus," *ZNTW* 44 (1952–3): 157–198. On cosmology see esp. 165–6, endorsed by L. W. Barnard, *Justin Martyr* (Cambridge: CUP, 1967), 35–7. The cited Hellenistic passages are: Albinus (=Alcinous), *Didascalia* 25; Antiochus, *apud* Ciceronem, *De Fin.* V.21.59; Cicero, *De Fin.* IV.7.18; Origen, *Contra Celsum* IV.25.
32. Holte, "Logos Spermatikos," 110–168.
33. J. A. Cramer, "Die Logosstellen in Justins Apologien kritisch untersucht," *ZNTW* 2 (1901): 311 and 313; I. M. Pfättisch, *Der Einfluss Platons auf die Theologie Justins des Martyrers*, Forschungen zur christliche Literatur und Dogemengeschichte 10.1 (Paderborn, 1910).
34. Andresen, "Justin und die mittlere Platonismus," 177–8.

A third position might embrace these theories, while observing that they do not in every case conflict with those that turn to Jewish sources for a doctrine of the Logos.[35] The Stoics could give their own meaning to the statement that the Logos is a Nomos; and, whatever the antecedents of the name Logos in Philo's writings, it was surely the Hellenistic schools that taught him to define it by the term *spermatike ousia*.With such a mediator—a Jewish mediator in his own view, as we have stated—could not Justin have taken his doctrine indirectly from a Greek source, while believing that he stood squarely in the Biblical tradition?

Against all these positions, I shall argue in the remainder of this paper that they entail at least six special difficulties which a theory based entirely on the current understanding of the Scriptures would forestall.

1. Whatever Justin learned from his early schooling with the Platonists, it was not the use of Logos as a name for the cosmic demiurge or the intellect of man. It was the Stoics who spoke of *logos* where the Platonists spoke of *nous*; yet Justin is either singularly ignorant of their views or strangely ungenerous, since, while he admires their virtues, he says little of their tenets, except to endorse their prophecies of a terminal conflagration or *ekpurosis*, while deploring their belief in the omnipotence of fate and the perpetual restitution of the past.[36] The notion that he borrowed from Stoics and Platonists unconsciously must be taken, in the present state of knowledge, as a claim that he read Philo; and Goodenough's convictions on this subject have been met by criticisms which have hitherto been found unanswerable.[37]

2. Holte, in attributing to Justin a belief that makes the knowledge of God ubiquitous by nature, does little to reconcile this with the more famous and influential claim advanced in the *First Apology*: namely, that the knowledge of divine things in pagan circles, and especially in Plato, was entirely derived from casual acquaintance with the Scriptures.[38] Justin nowhere shows himself aware that he holds two theories, or adopts the simple measures that would suf-

35. A referee points out to me Cicero, *De Resp.* III.22.33 and Clement, *Strom.* I.(25).165–6 on law as the *orthos logos* in some philosophers (though Clement himself formulates this notion, and adds that they stole it from Moses). As will be pointed out below, Cicero's concept of *ratio* hardly matches that of the speaking *logos* in Christianity.

36. See, e.g., Andresen, "Justin und die mittlere Platonismus," 185–7.

37. E. R. Goodenough, *Theology of Justin*, 168–173, answered by Barnard, *Justin Martyr*, 93–5.

38. Though Holte, "Logos Spermatikos," discusses the loan theory at 159–165.

fice to reconcile them. Both charity and economy should dispose us to conclude that he intended to state, not two—not even two complementary—theories, but one.

3. The theory of a congenital intuition of sacred truth implies a natural affinity between the mind of man and his Creator. In Aristotle, Plato and the Stoics this is an axiom, but for Justin it is not merely an unknown but an alien principle. Although the *Second Apology* declares that the enlightened mind enjoys a partial vision through the Logos of *to suggenes* (2 *apol.* 13.3 above), the grammar does not determine whether this kinship in the object is with the seer or with the Logos.[39] This question is determined, on the other hand, by the *Dialogue with Trypho*, where the old man, who is the mouthpiece of paternal revelation, forces Justin to renounce his Platonism and confess that the mind has no innate communion with God (*Dial.* 4.2). No doubt a shrewd apologist would allow a pagan audience to retain some false assumptions that he would hasten to repudiate in the presence of a Jewish one; but was it not the stated aim of every second-century apologist to convince his pagan neighbors that no god could be identical with a portion of the world?

4. The formula *emphutos logos*, used of our means of apprehending Christ at 2 *apol.* 13.5 is thought to be of Stoic provenance by many,[40] yet, notwithstanding a certain number of comparable phrases in Stoic literature, there is no true case of this.

5. Theories of a kinship between mankind and God would usually entail an understanding of salvation as the attainment of a likeness to, or union with, the Deity. "To be like God" is the goal of life in Plato, and in later times his school bent all its thought and discipline to the consummation of this end. While Christian thought could not gainsay the insuperable divorce between the creature and its Creator, Irenaeus and Origen conceive the work of grace as the imparting of that spiritual perfection which was lost or pre-emoted in the fall of Adam.[41] The reason for the muted praise of Justin in Nygren's *Agape and Eros*, on the other hand, is that he ignores such hopes and grounds his faith in the imitation of Christ's ac-

39. Against Holte, "Logos Spermatikos," 147–148. See n. 30 above.
40. See Holte, "Logos Spermatikos," 133–136. J. von Arnim notes only *emphutos prolepsis* at *Stoicorum Veterum Fragmenta*, vol III (Leipzig: Teubner, 1903), 17.14, i.e., Plutarch, *Stoic. rep.* 1041e.
41. See Irenaeus, *Adv. haer.* V.6; Origen, *De princ.* III.6.1 etc.

tions, not the sharing of his nature, in the righteousness of service, not the confidence of growth.

6. The work of Christ as Logos, in the *Apologies* as in the *Dialogue with Trypho*, is effected by continual activity; both the means and the time of his revelation are in the mystery of his will.[42] As Basil Studer observes in a recent study, Justin frequently describes his Logos as a power or *dunamis*;[43] and, whereas a Stoic or Platonist might have given the name of Logos to an ever-active potency that works without choice or feeling, the power of Justin's Word is manifested in spontaneous and momentary acts of revelation. In short, as Studer emphasises, he *teaches* and he *speaks*.[44] Stoic pantheism, and even the Platonic theory of emanation, leave no room for anything so personal or elective in the ruling principle, making it more a permanent ground of virtue and felicity than a temporal cause of either.

Holte, paying little heed to this dynamic working of the Christian Logos, illustrates the insufficiency of his own solution by proposing that the Stoic Logos was combined in Justin's theory with the parable of the Sower.[45] In Stoic and Platonic metaphor the salient characteristic of the seed is its potential for maturity; it is an origin, a portion, a proleptic adumbration of the plant. Since, however, *sperma* is cognate with the root of *speirein,* etymology defines it, less as something that will *grow*, than as something *sown.* Justin uses *sperma* interchangeably with *spora*, which betrays its derivation still more clearly.[46] In so far as *sperma* is connected in his *Apologies* with the activity of Christ, we have no reason to think that he would separate the sowing from the seed, any more than he elected to separate speaking from the word.

A theory which avoids these criticisms has already been unveiled. The kernel of Justin's *Dialogue with Trypho* might be stated, in the words of his contemporary Melito, as "*Nomos* into *Logos*"; might not this current

42. See especially *1 apol* 63.4–5: "The word of God is his Son, as we have said. And he is called messenger (angel) and apostle, because he announces what is to be known and is sent out to show forth whatever is announced, as our own Lord said, 'He who hears me hears him that sent me.'" As subsequent remarks make clear, Justin has in mind particularly the apparition of God to Moses and the Israelites at Sinai, i.e., God in his role as Lawgiver.

43. B. Studer, "Der apologetische Ansatz zur Logos-Christologie Justins der Martyrers," in Ritter, *Kerygma und Logos*, 435–448. On special manifestations of Christ's *dunamis*, see *Dial.* 30.3 etc.

44. Studer, "Der apologetische Ansatz," 443: "Gott in ihn *redet* und *spricht*".

45. See Holte, "Logos Spermatikos," 128.

46. Cf *2 apol.* 13.5 and *2 apol.* 8.1.

slogan shed as much light on his two *Apologies*? We observed elsewhere that epithets of *logos* from the *Dialogue* recur in the *Apologies*; it only remains to show that an explanation of this term in the *Apologies* which is based upon Christ's personal inspiration and fulfilment of the Scriptures is as strong on all six points as its competitors are weak.

1. Justin's perfect acquaintance with the Septuagint is beyond all need of proof. We have seen above that this thesaurus yielded to ancient seekers a composite notion of the Logos which fell only one step short of a Christology. Melito and the Fourth Gospel take this step when they affirm that the incarnation of the Saviour turned the Law into the Word. Justin required no precedent in pagan thought for his doctrine of a Word who was the agent of creation and its governor, the Son of God and teacher of humanity, the record and the instrument of grace.

2. From current expositions of his doctrine, one would never guess that the passage in which Justin traces the better thoughts of pagans to the Bible is also one of the most important witnesses to the meaning of his "seed":

    And whatever both philosophers and poets said about the immortality of the soul or punishments after death or the contemplation of the heavens or other such doctrines, they contrived to know and expounded by beginning from the prophets; hence there appear to be seeds of truth among all (*1 apol.* 44.9–20).

    Here at least the theory of dissemination is also a theory of plagiarism; we have to do, not with two competing theories, but with complementary statements of the same one. Not nature, but the written text, is the vehicle of enlightenment, and the point of the metaphor lies not so much in any latent properties of the seed as in the fact that it is sown.

3. The seed in Justin's thought is both a portion and an image of the Logos, but is nowhere consubstantial with the believer, who requires it both as object and as guide of his mental eye if he is to imitate the one of whom the seed itself partakes. The seed can be a medium of truth to him without being an inherited constituent of his nature, since, even when he dwells upon the metaphor from nature, the seed in Justin seems to be related to its archetype in the manner of a symbol. At *1 apol.* 19.1, where Justin finds a simile for the posthumous resurrection of the body in the growth of the human foetus from the semen, he makes no use of theories of gesta-

tion or heredity, but only of the principle that the seed is as an *eikon grapte*, a written or graven image, of the supervenient form.

4. The phrase *emphutos logos* is a proof that Justin's language is continuous with early Christian preaching: it is first attested at James 1.21: "receive in meekness the *emphutos logos* that is able to save your souls." Here the seventeenth-century's "engrafted word" is still the best translation, since the meaning is that life comes by the Gospel, not by anything held in common with the world.

5. Our thesis is that the whole of Justin's work propounds the Christology which Melito reduces to the catchword "Law become Logos." His equation of "Law and Logos" with the Saviour in his *Dialogue with Trypho* is confirmed by the citation of the same text in the *First Apology* (39.1). He urges that the Christians do not break the laws of men (68.10), though he also intimates that these are not so profitable as the *theios logos*:

> For that which human ordinances were powerless to effect, the *theios logos* would have done, had not the base demons scattered many lies and impious allegations, taking into alliance the bad and variable nature in every man towards all evil (*1 apol.* 10.6).

The formula *theios logos*, which is a proper name of Christ in the *Apologies*,[47] must connote here the commandments given to Israel, which are contrasted on the one hand with the Gentile codes and on the other with the lies of demons. Nothing is granted to human beings by nature but their vices; Justin states elsewhere that both the motion of the heavens and human chastity are in the course of nature (*2 apol.* 2.4, 4.2), and that human beings have an innate capacity to choose between good and evil (*2 apol.* 14.2), but without presuming anywhere that knowledge of divine truths is inborn. His references to partaking or *methexis* of the *logos,* though they are often thought to bespeak his pagan schooling, are amply covered by our thesis. Propositional truth "partakes" of Scripture, since the Scripture itself contains all revelation; when human beings partake, it is according to an idiom, familiar since Herodotus, whereby hearers are called partakers of what they hear.[48]

6. In his *Apologies* Justin mentions passages from Scripture, in which

47. See Pfättisch, *Der Einfluss Platons*, 110; Holte, "Logos Spermatikos," 94; *2 apol* 13.3.

48. See Herodotus, *Histories* I.127, where the sense is that of being party to a secret.

sperma is definable as "that which supervenes on propagation."[49] The blessings pronounced upon the seed of Abraham were contingent, not on any inchoate merit, but on paternity, and even in the New Testament, it is chiefly as the recipient of these promises that Christ is called the seed of Abraham.[50] The germination of seeds is a frequent subject in the parables,[51] but the seed does not originate in any natural environment; it is the gift of a peculiar dispensation, which occurs at a point in history and is mediated only by the Gospels which contain the parables.

The parable of the Sower, as it is glossed in the Synoptics (Matt 13.8ff and par), is for us a parable of interpretation. The seed is at first the propositional word, but then, as it flourishes or withers, it takes on the situation of the hearer. The word is therefore all but identical with its recipient, yet this is no result of our original constitution, but only of the historical embodiment of truth in Jesus Christ. The Sower is the Word of God, according to Luke (8.11), so that the term *spermatikos logos* was no more than a description of his parabolic role.

That this phrase must denote the sowing agent, not the sown, is proved by Holte, who also demonstrates that the Stoics were the first to coin it.[52] But this is not to say that they defined all subsequent usage, as it could easily be adopted either in ignorance or in defiance of their intention. The latter is most probably the case when Justin avers that the Stoics themselves, who posit an implanted seed (*emphuton sperma*) of wisdom in all humanity (*2 apol.* 8.1), had only partial knowledge of the whole spermatic Logos (8.3). He evidently does not wish to endorse the term *emphuton sperma* in their sense, but by this discreet allusion he insinuates that the true spermatic Logos, though accessible to all Christians, had reached the Stoics in a fragmentary and mediated form.

Justin imitates the shift of meaning which we noticed in the parable of the Sower when he contrasts the word of Socrates with the perfect revelation:

For not only were these [falsehoods] refuted among the Greeks by the *logos* of Socrates, but also among the barbarians by the *logos* itself transformed, made man and called Christ Jesus (1 *apol.* 5.4).

49. Thus Isaiah 54.3 is cited at *Dial.* 13.8; Genesis 21.12 at 56.7; Genesis 24.4 and 28.14.
50. Thus the discussion at *Galatians* 3.16–17 is entirely with respect to *kleronomia*, not germinative properties.
51. See, e.g., Mark 4.6–9; Matthew 13.24–30 and 13.31–2 etc.
52. Holte, "Logos Spermatikos," 136ff.

This is no pun, no sophistry, no equivocation: among the Jews, the most intractable of all barbarians, Christ is indeed the written Word made flesh.

IV

These criticisms of Andresen and Holte are intended as an original contribution to the study of Justin Martyr; they should none the less commend themselves to those distinguished scholars who have already urged that Justin is primarily a Christian, that he did something more than pump the veins of Scripture with Stoic ethics and Platonic metaphysics. Even while this view was being allowed to stand in the *Oxford Classical Dictionary*,[53] Henry Chadwick wrote that there was no pejorative sense in which he was either an eclectic or a syncretist, and E. F. Osborn rightly approves his dictum that "Justin does not merely use Greek philosophy. He passes judgment on it."[54] Our study, however, goes a little further in suggesting that, so far as one who wrote in Greek could do so, he avoided even the use of that philosophy with which he was so thoroughly acquainted.

We must, for example, question Chadwick's statement that the Martyr entertained a Platonic doctrine of the natural affinity between the soul and God.[55] When he puts this teaching into his own mouth as a Platonist, it is immediately rejected by the old man. Nor can we infer that he had already found his Logos in the Academy because we hear him express the ambition of "mounting the *logos* that governs all, and looking down on others and their pursuits."[56] This is the common idiom of Platonists, who aspired to an exalted state of reason which would make them friends of God and the unrecognised superiors of all their fellow-mortals; but it is only an ironic contiguity of language that enables the young philosopher to speak as though he already understood the ruling Principle whom only Christians know.

Even where Justin makes the greatest possible concession to philosophy, we must be careful to observe what is withheld. Though some, like Socra-

---

53. Article, "Justin," by W. H. C. Frend in the *Oxford Classical Dictionary*, 2nd ed. (Oxford: OUP, 1970), 570, now revised for the new edition (1995).

54. E. F. Osborn, *Justin Martyr*, 42, citing H. Chadwick, *Early Christianity and the Classical Tradition* (Oxford: OUP, 1966), 20.

55. Chadwick, *Early Christianity*, 12, citing *Dial.* 4.2.

56. *Dial.* 3.3, playfully replying to the imputation of being a *philologos*. Van Winden, *Early Christian Philosopher*, 57, notes the relevance of Plato, *Phaedo* 85c8, to which one might add other passages collected in my "Treading the Aether," *CQ* 40 (1990): 465–9.

tes, lived *meta logou*, they did not live *meta tou logou*;[57] they had their critical faculties by nature, but, except through plagiarism, no acquaintance with the Word. Just as in the parable of the Sower, there is one soil that is better prepared than others, yet there is none that is so prepared as to contain the seed already. Scripture is the necessary bridge between philosophy and Christ.

Our conclusion, therefore, is that in the two *Apologies*, no less than in the *Dialogue with Trypho*, Christ is the Logos who personifies the Torah. In Jewish thought the Word was the source of being, the origin of Law, the written Torah and a Person next to God. Early Christianity announced the incarnation of this Person, and Justin makes the further claims that Scripture is the parent of all truth among the nations, and that the Lord who is revealed to us in the New Testament is the author and the hermeneutic canon of the Old.

Is it, we may ask, a strong objection to our theory that it makes the apologist speak with the same intent to Greek and Jew? How could he expect a pagan audience to comprehend a doctrine based on an esoteric key that, once mislaid, took Christian scholarship some centuries to recover? This objection is based upon a widespread but fallacious modern axiom that an author must address himself entirely to the comprehension of his present audience. No seminal interpretation of Homer, Virgil or Shakespeare has subscribed to such a premiss in our century, and we can no more hope to extrapolate the audience from the work in ancient times than we could estimate the character of an eighteenth-century reader from the poems of William Blake. Every genius has to create the audience that will be able to comprehend him, and even a mind of the second rank, like Justin's, may be driven a little way beyond its period by the force of the world's most influential book.

In any case we cannot lightly assume that all apologies were written for the putative addressees. Most speeches in the ancient world have an epideictic quality, so that, if they fail to convince another party, they may none the less enhance the author's credit with his own. Arnobius wrote his learned and unusual book to prove that his conversion was sincere; Origen expounded his mature beliefs by arguing against a pagan author who had been dead for half a century, and appears to have been forgotten by his co-religionists. Can anyone believe that all twenty-two books of Augustine's *City of God* were inspired by the calamities of a city that he hardly knew, and the feeble possibility of a pagan restoration? It is often assumed that in

---

57. 1 *Apol.* 46.3. Cf. 1 *apol.* 5.3, and, for the relevance of the definite article, 5.4, cited above.

the second century apologies still aspired to have an effect upon their putative recipients, and yet the evidence that pagans read them is nugatory. Robert Grant invents a bold itinerary that would allow one patient autocrat to hear all five apologies that invoked his name;[58] but no one has located the Areopagus from which Tatian could have delivered his *Oration to the Greeks.*

Justin's knowledge of Greek philosophy is not in doubt; and neither— most uncommon though it was for a Christian writer of this epoch—is his martyrdom. We need not, then, deny that he might crave a pagan audience and hope to effect conversions by his preaching. We may, and should, deny that he would let his thoughts be fettered by the likely understanding of a pagan readership, and we may reasonably imagine that at all times he was writing, as he died, for the instruction of the Church.

M. J. Edwards teaches at Christ Church, Oxford University

58. R. M. Grant, "Five Apologists and Marcus Aurelius," *VigChr* 42 (1988): 1–17. For further remarks, see my "Aristides of Athens and the Origins of Christian Apologetic," forthcoming in *ANRW* 27.2.

Vigiliae Christianae 48 (1994), 1-24, © E. J. Brill, Leiden

ARGUMENTS FOR FAITH IN CLEMENT OF ALEXANDRIA

BY

ERIC OSBORN

In the history of ideas, the defence of faith, which is offered by Clement of Alexandria, ranks beside that of Paul who, in Romans 4, sought to prove the primacy of the faith of Abraham over the law of Moses. Paul was supported by the Letter to the Hebrews, which claimed that not only Abraham, but all the notables of Jewish scripture were persons of faith. Yet faith found its first principle and perfection in Jesus. For Clement, just as the law was a *paidagogos* to the Jews, so philosophy was a *paidagogos* to the Greeks to bring them to Christ. In the second century, both *paidagogoi* were unhappy at their compulsory retirement, especially since they were required to leave their books behind for use by their younger replacement. Justin made it clear that the scriptures now belonged to Christians; Tertullian warned all that the scriptures were Christian property.

In philosophy, Justin and Clement used an identical formula to assert that whatever had been well said, belonged to Christians. Justin's *logos spermatikos* claimed Socrates and Heraclitus as Christians before Christ. Clement, in his *Stromateis*, claimed that the Greek schools had torn the limbs of truth apart; Christ brought them all together. The need for philosophical argument was self-evident for it would have to be used to prove itself unnecessary. The protest against the Christian acquisition of Greek philosophy was strong and found its centre exactly where Jewish protest against Paul was fixed—the inadequacy of faith. Clement's reply defended faith with philosophical arguments which he connected to the arguments which Paul and the Epistle to the Hebrews had used against a different opponent.

The move from the New Testament to Christian theology through the joining of New Testament ideas to Greek philosophy was, I think, the beginning of European thought, and the argument about faith stands in the centre of that development. Faith became an object of attack from philosophers because it claimed too much and from Gnostics because it achieved too little. Clement of Alexandria's plea for the faith, which he had learned from his much-quoted Paul, is pervasive and of many strands. These strands have sometimes been separated between bible and philosophy[1] and subjected to limited scrutiny. My concern is to let the two sources speak together, to look at them in the light of recent discussion concerning Greek philosophy, and to solve a long-standing problem of false attribution, where Zeno is supplanted by Aristotle.

Christians were, according to the Platonist Celsus, always saying, 'Only believe', and never offering rational grounds for the acceptance of their creeds. Origen replied that not everyone could be a full-time philosopher, and that the scriptures were studied with logical rigour. Further, most people had neither time nor ability for rational inquiry and they must be helped (*Cels.* 1.9). Indeed, philosophers choose their school of philosophy on non-rational impulse, either because they have met a certain teacher or believe one school to be better than the rest (*Cels.* 1.10). Faith in the supreme God is a commendable thing, the writers of the Gospels were plainly honest men and Christian doctrines are coherent with the common notions of human reason (*Cels.* 3.39f.).

Clement's reply to the same criticism had been more complex. He needed more argument to meet the objections of Gnostics as well as philosophers to the high place which Christians gave to faith in their preaching, worship and discipline. He drew his account of faith from Paul (to whom he attributed the Epistle to the Hebrews), John, Plato, Aristotle, Theophrastus, Stoics, Epicurus and others. The philosophy of Clement's day, Middle Platonism, mixed Plato with Aristotle and the Stoics.

Faith was anticipation, assent, perception, hearing God in scripture, intuition of the unproved first-principle, discernment by criterion, dialectic and divine wisdom, unity with God.

Despite diversity of origin, all these moves in ancient epistemology had served a common end, that of finding a basis for knowledge and avoiding 'infinite regress'.

Clement was a Stromatist, not simply to hide things from unthinking Sophists, but because he wanted his different readers to learn from the similarities between their own ideas and Christian faith. 'To those who ask for the wisdom which is in us, we must present what is familiar to them so that, as easily as possible, through their own ideas (διὰ τῶν ἰδίων), they may reasonably arrive at faith in the truth' (*str* 5.3.18).

For Clement, as he begins the discussion in *Stromateis* 2 and takes it up again in *Stromateis* 5, argument and faith are necessary to one another. Argument for faith is still argument. His introduction indicates his approach. Philosophical proof is a benefit to minds rather than to tongues (*str.* 2.1.3). Just as fowls which scratch vigorously for their own food have the best flesh, so there is need for pain and effort by those who search for truth (*str.* 2.1.3). We need wisdom in all our ways (Prov. 3:5f.). Faith is the way and the fear of God is foremost (*str.* 2.2.4). The barbarian or biblical philosophy is perfect and true. Wisdom is the unerring knowledge of reality, of virtues and of the roots of things (Wisd. 7:17ff.; *str.* 2.2.5). Clement begins from the fear of the lord, as extolled in the Wisdom literature, which had already joined the faith of the Old Testament to Hellenistic philosophy (*str.* 2.2.4).

Divine wisdom is the universal guide. She requires rejection of earthly wisdom, conformity to reason, discriminating use of secular culture, departure from evil and, supremely, the fear of God (Prov. 3:5,6,7,12,23). Through wisdom God gives true understanding of existing things: 'a knowledge of the structure of the world and the operation of the elements; the beginning and end of epochs and their middle course; the alternating solstices and the changing seasons; the cycles of the years and the constellations; the nature of living creatures and behaviour of wild beasts; the violent force of winds and the thoughts of men; the varieties of plants and the virtues of roots. I learnt it all, hidden or manifest, for I was taught by her whose skill made all things, wisdom' (Wisd. 7:17-21). With these verses, Clement summarises 'barbarian philosophy' and the wisdom which leads to God who, although remote in essence, has come near to men (Jer. 23:23).[2] The riddles of divine utterance and the deep things of the spirit, he says, are secrets which exclude the unworthy. What is holy must be kept from the dogs. Heraclitus limited understanding to the few and seems to rebuke the many who do not believe; the prophets tell us that the righteous live by faith and without faith there can be no understanding. Without faith, said the writer to Hebrews, it is impossible to please God (*str.* 2.2.4-8).

Clement's eight arguments are the following:

First, *faith is preconception*, the substance of things hoped for.

Second, *faith is assent or decision*, and never a natural possession.

Third, *faith is hearing and seeing*, as the definition and narrative of Hebrews 11 make clear.

Fourth, *faith is listening to God in the scriptures.*
Fifth, a first principle *is to be unproved and unprovable.* To avoid
infinite regress, there has to be a starting point which is grasped by
faith.[3]
Sixth, *faith is the criterion* which judges that something was true or
false.
Seventh, *faith is always on the move, from faith to faith,* moving up the
ladder of dialectic. It is the grain of mustard seed which stimulates the
soul to grow.
Eighth, *faith is fixed on God and in some way divine,* a source of *power
and stability.* From the shifting sands of error, it moves to the firm
ground of truth and there it remains.

All these arguments raise problems which show that they never were
without ambiguity. In order to use them Clement had to decide what
they meant; their close examination shows how many questions had to
be faced in order to give an account of faith. The eight points also show
how intricately scripture and philosophy are joined. Today it seems
natural to divide the language of philosophy and the language of the
bible.[4] For Clement the bible was the barbarian philosophy and logos
linked the text of scripture to human reason. It was not possible to pluck
instant fruit from the vines; there had to be planting, weeding, watering
and all sorts of farming. It is a mistake, in the elucidation of Clement's
complex ideas, to isolate philosophical argument from evangelical
exhortation. Clement quotes Plato 600 times and Paul 1200 times; frequently they are quoted together.

1. *Preconception and hope*

Faith, says Clement, is denigrated by the Greeks but it is what they
recognise as a deliberate preconception or anticipation (πρόληψις
ἑκούσιος). Hebrews 11 has offered the same defence of faith: faith gives
substance to our hopes (*str.* 2.2.8).

'Epicurus supposes faith to be a preconception of the mind, He
explains this preconception as attention directed to something clear and
a clear concept of something. He declares that no one can make an
inquiry, confront a problem, have an opinion and indeed make a refutation without a preconception' (*str.* 2.4.16). Epicurus saw that without
an anticipation one cannot inquire, doubt, judge. Isaiah insisted that
there could be no understanding without faith (7:9) and Heraclitus

wrote 'Except one hopes for what is beyond hope, he will not find it, for it will remain impossible to examine and to understand' (Diels 18). This means that the blessed and happy man must be from the beginning a partaker of truth, believing and trustworthy (Plato, *Laws* 730bc). The *apistos* is hopeless in the arena of truth and is a fool (*str.* 2.4.16).

Hope depends on faith. Even Basilides, the Gnostic, saw that faith is the assent of the soul to things which are not present to the senses (*str.* 2.6.17). Basilides went wrong when he denied the freedom of faith and the decision which it involved. Faith is a wise preconception prior to comprehension (πρόληψις εὐγνώμων πρὸ καταλήψεως). It is an expectation and confidence in the only and all-sufficient God, whose beneficence and kindness are turned to us (*str.* 2.6.28).

The *function* of Epicurean preconceptions is to make knowledge possible, when the perceiver is confronted by a mass of sensations.[5] Preconceptions are 'a kind of ἐπιβολὴ τῆς διανοίας, distinguished from other mental visions by their generic content.'[6] They claim to generate universals from streams of phenomena. By means of preconception we recognise different kinds of things. The mind selects from streams of atomic images to form the preconception which enlarges the act of perception.[7] Preconceptions become indispensable starting points. 'It is as a matter of fact, from Epicurus on, a philosophical commonplace that preconceptions are what make inquiry possible'.[8] Regrettably, they were no more impregnable against Skeptics than were other starting points, for the Skeptic simply claimed that he had different preconceptions and could not choose between them.[9]

There are three different theories concerning the *origin* of preconceptions. In the first account they are due to repeated sensation, in the second they are innate, and in the third they are ingrained.

(i) Preconceptions come from what has frequently been evident to the sense (D.L. 10.33). Each word brings to the mind a clear delineation which is a self-evident starting point, and which removes the danger of infinite regress (cf. *Ep.Hdt.* 37f.). We do not inquire about anything of which we have no prior knowledge. Sensations are marked off from one another and classified by means of preconceptions, which have been gained through repeated experiences of particular objects (D.L. 10.33). Other concepts may also be derived from preconceptions; even the gods are objects of refined perception.[10]

(ii) The late Stoicizing Academy speaks of innate preconceptions. For example, every race of men possesses, in its untaught state, a preconception of the gods. 'Epicurus' word for this is *prolepsis*, that is what we may call a delineation of a thing, preconceived by the mind, without which understanding, inquiry and discussion are impossible' (Cicero, *ND* 1.44).[11] These preconceptions are *insitae* and *innatae*.

(iii) In between these positions is that of the Old Stoa. Chrysippus considered preconceptions to be ingrained (ἔμφυται) rather than innate, and was credited with clearing up confusion between preconceptions and conceptions (Plutarch, *Comm. not.* 1059C). 'There is no other "evidence" in the Old Stoic writers for a theory of any kind of "inborn" belief; their philosophy needs no such beliefs and should not be saddled with them.'[12]

Attempts to harmonise the different accounts of origin have been unsuccessful.[13] The first belongs to Epicurus, the second to the late Stoicizing Academy and the third to the Old Stoa. For the Epicurean, the world is perceived as divided into natural kinds which we recognise, for the Stoic, definition is a prerequisite for any inquiry. The Stoic idea aims to represent the world. The Epicurean idea simply responds to a stimulus in the world. The scholarly consensus that Stoics merely took over Epicurean preconception is seriously wrong.[14] We have no Epicurean text which sets out exactly the nature of preconception; but the empiricist, materialist position of the Epicureans should prevent them being assimilated by Stoicizing commentators. *Prolepseis* are concerned, not with mental states, but with states of affairs in the world.[15] *Prolepseis* organise *phainomena* either into natural kinds or into persistent conditions.[16] Anything more must be a conceptual invention. There is a difference between recognizing something in the world and conceiving something which represents it.[17]

The 'substance of things hoped for' in Hebrews 11 is a simple development from Pauline theology. Just as Abraham was justified by faith, so all Old Testament notables are heroes of faith.[18] The notion of anticipation (*vorauseilen, vorangehen, vorausnehmen*) is stressed by Bultmann in his sermons. 'To be a Christian, to believe, means to have hurried on ahead of the time of this world. It means to stand already at the end of this world.'[19] In this way faith becomes that victory which overcomes the world (1Jn 5:4).[20] As so often for Clement, Heraclitus, for whom hope is essential to understanding,[21] provided the link between philosophy and the bible.

Clement's adoption of *prolepsis* is not a blind appropriation, because there are different theories between which he must choose. For his own reasons, Clement gives Epicurus a more Stoic doctrine than he had propounded; but he cannot (for anti-Gnostic reasons) concede that preconceptions are innate. Faith is *hekousios* and it is a clear vision of the future which links faith and hope. These claims lead on to the next two arguments.

2. Assent and choice

The preconception of faith is chosen. It is the assent of godliness, or saying 'yes' to God (θεοσεβείας συγκατάθεσις *str.* 2.2.8). Faith (*str.* 2.2.9) is an assent which unites[22] the believer to God. Faith provides a foundation by rational anticipatory choice. The decision to follow what is better is the beginning of understanding. Unswerving anticipatory choice (προαίρεσις) provides the movement towards knowledge (*str.* 2.2.9). Choice and decision had been important for Plato and especially for Aristotle (*Nic.Eth.* 1139a 31ff.).[23] Here Clement is concerned both to attack Gnostics and to convince philosophers. For Basilides, faith is innate and, as for Valentinus, inferior to knowledge. Both deny that faith is a matter of free choice (*str.* 2.3.10). For Clement, faith must be voluntary (*str.* 2.3.11).

The scriptures tell of free choice, and the scriptural command to believe is an invitation to assent or choose. With a willing spirit we choose life and believe God through his voice (*str.* 2.4.12). Following Hebrews 11, the faith of Abel, Enoch, Noah, Abraham, Isaac, Jacob, Sarah, is celebrated. Clement continues with Joseph and Moses who also chose God's way of faith. Faith is in our power and shows its effects in a repentance which is freely chosen (*str.* 2.6.27). Both Platonists and Stoics say that assent is in our power (Chrysippus *frag.phys.* 992) (*str.* 2.12.54). Indeed all opinion, judgement, conjecture and learning is assent, which is faith. Unbelief shows that its opposite (faith) is possible, while it remains a mere privation and has no real existence (*str.* 2.12.55). Faith as the voluntary assent of the soul produces good works and right action (*str.* 5.13.86). We may note, in contrast (*str.* 5.5.28), that David says 'Be angry and sin not' (Ps. 4:5). This means, says Clement, that we should not give our assent to the impression of anger or confirm it by action.

Confession (*homologia*) to God is martyrdom (*marturia*). The soul which has lived purely, known God and obeyed his commandments is a *martus* by life and word. It sheds blood all along the way of life until

111

it goes from earth to be with God (*str.* 4.4.15). However, those (Marcionites or others) who choose martyrdom out of hatred for their creator, do not qualify as 'believing martyrs'. They have not known the only true God and die in futility. Nor are words enough. The true confession of martyrs is not what their voice utters, but the deeds and actions which correspond to faith (*str.* 4.9.71).

Knowledge, for Zeno (*SVF* i 68), is a form of grasping or comprehension, a *katalepsis* which cannot be overthrown by any argument. External objects produce impressions, which reach the governing-principle of the perceiver (*SVF* ii 56), who *assents* or judges that his impression corresponds to fact. Then, he grasps the impression and finally he knows. Zeno described the four stages, by extending his open hand which received the impression, then partly closing his hand to show assent, then clenching his fist to show cognition and finally grasping his fist with his other hand to show what knowledge was like (Cic.*Acad.* 2.145). Many things may be grasped and known by the senses, but never without assent, which we may give or withhold. Yet the living mind must admit what is self-evident as surely as scales sink under weights (Cic.*Acad.* 2.37f.). Some impressions are immediately certain; these cognitive or recognizable impressions virtually take us by the hair and drag us to assent (Sextus, *Adv.math.*, vii, 257).

Sense perceptions are like blows from outside to which the assent of the mind must be given from within (Cic.*Acad.* 1.40f.). The senses send their impressions to the mind which assesses their testimony. The wise man gives assent only to impressions which are cognitive and consequently he does not err. Ignorance is changeable and weak assent. While the wise man supposes nothing weakly, but securely and firmly (ἀσφαλῶς καὶ βεβαίως), the inferior man is precipitate and gives assent without cognition.[24]

Assent is given by the ruling faculty of the soul (Aetius 4.21) mediating between impressions and impulses. 'Without assent there is neither action nor impulsion'.[25] Such assent means 'going along with' or 'committing oneself to' the truth of an impression. For the New Academy, assent was not an acceptable theory. Carneades had driven it as a wild and savage monster from their minds (*Acad.* 2.108). Arcesilaus denied the propriety of assent to any truth (*Acad.* 1.43-6). Assents are bad; suspension of judgement is good (Sext.Emp.*Pyrr.* 1.232-4). As well as assent, Clement gives an account of faith as choice, when reason fails. We do not inquire into questions which are obvious, opaque, ambivalent, or which have one irrefutable side. If the cause for inquiry is removed in any of these ways, then faith is established, πίστις ἐμπεδοῦται (str. 5.1.5).

3. Perception, hearing, seeing and believing

Faith needs to perceive that to which its assent may be given. Faith is the scrutiny of things not seen (Heb. 11:1). Moses endured as seeing him who is invisible (Heb. 11:27). He who hopes, as he who believes, says Clement, sees with his mind both mental objects and future things. What is just, good, true is seen with the mind and not with the eyes (str. 5.3.16). Faith is prior to argument, and may be considered as a form of perception. For Theophrastus, Clement tells us, aisthesis is the arche of faith. From perception the archai come to our logos and dianoia (str. 2.2.9). While truth is found in aisthesis, nous, episteme and hupolepsis, nous is first by nature, even if for us aisthesis is first in the order of our experience. Sensation and nous are the essence of knowledge, sharing what is enarges. Sensation is the ladder to knowledge. Faith advances through things which are perceived, leaves assumptions (ὑπολήψεις) behind and comes to rest in truth (str. 2.3.13). While materialists grasp rocks and oaks in their hands to argue with idealists (Sophist 246a), faith provides a new eye, new ear and new heart which apprehend what eye has not seen nor ear heard nor has entered in to the heart of man (1 Cor. 2:9; Is. 64:4). By faith comes the quick comprehension of the disciples of the lord. They discern the false from the genuine, like money changers, who tell others what is counterfeit but who do not try to explain why, because only they have learnt the difference (str. 2.4.15).[26] Those who have ears to hear should hear. Epicharmus explains further that it is mind which sees and hears, while all else is deaf and blind. Heraclitus describes unbelievers as ignorant of how to hear or to speak, while Solomon (Sir. 6:33) links hearing with comprehension and wisdom (str. 2.5.24).

Such hearing comes from the son of God through the word of the lord and the preaching of the apostles; it ends in faith (Is. 53:1; Rom. 10:17, 14, 15). Word and preaching need cooperation. As in a game of ball the thrower must have someone to catch, so faith catches what it hears and is a cooperating cause in the gaining of truth (str. 2.6.25).

113

Faith is the ear of the soul, whereby he who has ears to hear may hear, and comprehend what the lord says.[27] Faith of teacher and of hearer work together to the one end of salvation. Paul speaks of the mutual faith which he shares with the Romans (Rom. 1:11f.).

Faith directs the sight of the soul to discovery. Obstacles like jealousy and greed must be cleared away (*str.* 5.1.11). So there are to be no pearls cast before swine; the natural man does not receive the things of God (*str.* 1.12.56 also 5.4.25). All, both barbarians and Greeks, who have spoken of divine things, have veiled their account of first principles in riddles, symbols, allegories, and metaphors (*str.*5.4.21). The common crowd will stay with their five senses; but we must go within the veil. Plato excluded the uninitiated who thought that all existence could be grasped by their hands. God cannot be known by those who are limited to their five senses. The son revealed the father in the flesh but he is known only in the spirit. We walk by faith, not by sight (*str.* 5.6.34).

Earlier, in Justin, we may note how the transition from Platonism to the prophets is made by the certainty that νοῦς νοητὰ ὁρᾷ καὶ νοητῶν ἀκούει.[28] In scripture the language of seeing and hearing is present on every side. Paul speaks of the new eye and ear, of looking to things unseen and eternal, even of visions in the third heaven. Hebrews 11 is full of the evidence of what is unseen. Blindness and deafness are the epistemological illnesses of the Gospels. At the last judgement, condemnation is pronounced on those who did not see, in the hungry, thirsty, lonely, naked, sick and prisoner, the presence of their lord.[29]

4. Faith and scripture

Perception leaves us with the question: where is God to be seen and heard? God is the first object of faith and the arguments for faith only work because God has spoken in scripture. Here we receive the voice of God as irrefutable proof. The strength of scripture is, like the call of the Sirens, greater than human power; it disposes hearers, almost against their wills, to receive its words (*str.* 2.2.9).

Plato (*Tim* 40de), says Clement, claims that it is possible to learn the truth only from God or from the offspring of God. We are confident in the divine oracles which we possess and the truth we learn from the son of God, a truth which was first prophesied and then made clear (*str.* 6.15.123).

The disciples of Pythagoras found in his αὐτὸς ἔφα a sufficient ground for faith. Therefore the lovers of truth will not refuse faith to a master worthy of faith, the only saviour and God (*str.* 2.5.24). From him come the word of the lord, the preaching of the apostles, and the hearing which turns to faith (Is. 53:1; Rom. 10:17,14,15) (*str.* 2.6.25).

In general, faith and proof may depend on either knowledge or opinion. From the scriptures we have proof based on knowledge in an obedience which is faith in God (*str.* 2.11.48). Even the simplest faith has this knowledge or rationality. The highest proof produces *episteme* through scriptures and leads on to *gnosis* (*str.* 2.11.49). Faith cannot be overthrown because God comes to our help in scripture (*str.* 5.1.5). It would be wrong further to disbelieve God and ask for proofs from him (*str.* 5.1.6).

Clement's strong claims for scripture might be assisted in two ways. First, it was common in the ancient world to look to literature as a source of all knowledge.[30] Secondly, Christians (notably Justin) took over Jewish scriptures which were studied as the oracles of God, a complex totality of truth. These had ceased to belong to the Jews and had become Christian property. Irenaeus, Clement and Tertullian saw them as crowned by the writings of the New Testament. The central problem, which Clement raises with striking clarity, is the relation between divine oracle and the philosophy, which for him means argument. Plato, he shows, had established the conjunction. In Philo, oracle almost swallows philosophy, and in the Gnostics there is nothing but oracle. Clement stays close to Plato and insists that we should follow the wind of the argument wherever it leads. Philosophical argument is never optional: we should have to argue in order to show it to be unnecessary (*str.* 6.18.162).

For Clement the divine oracles are alive. His enthusiasm for scripture is enhanced by its novelty. He writes with the wonder of the poet John Keats, 'On first looking into Chapman's Homer'. Faith, says Clement, is active through love in writing or speaking the word (*str.* 1.1.4). The prophets and disciples of the spirit knew by faith (*str.* 1.9.45). We are taught by God, instructed by the son of God in the truly 'sacred letters which are the scriptures' (*str.* 1.20.98). Faith in Christ and the knowledge of the gospel provide explanation and fulfilment of the law. As Isaiah says, unless we believe, we do not understand. We must believe what the law prophesies and delivers in oracles in order to understand the Old Testament, which Christ, by his coming, expounded.

Indeed faith in Christ and the knowledge of the gospel are the exegesis of the law and its fulfilment (*str.* 4.21.134).

At the same time philosophy is at least as important as oracle. The scriptures provide the real philosophy and true theology if we read them often, put them to the test by faith and practise them in the whole of our lives (*str.* 5.9.56). He who believes scripture and the voice of the lord may be trusted. Scripture is the criterion and first principle, and not subject to criticism. It is reasonable to grasp by faith the unprovable first principle and to receive from it demonstrations about the first principle. In this way we are trained to know truth by the voice of the lord (*str.* 7.16.95). We have already arrived at the next argument.[31]

5. *Faith and proof*

Scripture makes claims about God and salvation. How can these be rationally accepted? The faith of Abraham points to one cause and principle of all things, to the self-existent God, who justifies the ungodly, raises the dead and creates out of nothing. God, says Clement, who is remote in his being, has come near to us (Jer. 23:23f.). Moses, on the mountain, entered into the darkness, into the inaccessible ideas about existence (*str.* 2.2.6). Hidden truth may now be learnt (Prov. 1:2-6; *str.* 2.2.6). With the Holy Spirit, it is possible to search the deep things of God (1 Cor 2:10). That which is holy is not for dogs (*str.* 2.2.7). Understanding follows faith (Is. 7:9).[32]

For the first-principles of things are not proved or provable. They are not known by practical *techne* or by *phronesis* which handles changeable things: the first principle or cause of all things is known by faith alone.[33] All knowledge may be taught, and what is taught is based on previous knowledge. The first principle was not known to Greeks like Thales or Anaxagoras. Since no one can know and teach first principles, we must call no man our master on earth (*str.* 2.3.13). Wisdom, which begins from the fear of the Lord, the grace and word of God, is faith.

God, we are told later, in *Stromateis* 5, gave us life and reason; he wished that our life be both reasonable and good. From Justin's *logos spermatikos* onwards, this was the dominant theme of early Christian thought: reason and goodness stand together. The logos of the father of all things is not just a spoken word but his wisdom and transparent goodness, his divine and sovereign power, his almighty will, conceivable even for those who do not confess him (*str.* 5.1.6). Man's own rational power is limited. Paul declared God's judgement on the fragile wisdom of the disputers of this world. In similar vein Numa, king of the Romans, rightly built a temple to faith and peace, which are the opposites of the worldly debate. Abram was justified by faith, recognised God as superior to creation and scored an extra Alpha to be called Abraham. He had always been interested in the heavens; when he grasped the simplicity and unity of God, he received a second Alpha and a new name. The link of justification and the indemonstrable first principle is an important clue to the meaning of faith (*str.* 5.1.8). While Empedocles claimed truth in his myths, he declared that the inclination to faith (πίστιος ὁρμή) is resisted by the mind (*str.* 5.1.9). So Paul put his faith not in the wisdom of men, but in the power of God, which alone and without proofs can save.

In his logic note-book of *Stromateis* 8, Clement expands his claim that first principles cannot be proved or else they would not be first principles but dependent on something prior to them. This is the simplest argument for faith. It is not a proof of God's existence, but a proof that God, because he is God and ultimate first principle, is only accessible to faith (*str.* 8.3.6f.). An account of unprovable first-principles had been central to the logic of Aristotle, as stated in the Metaphysics. 'There cannot be demonstration of everything alike: the process would go on to infinity so that there would still be no demonstration' (*Met* 1006a6), and elaborated in *Posterior Analytics* 2.19.100a,[34] where it is insisted that there must be unproved first-principles. These are of two kinds: principles on which reasoning works (non-contradiction and excluded middle) and axioms (mathematical and ethical).

The final chapter of *Posterior Analytics* bases all knowledge on *sensation*, which is an 'innate discriminatory capacity', distinguishing one thing from another. From memory and experience, we come to know the 'whole universal that has come to rest in the soul (the one apart from the many, whatever is one and the same in all those things)' (*Post.an.* 2.19.100a); beginning from particulars, we perceive universals, then categories which are 'the ultimate first principles of all that exists, *qua* existing' (*Met* 1005b10). In the end 'Now besides *episteme* only *nous* infallibly gives truth, therefore *nous* is the source of all knowledge, the *arche* of the *archai*'.[35]

Aristotle's account of dialectic and first principles has been explored in a recent study.[36] Dialectic cannot find the first principles of science, which must be self-evident, and be grasped as true and necessary in themselves. First principles are grasped by *nous* (*Post.An.* 100b5-17). The self-evident will not seem self-evident to us before we grasp it. Empirical inquiry, induction, dialectic are ways to first principles; but they do not make a first principle self-evident. They may serve as stimuli or occasions for intuition. For Plato, dialectic, through its coherence, could justify first principles;[37] Aristotle denies this because dialectic is shaped by the common beliefs from which it starts and these beliefs are always open to challenge. 'Aristotle's assumptions about knowledge and justification do not seem to yield a solution to the problems he has raised for himself; either the sort of intuition he advocates is indefensible or (if the right defence is found) it is superfluous'.[38]

However Aristotle seems to take a new direction in *Metaphysics* 4. In his account of first philosophy he uses a new method, which may be described as 'strong dialectic' and 'which differs from pure dialectic in so far as it selects only some of the premises that pure dialectic allows'.[39] Strong dialectic considers that the right kind of coherence can justify the truth of a belief and will explain the kind of argument which Aristotle assigns to first philosophy. While Aristotle never explicitly renounces his early foundationalism (which is inconsistent with strong dialectic), 'the anti-sceptical arguments in *Metaphysics* IV show that at any rate he does not consistently adhere to the foundationalism of the *Analytics*'.[40] His practice of strong dialectic may be defended on the ground that his first principles and methods provide a basis for the criticism of his own conclusions. However the problem remains for us today: if we have no alternative to dialectic as a method, we face his difficulties about first principles.[41] Clement is close to the central puzzle, since together with faith and dialectic, he states the need for 'true dialectic, which is philosophy mixed with truth' (*str.* 1.27.177).

By argument and faith, Clement continues, we reach the first principle of all things (*str.* 2.4.14); the errors of Thales show that there is no other way. Faith is a grace which goes beyond the indemonstrable principle to what is entirely simple, and in no way material. The point of Clement's argument is that it shows how faith and God are correlative. For Paul, faith depends on the God who justifies the ungodly (Rom 4:5), raises the dead and creates out of nothing (Rom 4:17). Such a God is the ultimate first principle and not accessible except by faith.

6. *Judgement and criterion*

The first principles which faith grasps are the elements of truth. They may therefore be used to test other claims to truth. The faith which holds them becomes the criterion for which Hellenistic philosophy sought.[42]

Aristotle, according to Clement, says[43] that the *krima* which follows the knowledge of a thing and affirms it to be true is faith. Faith, then, is the criterion of knowledge and greater than knowledge because it determines whether knowledge is true or false (*str.* 2.4.15). The only possible reference in Aristotle seems to be in *Top.* 4.5,126b: 'Similarly also the belief will be present in the opinion since it is the intensification of the opinion; so the opinion will believe. Further the result of making an assertion of this kind will be to call intensification intensified and excess excessive. For the belief is intensified; if therefore, belief is intensification, intensification would be intensified'.[44] This is an unlikely source for Clement's simple claim.

There remain four possibilities behind Clement's account. First, it may refer to a lost text of Aristotle. Secondly, it may be a development from what Aristotle said about the importance of a canon. When speaking of the construction of the soul, he talks of the carpenter's straight rule which can test both straight and curved lines, while a curved rule can test nothing (*anima* 1.5,411a). Thirdly, the claim may come from a rhetorical source. When an orator offers an argument, we call it a *pistis*, because we are intended to *pisteuein* the conclusion after being convinced by the argument. It is from our *pistis* that we judge the strength of the argument and the *episteme* of its author.[45] Finally, because the argument is strongly Stoic, it is probable that a Stoic argument has simply been attributed to Aristotle in error. Inaccurate citation was common in Clement's day.[46]

The Stoic origin of the argument can now be asserted with confidence.[47] The same argument, in an extended form, is attributed by Cicero to Zeno (*Acad.* 1.41f.) and set out in these terms:

1. Assent is a voluntary act.
2. Not all sensible presentations are worthy of faith (*fides*).
3. Only those, which possess clarity and are recognisable presentations, are worthy of faith.
4. Sensation, firmly grasped or recognisable, is knowledge (*scientia*), irremoveable by reasoning. All other sensation is ignorance (*inscientia*).

5. The stage between knowledge and ignorance is *comprehensio*, and it alone is credible *'sed solum ei credendum esse credebat'* (*Acad.* 1.42). 6. Hence Zeno granted *fides* also to the senses, because it let go nothing which was capable of being its object, and because nature had given a *canon* (or *criterion*) and a first principle of itself from which the first principle of a thing might be impressed on the mind.

Finally, Cicero, following Antiochus, remarks that 'the Stoic system should be considered a correction of the Old Academy rather than another new teaching' (*Acad.* 1.43). This makes the attribution to Aristotle easy to understand.

Clement's summary of this argument, which he would have learnt from a Greek source similar to that of Cicero, is brief: the judgement concerning the truth of a presentation judges whether it is faithful and this verdict is reached by faith, using its own criterion. Here the argument from assent seems to be repeated, using κρῖμα instead of συγκατάθεσις, so that faith becomes criterion.

Canon and *criterion* dominated Hellenistic philosophy, for they indicated the way in which objective truth might be tested.[48] The canon of Epicurus set out criteria to test truth and falsity. Clement speaks similarly of the canon of the church which is the confession of the essential articles of faith (*str.* 7.15.90). For example, the criterion of faith works at scripture to present a coherent account which follows from faith's first principle. The lover of truth must exercise strength of soul, strict adherence to faith's rule, critical discrimination between true and false, and a sense of what is essential. Heretics do not follow logical rules and plain argument. The believer will not abandon the truth to which the Word has appointed him, but stands firm, grows old in the scriptures, lives by the gospel and finds proofs in the law and the prophets. He must never defile the truth or canon of the church. Heretics do not enter by the main door of the church, the tradition of Christ, but cut a side door through the wall (*str.* 7.17.106). The pious forger of the 'Secret Gospel of Mark' took this reference to a hole in the wall literally and one modern writer has tumbled in after him.[49] The failure of the heretic is a twofold logical error, through failure to use a true criterion and failure to observe simple rules of argument.[50]

7. *Faith, knowledge and love*

Faith as criterion could have a negative function. For Clement, its use was primarily positive. Faith was needed as the beginning of exuberant growth, strenuous thought and virtuous living. Clement attacks those who want bare faith alone, who are not prepared to cultivate and farm the vines they plant, but wish to harvest fruit immediately (*str.* 1.9.43). In contrast, the true dialectic, which is philosophy mixed with truth, ascends and descends (*str.* 1.28.177).

(i) Faith and dialectic

Faith becomes knowledge (*gnosis*) for which it has provided a good foundation. It moves on towards knowledge by a process of dialectic. Clement has been well known for his account of the way in which faith grows to knowledge in his Christian savant, the true gnostic. Intellectual progress comes through dialectic and scripture. For Justin and Clement, scripture is the mind and will of God (*dial.* 68); it replaces the Platonic forms.

We have noted differences between Plato and Aristotle on the use of dialectic. Plato believed that dialectic could reach the highest first principle; Aristotle did not. Yet for both, intuition was needed at the top of the logical ladder, so Clement used both Plato and Aristotle. Plato took him to the unknown and ineffable God who, according to Acts 17, was declared in Jesus Christ (*str.* 5.12.81f.); in another place the via negativa is taken to the monad, then to the dimension of Christ, then to the void, and then to a perception of the Almighty (*str.* 5.11.71).

For later Platonism, dialectic is concerned with the upward movement of the *Republic*, where hypotheses are destroyed to be replaced by more ultimate principles.[51] This is what Clement means when he speaks of the true dialectic, which is applied to scripture: universal principles like the Sermon on the Mount and the love commandment would stand at the top, while particular injunctions would stand at the bottom. Yet at the same time there is downward movement to particular points, as in the demolition of Gnostic *koinonia* (*str.* 3.5.42). In *Phaedrus, Politicus, Sophist*, and elsewhere, dialectic is also concerned with dividing and joining specific kinds. Definitions are ladders which proceed downwards to these kinds.

(ii) Faith as a virtue

As indicated earlier, the theme of early Christian thought was that God required both reason and goodness. Faith is the royal wisdom described by Plato.[52] Those who have believed in Christ are *chrestoi*, as those cared for by the true king are kingly. What is right is lawful because the law is right reason. Law is the king of all (Pindar, fr. 169). For Plato and the Stoics, only the wise man is king and ruler (*str.* 2.4.18).

Plato (*Laws* 630bc and *Rep* 475bc) commends faithfulness. Faith is the mother of virtues (*str.* 2.5.23). Faith is divine and cannot be eroded by worldly friendship or fear. Love makes men believers, and faith is the foundation of love (*str.* 2.6.30). Faith is the first movement to salvation. It is followed by fear, hope, repentance, temperance, patience and finally love and knowledge (*str.* 2.6.31). The sequence of the virtues may also be seen as faith hoping through repentance, fear through faith: patience and practice lead on to love (*str.* 2.9.45). Both faith and gnosis look to the past in memory and to the future in hope (*str.* 2.12.53).

Hermas (*Vis.* 3.8.roughly), Clement continues, describes faith as the virtue by which the elect are saved; it is followed by continence, simplicity, knowledge, innocence, modesty, love, all of which are the daughters of faith (*str.* 2.12.55).

God (*str.* 5.1.13) is love, and known to those who love; he is faithful and known to those who are faithful. We are joined to him by divine love, so that by like we may see like. God's temple is built on the threefold foundation of faith, hope and love (*str.* 5.1.13).

After having presented testimonies from the Greeks about faith Clement adds only a few about hope and love. Plato speaks of hope about life after death in several places: *Crito* 48b, *Phaedrus* 248f, *Symp.* 206c-208b; *Theaet.* 150bc (*str.* 5.2.14).

(iii) Faith to faith

Faith and knowledge are inseparable, as are the father and the son (*str.* 5.1.1). Faith is twofold, for Paul speaks of righteousness which is revealed from faith to faith (Rom. 1:17). A common faith, says Clement, is the foundation; this is indeed what Paul is saying. Paul is concerned with unbroken continuity and the dimensions of a new world,[53] rather than with two separate stages of development. The perfection of faith comes from instruction and logos. Faith saves men and removes mountains (*str.* 5.2.1). Faith stimulates the soul like a grain of mustard and grows to greatness in it, so that the words about things above rest on it (*str.* 5.2.1). Faith (*str.* 5.1.11) is not inactive (ἀργή) and alone. It seeks and finds. Sophocles says that what is sought may be captured but what is neglected escapes. The sight of the soul must be directed towards discovery and freed from the obstacles in its way (*str.* 2.2.9).

The just live by faith. We must not hold back, but believe so that our souls are saved (Heb. 10:32-9). The endurance of faith (Heb. 11:36-40; 12:1,2) looks to Jesus the pioneer and perfecter of faith (*str.* 4.16.103). The faith which by love ascends to knowledge is desirable for its own sake. If we had to choose between the knowledge of God and eternal salvation we should choose knowledge. The soul never sleeps. The constant exertion of the intelligence is the essence of an intelligent being (*str.* 4.22.136); this is the divine perfection to which we are called.

(iv) Perfection of faith (*paid.* 1.6.25-52)

Faith brings life and is perfect in itself. For the believer after death there is no waiting, since, through the pledge of life eternal, he has anticipated the future by faith. Faith goes from promise to enlightened knowledge to final rest. Instruction leads to faith, which goes on to baptism, and then to the training of the holy spirit. Faith is the one salvation of all men and guarantees equality in communion with God. As Paul says, we had the law as our *paidagogos* until faith came; now as God's children through faith, we are all one in Christ. There is no distinction between those who are enlightened and those who are at an animal or psychic level. All who have abandoned carnal desires are equal and spiritual in the presence of their lord. They have been baptised by one spirit into one body (1 Cor. 12:13). Paul explained Christian maturity when he told us to be children in wickedness, but men in understanding (1 Cor. 14:20). The childish things which he has put away (1 Cor. 13:11) are not smallness of stature or age. Because he is no longer under the law (Gal. 4:1-5), he has lost the fear of childish phantoms of the mind. To be a grown man is to be obedient to the word, master of oneself, to believe and be saved by voluntary choice, to be free from irrational fear, to be a son and not a servant (Gal. 4:7). Childhood in Christ is full maturity, instead of infancy under the law. The infant milk of children in Christ (1 Cor 3:2) is difficult to relate to the perfection of milk and honey (*paid.* 1.6.24f.). Clement finally goes into physiology to explain the link. The Christian life in which we are being trained is a system of rational[54] actions and an unceasing energy which is faith.

Greek philosophy cleanses and prepares the soul for faith. Then truth builds knowledge on the foundation of faith (*str.* 7.3.20). Faith does not search for God, but confesses and glorifies him. Knowledge starts from faith and goes on to love, the inheritance and the endless end (*str.* 7.10.55). Faith is a comprehensive knowledge of the essentials; knowledge proves what it receives from faith and goes on to certainty (*str.* 7.10.57). Yet faith remains supreme, although some have deviated from the truth in their zeal to surpass common faith (*str.* 7.16.97).

8. Strength and stability

For critics like Celsus, faith was a weaker thing and the affliction of feeble minds.

(i) Power of God.

Faith is the power of God (cf. 1 Cor. 2:5) and the strength (ἰσχύς) of truth. It moves mountains and determines what we receive. According to our faith, we receive (*str.* 2.11.48). Paul, says Clement, pointed faith away from the wisdom of men to the power of God, which alone and without proofs, can save (*str.* 5.1.9).

(ii) Stability and blood.

The mature Christian (the true 'gnostic') is fixed firmly by faith (πέπηγεν) (*str.* 2.11.51) while the man who thinks that he is wise and does not willingly attach himself to truth, is moved by uncertain and capricious impulses (*str.* 2.11.51). While faith and knowledge make the soul constant and uniform, error brings instability and change. Knowledge brings tranquillity, rest and peace (*str.* 2.11.52). 'Therefore also to believe in him and through him is to become a unit, being indivisibly made one in him; but to disbelieve means separation, estrangement, and division' (*str.* 4.25.157). Here the drive to unity with the One has clear Platonic overtones. To those who believe and obey, grace will overflow and abound (*prot.* 9.85). 'Your faith has saved you' was said to Jews who had kept the law; those who lived blamelessly needed only faith in the lord (*str.* 6.14.108). Faith is the *stasis* of the soul concerning what is (*str.* 4.22.143). Yet it is a strange stability. The crown of thorns which the lord wore is a type of our faith, of life because of the tree, of joy because it is a crown, of danger because of thorns. No one can approach the word without blood (*paed.* 2.8.73).

(iii) God in us

The aim of faith is assimilation to God, as required by Plato, and the end is the restitution of the promise effected by faith (*str.* 2.22.136). Faith grants divinity to the believer. Those, who are taught by the son of God, possess the truth, for he is the person of truth (*str.* 6.15.122). On the believer rests the head of the universe (we have the mind of Christ, 1 Cor. 2:16), the kind and gentle word who subverts the craftiness and empty thoughts of the wise (*str.* 1.3.23; 1 Cor. 3:19f.).

Conclusion

The concept of faith aims at simplicity. Hope, assent, perception, hearing, testing, and the mustard seed which grows—all these seem straightforward ideas. Yet the concept is tied at every point to interesting philosophical problems and there is always a variety of interpretations between which Clement has made a rational choice. To these Clement adds his own contemporary controversy with Basilides, who wants faith to be a natural endowment, and Gnostics, who divide faith from knowledge. It is not the case, as some *Quellenforschung* has suggested, that Clement has collected unambiguous arguments from different sources. Clement's arguments make at least one good point. Preconception is a proper part of epistemology. Assent or choice is essential to Christian faith, which is always a matter of confession. Perception of God is a part of faith. There is a tension between the claim that faith is concerned with what is not seen but anticipated and the claim that God is indeed heard and perceived; this is inescapable if the Christian message of both present and future eschatology be understood. Scripture stands as the rational link with God; yet as divine oracle it has symbolic content. The argument to an unproved *arche* does not prove God, but shows why Pauline faith and God go together. Faith serves as a criterion to discern true from false. The growth of faith follows the word where it leads. The final link of faith and God guards against triumphalism and preserves the dialectic of Christian existence which lives by dying. Clement has no trouble joining the faith of the scriptures with the faith of philosophers. A unity had already been achieved within the Wisdom literature; he added, to the concept of the bible as the barbarian philosophy, the theology of Paul, the wisdom of Christ crucified. Like all second century theologians, Clement thought that a God, who had become incarnate in Jesus, was more credible than a creator who had not cared enough to redeem the world he had made. Hellenistic philosophers were concerned to find arguable alternatives to the negative arguments which Skeptics produced and the rivers of words which flowed from Sophists. Epistemology had a continuing urgency in their studies. Their several proposals were taken up by Clement, fortified by Plato and Aristotle, linked with scripture and turned into arguments for faith. Faith remained central to Clement in his deep dependence on Paul. 'Faith is strength to salvation and power to eternal life' (*str.* 2.12.53). Abraham's faith, as Paul indicated, was in the only God who showed his absolute sovereignty in the justification of the ungodly, creation out of nothing and the resurrection of the dead. This God is the first cause of all that exists, the ultimate first principle. Faith is not inferior to other ways of knowing, but the only way to know the sovereign God[55].

NOTES

¹ As in my *The philosophy of Clement of Alexandria* (Cambridge, 1957) and S.R.C. Lilla's *Clement of Alexandria, A study of Christian Platonism and Gnosticism* (Oxford, 1971).
² While drawing on Philo, his main point (on the coming near of the unapproachable God) is not from Philo.
³ Much ancient theory of knowledge was deductive and took geometry as its model. There had to be axioms.
⁴ Herein lies the limitation of K. Prümm's useful study, Glaube und Erkenntnis im zweiten Buch der Stromata des Klemens von Alexandrien, *Scholastik* 12 (1937), 17-57. The same weakness in other work has already been noted above.
⁵ A. Manuwald, *Die Prolepsislehre Epikurs* (Bonn, 1972), 103.
⁶ D.K. Glidden, *Epicurean prolepsis*, Oxford studies in ancient philosophy, III, (Oxford, 1985), 194.
⁷ Ibid., 205.
⁸ Long and Sedley, *The Hellenistic philosophers*, 1, 89.
⁹ Sextus Empiricus, *adv. math.*, 8.331f. See Long and Sedley, 1, 249.
¹⁰ A.A. Long, *Hellenistic philosophy* (London, 1974), 25.
¹¹ Translation, Long and Sedley, *Hellenistic philosophers*, 1, 141.
¹² J.M. Rist, *Stoic philosophy* (Cambridge, 1969), 139. F.N. Sandbach shows that ἔμφυται here means 'ingrained' or 'implanted'. See Ἔννοια and πρόληψις in the Stoic theory of knowledge, CQ 24(1930), 44-51.
¹³ A. Manuwald, *Die Prolepsislehre Epikurs* (Bonn, 1972), 39.
¹⁴ D.K. Glidden, *Epicurean prolepsis*, 179f.
¹⁵ Ibid., 201.
¹⁶ Ibid., 210.
¹⁷ Ibid., 212.
¹⁸ They were not made perfect, nor did they receive the promise. The new situation of Christian hope is set out in 2 Cor. 3.1-18. Paul's hope belongs to a minister of the new covenant which is marked by freedom, boldness and boasting. See R. Bultmann, *TWNT*, 2, 528.
¹⁹ R. Bultmann, *Marburger Predigten* (Tübingen, 1956), 170f.
²⁰ Anticipation is also the theme of J. Moltmann, *Theologie der Hoffnung* (München, 1964), 9-30.
²¹ The influence of Heraclitus on Clement is strong. See for an introductory statement P. Valentin, Héraclite et Clément d'Alexandrie, *RSR*, 46 (1958). Heraclitus was important for, and transmitted by, the Stoics.
²² ἐνωτικὴ συγκατάθεσις. Declining Stählin's emendation ἐννοητική, as do Mondésert and Prümm.
²³ Prümm, Glaube 23.
²⁴ Stob. 2.111f., Long and Sedley, *The Hellenistic philosophers*, 1, 256.
²⁵ Plutarch, *Stoic. Repug.* 1057A, Long and Sedley, *The Hellenistic philosophers* 1, 317.
²⁶ 'The artist makes us see what is, in a sense manifestly and edifyingly *there* (real), but unseen before, and the metaphysician does this too'. I. Murdoch, *Metaphysics as a guide to morals* (London, 1992), 433.
²⁷ Homer, says Clement, uses 'hear' instead of 'perceive', a specific form of perception instead of the generic concept.

²⁸   Dial. 4; see Osborn, *Justin Martyr* (Tübingen, 1973), 26 and W. Schmid, Frühe Apologetik und Platonismus, *Hermeneia*, FS Otto Regenbogen (Heidelberg, 1952), 181.

²⁹   A useful philosophical treatment of this kind of perception is found in, William P. Alston, *Perceiving God, the epistemology of religious experience* (Cornell University Press, Ithaca and London, 1991).

³⁰   Poetry was 'a massive repository of useful knowledge, a sort of encyclopedia of ethics, politics, history and technology'. E.A. Havelock, *Preface to Plato* (Oxford, 1963), 27, cited by R. Bambrough, *Reason, truth and God*, 122. While this might not help strict folllowers of Plato, who banished poets from his city, Clement quotes poets incessantly.

³¹   Before moving on, we should note that the distinction between divine oracle and true philosophy was and remains central to the Christian use of scripture.

³²   Clement turns the virtue of faith into a necessity for knowledge. God is not to be found except by abstraction from earthly things and by entering the abyss of faith and the dimension of Christ (*str.* 5.11.71).

³³   For Aristotle, a first principle is also a cause. See Guthrie, *History*, 6, 178. Prümm does not see why for Clement, as a Platonist, the ground of knowledge has to be the ground of being. See Prümm, Glaube, 28.

³⁴   'The last chapter of the *Posterior Analytics* is ... a confession of his epistemological faith, a statement of the source from which in the last resort all knowledge springs.' W.K.C. Guthrie, *A history of Greek philosophy*, 6, *Aristotle, an encounter* (Cambridge, 1981), 179.

³⁵   Guthrie, *Aristotle*, 184.

³⁶   T.H. Irwin, *Aristotle's first principles* (Oxford, 1988).

³⁷   Plato's dialectic had gone on to the form of the good; but Aristotle would not do this (*EN* 1095 a 26-28).

³⁸   Irwin, *First principles*, 149.

³⁹   Ibid., 476. Aristotle, says Irwin, gives an inversely proportional amount of space to problems which he regards as important.

⁴⁰   Ibid., 482.

⁴¹   Ibid., 484.

⁴²   See Sext. Emp. 7.29 and J.M. Rist, *Stoic Philosophy* (Cambridge, 1969), 133-51.

⁴³   Theodoret attributes this formula to Aristotle (*Graec.affect.cur.* 1, 90). Stählin points out that it cannot be found in the text. Mondésert suggests *Top.*, IV, 5, 126b.

⁴⁴   Loeb translation.

⁴⁵   I owe this comment to Prof. H.A.S. Tarrant. See on this point Frances Young, *The art of performance* (London, 1990), 123ff., and 131; also see J.L. Kinneavy, *Greek rhetorical origins and Christian faith* (Oxford, 1987), 26-53.

⁴⁶   See C. Collard, Athenaeus, the Epitome, Eustathius and quotations from tragedy, *RFIC* (1969), 157; also E. Osborn, Philo and Clement: Citation and influence, in *Lebendige Überlieferung* (Beirut and Ostfildern, 1992), FS H.-J. Vogt, ed. N. El-Khoury et al., 231.

⁴⁷   For the place of the criterion in Stoic epistemology see J.M. Rist, *Stoic Philosophy* (Cambridge, 1969), 138-42.

⁴⁸   See Osborn, Reason and the rule of faith, in the second century AD, in *The Making of Orthodoxy*, FS H. Chadwick (Cambridge, 1989), 40-61.

⁴⁹   Morton Smith, *Clement of Alexandria and a secret Gospel of Mark* (Cambridge, Mass., 1973). See my rejection of this hypothesis in an article, Clement of Alexandria: a

review of research, 1958-1982, *The Second Century*, 1985, 219-24, especially pages 223-5.
[50]   Osborn, Reason and the rule of faith, 51-53.
[51]   Albinus (*Did.* 5) describes three types of analysis: (i) the upward movement from sensible things to 'primary intelligibles' (as in *Symp.* 210a ff.), (ii) the upward move from demonstrable to indemonstrable propositions (as in *Phaedrus* 245c ff.), (iii) the move from hypothetical to non-hypothetical principles (as in *Rep.* 6, 510b ff.). We cannot be sure when this organisation of Plato's ideas took place; but it probably occurred in the Old Academy and was taken over by Albinus. See John Dillon, *The Middle Platonists* (London, 1977), 277f.
[52]   In *Euthydemus* 291D and *Politicus* 259AB.
[53]   E. Käsemann, *Commentary on Romans* (Grand Rapids, 1980), 31.
[54]   Taught by the logos.
[55]   I wish to thank Dr. Robin Jackson of Ormond College and the University of Melbourne for discussion and help at several points of ancient Greek and Hellenistic philosophy.

P.O. Box 20, *Point Lonsdale*, Vic 3225 Australia

STOIC LOGIC AS HANDMAID TO EXEGESIS AND THEOLOGY IN ORIGEN'S COMMENTARY ON THE GOSPEL OF JOHN

In his letter to Gregory, Origen advises his student to take what is useful from Greek philosophy as preparatory studies for Christianity, so that just as the followers of the philosophers speak of the other disciplines of learning as ancillary to philosophy, so the Christian student may say the same about philosophy itself in relation to Christianity.[1] Origen then illustrates his meaning by his metaphor of 'spoiling the Egyptians',[2] a figure that was to become common coin among the later Fathers of taking things from secular learning and applying them to the disciplines of theology.

Origen's advice to Gregory shows that he took the study of philosophy seriously, both for himself and for his students. It also suggests that he was not committed to any one philosophical school, but ranged through them all looking for that which he could use as a Christian scholar. One of the philosophical schools in which Origen found much that was helpful, as a few modern studies have shown, was that of Stoicism.

In 1947 H. Chadwick called attention to Origen's extensive knowledge of Stoicism in an article dealing primarily with Origen's polemic against the Stoic doctrines of fate and the corporeality of God in the *Contra Celsum*.[3] In 1962 H. Crouzel commented on Origen's familiarity with 'le milieu de la Stoa', but noted that his Stoicism had not yet been thoroughly studied.[4] In 1970 L. Roberts complained that the extent of Origen's debt to Stoicism had 'not yet been determined', and that his use of Stoic logic had been 'almost entirely ignored'.[5]

---

[1] *Philoc.* 13. 1.

[2] Ibid. 13. 2.

[3] 'Origen, Celsus, and the Stoa', *JTS* 48 (1947), 34–49.

[4] *Origène et la philosophie* (Aubier, 1962), 35. Crouzel surveys some of the more obvious contacts of Origen with Stoicism, especially in the *Contra Celsum*, but makes no mention of Origen's use of Stoic logic (pp. 35–45).

[5] 'Origen and Stoic Logic', *Transactions of the American Philological Assn.* (1970), 433–44. Roberts himself has worked at eliminating this ignorance. See his *Philosophical Method in Origen's Contra Celsum*. Dissertation State University of New York at Buffalo, 1971; and the short note, 'Contra Celsum 1, 48', *Mnemosyme* 26 (1973), 286. Some notice is also taken of the role of Stoic logic in Origen in R. M. Berchman, *From Philo to Origen: Middle Platonism in Transition*. Brown Judaic Studies 69 (Chico, California: Scholars Press, 1984), 201–14. The book by M. Spanneut, *Le stoïcisme des pères de l'eglise* (Paris, 1957), ends with Clement of Alexandria, and the excellent study by M. L. Colish, *The Stoic Tradition from Antiquity to the early Middle Ages*, 2 vols. (Leiden: E. J. Brill, 1985), treats Stoicism in Christian literature only in the literature of the Latin West.

© Oxford University Press 1993

[Journal of Theological Studies, NS, Vol. 44, Pt. 1, April 1993]

J. M. Rist published an article in 1981, largely in response to some of the points in Roberts's article, which confirms Origen's extensive knowledge of Stoic logic.[6] Rist comments, however, that

> a reader of almost any modern study of Origen ... would get the impression that Stoic logic was not one of Origen's main concerns and that nothing fundamental about Origen could be discovered in this quarter. He might even get the impression that ... Origen took virtually no interest in questions of logic and knew little about them.[7]

The studies of Roberts and Rist have established unquestionably that Origen had a thorough knowledge of Stoic logic. This should come as no surprise, since, in his delineation of Origen's school curriculum at Caesarea, Gregory Thaumaturgus describes dialectic as the first stage of his education with Origen,[8] and the logical part of philosophy, for the Stoics, consisted of rhetoric and dialectic.[9] Since Origen considered the study of logic to be of fundamental importance for his students, he must have been well versed in it himself. Furthermore, as Rist has pointed out, in antiquity 'it was generally Chrysippus, not Aristotle, who was regarded as the prince of logicians'.[10] Rist thinks Origen probably knew the works of Chrysippus on logic at first hand, and suggests that he may even have studied with Stoic teachers during his youth at Alexandria.[11]

Despite the significance and helpfulness of the works of Roberts and Rist, our knowledge of the extent of the influence of Stoic logic on Origen's thought and works is only in its beginning stages. Both Roberts and Rist, as indeed nearly everyone who has worked on Stoicism in Origen's thought, have focused almost exclusively on the *Contra Celsum*.[12] It is in this treatise that Origen's explicit discussions of certain points of Stoic logic occur, and where vari-

---

[6] 'The Importance of Stoic Logic in the *Contra Celsum*', in *Neoplatonism and Early Christian Thought*, ed. by H. J. Blumenthal and R. A. Markus (London: Variorum Publications, 1981), 64–78. Rist's article, 'Beyond Stoic and Platonist: A Sample of Origen's Treatment of Philosphy (Contra Celsum: 4. 62–70)', in *Platonismus und Christentum: Festschrift für Heinrich Dörrie*, ed. by H. Blume and F. Mann, JbAC Erg. 10 (Münster: Aschendorffsche Verlagsbuchhandlung, 1983), 228–38, further shows Origen's mastery of Stoic thought, though it does not deal with the subject of logic.

[7] 'Importance of Stoic Logic', 64.

[8] *Pan. Or.* 7. 99–8. 109. Gregory uses the term διαλεκτική in 8. 109.

[9] D.L. 7. 41–4.

[10] 'Importance of Stoic Logic', 69. See Clem. *Str.* 7. 16. 101. 4, and D.L. 7. 180. Even Dionysius of Halicarnassus recognizes the importance of Chrysippus as an author of logical treatises, though he thinks his style of writing atrocious (*Comp.* 4).

[11] Ibid. 76.

[12] Roberts does have some cross references in footnotes to a few passages in Books 1 and 2 of Origen's *Jo.* and to a few fragments of the same work.

ous Stoics, including Chrysippus, are named.[13] I shall attempt in this essay to take our understanding of the influence of Stoic logic on Origen a step further by showing that and how he employs aspects of Stoic logic in his exegetical work on the Gospel of John.

There is no mention of Chrysippus nor of the Stoics in general in the commentary on John,[14] nor are there any formal discussions of logic in the commentary. Origen's knowledge of Stoic logic is never brandished, even in the *Contra Celsum*. What we find in the commentary on John is that Origen sometimes thinks and works as one trained in Stoic logic.

I. THE RELATIONSHIP BETWEEN GOD AND THE WORD:
COMMENTARY ON JOHN 1: 90–2. 69 ON JOHN 1: 1–2

Origen considers John 1: 1–2 to consist of four propositions.

Perhaps John, seeing some such order in the argument, did not place 'the Word was God' before 'the Word was with God', so that we might not be hindered in seeing the individual meaning of each of the propositions [ἀξιωμάτων] in the affirmations of the series. For the first proposition [ἀξίωμα] is this: 'In the beginning was the Word'; and the second: 'The Word was with God'; and the next: 'And the Word was God.'[15]

The fourth proposition is in John 1: 2.

After the evangelist has taught us the three orders through the three propositions [προτάσεων] which were previously mentioned, he sums up the three under one head, saying, 'This one was in the beginning with God.' ... It is as if ... he indicates the previously mentioned God the Word by the expression 'this one', and gathers the three ... into a fourth proposition [πρότασιν] and says: 'This one was in the beginning with God.'[16]

Origen uses the terms ἀξίωμα and πρότασις as synonyms. He states this explicitly a little later, when he says that there are 'four

---

[13] The latter is never mentioned, however, in connection with discussions of logic in the *Cels.*, nor are any of his logical treatises mentioned. Ioannes ab Arnim, *Stoicorum veterum fragmenta*, 4 vols. (Stuttgart: B. G. Teubner, 1964), lists fifty-four passages from *Cels.* dealing with Stoicism, with only a few passages coming from other treatises. There are four from *Jo.*, but none dealing with logic.

[14] No one is named in the *Jo.* who might be considered a contemporary or near contemporary of Origen except Ambrose, for whom Origen was writing the commentary, Heracleon, the Gnostic whose work on John Origen was writing against in certain passages, at least, and the Gnostic Valentinus.

[15] *Jo.* 2. 11; translation R. E. Heine, *Origen: Commentary on the Gospel according to John, Books 1–10*, FOTC 80 (Washington, D.C.: The Catholic University of America Press, 1989), 97.

[16] *Jo.* 2. 34–5; trans. FOTC 80: 103.

ἀξιώματα here, which some call προτάσεις'.[17] His more usual term in the Commentary is πρότασις; that of the Stoics was ἀξίωμα.[18] The ἀξίωμα was 'the basic material of Stoic logic'.[19] It consists of 'a complete expression which can be asserted in and of itself'.[20] Chrysippus asserted, in addition, that every proposition is either true or false.[21] To be true, the predicate ascribed to the subject must correspond to the actual state of affairs in the world,[22] i.e. the proposition, 'Dion is walking', is true whenever Dion is, in fact, walking. The proposition could also be either simple or non-simple.[23] Origen treats both kinds in the Commentary, though he never so designates them. The four propositions he discusses here fall under the Stoic category of simple propositions. The first three are assertoric propositions; the fourth is a demonstrative proposition. An assertoric proposition consists of 'a nominative case and a predicate, e.g. "Dion is walking"'; 'a demonstrative proposition consists of a nominative demonstrative case and a predicate, e.g. "This one is walking."'[24] The four propositions Origen perceives in John 1: 1–2 would then be analysed as follows:

Subject	Predicate
P1: The Word	was in the beginning.
P2: The Word	was with God.
P3: The Word	was God.
P4: This one	was in the beginning with God.

P1–P3 each ascribe a different predicate to the Word. Before proceeding to show what Origen concludes from this analysis of John 1: 1–2, we must note another aspect of Stoic thought which affects the way in which Origen works on these verses.

The Stoics divided dialectic into subjects of discourse and language. Subjects of discourse included such things as propositions, arguments, and syllogisms. Language included, among other things, verbal ambiguity.[25] The Stoics held that words are capable of having several meanings. 'Chrysippus said that every word is

---

[17] Jo. 2. 65.

[18] See the note on these terms in M. Frede, Die Stoische Logik (Göttingen: Vandenhoeck & Ruprecht, 1974), 32–3.

[19] A. A. Long and D. N. Sedley, The Hellenistic Philosophers, vol. I (Cambridge: Cambridge University Press, 1990), 205.

[20] S.E., P. 2. 104. Cf. D.L. 7. 65, and the discussion in Frede, 32–40.

[21] D.L. 7. 65; Cic., Fat. 38.

[22] S.E., M. 8. 100; D.L. 7. 65.

[23] D.L. 7. 69–74. We shall discuss non-simple propositions in a later section.

[24] D.L. 7. 69–70; trans. in Long and Sedley, The Hellenistic Philosophers, vol. I, 205.

[25] D.L. 7. 43–4.

ambiguous by nature, since two or more meanings can be understood from it.'[26] He is reported to have written seven treatises on ambiguity [ἀμφιβολία], none of which have survived.[27] Origen seems to have been well-versed in Stoic teaching on this subject. For example, in Book 6 he complains that Heracleon has misinterpreted Luke 7: 28 because he does not know how to treat an ambiguity [ἀμφιβολίαν].[28] Again, in Book 32, Origen asserts that the 'testimony' referred to in John 13: 21 is ambiguous [ὁμώνυμος] because the verb 'to testify' must have a different meaning when it is used in reference to the statement made of Judas, 'One of you will betray me', and when it is used in general of testifying and dying on behalf of religion. Ὁμωνυμία, or ambiguity arising from individual words, was one of the kinds of ambiguity recognized by the Stoics.[29]

Origen begins his exposition of John 1: 1–2 with the statement, 'It is not only the Greeks who say that the noun "beginning" has many meanings.'[30] Most of the space in the Commentary devoted to John 1: 1–2 is taken up with examining the possible meanings, not only of 'beginning', but of each significant term in the four propositions.[31]

[26] Gell. 2. 12. 1; trans. Long & Sedley, *The Hellenistic Philosophers*, vol. I, 227; cf. D.L. 7. 62; 104–5; 137; Stob. 1. 129, 2–130, 13.

[27] D.L. 7. 193. We are dependent almost exclusively on chapter 4 of Galen's work on ambiguity for our knowledge of the views of the Stoics. See R. E. Edlow, *Galen on Language and Ambiguity: An English Translation of Galen's 'De Captionibus (On Fallacies)' with Introduction, Text, and Commentary.* Philosophia Antiqua, Vol. XXXI, ed. by W. J. Verdenins and J. H. Waszink (Leiden: E. J. Brill, 1977). Edlow thinks Galen had a Stoic source in hand as he wrote, possibly even one of the seven composed by Chrysippus (pp. 132–3).

[28] 6. 116. Origen argues that ' "Among those born of women, no one is greater than John", is true in two ways. It is true not only in his being greater than all, but also in some being equal to him.' The ambiguity, as Origen perceives it, seems to lie in the word 'greater', which Origen asserts can mean either (*a*) having no equal, or (*b*) although having some equals, having no one who exceeds one. If this understanding is correct, then Origen must have understood this to have been a case of what Galen classes as second in the eight kinds of ambiguity recognized by the Stoa, i.e. that arising from homonymy in simple words (Gal., *Capt.* 4; cf. the definition of ambiguity in D.L. 7. 62).

[29] Gal., *Capt.* 4.

[30] *Jo.* 1. 90. Origen may also be said to be using terminology from Stoic grammatical works in this paragraph, though he does not use it so precisely as the Stoics had. He uses both προσηγορία and ὄνομα to mean noun in reference to 'beginning'. The Stoics distinguished between the two terms, using the former of a common noun and the latter of a proper noun (D.L. 7. 57–8, cf. R. H. Robins, *A Short History of Linguistics* (Bloomington, Indiana: Indiana University Press, 1967), 28).

[31] The basis of Origen's examination of each word in the propositions seems to be what Galen called the second mode of ambiguity, i.e. that arising from homonymy in simple words. Galen cites 'manly' as an example, which can be used either of a chiton or of a man (Gal., *Capt.* 4).

Origen discusses six possible meanings of the noun ἀρχή.[32] He is not so clear, however, on which meaning of 'beginning' he thinks is applicable to John 1: 1. What he ultimately settles on, though it is not very explicit until much later in the Book, is that the beginning in John 1: 1 must be understood in relation to Prov. 8: 22, where Wisdom is called 'the beginning' of God's ways. 'Since, then', he says,

our purpose is to perceive clearly the statement, 'In the beginning was the Word', and wisdom, with the aid of testimonies from the Proverbs, has been explained to be called 'beginning', and wisdom has been conceived as preceding the Word which announces her, we must understand that the Word is always in the beginning, that is, in wisdom.[33]

He equivocates later, however, and adopts a temporal meaning for beginning in relation to the rest of the cosmos.[34]

After examining the possible meanings of 'beginning', Origen turns to 'the Word', the subject of the first three propositions. He examines this noun from three perspectives. First, he wants to show that those who treat this term as the only, or even most important, designation of the Christ are in error. He does this by citing and discussing, in a lengthy section which we shall pass over (1. 125–266), the many titles applied to Christ in the Bible. Second, he examines what the noun Word means when applied to Christ, and third, he shows why John 1: 1–2 uses the expression 'the Word', and not the phrase, 'the Word of God'.

In examining what 'the Word' means in these propositions (1. 266–92) Origen stresses the rational aspect of the term.

He is called 'Word' [λόγος], because he removes everything irrational [ἄλογον] from us and makes us truly rational [λογικούς] beings who do all things for the glory of God ... so that we perform both the more common and the more perfect works of life to the glory of God because of reason [λόγον].[35]

This is the meaning Origen wants to be understood in these verses. The meaning of 'Word' which he wants to eliminate is that based on Ps. 44: 2, 'My heart has uttered a good word', which other interpreters had used to show what 'Word' means in John 1: 1.[36]

---

[32] Jo. 1. 91–118.

[33] Jo. 1. 289; cf. 1. 111, 222, 243–6.

[34] Jo. 2. 36. The basis for this equivocation appears to lie in the strong distinction Origen perceives between the verbs ἦν and γίνεσθαι (see our discussion of this distinction below). It is because the Word 'was' in the beginning, i.e. was in existence prior to the beginning that Origen adopts the temporal meaning of beginning here.

[35] Jo. 1. 267; trans. FOTC 80: 88–9.

[36] Jo. 1. 279–87.

These other interpreters had taken Ps. 44: 2 in a literal sense,[37] and applied it to John 1: 1 as though the Son of God were 'an expression of the Father occurring in syllables'. Consequently, they failed to ascribe a separate substance to the Son, and to acknowledge any real separation of the Son from the Father.[38] Origen recognizes that his own analogy between the 'Word', meaning Reason, being with God, and the reason that is in us, breaks down in that the reason in us 'has no individuality apart from us' and does not possess substance, both of which he takes to be true of 'the Word' which 'was in the beginning'.[39]

The final perspective from which Origen attempts to define the meaning of 'the Word' in John 1: 1 is that of contrasting it with the fuller phrase, 'the Word of God', which appears as a designation of the Christ in Rev. 19: 13. He assumes that someone will raise the question, 'Why it was not said, "In the beginning was the Word" of God, "and the Word" of God "was with God and the Word" of God "was God".'[40]

What Origen wants to establish at this point is that 'the Word' of John 1: 1 is unique and that there are no other similar Words.[41] To have used the phrase, 'the Word of God', he argues, would have left open the possibility that there might be other such Words, for example, 'the word of angels', or 'the word of men'. Origen makes his point by using the first and second non-demonstrable arguments of the Stoics.[42] He begins with the second, which, according to Sextus Empiricus, 'deduces the opposite of the antecedent from the major premiss and the opposite of the consequent, as for example "If it is day, it is light; but it is not light; therefore it is not day." '[43] Origen argues that if there is a plurality of Words, then there may also be a plurality of wisdoms and justices. But to think the second is absurd, therefore, there is not a plurality of Words.[44] He repeats the same form of argument

[37] *Jo.* 1. 281–2.
[38] *Jo.* 1. 151–2. It was actually this view that called forth Origen's lengthy discussion of the various titles of Christ in the Bible (1. 153).
[39] *Jo.* 1. 291–2.
[40] *Jo.* 2. 37.
[41] *Jo.* 2. 44.
[42] The Stoics had five such arguments (S.E., P. ii. 157–8). They were called non-demonstrable because it was assumed that they did not require any demonstration of their validity (J. B. Gould, *The Philosophy of Chrysippus*, Philosophia Antiqua XVII, ed. by W. J. Verdenius and J. H. Waszink (Leiden: E. J. Brill, 1971), 83.
[43] S.E., P. ii. 157; trans. R. G. Bury, *Sextus Empiricus*, vol. I, (London: Heinemann, 1967), 253.
[44] *Jo.* 2. 38. Origen uses the form of the second non-demonstrable argument again in *Jo.* 2. 140, where he wants to establish that Christ is not the light of men only (John 1: 4), but is the light of all creatures.

in relation to truth and wisdom.[45] Finally, he concludes by using the form of the first non-demonstrable argument of the Stoics, which 'deduces the consequent from the major premiss and the antecedent, as for example "If it is day, it is light; but in fact it is day; therefore it is light." '[46], 'If truth is one and wisdom is one,' Origen argues, 'the Word also, who announces the truth and wisdom ... would be one.'[47]

Next Origen considers the meaning of the verb 'was' [ἦν] which occurs in the predicate of each of the four propositions in John 1: 1–2. He contrasts the meaning of this verb with that of γίνεσθαι, 'to come to be'. The latter verb implies a time of 'not being' followed by 'being'; the former implies a continuous state of 'being', without an understood beginning point. Origen shows the contrast between the two verbs by choosing three examples from the LXX which parallel the second proposition in John 1: 1, except that the verb in each case is γίνεσθαι.[48] He concludes the following from this comparison.

The Word *comes to be* ... with men who could not previously receive the sojourn of the Son of God who is the Word. On the other hand, he does not *come to be* 'with God' as though previously he were not with him, but because he is always with the Father, it is said, 'And the Word *was* with God', for he did not *'come to be* with God'. And the same verb, 'was', is predicated of the Word when he *'was* in the beginning' and when he *'was* with God'. He is neither separated from the beginning nor does he depart from the Father. And again, he does not *come to be* 'in the beginning' from not being 'in the beginning', nor does he pass from not being 'with God' to *coming to be* 'with God,' for before all time and eternity 'the Word *was* in the beginning,' and 'the Word *was* with God'.[49]

Finally, Origen discusses the ambiguity in the term God in the second and third propositions (2. 12–8). He shows that there are four possible meanings of the noun God, and that it is used with

[45] *Jo.* 2. 39–40.

[46] S.E., P. ii. 157; trans. Bury, *Sextus Empiricus*, vol. I, p. 253.

[47] *Jo.* 2. 40. The form of the first non-demonstrable argument appears twice in *Jo.* 2. 141–3.
Origen uses the first and third non-demonstrable arguments in *Jo.* 32. 145–51 to show that Judas was not an apostle when he betrayed Jesus. The third non-demonstrable argument 'deduces from the negation of a coupled premiss and ⟨the affirmation of⟩ one of its clauses the opposite of the other clause, as for example, "It is not both night and day; but it is day; therefore it is not night" ' (S.E., P. ii. 158; trans. Bury, *Sextus Empiricus*, vol. I, p. 253). See my note at *Jo.* 32. 148 in my forthcoming translation of books 13–32 of the Commentary.

[48] *Jo.* 2. 1–11, esp. 2. 2–3, and 10. The three Old Testament examples are Hos. 1: 1, Isa. 2: 1, and Jer. 14: 1. In each example λόγος is the subject, and the verb γίνεσθαι is followed by the preposition πρός with a personal object.

[49] *Jo.* 2. 8–9.

two different meanings in these propositions. He notes that God is used with the article in the second and fourth propositions, when the Word is said to 'be with *the* God', and that it appears without the article in the third proposition, when it is said that 'the Word was God'. He takes '*the* God' to mean 'the uncreated cause of the universe' (2. 14), or 'the very God' (2. 17), or 'the true God' (2. 18), all of which are equated with 'the Father' (2. 19). On the other hand, all those beings, of whom the Word is the highest, who are made God by participation in the divinity of '*the* God' are properly termed 'God' without the article.[50]

Having surveyed Origen's discussions of the meanings of the terms used in John 1: 1–2, we are now ready to consider the conclusions he draws from his observation that these verses consist of four propositions. He considers the order of the four propositions to be significant. 'Perhaps John, seeing some such order [τάξιν] in the argument did not place "the Word was God" before "the Word was with God." '[51] And again, 'Since the proposition, "In the beginning was the Word", has been placed first, perhaps it indicates some order [τάξιν].'[52] Τάξις, 'order' or 'arrangement', was more important as a rhetorical term than as a logical term.[53] One might question, then, whether Origen was thinking as a logician or a rhetorician in his analysis. On the other hand, since rhetoric and dialectic were joined by the Stoics as the two branches of the logical part of philosophy, one might best say that he was thinking as a Stoic.[54]

What Origen makes of the order of the propositions is this. P1 establishes that the Word always was, and that He always was in Wisdom (1. 289; 2. 9, 36). P2 distinguishes the Word from God the Father, while at the same time establishing that the Word was always with God the Father (1. 289; 2. 12). Because P3 follows

---

[50] The other two meanings of the noun God, which are not significant for the propositions in John 1: 1–2, are (*a*) the heavenly bodies which were given to the nations as gods (Deut. 4: 19–20), and (*b*) idols, which, while named gods are not gods (*Jo.* 2. 27).

[51] *Jo.* 2. 11.

[52] *Jo.* 2. 12, cf. *Jo.* 2. 131, 153.

[53] See, for example, Arist., *Rh.* 1414a 29. The word appears only once in Arnim's index, where it refers to D.L. 7. 43, which is a brief statement about the four parts into which the Stoics divided rhetoric, one of which was τάξις.

[54] D.L. 7. 41. For the Stoics, as Long and Sedley point out, logic includes the 'study of everything to do with rational discourse', including 'the phonetic and semantic aspects of language, phraseology and stylistics, analysis of sentences and arguments, and also epistemology' (i, p. 188). See also Roberts, 'Philosophical Method', 86–7, where he notes Origen's consideration of the order of words and propositions in *Cels.* Roberts also notes 'the close relation between dialectic and rhetoric in Origen's method' (ibid., and cf. p. 40).

P2, it shows that the reason the Word is God is because He is with *the* God (2. 12, 18). The first three propositions teach, then, 'in what the Word was, namely "in the beginning", and with whom he was, namely "with *the* God", and who the Word was, namely "God".'[55] P4 combines the previous three propositions into one. The demonstrative pronoun, 'this one', which is the subject of P4, sums up P3. A demonstrative pronoun is the equivalent of pointing to something. Origen takes the demonstrative in P4 to point to the immediately preceding proposition (P3), so that 'this one' is equivalent to saying 'God the Word'.[56] The predicates of P1 ('was in the beginning') and P2 ('was with God') are then ascribed to the demonstrative in P4. Origen describes the significance of P4 as follows.

Insofar as 'the Word was in the beginning', we had not learned that he was 'with *the* God', and insofar as the Word was 'with *the* God', we could not have known clearly that he was in the beginning with *the* God, and insofar as 'the Word was God', it could not be revealed that he was 'in the beginning' nor that he was 'with *the* God'. But in the statement, 'This one was in the beginning with *the* God', the expression 'this one' being considered with reference to the Word and God, and the phrase 'in the beginning' being thus attached, and the phrase 'with *the* God' being added, nothing is lacking of the things in the three propositions which is not summed up when they are gathered into one.[57]

The point of Origen's lengthy exegesis of John 1: 1–2 seems to have been primarily to refute the Monarchian view of God, especially that called the modalistic view, which did not hold to any real distinction or separation between God the Father and God the Son. Origen sets forth their view clearly when he refers to those who 'are afraid that they may proclaim two Gods', and consequently 'deny that the individual nature of the Son is other than that of the Father'. He proceeds then to those commonly called the dynamic Monarchians in his statement that others 'deny the divinity of the Son and make his individual nature and essence as an individual to be different from the Father'.[58] The latter usually held some form of adoptionist Christology. The modalistic Monarchians appear to have been more on Origen's mind than the dynamic Monarchians. He expressly attempts to answer the former by his analysis of the use of the article with God in John 1: 1.[59] Nevertheless, it is possible to see P1 as a refutation of the

[55] *Jo.* 2. 35.
[56] *Jo.* 2. 35.
[57] *Jo.* 2. 67–8.
[58] *Jo.* 2. 16; cf. 1. 151–3, and our discussion at n. 38.
[59] *Jo.* 2. 17.

views of the dynamic Monarchians, P2–P3 as a refutation of the
views of the modalists, and P4 as a refutation of both Monarchian
positions.

Origen's methodology in this section of the Commentary owes
much to Stoic logic. He has spoken of simple propositions and
ambiguity, and used undemonstrated argument forms. This is not
to suggest that Origen has written in the compact style of a
logician. His style is discursive and digressive, as he himself
admits. Nevertheless, there is a structure beneath the discurs-
iveness, and the structure comes from Stoic logic. He perceives
all his work in this section to be related to the elucidation of the
four propositions he finds in John 1: 1–2.

II. THE GNOSTIC DOCTRINE OF NATURES: COMMENTARY ON JOHN 20

Book 20 of the Commentary covers John 8: 37–53. There are
four sections in this Book in which Origen employs aspects of
Stoic logic. Common to all four sections is the fact that in each
he is arguing against some form of the doctrine of 'natures' put
forward by Heracleon, i.e. that some beings have been created
with different natures than others, and these natures determine
what the particular beings are capable of doing.

Commentary on John 20: 96–127 on John 8: 41a

"You do the works of your father."

Origen's purpose in this section is to refute 'those who think
they can prove from this source that some are sons of the devil as
the result of creation'.[60] He joins John 8: 44a and 1 John 3: 8–10
with John 8: 41a and interprets the latter in conjunction with the
former two passages.

Origen begins by noting that it is not clear who is meant by the
word father in John 8: 41a.[61] He is here again working with the
Stoic principle of ambiguity, though the technical terminology
does not appear in the passage.[62] The fourth kind of ambiguity
recognized by the Stoics was that which arises from ellipsis or
omission.[63] The identification of father in John 8: 41a has been
omitted. In the context the word father is used of Abraham, God,

---

[60] *Jo.* 20. 127. Cf. 20. 168–70, where a similar view is explicitly ascribed to
Heracleon.
[61] *Jo.* 20. 96–8.
[62] See nn. 26–9 above. At *Jo.* 20. 171–2 he does use the technical term ἀμφί-
βολος in discussing John 8: 44a, 'You are of the father of the devil'.
[63] Gal., *Capt.* 4.

and the devil. Origen takes John 8: 44a to identify who is meant by 'your father' in John 8: 41a, i.e. 'the devil'.

After establishing the meaning of father, Origen turns to 1 John 3: 8–10 to prove that John 8: 41a does not support the gnostic doctrine that some are children of the devil by their nature from creation. He considers 1 John 3: 8–10 to contain two propositions. 'Give careful attention to the differences in the propositions [προτάσεων]', he says, 'and note how John has proposed them very precisely [μετὰ πάσης ἀκριβείας] so that one might marvel at how accurately and, as some would say, dialectically [διαλεκτικῶς], he has set them forth.'[64] The two propositions, found in 1 John 3: 8–9, are simple assertoric propositions, consisting of a nominative case and a predicate.[65]

Subject	Predicate
P1: He who commits sin	is of the devil.
P2: Everyone who has been born of God	does not commit sin.

Prior to this specific reference to the propositions in the Biblical text, Origen has himself constructed several non-simple propositions from the statements in 1 John 3: 8–10 in his argument against the doctrine of natures. He has, for example, used the conditional proposition repeatedly. Chrysippus defined a conditional proposition as 'one linked by the conditional connective "if". This connective declares that the second follows from the first. For example, "If it is day, it is light."'[66] P1, which Origen takes to mean that it is committing sin that causes one to belong to the devil, is the basis for his argument, but he amplifies this by means of conditional propositions. He argues, for example, 'If everyone "who commits sin is of the devil", everyone who is not of the devil does not commit sin.'[67] On the basis of 1 John 3: 8b, 'the reason that the Son of God appeared was that he might destroy the works of the devil', Origen argues by means of another conditional proposition: If 1 John 3: 8b is true, 'to the extent that he has not yet destroyed the works of the devil in us, because we have not presented ourselves to him who destroys the works of the devil, we have not as yet put aside being children of the devil'.[68] Underlying both of these propositions is Origen's assumption that one

---

[64] Jo. 20. 115. Cf. the discussion of this statement in C. Blanc, Origène: Commentaire sur saint Jean IV, SC 290 (Paris: Les éditions du Cerf, 1982), 378–81.
[65] See n. 24 above.
[66] D.L. 7. 71; trans. Long and Sedley, The Hellenistic Philosophers, vol. I, p. 208.
[67] Jo. 20. 104.
[68] Jo. 20. 105. Cf. the similar argument in 20. 126.

becomes a child of the devil or of God by one's own choice and deeds. He then adduces Matt. 5: 45 to prove that one who was not a son of God may become such.

He carries his argument further by means of two disjunctive propositions. The Stoics defined a disjunctive proposition as 'one which is disjoined by the disjunctive connective "either". For example, "Either it is day, or it is night." This connective declares that one or other of the propositions is false.'[69] Origen argues, 'Every person, on attaining the age of reason, is either a child of God or a child of the devil.' And again, 'One either commits sin or does not commit sin.'[70] The latter, of course, he assumes is what makes one either a child of God or a child of the devil.

After the disjunctive propositions, Origen returns to a series of conditional propositions. 'If one commits sin, he is of the devil.' 'If one does not commit sin, he has been born of God.'[71] Then, on the basis of 1 John 3: 6, he argues, 'If ... everyone who abides in him does not sin, he who sins does not abide in the Son.' 'If everyone who sins has not seen him, he who has seen him does not sin.'[72]

At this point Origen sees the possibility that someone may object that he has proven too much in his argument that being sons of the devil or sons of God is dependent on whether one commits sin or not. Might not one then be both a child of God and a child of the devil because he does good and bad alternately? To answer this objection Origen calls attention to the precise way in which John has stated P1 and P2. He emphasizes the differences between the two propositions. John has not said 'the same things concerning those who are of the devil, and those who are of God'.[73] He did not write, 'He who does justice is of God' on the pattern of P1, nor did he write, 'Everyone who has been born of the devil does not do justice' on the pattern of P2.[74] Origen notes that two different verbs have been used in the two propositions. To say 'has been born' of the one who is of God exalts this person, but to say this of the one who is of the devil would mean something worse than saying 'he is of the devil'.[75] On the other hand, 'to

---

[69] D.L. 7. 71–4; trans. Long and Sedley, *The Hellenistic Philosophers*, vol. I, p. 208.
[70] *Jo.* 20. 107.
[71] *Jo.* 20. 107.
[72] *Jo.* 20. 109.
[73] *Jo.* 20. 115.
[74] Ibid.
[75] On 'being born of the devil', cf. Or. *hom. in Ex.* 8. 6.

have been born of God is much better than to be of God',[76] presumably because the former involves one's personal choice.

Origen then provides two reasons why the one born of God does not commit sin. The first, based on 1 John 3: 8, is that he has God's seed within him, and this seed makes it possible for him no longer to sin.[77] The second, based on 1 John 5: 18, is that such a person guards himself so that the wicked one may not touch him.[78]

Origen rounds off his argument by combining a conditional proposition with a conjunctive proposition, a combination which he himself later describes in his analysis of John 13: 32.[79] For the Stoics, 'a conjunctive proposition is one which is conjoined by certain conjunctive connectives. For example, "Both it is day, and it is light."'[80] Origen's argument is as follows (A = the conditional proposition; B = the conjunctive proposition).

(A) 'If the one who is born of God guards himself and the wicked one does not touch him', (B) the one who does not guard himself that the wicked one may not touch him has not been born of God, and everyone whom the wicked one touches has not been born of God, but the wicked one touches those who do not guard themselves.'[81]

Origen has answered the objection that he assumed someone might raise, that one might, by doing good and bad alternately, be both a child of God and a child of the devil, by constructing an argument from Scripture with the tools of Stoic logic. His conclusion is that the one who has been born of God does not sin, and, therefore, cannot be also a child of the devil.

Commentary on John 20: 135–140 on John 8: 42a

'If God were your Father, you would love me.'

Origen asserts that 'those who introduce the natures use this saying, and explain it to mean that if God were your Father you would have recognized me as one of your family ... and furthermore you would have loved me as your own'.[82] He wants to prove that one is not a child of God by nature, but becomes one when he keeps his commandments.[83] He takes Paul as an example, and

---

[76] *Jo.* 20. 118.
[77] *Jo.* 20. 120. Origen may be assuming here some of the things he had said in his earlier lengthy discussion of seeds in relation to souls (*Jo.* 20. 1–45).
[78] *Jo.* 20. 121–2.
[79] *Jo.* 32. 330. We shall discuss this passage in the final section of the essay.
[80] D.L. 7. 72; trans. Long and Sedley, *The Hellenistic Philosophers*, vol. I, p. 208.
[81] *Jo.* 20. 122.
[82] *Jo.* 20. 135. Cf. 20. 168, where such a view is ascribed to Heracleon.
[83] *Jo.* 20. 140.

by three successive questions, all of which, on the basis of the account about Paul in the Bible, must be answered in the affirmative, establishes that there was a time when Paul hated Jesus. He then builds his case concerning Paul by using a series of Stoic arguments. Sextus defines the Stoic concept of an argument as 'a system composed of premisses and an inference. The premisses of it are ... the *propositions adopted by consent* [emphasis mine] for the establishment of the inference, and the inference is the proposition established by the premisses.'[84]

There are several terms in the section which are derived from Stoic logic. He uses ὑγιής and ἀληθής interchangeably of the truth or correctness of propositions;[85] he uses τὸ ἀκόλουθον for the consequent which follows from the antecedent in the συνήμμενον (conditional proposition);[86] he uses ἄρα in the conclusions of arguments;[87] and he uses ἀλλὰ μήν twice to introduce either the acceptance or denial of one of the premisses in a demonstrative argument.[88]

Because the reasoning in this section is very tight, and the section is not so long, I offer the following translation of the passage before analysing it.

If, therefore, (the conditional proposition) is true [ἀληθές], 'If God were your Father, you would love me', it is clear that the (conditional) contrary to this is also true [ὑγιές], 'If you do not love me, God is not your Father.' Therefore, God is not Father of those who do not love Jesus, and there was a time when Paul did not love Jesus. Therefore [ἄρα] there was a time when God was not Paul's Father. Therefore [ἄρα] Paul was not a son of God by nature, but he later became a son of God, since we would also consider true [ὑγιῶς] the consequent [τὸ ἀκόλουθον] which is derived from the conditional proposition [τοῦ συνημμένου], namely,[89] 'But in truth [ἀλλὰ μήν] God is your Father, Paul, therefore [ἄρα] you love Jesus.' But since the (conditional), 'If God were your Father, you would love me', was true [ὑγιῶς] also prior to Paul's faith, it is fitting to admit

---

[84] S.E., P. 2. 135–6; trans. Bury, *Sextus Empiricus*, vol. I, pp. 237–9, adapted.

[85] See B. Mates, *Stoic Logic* (Berkeley and Los Angeles: University of California Press, 1961), 136.

[86] See ibid. 132, 135.

[87] Ibid. 133, notes that the Stoics used ἄρα 'to introduce the conclusion of an argument, never the consequent of a conditional'. Origen uses it four times in this correct Stoic manner in this passage.

[88] See S.E., P. 2. 136, 142.

[89] Λέγοντος should perhaps be emended to λέγον, since the participle must have reference to τὸ ἀκόλουθον and not to τοῦ συνημμένου. The error can be explained as assimilation to the case of the immediately preceeding word. The 'conditional' must refer back to the Biblical words, 'If God were your Father', which Origen quotes prior to introducing the conclusion to the next argument.

that Jesus said (then) as it were, 'But in truth [ἀλλὰ μήν] you do not love me, Paul, therefore [ἄρα] God is not your Father.'[90]

Origen begins with the first non-demonstrable argument.[91] Both he and the Gnostics would have agreed, though on different bases, on the truth of the two premisses in this argument and the conclusion derived from them. This argument takes the form: If the first, the second. The first. Therefore, the second. Origen argues:

First: (P1) 'If ... the statement is true [ἀληθές], "If God were your Father, you would love me,'"
Second: (P2) 'it is clear that the converse to this is also true [ὑγιές], If you do not love me, God is not your Father.'
The first.
Therefore, the second: 'God is not the Father, therefore, of those who do not love Jesus.'[92]

Next, Origen builds a chain of syllogisms using the conclusion from each preceeding syllogism as the implicit premise for the next.[93] The pattern may be diagramed as follows, where P* = the implicit premiss which was the conclusion of the preceding argument, and (+) = a proposition Origen joins to the implicit premiss with 'and'.

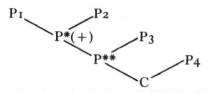

P1 and P2 in the first non-demonstrable argument described above yield the conclusion P*, 'God is not the Father ... of those who do not love Jesus.' This conclusion is then joined by 'and' to the conclusion he reached earlier about Paul hating Jesus at one time, and the two so joined form the premiss for the next argument in the chain. The type of arguments used in the chain are what the Stoics called a demonstrative argument, i.e. an argument which from pre-evident premisses deduces something non-evident. Sextus illustrates this as, 'If sweat pours through the surface, there are insensible pores; but in fact [ἀλλὰ μήν] sweat does pour through the surface; therefore [ἄρα] there are insensible pores.'[94]

[90] Jo. 20. 137–9.
[91] See n. 46 above.
[92] Jo. 20. 137.
[93] See Frede, Die Stoische Logik, 174 ff.; Mates, Stoic Logic, 77 ff.; S.E., P. 2. 135–43; M. 8. 228–41; Alex. Aphr., in APr 278. 8–11.
[94] S.E., P. 2. 140; trans. Bury, Sextus Empiricus, vol. I.

The argument, with the implicit premiss, is in the form of the first non-demonstrable argument again.

First: (P*+) [(If) 'God is not the Father of those who do not love Jesus']
'and there was a time when Paul did not love Jesus,'
Second: (P3) 'Then [ἄρα] there was a time when God was not Paul's Father.'
The first.
Therefore, the second.

This conclusion then becomes the implicit premiss of the next demonstrative argument, which takes the same form as the previous.

First: (P**) [(If) 'there was a time when God was not Paul's Father']
Second: (P4) 'Then [ἄρα] Paul was not a son of God by nature, but later became a son of God.'
The first.
Therefore, the second. 'Paul was not a son of God by nature, but later became a son of God.'

The basis for asserting that Paul later *became* a son of God is then shown in two additional demonstrative arguments, both of which take the words of the biblical text used in the first argument in the series as their premisses, the first implicitly, the second explicitly.

First: ['If God were your Father,'
Second: 'you would love me.']
The first: 'But in fact [ἀλλὰ μήν] God is your Father, Paul,'
Therefore the second: 'therefore [ἄρα] you love Jesus.'

Nevertheless, there was a time when the contrary was also true.

First: 'If God were your Father',
Second: 'you would love me'.
Not the second: 'But in fact [ἀλλὰ μήν] you do not love me.'
Therefore not the first: 'Therefore [ἄρα] God is not your Father, Paul.'

C. Blanc refers these last two arguments to the Stoic argument from two conditionals discussed by Origen in *Cels.* 7. 15, whereby contrary conclusions are deduced from the same condition thereby rendering the condition false or meaningless.[95] Origen gives the formula for this argument as: 'If the first, also the second. If the first, not the second. Therefore, not the first.' He also provides the example the Stoics used, 'If you know that you are dead, you are dead. If you know that you are dead, you are not dead. Therefore you do not know that you are dead.' There are, however,

---

[95] *Origène* iv. 383. See the exposition of *Cels.* 7. 15 by Roberts, 'Origen and Stoic Logic', 441–2, and Rist, 'Stoic Logic in the *Contra Celsum*', 73–5.

some important differences between the arguments here, and that of two conditionals. Here the 'first' *and the* 'second' are identical in both arguments. In *Cels.* 7. 15 'the second' is different in the two propositions, i.e. 'you are dead', and 'you are not dead'. Here Origen switches argument forms between the two. The first argument is in the form of the first non-demonstrable, which affirms the first, and, therefore also the second. The second argument has the form of the second non-demonstrable argument, which denies the second and thereby denies also the first. Origen definitely does *not* intend to render the premiss false in both arguments, which is what the argument from two conditionals would do. He wants the premiss to be false only prior to the time of Paul's faith. Had he used the argument from two conditionals, he would have established thereby that God was never Paul's Father.

Commentary on John 20: 237–255 on John 8: 44b

'He did not stand in the truth, because truth is not in him.'

Heracleon had said of these words,

For his nature is not of the truth, but is of the opposite to the truth, namely of error and ignorance. For this reason ... he can neither stand in the truth nor have truth in himself, because he possesses falsehood as his own from his own nature and is unable by nature ever to speak truth.[96]

In his argument to show that the devil is not, by nature, incapable of having truth in himself, Origen asks what the statement, 'Truth is not in him', means. He offers three possible answers. (*a*) He never holds a true opinion, but everything he ever thinks is false. (*b*) He does not participate in Christ, since those who participate in Christ participate in the one who said, 'I am the truth'. As a final alternative, he says, (*c*) 'Some will wonder if it is necessary to say that truth is not in one who admits a lie at any time, even if he should hold the lie along with many things that are true.'[97]

The third suggestion is based on the Stoic criterium for a conjunctive proposition [συμπεπλεγμέμον]. Such a proposition consisted of several propositions joined together by the conjunction 'and'. Gellius defined the criterium for the truthfulness of such a proposition as follows: 'If in the whole conjunctive proposition there is one falsehood, even if the others are true, the whole is said to be false.'[98] Origen is clearly aware of such a definition when he says of the third option which he lists, 'For as that which

[96] *Jo.* 20. 252–3.
[97] *Jo.* 20. 245–6.
[98] 16. 8. 10–11.

consists of countless things which are true is false if even one falsehood is combined [συμπεπλεγμένου], so in the case of him who holds one false opinion along with many true ones, as if such is combined [συμπεπλεγμένον], one would say, consequently that truth is not in this person.'[99]

Origen thinks any of the three possible answers he has provided may be the correct one, and that any one of them or a combination of the first and second is sufficient to disprove Heracleon's interpretation. He does note that some might not find the third suggestion convincing.[100]

Commentary on John 20: 287–309 on John 8: 47

'He who is of God hears the words of God; you do not hear them because you are not of God.'

'Those who introduce the fable concerning different natures', Origen says, 'and say that there are sons of God by nature who also ... are uniquely capable of receiving the words of God because of their kinship with God, appear to prove their point from this passage too.'[101]

Origen begins his interpretation of John 8: 48 by constructing a demonstrative argument[102] in the form of a first non-demonstrable argument, i.e. If the first, the second. The first. Therefore the second. His argument is as follows.

First: 'If indeed [εἴπερ] as many as received "the true light which enlightens every man coming into this world" [John 1: 9] have not received it because they are of God, ...'
Second: 'then it is clear that [δῆλον ὅτι] those who are not of God do not have any power at all to become children of God before they have received the true light, and [δέ] once they receive it, do not yet become children of God, but receive power to become children of God because they have received the light.'[103]

The premiss in this argument is, of course, not something that is self-evident, nor is it something someone would necessarily agree to without further proof. Origen realizes this, and supplies the proof for the truth of his premiss in a parenthetical contrary-to-fact conditional sentence. 'For if they have received it [i.e. the light] *because they are of God* [emphasis mine], it would not have been written of them, "But as many as received him, he gave them power to become children of God ..."' (John 1: 12). The fact that

[99] *Jo.* 20. 247.
[100] *Jo.* 20. 251.
[101] *Jo.* 20. 287.
[102] See n. 94 above.
[103] *Jo.* 20. 288.

it has been so written proves for Origen that 'they have not received it because they are of God'. Whether Origen could justly assume that Heracleon would also admit the truth of this assertion based on John 1: 12 is difficult to say. Heracleon had, it seems, written a commentary on the Gospel of John, and therefore, must have held its words in esteem. Origen could, nevertheless, assume that his own students and Ambrose, at whose instigation he was writing the commentary, would have been convinced by this argument, and would, therefore, have agreed with the premiss. Origen then joins a conjunctive proposition to the conditional as the conclusion to the argument.[104]

Origen assumes that every man *qua* man receives the true light, and that this reception is the precondition for *becoming* a child of God. All, however, do not 'aspire to be such', and therefore, 'do not become children of God, nor do they come to be of God, and this is why they do not hear his words'.[105] Consequently, John 8: 48 cannot be used to prove that there are sons of God by nature, who because of this special kinship with God, are capable of hearing his words. Origen repeats the same form of argument to the same effect a little later, but uses Matt. 5: 44–5 as the basis for the premiss.[106]

Next Origen asks, perhaps again using the Stoic principle of ambiguity arising from, homonymy,[107] what it means '*to hear* the words of God'. He suggests three possibilities which he immediately rejects,[108] and then, on the basis of a proof from contraries, argues for a fourth meaning.

Origen's proof from contraries may have been derived from Aristotle, and not the Stoics.[109] Aristotle states that 'one topic of demonstrative enthymemes is derived from opposites'.[110] It is perhaps important to note, however, that Origen uses the word paradox twice when speaking of this argument.[111] While no example of a Stoic argument like that used by Origen here has been preserved, we do know, on the basis of several brief fragments, that Chrysippus was interested in opposites and para-

---

[104] See nn. 79 and 80 above.
[105] *Jo.* 20. 289.
[106] *Jo.* 20. 292.
[107] See n. 29 above.
[108] *Jo.* 20. 294–7.
[109] See C. Blanc, *Origène*, iv. 383.
[110] *Rh.* ii. 1397a; trans. J. H. Freese, *Aristotle. XXII. The 'Art' of Rhetoric* (London: Heinemann, 1975), 297; cf. *Rh.* ii. 1392a.
[111] *Jo.* 20. 298.

doxes.[112] It is not impossible, therefore, that Origen knew this argument from the Stoics.

What Origen wants to prove with this argument is that the words 'to hear the words of God' in John 8: 48 refer to a graduated hearing. One advances in the capacity to hear until finally he can 'receive all the words of God, or as many, at least, as it is possible for those considered worthy of the spirit of adoption to receive both now and later'.[113] 'The paradox', he says, 'is this, that someone is more a son of God than is another son of God, and that someone is twice as much a son of God as another.'[114] He begins by citing Matt. 23: 15, where Jesus accuses the scribes and Pharisees of making their converts 'twice as much a son of hell as' themselves. This shows, Origen asserts, (*a*) that there are no sons of hell by nature, and (*b*) that all the sons of hell are not equally sons of hell. But if one can be twice as much a son of hell as another, why not also twice as much a son of light, or life, or son of God? This can be the case, Origen argues, and the reason one is more a son of God than another is that one hears more words of God than another. He has also shown that 'more' has a qualitative as well as a quantitative meaning, i.e. one hears the secret words of God as well as 'those which have been recorded'.[115] Heracleon cannot, therefore, use John 8: 48 to prove that it is because some are sons of God by nature that they hear the words of God.

III. THE GLORIFICATION OF THE SON AND THE FATHER IN THE ECONOMY OF SUFFERING: COMMENTARY ON JOHN 32: 318–367 ON JOHN 13: 31–2

Origen sees the departure of Judas to betray Jesus as the beginning of the economy of suffering of the Son of man.[116] This economy [οἰκονομία] results in the glorification of the Son of man, and in the glorification of the Father in him. John 13: 31–2 are important verses for Origen, and he treats them accordingly. A cluster of scriptural texts are brought to bear on their interpretation. He reads the verses themselves as Stoic propositions, and makes a sophisticated analysis of one of the propositions in the technical vocabulary of the Stoics.[117]

The discussion in this section revolves around three figures

[112] See Gould, *Philosophy of Chrysippus*, 87–8.
[113] *Jo.* 20. 308.
[114] *Jo.* 20. 298.
[115] *Jo.* 20. 298–304.
[116] *Jo.* 32. 25, 34, 84, 295, 320, 359, 391.
[117] Cf. C. Blanc, *Origène*, iv. 383.

whom Origen manages, usually, to keep distinct. First is *the human Jesus*. This is always the meaning of the phrase 'the Son of man' (John 13: 31) in this section, who is also identified as the one 'born of the seed of David according to the flesh' (Rom. 1: 3), the 'man' whom some were seeking to kill (John 8: 48), and the one whom God highly exalted 'when he became obedient unto death' (Phil. 2: 8). Origen's use of the term 'Son', however, in this section is not consistent, and is not always completely clear. It usually refers to God the Word, but sometimes seems to mean the human Jesus.

The second key figure in the discussion is *God the Word*. Origen makes a clear distinction between the Word and the human Jesus. The former 'by nature, does not die', nor is he 'capable of being highly exalted', both of which the man Jesus experiences.[118]

The third figure in the discussion is *God the Father*. God with the article [ὁ θεός] in John 13: 31–2 is taken to mean the Father. This is consistent with Origen's earlier discussion of God with the article.[119] This identification is made explicit in his comment on John 13: 31b, 'And God [ὁ θεός] is glorified in him', when he says of these words, 'It is not possible that the Christ be glorified if the Father is not glorified in him.'[120]

Origen analyses John 13: 31–2 with the tools of Stoic logic in the following manner.

Now for the sake of clarity, let us give careful attention to what is said in the first proposition, 'Now is the Son of man glorified'; and in the second, 'And God is glorified in him'; and in the third, which is a conditional proposition [συνημμένῳ], as follows, 'If God is glorified in him, God will also glorify him in himself'; and in the fourth, 'And he will glorify him immediately.'

One might perhaps construe this latter proposition as a conjunctive proposition [συμπλοκήν] which is the consequent [τὴν ἐν τῷ λήγοντι] of the conditional [συνημμένου], so that the conditional [τὸ συνημμένον] begins after the proposition, 'God is glorified in him', and concludes [λήγῃ] with the conjunctive proposition, 'And God will glorify him in himself, and he will glorify him immediately.'[121]

Origen has suggested two possible ways of reading John 13: 31–2. The first takes the text to contain four propositions.

---

[118] *Jo.* 32. 322, 324.

[119] *Jo.* 2. 12–19. The text of John 13: 32 printed in Preuschen (p. 469) must be in error, for it omits the article before θεός. The critical apparatus in Nestle-Aland shows several witnesses which omit the entire conditional clause, but none of those that have it omit the article. Furthermore, Origen read the text with the article, for he quotes it with the article in 32. 329.

[120] *Jo.* 32. 321.

[121] *Jo.* 32. 329–30.

Propositions one, two, and four are simple assertoric propositions.[122]

Subject	Predicate
P1 The Son of man	is glorified now.
P2 God	is glorified in him.
P4 He [i.e. God]	will glorify him immediately.

The third proposition is a conditional proposition.[123] Sextus Empiricus describes the parts of a conditional as follows: 'Of the propositions in the conditional [συνημμένῳ], the one that immediately follows the connective "if" is called "the antecedent" and "the first," and the other one is called "the consequent" [τὸ λῆγον] and "the second".' Origen's vocabulary, noted above in his description of the third proposition, reveals his knowledge of such a description. Sextus goes on to say, 'Such a proposition seems to announce that the second part of it follows from the first: that is, if the antecedent holds, so will the consequent. Hence, if this sort of announcement is fulfilled, that is, if the consequent does follow from the antecedent, then the conditional is true; otherwise it is false.'[124] The third proposition, according to Origen's first suggestion for reading the text, then, is as follows.

Condition	Consequent
P3 If God be glorified in him	God will also glorify him in himself.

The other way Origen proposes for reading the text affects only P3 and P4. He suggests that one might consider the consequent of the conditional to be a conjunctive proposition, i.e. two propositions joined by 'and',[125] so that P4 becomes a part of the consequent of P3. The text would then consist of only three propositions.

Condition	Consequent
P3 If God be glorified in him	God will also glorify him in himself, and he will glorify him immediately.

Origen does not say explicitly which way he himself reads the text, but it appears to be in the second way, as we will note later in our discussion.

---

[122] See n. 24 above.
[123] See n. 66 above.
[124] S.E., M. 8. 108–11; trans. Mates, *Stoic Logic*, 97. The proof of a conditional proposition, however, was strongly debated, even among the Stoics themselves. See, for example, S.E., M. 8. 112 ff.
[125] See n. 80 above.

We shall now examine what Origen takes these propositions to mean. The 'now' in P1 refers to the beginning of the 'economy' in which Jesus was to die, and this beginning is activated by Judas' departure 'to transact his business against Jesus'.[126] 'The Son of man', as I have shown above, means the human Jesus. The glorification of the Son of man in P1 is taken to be virtually equivalent to the exaltation referred to in Phil. 2: 9, 'Wherefore [i.e. because he became obedient unto death] God has highly exalted him.'[127] This exaltation (=glorification) of the Son of man 'consisted in the fact that he was no longer different from the Word, but was the same with him', i.e. 'the humanity of Jesus became one with the Word'.[128]

P2 follows P1 'because it is not possible that the Christ be glorified if the Father is not glorified in him'. Origen joins John 12: 32 and 21: 19 to show that the Son of Man 'glorified God in dying'.[129] Col. 1: 15 and 1: 20 are also quoted to show that Jesus 'glorified God in death' by his victory over the principalities and powers.[130]

Origen interrupts his discussion of the propositions to investigate the meaning of the noun glory. This investigation may reflect the Stoic principle of ambiguity by homonymy. The investigation is prompted by what he considers to be the inadequate definition of glory held by 'some of the Greeks'.[131] He considers the meaning of glory in several Biblical passages,[132] from which he concludes that it means, anagogically, that which can be known of God by that mind which has been purified so that it can contemplate *the* God, i.e. the Father. This contemplation of *the* God in turn makes the one who contemplates Him divine.[133]

Origen then returns to P1 and P2[134] and attempts to flesh out the meaning of 'glorified' in these propositions on the basis of this understanding of glory. 'The Son', he says, is glorified (*a*) by knowing the Father, (*b*) by knowing himself, which 'does not fall far short of the former', and (*c*) by knowing the universe, which may be what it means 'for the so-called very Son of man to be made one with wisdom.' The latter, of course, is inseparable from

[126] *Jo.* 32. 320; cf. 32. 318–9.
[127] *Jo.* 32. 324; cf. 32. 354.
[128] *Jo.* 32. 325–6.
[129] *Jo.* 32. 319; cf. 32. 325. John 21: 19 is a statement made in reference to Peter's death in the Gospel, and not about the death of Jesus.
[130] *Jo.* 32. 327.
[131] *Jo.* 32. 330.
[132] *Jo.* 32. 331–43.
[133] *Jo.* 32. 338.
[134] *Jo.* 32. 344.

the Word in Origen's mind.[135] The Son of man is glorified when the Father bestows all this glory on him.[136]

The Father, in turn, is glorified (*a*) not only 'by being known by the Son, but ... in the Son', and (*b*) by contemplating himself.[137] The latter provides a greater glorification for God than the former.

Origen is concerned especially with how God is glorified in the economy of suffering. Heb. 1: 2–3 and 2: 9 play significant roles in his understanding. 'The Son' (Heb. 1: 2), he says, 'is the reflection of the total glory of God himself' [τοῦ θεοῦ αὐτοῦ, Heb. 1: 3]. No one but the Son 'can contain the whole reflection of the full glory of God'.[138] On this basis, then, 'when the economy of the suffering of the Son of man for all men occurs, it is not *without God*' (Heb. 2: 9, emphasis mine).[139] Origen has here used the variant reading of Heb. 2: 9, which he often uses, though he knows the other reading as well. R. A. Greer has noted that Origen usually takes Heb. 2: 9, with the variant reading, to mean: ' "He tasted death for all rational beings except God." '[140] He obviously does not take it to mean that here. The negative clearly points the phrase away from meaning that God is an exception. He means that God is involved in the economy of suffering of the Son of man. But how? There is certainly no Patripassianism here.

The νῦν οὖν with which the sentence begins makes it dependent on the preceding sentence in which Origen has asserted, on the basis of Heb. 1: 3, that the Son alone contains 'the whole reflection of the full glory of God'. In this statement Origen uses the noun God with the article, and consequently, means God the Father.[141] In the statement that the economy of suffering does not occur 'without God', there is no article with the noun God. The article is absent in the biblical text. Given Origen's understanding of the distinction indicated by the presence or absence of the article with the noun God, he must have understood this phrase to mean God the Word who is God 'because he is "with the God" ',[142] and who alone, consequently, can be a reflection of 'the full glory of God'.

---

[135] See n. 33 above.

[136] *Jo.* 32. 345–7.

[137] *Jo.* 32. 348–50. The concept of God contemplating himself derives ultimately from Aristotle (*Nic. Eth.* 10. 8 1178b 20–2; *Met.* 12. 9). However, as E. A. Clark has noted, these Aristotelian motifs 'had been absorbed into Middle Platonic theology prior to the time of Clement' (*Clement's Use of Aristotle* (New York: The Edwin Mellen Press, 1977), 79, 85).

[138] *Jo.* 32. 353.

[139] *Jo.* 32. 354.

[140] *The Captain of Our Salvation* (Tübingen: J. C. B. Mohr, 1973), 51.

[141] See nn. 119, 120 above.

[142] *Jo.* 2. 12, 14, 18.

It is on this basis that Origen says the economy of suffering does not occur 'without God'. It is God the Father, however, whose glory is reflected in the Son, who is glorified in the suffering of the Son of Man. This conclusion is based on the juxtaposition of P1 and P2, for Origen says, 'It does not say "the Son of man is glorified", alone, for indeed "*the* God is glorified in him."'[143]

Origen then suggests two possible ways of understanding how the Son of man is glorified and how the Father is glorified in him in P1 and P2. The alternatives are introduced by nearly parallel statements. 'One might interpret the matters in this passage as follows' [καὶ οὕτως δ᾽ ἂν τὰ κατὰ τὸν τόπον τις διηγήσαιτο],[144] and, 'But the matters in this passage might be understood even more clearly as follows' [ἔτι δὲ καὶ οὕτως σαφέστερον ἂν τὰ κατὰ τὸν τόπον λαμβάνοιτο].[145]

Origen's first suggestion uses Matt. 11: 27a and 16: 17 to show that only the Father knows the Son. The world, therefore, did not know the Son (John 1: 10) and, consequently, did not glorify him. Those from the world to whom the Father revealed 'knowledge of Jesus' did glorify him, which brought about a consequent glory for them also, for they were transformed into the same image (2 Cor. 3: 18). It is, however, because Jesus knows that in the economy of suffering he will be glorified by the Father over and above 'the glory of those glorifying him, that he said, "Now is the Son of man glorified."'[146]

Origen then uses Matt. 11: 27b to show that only the Son knows the Father, 'and he to whom the Son may reveal him'. On this basis, when the Son was about to reveal the Father by means of the economy of suffering [ἐκ τῆς οἰκονομίας], he said, 'And God is glorified in him'.[147] Or, P2 can be compared with the words, 'He who has seen me has seen the Father who sent me' (John 14: 9; 12: 45). Origen's thought has shifted, however, from the human Jesus to God the Word, for he says, 'For he who begot him is contemplated in the Word, since the Word is God [ὄντι θεῷ] and the image of the invisible God [τοῦ θεοῦ], and he who beholds the image of the invisible God is able to behold the Father directly too.'[148]

The second approach that Origen offers to understanding these first two propositions is a moral approach. He begins with another

[143] *Jo.* 32. 354.
[144] *Jo.* 32. 354.
[145] *Jo.* 32. 360.
[146] *Jo.* 32. 357–9.
[147] *Jo.* 32. 359.
[148] *Jo.* 32. 359.

argument from contraries, although he calls no attention to it.[149] 'Just as the name of God is blasphemed among the Gentiles because of some (Rom. 2: 24), so because of the saints whose good works are seen ... before men, the name of the Father ... is glorified' (Matt. 5: 16).[150] Approached in this way, no other has glorified God to the extent that Jesus has, 'since he committed no sin'.[151] Consequently, 'the Son is glorified [P1], and God is glorified in him [P2].'[152]

Origen then takes up the conditional in P3: 'But if God is glorified in him.' He argues that what the Son of Man receives from the Father is greater than what the Father receives from the Son of Man. This is based on the consequent of P3, i.e. that 'the Son of man is glorified in God, the lesser in the greater'.[153]

Finally, Origen takes up P3 in its entirety, i.e. the conditional with the conjunctive consequent, and shows how the Father is the source of all the glorification discussed in the proposition. 'It is fitting indeed that the one who is greater ... grants to the Son what he said, namely, to glorify him in himself [P3a], that the Son might be glorified in God [P3b]. Since, then, these things were not yet to take place (I mean for the Son to be glorified in God), he adds, "And he will glorify him immediately [P3c]"'.[154]

The significance of P3c, for Origen, appears to lie in the Stoic concept of the truth of a proposition. For example, the proposition, 'Dion is walking' is true only if Dion is walking at the time the proposition is uttered.[155] On this basis, the proposition, 'God will glorify him in himself', alone might have been considered false when Jesus uttered it, since God was not then glorifying him. It is true that the verb in John 13: 32 is future: ὁ θεὸς δοξάσει αὐτὸν ἐν αὐτῷ. When Origen quotes the propositions, he uses the future tense in P3b as it appears in the text of John (32: 330). When he discusses P3, however, he refers to P3b either with the aorist tense or the present tense (32: 363–5). He refers to P3b first in the following phrase with the aorist infinitive: τὸ δοξασθῆναι τὸν υἱὸν τοῦ ἀνθρώπου ἐν τῷ θεῷ (32: 363). The phrase, τὸ δοξάσαι αὐτὸν ἐν αὐτῷ, is another reference to P3b, again with an aorist infinitive (32: 365). This latter reference is then explained

[149] See nn. 109–112 above.
[150] *Jo.* 32. 360.
[151] *Jo.* 32. 361.
[152] *Jo.* 32. 362.
[153] *Jo.* 32. 363. Origen takes αὐτῷ in the consequent of P3 to refer to God the Father: τὸ δοξασθῆναι τὸν υἱὸν τοῦ ἀνθρώπου ἐν τῷ θεῷ.
[154] *Jo.* 32. 365.
[155] See n. 22 above.

by a purpose clause with the verb in the present subjunctive, ἵν' ὁ υἱὸς ᾖ ἐν τῷ θεῷ δοξαζόμενος. But, Origen says, 'these things' were not yet to occur. To clarify what he means by 'these things', he refers parenthetically once more to P3b, using a present infinitive: λέγω δὲ τὸ δοξάζεσθαι τὸν υἱὸν ἐν τῷ θεῷ. It is P3c, then, which shows that the glorification of the Son in the Father (P3b) would be subsequent to the time the proposition was uttered, and which, therefore, allows the conjunctive proposition to be true.[156]

Stoic logic plays a significant role in Origen's exegesis of the Gospel of John. It is particularly evident in connection with theological points that are made in the commentary. It provides the structure for his refutation of the Monarchian view of God in Books 1 and 2, and also for his attempt to explain the relation between the Father and the Son in the economy of suffering in Book 32. It is an important tool as well in his refutation of Heracleon's doctrine of natures, and the establishment of his own doctrine of freedom and choice.

In his use of Stoic logic, Origen has employed some of the most sophisticated tools of his day for the analysis of thought. The unobtrusive way in which he uses it shows that he has internalized the subject so thoroughly that it shapes the way he thinks about texts and about the way others have interpreted those texts.

RONALD E. HEINE

[156] See n. 98 above.

The Philosophy in Christianity: Arius and Athanasius[1]

MAURICE WILES

Cui bono? Cherchez la femme! These ancient maxims offer counsel to the investigator of an unsolved murder or some inexplicable pattern of behaviour. They advise the pursuit of what has come more recently to be known as a form of lateral thinking. The puzzle may not best be solved by an intensification of the examination of the immediate data. The primary clue may lie out of sight somewhere further back. Financial advantage or sexual attraction, which does not show up as a feature of the immediate situation, may be the hidden motive of the traditionally male agent's actions. When that is recognized, the otherwise inexplicable phenomena may become intelligible.

The early Church, particularly under the influence of the third-century writer Hippolytus, had a somewhat similar view of how to achieve an understanding of heresy. Orthodox belief was generally regarded as so clearly the correct embodiment of God-given revealed truth that the emergence of heresy was a puzzle in need of explanation. Evil motives, such as private antagonism or personal ambition, were often alleged. But more intellectual explanations were also called for. Why should the heretic's hatred of the truth have taken the particular form that it did? The key to answering that question, they maintained, often lay in the heretic's undue dependence on the teachings of philosophy. It was there that one needed to look to account for the particular form that the heretic's distortion of Christian truth had taken. The epistle to the Colossians (2:8) had warned the Church of the danger of being taken prey by philosophy, and heresy was the outcome of failing to heed that warning.

In the light of this general theory the roots of Arianism have often been ascribed to Aristotelian philosophy. Arius, who was a presbyter in the church of Alexandria at the time of the outbreak of the controversy, is described by one of the early Church historians, Sozomen (*HE* 4:5), as διαλεκτικώτατος—an acute reasoner, a highly dialectical man. This has, sometimes, been understood to imply a deep commitment to the precise forms of Aristotelian logic and their application to Christian

[1] I am grateful to Dr Rebecca Lyman for helpful comments on an earlier draft of this paper.

theology. Moreover adherence to a specifically Aristotelian understanding of οὐσία (substance) has been seen as a source of confusion in
the interpretation of the credal term ὁμοούσιος (of one substance) and
of the Arian refusal to accept it as defining the relation between the
Father and Son. But a more careful examination of the evidence does
not bear out an explanation along these lines. Although different
philosophical schools still existed, there had been a good deal of cross-
influence between them. There is scant sign in the case of the Arian
controversy of any strictly Aristotelian influence at work, of the sort
that such a theory presupposes. Arius and Athanasius, his chief
orthodox opponent, shared a common background of a broadly eclectic
Platonist kind. Moreover it is clear that the introduction of substance
language into the debate, and thereby into the Nicene creed, was not
done with any precise philosophical connotation in mind. Neither
differing philosophical allegiance nor differing evaluation of the
importance of philosophical reasoning was a crucial factor in the split
between Athanasius and the Arians. The role of philosophy in that
essentially Christian debate was of a less straightforward and less
external kind.

Arius is not only described by the Church historians as an acute
reasoner; he is also described as an expositor of scripture (Theodoret
HE 1:1). Although we have very little of his work on which to base our
judgment, it is clear enough that he draws thoughtfully and extensively
on the teaching of scripture. On that score there is again no significant
difference between him and Athanasius. Neither has any doubt that
Christ is Son of God in a unique sense. But the ways in which scripture
speaks about Christ as Son of God are immensely varied. It is as Son
that Jesus prays to his Father in Gethsemane, struggling to align his
will with that of the Father in an act of filial obedience (Mk. 14:36). But
it is also the Son who is spoken of as in the bosom of the Father and thus
alone able to reveal him (Jn. 1:18). He and his Father are one (Jn.
10:30); yet the Father is greater than he (Jn. 14:28). Such language
cries out for further elucidation and clarification. Arius and Athanasius
were at one in believing that scripture, rightly understood, conveyed a
single, uniform saving truth about God. Any attempt to show that it
does so in the face of its apparently diverse teaching requires some kind
of overall framework of understanding. And was that not precisely what
the philosophers of the time were already seeking to provide in relation
to the equally diverse and puzzling phenomena of human life as a
whole?

In using the insights of philosophy to present a coherent account of
the scriptural witness, Arius and Athanasius were not pioneers in the
fourth century. Christians of the second and third centuries had been
doing it already. Philosophy was not, therefore, something wholly

external, a feature exclusively of the surrounding pagan world. It also came to Arius and Athanasius embedded within the Christian tradition that they inherited, and to which they both sought to be loyal as well as being faithful interpreters of scripture.

Philosophy was certainly an important element in the Alexandrian scene to which both Arius and Athanasius belonged. There is no way of telling whether either of them had very close contact with the philosophical school at Alexandria. It is not very likely that they did, but it is reasonable to suppose that they would have had some general idea of the issues being discussed there. In any event we have little knowledge of the Alexandrian school at that time. 'It is', says A. C. Lloyd, 'clouded in obscurity from the time Plotinus was there [c. 233–244] till about 400.' In trying to assess the philosophical climate to which they would have been exposed, we need therefore to draw more generally on the philosophical literature available to us from the immediately preceding centuries.

I have already spoken of that general philosophical tradition as Platonist in basic character, but affected by the influence of both Aristotelian and Stoic thought. It was not a static tradition but a living, changing one. Looking back on it as historians, we classify it into distinct periods with their distinct titles: Middle Platonism and Neo-platonism. But it is important that we don't think of them as discrete entities, replacing one another at a particular moment like frames in a slide-show. The most distinctive characteristics of Neoplatonism with its increased emphasis on transcendence were already recognizable tendencies in the later Middle Platonic period. Recent discussion of the philosophical background to the thought of Arius has laid a good deal of stress on whether or not he knew the work of Plotinus, the founding father of Neoplatonism. Plotinus, as we have already observed, had been in Alexandria some seventy-five years before the outbreak of the Arian controversy, but it was some time before his work began to be at all widely disseminated. It is questionable whether the issue can be settled with any confidence, one way or the other. But it is perhaps not as important as is sometimes claimed. It is the nature of the issues that were being debated at the time that is crucial for our purpose. And these included many of the most problematic features of Platonism, especially ones that related to the contemporary emergence of Neo-platonic thought. Moreover many of these questions which philo-sophers were subjecting to careful critical scrutiny and for which a variety of solutions were being put forward, had important points of affinity with the issues which were troubling Christian theologians at that time. What is the relation between unity and the multiplicity of experience, between the eternally changeless and the phenomenal realms? Is there some mediation between the two, and if so what is the nature and status of any such mediatorial entities? And how does the Demiurge of Plato's *Timaeus* relate to Plato's account of the ideal forms? As background to any attempt to assess the place of philosophy within the Arian debate, I propose to outline five areas of philosophical discussion, current at the time, which are, even if only indirectly, significant for the understanding of the issues involved in that debate.[2]

(1) Perhaps the most fundamental problem for a Platonist philosophy is the relation between the ideal forms and the phenomenal world. The logic of the basic Platonist position requires a sharp contrast between the timeless and the temporal, the changeless and the changing, the immutable and the mutable. Yet for all the directness of the contrast, the chasm between the two cannot be unbridgeable. For the ideal world is the ground of the existence of the phenomenal. There must be some positive relation between the two. How is that relation to be described? Is our world simply a copy of the ideal world—or does the relation go deeper so that the lower can be spoken of as participating in the higher? When the notion of transcendence is most strongly affirmed, the relation of the this-worldly to the higher reality will be spoken of primarily in the negative terms we have been using. That higher reality can be defined only in terms of what it is not—it is time*less*, change*less,* im*mutable. In religious terms a conception of that kind finds its expression in mystical or apophatic ways. God is to be defined by what he is not. Where, on the other hand, perhaps under Stoic influence, more weight is given to the presence of an immanent logos or rationality within our world, a more positive relation can be affirmed. God is intellect or goodness itself, in which we as rational beings can in some measure participate. The way is then open for a more positive use of language applied analogically to God and for a more sacramental apprehension of the world. But the dominant tendency of the time, which was to find its culmination in Neoplatonism, was to lay increasing emphasis on the transcendent or negative pole.

(2) In the *Timaeus* (28c) Plato had spoken of God as 'Father and Creator of all'. Was that phrase to be taken, as would seem most natural, as referring to the same single reality? Some philosophers, like Atticus, understood it in that way. There was a single divine, creative reality, who was both Father and Creator. But others, like Numenius, took Plato's words as referring to two distinct realities—a first God who is Father and a second God who is Creator. Thereby a greater distance was maintained between the supreme reality and the world that derives from it. So the divine is conceived as existing in the form of more than

---

[2] For a much more detailed account of the most relevant features of this second- and third-century philosophical discussion, see John Dillon, 'Logos and Trinity: Patterns of Platonist Influence on Early Christianity', above.

one entity, ordered in a hierarchical sequence. Such hierarchies were often threefold, as with Plato himself and also with Plotinus' conception of the One, the world mind and world soul. There was a gradual progression from pure unity to the realm of the ideas and then to the animating power of the world. Such hierarchies were variously named and variously understood. But there was much discussion of a mediating process between the highest reality and the created world. The issue was one of increasing significance in the philosophical thought of the time.

(3) Various names were given to these higher levels of divine reality—unity (τὸ ἕν), being (οὐσία), intellect (νοῦς), the good (τὸ ἀγαθον). In psychology and ethics, which were important features in the teaching of the philosophical schools, much attention was also given to the concept of the will. As is to be expected in a scheme of thought in which the divine is not conceived in personal terms, will is not a concept much used in relation to the supreme divine reality. But it is not wholly absent. Platonists were concerned not merely to give some account of the emergence of a world, but also to affirm some form of providence clearly distinguishable from Stoic conceptions of fate or other prevalent forms of fatalist teaching. That concern with cosmology, and still more with providence, led to the occasional introduction of the idea of will into philosophical discussion of the divine. The relation of will to intellect or being with reference to God was an emerging issue of concern.

(4) The contrast between the divine as eternal and changeless and the world as temporal and changing poses a problem about the temporality of the world. If we say that the world itself is eternal, do we not deny its fundamental character as temporal and contingent? But if we affirm its creation to be in time, do we not deny the eternal and changeless character of the divine, which must at some time have changed and begun to give rise to a world? Some, like Plotinus, saw no objection to the idea of an eternal process of emanation, an eternal dependence of the world on the changeless One. But for others, both before and after him, the act of creation, the bringing of order out of formless matter, could not be reckoned eternal—whatever might be true of the formless matter itself. So careful discussion was called for about the different senses of 'creation', and still more about the different senses of 'time'. The creation of the world could not be unequivocally affirmed either as timeless or as within time. As an illustration of the type of distinction being proposed, one can take the words of Atticus that 'there was time before the creation of the world, but there was not measured (τεταγμένος) time'.

(5) Philosophy concerned itself not only with the origin of things but also with the goal of human life. Plato had spoken of the ideal of

'likeness to God', and that goal was espoused not only by Platonists but by some Stoics also. Both saw it as something that could only be attained by moral training and endeavour. But there were differences between them, particularly concerning the role of the emotions in the moral life. Moreover for the Platonist, for whom God was clearly distinct from nature and yet for whom some form of participation in the divine was possible, such a formulation of the goal in terms of likeness to God served to link ethical progress with a religiously conceived participation in God—at least, as Albinus is careful to add, with the second if not the supreme God.

These contemporary issues in all their diversity provided the intellectual and religious climate in which Christian reflection was being carried on. Whether or not Christian authors can be shown to hold particular opinions on specific issues of philosophical debate, their own reflections bear the imprint of contemporary philosophical vocabulary and perspectives. In the case of Arius and Athanasius, that philosophical environment certainly contributed to the ways in which they responded to the central theological issue of their day. But that is a far cry from seeing them as philosophers or direct participants in a specifically philosophical debate. A contemporary scholar's approach to his subject today, for example, can be much influenced by the concepts and vocabulary of evolution without him or her having had any direct involvement in either biology or the philosophy of science. It is in this generalized, but none the less highly significant way, that we need to envisage the role of philosophy in the great theological controversy of the early fourth century.

What then was the nature of the theological issue at the heart of that controversy? The evidence available to us does not enable us to offer a confident answer to that question, which is much debated among historians of theology at the present time. I shall begin by giving a very brief survey of the way in which the Church's thought about the person of the Son had been developing up to that time. Both scripture and the worshipping practice of the Church pointed to the existence of one who was the divine source of revelation and salvation, but who could not be simply identified with God, the one whom he himself called Father. So Christians spoke of a second divine being, whom they called not only Son (with the risk of crude misunderstanding in a world of Greek myths) but also Word and Wisdom. Those latter designations had firm roots in the Old Testament, but for educated Christian apologists deliberately seeking points of contact between their Christian faith and the surrounding culture, they were also strongly suggestive of that second divine reality in philosophical thought, where the pure transcendent unity gives rise to rationality and to the realm of the ideas. This second divine being was clearly derivative from God—even if, as in

Origen's view, eternally derivative as was the world from the One in the Plotinian scheme. Understood within such a context, the existence of a second divine being was not felt to constitute any threat to monotheistic faith, for the Father remained the one source of all else. Furthermore, such an approach did not only help to make sense of the idea of the Word or Son as the agent of God's providence in creation and history; it was also of help in enabling Christians to conceive and speak of him as actually embodied in a full and unique manner in the person of Jesus Christ. At the same time his perfect reflection of the Father's rationality and goodness and also the devotion offered to him in the worship of the Church led Christians to speak of him and to address him in language almost as exalted as that used of the Father. A framework might have been provided for containing the tension that we referred to earlier as inherent in the language of the New Testament, but the tension itself was still there. Such a tension was a perpetual invitation to crisis and dispute.

Meanwhile Christian teaching about the creation of the world was moving in a direction that took it further away from that of the philosophical schools, and at the same time exacerbated the tension inherent in Christian teaching about the Son. Earlier Christian teachers had not clearly differentiated their view of creation from the characteristic Platonic view of creation as the ordering of formless matter. Moreover for Origen human souls had an eternal kinship with the divine Word, which while not undermining their dependent created status, enabled him to conceive the Word as a bond or mediating nature between God and the lower level of the created, yet kindred, spiritual order. But increasingly the stress came to be laid on the absoluteness of God's creative work as creation out of nothing. The great divide was not between the spiritual realm (God, the Word, angels, human souls) and the phenomenal; it was between God and the created order, between God and everything else. The tension always inherent in Christian understanding of the Son was being stretched to breaking point. How in such an altered framework was the person of the Son to be understood?

In trying to see how Arius and Athanasius responded to this issue, I shall base my account of Arius somewhat narrowly on the two short letters of his, that have come down to us from the earliest period of the debate—the one a confession of faith to his bishop, Alexander of Alexandria, with whom he was in conflict and the other a request for support from his most powerful ally outside Alexandria, Eusebius of Nicomedia.[3] The letters have a clear polemical purpose and may not

---

[3] The text of these two letters in English translation is most readily accessible in J. Stevenson, *A New Eusebius*, revised edn (SPCK, 1987), Extracts 283 and 284 (pp. 324–327).

necessarily give a balanced account of Arius' overall position. But there is no reason to doubt that they do express beliefs that he felt to be important and to be under threat in the dispute with his bishop.

If we analyse the contents of those two letters, they can be summarized as embodying seven affirmations or points of teaching:

(1) God, more specifically God the Father, is uniquely transcendent.

(2) The Son is the product of God's will.

(3) The Son is 'from what is not', because the only conceivable alternatives (that there are two ultimates; that he is a part of the Father; that he is from some lower essence) are all unacceptable.

(4) He is a creature, but unlike any other creature since he is God's agent in the creation of all other creatures.

(5) His existence is pre-temporal, but he is not without beginning, as the Father is.

(6) He is unchangeable.

(7) He is god (θεός).

The centrality of these issues to the initial debate is further witnessed by the fact that nos. 3–6 are all directly contradicted in the anathemas attached to the creed accepted at the Council of Nicaea, and nos. 2 and 7 are clearly repudiated or shown to be inadequate in the text of the creed itself.

Our task then is to try to gain from their fragmentary evidence a coherent picture of Arius's answer to the aporia with which Christian theology was faced, and to determine how philosophy has entered into the construction of that answer.

One of the Church historians, Socrates, tells us that it was Alexander's insistence on the full coeternity of the Son with the Father that so offended Arius as to provide the igniting spark for the bitter controversy. Intelligible though such a concept might have been within an Origenist view of an eternal spiritual world, in the changed climate of thought of Arius's day it appeared to Arius to carry drastic and unacceptable implications. To place the Son coequally alongside the Father, particularly if that was expressed in terms of sharing the οὐσία or being of the Father, must, it appeared to him, involve either the denial of the oneness of God as supreme reality or the denial of the distinct existence of the divine Son. The tension inherent in Christian tradition had been lost.

Arius's alternative account begins with an insistence on the unique transcendence of God. The developed Christian understanding of creation combined with the more radically transcendent strain in Platonism to convince him that no other reality could exist as derived from God, except on the basis of God's will. Any other relation would be an

unacceptable qualification of the unity of God and of the absoluteness
of his creative work. So it must be that the Son is the product of God's
will. Such a stress on the will derives primarily from the more personal-
ist Christian tradition, but it had also, as we have seen, its precedent
within the philosophical tradition. But Arius has no desire or intention
to play down the unique mediatorial role of the Son, as the divine agent
in creation, revelation and incarnation. That was an integral element in
the traditional faith to which he was fully committed. The question was
how such a unique status was to be defined, if the Son's existence was
understood to be, like all other creatures, dependent wholly on God's
will. And here the philosophical discussions about different senses of
'creation' and 'time' in relation to the world offered a useful guide. In
affirming that the Son was a 'creature but not like any other of the
creatures' and that his creation was outside time but not without
beginning, Arius was not simply indulging in tortuous equivocation.
However difficult the concepts, they stood within a tradition of
philosophical reflection on the relation of the cosmos to God. That
tradition could well appear to Arius as one that offered a way of giving
reasoned expression to the ambivalence inherent in scripture and traditional language about the Son.

At first hearing Arius's two final propositions—that the Son is
changeless and that he is θεός—may seem to involve some going back
on his earlier insistence on the radical uniqueness of the Father and the
created status of the Son. It is not easy to determine just from the letters
themselves how they are to be understood in relation to the earlier
propositions. A contemporary letter of his bishop, Alexander, provides
a clue. In it he complains that Arius inconsistently shifts his ground
under pressure of argument, sometimes acknowledging the Son to be
unchangeable while at others affirming him to be changeable. It seems
pretty clear that the unchangeableness which Arius affirms is not to be
identified with the unchangeableness that applies to the Father. It is a
moral rather than a metaphysical unchangeableness, an unchangeableness sustained by the Son's freely chosen will and obedience rather than
an unchangeableness inherent in his nature as such—as is the case with
the Father. And it is that too that constitutes him θεός—his perfect
moral likeness to and unity with the Father.

These final constituents of the outline position that emerges from
these two brief letters of Arius are not merely consistent with what has
gone before; nor do they simply give positive content to the uniqueness
of the Son, justifying the Christian acknowledgment of him as divine.
Set them in the context of philosophical discussions of ethics, and they
add a dimension to Arius's position which is probably more important
than would appear from the texts at first reading. For both Platonist
and Stoic in their different ways a likeness to God that needed to be

learned the hard way through moral endeavour and progress was the true goal of human life. A Son, whose unchangeable divinity was the fruit of his own consistent moral choosing was thus not merely a Son who could be intelligibly envisaged as the subject of the life of Jesus. He was a potential savour whose 'learned obedience' (Heb. 5:8) could be a source of salvation, intelligible both in terms of Christian discipleship and of that growth in 'likeness to God' which philosophy aspired to teach.

Why then did Athanasius react so violently to such a vision? What part did philosophy play in determining his contrasting response to the theological problem before the Church? I have already insisted that there was no major difference of philosophical approach between them. But there were differences of philosophical emphasis, which contributed to the different theological positions they embraced. Two such differences are particularly significant.

Free will is a difficult and contentious issue, even in its application to human persons without the added complication of its reference to God. Its relation to necessity was, as it still is, a matter for dispute. In Athanasius' eyes the concept of will as Arius used it, both in relation to the Father in his work of creation and in relation to the Son, was an unsatisfactory one. He was wrong philosophically to separate it so sharply from being. By doing so he had unnecessarily and damagingly separated the Son from the Father, and introduced an element of arbitrariness, and therefore of unreliability, into the ways of the God on whom we rely for our salvation.

Arius had used the category of will to bridge the gap between the transcendent God and the created order which was radically other than God in being. Athanasius' rejection of the dichotomy between will and being goes hand in hand with a more sympathetic attitude towards the old Platonic notion of the created order's participation in the divine. Although God is radically other than his creation, that does not cut him off from his creation. It is God, and not some lower order of created divine being, with whom Christians have to do in revelation and the life of the Church. More significantly still the goal of 'likeness to God' is not just a matter of moral likeness, though that it certainly is; it is participation in the divine, something that can even be spoken of as θεοποίησις (divinization), which is the destiny of the Christian. And Christ can convey it, because as truly divine and also incarnate, his very nature constitutes the bridge which makes participation in the divine a possibility for us. The Arian Christ could not be the source of a salvation thus conceived. His status as creature but not like any other of the creatures and as outside time yet not without beginning is, in Athanasius' eyes, religiously inadequate, and also intellectually equivocal and incoherent. But Athanasius' alternative vision deriving much of its framework and plausibility fron an older, less transcendental Platonism, had its own *prima facie* incoherences to face. How can Father and Son be coequal and distinct, and still constitute the one transcendent God? And how can the supreme, transcendent God be incarnate as the person of Jesus Christ? There is no sign that Athanasius used his philosophical resources in any very specific way to illuminate either of those questions. The implications of the word 'homoousios' (of one substance) were later explored in some detail in the search for philosophical illumination of the problem, but the term in itself brought no such illumination at the outset. Its introduction into the creed at Nicaea seems to have been designed more to exclude Arius and his most determined supporters than to provide clarification of an alternative orthodox view. It was only many years after the Council that Athanasius began to use it for the expression of his own theological convictions. So too the union of the fully divine and the fully human in the person of the incarnate Christ was later illuminated by analogy with philosophical explorations of the mysterious relation between the immaterial soul and the physical body. But that also was something that was to come only later.

So different philosophical emphases within the same overall philosophical view gave expression to conflicting configurations of Christian belief. But significant though those distinguishable philosophical affiliations are, they do not seem to me to be the primary determinant of either position or to be the main cause of the division between them. That role is probably better ascribed to differing styles of piety and differing understandings of salvation. But even to say that is probably to offer a false contrast. For conceptions of piety and salvation are not wholly independent of philosophical considerations. They involve giving differing weight to different aspects of Christian faith and experience. And those different religious judgments may themselves be, in part at least, caused by already existing philosophical preferences, and may also help to determine what philosophical option a religious thinker will choose to adopt for the elaboration of his or her beliefs.

In short, the role of philosophy in this fourth-century debate is to be seen primarily in the way in which the debate as a whole was couched rather than in its influence on the particular answers given. It is in the posing of the questions about the person of the Son and about human salvation in the terms of a Platonic ontology that the most lasting contribution of philosophy is to be found. And a lasting one it has certainly been. Its effect is still very much with us, because the Nicene creed which embodies answers to that particular way of putting the questions now stands as a normative statement of Christian truth. Part, but admittedly only part, of the difficulty that many people today find in such traditional statements of faith coming down to us from the past is that our contemporary questions and frameworks of understanding are likely to have been formed by very different styles of philosophical thought from those which underlay and permeated all forms of fourth-century Christian belief, orthodox and heretical alike.

Vigiliae Christianae 44 (1990), 136-167, E. J. Brill, Leiden

NON-BEING AND EVIL IN GREGORY OF NYSSA

BY

ALDEN A. MOSSHAMMER

"No evil exists in its own substance (κατ' ἰδίαν ὑπόστασιν) lying outside the faculty of free choice (ἔξω προαιρέσεως κείμενον)."[1] So says Gregory of Nyssa in the *De Virginitate*, his earliest work.[2] This statement Gregory repeats, almost verbatim, in works of every period of his career, whenever he discusses the origin and nature of evil.[3] The idea that evil has no reality of its own had become a commonplace both in the Greek philosophical literature of Gregory's time and in Christian teaching.[4] Gregory knew such a doctrine, if from no other source, then from his brother Basil, who describes evil as "not a living essence (οὐχὶ οὐσία ζῶσα), but a disposition of the soul opposed to virtue, resulting through a falling away from the good." Basil adds, however, "that evil certainly exists, no one living in the world will deny."[5]

Basil's juxtaposition of these two statements points to the difficulty that confronts early Christian writers in trying to reconcile the reality of sin with the omnipotence and benevolence of God. If evil has no substance in the structure of things, then it is difficult to understand how it can be said so confidently to "exist". Gregory of Nyssa faces this problem more resolutely than his predecessors. Not satisfied with exempting God from responsibility for evil, Gregory wishes to show how evil is not only an absence of the good but a peculiar kind of absence that does in fact "exist" in dependence on the powers of the created will. As he puts it in the homilies on the Beatitudes (PG 44, 1256B), "evil takes subsistence as soon as we choose it, coming into being at the very moment of choice, for by itself in its own hypostasis outside of prohaeresis evil is nowhere to be found existing."

Gregory does not systematically explore all of the implications of such statements, nor does he anywhere present a comprehensive summary of his teaching as a whole. Nevertheless, the several components of Gregory's understanding of the nature of evil do constitute a more coherent and more philosophically interesting set of teachings than his commentators—or even, perhaps, Gregory himself—seem to have recognized. For Gregory, evil is not simply the absence of the good, but the not-being of the good—a form of non-being that the created will causes to "exist" as the absence of the good. All created reality is subject to constant motion and change because, according to Gregory, creation itself is a change and a motion from non-being toward being. Created goodness, especially the goodness in which God calls upon created intelligence to participate, is a positive motion, a potentially unlimited course towards the inexhaustible being of the divine nature. Evil is the failure of created intelligence to respond to this vocation for motion in the good. Evil is therefore a motion of created intelligence in withdrawal from the being of God, a course towards non-subsistence. As a motion of withdrawal, the course of evil is not unlimited, but must end in the death of the created will that is its progenitor and, perhaps, in the "death" of created intelligence as a whole. It is only because Christ has entered into and transformed the non-being towards which evil moves that created intelligence has been saved from its suicidal course. With this set of teachings Gregory both explains how evil does in fact exist as a thing outside of God and makes the philosophical definition of evil as absence a vehicle for the expression of a Christian understanding of sin and grace.

Evil as non-being

Gregory begins from Basil's position that evil does not proceed from God and therefore has no existence of its own, but is defined by the absence of the good. In the *De Virginitate*, he uses the analogy of darkness produced by the voluntary closure of the eye or by the negligent failure to build windows into a house. The darkness is not the responsiblity of the sun. It is an absence of light resulting from the failure of sight. Even so, Gregory says, evil arose when the first men chose to withdraw from the good.[6] In the commentary on the inscriptions to the Psalms (GNO V, 63,1-6), he goes farther. Evil is not only a withdrawal from the good, but a fall into non-being. Commenting on the phrase (Psalm 107, 40) "nothingness (ἐξουδένωσις) was poured out on their princes," Gregory says that to be in evil is not properly (κυρίως) to be, because there is no evil in itself—the nonsubsistence of the good is the genesis of evil. As we say wine when poured into water is "watered" or iron when smelted "fired", so whoever falls into the nothingness that is evil is "nihilized" (ὁ ἐν τῷ οὐδενὶ γενόμενος—τοῦτο δέ ἐστιν ἡ κακία—ἐξουδένωται). It was nonsubsistence (ἀνυπαρξία), Gregory says, that "came upon the inventors of evil, the first men, like a foul flood, and it poured itself out upon their whole succession."

It is partly the scriptural phrase under exegesis that prompts this identification of evil with non-being, but Gregory more formally defines evil elsewhere in the work (GNO V, 155,6-8) as a "thing outside of being whose essence has substance (or "whose nature has definition") not in being, but in not being good (εἰ δέ τι ἔξω τοῦ ὄντος ἐστίν, οὗ ἡ οὐσία οὐκ ἐν τῷ εἶναι, ἀλλ' ἐν τῷ ἀγαθὸν μὴ εἶναι τὴν ὑπόστασιν ἔχει). The same definition appears in Gregory's most comprehensive statement, a passage of the homilies on Ecclesiastes (GNO V, 406,7-407,15) where he offers his own "higher philosophy" about the nature of reality.

> The really real (τὸ ὄντως ὄν) is the self-good... This good, therefore, or, rather, this beyond the good, both itself truly is and by means of itself has given and continues to give to the things that exist the ability to become and to remain in being; whatever is found outside of it is nonsubsistence (ἀνυπαρξία), for whatever is outside of the real is not in being. Now since evil is understood as the opposite of virtue and since the perfect virtue is God, evil is therefore outside of God; its nature is conceived not in its being anything itself, but in its not being good. For to the conception "outside the good" we have given the name "evil". Evil and good are opposite in conception in the same way that not-being is distinguished as the opposite of being. When therefore by our own sovereign movement we have fallen away from the good—just as those who shut their eyes in the light are said to see the dark, for to see darkness is precisely to see nothing—it is then that the nonsubsistent (ἀνύπαρκτος) nature of evil is given being (οὐσιώθη) in those who have fallen away from the good; and it exists for just as long as we are outside the good. If the sovereign motion of our will again tears itself away from its company with the nonsubsistent and is grafted to the real, then that which no longer has its being within me will no longer have being at all. For evil subsisting (κείμενον) by itself outside of prohaeresis there is not.

Gregory here seeks to distinguish between the subsistence of created being by the power of God and the nonsubsistence which is evil as a thing outside of being. Whatever exists does so by the power of God, and whatever is not sustained by the power of God does not exist.[7] Since evil is the opposite of goodness and God is goodness iself, evil must somehow be a "thing" outside of God and therefore outside of being. Gregory tries to explain this not-being of evil by defining evil as something whose nature consists entirely in its not being good. Just as one cannot really "see" darkness, but must understand blindness as the not-seeing of the light, so one conceives of evil only as the not-being of the good. Neither "darkness" nor "evil" is the name of a thing that exists in its own right, but rather the word we use to refer to the non-existence of the opposite thing. Furthermore, since God is the author of all being and being therefore is good, evil must be conceived not only as the not-being and absence of the good, but somehow also as the not-being of being. Gregory goes on, however, to say that this nonexistent nature of evil "takes being" in those who have fallen away from the good, just as darkness is an "absence" constituted by one who has shut his eyes. Thus evil is not a "thing outside of being" in the sense of what does not exist at all, but some mode of existence that can be conceived of only as the absence of its opposite.

We find a similar definition in the catechetical oration (PG 45, 28C), where we also meet one of Gregory's many definitions of created reality as a passage from non-being to being, so that it becomes even clearer that evil must be non-being in a sense quite different from nothing-at-all.

> The distinction between virtue and evil is not an opposition of two things appearing by hypostasis. But rather, just as the nonexistent is the opposite of the existent (ἀντιδιαιρεῖται τῷ ὄντι τὸ μὴ ὄν) and it is not possible to say that the nonexistent stands as an hypostasis over against the existent, but instead that the absence of existence (ἀνυπαρξία) is the opposite (ἀντιδιαιρεῖσθαι) of existence (ὕπαρξις), so also evil is the opposite of virtue, not being anything by itself but conceived only by the absence (τῇ ἀπουσίᾳ) of the better. As we say that blindness is the opposite of vision, not that blindness is anything by nature in itself, but a privation of a previous condition (προλαβούσης ἕξεως στέρησιν), even so we say that evil is understood in the privation of good, like a shadow following the passage of the sunbeam. Now the uncreated nature is unreceptive of any motion of change or variation, while everything that subsists (ὑποστάν) by means of creation is akin to change, because the very hypostasis of creation begins with a change, non-being having been transformed into being by a divine power."

Gregory goes on to discuss at length how envy was born by a sovereign movement of the created and therefore mobile will of the angelic inventor of evil, who then deceived man into making an equally free choice of evil. He concludes (PG 45, 32C) by recapitulating his definition of evil as the nonsubsistence of the good.

> Evil has its character in being the absence of good, not being a thing of itself nor conceived of as hypostasis. For no evil exists by itself outside of

prohaeresis, but is so called by its not being the good. That which is not (τὸ δὲ μὴ ὄν) has no hypostasis (οὐκ ὑφέστηκε), and of that which has no subsistence the maker of the subsistent cannot be the maker".

Here again Gregory defines evil as a negative conception, opposed to the good in the same way that non-being is opposed to being. Evil is a μὴ ὄν, a non-being without subsistence of which God cannot be the author, a name for the absence of the good. Yet Gregory speaks of this μὴ ὄν as "that which has no subsistence" in such a way as to suggest that it does exist, although God cannot be its author. Furthermore, in this same passage Gregory also uses "non-being" to characterize the absence from which God created being. If we are not to understand "evil" as a name for the absence of being out of which God brought all things into existence, we must somehow distinguish between a non-being that is pure nothingness without quality in the absence of the good and the non-being to which we give the name "evil" whenever there is a withdrawal from the presence of the good. Such a distinction follows from Gregory's characterization of evil not only as the "not-being" or absence of the good, but also as the deprivation (steresis) of the good that follows upon a previous state of presence. Gregory is using "steresis" in the Aristotelian sense of an absence of what ought to be present, not a complete void.[8] Basil too had characterized evil as "steresis," but Gregory goes beyond Basil in his understanding of this state of privation. As a failure of what ought to be—and in fact was—present, the non-being of evil is not an absence in the sense of nothingness, like the non-being out of which God called the creation into being, but a negative condition within being that results from a withdrawal from a being that is already present. That is, the non-being which is evil depends on the being of which it is the deprivation and which it therefore presupposes. Evil is then not simply the logical opposite of being that Gregory's definition seems to imply, a mere locution equivalent to the predication of non-existence, but some kind of existence that can be defined only by negation. Gregory has Macrina state the case most succinctly when she says (De Anima PG 46, 93B) there is nothing outside of the divine except evil, which, "paradoxical as it may sound, has its being in not being (ἐν τῷ μὴ εἶναι τὸ εἶναι ἔχει).

Evil as being

Gregory, then, defines evil as non-being, while also suggesting that evil nevertheless "exists" in the absence of the good. An existence of some kind for evil also follows from the numerous passages in which Gregory affirms the Christian's constant prayer and expectation for the banishment of evil to non-being. A few examples will suffice for the point. In the dialogue on the soul, referring back to her paradox that evil has its being in non-being (PG 46, 93B), Macrina says (PG 46, 101A) that evil must, in the end, be removed from being (ἐκ τοῦ ὄντος), because that which does not truly exist does not exist at all.⁹ "Thy kingdom come" is a prayer for the withdrawal of all the forces of evil, indeed for their removal into non-being (εἰς τὸ μὴ ὄν, De Oratione PG 44, 1156D). It was to force the withdrawal of evil into non-subsistence (εἰς ἀνυπαρξίαν, De Tridui Spatio GNO IX, 283,6), that Wisdom entered into the bowels of the earth.¹⁰

Since evil must withdraw into non-being and nonsubsistence in the end, it cannot be characterized as non-being and nonsubsistence, at least not in the same sense, in the interim. If evil must be removed from being, then it must also be understood in some sense as existing. Gregory uses "non-being" in two quite different senses, between which he is not very careful to distinguish. The first is non-being as nothingness and non-existence. Created reality arose out of such a non-being and would revert to that nothingness without the sustaining power of God. It is also in this first sense that evil will be banished to non-being in the end—evil will simply not exist, and there will be no impediment to created wills in their movement toward being. The second sense is the non-being that describes evil during the present historical situation, a condition of absence and privation within being. Unlike the non-being from which God brought all things into being, the non-being of evil presupposes the existence of created being, and evil itself "exists" as the privation of that being which it presupposes. Gregory's conception of evil as "that which has its being in non-being" (De Anima PG 46, 93B) is reminiscent of Plato's claim in the Sophist (258) that the non-being which truly "is" non-being is not the opposite of being, in the sense of a thing that does not exist, but that form of being which is defined by its otherness than being.¹¹ For Gregory, evil is not the total absence which is the opposite of being, but a privation which is an otherness than being, the presence of non-being within being. Created existences rise from non-being toward being, taking substance by the power of God. Evil arises from within created being as a non-being defined by the privation of substance. Thus goodness has its substance from being so as to rise from non-being. Evil, on the other hand, is a fall from being, so that its "substance" must be from non-being. As Gregory puts it in *On Ecclesiastes* (GNO V, 300,22), evil is a thing without substance, precisely because it has its substance from non-being (τὸ γὰρ κακὸν ἀνυπόστατον, ὅτι ἐκ τοῦ μὴ ὄντος τὴν ὑπόστασιν ἔχει).

Evil and free choice

It is the power of God that creates being from non-being. The question remains by what power non-being comes to existence from within being. Gregory answers this question by suggesting that evil is not a self-existing condition that presents itself to the soul as a false object of choice, but an otherwise nonexistent condition that the soul constitutes as a possibility for choice by the very act of choosing it. This suggestion appears first in the passage from the homilies on the Beatitudes already cited (PG 44, 1256B), where Gregory says that "evil takes subsistence (ὑφίσταται) as soon as we choose it, coming into being (εἰς γένεσιν) at the very moment of choice, for by itself in its own hypostasis outside of prohaeresis evil is nowhere to be found existing (κείμενον)." In his formal definition of evil as the nonsubsistence of the good (*In Eccles.* GNO V, 407,8-11), Gregory says that this nonsubsistent nature takes being in those who have fallen away from the good and remains in being for as long as that withdrawal from the good continues. Similarly, in the catechetical oration (PG 45, 24D), Gregory says that evil grows from within, coming to subsistence in the prohaeresis (τῇ προαιρέσει τότε συνιστάμενον) whenever there is any withdrawal of the soul from the good. In the *De Anima (PG 46, 101A)*, after assuring us that evil must disappear into non-being in the end, Macrina explains that "since outside of prohaeresis evil has no nature, when all prohaeresis is in God, evil will vanish, there being no receptacle (δοχεῖον) left for it." For Gregory, then, evil is neither a nothingness that has no existence at all nor a "true" form of being in the sense that it is brought into existence by the will of God and therefore enabled to subsist in its own right as a constituent of created reality, but rather a non-subsistence that depends for whatever existence it has on the created will that produces and sustains it within its own "receptacle." When Gregory says that no evil exists in its own hypostasis "outside" (ἔξω) of prohaeresis, he means that phrase quite literally—evil exists somehow "in" the prohaeresis.

This notion of evil as a spurious existence clinging to being in dependence on the powers of the created will informs some of Gregory's most suggestive metaphors. Whatever is outside of being, he says, existing only in the not-being of the good, is like a false growth, rootless and unsown, whose apparently abundant crop is without real substance (*In Psalm*. GNO V, 155,5-10). Evil is like an intestinal parasite that the soul nourishes within itself to its own destruction (*In Eccles*. GNO V, 384,3-15). In one of his most interesting analogies (*In Psalm*. GNO V, 134,14-28) Gregory likens evil to the mule, a creature outside of creation existing by a mockery of nature.

> Mules cannot generate their own succession one from another; nature must always make the mule anew, contriving by a clever distortion what does not exist in creation (τὸ μὴ ὂν ἐν τῇ κτίσει παρασοφιζομένη). ... Similarly, evil does not have its existence (ὕπαρξιν) from God, nor can it continue by itself in its own hypostasis. Like the mule, evil cannot preserve and propagate itself; it must always be generated by another, whenever the noble steed in our nature, haughty and exultant, conceives the desire for an asinine union.

Gregory goes on to identify the muleherd as the jealous angel who draws human nature into evil; but the point remains that evil is a form of non-being generated from within being by the created will, whether human or angelic. Gregory develops the idea in one of his most famous metaphors, that of the two trees in the sixth homily on the Song of Songs (GNO VI, 348,12-352,1). Two things of opposing power—the tree of life and the tree of death—cannot occupy the same point at the same time. Scripture (Genesis 2,9) describes both trees as being in the same center in order to teach us that "the center of God's planting is life, while death is unplanted and rootless by itself. Death has its own space nowhere, but implants itself in the privation of life, whenever participation in the better lies fallow for living things. Because life is in the middle of the divine plantings, and by its withdrawal the nature of death takes substance (ἐνυφίσταται), for that reason the one who through enigma philosophises this teaching says that the death-bearing tree is also in the middle of the garden" (GNO VI, 349,19-350,6). The one tree exists by nature, Gregory continues, the other succeeds the existent one by privation; for it is from the same tree and in the same space by means of participation and privation (ἐκ γὰρ τοῦ αὐτοῦ ἐπὶ τοῦ αὐτοῦ διὰ μετουσίας τε καὶ στερήσεως) that the interchange of life and death takes place (GNO VI, 351,15-18). As he says elsewhere in the same work (GNO VI, 56,3-6; cf. *De Vita Moysis* (GNO VII.1, 59,21-23), all being is of one nature, but the prohaeresis has divided it into friend and foe.

Evil cannot exist in its own nature, nor can it occupy its own space.[12] Evil is neither a total emptiness in the absence of the good nor an entirely alien presence that comes from outside to invade a space left void by the withdrawal of the good. Rather, the prohaeresis confronts but one reality which it is capable of rendering either good or evil by the exercise of its powers of choice. The non-being of evil is a perverted form of created being, an otherness brought into subsistence by the created will. Although evil is the absence of being and goodness, it is dependent for its subsistence on what is by nature real and good. One may compare Augustine's teaching (*Civ.Dei* 12,3) that evil is possible only in a nature that is good. Paul Tillich's definition of evil as the "structure of destruction" captures Gregory's view particularly well—"destruction has no independent standing in the whole of reality but is dependent on the structure of that in and upon which it acts destructively—non-being is dependent on being, the negative on the positive, death on life."[13]

Being and non-being as products of will

One of the most interesting aspects of Gregory's teaching that "no evil exists in its own substance outside of free will" is its relationship to his doctrine that nothing at all exists apart from the divine will. Evil is a less-than-absolute form of non-being that the created will brings to subsistence from within being, while (created) goodness is a less-than-absolute form of being that the divine will brings to subsistence from non-being. Gregory's description of the created will (or "the soul" or "man" in general) as being "in a certain sense the demiurge" (*De Virg.* GNO VIII.1, 298,20) and receptacle (*De Anima*, PG 46, 101A) of evil suggests that created intelligence, in giving being to evil, acts as a false image of God, able by the exercise of its freedom to alter the structure of reality. For God created man in the divine image, and the greatest of the gifts constituting that image is sovereign freedom of the will (*Or.Cat.* PG 45, 24C; cf. *De Hominis Opificio* PG 44, 136B-C). This freedom of the will, since it is an image of the creative freedom of God, entails an inventive power, Gregory says (*In Cant.* GNO VI, 55,3-11), adding that there was found one who used this power wrongly and became the inventor of evil.[14] Gregory might well have agreed with Augustine (*Confessions* 2,6.14) that those who rebel against God merely copy Him in a perverse way.

Although no evil can exist in its own hypostasis, evil nevertheless has reality in dependence on the created will in a manner that is the negative analogy of the hypostasis of being from non-being as an actualization of the divine will. Just as God requires no external substratum, either of matter or of spirit, for His creative act, so no independent principle of evil need be posited to account for its reality in human experience. The powers of a sovereign freedom are sufficient in both cases, except that the production of evil presupposes the structure of created being so as to be its privation, while the divine will supplies its own substratum so as to bring being from non-being.

The total dependence of created being on the divine will is one of the best known features of Gregory's teaching.[15] The will of God by itself, unassisted by any external substratum, gives hypostasis to the nonexistent (*De Opificio* PG 44, 212B; cf. *In Eccles.* GNO V, 416,1-5; *Tunc Ipse Filius* PG 44, 1312A). The motion (ὁρμή) of the divine decision (προαίρεσις), whenever it wills (ἐθέλει) to do so, becomes act and so its wish becomes substance (οὐσιοῦται, *De Anima* PG 46, 124B). God in one and the same instant both wills that things should be and furnishes the substance of their existence—all things, including the bodily nature, take hypostasis immediately in the first movement of the divine will (*De Opificio* PG 44, 212B).[16] It is not only by the will of God that existing things rise from non-being to being and take their subsistence, but indeed from the will of God.[17] Macrina puts the case most succinctly when she defines οὐσία as the ὕπαρξις of the divine will (*De Anima* PG 46, 124B). If it is necessary to speak at all of a substratum for existing things, then, as von Balthasar has suggested, that can be nothing other than the will of God, taking hypostasis in the act of his speech.[18]

All things take substance by an act of the divine will, rising from non-being to being in the actualization of God's Word and command. Evil is a deformation of being, a form of non-being that the created will brings to subsistence from within being. Although good and evil, being and otherness-than-being are opposites, they are also analogous in that each is dependent for whatever existence it has on an act of will. While Gregory makes it clear that evil is a perversion of God's gift of freedom, he offers little discussion of the positive powers of created will. His theory that God created man as a mediator between the intelligible and the sensible, intended to communicate intelligible being to the bodily nature and so to bring all things into participation of the divine life certainly suggests such powers.[19] Whatever his view of the positive powers of created intelligence, Gregory does show that the production of evil as a perversion of its powers is possible because created intelligence is but an image of the divine power, not possessed of the full freedom or being of the divine nature itself. The essential difference between the two is that the divine will contains real being within itself, while the created will must derive being from outside of itself. God exists absolutely; but the creature is a nature in passage from non-being toward being and exists only by free participation in the being of God. Thus God can will only being, but it is possible for the creature to will non-being by failing to choose being.

Although Gregory observes no rigid distinctions in vocabulary, the qualitative difference between created and uncreated freedom is clear throughout his works and emerges particularly from his usage of "prohaeresis" in reference to the creature. Gregory sometimes uses this word in speaking of the divine will (e.g. *De Anima* PG 46, 124B), in order to emphasize that God's creative grace is a deliberative act, not a natural necessity; but in general "prohaeresis" is a property of the created nature.[20] "Prohaeresis" is the faculty of deliberate choice and most especially of the choice between two opposite objects. This is a faculty of which the intellectual creature is capable because he is endowed with freedom, but it is also one which he must continuously exercise because his being is dependent and his nature mobile. The creature must exercise his freedom in order to remain in participation of being. The divine will, on the other hand, expresses in the act of creation the being it already possesses. Thus the divine will is free in a more absolute sense than is the created prohaeresis, precisely because God exists and is good by nature and not by choice. The creature is free to choose between something and something (or, in the case of evil, perhaps, between something and nothing), but he is not free not to choose at all.

These relationships between being and willing are most explicit in the books against Eunomius. In the first book (GNO I, 106,23-107,10), Gregory defines the difference between the created and the uncreated natures as consisting in the fact that the uncreated nature both exists and is good absolutely, while the created nature has no necessary qualities of its own, but stands on the borderline (ἐν μεθορίῳ) of better and worse, participating in being and goodness in accordance with the inclinations of its own sovereign prohaeresis.[21] In the third book (GNO II, 45,17-46,7), Gregory excludes the divine nature from any such borderline status, stating that a man can choose to become either a son of God or a child of perdition, while God ever looks in the same direction and is never changed by such motions of prohaeresis. The divine nature always is what it wills and wills what it is, with no separation between will and act, while the creature is always in motion, possessed of no being of its own, seeking to become what it is not yet (GNO II, 46,1-3; 191,16-192, 4; 213,1-5).

The divine will possesses—indeed is—real, unchanging being and it lends being to its products by an actualization of its power that leaves its own substance undiminished. The created will has no being of its own, but exists only by free participation in the divine life. The uncreated nature is unchanging and self-existent. The created nature is always in motion, creation itself being a change from non-being, so that the creature must continuously choose the good in order to remain in being. When the prohaeresis does will the good, it draws itself into the being of the divine life. When it wills the opposite—or, rather, when it fails to will the good—the prohaeresis diminishes itself in the being that it draws from the good and thereby becomes the author and receptacle of nonbeing and evil. Furthermore, since the created nature derives its qualities from the goal toward which it moves, the soul now takes on the qualities of the non-being it has produced and is further diminished. For human nature is like a mirror, Gregory says (*Cant.Cant.* GNO VI, 103,15-104, 4), changing its image in accordance with what the prohaeresis chooses to reflect.[22]

The necessity of choice and the possibility for error Gregory attributes to the mobility inherent to the creature as a nature in passage from non-being toward being. He makes the point repeatedly in the catechetical oration (e.g., PG 45, 28D, 40A, 57D, 100D), but adds that mobility itself and the God who set the creation in motion from non-being toward being are not to blame. For there are two kinds of motion, Gregory says (PG 45, 60A)—motion toward the good, which is a continuous progress through an unlimited course, and motion towards the opposite, towards that whose substance is in what has no substance (οὗ ὑπόστασις ἐν τῷ μὴ ὑφεστάναι ἐστίν).[23] Motion in the good is an unlimited course towards life sustained by the creative power of God. Motion in evil is a course towards nonsubsistence that cannot therefore be sustained indefinitely. For goodness has a real existence as a product of the divine will, but evil exists only as an absence of the good within the created will in withdrawal from being.

Non-being as the limit of evil

Motion in the good is an upward course of expansion toward the inexhaustible being of God and can therefore be without limit. Motion in evil, however, is a downward course of diminution towards "that whose substance is in what has no substance," so that non-subsistence is a kind of "absolute zero" beyond which no further such motion of withdrawal is possible. In discussing the origins of evil in the catechetical oration, Gregory describes the angelic inventor of evil as plunging like a rock from a precipice "towards the ultimate limit of evil" (πρὸς τὸν ἔσχατον τῆς πονηρίας ὅρον PG 45, 29A). While this idea of an absolute limit to evil is no more than implicit in Gregory's discussion of the nature of evil as non-being, he does in fact maintain in other contexts that progress in evil reaches an outer limit beyond which it can expand no further and that it was at this "akme of evil" (*De Die Natali* PG 46, 1132A) that Christ intervened. Many commentators have found little relationship between Gregory's definition of evil as a thing without substance and his teaching that Christ overcame evil when it had reached its akme. If evil is defined simply as absence, then it is indeed difficult to understand how it can be said to "increase" at all, much less reach a maximum "extent." Gregory's teaching, however, is not that evil is a "state" of absence and nonsubsistence, but a motion towards nonsubsistence, a reversal of the course towards being. As created goodness is a motion out of non-being toward being, so evil is a reversion back towards non-being—a motion of withdrawal towards that which has no hypostasis (*Or.Cat.* PG 45, 60A).[24] Created goodness can increase without limit towards the infinity of the divine life. Evil can continue to exist only so long as its host in created intelligence remains in some minimal participation of being. Tillich's words again express the implications of such a view in its most radical consequences—"it aims at chaos; but, as long as chaos is not attained, destruction must follow the structures of wholeness; and if chaos is attained, both structure and destruction have vanished."[25] Gregory does not pursue the matter to this radical conclusion. He does not describe the course of evil as leading to a complete dissolution of all created existence, but rather as culminating in the complete corruption and enslavement of created intelligence—deprived of real life and being, but nevertheless existing in thrall to the "archon of evil."[26] Gregory does not conceive of evil as an attack on the whole created order leading to an annihilation of all created substance, sensible as well as intelligible, but as a withdrawal of the intellectual creation from the being of God. His teaching (*De Opificio* PG 44, 144B-149A, *Or.Cat.* PG 45, 25D) that man was intended as a bridge between the intelligible and the sensible, in order to bring the sensible also into participation of the divine life, might perhaps imply that the self-destruction through evil of this critical link has disastrous consequences for the whole of creation. As we have already noted, however, Gregory does not develop this idea of man as an ontological link. However that may be, for Gregory it is simply unthinkable that God would not have intervened when evil reached its akme, and he does not speculate on what might have been the case otherwise. Although Gregory does not therefore describe evil as ending in a great catastrophe in which "both structure and destruction have vanished," he does nevertheless see evil, with Tillich, as limited by its own nature as evil and not only by the intervention of Christ.

Gregory's thoughts on the increase and limit of evil undergo considerable development. Jean Daniélou has discussed all of the relevant passages in detail.[27] The present discussion is confined only to suggesting how Gregory's understanding of evil as a motion away from being is connected, at least logically, both to his teaching that evil must reach a maximum extent and to his soteriology.

In his earlier works, Gregory emphasizes the dire consequences of the first sin—evil spreads and propagates in each successive generation until it has infected the whole of humanity and manifested itself in every imaginable permutation of depravity.[28] Gregory characterizes this spread of evil as "boundless" (εἰς ἄπειρον, *De Virg.* GNO VIII.1, 299,18; *In Psalm.* GNO V, 158,8); but he also maintains that the increase of evil cannot be without limit. He offers three different reasons. Evil, like everything else outside the godhead, is not eternal; evil had a beginning and must therefore also have an end (*In Psalm.* GNO V, 101,2-4). Second, the goodness and mercy of God are more powerful than any evil, however great its increase (*In Psalm.* GNO V, 158,8-10). There is little in these first two arguments to distinguish the limitations of evil from the finitude of the created order in general. More interesting is Gregory's third argument—that motion in evil is contained within definite boundaries that do not apply to created motion toward the good. We meet this third argument first in the *De Opificio* (PG 44, 201B-C), where Gregory says that the mobility of the created nature prevents it from remaining fixed anywhere, not even in evil.

That which is always in motion, if it direct its course toward the good, need never stop its forward progress, because of the infinite nature of what is traversed. For it will find no end of what is being pursued, where it might take a hold and stop from moving. But if it directs its motion toward the opposite, when it has finished the course of evil and arrived at the utmost measure (ἀκρότατον μέτρον) of evil, then, since its nature knows no stopping, having traversed the expanse (διάστημα) of evil, it will of necessity turn its motion toward the good. Because the progress of evil is not infinite, but contained within fixed bounds (ἀναγκαίοις πέρασι), good necessarily succeeds the boundary (πέρας) of evil. So it is that our mobile nature turns its course at last to the good, chastened by its misfortunes so as not again to suffer their like.

Gregory illustrates this teaching with an astronomical analogy (PG 44, 201D-204A). The universe is all light; and darkness results only from the interposition of the earth, whose sphere casts a conical shadow within the rays of the sun. Since the sun is many times larger than the earth, a circle of light surrounds the shadow, and the rays of the sun everywhere form the border of the cone. Now if someone were able to traverse the measure (μέτρον) of the shadow, he would arrive again at the light. So it is with us, Gregory says, having passed through the boundary (ὅρος) of evil, when we arrive at the edge of the shadow of sin, we will again live in the light, since the nature of good exceeds the measure of evil by countless numbers of times.

Here Gregory is relying primarily on his second reason for believing that evil is limited, because overwhelmed by the goodness of God; but the astronomical analogy does suggest that evil occupies a definite "space" beyond which it can expand no further. In later works, Gregory argues that God waited until evil had filled its own limited space before intervening to banish it to non-being. The earliest example appears in the *De Tridui Spatio* (GNO IX, 283,13-284,8). As before, Gregory speaks of the increase of evil from its beginnings with the first men, spreading and increasing in each successive generation. Thus evil expanded indefinitely to its extremity (πρὸς ἄπειρον, ἕως εἰς τὸ ἀκρότατον) and ruled all of human nature. It is at this greatest extent of evil that God intervened; and it is the supreme miracle, hardly grounds for complaint of delay, that Christ within just three days destroyed the whole mass of evil. Other passages make it clear that the course of evil reaches an extremity beyond which it can expand no further independently, and not simply because Christ has intervened. In the catechetical oration, using the analogy of the physician (PG 45, 76A-B), Gregory says that the healer of all waited for the full completion of evil—"when evil arrived at its utmost measure and there was no form of wickedness that had not been dared among men, so that the cure might proceed through the whole of the malady, for this reason not at its beginning, but at its completion (τελειωθεῖσαν), he cured the disease."[29]

Most commentators have argued that Gregory sees evil as limited either because it is contained within the limits of the created order or because Christ has intervened to set a limit to an otherwise boundless increase of evil. Following von Ivánka, Jean Daniélou argues that the notion of a necessary limit to the increase of evil is an integral part of the contrast between the infinity of God and the finitude of created being that is central to Gregory's thought. The space that evil occupies, according to Daniélou, is the temporary historical space of creaturely development, bounded by the apocatastasis of all things to their state of original perfection. Paul Zemp agrees; and he suggests that evil is limited not because of its ontological nature as non-being, but because of its setting within the limited diastema of created being. Mariette Canévet emphasizes the importance of the incarnation to interrupt the progress of evil and bring salvation to the created order. That there is a limit to evil Canévet attributes to the intervention of God, not to the mobility of nature or the finitude of evil, which she considers unlimited in historical time except for the grace of the incarnation.[30] Daniélou and Zemp are right to argue that evil is limited because it is confined to the finite space and time of the created order; but to suggest that evil is limited only because it shares the limitations of the created order is to put evil on a par with created being rather than to understand evil, with Gregory, as a failure of created intelligence, a motion of withdrawal from being. Canévet is right to emphasize the divine intervention, but this intervention is salvific precisely because evil had reached a critical limit. For Gregory, evil is limited not just because it is confined to the limited diastema of created being, but more importantly because it represents the withdrawal of created intelligence from the being that should sustain it. Growth in being is a potentially unlimited course towards life, but the course of withdrawal must come to an end when the separation from being is complete.

In the *De Tridui Spatio* (GNO IX, 283,21-284,3), Gregory defines what he means by the maximum extent of evil and explains why it was necessary for Christ to intervene at just this point. For evil had spread and increased with each successive generation, he says, so that "having arrived at its maximum extent, evil dominated all of human nature and, as the Prophet says (Psalm 14,3), 'all had gone astray, all were corrupt,' and there was nothing among existing things that was not an instrument of evil.'' The maximum extent of evil, according to this passage, is all of created being, or at least all of created intelligence. Evil reaches a limit beyond which it can expand no further for two reasons. First, evil is a product of created intelligence and when all such intelligence has become its instrument, there can be no further source for its expansion. Thus, as Daniélou has argued, evil is bounded by the created diastema and can expand no further. But since evil can be conceived in Gregory's terms as existing only as the absence of (or the withdrawal from) being, then evil is limited for a second reason. For evil is not only the "product" of created intelligence, but also its destruction. The "being" of which evil is the absence is the participated being of the created soul itself. The archon of evil induced man to become his own murderer, Gregory says (Or.Cat. PG 45, 29B). Whoever falls into evil is "nothingized" (In Psalm. GNO V, 63,1-6). As the choice of the good causes the soul to expand and increase its capacity for the reception of the good (De Anima PG 46, 105B), so the choice of evil represents a diminution and leads to an ever decreased capacity for goodness and therefore also for being (In Eccles. GNO V, 380,20-21). Thus the akme of evil is not so much coextensive with created life as it is its dissolution. This Gregory expresses metaphorically in the De Tridui when he identifies the akme of evil with death. Christ entered the heart of the earth "in order that evil might recede into nonsubsistence when the last enemy has been destroyed, which is death" (GNO IX, 283,6-8). Christ's intervention is salvific because the akme of evil represents the death of created intelligence.

Gregory frequently associates evil with death, and sometimes he speaks of "evil", "non-being", and "death" as if they were synonymous. But he speaks of evil as death in two senses. In the first sense, "to be in evil is not properly to be" (In Psalm. GNO V, 63,1-6), so that evil is a form of death inasmuch as the soul that has chosen evil has chosen to separate itself from the true life that follows only from communion with God. In the second sense, death is the retribution for evil and the end toward which the course of evil moves. The choice of evil by the first men entailed a loss of immortality; and as a result not only does the individual man face physical death,.but mankind as a unit has been set on a course towards death (Or.Cat. PG 45, 33B, 52C;

Cant.Cant. GNO VI, 147). This is why Death is the last enemy. "Death" in the first sense is an unauthentic existence; "death" in the second sense is annihilation. Evil is a motion of the soul in withdrawal from being. The soul which has chosen evil is already "dead" in the first sense, but also moving towards death in the second sense. In the third book against Eunomius (GNO II, 213,5-29; cf. *Or.Cat.* PG 45, 36B), Gregory distinguishes between these two senses of death. The text is unfortunately corrupt at a critical point (indicated here by asterisks), but the passage is sufficiently comprehensive to show that Gregory does conceive of evil as a motion that leads towards a limit in non-being and death.

> If that which is truly life is found in the divine and supernal nature, the falling away from this will surely end in what is entirely opposite. The meaning of life and death is multiple and not understood in the same way. For the flesh, the activity and motion of the bodily senses is called life and the opposite, the extinction and dissolution of these things, is named death. For the intellectual nature, assimilation to the divine is life, and the falling away from it has the name death. ... The meaning of death being twofold therefore in the scriptures, that which is truly unchangeable and immutable alone has immortality. ... As many things as participate in death, being removed from immortality because of the tendency in the opposite direction***but if it should fall away from participation in the good, it would receive because of the mutability of its nature community with the opposite, which is nothing other than death, being somewhat analogous to the bodily death. As in the one case the extinction of the natural energies is called death, so also for the intellectual nature the lack of motion (ἀκινησία) towards the good is death and withdrawal from life.

What is significant about this passage for the present argument is that Gregory speaks of evil as a motion (or a lack of motion ἀκινησία) that leads towards an end in death. To be in evil is both to lack the true life and to move towards an end in what is the opposite of true life—a death analogous to the total extinction of bodily sense and activity. We can distinguish between the death and non-being that describes evil as a blight upon created life and the death and non-being towards which evil moves as it "expands." Evil as a false presence within being is a form of non-being, existing as an absence of the good. Evil as a process is a motion of withdrawal from being and goodness. "Death" and "Non-Being" can therefore be names both for evil as it exists and for the dissolution of life towards which it moves. In the refutation of Apollinarius (GNO III.1, 221,21) Gregory equates the climax of evil with the end of human life (ἐπὶ τέλει τοῦ ἀνθρωπίνου βίου ἤδη τῆς κακίας ἡμῶν πρὸς τὸ ἀκρότατον αὐξηθείσης), stating that Christ acted at just this point so as to save humanity from death once and for all, "leaving nothing of evil uncured."

The point at which evil has filled the whole of created being is also the point at which created intelligence has been emptied of life and nothing but death would "exist" except for the intervention of the Christ. Although Gregory does of course maintain the doctrine of the immortality of the soul, evil nevertheless moves towards and climaxes in a state of death, the "enslavement of being to non-being" (In Eccles. GNO V, 301,4-5). As physical death is not destruction, according to Gregory (Or.Cat. PG 45, 33D), but dissolution of the elements, so also it is possible for the immortal soul to "exist" even in non-being and death.

In all of the passages where Gregory speaks of the "maximum" extent of evil it is the work of Christ, rather than the metaphysics of evil, that is his main focus. It is nevertheless clear that evil reaches its maximum extent independently—that Christ intervenes because evil has reached its akme, not that evil reaches its akme because Christ has intervened. More importantly, the maximum extent of evil represents for created intelligence a withdrawal from being so complete as to be irreversible, except for the intervention of Christ. Christ's act is truly salvific precisely because he intervened at that critical moment "at the end of human life" (Contra Apollin. GNO III.1, 221,21), "in the last days" when all lay "in the shadow of death" (In Diem Natalem PG 46, 1132C).

Gregory's definition of evil as the withdrawal of created intelligence from being implies an absolute limit to the course of evil independent of divine intervention and his description of the akme of evil as a state of death and corruption involving the whole of created life is at least consistent with such a definition. The significance of this conclusion is twofold. First, we must distinguish between the limitations inherent in created being and the limit to evil that follows from its definition as the withdrawal of created intelligence from the being that sustains it. Created goodness is finite, but because it is a motion from non-being towards being it proceeds on a potentially unlimited course. The course of evil is limited because it is a failure of that motion—a withdrawal from being to non-being, a motion towards nonsubsistence (Or.Cat. PG 45, 60A). Second, the dissolution that evil causes is irreversible, except for the intervention of the Christ. Mariette Canévet has rightly emphasized this point. It is because Christ did in fact "enter upon the akme of evil" (*Tunc Ipse Filius* PG 44, 1316A) that there is cause for rejoicing and a "new epinician" (*In Sanctum et Salutare Pascha* GNO IX, 311,11).

Gregory's teaching contains a clear distinction between "nature" and "grace." Left to its own resources, once it has rebelled against the sustaining power of God, created intelligence can arrive only at death and non-being. It is the grace of God, not the mobility of nature, that has prevented the dominance of non-being over being (cf. *In Eccles.* GNO V, 301,3-6 and 305,9-13). Nevertheless, the idea that motion in evil must reach a limit in immobility and death seems inconsistent with what Gregory says in the *De Opificio* (PG 44, 201B-C) that because of the constant mobility of the created nature the limit of evil is necessarily followed by a return to the good—when it has reached the outer boundary of evil, it turns its motion by necessity (κατ' ἀνάγκην) to the good, chastened by the memory of what it has suffered so as not again to experience the like. In the *De Mortuis* (GNO IX, 54,5-57,28) Gregory similarly states that the desire for what is alien is not permanent in our nature, and he suggests that God permitted the choice of evil in the first place, so that man might learn a lesson from the experience and make a free return to the good.

By our thesis, the arrival at the outer boundary of evil ought to mean death and immobility, rather than a return to the good necessitated either by the mobility of the created nature or by the finitude of evil. In fact, Gregory's point both in the *De Opificio* and in the *De Mortuis* is not that man can expect by his own nature or resources to cross the boundary of evil and return to the good, but that the life-sustaining love of God is more powerful than the death-bearing grip of evil. The point of the astronomical analogy in the *De Opificio* is, as Gregory explicitly says, to show that, just as the realm of the sun's light is many times greater than the cone of the earth's shadow, even so the might of God's goodness is vastly superior to the power of evil, however great its increase. Likewise, in the *De Mortuis*, although Gregory says that the desire for what is alien is not permanent in our nature, he makes it clear that the removal of the impurities is the work of the potter, not the pot.[31] Gregory emphasizes the point in many contexts—man's return to the good is free only because Christ has purchased that freedom and restored to created intelligence its lost mobility. We needed no helper to fall into evil, Gregory says (*Or.Dom.* PG 44, 1165A), but human nature as a consequence of that fall is unable to save itself—that is why we must pray for the will of the Father to be done. "We cannot repair our nature ourselves" (*Or.Cat.* PG 45, 40B-C); "we supply of ourselves no cause for the good" (*In Psalm.* GNO V, 53,19-20). Christ did not appear simply as an example of virtue to invite man across the boundary of evil; for if human nature were sufficient in itself for the acquisition of the good, the mystery would be superfluous (*Contra Apollin.* GNO III. 1, 217, 12-17). Created for motion in the good, human nature instead lay immobilized in the frozen image of what it chose to worship, stone instead of man, unable to move toward the good; that is why the sun of righteousness has risen (*Cant.Cant.* GNO VI, 147,6-19).

Christ as the limit of evil

Left to its own course, evil moves towards non-being and death. Since death is the end towards which the choice of evil moves and since God wished to preserve the creature's freedom, God permitted evil to take its own course and acted in such a way as to make death an instrument of grace. By bringing the whole of mankind with him through its gate, Christ has made death a vehicle for mobility beyond the boundary of evil. The structure of Gregory's thought in its most mature form exhibits an elegant simplicity. Motion in evil must end in death, so that it is by means of death that the course towards the good must be renewed. God brought creation into being from non-being in the beginning, and it is from non-being that He creates being anew. The death of men and of man represents the victory of death over life. The death of Christ represents the victory of life over death, because His death is of an entirely different order. Man only participates in being and can therefore lose it. Christ, however, since he is life and being, destroys death by embracing it (*De Tridui* GNO IX, 285,3-6). Thanks to the grace of God, the death of Christ rather than the final enemy, whose name is Death, stands waiting for the consummation of evil. So it is that there is now "another birth, a different living, another kind of life, a restructuring of our very nature" (*De Tridui* GNO IX, 277,21-278,1).

Again, Gregory's views reflect considerable development. In his earliest works, he describes death as a release from evil in a sense that has little specifically Christian content. Sin is born with us, grows with us, ceases only with death.[32] In later works, he describes death as an instrument of the divine providence for the cleansing of the soul from taint by the dissolution and reconstitution of the elements.[33] Even when this idea is combined with the doctrine of the resurrection of Christ as the dissolution and remaking of all mankind, it remains on a literal level that, apart from the denial of metempsychosis, is of a piece with Plato's myth of Er at the end of the *Republic* or Vergil's picture of the purified soul in *Aeneid* 6. In his most mature works, Gregory introduces a sacramental theme according to which the individual participates in the death and resurrection of Christ not only at his own physical death or at the end of time, but also in his own life and world through the symbolic death of baptism and, more importantly, through a spiritual death and resurrection that Christ has made an object of choice for the Christian soul at every moment. This sacramental death as a member of the mystical body of Christ corresponds, on the positive side, to the spiritual death that each member of the human race suffers in participation with Adam (*Or.Cat.* PG 45, 52C). Evil works both on the cosmic and the individual level, infecting the whole human race as the result of the first sin, yet presenting itself anew to each individual. As evil was complete in Adam, yet reveals itself in an historical expansion toward death, so the redemptive death and resurrection of all mankind is complete in Christ, yet accomplished in each individual in an historical struggle with evil. So it is that evil appears still to hold being in its grasp, even after the decisive intervention of Christ.[34] Although the sin of Adam brought death to the entire human race, nevertheless each man freely chooses to participate in that death. Likewise, although Christ entered upon the akme of evil to reunite the whole of humanity to God, each one must freely choose to halt the course of evil by participating in the death and resurrection of Christ.[35] The moment of Adam's sin, of evil's akme, of Christ's transformation of death to life—all are simultaneous in the perspective of God, and all are present at every moment to the created prohaeresis at the boundary of good and evil.

This transition from a physical to a sacramental understanding of death as the end of evil is evident most clearly in the catechetical oration. This labyrinth of living death can neither be traversed nor escaped, Gregory says, except by doing as Christ did—passing through death to new life (PG 45, 88B). Gregory refers to his earlier argument (PG 45, 36D-37C, 52B-C) that the individual participates physically in the death and resurrection of Christ at his own death, passing through the purifying fire if necessary, waiting for that great day when the general resurrection will restore all to their original state. The Christian imitates and participates in this act of "doing as Christ did," Gregory now adds (PG 45, 89B), through the sacrament of baptism, when rightly received. The symbol of death in the water represents for us even now a break in the continuity of evil.

Gregory takes the final step in the commentary on the Song of Songs. The actual ritual of baptism, performed but once, represents a sacramental passage through death to life that Christ performs for his members—and to which they must freely respond—at every moment. When the first man chose the fruit of that death-bearing tree, death invaded the whole human nature; as man brought death by dying to life, so now it is by dying to death that he must again be made alive. Hence the Singer describes the bride as dripping with myrrh, the symbol of death (GNO VI, 350,19-352,5). Like the apostle, she must be a myrrh-bearing tree, dying each day and becoming an aromatic source of salvation to others (GNO VI, 307, 9-13). What is possible in the earlier works only once, only in the eschatological perspective or only through the purifying fire of physical death, now becomes eternally present to every soul who has chosen by dying to live. Through the building of his body in the Church Christ enters daily upon the akme of evil and restores dead humanity to life (GNO VI, 381,19-382,7).

The course of evil leads from being back toward non-being and ends in death. Christ, by entering into and conquering death, once again as in the beginning sets in motion the course toward being. The created prohaeresis becomes what it was intended to be, a power for the unification and uplifting of being, instead of the demiurge of non-being. There is no danger of recidivism, no cyclical alternation of being and non-being, for all of this transpires in the same eternal moment, the end coinciding with the beginning.

Christianity and Hellenism

Gregory of Nyssa accounts for the very real power of evil in the world, without compromising either the benevolent omnipotence of God or the freedom and responsibility of man, by conceiving of evil as having a status analogous, but contrary, to that of created goodness. As created goodness has no existence except in dependence on the divine will, so no evil exists except in dependence on the created prohairesis. What subsists by the divine act of creation has a real existence, inasmuch as it is a product of that which alone can be said truly to exist. Since evil results from the privation of being, it cannot exist in its own nature as absence. But this does not mean that evil does not exist at all. Evil is a powerful and dangerous force in the world, because of the negative character of its motion, not because of the negative definition of its essence. The non-being which is evil is not the opposite of created being, but the opposite of the motion of created being toward the good. For Gregory, only the uncreated, divine nature exists immutably as being itself. Whatever things come into subsistence from non-being, he says (Or.Cat. PG 45, 40A-B, cf. 100A), proceed always by means of change. If they act according to nature, that change is always towards the better, but if they turn aside from the straight path, change towards the opposite takes over. This applies especially to man, he adds, for whom withdrawal from the good entails every kind of evil as its opposite. Thus created reality and, especially, the goodness of created intelligence do not exist as a state of being, but as a process, a motion from non-being toward being. Similarly, evil is not a "state" of non-being, but a regress from being toward non-being. Good exists in inexhaustible abundance in the divine nature and the motion of created intelligence towards being is therefore a potentially infinite process that draws energy from its motion toward the source. Evil is a thing without substance, and motion in evil is therefore a course toward nonsubsistence that must come to an end in death and non-being. By entering upon the akme of evil, God has transformed the non-being toward which evil inexorably moves, making the end of evil a new beginning for a course toward life in the Body of Christ.

With this doctrine, which is fully consistent in its internal logic, even if not always in its expression, Gregory succeeds—perhaps unconsciously—in affirming two opposite ways of responding to the world. The first we may call the typically Greek response to evil. Evil is inherent in the nature of the world; it is the principle of disorder and danger that prevents man from exercising his freedom and realizing his ambitions, whether that be perfection in a moral sense or the ἀρετή of a traditional nobility. The source of this disorder may be identified with an actively hostile power, such as the ἄτη of Homer, or with a passive, but resistant, barrier to freedom, like the ἀνάγκη of Plato's Timaeus. In either case, this alien element is fundamental to the nature of things, and neither the gods nor men have finally any control over it. Men seek to minimize its influence, by carving out a space of order within the polis and setting boundaries between law and the wilderness, by apotropaic ritual, or by a philosophical pursuit of an unseen mode of being reliably permanent, continuous, and rational. This attitude takes full account of the danger, failure, and suffering of human life in the world; but it fails in its inability to account for the source of man's resistance to this power, to explain why evil should be regarded as "alien," rather than normative.

The second attitude we may call the "Biblical." Evil is experienced as a human failure to respond, rather than as a flaw in the way things are. Evil results from convenantal faithlessness, a refusal to acknowledge the power and sovereignty of what really exists and what the Law and the Prophets have clearly revealed. Evil is a rebellious self-destruction, a sin that represents not a missing of the mark, but a wilful and defiant choice of the wrong target. This mode of response accounts for the source of man's vocation to order; but it fails in its inability to explain how a mode of reality totally dependent on a superior power can act in defiance of its own source and become in fact so evil as to invite destruction.

The Greek feels himself confronted with danger and forced to seek for a principle of order to control it. The prophet feels himself confronted with the power and judgment of the divine and forced to seek an explanation for human faithlessness. In identifying these modes of response as "Greek" and "Biblical", we of course oversimplify and perhaps identify as "typical" attitudes that others who have sought to make such generalizations would be unable to recognize. Both cultures can be shown to evidence the whole range of responses between these extremes, as indeed does Gregory of Nyssa himself. But even if Gregory does not always succeed in rising above the tensions between them, his view of creaturely good and evil exhibits a logical structure that is able to accommodate both points of view. By understanding reality as a process, rather than a state, intentionally good, but neutral except as actualized in creaturely experience, Gregory avoids characterizing the phenomenal world as fundamentally good or evil or even as having any essence at all. The world is what experience chooses to make of it. Evil is simultaneously a rebellion against the sovereign power of being manifest in the very fact that experience, rather than nothingness, is even possible, and an alteration of the structure of experience so that it appears—and, in fact, is—hostile. The source of the drive for order is explained in that anything exists at all; the source of the rebellion is explained in that nothing exists in itself. Reality is suspended between being and non-being. The rebellion of sin is not the assertion of an opposite power with a nature of its own, but an assertion of the nothingness from which the creature arose. The alien structures that oppose man represent an absence of structure, but by the very fact that this absence is manifest as destruction, rather than as an emptiness, the "assertion" of non-being points to the being on which it depends. There can be no dualism, because failure and non-being are intelligible, as Gregory says, only as the absence of their opposites. Thus the experience of nothingness and death at the akme of evil brings an awareness of being and opens the way for the entrance of a grace that can overcome non-being by embracing it.

Gregory's doctrine of sin, evil, and redemption builds upon established foundations. Origen (*In Joh.* 2, 13) had already denied that evil has any substantial reality, and Basil's teaching that evil is a condition of a diseased soul, without hypostasis of its own, contains the heart of Gregory's view. Athanasius (*De Incarnatione Verbi* 4-6) anticipates the theory that sin is a return to the non-being from which the creature arose. Gregory's own contribution is his understanding of created being as process and of evil as a regressive motion that undermines that process. In formulating this set of teachings, Gregory is motivated primarily by his own developing understanding of the nature of created reality as an infinite progress from non-being toward an unlimited and inexhaustible good, seeing evil as its opposite. Nevertheless, although Gregory's teaching is both distinctively Christian and distinctively his own, many of his ideas bear a strikingly similarity to what Plotinus has to say about the nature of evil as non-being.

Jean Daniélou has suggested that Gregory's doctrine of evil shows the influence, perhaps directly, of Plotinus.[36] Daniélou sees the agreement primarily in a common view that evil, although defined as privation, has an objective reality that positively prevents the soul from realizing its natural capacities, and the disagreement in that Plotinus locates the source of evil in matter, while Gregory attributes the prior existence of evil to the bad will of the demons. Gregory certainly acknowledges the power of demons over human life, but this is neither what is most distinctive about his doctrine nor what is most interesting about the relationship of his thought to that of Plotinus.

The principal point of contact between Gregory and Plotinus is their agreement in the technical defintion of evil as non-being, an absence of being that is inconceivable in itself and whose whole nature consists in its being conceived as the opposite of something else. Gregory formally defines evil as "having its being in non-being" (*De Anima* PG 46, 93B), as a thing outside of being "whose ousia has its hypostasis not in being, but in not being good" (*In Psalm.* GNO V, 155, 7-8), "whose nature is conceived not in its being something, but in its not being good (*In Eccles.* GNO V, 407,2-3), an opposition understood "not as existing in itself, but in the absence (ἀπουσία) of the other" (*Or.Cat.* PG 45, 28C). These statements recall Plotinus's definition of evil as some "form or mode of non-being" (I,8.3), that is not merely different from being but whose whole nature is constituted by its non-beingness, its otherness than being (I,8.6; cf. II,4,16, II,5.5). Gregory and Plotinus agree in understanding ordinary reality as suspended between being and non-being and in describing the proper life of the soul as an ascent toward being. Although for Plotinus evil has an objective existence as matter, nevertheless evil in the soul results for him, as for Gregory, in the soul's failure to incline toward its superiors. Gregory's teaching that evil is a production of the created prohaeresis has its counterpart in Plotinus's statement (III, 9.3) that "motion toward the lower is toward non-being; and this is the step the soul takes when it is set upon itself; for by willing toward itself it produces its lower, an image of itself, a non-being, and so is wandering into the void."

For Plotinus, this "authentic nonexistence" of evil is the limit of being, the furthest extent to which being can reach, the point at which the overflowing of the Good is exhausted and must end. This non-being, which Plotinus tends to associate with matter, is not an evil principle that exists outside of and in opposition to the good. It is rather a necessary consequence of multiplicity and, in a sense therefore, good (I, 8,7; II,9,3). Nevertheless, this utter formlessness infects everything with which it comes into contact and is therefore the source of evil. Plotinus insists (I,8) that evil comes into the soul from the outside, yet matter itself is a production of the soul and is good, inasmuch as it is the necessary consequence and limit of being. Although matter is the source of evil, the manifestation of evil requires the activity of the partial soul when it turns away from its source and toward its own inferior products. Plotinus is unable to explain how that which must necessarily exist as the outer limit of being can be the principle of evil or how it is that the soul's own product at the last stage of being can be said to have a prior existence as the cause of the soul's fatal weakness in its declension to evil.[37]

Gregory both brings his own Christian understanding of evil to expression and explains what Plotinus cannot by standing the whole Plotinian system on its head. For Plotinus, reality is a process of unfolding from the higher to the lower, a motion from being toward non-being. Being has no boundary in space or time, but it does have a limit in non-being as its own most minimal product. This non-being is not non-existence, but an existence conceived as utter lack. Being consists in definition, so that the ultimate Beyond-Being is so fully defined as to be the One, while lower modes of being spread out toward multiplicity and absence, so that the ultimate limit of being is not nothingness, but the utter darkness of the indefinite (τὸ ἀόριστον). The concept of non-being as nothingness is precisely what such a system cannot embrace, and Plotinus specifically denies its possibility (II,4,6). Gregory reverses this understanding of reality in two significant ways. First, the unlimited (τὸ ἀόριστον) is the characteristic of the truly real, instead of the truly unreal.[38] The opposite of being-itself is therefore a finitude so absolute that it is nothing at all. Second, created reality is a process of filling the emptiness, rather than a progressive production of the inferior. Being can therefore grow without limit toward the infinite goodness, instead of diminishing toward an indefinite absence. The non-being of evil is a failure of this growth toward being that must therefore come to an end, instead of a necessary consequence of being that is therefore eternal. Because he is able to conceive of nothingness and non-being in the most radical sense, Gregory avoids the Plotinian implication of the good in the production of a non-being that becomes the source of evil. Since Gregory understands created being as rising from nothingness, instead of flowing from the One, the soul is divine only by participation, not by nature. Because the soul is nothing in itself, how the soul can produce an image of itself in non-being becomes intelligible. Since evil is the privation of the good, it can exist only in dependence on the good—here Gregory and Plotinus agree—but for Plotinus non-being is the limit of the good so that non-being must be as eternal as being, while for Gregory non-being is the limit of evil, so that progress in evil must come to an end.

What is interesting about these relationships between Gregory and Plotinus, between Gregory the speculative thinker and Gregory the evangelical preacher—and what demands a much fuller analysis than is possible here—is the way that a philosophical analysis about the nature of being and non-being can inform a Christian understanding of sin and redemption, while that Christian understanding in turn alters the structure of the philosophical system that has given it expression. The relationship between Christianity and Hellenism, between biblical thought and Greek philosophy, is a dialectic in which each side rediscovers in the other its own most deeply held truths.

NOTES

¹ Gregory understands προαίρεσις as the faculty of freely willed, deliberative choice. He sometimes uses the word in reference to God (i.e. *De Anima* PG 46, 124B); but in general Gregory understands προαίρεσις as the faculty of choice between two opposite, especially two morally opposite, courses of action, and he therefore most frequently uses the word in reference to created freedom. The best translation would probably be "free choice," but I have frequently rendered the term simply as "prohaeresis" throughout this essay. Similarly, I have frequently used "hypostasis" as if it were an English word, rather than translating it as "substance." Gregory uses "hypostasis" in a wide variety of senses. In the context of his discussion of evil the word can be taken as referring sometimes to the definition of a thing's nature and sometimes to the actual presentation of a thing in the world as an individuated expression of the qualities that define its generic essence. In the latter sense, since its essence is absence, evil cannot present itself in its own hypostasis as a specific instance of what is not; in the former sense, evil can have no hypostasis ("definition") of its own since it can be defined only as the opposite of something else. But Gregory nowhere defines his terms very precisely. On Gregory's use of "hypostasis" more generally and on his lack of precision and consistency in his technical vocabulary see Christopher G. Stead, 'Ontology and Terminology in Gregory of Nyssa,' *Gregor von Nyssa und die Philosophie*, ed. H. Dörrie et al. (Leiden 1976), 107-127, reprinted in *Substance and Illusion in the Christian Fathers*, London 1985. A good summary of the many different senses in which Gregory uses the word can also be found in Javier Ibañez and Fernando Mendoza, 'El valor del término 'hypostasis' en il libro I contra Eunomio de Gregorio de Nisa,' *El "Contra Eunomium I" en la producción literaria de Gregorio de Nisa,* ed. L. F. Mateo-Seco (Pamplona 1988) 329-337.
² GNO VIII.1, 299,12-14. Gregory's works are cited by the Jaeger edition *Gregorii Nysseni Opera*, where available, or after the texts as published in *Patrologia Graeca* (PG), volumes 44-46. On the chronology of Gregory's works see especially Jean Daniélou, 'La chronologie des sermons de Grégoire de Nysse,' *Revue des sciences religieuses* 29 (1955) 346-71, 'La chronologie des oeuvres de Grégoire de Nysse,' *Studia Patristica* 7 (1966) 159-69, Gerhard May, 'Die Chronologie des Lebens und Werke des Gregor von Nyssa,' *Écriture et Culture Philosophique chez Grégoire de Nysse* (Leiden 1971) 51-67. The *De Virginitate* is generally acknowledged among Gregory's works, written sometime in the early or mid-370's, although the evidence for dating the work to 371 and considering it in fact the earliest is no longer regarded as compelling.
³ *De Beatitudinibus* PG 44, 1256B; *De Anima* PG 46, 101A; *In Ecclesiasten* GNO V, 407,14-15; *Oratio Catachetica* PG 45, 32C; *De Vita Moysis* GNO VII. 1, 59,24.
⁴ For a brief survey of the history of this idea in Christian thought before Gregory see W. Völker, *Gregor von Nyssa als Mystiker* (Wiesbaden 1955) 89-90; on evil as non-being

in Athanasius see E. P. Meijering, *Orthodoxy and Platonism in Athanasius* (Leiden 1968) 10-18.

⁵ *In Hexaemeron* II,4, PG 29, 37C-D; cf. the homily *Quod Deus non est auctor malorum* PG 31, 341B, where Basil says there exists no proper substance (ἰδίαν ὑπόστασιν) of evil.
⁶ GNO VIII.1, 298,21-229,6. For detailed discussion of the analogy of the eye see Jean Daniélou, 'Aveuglement,' *L'être et le Temps chez Grégoire de Nysse* (Leiden 1970), 133-153 (hereafter cited as *L'être*). Gregory tends, in this passage and elsewhere, to diminish somewhat the responsibility of the first men by blaming "him who first begot evil in the man." Our focus in the present essay is on the metaphysics of evil, and we cannot discuss the problem of the primordial fall or the relative responsiblity of the protoplasts and Satan in what is already too lengthy a paper. See, with perhaps too much emphasis on the Satanic responsiblity for evil, E. J. Philippoi, 'The Doctrine of Evil in St. Gregory of Nyssa,' *Studia Patristica* 9 (1966) 251-56.
⁷ On the theme of participation in the being of God, see David Balás, *Metousia Theou: Man's Participation in God's Perfections according to St. Gregory of Nyssa*. Studia Anselmiana 55, (Rome 1966).
⁸ Aristotle, *Categories* 12A. Cf. Jean Daniélou, 'Aveuglement,' *L'être*, 138, who suggests that Gregory is following a Stoic adaptation of the Aristotelian usage.
⁹ Macrina adds that since evil does not have a nature to exist outside of prohaeresis, it will necessarily vanish when every prohaeresis is in God, there being no receptacle left for it. This passage is discussed further below.
¹⁰ Cf. *De Mortuis* GNO IX, 57,25-26; *In Eccles.* GNO V, 297,13-298,3; *Tunc Ipse Filius* PG 44, 1316A; *In Psalm.* GNO V,113,12-13; 155,10-14; *In Sanctum et Salutare Pascha* GNO IX, 311,15.
¹¹ On this passage see Edward N. Lee, 'Plato on Negation and Not-Being in the *Sophist*,' *Philosophical Review* 81 (1972) 267-304. On the similarities between Gregory and Plotinus in this matter, see below.
¹² Cf. *Contra Arium et Sabellium*, GNO III.1, 84,9-24, "there is not where God is not, even if the archon of evil happens to be somewhere." On the authenticity of this work, which K. Holl, 'Über die Gregor von Nyssa zugeschriebene Schrift Adversus Arium et Sabellium,' *Zeitschrift für Kirchengeschichte* 25 (1904) 380-398 (*Gesammelte Aufsätze* II, Tübingen 1928, pp. 298-309), sought to attribute to Didymus the Blind, see Jean Daniélou, 'L'Aduersus Arium et Sabellium de Grégoire de Nysse et l'Origénisme Cappadocien,' *Recherches de science religieuse* 54 (1966) 61-66, who defends Gregorian authorship, and Reinhard Hübner, 'Gregor von Nyssa und Markell von Ankyra,' *Écriture et Culture Philosophique chez Grégoire de Nysse* (Leiden 1971) 199-229 (especially 211, note 1), who argues against its authenticity.
¹³ Paul Tillich, *Systematic Theology* (Chicago 1957) II,60.
¹⁴ Again, Gregory tends to blame the jealous archangel; but again the essential point remains that, as he says in the same passage (GNO VI, 56,3-10), there is but one mother and cause for existing things and it is the prohaeresis that has rent nature asunder—those who stand off from the good thereby give substance to evil, for there is no other hypostasis of evil except the withdrawal from the better.
¹⁵ See Ekkehard Mühlenburg, *Die Unendlichkeit Gottes bei Gregor von Nyssa* (Göttingen 1966) 138-141; Paul Zemp, *Die Grundlagen heilsgeschichtlichen Denkens bei Gregor von Nyssa* (Munich 1970) 38-51.

16   Cf. *In Hexaemeron* PG 44, 69A-C. On the status of corporeal existence see A. H. Armstrong, 'The Theory of the Non-Existence of Matter in Plotinus and the Cappadocians,' *Studia Patristica* 5 (Berlin 1962) 427-29, and Hans U. von Balthasar, *Présence et Pensée: Essai sur la philosophie religieuse de Grégoire de Nysse* (Paris 1942) 20-23.

17   Cf. Harry Wolfson, 'The Identification of *ex nihilo* with Emanation in Gregory of Nyssa,' *Harvard Theological Review* 63 (1970) 53-60. Wolfson's suggestion that Gregory thinks of non-being as an apophatic description of the divine seems implausible, however.

18   H. U. von Balthasar, *loc. cit.*

19   See *De Opificio* PG 44, 144B-149A, *Catechetical Oration* PG 45, 25D, *De Infantibus* GNO III.2, 78,16-79,2, and for discussion Eugenio Corsini, 'Plérôme humain et plérôme cosmique chez Grégoire de Nysse', *Écriture et Culture Philosophique chez Grégoire de Nysse* (Leiden 1971) 111-26, and R. Gillet, 'L'homme divinisateur cosmique dans la pensée de saint Grégoire de Nysse,' *Studia Patristica* 6 (1962) 62-83.

20   On the usage in Gregory, see Jérome Gaïth, *La conception de la liberté chez Grégoire de Nysse* (Paris 1953) 45-72; on the word more generally, see John M. Rist, '*Prohaeresis*: Proclus, Plotinus, et alii,' *De Jamblique à Proclus* (Geneva 1975) 103-117.

21   On the theme of the created soul as μεθόριος of good and evil (e.g. *De Anima* PG 46, 57C, *Contra Eunomium* GNO I, 106,24; II, 45,) see Jean Daniélou, 'Frontière', *L'être* 116-132.

22   Compare the Aristotelian theory (*De Anima* 429A) that the soul becomes what it thinks.

23   On the significance of Gregory's positive view of motion and change see Jean Daniélou, 'Changement,' *L'être*, 95-115, and Brooks Otis, 'Gregory of Nyssa and the Cappadocian Concept of Time,' *Studia Patristica* 14 (1976) 327-57.

24   Cf. Gaïth (op. cit. p. 78), who speaks of evil as "une régression vers le néant."

25   Paul Tillich, *loc. cit.*

26   On the problem of angelic sin as a source of "illogic" in Gregory's thought, see the comments of Brooks Otis, 'Cappadocian Thought as a Coherent System,' *Dumbarton Oaks Papers* 12 (1958) 97-124.

27   Jean Daniélou, 'Comble,' *L'être*, 186-204.

28   See, for example, *De Virg.* GNO VIII.1, 299,16-23, *De Beat.* PG 44, 1201A, *In Psalm.* GNO V, 63,13-15; for discussion, Jean Daniélou, 'Enchaînement,' *L'être* 18-51.

29   Gregory frequently uses the analogy of the physician when speaking of the intervention of Christ at the akme of evil; cf. *Contra Apollin.* GNO III.1, 171,21-24, 221,21-23; *De Die Natali* PG 46, 1132A.

30   Jean Daniélou, 'Comble,' *L'être* 186-204; Endre von Ivánka, *Hellenisches und Christliches im frühbyzantinischen Geistesleben* (Vienna 1948) 52-55; Paul Zemp, *Die Grundlagen heilsgeschichtlichen Denkens bei Gregor von Nyssa* (Munich 1970) 186-87; Mariette Canévet, 'Nature du Mal et Économie du Salut chez Grégoire de Nysse,' *Recherches de science religieuse* 56 (1968) 87-95.

31   Cf. M. Canévet, *art. cit.*, 93-95.

32   *De Beat.* PG 44, 1273A.

33   *De Mortuis* GNO IX, 59,23-60,2; *Or.Cat.* PG 45, 33C; cf. *In Pulcheriam* GNO IX, 472, 1-15. See Jean Daniélou, 'Mortalité,' *L'être*, 154-85.

34   Gregory uses the analogy of the snake whose head has been cut off, yet whose coils still move and threaten, to try to explain how it is that evil can be both dead and alive (*Or.Cat.* PG 45, 76C). See Jean Daniélou, 'Comble,' *L'être* 186-204.

[35]   See, for example, *Contra Apollin.* GNO III.1, 177,3-5, 227,1-6.

[36]   Jean Daniélou, 'Aveuglement,' *L'être* 133-53. See also Harold Cherniss, *The Platonism of Gregory of Nyssa* (Berkeley 1930; reprint New York 1971) 49-54.

[37]   On Plotinus's various theories about matter and evil see John M. Rist, 'Plotinus on Matter and Evil,' *Phronesis* 6 (1961) 154-66, and *Plotinus: The Road to Reality* (Cambridge 1967) 112-29, to which the present discussion is much indebted.

[38]   See especially Ekkehard Mühlenberg, *Die Unendlichkeit Gottes bei Gregor von Nyssa* (Göttingen 1966).

University of California, *San Diego*, La Jolla, CA 92093

Augustinian Studies 23 (1992) 7–32
Roland Teske, S.J.

The 1992 Saint Augustine Lecture

Saint Augustine as Philosopher: The Birth of Christian Metaphysics

A distinguished Augustine scholar, Goulven Madec, has said, "The history of patristic philosophy has only a precarious status. It lacks a principal object; for there is no 'patristic philosophy' . . . ." He immediately adds, "and the Fathers of the Church are not 'philosophers' in the commonly accepted sense."[1] Certainly, he is correct in maintaining that the Fathers of the Church are not philosophers in the sense commonly accepted today. However, it is not nearly so clear that the Fathers of the Church were in no sense philosophers or that there is no philosophy to be found in the Fathers of the Church. Regardless of the claim about the Fathers of the Church in general, I shall argue that Augustine of Hippo was a philosopher in some sense and that there is an Augustinian philosophy, even in the sense of philosophy commonly accepted today. I shall first examine what Augustine understood by philosophy; then I shall ask whether there is in Augustine a philosophy in the contemporary sense. Finally, I shall suggest what I consider the principal features of Augustine's legacy to Western philosophy.

I. *What Augustine Meant by Philosophy*

Augustine provides a nominal definition of philosophy as "the love of wisdom" or "the pursuit of wisdom."[2] While a philosopher of the late twentieth century certainly recognizes and can probably accept such a definition, if one listens further to what Augustine says about philosophy, one finds the *philosophia* of which he speaks to be something both familiar and also something quite unfamiliar, something much the same and something quite different from what is today meant by philosophy. I will suggest one reason why at least some today find themselves at home with what Augustine meant by philosophy; then I want to point out two ways in which what Augustine meant by philosophy differs from what most of us take philosophy to be.

I suggest that we find the *philosophia* of which Augustine speaks something familiar, because he saw philosophy as a continuation of classical Greek philosophy, as something rooted in and carrying on the very best of Greek philosophy. Augustine began to burn with the love of wisdom from the time of his reading Cicero's *Hortensius* which contained an exhortation to this love of wisdom.[3] He tells us that he began to desire "the immortality of wisdom with an incredible ardor of heart" and "began to rise up to return to" his God.[4] This conversion to philosophy, begun with the reading of the *Hortensius*, reached a high point in the momentous encounter with the *libri platonicorum* in 386 when the fire kindled by the *Hortensius* flamed out incredibly.[5] But what was this *philosophia* that so aroused Augustine's love? In the closing sections of *Contra academicos*, he presents a brief history of philosophy, beginning with Socrates and Plato, through the later Academy and Plotinus, and continuing down to his own time. Plato, he tells us, added to the moral teaching of Socrates a knowledge of natural and divine reality, derived from Pythagoras and other wise men, and crowned it with dialectic, which is either itself wisdom or its indispensable condition. Hence, Augustine adds that "Plato is said to have put together the complete discipline of philosophy."[6] Augustine singles out the features of the Platonic system that are for his purposes most significant:

> that there are two worlds: one the intelligible world in which Truth dwells, and this sensible world, which, it is clear, we perceive by sight and touch. The former is the true world; this one is similar to it and made in its image. From the intelligible world the Truth, so to speak, shines forth and becomes, as it were, clear in the soul that knows itself. But of this world, not

knowledge, but only opinion can be generated in the minds of the foolish. . . .[7]

Later in his history of philosophy, Augustine points out that "the doctrine of Plato, which is purest and brightest, has banished the clouds of error and has shone forth, especially in Plotinus." Plotinus was so kindred a soul to Plato that he seemed to be Plato come back to life.[8] By his own time Augustine claims that there has

been filtered out one teaching that is the true philosophy. It is not the philosophy of this world, which our sacred mysteries rightly detest, but of the other intelligible world. . . .[9]

Furthermore, in *De ordine* Augustine makes it quite clear that Christ himself taught what was for Augustine the core of Platonic philosophy, namely, that there was another intelligible world besides this world known to the senses. He says, "Christ himself does not say, 'My kingdom is not of the world,' but 'My kingdom is not of this world,'" thus indicating that "there is another world far removed from these eyes."[10]

Through his brief history of philosophy Augustine clearly indicated that what he calls the true philosophy, the philosophy of the intelligible world, is in continuity with the best in Greek thought, namely, that of Plato and Plotinus. Later in *The City of God*, Augustine's appraisal of the achievements of the Platonic philosophers is no less laudatory. They recognized, he tells us, that "the true God is the author of reality, the source of the light of truth and the bestower of beatitude."[11] The Platonists "saw that God was not a body, and, therefore, transcended all bodies in their search for God." They "saw that nothing subject to change is the highest God and, therefore, transcended every soul and all spirits subject to change in their search for the highest God."[12] Plato taught that the wise man imitates, knows and loves this God and becomes blessed by participating in him.[13] There is no need to look at the position of any other philosophers; none of them have come closer to us than the Platonists.[14] Most of us, I suspect, can agree with Augustine that Plato and Aristotle and Plotinus were philosophers and that we too mean by philosophy the sort of thing that Plato, Aristotle and Plotinus did.[15]

But what we mean by philosophy also differs from what Augustine meant in at least two very important ways. First, philosophy for Augustine meant a whole way of life. When Augustine said that "a human being has no other reason for philosophizing except to be happy,"[16] he meant by *philosophari*, not the pursuit of a particular academic discipline, but a whole way of life dedicated to the pursuit of wisdom. With an exaggeration perhaps needed to prevent us from assuming that we know what the ancients meant by *"philosophia,"* one scholar has said that "philosophy means something entirely different in Graeco-Roman antiquity from what it does today."[17] Following what Pierre Hadot has written, A. H. Armstrong has put it this way with greater balance:

> for most ancient philosophers, philosophy was a comprehensive and extremely demanding way of life, requiring, certainly, the intense study of the whole of reality, but designed to lead, not simply to what we should call an "intellectual" or "scientific" understanding of the nature of things, but to the attainment of that human goodness, including or consisting in wisdom, but a transforming wisdom, which can alone bring about human well-being.[18]

With such a view of philosophy in mind, Augustine reminds Romanianus of his frequent insistence that he "regarded no fortune as favorable save that which bestowed the leisure to philosophize (*otium philosophandi*), no life as happy save that which is lived in philosophy."[19]

A life lived in philosophy required *otium* which we correctly, but very inadequately, translate as "leisure." André Mandouze says that, besides leisure and the material resources needed to assure it, *otium* requires "above all the interior availability (*disponibilité*) without which there is neither tranquillity of soul nor peace of mind, two things indispensible for withdrawal into oneself and the recollection of God."[20] It was for the sake of such *otium* that Alypius kept steering Augustine away from marriage, warning that "we could by no means live together a life of secure leisure in the love of wisdom, as we had long desired," if Augustine took a wife.[21] Years later, in looking back on the time at Cassiciacum, Augustine described it as: *Christianae vitae otium*: the Christian life of leisure.[22] And soon after his return to Africa, in writing to Nebridius, Augustine used the marvelous phrase: *"deificari in otio*: to become God-like in leisure"[23] to describe his aim in withdrawing from the troubled journeys of this world in order to "think of that one last journey which is called death."[24] Georges Folliet claims,

> Augustine speaks as a Christian convert, but the description of the asceticism he envisages and the expressions he uses make one suspect that his present ideal for life is much closer to that of the wise man presented by the Neoplatonic philosophers than to that of the Gospel.[25]

Folliet has perhaps overemphasized the Neoplatonic influence upon Augustine's ideal for the life he and his companions were beginning to lead at Thagaste, a life which others see as the cradle of Western monasticism.[26]

Later in his life Augustine said that "the true philosopher is a lover of God,"[27] for the true philosopher loves that Wisdom which or, rather, who is God. We must remember that for Augustine what one loves necessarily transforms the lover into itself.[28] Thus in loving God, one is transformed into or becomes God.[29] Hence, Augustine's goal at Thagaste of "becoming God-like" is simply the goal of the life of philosophy. The life of philosophy is, after all, a life in love with wisdom, "but of a transforming wisdom" — to use Armstrong's words — of that Wisdom that transforms one into God, into children of the Most High.

Certainly, the *otium* of Thagaste is Christian and monastic, but it is also, I believe, clearly in continuity with the dedication to the life of philosophy envisioned at Cassiciacum. In any case, to dedicate oneself to philosophy, in order to become God-like in leisure, was far more like entering monastic life than selecting a major in college or even a program of graduate studies. This is the first respect in which the *philosophia* of Augustine is quite different from the contemporary meaning of philosophy.

The second way in which what Augustine called philosophy differs from what most moderns understand by philosophy has to do with the task and the content of philosophy. In one passage Augustine tells us that philosophy has a twofold question:

> one about the soul, the other about God. The first makes us know ourselves; the other that we know our origin. The former is sweeter to us; the latter more precious. The former makes us worthy of happiness; the latter makes us happy.[30]

That is, as aiming at the happy life, philosophy has no concern with this world of bodily things, but only with God as our goal and ourselves as returning to him.[31] Philosophy is not the path for everyone, but for the very few. Philosophy promises reason to these few, setting them free and teaching them, "not only not to hold those [i.e., the Christian] mysteries in contempt, but to understand them, and them alone, as they should be understood."[32] Thus the content which philosophy brings the very few to understand is identical with the mysteries of the Christian faith. The true and genuine philosophy has, Augustine claims, no other task than to teach what is the principle without principle of all things and how great an intellect remains in it and what has flowed forth from there for our salvation without any lessening of its being. . . .[33]

Augustine explicitly identifies these three with the Father, Son and Holy Spirit, which "the venerable mysteries . . . proclaim, neither confusing them, as some do, nor treating them unjustly, as many do."[34]

Thus, the whole task of philosophy is to understand the Christian Trinity as the source of being, of truth, and of salvation. It does not take too much stretching to see in this early text the *"rerum auctorem, ueritatis inlustratorem et beatitudinis largitorem"* of *The City of God.* Thus the whole content of philosophy for Augustine is the triune God of Christianity.

Philosophy is the love of wisdom, and as early as the *Contra academicos* Augustine appeals to Cicero's definition of wisdom as "the knowledge of things human and divine."[35] In the *De trinitate*, following St. Paul in 1 Corinthians 12:8, Augustine distinguishes wisdom and knowledge so that wisdom (*sapientia*) is the knowledge of things eternal and knowledge (*scientia*) is knowledge of things temporal. *Scientia* is not knowledge of just anything temporal, but only of that "by which the saving faith, which leads to true happiness, is born, nourished, defended and strengthened."[36] Madec has noted that this distinction between *sapientia* and *scientia* "is not without analogy with the double function that Cicero assigns to philosophy in the *Hortensius*: the practice of the virtues and contemplative wisdom."[37] Thus, in *Contra academicos* I,vii,20, the knowledge of things human is "that by which one knows the light of prudence, the beauty of temperance, the strength of courage, and the holiness of justice."[38]

It is, I suggest, Augustinian wisdom in the proper sense, which is the content of philosophy, that is, knowledge of the eternal God: Father, Son and Holy Spirit, while knowledge in the proper sense embraces the means of the soul's return to God, the temporal dispensation by which God has offered us salvation.[39] Or, as Augustine has often expressed it, the great Neoplatonists have seen from afar the Fatherland to which we must return.[40] They have come to know the eternal reality of God, but in their pride they have failed to know the way to attain the Fatherland.[41] That way is the humanity of Christ, who as God is also the goal. As human, he is our knowledge, as divine he is our wisdom. What philosophy can attain, and what the great Platonists have attained is the knowledge of God's eternal reality; what philosophy cannot attain is the knowledge of the temporal dispensation and the humanity the Word has assumed, which is also the way, indeed the only way of return.[42] Thus from his earliest writings Augustine saw the need for the Incarnation of the Word if souls, "blinded by the abundant darkness of error and stained with the deepest filth of the body," were to be "able to return to themselves and see again their fatherland."[43]

We have seen that *philosophia* for Augustine was a wisdom in continuity with the best in classical Greek thought, but that it differed from what it means for us in the twentieth century insofar as it involved a whole way of life aimed at true happiness and embraced as its content only the Christian mysteries. On the other hand, Augustine is quite clear that, if philosophy can know the eternal God as the source of our being, knowledge and beatitude, philosophy cannot provide the way of attaining God. For that we need faith in Christ, our knowledge, who is also our wisdom.

II. Can There Be An Augustinian Philosophy?

The most serious objections to the claim that there is such philosophy in Augustine stem from Augustine's clear claim that one must first believe in order to understand.[44] Etienne Gilson has made the strong claim that "we know of no single instance where Augustine allowed reason to dispense with faith as its starting point . . . . This is the reason why belief in God precedes even proof of His existence. . . ."[45]

Augustine's insistence that one must first believe in order to understand would seem to prejudice the case against anything like an autonomous philosophy within his thought. "Faith seeking understanding" is, after all, the classical description of the movement of theology rather than of philosophy.

Moreover, the case for an independent philosophy, is aggravated by an important change in Augustine's thought. Scholars frequently speak of Augustine's conversions in the plural.[46] Besides the momentous events of 386-387 that led to his baptism and becoming a servant of God, there is Augustine's conversion to Manichaeism in 373. But there is another turning point in Augustine's life which has been described as his final conversion.[47]

In 396, while writing to Simplician, Augustine came to realize that faith is a gift of God. Much later, in writing to the monks of Hadrumentum, Augustine admits that he had "other thoughts on this question. . . ." and that God

211

"revealed to me the means of solving the problem, when . . . I was writing to bishop Simplician."[48]

Prior to the time of *De diversis quaestionibus ad Simplicianum,* he thought "that the faith by which we believe in God is not a gift of God, but something that we have from ourselves. . . ."[49] At that time he thought that we needed grace in the sense that we needed to have the Gospel preached to us, but "I thought that it was entirely up to us that we should consent to the Gospel preached to us, and that we had it from ourselves."[50] Hence, from 396 on Augustine regarded the assent of faith to the Gospel as a gift of God, while prior to that time he thought of the assent as merely a reasonable act of human practical reason. Prior to 396 Augustine had distinguished human authority and divine authority as grounds for belief, and he had distinguished divine and human objects of belief.[51] But he had not distinguished the assent of belief that is a gift of God from the assent which is merely a reasonable human act.

What then is the relevance of this final conversion to my topic? Prior to 396 believing was, in Augustine's eyes, a matter of reasonable human assent, whether one relied upon divine or human authority, whether what one believed was what God spoke or what another human spoke. Hence, believing in order to understand was a method open to every reasonable human being and, for that reason, a philosophical method. Masai describes Augustine's pre-396 position as a philosophical fideism in the sense that one must begin with faith, albeit a philosophical faith.[52] Masai sees in the revelation of 396 the birth of theology and refers to Augustine's position after 396 as a theological fideism, because one begins with faith, but a faith that is a gift of God and not, therefore, something entirely up to us or that we have from ourselves as human beings. Masai concludes,

> Beginning in 396, Augustine acknowledged in the act of faith as well as in its object a divine origin and nature. But *ipso facto* the philosophical character of Augustinian thought is found to be compromised. As it rests entirely upon the foundation of a light freely given by God, it cannot keep the pretense of addressing human reason as such; it becomes necessarily a knowledge reserved for the faithful alone. In brief, the philosophy of Augustine has from that time been transformed into theology.[53]

Obviously the question of whether there can be an Augustinian philosophy becomes more difficult once the act of believing is seen to be a free gift of God and not something up to us so that we can believe if we want to do so. It is not merely that prior to 396 Augustine did not consider the question of our beginning to believe as a grace; rather, he tells us that he had regarded beginning to believe as something within our power.

In a footnote Masai wonders whether it is conceivable to restore within the strictly Augustinian perspective a Christian philosophy along side theology.[54] He dodges an answer, while noting that an answer to this question depends upon the solution of other problems raised by divine illumination and, more generally, the relation between nature and grace.

On the other hand, the existence of philosophy in Augustine has also had its defenders. In the second Bibliothèque Augustinienne edition of *De magistro* and *De libero arbitrio*, F. J. Thonnard, while admiting that Augustine did not formally create a philosophical system, holds that it is possible to make explicit Augustine's philosophy. He points to three conditions of an Augustinian philosophy that were articulated by Fulbert Cayré:

1) if the philosophical questions that Saint Augustine has dealt with were studied by him in a rational manner and not merely from the perspective of faith; 2) if these questions include all the major problems posed by every philosophy worthy of the name; 3) if the solutions that he brings to them are tied together by common principles capable of giving to the whole a solid coherence. If these are fulfilled, there is in Saint Augustine a true philosophy that can be separated from his theology, even if he himself has not separated them.[55]

I agree with F. Cayré that the three conditions for the existence of philosophy are sufficient and sufficiently met in the works of Augustine for one to speak of an Augustinian philosophy. But I think one can go further and say that there has to be within Augustine's strictly theological thought an autonomous philosophy that is an indispensable condition of the possibility of his theology. Masai is surely correct that a proper solution to the question of whether there can be an Augustinian philosophy depends upon the wider questions of nature and grace, or of reason and faith.

There was a time in the not so distant past when in Catholic circles philosophy and theology were sharply distinguished, so much so that philosophical ethics, for example, was said to be the sort of moral guidance that would have been applicable, if we were living in a state of pure nature, that hypothetical state which has never existed, but would have existed if human beings were not destined for a supernatural end. Theologians, such as Karl Rahner and Henri de Lubac, have done much to correct the view that revelation and grace are purely extrinsic additions to nature.[56] Rahner has argued that the possibility of revelation requires that man, as the hearer of the word of God, have a natural self-understanding independent of special revelation in order to be able to hear and understand God's word. He claims that theology "necessarily implies philosophy, i.e., a previous . . . self-comprehension of the man who hears the historical revelation of God."[57] Furthermore, he maintains that "that self-clarification of man's existence which we call philosophy can certainly be 'pure' philosophy in the sense that it does not take any of its material contents and norms from . . . revelation. . . ."[58]

But even apart from such a transcendental deduction of the necessity of a philosophy for understanding the revealed word of God, one can, I believe, argue that in Augustine there are philosophical truths that human reason can know independently of accepting in faith God's revelation of those truths. These truths would be analogous to what Thomas Aquinas called the *praeambula fidei*. Let me briefly sketch my reasons for this claim. First, even after 396 when God revealed to Augustine that the act of believing is a gift of God and not something within human power, it does not seem to be the case that every act of believing is a gift of God. Indeed Augustine implies that faith need precede reason only "in certain things pertaining to the doctrine of salvation which we cannot yet perceive by reason."[59] Second, Augustine groups the objects of belief (*credibilia*) into three classes. He speaks of things which must always be believed and can never be understood, of things that are understood as soon as they are believed, and of things which are first believed and later understood,. The first class of objects of beliefs includes all historical events of which we were not ourselves witnesses. The second class includes "all human reasonings either in mathematics or in any of the disciplines." The third class of objects of belief includes truths about "the divine realities that can only be understood by the pure of heart.[60] Augustine thought that one understood, for example, a theorem in geometry as soon as one accepted it as true. Certainly, the second class of *credibilia* are supernatural in terms neither of the object believed nor of the authority one believes nor of the act of believing as a special gift of God.[61] Third, Augustine credited the great Greek philosophers with having come to a knowledge of God and of human destiny. Though he entertained the idea that Plato had come into contact with God's revelation to the Jewish people, he clearly stated that they came to a knowledge of the eternal reality of God from the things God had made.[62]

Hence, I believe that one can maintain that there is in Augustine—and indeed there must be in Augustine—a philosophy, and a philosophy that can be recognized as philosophy even in the sense in which we speak of philosophy today. One could, of course, so define philosophy that Augustine's thought is automatically excluded. But any such definition could, I fear, banish from the realm of philosophy the works of Hegel and Aquinas, Kierkegaard and even Descartes as well.

III. Augustine's Legacy to Western Philosophy

Any attempt to sum up the core of Augustine's legacy to Western philosophy is bound to be incomplete and perspectival. I intend to touch upon three topics, one an attitude, the other two matters of doctrine.

The attitude that I want to single out is a deep appreciation for human intelligence. Prior to Augustine, at least in the African Church, the spirit of Tertullian was still regnant—Tertullian who asked what Athens has to do with Jerusalem, what the Academy has to do with the Church, Tertullian who claimed that we have no need for a curiosity going beyond Christ Jesus or for inquiry going beyond the Gospel.[63] When Augustine warns of bishops and priests who "avoid unveiling the mysteries or, content with simple faith, have no care to know more profound truths," he indicates the anti-intellectual atmosphere within the *Catholica* that helped push him into the Manichaean fold.[64] From his own conversion to Manichaeism Augustine learned how dangerous it could be to meet the human desire to know with ridicule instead of respect.[65] In his *Literal Commentary on Genesis* he again and again indicates his respect for the inquiring mind by refusing rashly to claim knowledge or to give up on its pursuit.[66]

Let me offer two examples of Augustine's respect for the human intellect's desire to know. First, years after Augustine's ordination to the episcopacy, Consentius wrote to Augustine that he thought "that the truth about God's reality ought to be grasped by faith rather than by reason."[67] Otherwise, Consentius suggests, only the likes of philosophers would attain beatitude, and he argues that "we should not so much require a rational account of God as follow the authority of the saints."[68] In response Augustine warns with regard to the Trinity against following the authority of the saints alone without making any effort to understand. "Correct your position," he says, "not so that you reject faith, but so that what you already hold by solid faith, you may also see by the light of reason."[69] Augustine adds, "Heaven forbid that God should hate in us that by which he made us more excellent than the animals. Heaven forbid, I say, that we believe so that we do not accept or seek a rational account, since we could not believe unless we had rational souls."[70] He cites St. Peter's warning that we should be ready to give an account of our faith and urges Consentius to "a love of intelligence" (*ad amorem intelligentiae*). His words, "*Intellectum uero ualde ama*: Have a great love for the intellect," echo down the centuries as a charter for Christian dedication to intellectual pursuits, first of all, in theology, but also in what we today identify as philosophy and the sciences.[71]

Second, no one would claim that Augustine was a philosopher of science, but his care to interpret Scripture in such a way as to avoid a contradiction with what has been scientifically proven has been admired by a scientist as great as Galileo. In *The Literal Interpretation of Genesis*, while dealing with the shape of the heavens, Augustine manages to ask a question that cannot on the surface fail to strike us, who live in the age of space exploration, as naive. "What does it matter to me," he asks, "whether the heaven encloses the earth like a sphere . . . or only covers it from above like a lid?"[72] Yet he worries that someone might find in the Scripture what seems opposed to clearly seen rational arguments and, as a result, give up all belief in the Scriptures. He warns that "the Holy Spirit who spoke through the [authors of Scripture] did not intend to teach human beings matters of no use for their salvation."[73] He faces the Psalm text that God "has stretched out the heaven like a skin" (Ps. 103:2), which seems contrary to the view that the heaven is spherical. Augustine even envisages the case in which some are able to prove with indubitable arguments that the heaven is spherical and says,

> Then we must prove that what our books say about the skin is not contrary to those rational truths; otherwise, there will be another contradiction between this text and the other passage of Scripture in which it says that the heaven was hung as a vault (Is 40:22).[74]

In writing to Christine of Lorraine, Galileo cites the text from Augustine and adds,

> From this text we see that we need no less care to show how a passage of Scripture is in agreement with a proposition demonstrated by natural reason than to show how one passage of Scripture agrees with another contrary to it. . . . one must admire the circumspection of this saint who manifests such

216

great reserve in dealing with obscure conclusions or those of which one can have a demonstration by human means.[75]

Let me, then, turn to two points of philosophical doctrine. In writing to Caelestinus in 390 or 391, Augustine offers a brief, but important summary of his world view.

Accept this priceless, but tiny gem (*quiddam grande, sed breve*): There is a nature changeable in places and times, such as the body, and there is a nature not changeable in place at all, but changeable only in time, such as the soul, and there is a nature which cannot change either in place or in time. This is God.[76]

Robert O'Connell has pointed to this three-tiered view of reality with the utterly immutable God at the top and souls mutable only in time in the middle and bodies mutable in both time and place at the bottom as the controlling idea in Vernon Bourke's presentation of Augustine's view of reality.[77]

Contained in that "*quiddam grande et breve*" that Augustine offered to Caelestinus are two doctrines that lie, I suggest, at the heart of Augustine's philosophical legacy to the Western world: his concept of non-bodily realities, such as the soul and God, and his concept of non-temporal reality, such as, the utterly unchanging reality of God. As a nature that is immutable in place must be free from any spatial extension, so a nature that is immutable in time must be free from any temporal distension.

Prior to Augustine, at least in Western Christianity, there was no philosophical concept of incorporeal being, of being that is whole wherever it is (*totus ubique*). Once again the philosophical views of Tertullian and the corporealism of the Stoics were the common philosophical patrimony of the West.[78] In the West prior to Augustine, the term "spirit" was, of course, used in the Bible, in medicine and in philosophy. But when the meaning of spirit was spelled out, it seems to have meant a subtle kind of body, not something non-bodily. So too, we use "spirits" to refer to a beverage, and pneumatic tires are certainly bodily.[79] In holding that God and the soul were bodily, the Manichees were not being singular, but rather were in full accord with the common philosophical view of the age.[80] Even the Arians whom Augustine encountered seem to have thought of God as corporeal.[81] From Consentius' letter to Augustine already mentioned, we can see that even this budding theologian could not quite see how God was bodiless.[82] We also know that Augustine encountered in the young layman, Vincentius Victor, a convert from Donatism, a thinker who explicitly held that the soul was corporeal.[83] Even after Augustine's time the doctrine of the incorporeal nature of the soul was not universally accepted. Thomas Smith points to Faustus of Riez and Cassian as examples in fifth century Gaul of thinkers who held the corporealist position on the nature of the soul.[84] Augustine's spiritualist understanding of God and the soul, however, became the dominant view in the West for centuries to come. Indeed, the Augustinian revolution was so effective that many anachronistically suppose that the concept of spiritual reality is biblical and explicitly contained in the Christian revelation.[85]

The second philosophical doctrine that Augustine bequeathed to the West is the concept of eternity as timelessness, as a mode of existence that is whole all at once (tota simul), without past and without future.[86] Once again, as in the case of spirit, there is in the Bible the language of eternity in the sense of a duration that is everlasting, a duration without beginning or, at least, without end. So too, there was in earlier Greek philosophy the concept of a world without beginning or end.[87] Only with Plotinus do we find a philosophically articulated concept of eternity as timeless duration.[88] But prior to Augustine, at least in the West, there does not seem to have been a philosophically articulated concept of eternity as timeless presence in any Christian author.[89] Even if Gregory of Nyssa did anticipate Augustine in adopting the Plotinian concept of eternity into Christian thought, Augustine certainly remains the source of the concept for the Christian West.

Just as Augustine needed the philosophical concept of incorporeal reality if he was going to be able to deal with the Manichaean questions about the ontological status of evil, so he needed the concept of timeless eternity to handle their questions about what God was doing before he created the world.[90] Unless one has a concept of God as a reality not extended in length, breadth and depth, one cannot maintain that God is infinite and that evil is not in God, unless, of course, one takes the radical option of denying the reality of evil. So too, unless one can think of God's eternity as a duration not extended beyond the present into past and future, one is faced the prospect of an idle or sleeping God who wakes up and in a burst of energy creates the world.

Peter Brown speaks of Augustine's discovery of spiritual reality in reading the libri Platonicorum as "the evolution of a metaphysician."[91]Brown adds, "[A]nd his final 'conversion' to the idea of a purely spiritual reality, as held by the sophisticated Christians in Milan, is a decisive and fateful step in the evolution of our ideas on spirit and matter."[92] It was certainly that, but I suggest that it was also the birth of Christian metaphysics in the West, if one may use such an Aristotelian term for so Platonic an offspring. It was the philosophical doctrine of Augustine on the spirituality of God and the soul and on the eternity of God that pervaded Western Christian thought for centuries to come. Both of these doctrines were found in Neoplatonism prior to being taught by any Christian thinker, and the Christian faith was proclaimed and taught for the better part of four centuries before there emerged clear concepts of God and the soul as non-bodily and of God as timeless. Hence, these doctrines cannot have been derived from the Christian revelation; they must rather be philosophical doctrines independent of revelation, however useful they may have come to appear as means for articulating the word of God. Just as the desire to know, or the love for intelligence, is part of the nature of human beings, so the doctrine of the incorporeal nature of the human soul and of God and the doctrine of the eternity of God are matters of philosophical, not revealed knowledge.

IV. Conclusion

I have tried to show what Augustine meant by philosophy and have argued that there is in Augustine philosophy even in the contemporary sense. Finally, I have tried to show that Augustine's philosophical legacy to the West has been very rich, though there is, of course, much, much more in Augustine than philosophy and he is much more than a philosopher.

Notes

1. G. Madec, "La christianisation de l'hellenisme. Thème de l' histoire de la philosophie patristique," *Humanisme et foi chrétienne. Mélanges scientifiques du centenaire de l'institut catholique de Paris* (Paris: Beauchesne, 1976), pp. 399-406, here p. 399 (my translation).

2. Cf. *Contra academicos* II, iii, 7: *CC* XXIX, 21; *De ordine* I, xi, 32: *CC* XXIX, 105; *Epistula* CXLIX, 30: *CSEL* XLIV, 376.

3. *Confessiones* III, iv, 7: *CC* XXVII, 29-30. The *Hortensius* survives only in fragments, many of which are contained in the writings of Augustine. The fragments have been edited by Michel Ruch, *L'Hortensius de Cicéron: Histoire et reconstitution* (Paris: Belles Lettres, 1958). Cf. G. Madec, "L'*Hortensius* de Cicéron dans les livres XIII-XIV du *De Trinitate*," *Revue des Etudes augustiniennes* 15 (1969) 167-171, where Madec

argues that Augustine may have derived his definition of wisdom as "rerum humanarum divinarumque scientia" (*De trinitate* XIV, i, 3: *CC* L/A, 423) from the *Hortensius*, though it is clearly found in other works by Cicero.

4. *Confessiones* III, iv, 7: *CC* XXVII, 30: "immortalitatem sapientiae concupiscebam aestu cordis incredibili et surgere coeperam, ut ad te redirem." Cf. also, R. J. O'Connell, "On Augustine's 'First Conversion' Factus Erectior (*De beata vita 4*)," *Augustinian Studies* 17 (1986) 15-29.

5. *Contra academicos* II, ii, 5: *CC* XXIX, 20-21. In "Verus Philosophus Est Amator Dei: S. Ambroise, s. Augustin et la philosophie," *Revue des sciences philosophiques et théologiques* 61 (1977) 549-566, G. Madec has said, "*L'Hortensius* a lancé Augustin dans la quête de la sagesse; il a ouvert son esprit un espace de liberté."

6. *Contra academicos* III, xvii, 37: *CC* XXIX, 57: "Igitur Plato adiciens lepori subtilitatique Socraticae, quam in moralibus habüit, naturalium diuinarumque rerum peritiam, quam ab eis quos memoraui diligenter acceperat, subiungensque quasi formatricem illarum partium iudicemque dialecticam, quae aut ipsa esset aut sine qua omnino sapientia esse non posset, perfectam dicitur composuisse philosophiae disciplinam." Cf. also *De civitate dei* VIII, 4: *CC* XLVII, 220, where he again sketches in outline the history of philosophy and gives the same central position to Plato. While Pythagoras excelled in the contemplative part of philosophy, Socrates excelled in the active part. "Proinde Plato utrumque iungendo philosophiam perfecisse laudatur, quam in tres partes distribuit: unam moralem, quae maxime in actione versatur, alteram naturalem, quae contemplationi deputata est; tertiam rationalem, qua uerum discernatur a falso."

7. *Contra academicos* III, xvii, 37: *CC* XXIX, 57: "Sat est enim ad id, quod volo, Platonem sensisse duos esse mundos, unum intelligibilem, in quo ipsa ueritas habitaret, istum autem sensibilem, quem manifestum est nos uisu tactuque sentire; itaque illum uerum, hunc ueri similem et ad illius imaginem factum, et ideo de illo in ea quae se cognosceret anima uelut expoliri et quasi serenari ueritatem, de hoc autem in stultorum animis non scientiam sed opinionem posse generari. . . ."

8. *Contra academicos* III, xviii, 41: *CC* XXIX, 59-60: "Adeo post illa tempora non longo interuallo, omni peruicacia pertinaciaque demortua os illud Platonis, quod in philosophia purgatissimum est et lucidissimum, dimotis nubibus erroris emicuit maxime in Plotino, qui Platonicus philosophus ita eius similis iudicatus est, ut simul eos uixisse, tantum autem interest temporis, ut in hoc ille reuixisse putandus sit."

9. *Contra academicos* III, xix, 42: *CC* XXIX, 60: "sed tamen eliquata est, ut opinor, una uerissimae philosophiae disciplina. Non enim est ista huius mundi philosophia, quam sacra nostra meritissime detestantur, sed alterius intellegibilis. . . ."

10. *De ordine* I, xi, 32: *CC* XXIX, 106: "Esse autem alium mundum ab istis oculis remotissimum, quem paucorum sanorum intellectus intuetur, satis ipse Christus significat, qui non dicit: 'regnum meum non est de mundo', sed: 'regnum meum non est de hoc mundo.' Later in his *Retractationes* I, iii, 2: *BA* 12, 286, Augustine expresses his displeasure at this interpretation of Christ's words and sees that it would have been better to understand him as referring to the new heaven and new earth. However, he adds: "Nec Plato quidem in hoc erravit, quia esse mundum intelligibilem dixit, si non vocabulum, quod ecclesiasticae consuetudini in re illa inusitatum est, sed ipsam rem velimus attendere. Mundum quippe ille intelligibilem nuncupavit ipsam rationem sempiternam atque incommutabilem, qua fecit Deus mundum."

11. *De civitate dei* VIII, 5: *CC* XLVII, 221: "uerum Deum et rerum auctorem et ueritatis inlustratorem et beatitudinis largitorem esse dixerunt."

12. *De civitate dei* VIII, 6: *CC* XLVII, 222-223: "Viderunt ergo isti philosophi, quos ceteris non inmerito fama atque gloria praelatos uidemus, nullum corpus esse Deum, et ideo cuncta corpora transcenderunt quaerentes Deum. Viderunt, quidquid mutabile est, non esse summum Deum, et ideo animam omnem mutabilesque omnes spiritus transcenderunt quaerentes summum Deum."

13. *De civitate dei* VIII, 5: *CC* XLVII, 221: "Si ergo Plato Dei huius imitatorem cognitorem amatorem dixit esse sapientem, cuius participatione sit beatus, quid opus est excutere ceteros?"

14. *De civitate dei* VIII, 5: *CC* XLVII, 221: "Nulli nobis quam isti propius accesserunt."

15. Augustine knew that some had claimed that Plato and Aristotle held that same doctrine; cf. *Contra academicos* III, xix, 42: *CC* XXIX, 60: "non defuerunt acutissimi et solertissimi uiri, qui docuerunt disputationibus suis Aristotelem ac Platonem ita sibi concinere, ut imperitis minusque attentis dissentire uideantur. . . ." He is perhaps alluding to the lost work of Porphyry that bore such a title. Cf. "Porphyrios," by R. Beutler, in *Real-encyclopädie der classischen Altertumswissenschaft vol. 22, pt. 1 (Stuttgart: Metzler, 1953), cc. 284-285.*

16. *De ciuitate dei* XIX, i, 2: *CC* XLVIII, 659: "nulla est homini causa philosophandi, nisi ut sit beatus."

17. I. Hadot, "The Spiritual Guide," in *Classical Mediterrean Spirituality*. Volume 15 of *World Spirituality: An Encyclopedic History of the Religious Quest* (New York: Crossroad, 1986), pp. 436-59, here 444.

18. A. H. Armstrong, *Expectations of Immortality in Late Antiquity*. The Aquinas Lecture, 1987 (Milwaukee: Marquette University Press, 1987), p. 21. Armstrong refers to P. Hadot's *Exercises spirituels et philosophie antique* (Paris: *Etudes Augustiniennes*, 1981).

19. *Contra academicos* II, ii, 4: *CC* XXIX, 20: "nullam mihi videri prosperam fortunam, nisi quae otium philosophandi daret, nullam beatam uitam, nisi qua in philosophia uiueretur. . . ."

20. A. Mandouze, *Saint Augustin. L'aventure de la raison et de la grâce* (Paris: *Etudes Augustiniennes*, 1968), p. 194 (my translation).

21. *Confessiones* VI, xii, 21: *CC* XXVII, 87: "Prohibebat me sane Alypius uxore ducenda cantans nullo modo nos posse securo otio simul in amore sapientiae uiuere, sicut iam diu desideraremus, si id fecissem."

22. *Retractationes* I, 1: *BA* 12, 274.

23. *Epistula* X, 2: *CSEL* XXXIV, 24.

24. *Epistula* X, 2: *CSEL* XXXIV/1:23: "de illa una ultima, quae mors vocatur, cogitantis . . . ."

25. G. Folliet, "'Deificari in otio.' Augustin, *Epistula 10, 2*", *Recherches Augustiniennes* 2 (1962) 225-236, here 226 (my translation).

26. Cf. A. Mandouze, *Saint Augustin. L'aventure de la raison et de la grâce* (Paris: *Etudes Augustiniennes*, 1968), pp. 207-209, where the author emphasizes the advance represented by *deificari in otio* over the ideal of Cassiciacum and insists that the *otium* of Thasgaste includes the framework of religious life and communal sharing of goods. Cf. also George Lawless, *Augustine of Hippo and His Monastic Rule* (Oxford: Clarendon Press, 1987), p. 51, where Lawless says of the *otium* described in *De vera religione* XXXV, 65: *CC* XXXII, 229-230 that it "is a far cry from the leisure of the philosophers."

27. *De civitate dei* VIII, 1: *CC* XLVII, 216: "uerus philosophus est amator dei."

28. *De diversis quaestionibus octoginta tribus* XXXV, 2: *CC* XLIV/A, 52: "Et quoniam id quod amatur afficiat ex se amantem necesse est, fit ut sic amatum quod aeternum est aeternitate animum afficiat. Quocirca ea demum uita beata est quae aeterna est. Quid uero aeternum est quod aeternitate animum afficiat nisi Deus?"

29. *In epistolam Ioannis ad Parthos* II, 14: *PL* XXXV, 1997: "quia talis est quisque qualis eius dilectio est. Terram diligis? terra eris. Deum diligis? quid dicam? deus eris? Non audeo dicere ex me, Scripturas audiamus: 'Ego dixi, Dii estis, et filii Altissimi' . . . ." Cf. also *Sermo* CXXI, 1: *PL* XXXVIII, 678.

30. *De ordine* II, xviii, 47: *CC* XXIX, 133: "Cuius duplex quaestio est, una de anima, altera de deo. Prima efficit, ut nosmet ipsos nouerimus, altera, ut originem nostram. Illa nobis dulcior, ista carior, illa nos dignos beata uita, beatos haec facit."

31. Cf. *Contra academicos* I, i, 3: *CC* XXIX, 5: "Ipsa docet et uere docet nihil omnino colendum esse totumque contemni oportere, quidquid mortalibus oculis cernitur,

quidquid ullus sensus attingit. Ipsa uerissimum et secretissimum Deum perspicue se demonstraturum promittit et iam iamque quasi per lucidas nubes ostentare dignatur."

32. *De ordine* II, v, 16: *CC* XXIX, 115-116. "Philosophia rationem promittit et uix paucissimos liberat, quos tamen non modo non contemnere illa mysteria sed sola intellegere, ut intellegenda sunt, cogit . . . ." G. Madec, "A propos d'une traduction de *De ordine* II, v, 16," *Revue des Etudes augustiniennes* 16 (1970) 179-185, where Madec argues convincingly that "*sola*" modifies "*mysteria*" rather than "*philosophia*."

33. *De ordine* II, v, 16: *CC* XXIX, 116: "nullumque aliud habet negotium, quae uera et, ut ita dicam, germana philosophia est, quam ut doceat, quod sit omnium rerum principium sine principio quantusque in eo maneat intellectus quidue inde in nostram salutem sine ulla degeneratione manauerit . . . ."

34. *De ordine* II, v, 16: *CSEL* LXIII, 157: "quem unum deum omnipotentem, cum quo tripotentem patrem et filium et spiritum sanctum, ueneranda mysteria, quae fide sincera et inconcussa populos liberant, nec confuse, ut quidam, nec contumeliose, ut multi, praedicant." Here I find Madec's argument for following the edition of P. Knöll persuasive. I also agree with Madec's claim that "*confuse*" and "*contumelose*" refer to the doctrine of the Sabellians and of the Arians respectively; cf. G. Madec, "A propos d'une traduction," 182-184. F. Van Fleteren, however, suggests that it is Porphyry whom Augustine has in mind; cf. F. Van Fleteren, "Authority and Reason, Faith and Understanding in the Thought of St. Augustine," *Augustinian Studies* 4 (1973) 33-71, here 48-49.

35. Cf. *Contra academicos* I, vi, 16: *CC* XXIX, 12: "Non enim nunc primum auditis, 'Sapientiam esse rerum humanarum diuinarumque scientiam.'" Augustine repeats that definition four or even five times in the first book. Cf. G. Madec, "*L'Hortensius* de Cicéron dans les livres XIII-XIV du *De Trinitate*," *Revue des Etudes augustiniennes* 15 (1969), 169.

36. *De trinitate* XIV, i, 3: *CC* L/A, 423-424: "Verum secundum hanc distinctionem qua dixit Apostolus: 'Alii datur sermo sapientiae, alii sermo scientiae' (I Co 12:8), ista definitio diuidenda est ut rerum diuinarum scientia proprie sapientia nuncupetur, humanarum autem proprie scientiae nomen obtineat . . . huic scientiae tribuens, sed illud tantummodo quo fides saluberrima quae ad ueram beatitudinem ducit, gignitur, nutritur, defenditur, roburatur."

37. G. Madec, "*L'Hortensius* de Cicéron dans les livres XIII-XIV du *De Trinitate*," *Revue des Etudes augustiniennes* 15 (1969) 170 (my translation). Madec adds, "Mais la *scientia* augustinienne assume précisément la fonction pratique de la philosophie . . ." (p. 170).

38. *Contra academicos* I, vii, 20: *CC* XXIX, 14: "Illa est humanarum rerum scientia, qua nouit lumen prudentiae, temperantiae decus, fortitudinis robur, justitiae sanctitatem."

39. Madec claims that the true philosophy included the Incarnation of the Word. In "Connaissance de Dieu et action de grâce. Essai sur les citations de l'*Ep. aux Romains* 1, 18-25 dans l'oeuvre de saint Augustin," *Recherches Augustiniennes* 2 (1962) 273-309, here 283, he says, "Augustin a reconnu dans la doctrine du Verbe incarné la 'seule doctrine philosophique parfaitement vraie' et 'la philosophie véritable et authentique' qui a pour tâche l'intelligence des mystères." He refers to *Contra academicos* III, xix, 42: *CC* XXIX, 60, where Augustine says, referring to the intelligible world: "cui animas multiformibus erroris tenebris caecatas et altissimis a corpore sordibus oblitas numquam ista ratio subtilissima reuocaret, nisi summus deus populari quadam clementia diuini intellectus auctoritatem usque ad ipsum corpus humanum declinaret atque submitteret, cuius non solum praeceptis sed etiam factis excitatae animae redire in semet ipsas et resipiscere patriam etiam sine concertatione potuissent." I am in complete agreement with Madec that without humble faith in the Incarnate Word, souls could never attain the fatherland, even if they saw it from afar. The Platonists certainly did not know or were too proud to take the way, but faith in the Incarnation belongs to *scientia* as opposed to *sapientia*, to the way as opposed to the goal. *Philosophia* concerns the *aeternalia Dei*, not the temporal dispensation. Cf. my "The Link between Faith and Time in St. Augustine," *Collectanea Augustiniana* II, forthcoming.

40. *In Ioannis Evangelium tractatus* II, 4: *CC* XXXVI, 13 "Viderunt quo ueniendum esset. . . . Illud potuerunt uidere quod est, sed uiderunt de longe." *De trinitate* IV, xv, 20: *CC* L, 187: "nonnulli eorum potuerunt aciem mentis ultra omnem creaturam transmittere et lucem incommutabilis ueritatis quantulacumque ex parte contingere. . . . de longinquo prospicere patriam transmarinam."

41. *De trinitate* IV, xv, 20: *CC* L, 187: "Sed quid prodest superbienti et ob hoc erubescenti lignum conscendere de longuinquo prospicere patriam transmarinam? Aut quid obest humili de tanto interuallo non eam uidere in illo ligno ad eam venienti quod dedignatur ille portari?"

42. Cf. *Confessiones* VII, ix, 13-14: *CC* XXVII, 101-102, where Augustine contrasts what he found in the *libri Platonicorum* and what he did not find there. What he found there were the *aeternalia Dei*; what he did not find there was the temporal dispensation by which we are saved. Cf. also *De consensu euangelistarum* I, xxxv, 53: *CSEL* XLIII, 60: "Ipse est nobis fides in rebus ortis qui est ueritas in aeternis." *De trinitate* XIII, xix, 24: *CC* L/A, 416-417: "Scientia ergo nostra Christus est, sapientia quoque nostra idem Christus est. Ipse nobis fidem de rebus temporalibus inserit; ipse de sempiternis exhibet ueritatem. Per ipsum pergimus ad ipsum, tendimus per scientiam ad sapientiam; ab uno

tamen eodemque Christo non recedimus, 'in quo sunt omnes thesauri sapientiae et scientiae absconditi'" (Col 2:3).

43. *Contra academicos* III, xix, 42: *CC* XXIX, 60; cf. above note 39.

44. Augustine read in Isaiah 7:9, "Nisi credideritis, non intellegetis." He cites the text for the first time in *De libero arbitrio* I, ii, 4 and then again in *De libero arbitrio* II, ii, 6 and *De magistro* XI, 37.

45. E. Gilson, *The Christian Philosophy of Saint Augustine*, p. 34. Gilson points to *De moribus ecclesiae catholicae* I, ii, 3: *PL* XXXII, 1311-1312, where he claims Augustine uses the faulty method of beginning with reason—a method that Gilson oddly views as Manichaean. Gilson comments, "He only resigns himself to stoop to the madness of the Manichaeans by provisorily adopting their method, even as Jesus Christ submitted to death to save us." *The Christian Philosophy*, p. 265, n. 31.

46. Cf. J. LeBlond, *Les conversions de saint Augustin* (Paris: Aubier, 1950); F. Masai, "Les conversions de saint Augustin et les débuts du spiritualisme en Occident," *Le moyen âge* 67 (1961) 1-40; Leo C. Ferrari, *The Conversions of Saint Augustine* (Villanova: Villanova University Press, 1984).

47. Cf. Ferrari, pp. 70ff. A. Pegis refers to this conversion as Augustine's second. Cf. Anton C. Pegis, "The Second Conversion of St. Augustine," in *Gesellschaft, Kultur, Lituratur: Rezeption und Originalität im Wachsen einer europäisschen Lituratur und Geistigkeit* (Stuttgart: Anton Hiersemann, 1975), pp. 79-93.

48. *De praedestinatione sanctorum* IV, 8: *BA* 24, 488. Ferrari takes Augustine's use of *"revelare"* in this passage in a strong sense. He speaks of the revelation as "a tremendous transformation in the very foundations of Augustine's thought. Furthermore, it was no conclusion reached on the basis of mere human reasoning. Indeed, as Augustine tells us, it was a veritable revelation to him from God Himself, as he struggled to answer the question of Simplicianus . . ." (Ferrari, p. 77). However, Augustine uses *"revelare"* in the preceding paragraphs of *De praedestinatione sanctorum*, and he does so in dependence upon Paul's words, "And if on some point you think otherwise, God will reveal this to you as well; only, let us walk in the truth that we have already attained" (Phil 3:15-16). Augustine applies this text to the monks of Hadrumentum, saying that, if they cling to the truths they already hold which separate them from the Pelagians, "if they think otherwise with regard to predestination, God will reveal this to them as well" (1.2) Surely Augustine is not promising these monks an exceptional revelation from God, but simply the intellectual clarification that comes from prayerful pursuit of the truth, which is always for Augustine a divine gift. Cf. as well Augustine's use of this text in *Epistula* CXX, i, 4: *CSEL* XXXIV, 707, where Augustine can hardly be promising Consentius an exceptional revelation of the doctrine of the Trinity. On the other hand, Peter Brown's statement, "when Augustine speaks of an idea having been 'revealed' to him, he means only that he has reached the inevitable

conclusion of a series of certainties . . . — an experience not unknown to speculative thinkers today," (*Augustine of Hippo: A Biography* [Berkeley: University of California Press, 1969], p. 280, n. 2) seems to offer a too naturalistic interpretation that overlooks the fact that for Augustine it is God "who gives understanding" (cf. *De praedestinatione sanctorum* 1.2).

49. *De praedestionatione sanctorum* III, 7: *BA* 24, 478: "errarem, putans fidem qua in Deum credimus, non esse donum Dei, sed a nobis esse in nobis . . . ."

50. *De praedestinatione sanctorum* III, 7: *BA* 24, 478: "ut autem praedicato nobis Evangelio consentiremus, nostrum esse proprium, et nobis ex nobis esse arbitrabar."

51. Cf. *De ordine* II, ix, 27: *CC* XXIX, 122: "Auctoritas autem partim diuina est, partim humana, sed uera firma summa est, quae diuina nominatur."

52. The term "fideism" is, I believe, unfortunate; like the term "ontologism," it carries misleading historical overtones and recalls the fideism of Huet (1630-1721) or the traditionalism of Bonald (1754-1840) and of Lamennais (1781-1854) in accord with which all knowledge had to begin with an act of faith.

53. F. Masai, "Les conversions de saint Augustin," pp. 36-37.

54. F. Masai, p. 37.

55. Cf. the note complmentaire: "La philosophie augustinienne," in the second edition of *BA* 6, 514-517, here 517. In the third edition by G. Madec, this note is omitted, perhaps because of Madec's conviction that there is no patristic philosophy.

56. Cf. my "Rahner on the Relation of Nature and Grace," *Philosophy and Theology*, disk supplement 4, 4 (1989) 109-122.

57. Karl Rahner, "Philosophy and Theology," in *Theological Investigations*, vol. 6 (Baltimore: Helicon, 1969), p. 73.

58. Ibid., p. 78.

59. *Epistula* CXX, i, 3: *CSEL* XXXIV, 706: "Ut ergo in quibusdam rebus ad doctrinam salutarem pertinentibus, quas ratione nondum percipere valemus, sed aliquando valebimus, fides praecedat rationem. . . ."

60. *De diversis quaestionibus octaginta tribus*, XLVIII: *CC* XLIV/A, 75: "alia quae mox ut creduntur intelleguntur, sicut sunt omnes rationes humanae uel de numeris uel de quibuslibet disciplinis; tertium quae primo creduntur et postea intelliguntur, qualia sunt ea quae de diuinis rebus non possunt intelligi nisi ab his qui mundo sunt corde. . . ."

61. Thus in *Epistula* CXX, i, 5: *CSEL* XXXIV, 708, Augustine seems to say that there are some truths which we know to be true and cannot believe once an account has been given. "Sunt autem quaedam, quae cum audierimus, non eis accommodamus fidem et ratione nobis reddita uera esse cognoscimus, quae credere non ualemus."

62. *De civitate dei* VIII, xii: *CC* XLVII, 229: "Sed undecumque ista ille [Plato] didicerit, siue praecedentibus eum ueterum libris siue potius, quo modo dicit Apostolus, quia 'quod notum est Dei manifestum est in illis. . . .'"

63. Tertullian, *De praescriptione haereticorum* VII, 9 and 12: *CC* I, 193: "Quid ergo Athenis et Hierosolymis? Quid academiae et ecclesiae? . . . Nobis curiositate opus non est post Christum Iesum nec inquisitione post euangelium."

64. *De moribus ecclesiae* I, i, 1: *BA* 1, 136: "Nec, si ea discere cupiens, in aliquos forte inciderit vel episcopos vel presbyteros, vel cujuscemodi Ecclesiae catholicae antistites et ministros, qui aut passim caveant nudare mysteria, aut contenti simplici fide, altiora cognoscere non curarint, desperet ibi scientiam esse veritatis, ubi neque omnes a quibus quaeritur docere possunt, neque omnes qui quaerunt discere digni sunt." Cf. *De utilitate credendi* I, 2: *CSEL* XXV/1, 4, for Augustine's claim that it was the demand for belief prior to understanding that lured him into Manichaeism.

65. We perhaps have a reflection of such ridicule in Augustine's refusal to give the answer that someone gave to the question about what God was doing before he created the world, namely, that he was preparing hell for people who ask profound questions; cf. *Confessiones* XI, xii, 14: *CC* XXVII, 201: 'Alta, ' inquit, 'scrutantibus gehennas parabat.' Aliud est uidere, aliud ridere. Haec non respondeo."

66. Cf. the "note complémentaire": "Le charactère aporétique du De Genesi ad litteram," in *BA* 48, 575-580.

67. *Epistula* CXIX, 1: *CSEL* XXXIV, 699: "ego igitur cum apud memet ipsum prorsus definerim ueritatem rei diuinae ex fide magis quam ex ratione percipi oportere. . . ."

68. Ibid.: "si enim fides sanctae ecclesiae ex disputationis ratione, non ex credulitatis pietate adprehenderetur, nemo praeter philosophos atque oratores beatitudinem possideret."

69. *Epistula* CXX, i, 2: *CSEL* XXXIV, 706: "corrige definitionem tuam, non ut fidem respuas, sed ut ea, quae fidei firmitate iam tenes, etiam rationis luce conspicias."

70. *Epistula* CXX, i, 3: *CSEL* XXXIV, 706: "Absit namque, ut hoc in nobis deus oderit, in quo nos reliquis animantibus excellentiores creauit. absit, inquam, ut ideo credamus, ne rationem accipiamus siue quaeramus, cum etiam credere non possemus, nisi rationales animas haberemus."

71. *Epistula* CXX, i, 6 and iii, 13: *CSEL* XXXIV, 708 and 716. It is important to bear in mind that Consentius' principal difficulty was purely philosophical, namely, to conceive of God as an incorporeal being, as we shall see shortly.

72. *De Genesi ad litteram* II, ix, 20: *BA* 48, 174: "Quid enim ad me pertinet, utrum caelum sicut sphaera undique concludat terram in media mundi mole libratam, an eam ex una parte desuper velut discus operiat?"

73. *De Genesi ad litteram* II, ix, 20: *BA* 48, 176: "sed spiritum Dei, qui per eos loquebatur, noluisse ista docere homines nulli saluti profutura."

74. *De Genesi ad litteram* II, ix, 21: *BA* 48, 176: "demonstrandum est hoc, quod apud nos de pelle dictum est, ueris illis rationibus non esse contrarium; alioquin contrarium erit etiam ipsis in alio loco scripturis nostris, ubi caelum dicitur uelut camera esse suspensum."

75. Galileo Galilei, "Lettre Christine de Lorraine, Grand-Duchesse de Toscane (1615), traduction et présentation par Franois Russo," *Revue d'histoire des sciences et de leurs applications* 17 (1964) 332-366; cited from *BA* 48, 177, n. 20 (my translation). Galileo also cites *De Genesi ad litteram* I, xvii, 37; I, xix, 38-39, 41; II, x, 23; II, xviii, 38; VII, xxviii, 43.

76. *Epistula* XVIII, 2: *CSEL* XXXIV, 45: "Sane quoniam te noui, accipe hoc quiddam grande et breve. est natura per locos et tempora mutabilis, ut corpus, et est natura per locos nullo modo, sed tantum per tempora etiam ipsa mutabilis, ut anima, et est natura, quae nec per locos nec per tempora mutari potest, hoc deus est."

77. Robert J. O'Connell, S.J., *Imagination and Metaphysics in St. Augustine* (Milwaukee: Marquettee University Press, 1986). O'Connell is referring to Bourke's *St. Augustine's View of Reality* (Villanova: Villanova University Press, 1964).

78. Cf. G. Verbeke, *L'évolution de la doctrine du pneuma, du Stoïcisme à s. Augustin* (Paris and Louvain, 1945). Verbeke attributes the concept of spirit as incorporeal to the influence of Scripture. F. Masai more correctly, I believe, recognizes the term as biblical, but attributes the concept to Neoplatonism. Cf. F. Masai, "Les conversions de saint Augustin et les débuts du spiritualisme en Occident," *Moyen Age* 67 (1961) 1-40, here 17. For the Stoic view that whatever is is a body, cf. E. Weil, "Remarques sur le 'matérialisme' des Stoïciens," in *Mélanges Alexandre Koyré. II. L'aventure de l'esprit* (Paris: Hermann, 1964), pp. 556-572. Weil argues that corporealism more accurately describes the Stoic position than materialism. With Augustine too, the term "materialism" should be used with care, since matter is present in everything changeable, such as souls, though souls are not bodily. Cf. *Confessiones* XII, vi, 6: *CC* 14, 219.

79. Cf. Masai, pp. 15-23, for his account of the spiritualization of spirit. Just as most of us who are believers do not require a philosophical concept of non-bodily reality when we pray to God, so the Christians of the first centuries had no need for such a concept of God or of the soul in their lives. So too, prior to the Arian controversy, there was no need for a concept such as the consubstantiality of the Father and the Son, but once the question arose whether or not the Son was a creature, the technical term and concept were needed. In Augustine's case, it was the problem of evil that necessitated a concept of God as non-bodily. After all, if all that is is bodily, then God is an infinite body and evil is in God, or God is finite and evil is another body. The former view means that God is not all good; the latter approximates the Manichaean position.

80. Masai says, "La vérité est qu'avant Augustin, il est vain de chercher dans l'Afrique chrétienne un spiritualisme au sens moderne du terme: le Stoïcisme de Zenon y régna sans contest . . ." (p. 19). For the Manichaean position, cf. *Contra epistulam quam uocant Fundamenti* XX, 22: *CSEL* XXV/1, 216, where Augustine calls the Manichees "carnal minds" "qui naturam incorpoream et spiritualem cogitando persequi uel non audent uel nondum ualent. . . ." So too, he admits in *Confessiones* IV, xvi, 31: *CC* XXVII, 55, that he thought of God as a "bright and immense body" and that he was "a part of that body."

81. Cf., for example, *Contra Maximinum* II, ix, 2: *PL* XLII, 764, where Augustine accuses Maximinus of a carnal interpretation of "in sinu Patris" (Jn 1:18): "Sinum quippe tibi fingis, ut video, aliquam capacitatem majoris Patris, qua Filium minorem capiat atque contineat: sicut hominem corporaliter capit domus, aut sicut sinus nutricis capit infantem." Cf. my paper, "Heresy and Imagination in St. Augustine," *Studia Patristica* 11, forthcoming.

82. Cf. *Epistula* CXIX, 5: *CSEL* XXXIV, 702, where Consentius writes to Augustine, "ais non tamquam aliquod corpus debere cogitare deum . . . sed sicut iustitiam uel pietatem corpoream cogitare non possumus . . . ita et deum sine aliqua phantasiae simulatione, in quantum possumus, cogitandum." Cf. R. J. O'Connell, *The Origen of the Soul in St. Augustine's Later Works* (New York: Fordham University Press, 1987), p. 94.

83. Cf. *De anima et ejus origine* IV, xii, 19-xiv, 10: *BA* 22, 612-622. Cf. the notes to the text which show the linkage to Tertullian's position, as well as the "note complémentaire": "Une théorie stoïcienne de l'âme," pp. 837-843.

84. Cf. Thomas A. Smith, "Augustine in Two Gallic Controversies: Use or Abuse?" *Collectanea Augustiniana* II, forthcoming. Cf. also, E. Fortin, *Christianisme et culture philosophique au cinquième siècle. La querelle de l'âme humaine en Occident* (Paris: Etudes Augustiniennes, 1959).

85. Masai, for example, points to M. Testard who, in speaking of the young Augustine, mentions that he totally lacked certain beliefs fundamental to the Christian faith, such as the spiritual nature of God and the soul (M. Testard, *Saint Augustin et Cicéron* [Paris: Etudes Augustiniennes, 1958], I, p. 101; Masai, *art. cit*, p. 13).

86. For the texts on eternity in Augustine, cf. my 'Vocans temporales, faciens aeternos': St. Augustine on Liberation from Time," *Traditio* 41 (1985) 29-47.

87. Cf. Aristotle, *De caelo* II, c. 1, 283b26-32.

88. For the Plotinian source of the concept of timeless eternity, cf. W. Bierwaltes, *Plotin über Ewigkeit und Zeit* (Frankfurt a.M.: V. Klostermann, 1967), pp. 198-200, and also my 'Vocans temporales, faciens aeternos': St. Augustine on Liberation from Time," *Traditio* 41 (1985) 29-47.

89. The only Christian thinker prior to Augustine to have used the Plotinian concept of eternity in his speculative thought seems to have been Gregory of Nyssa. Cf. David L. Balás, "Eternity and Time in Gregory of Nyssa's *Contra Eunomium*," in *Gregor von Nyssa und die Philosophie*, ed. Heinrich Dörrie, Margarete Altenburger and Uta Schramm (Leiden: E. J. Brill, 1976), pp. 128-155. Balás concludes, "Most historians of philosophy would consider St. Augustine as the first Christian thinker who adopted [the strict notion of eternity]. Priority surely belongs to Gregory of Nyssa. In fact the famous definition of Boethius: 'interminabilis vitae tota simul et perfecta possessio' could easily be put together from Gregory's texts" (p. 147). The *Contra Eunomium* is dated between 380 and 383, but a direct influence of Gregory upon Augustine seems less likely than the dependence of Augustine upon Plotinus and the Neoplatonic Christians of Milan. B. Altaner concludes that Augustine knew no work of Gregory of Nyssa; cf. his "Augustinus und Gregor von Nazianz, Gregor von Nyssa," in *Kleine Patristische Schriften*, ed. G. Glockmann (Berlin: Akademie Verlag, 1967), p. 285.

90. E. Peters, "What was God doing before He created the Heavens and the Earth?" *Augustiniana* 34 (1984) 53-74.

91. P. Brown, *Augustine of Hippo. A Biography* (Berkeley: University of California Press, 1968), p. 86.

92. Ibid.

Augustinian Studies 23 (1992) 103–123

John Cavadini

The Structure and Intention of Augustine's *De trinitate*.[1]

Augustine often commented on the "extreme difficulty" of his work *On the Trinity*, repeatedly remarking that it would be comprehensible only "to few."[2] This may explain why, while there is a surfeit of modern discussions which draw upon material from the *De trinitate*, there are virtually no modern treatments of the work as a whole.[3] Perhaps this is because, of all of Augustine's works, the *De trinitate* appears to us to be the most moorless, an intractable mass of speculation floating oddly aloof from foundation in any particular social context. Peter Brown, commenting on the *De trinitate* in his biography of Augustine, warns us that we are wrong if we do not think that Augustine was capable of writing a book out of purely speculative motivation.[4] But perhaps this too is merely a polite way of suspecting that the work is essentially irrelevant, and indeed Brown immediately drops the work from further consideration, and others have followed suit. In this paper I would like to take an exploratory first step towards removing the stigma of pure speculation from this work by suggesting a location for it within a circle of discourse peculiar to Augustine's intellectual milieu, and I would like to propose that the key to such an enterprise will lie in a consideration of the *structure* of the work as a whole.

Despite Augustine's insistence, in the letter affixed by his design to the beginning of every copy of the work, that "the subsequent books are linked to the preceding ones by a continuous development of the argument,"[5] a standard interpretation of the unity of the work divides it in half, something like this: A

231

first "half" (usually construed as books 1-7 but sometimes given as 1-4 or 1-8) presents the teaching on the Trinity which constitutes the Catholic "faith," while the remaining "half" of the treatise presents an attempt to "understand," through the use of reason, the faith so presented.[6] Apart from the fact that Augustine does not divide the treatise this way, but rather conceives of the whole work as an attempt to bring the reader to understanding,[7] on this interpretation of the structure there remain in the work masses of material, both large and small, which are not accounted for. The long discussions of redemption in bks. 4 and 13, the discussion of contemplation in bk. 1 and in the prologues to books 1-5, the treatment of original sin and human renewal in bk. 14, as well as the sheer extent of the discussion of the theophanies of Genesis and Exodus in bks. 2-3, are not easily fit into the standard plan. Those who adhere to it will probably find themselves lamenting, with Stephen McKenna, that "the *De trinitate* of St. Augustine is not as systematically arranged as the medieval or modern studies of this dogma."[8] Probably we would do well to remember that it actually is not a medieval or modern study of the dogma, if it is a "study" of a "dogma" at all, and is therefore most likely not structured by the understanding of "faith" and "reason" and their relation which may inform these later works.

Nevertheless, we may be forgiven for going astray since we are not among the "few" whom Augustine expected would understand the treatise. These "few" can however be glimpsed in numerous other places in Augustine's writings. Augustine often stops to address specialized remarks to them in the course of his homilies.[9] We first meet these "few" in the earliest pages of Augustine's first writings, as those accomplished in or invited to the study of "philosophy." They would include the dedicatees of the early writings, e.g. Augustine's patron Romanianus, and the Christian Platonist Manlius Theodorus.[10] These people, some of whom can be glimpsed by name in the Letters,[11] would know (or in Augustine's view be capable of knowing) that "knowledge" or "understanding" of that which is uncreated and eternal consists in a sort of intellectual "seeing" or "vision" of it,[12] one which involved a mode of thinking completely free of images or of any mental construct applicable to the creature,[13] much as Augustine himself had learned from his first reading of Plotinus.[14] The "few" would also realize (or at least be expected to be able to grasp) that the mind could be "exercised"[15] in this image-free thought through a process of step-by-step ("gradatim") "ascent" from the consideration of physical things, to that of finite spiritual things, to the eventual vision of things eternal. Such an "ascent" would also represent a turning inward as one passes from bodily things to the things of the soul and mind.[16] In short, the "few" whom Augustine expected might understand his treatise would be those familiar with a standard Plotinian and especially Porphyrian characterization of the "return" of the soul to contemplation or *noesis*.[17]

Clearly, the *De trinitate* is predicated upon such a notion of understanding. The guided tour of the human mind which we receive in books 9-14 is nothing less than an attempt at a directed "ascent" (with several detours) from the consideration of that which is created to the contemplation — the Plotinian *noesis* — of the Creator. These books are, in effect, an extended exercise[18] of the mind in the "non-corporeal" mode of thinking with which the Trinity will ultimately be grasped. Perhaps, as a unit, they could be regarded therefore as one of the finest examples of what could be called Neoplatonic anagogy[19] that remains from the antique world. The question now becomes, what is it doing here in Augustine's *De trinitate*?

We can answer this question in part by remembering that the quest for the Neoplatonically conceived direct vision of God is not a new theme in the work of Augustine, and appears with particular strength in the early philosophical dialogues which Augustine wrote shortly after his conversion. These works are characterized by a frankly Neoplatonic agenda aiming at the contemplation of a Plotinian divine triad.[20] Augustine lavishes praise upon both Plato and Plotinus;[21] employs Cicero's *Hortensius* as his main instrument of the philo-sophical conversion of the youth attached to him;[22] and there is everywhere breathed an (almost insufferable) optimism regarding the capacity of "philos-ophy" to induct those converted to it into the vision of God's eternal light.[23] The only function which the Incarnation seems to have in this system is as an authoritative injunction to a faith in the ability of philosophy to lead one back to God, a faith which will serve to purify our minds so that the philosophical ascent may be successfully completed.[24]

Olivier du Roy has characterized this early relation between faith and reason as one in which the philosophical agenda remains definitive, essentially unaffected by a faith which serves only as a sort of extrinsic adjunct helpful to the process but not even, in every case, necessary.[25] However it is more difficult to agree when he (and others echoing him)[26] go on to remark that this relation remains characteristic of Augustine's work for the rest of his life, with minor variation.[27] In the first place, such a way of thinking ignores Augustine's pointed remarks, both in the *Confessions* and in the *Retractations*, about his earlier works in general, as well as the more specific observations made about each of the earlier works in the various chapters of the *Retractations*.[28] But what this view fails to take seriously above all is the *De trinitate*, and here we can begin to see the deleterious effect of regarding this work as separable into two "halves," essentially extrinsic to each other, one belonging in a general way to "faith" and one to "reason."

I would suggest, instead, that the *De trinitate* uses the Neoplatonic soteriology of ascent only to impress it into the service of a thoroughgoing critique of its claim to raise the inductee to the contemplation of God, a critique which, more generally, becomes a declaration of the futility of any attempt to come to any saving knowledge of God apart from Christ.

In Books 5-7, Augustine attacks the "Arians,"[29] as well as what he conceives to be an inadequate orthodox response to the Arian position. This discussion serves to point the reader to an awareness of the absolute uniqueness of the being of God and hence the necessity of a new sort of thinking which rises beyond images or categories appropriate only to creaturely life.[30] The language developed in book 5 for speaking about the Trinitarian relations is a way of constructing a vocabulary which will preserve rather than reduce (as the "Arians" do) the absolute uniqueness of the *esse* of God. And in book 7, with the failure to discover any positive content for the term *persona*,[31] we are forcefully pushed as it were to the brink of language itself, persuaded, finally, that any closer apprehension of the divine essence will have to be without words and without any mental pictures whatsoever. We are persuaded, in other words, of the necessity of the ascent, upon which, in Book 8, we immediately embark.

There are actually two consecutive attempts to tread the way of the ascent in the *De trinitate*, one coincident with Book 8, and the other developed off and on in the sequence of Books 9-14.[32] But the most striking point about both attempts is that they fail. Neither one of them delivers us to the contemplation of the Trinity which we have been expecting all along. Of course, there is nothing new in attempts at Plotinian ascents ending in failure. We can all recall that Porphyry reports that he completed the ascent only once, and that even Plotinus was not many times more successful.[33] But there *is* something new in structuring a work so that the whole is predicated upon a *deliberate* failure, especially when the work has already persuaded us that the ascent is necessary.

The failure of the first attempt is recorded in language very similar to Augustine's account of his own first encounter with the divine "light" in Book 7 of the *Confessions*.[34] What Augustine discovered there when he finally succeeded in making the ascent was not the secure contemplation of God, but rather the *distance* that existed between himself and God.[35] And we, reading book 8 of the *De trinitate*, also find from the very experience, that we are too "weak" to keep the "eye of our minds fixed" on the splendor we glimpse.

We should not be surprised to reach this point of failure, for Augustine had announced it as his intention from the opening chapters of Book 1 (chapters which were among the last to be written[36] and which therefore have some claim to reflecting Augustine's final view of the work). Pointing out how difficult it is to "see" and "fully know" the substance of God,[37] and that faith is necessary if we are to "see the ineffable ineffably,"[38] Augustine goes on to state that his treatise will serve to point out precisely this. His reasoned explanation of how the "Trinity is the one, only, and true God"[39] will function to show all who inquire, from their own "actual experience,"

> *both* that the highest good, which is perceived only by minds which are wholly purified, exists, *and* that they themselves are unable to see or to comprehend it . . . because the weak eye of the human mind cannot be fixed on a light so dazzling, unless it has been nourished and become stronger by the justice of faith.[40]

This is not a promise to deliver the reader to contemplation, but simply a promise to show us by our own experience that which we seek to contemplate does exist but that we are too weak to actually contemplate it.[41] And the rest of Book I, in the process of laying out exegetical rules for Trinitarian disputation,[42] develops into a discussion of contemplation as something which will be achieved only eschatologically, when Christ delivers the kingdom — that is, that body in whom he now reigns by faith — to God the Father.[43] Right from the outset, therefore, the ultimate context of the endeavor upon which we have embarked has been laid out as one which is eschatological.[44] *Noesis*, Plotinianly conceived, has receded to the limiting point of the eschaton, and, if it remains the goal, is only so eschatologically.

Even here, however, Augustine is to some extent echoing Porphyry, who also held that for most persons *noesis* would be postponed until after death.[45] But for Augustine, the difference between the two positions is made clear as we proceed upon the second, extended attempt, in Books 9-14, to slowly ascend to contemplation through a consideration of our own created minds. This attempt ends in an even more spectacular failure in Book 14, where we discover that the image of God which we bear in our minds has become radically disfigured through sin.[46] And thus, when the results are reviewed in bk. 15, and we attempt to rise to the direct consideration of the Creator, we find that we cannot.[47] Or, more precisely, we find that we have been contemplating an image which is more notable for its lack of similarity than for its similarity, even apart from the disfigurement caused by sin.[48] What we have discovered by making the ascent, by learning to think non-corporeally, is the painful awareness of our own *distance* from God, and that our coming to contemplation will be an onerous lifetime project of seeking, if it is possible at all.

But we have also discovered that to continue the purely introspective Neoplatonic ascent is to continue a process which has not only failed but which *cannot but fail*, for the more we persist in contemplating a disfigured image as though it were not disfigured, as though it were, so to speak, an accurate image of God, the more we persist in furthering the disfigurement. For Augustine it is this second failure, impossible to avoid, which is meant to definitively break open the absolutely introspective character of the soteriology of ascent. For what is necessary now is not so much an uninterrupted consideration of the image but a "renewal" of the image. And this consists not in the static regard of an essentially unchanging intellect or in the eschatological cleansing of that image from extrinsically accrued bodily taint at death, but in the genuine "growth" of that image itself in, as Augustine puts it, a "gradual," "day by day" "progress," one which is accomplished "holding fast to the faith of the Mediator."

This faith, for Augustine, is what enables us to break the impasse of the introspective soteriology of ascent, and Augustine has already prepared us for this realization. The discussion of the economy of redemption in books 2-4[49] serves to make the point that if we can see God in this life, it is only, like Moses, the "backparts" of God ("posteriora," Ex. 33.11-23) which we see, namely the flesh of Christ in which he was crucified.[50] And in Book 13, in more direct preparation for the failure of Book 14, Augustine's lengthy discussion fixes our regard even more firmly outward, on the blood of Christ. He asks, "What is the meaning of *justified by his blood*? What power is there in this blood that believers are justified by it?"[51] Faith in Christ, Augustine insists, means clinging to his blood as the price paid for our redemption, and, subsisting on the confidence in the love of God which it reveals. "For what," Augustine asks, "was so necessary for raising our hopes and for liberating the minds of mortals . . . than to show how highly God esteemed us and how much God loved us?"[52] Our minds are liberated by this faith because in faith the awareness of the absolute distance separating God and ourselves – an awareness which we necessarily come to on our ascent to contemplation – becomes a coincident awareness of the love of God which crossed that distance. And the greater and more painfully aware we are of the distance, the more we become aware of the love of God. Thus we are freed from the necessity of what Augustine regards as stop-gap, self-generated, and self-defeating philosophical measures which serve to remove the painful awareness of distance by in effect denying it rather than actually bridging it.[53]

But what it is important to note here is not simply that we have a new "way" for completing an ascent which remains definitively Neoplatonic in its goal, but that the goal – *noesis* itself – has acquired a new character. Our contemplative regard is pushed outward, from the consideration of a static metaphysical self essentially disconnected from the uncomfortable realm of the bodily and historically contingent – that realm which defines our ontological distance from God – to that very realm itself and to the blood, irreducibly contingent and irreducibly historical, which for Augustine became its central node. "Faith" is thus revealed not merely as a propaedeutic to vision, but as a redirecting of the noetic regard to a decidedly un-noetic realm, and "understanding" becomes the position of the self constituted by a growth wholly defined in that realm – it becomes, that is, a "seeking." We come to learn then, by Book 15, why the Psalmist could say, "Seek his face evermore" (Ps. 104.4):

> If therefore, He who is sought can be found, why was it said, *Seek his face evermore*? Or is He perhaps still to be sought even when He is found? For so we ought to seek incomprehensible things, lest we should think that we have found nothing, when we find how incomprehensible is the thing which we are seeking. . . . Faith seeks; understanding finds; and therefore the prophet has said, *Unless you believe, you shall not understand*. And again the understanding still seeks Him whom it has found: . . . for this reason, then, humans ought to attain understanding in order that we may seek God.[54]

Noesis itself has become, or at least has been replaced by, an "understanding" which is itself a seeking. In bringing us to this point, Augustine has discharged the intention first announced in the prologue to Book 1, and he has created a work which is in effect a re-issuing of the earlier philosophical dialogues, but here radically redone, as a critique of the position that there is any accurate or saving knowledge of the Trinity apart from faith in Christ.[55]

And thus the *De trinitate* is not in the first instance a purely "speculative" work inquiring into the mystery of the Trinity for the sake of systematizing Christian dogma, but finds its context rather in a polemical dialogue, visible in other, more familiar parts of the Augustinian corpus, against Neoplatonic views of salvation and also against (as Augustine sees it) overly Platonizing Christian views.[56] I would agree with Emilie Zum Brunn when she notes in a related context that

> the problem that faces us . . . appears to be that of the interpenetration of two spiritualities and of two cultures more than that of reason and Revelation, philosophy and faith.[57]

I would add however that from Augustine's point of view, he is in the *De trinitate* arguing on behalf of one particular faith and spirituality over against another,[58] and of the modification of the notion of "understanding" which that faith, as he sees it, entails.

Notes

1. Earlier versions of this paper were presented at the Patristic, Medieval, and Renaissance Conference ("PMR", 1988) and the Annual Meeting of the North American Patristics Society ("NAPS", 1990). I would like to thank Kathryn Johnson, Robert Markus, Nicholas Lash, and J.J. O'Donnell, who all read earlier versions of this paper and provided helpful comments. In addition I would like to acknowledge helpful conversations with Celia Chazelle, Anthony Godzieba, and Robert Wilken, and with my colleagues David Burrell, Catherine LaCugna, and Blake Leyerle.

2. In *Epistolae* 169 (late 415; all letters cited in the edition of A. Goldbacher, *CSEL* vols. 33, 34, 44, 57, 58), Augustine tells Evodius " . . . nec libros de trinitate, quos diu in manibus verso nondumque complevi, modo adtendere velim, quoniam nimis operosi sunt et a *paucis* eos intellegi posse arbitror (*Epistolae* 169.1.1, p. 612.6-9). He thought of the *City of God* as a more pressing work, likely to be of benefit, by contrast, to many. Five years earlier, he had written a reply to the monk Consentius (*Epistolae* 120.3.13), where Augustine noted the "extreme difficulty" of the subject of the Trinity: " . . . volo, ut leges ea, quae ad istam quaestionem pertinentia iam multo conscripsimus, illa etiam, quae in manibus habemus et propter magnitudinem tam difficilis quaestionis nondum possumus explicare" p. 715.18-21). Cf. also *Epistolae* 143.4 (*ca.* 412, to Marcellinus).

3. Still standard is *Die psychologische Trinitätslehre des hl. Augustinus* (Münster: Aschendorff, 1927), as well as A. Schindler, *Wort und Analogie in Augustins Trinitätslehre* (Tübingen: Mohr, 1965). Anne-Marie La Bonnardière, *Recherches de chronologie augustinienne* (Paris: Etudes Augustiniennes, 1965) and E. Hendrikx, O.E.S.A. (in pp. 9-14 of the Introduction to *Bibliothèque Augustinienne: Oeuvres de Saint Augustin* [hereafter, *BA*] vol. 15, *La Trinité, Première Partie: La Mystère*, edited and translated by M. Mellet, O.P., and Th. Camelot, O.P. [Paris: Desclée de Brouwer, 1955]) provide the best chronology of the *De Trinitate*, at which Augustine worked on and off for some twenty years (finished *ca.* 420) finally publishing it in a version less polished than originally planned — the unfinished work had previously been stolen and circulated in an unauthorized version, and Augustine did not want the final version to differ too drastically from what was already circulated (see *Epistolae* 174, the prologue to *De trinitate* (edited by W.J. Mountain and Fr. Glorie, *CCSL* vols. 50-50A [Turnhout: Brepols, 1968]). Since Book 15 and the prologues to the earlier books were the last parts to be written, these have a special claim on our attention as representing Augustine's final understanding of the work as a whole.

4. Peter Brown, *Augustine of Hippo* (Berkeley: University of California Press, 1967), 277.

5. *De trinitate* Prologue : " . . . praecedentibus [libros] consequentes inquisitione proficiente nectuntur" (lines 9-10). All translations, with occasional modification, are taken from *Saint Augustine: The Trinity*, translated by Stephen McKenna, C.SS.R., vol. 45 of *The Fathers of the Church* (Washington: The Catholic University of America Press, 1963).

6. Thus, for example, E. Hendrikx in his Introduction to the *BA* edition and translation, divides the work into part I, "The Truth of the Church's Dogma Demonstrated from Scriptures," and part II, "The Explication and Deepening of the Dogma by Specula-tion," while the edition itself is divided into two volumes, Books 1-7 corresponding to "*La mystère*," and Books 8-15 to "*Les images*" (*BA* vol. 16, edited and translated by P. Agaësse, S.J. and J. Moingt, S.J.). Even as recently as 1986, Henry Chadwick essentially repeats this standard conception of the work (*Augustine* [Oxford: Oxford University Press, 1986], 91), which has authoritative defenders all the way back to Marrou (who keeps bk. 8 with the first seven books: *Saint Augustin et la fin de la culture antique* 4th edition [Paris: Editions E. de Boccard, 1958], 315-27). E. Hill, in the introduction to his new translation of the *De trinitate* (*The Trinity*, part I, vol. 5 of *St. Augustine: A Translation for the Twenty-First Century* [New York: New City Press, 1991], notes that "the *De Trinitate* divides itself fairly obviously into two parts, Books I-VII . . . and Books VIII-XV" (p. 21). Hill, however, modifies this by describing a chiastic structure (pp. 26-27) and pointing to the "dramatic" character of the *De trinitate* (pp. 18-19), linking Books 9-14 with the economy of salvation (pp. 25-26, 258-263).

7. It is true that Augustine marks Book 8 as a turning point in the work, both in the course of the text itself (8.P) and in the review given at 15.6.10 and at 15.3.5, and I do not wish to underestimate these markers. But the standard interpretation tends to overinterpret them, holding the two "halves" apart to the point where their relation becomes almost purely extrinsic, as though the two "halves" could almost be separate works (or at least separate volumes), and thus the "understanding" of what one "believes" becomes a moment formally separable from faith itself (as perhaps in some later scholastic treatments of "faith seeking understanding"). Surely one of the reasons these two halves are placed together – one of the reasons for Augustine's special insistence on the "continuous development of the argument" – is precisely to qualify any claims, philosophical or otherwise, that what one knows in faith and what one knows by understanding are different, or that what one learns by philosophical introspection is different and over and above what one learns from exegesis (see n. 42 below). In book 8 we are informed that we are now proceeding "modo interiore," but this does not mean that we have not been operating on the basis of "reason" before this; actually it implies a continuity of process, only in a different "style." In the summary of the treatise given at Book 15, Book 8 is marked as that book where the Trinity began "to dawn on us," but this once again can signify the term of a process, not a new process.

8. McKenna, p. xii.

9. As, e.g. in the *Tractates on John* (best edition by D.R. Willems, O.S.B., *CCSL* vol. 36 [Turnhout: Brepols, 1954]), a project that Augustine was working on concurrently with the *De Trinitate*. See for example *Tractatus* 1.1.13-17. For other passages, and on the distinction between the *animales* and *spirituales*, see R.J. Teske, "Spirituals and Spiritual Interpretation in Augustine," *Augustinian Studies* 15 (1984), 65-81.

10. At *Contra academicos* 2.1 (best edition by W.M. Green, *CCSL* vol. 29 [Turnhout: Brepols, 1970]), Romanianus is invited to join the "few" (2.1.1.14) for whom philosophy will bear fruit in the knowledge of the truth (2.3.9.56-58). In the *De beata vita* (best edition by W.M. Green, *CCSL* vol. 29) the "few" ("pauci," 1.1.6) are those who make it to the "port of philosophy" (1.1.1), some of whom go on to arrive at the happy life, where, Augustine presumes, Manlius Theodorus has already arrived (1.5.118-19; cf. *De ordine* [best edition by W.M. Green, *CCSL* vol. 29] 1.11.31.18-23).

11. A full scale study of this issue will have to await another article, but among correspondents from the period during the composition of the *De trinitate*, surely we can include Evodius. In *Epistolae* 169 (see n. 2 above), Augustine discusses with Evodius all of the issues which, from his point of view, will limit the appeal of the *de Trinitate* to only a "few," and he fully expects Evodius to understand the discussions in the *de Trinitate* when it is finally published. In *Epistolae* 162, Augustine identifies the issues which Evodius has repeatedly raised (in *Epistolae* 158, 160, and 161) as those which will be treated in the *De trinitate* and the *De Genesi ad litteram* (*Epistolae* 162.2,

p. 512.18-513.3). At *Epistolae* 159.2, p. 499.17-18, Augustine refers Evodius to *De Genesi ad litteram* 12, a highly sophisticated discussion of visions and the seeing of God such as only the "few" would understand. The list of correspondents would also include the lady Paulina, who has asked Augustine about how God is seen. Augustine's answer is a small treatise (*Epistolae* 147), denoted "On the Vision of God" at *Retractiones* 2.67, where Augustine also notes that its subject is "truly most difficult." If anything, it is treated more thoroughly than the corresponding treatment given for Evodius in *Epistolae* 162. Chapters 3-4 and 41-44 are typical of the exhortation to vision and spiritual ascent which are reserved for the "few" and are reminiscent of many passages in the *De trinitate*. Our list must also include Dardanus, praeterian prefect of Gaul and recipient of *Epistolae* 187, the treatise "On the Presence of God" (*Retractationes* 2.75). Prompted by Dardanus' request, and prefaced by a compliment on Dardanus' powers of reflection (a compliment which Augustine only rarely gives out, *Epistolae* 187.1.2, p. 83.4-5), it is a complex treatment of issues related to how to think about the non-corporeal omnipresence of God who is "everywhere wholly present" (see n. 56 below for further treatment). A preliminary list would also have to include Paulinus of Nola, as well as Marcellinus, frequent correspondent and the dedicatee of the *City of God*, and Marcellinus' friend Volusianus, who deftly raises explicitly philosophical questions for discussion by Augustine (see *Epistolae* 135 and 136), and whom Augustine answers in the complex *Epistolae* 137. The monk Consentius (of *Epistolae* 119 and 120) may also be included, although his understanding is not accorded the same esteem that Augustine cedes to those already mentioned. Among Augustine's correspondents before the period of the composition of the *De trinitate* (and not already mentioned here), we can recognize Nebridius (*Epistolae* 3-14; note especially *Epistolae* 11, an early letter on the Trinity), Zenobius (*Epistolae* 2, to whom the *De ordine* is dedicated), Romanianus (*Epistolae* 15, cf Paulinus and Therasia's letter to him at *Epistolae* 32), and perhaps Hermogenianus (to whom Augustine has submitted the *Contra academicos* for correction or comment, *Epistolae* 1).

12. For example, in the *De beata vita* Augustine explains that this is what he learned from Ambrose and Manlius Theodorus (1.4.91-94), and in the *De ordine* Augustine explains that a "few" healthy intellects "behold" the invisible, spiritual world: "Esse autem alium mundum ab istis oculis remotissimum, quem paucorum sanorum intellectus intuetur" (*De ordine* 1.11.32.44-46). By the time of *Epistolae* 169 to Evodius, what is "discerned" by the "few" (*Epistolae* 169.1.2, p. 612.17) is much more specific, namely the "ineffabilem trinitatis unitatem, sicut discernitur in animo nostro memoria, intellectus, voluntas" (*Epistolae* 169.1.2, p. 612.13-15). The parallels with the subject of Books 9 and 10 of the *De trinitate* are obvious. Further, it is clear from Evodius' own letter (*Epistolae* 158.6) that he is himself in the habit of thinking about just these issues, including the incorporeal oneness of memory, understanding, and will (p. 492.3-7).

13. See, e.g., his instructions to Paulina at *Epistolae* 147.43; the long instruction to Consentius in *Epistolae* 120.2.9-12 (followed by the recommendation to read the *De trinitate* when it is finished, 120.3.13, p. 715.18-21); and that to Volusianus at *Epistolae* 137.2.4-8 (in the *De Trinitate* compare, e.g., 1.1.1, 5.1.1-2, 10.10.16).

14. In the *Confessions*, as a result of reading the "Platonic books" (*Confessiones* 7.9.13.5-6, best edition by Luc Verheijen, O.S.A., *CCSL* vol. 27 [Turnhout: Brepols, 1990]), Augustine can say, "'Numquid nihil est veritas, quoniam neque per finita neque per infinita locorum spatia diffusa est?'" (*Confessiones* 7.10.16.22-23). The *De beata vita* (1.4.99) specifies Plotinus as the source (following Green's text, which defends the reading "Plotinus" as opposed to "Plato").

15. See Marrou's classic treatment of this theme, *Saint Augustine et la fin*, pp. 298-327, and also *BA* vol. 16, pp. 612-14 ("note complémentaire" 30). For a parallel idea in Plotinus, see Jean Trouillard, *La purification plotinienne* (Paris: Presses Universitaires de France, 1955), 163-65 ("Sciences et dialectique purificatrices"). On the ascent in general see also Frederick E. Van Fleteren, "Augustine's Ascent of the Soul: A Reconsideration," *Augustinian Studies* 5 (1974), 29-72.

16. Note, e.g., the expression at *De Trinitate* 12.8.13.1, "Ascendentibus itaque introrsus quibusdam gradibus . . . ," cf. *De trinitate* 14.3.5.29-30, where "ab inferioribus ad superiora ascendentes" is parallel to "ab exterioribus ad interiora ingredientes."

17. On *noesis* in Plotinus and Porphyry see Andrew Smith, *Porphyry's Place in the Neoplatonic Tradition* (The Hague: Martinus Nijhoff, 1974), esp. pp. 20-39. The philosophical "few" of Augustine's early dialogues are the same "few" to which Porphyry thought high philosophical vision would be limited. See, for example, Augustine's citation of him at *De civitate Dei* 10.29 (=Bidez fragment 10, in J. Bidez, *Vie de Porphyre, le philosophe néoplatonicien* [Hildesheim: Georg Olms, 1964) p. 37* lines 12-13): "'ad Deum per virtutem intellegentiae pervenire paucis' dicis esse concessum." On Porphyry and Augustine see Eugene TeSelle, "Porphyry and Augustine," *Augustinian Studies* 5 (1974), 113-147.

18. With reference to the preceding six books: "Volentes in rebus quae factae sunt ad cognoscendum eum a quo factae sunt exercere lectorem iam pervenimus ad eius imaginem quod est homo in eo quo ceteris animalibus antecellit, id est ratione vel intellegentia . . . " (*De trinitate* 15.1.1.1-4; see also 15.6.10.55-58, cited below, n. 46).

19. On the word "anagogy" see Emilie Zum Brunn, *St. Augustine: Being and Nothingness* (New York: Paragon House, 1988), 4. She takes the expression over from Olivier du Roy, *L'Intelligence de la Foi en la Trinité selon Saint Augustin* (Paris: Etudes Augustiniennes, 1966), who explains his usage at p. 170, n. 6.

20. See Du Roy, pp. 147-48. Note, for example, at *De ordine* 2.9.26 what makes the "few" the "few" is that they can contemplate Intellect and the First Principle (=Nous

and the One): Those eager to learn ("studiosi," line 1) will in fact eventually learn "quid [sit] intellectus, in quo universa sunt — vel ipsa potius universa — et quid praeter universa universorum principium. Ad quam cognitionem in hac vita pervinire *pauci*, ultra quam vero etiam post hanc vitam nemo progredi potest" (lines 17-20). See also *De ordine* 2.5.16.2-3, 47-50: "philosophia rationem promittit et vix paucissimos liberat . . . . Germana philosohia est, quam ut doceat, quod sit omnium rerum principium sine principio quantusque in eo maneat intellectus quidve inde in nostram salutem sine ulla degeneratione manaverit . . . ."

21. E.g. *Contra academicos* 3.18.41.41-46: " . . . os illud Platonis, quod in philosophia purgatissimum est et lucidissimum, dimotis nubibus erroris emicuit mauime in Plotino, qui Platonicus philosophus ita eius similis iudicatus est, ut simul eos vixisse, tantum autem interest temporis, ut in hoc ille revixisse putandus sit" (cf. also *Contra academicos* 3.17.38.42, which refers approvingly to "Platonica illa velut sacrosancta decreta"). Augustine retracts this praise at *Retractationes* 1.1.4.99-102 (best edition by A. Mutzenbecher, *CCSL* vol. 57 [Turnhout: Brepols, 1984): "Laus quoque ipsa qua Platonem vel Platonicos sive Academicos philosophos tantum extuli, quantum impios homines non oportuit, non inmerito mihi displicuit, praesertim contra quorum errores magnos defendenda est christiana doctrina." This sentence could sum up the *De trinitate* as itself a kind of *retractatio* of the ealier dialogues (see below, n. 55).

22. For example, the whole agenda of the *De beata vita* derives from the *Hortensius*, the beginning ("Beatos nos esse volumus," see *De trinitate* 13.4.7.32-35) of which is cited as the announcement of the argument of the *De beata vita* (2.10.85; note how prominent the *Hortensius* is in Augustine's account of his conversion just above, at *De beata vita* 1.10.85). See also *Contra academicos* 1.1.4.97-98, which shows that Augustine is still using Cicero's *Hortensius* as a kind of textbook, useful for helping people begin their study of philosophy.

23. As, e.g., at *Contra academicos* 1.3.77-80.

24. On Augustine's early view of the role of the Incarnation, see R.J. O'Connell, *St. Augustine's Early Theory of Man* (Cambridge MA: Harvard University Press, 1968), 265-78. In Du Roy, see pp. 109-148, where he notes "Les dialogues de Cassiciacum nous confirment aussi que, dès sa première théologie, il a tiré les conséquences de l'ordre des mystères chrétiens qui fut celui de sa découverte: la Trinité peut être connue avant même l'Incarnation, et sa connaissance, quoique confuse et orgueilleuse, se trouve déjà chez les philosophes païens. L'autorité ou la foi n'est là que pour nous purifier de la convoitise des sens et de l'orgueil de l'esprit" (148).

25. See e.g. Du Roy, 125, commenting on *De ordine* 2.5.16, p. 157.16-20.

26. E.g. Zum Brunn, 93, and 95, n. 8.

27. There is a particularly damning judgment on p. 105: "Si le mode suprême de connaissance a pu être atteint en quelque mesure par les philosophes païens sans la foi, si donc l'illumination suprême n'est pas transformée intrinsèquement par la foi, si c'est seulement le degré et la stabilité qui diffèrent, alors le Dieu révélé, le Dieu Trinité, peut être connu en dehors de l'économie de la révélation. . . . On conçoit que, la foi ne modifiant pas radicalement (ni explicitement, ni consciemment du moins) le mouvement propre de l'*intellectus* . . . . " The "anteriority" of knowledge of the Trinity to knowledge of the Incarnation is a "fundamental articulation" of Augustinian theology (p. 97), and as such it constitutes Augustine as a kind of crypto-gnostic (see especially p. 419). In Augustine, the relation between faith and understanding always remains "extrinsic" (p.456).

28. In the *Confessions* Augustine notes of his literary activity at Cassiciacum, "Ibi quid egerim in litteris iam quidem servientibus tibi, sed adhuc superbiae scholam tamquam in pausatione anhelantibus testantur libri disputati cum praesentibus et cum ipso ne solo coram te . . . " (*Confessiones* 9.4.7.4-7). One need only peruse the early chapters of the *Retractationes* to provide specification for this observation. Many of the comments are directed against excessive praise of philosophers or of philosophy itself.

29. Eunomius is mentioned at *De trinitate* 15.20.38.1-2, but it is not clear that the "Arians" refuted in Books 5-7 (*De trinitate* 5.3.4.3; 6.1.1.8; 6.9.10.11; cf. 2.15.25.15) are Eunomians. On the identity of these "Arians," see Michel Barnes, "The Identity of the Arians in Book Five and the Genre of Augustine's *De trinitate*," forthcoming in *Journal of Theological Studies*.

30. See especially *De trinitate* 5.1.1.1-6, 39-46, and note the specification of this in terms of the ten categories (given at *De trinitate* 5.7.8), some of which apply only metaphorically to God (*De trinitate* 5.8.9), and the rest of which, except for the category of substance (and at *De trinitate* 7.5.10 even this is suspect, so that God, and God alone, should rather be called "essentia") must be applied only in an accomodated sense, since there is no accident in God (*De trinitate* 5.4-5). In particular, there are no accidental, but only eternal, relations (*De trinitate* 5.5.6).

31. *De trinitate* 7.4.7.1-5; 7.4.9.117-120.

32. This is clear from the summary Augustine gives at *De trinitate* 15.6.10. Book 8 attempted to "raise" ("erigere," *De trinitate* 15.6.10.34) our minds to the unchangeable nature which is not our mind, but this failed because we could not keep the eye of our mind fixed firmly on the brilliance of its ineffable light (*De trinitate* 15.6.10.46-48), and thus we turned in Books 9-14 (*De trinitate* 15.6.10.54) to a consideration of the image, in order that, with Romans 1.20 — Augustine's favorite biblical description of the ascent — we might understand the invisible things of God through those which are made.

33. *Vita Plotini* 23 (text of P. Henry and H-R Schwyzer given with emendation by A.H. Armstrong in the Loeb Classical Library, vol. 440 (Cambridge, MA: Harvard University Press, 1966).

34. At *De trinitate* 15.6.10.34-30, Augustine points out that in the eighth book "erigere temptavimus mentis intentionem ad intellegendam illam praestantissimam immutabilemque naturam quod nostra mens non est. Quam tamen sic intuebamur ut nec longe a nobis esset et supra nos esset, non loco sed ipsa sui venerabili mirabilique praestantia ita ut apud nos esse suo praesenti lumine videretur. In qua tamen nobis adhuc nulla trinitas apparebat quia non ad eam quaerendam in fulgore illo firmam mentis aciem tenebamus" (cf. *De trinitate* 15.6.10.46-48; and see also 8.2.3.28-40). These passages may be usefully compared to *Confessiones* 7.17.23.27-32 and similar passages.

35. Of course *Confessiones* 7.10.16.17 ("et inveni longe me esse a te in regione dissimilitudinis") comes to mind, but see also, e.g., *Confessiones* 11.9.11.4-15.

36. See La Bonnardière, *Recherches*, 176.

37. *De trintate* 1.1.3.69-71.

38. *De trinitate* 1.1.3.72-75.

39. *De trinitate* 1.2.4.3.

40. " . . . suscipiemus . . . reddere rationem, quod trinitas sit unus et solus et verus deus . . . ut non quasi nostris excusationibus inludantur sed reipsa experiantur et esse illud summum bonum quod purgatissimis mentibus cernitur, et a se propterea cerni comprehendique non posse quia mentis humanae acies invalida in tam excellenti luce non figitur nisi *per iustitiam fidei* (Rom. 4.13) nutrita vegetetur" (1.2.4.1-2,3,6-11).

41. Augustine goes on to give a hint about those for whom this service will be accomplished: " . . . si voluerit et adiuverit deus, istis garrulis ratiocinatoribus, elatioribus quam capacioribus atque ideo morbo periculosiore laborantibus, sic fortasse serviemus ut inveniant aliquid unde dubitari non possint, et ob hoc in eo quod invenire nequiverint, de suis mentibus potius quam de ipsa veritate vel de nostris disputationibus conquerantur. Atque ita si quid eis erga deum vel amoris est vel timoris, ad initium fidei et ordinem redeant . . . " (*De trinitate* 1.2.4.13-20). Can we begin to put faces on "these chattering reasoners," for whom Augustine says he will render this service? Certainly they are a part of the "discerning few" in *Epistolae* 169 to Evodius (169.1.2), those in particular about whom Augustine complains later in the letter: "nonnulli a corporibus incorporea discernentes, cum sibi ex hoc magni videntur et inrident *stultitiam praedicationis* (1 Cor. 1.21), qua salvi fiunt credentes, ab unica via longe exerrent, quae ad vitam aeternam sola perducit" (*Epistolae* 169.1.4, p. 614.10-13). It is these whom the *De trinitate* promises to "return" to the "initium fidei." Perhaps one may think, in this connection, of Manlius Theodorus, to whom Augustine dedicated the *De beata vita*

but later regretted the dedication (or at least the praise with which it was given — see *Retractationes* 1.2). Did Augustine come to regard him as overly Platonizing? Pierre Courcelle describes Manlius Theodorus as Augustine's "maître" after Ambrose, and explains Augustine's later severity towards Theodorus as follows: "la raison de cette sévérité tient à ce que, vers la date de rédaction des *Confessions*, Theodorus venait de reprendre une vie mondaine et quasi-païenne: Symmaque dans ses lettres, Claudien dans un panégyrique en vers, le félicitent d'avoir obtenu le consulat pour l'an 399 et de fournir aux Romains des jeux à grands spectacles" (*Recherches sur les Confessions de Saint Augustin* [Paris: E. de Boccard, 1950], 154; see pp. 153-56 on Theodorus in general). Such a Theodorus, Augustine might think, would need to be returned to the "initium fidei." One may also think of the relatively innocuous but obnoxious Dioscorus of *Epistolae* 117 and 118, for whom Augustine points out the errors of the philosophers, the "Platonists" included, in the context of the sort of discussion of God's incorporeality which he might have with a member of the "few" (in this case, a would-be member).

42. The best article on these rules is Jaroslav Pelikan, "*Canonica Regula*: The Trinitarian Hermeneutics of Augustine," *Proceedings of the PMR* 1987-88 (12 & 13), 17-29. Pelikan points out quite rightly that the first, "exegetical," half of the *De Trinitate* is often ignored by scholars despite its importance to Augustine. But if, as Pelikan points out (25), the "immediate source" for the *canonica regula* is Phil. 2.5-11, this implies that Trinitarian hermeneutics, or any attempt to "understand" Scriptural teaching on the Trinity, will consist in and arise from a sustained reflection on the mysteries of God's saving work in Christ. This is why the two "halves" are placed together: one's coming to understand the Trinity is not separable from reflection on the economy of salvation (*pace* Colin Gunton, "Augustine, The Trinity and the Theological Crisis of the West," *Scottish Journal of Theology* 43, 33-58, esp. p.48, italicized passage) but is in fact coincident with such reflection. It is Scripture itself which, as Augustine points out at the very beginning of the treatise (*De Trinitate* 1.1.2; cf. *Epistola* 137 to Volusianus), mandates and engages us upon the ascent to understanding. The ascent *is* exegesis of the text, but it is an exegesis governed by *canonica regula* which forms the ascent, and thus the ascent itself occurs as a reflection upon the economy of salvation in which the Son of God "emptied himself". The point of placing the two "halves" together is that when in Book 8 we come to tread the path "modo interiore," we do not depart from reflection on the economy of salvation, but, on the contrary, we find its absolute priority demonstrated. The *Tractates on John* would be another good example of the coincidence of exegesis and ascent.

43. 1 Cor. 15.24; see e.g. *De trinitate* 1.18.17.80-95.

44. Note that the stages of this drama are marked by Scriptural citations which are introduced in Book I, and which serve, at crucial points in the narrative, as reprises of the eschatological themes laid out in Bk. 1. These include Ps. 104.4 ("Seek His face evermore . . . "; *De trinitate* 1.3.5.5); 1 Jn. 3.2 ("We shall be like Him, since we shall

see Him just as He is"; *De trinitate* 1.13.31.172); 1 Cor. 13.12 ("We see now in a glass darkly, but then face to face," *De trinitate* 1.8.16.63, cited 14 more times in Book I alone, and then in every succeeding Book except Book 11); 2 Cor. 5.7 ("For we walk by faith, not by sight," *De trinitate* 1.8.17.114-115).

45. *De civitate Dei* 10.29 = Bidez fr. 10, p37*, lines 17-19: "nec ipse dubitas 'in hac vita hominem nullo modo ad perfectionem sapientiae pervenire . . . .'"

46. Scripture teaches and "has pity upon" the deformed divine image ("deformitatem dignitatis eius miserans divina scriptura," *De trinitate* 14.4.6.13-14) which is the mind, and of which the reader is about to ascend to consideration (*De tinitate* 14.8.11.1-7). In fact, however, we were already at this point earlier: we *had* ascended to the consideration of this image in Book 10, and were about to ascend to consideration of that immutable nature (God) of which the mind is an image ("Iamne igitur ascendendum est qualibuscumque intentionis viribus ad illam summam et altissimam essentiam cuius impar imago est humana mens sed tamen imago?" *De trinitate* 10.12.19.1-3; equivalent to the step about-to-be-taken yet another time in Book 15: see *De trinitate* 15.1.1; 15.4.6), when we were prevented from doing it because of the way in which the mind tends *not* actually to stay in self-awareness, as it would if it were truly philosophic and able to think incorporeally, but to picture itself in a "phantasy," as extended, etc. (*De trinitate* 10.5,6,7,10). This inability is really a kind of failure of the ascent, and it causes the long detour of Books 11-13, in which Augustine attempts to help the reader distinguish between the trinities of sense and the mind's knowledge of itself (*De trinitate* 10.12.19.6-12,18-22; 14.6.9.55-61; 14.7.10.58-61). But this detour essentially comes back to the point of failure, as though we now learn the mind's inability to be aware of itself was a more serious problem than first thought, and in fact reflects the deformity of the image of God itself, and thus of its radical need for transformation by God's love. *De trinitate* 14.14.20 and 16.22 describe the mind's inability to know and love itself as due to an undue attachement to and thus conformation to lust for things beneath it, and that it is our job to "turn away" from this disfigurment or conformation to the world (*De trinitate* 14.16.22.1-4), but that this "reformation" (cf. Rom. 12.2) must be God's work (*De trinitate* 14.16.22.5-7), does not occur in the one moment of conversion but is a long course of healing (*De trinitate* 14.17.23.1-11), of day by day progress and growth in clinging to the faith of the Mediator, and full vision will only come after death ("In quo provectu et accessu tenentem mediatoris fidem cum dies vitae huius ultimus quemque compererit, perducendus ad deum quem coluit et ab eo perficiendus . . . ; in hac quippe imagine tunc perfecta erit dei similitudo quando dei perfecta erit visio," *De trinitate* 14.17.23.26-29,31-32). Awareness of the need for reformation is the true fulfillment of the Delphic "Know Thyself" (*De trinitate* 10.9.12.4,7,16), and love of God and neighbor in faith (*De trinitate* 14.14.18.26-31) is the true delivery from misery to happiness, the true love of wisdom, or "philosophy"

(*De trinitate* 14.1.2.32-38), which will, unbeknownst to Cicero, be the fulfillment of the exhortation in the *Hortensius* (*De trinitate* 14.19.26).

47. *De trinitate* 15.6.10.55-58: "Et ecce iam quantum necesse fuerat aut forte plus quam necesse fuerat exercitata in inferioribus intellegentia ad summam trinitatem quae deus est conspiciendam nos erigere volumus nec valemus"; cf. *De trinitate* 15.27.50.71-74, 89-91.

48. *De trinitate* 15.7.11-13 is an extended discussion of the unlikeness of God and God's image in us (cf. the parallel discussion in *Epitolae* 169.2.6, to Evodius, some five years earlier than Book 15; note also the "ontological gap" mentioned by Frederick E. Van Fleteren, "Thematic Reflections on the *De Trinitate*," *Proceedings of the PMR* 1987-88 [12 & 13], p. 224). Du Roy notices and comments upon the failures of ascent (of Book 8 and Book 15) and the discussions of the unlikeness of the image, but he can see them only as a "betrayal" of the "most profound aspirations" of Augustine's *intellectus fidei* (p.447), and he dissociates them from the overall anagogy of the *De Trinitate*: "Le livre XV va consacrer cet échec de l'anagogie en s'installant résolument dans l'analogie et en faisant le bilan des livres VIII à XIV. Il commence donc par les résumer. Puis il invite à s'élever jusqu'à la Trinité divine. Mais ce n'est plus par une méthode anagogique, c'est par une attribution analogique des perfections créés au Créateur" (p. 446). But Augustine, by reviewing the plan of the whole work, presents this moment as the culmination of the anagogy: it is the last "step," the one "above" (*De trinitate* 15.1.1.9) our nature, and it is our attempt to take this step which is analyzed. The language about "like" and "unlike," "higher" and "lower," "better" and "best" (in this context see especially *De trinitate* 15.4.6) is constitutive of the disimilarities (e.g. eternal *vs.* temporal, immutable *vs.* changeable, spiritual *vs.* corporeal) which enable the ascent to proceed. The point is not that at the end of anagogy we come to "analogy," but rather that *the same logic which defines the ascent also defines its failure*, i.e. that the spirituality of introspective ascent is inherently self-defeating. The anagogical path itself becomes a demonstration of the need for transformation and grace (explained in *De trinitate* 15 at 15.8.14, immediately following the failure of the ascent and the discussion of the dissimilarity of the image). Du Roy's distinction between anagogy and analogy here seems without textual warrant, imported from another (Thomistic?) world of thought in order to preserve his contention that Augustine believes there is (natural?) knowledge of the Trinity available independent of faith. Thus when the anagogy fails to raise us to understanding of the Trinity, the failure cannot be part of Augustine's own fundamental intentions – as a *critique* of the anagogical spirituality – but must instead be a "betrayal" of Augustine's intentions.

49. With prologues which Augustine added later to ensure that we do not lose sight both of the request for vision which he is entertaining and of its limitations. Books 2-4 of the *De trinitate* may be usefully compared to *Episotlae* 137 to Volusianus, where the discussion of the theophanies and the Incarnation, in connection with a discussion on

how we see God, is a response to a (Porphyrian?) critique that Christians localize God in a body.

50. "Non incongruenter ex persona domini nostri Iesu Christi praefiguratum solet intellegi ut posteriora eius accipiantur caro eius in qua de virgine natus est et mortuus et resurrexit . . . . Facies autem eius illa dei forma . . . Illa est ergo species quae rapit omnem animam rationalem desiderio sui tanto ardentiorem quanto mundiorem et tanto mundiorem quanto ad spiritalia resurgentem, tanto autem ad spiritalia resurgentem quanto a carnalibus morientem. Sed *dum peregrinamur a domino et per fidem ambulamus non per speciem* (2 Cor. 5.6-7), posteriora Christi, hoc est carnem, per ipsam fidem videre debemus . . . " (*De trinitate* 2.17.28.1-4,6,37-43). Aspiring to this contemplation means "building up" the neighbor in love (*De trinitate* 2.17.28.29-30).

51. *De trinitate* 13.11.15.1-3, "Sed quid est *iustificati in sanguine ipsius*? (Rom. 5.9). Quae vis est huius sanguinis obsecro ut in eo iustificentur credentes?"

52. *De trinitate* 13.10.13.11-15: "Quid enim tam necessarium fuit ad erigendam spem nostram mentesque mortalium conditione ipsius mortalitatis abiectas ab immortalitatis desperatione liberandas quam ut demonstraretur nobis quanti nos penderet deus quantumque diligeret?"

53. In the *De Trinitate* see 4.15.20 (especially lines 1-3, 10-17: "Sunt autem quidam qui se putant ad contemplandum deum et inhaerendum deo virtute propria posse purgari, quos ipsa superbia maxime maculat. . . . Hinc enim sibi purgationem isti virtute propria pollicentur quia nonnulli eorum potuerunt aciem mentis ultra omnem creaturam transmittere et lucem incommutabilis veritatis quantulacumque ex parte contingere, quod christianos multos [as opposed to the "few"] ex fide interim sola viventes nondum potuisse derident. Sed quid prodest superbienti et ob hoc erubescenti lignum conscendere [the only "ascent" which works] de longinquo prospicere patriam transmarinam?" Also see *De trinitate* 13.19.24.32-55 ("sine mediatore, id est sine homine Christo philosophati sunt," lines 40-41, cf. 14.19.26.64-68, where Books 4 and 13 are mentioned).

54. "Si ergo quaesitus inveniri potest, cur dictum est: *Quaerite faciem eius semper* (Ps. 104.4)? An et inventus forte quaerendus est? Sic enim sunt incomprehensibilia requirenda ne se existimet nihil invenisse qui quam sit incomprehensibile quod quaerebat potuerit invenire. . . . Fides quaerit, intellectus invenit; propter quod ait propheta: *Nisi credideritis, non intellegetis* (Is. 7.9). Et rursus intellectus eum quem invenit adhuc quaerit . . . . Ad hoc ergo debet esse homo intellegens ut requirat deum" (*De trinitate* 15.2.2.13-17, 27-29, 31-32).

55. Augustine directs the reader of the *Retractationes* specifically to the *De trinitate* for a correction of views expressed in the earlier dialogue literature (the *Soliloquia*, at *Retractationes* 1.4.4, cf. the comments on the *De animae quantitate*, *Retractationes* 1.7.2). The *De trinitate* is the only work mentioned by name as actually correcting

earlier books (of those written up to the time of his priesthood). Also, Augustine returns to his earliest practice of using Cicero's *Hortensius* to set his own agenda. The opening gambit of the *Hortensius* sets the agenda of Book 13 in much the same way it also set the agenda for the *De beata vita* (see above, n. 22), as though Augustine were almost rewriting or reissuing that treatise but from a new perspective. For if it is true that *beate vivere omnes homines velle* (*De trinitate* 13.4.7.24-25, 29-30, 35-36, 42-43, with the source actually cited at lines 33-34; 5.8.6, with long citations and attribution at 9-16; etc.), the question becomes what *is* the happy life? The ultimate conclusion is the same – contemplation of the Trinity ("Iam ergo in ipsis rebus aeternis, incorporalibus et immutabilibus in quarum perfecta contemplatione nobis beata quae non nisi aeterna est vita promittitur trinitatem quae deus est . . . " [*De trinitate* 15.4.6.1-4]; on the Trinitarian implications of the *De beata vita*, which ends with a citation of the Ambrosian verse, "Fove precantes Trinitas," see Du Roy, 149-171). But unlike the *De beata vita*, Book 13 argues that inquiry into the happy life requires not simply an exhortation to philosophy but a discussion of a very unphilosophical topic, the blood of Christ, as the only liberation of human beings from "unhappiness" (*De trinitate* 13.10.13.2). Faith (*De trinitate* 13.20.25) is the beginning of the reformation of the image of God in charity (see 13.20.26.64-74, where the mind ["animus"], memory and will, is formed by faith in the blood of the mediator and by *the sort of life* [lines 71-71] which results). This sets the stage for the discussion of renewal in Book 14, which continues to refer to the *Hortensius* and which ends by citing the end of the *Hortensius* (*De trinitate* 14.19.26.31-45), but qualifying its exhortation to philosophy: "Sed iste cursus qui constituitur in amore atque ivestigatione veritatis non sufficit miseris, id est omnibus cum ista sola ratione mortalibus sine fide mediatoris, quod in libris superioribus huius operis, maxime in quarto et tertio decimo quantum potui demonstrare curavi" (*De trinitate* 14.19.26.64-68). One could think of Books 13 and 14 – a discussion whose beginning and end coincides with the beginning and end of the textbook Augustine used at Cassiciacum – as a revision of that textbook and of the works which drew their inspiration from its use.

56. In many cases what the "few" of the letters and the homilies from the period of the composition of the *De Trinitate* finally learn is the impossibility of seeing God apart from faith and the works of charity. In the *Tractates on John* the distinction between the few and the many, the milk-fed and those capable of solid food, tends to be sublated by the mere fact that Augustine addresses the same homilies to both, and also by Augustine's tendency to collapse both into an inclusive "we" (see e.g. *Tractatus* 21.1; 22.1), none of whom can be saved apart from faith in the Incarnation and Passion (*Tractatus* 2.3-4). What purifies the eye is not introspection but the works of mercy; love of neighbor is the way in which God may be seen (*Tractatus* 17.8, 18.11). In the letter to Dardanus "On the Presence of God" (417), there is a progressive erosion of the idea of the philosophical few. God's metaphysical presence is "everywhere whole" ("ubique totus"), and awareness of it as such would be restricted to the few who can

think "incorporeally" (see e.g. *Epistolae* 187.1.2, p. 83.4-5; 187.4.11, p. 90.2-15; 187.6.18, p. 96.4-5; note the implications for Trinitarian speculation carefully laid out at *Epistole* 187.4.15). But, under the increasing exigencies of the polemic against Pelagius (see *Retractations* 2.75), this presence is in the course of the letter distinguished from God's "indwelling" by grace (see e.g. *Epistolae* 187.5.16, p. 93.18-19; p. 94.6-7: "Verum illud est multo mirabilis, quod, cum deus ubique sit totus, non tamen in omnibus habitat. . . . unde fatendum est ubique esse deum per divinitatis praesentiam sed non ubique per habitationis gratiam"; cf. *Epistolae* 187.5.17, p. 94.19-20 and 187.13.58, p. 116.4-8). But if the philosophical few and those in whom God dwells by grace are not coincident groups (see *Epistolae* 187.9.29), this hugely qualifies any efforts to know God through philosophical introspection and greatly relativizes claims to know God from God's (mere) metaphysical presence. Finally, and this is the most exhaustive qualification, it is only Christ in whom the *fulness of Godhead dwells bodily* (Col. 2.9, *Epistolae* 187.13.39, p. 116.9-10), and this is a grace different from and greater than that of any of the saints *quantalibet sapientia et sanctitate praestantibus* (*Epistolae* 13.40, p. 117.16), i.e. no matter how exclusive a group you choose to select, no matter what the criterion. The *few* have shrunk down to *One*, and it is only by being joined to his Body that anyone has any claim on God's indwelling presence. This means that when we think of God's presence, we are, as usual, not to think of masses and extension (*Epistolae* 187.13.41), but now the substance of our vision, its content, and the direction of our gaze is outward, at the unity and charity of the Body of Christ ("Deus caritas est, cum vero eius habitationem cogitas, unitatem cogita congregationemque sanctorum . . . " [*Epistolae* 187.13.41, p. 118.9-11]) and our knowledge of God, while not a matter of images or extension (c. 11, c. 40) is our growth in charity (*Episotlae* 187.13.40). Paulina, too, discovers that seeing God will mean ascending from corporeal images, but that this ascent is accomplished not by introspection but in the renewal of the image of God in acts of charity (*Epistolae* 147.43; Augustine makes sure that the passage he cites from Ambrose is not understood as meaning that we have any knowledge now apart from faith [*Epistolae* 147.35] — whether or not Ambrose did mean that is another, and very interesting, question). One could think of the beginning of this process of sublating the "few" as extending back to Augustine's inclusion of his mother — a most unphilosophical figure — in the philosophical discussions of Cassiciacum (see especially *De ordine* 1.11.31-33, where Augustine includes Monica as one of the few in whom "philosophy" is advanced even to the point of the fearlessness of death, while at the same time he has to explain to her what the word means).

57. Zum Brunn, 116.

58. See, e.g., *De trinitate* 13.20.25.

Revue des Études Augustiniennes, 40 (1994), 375-388

Augustine on magic :
A neglected semiotic theory

I. — INTRODUCTION

Historians should take heed of the anthropologist's warning : « To try to understand magic as an idea in itself, what is the essence of it, as it were, is a hopeless task. It becomes more intelligible when it is viewed not only in relation to empirical activities but also in relation to other beliefs, as part of a system of thought...[1] » Especially in the case of magic in Antiquity : for as A.D. Nock once remarked, « In [the modern] sense it [magic] means the attempt to divert the course of nature by methods which to our science appear to be of a non-rational kind, or which to the user appear to rest on some peculiar wisdom : the charming of warts we call magic, birth-control we do not. We distinguish it from science which proceeds by rational methods, and from religion which if it seems to influence the course of events does so by asking some superior being or beings to do what is needed either by operating directly by some kind of sympathetic action or again compelling the superior being or beings. » But, Nock insisted, this modern use of ' magic ' « does not fit the ancient world... There is not, then, as with us, a sphere of magic in contrast to the sphere of religion[2] ».

It may be that ' magic ' occupied a different place in antiquity on the map of human activities than it does in modern times, especially in relation to ancient science — at least on the comparatively rare occasions when ancient science emerges into clarity from the mists of magic, as, for instance in the case of Hippocrates[3] — and to ancient religion. Modern anthropological discussions have made such exercises in mapping very hazardous. The sharp distinction that used to be drawn between religion and magic has become increasingly untenable ; the two must be located on a continuous scale. The distinction between magic and religion has generally come to be seen not in terms of two different forms of

---

1. E.P. EVANS-PRITCHARD, *Theories of primitive religion* (Oxford, 1965), 111.

2. A.D. NOCK, « Paul and the magus », *Essays on religion and the ancient world*, 1 (Cambridge, Mass., 1972), 308-30, at 313-4. Nock refers (215 n. 32) to F. Pfister's ' admirable article ' in *RE* Supp. iv. 323 ff. in this connection. Cf. also his n. 43.

3. *Ibid.*, 317.

activity, or two different kinds of relation to the supernatural, but rather as the distinction between socially approved and socially disapproved, deviant, forms of ritual behaviour. Magical activity takes place within the framework of a particular religious tradition, and is, so to speak, parasitic upon it, lives within it as its matrix[4].

I shall be attempting to describe not ancient magic itself, but something much simpler, and also much rarer in antiquity : some of the attempts made by some ancient thinkers to understand the magic current in their own society. It will cause us no surprise that the ancients did not generally consider magic in the manner that sophisticated twentieth century anthropologists would prefer ; but we must put up with that.

As a working definition we may start with one given in a recent discussion of early medieval magic : « Magic may be said to be the exercise of preternatural control over nature by human beings, with the assistance of forces more powerful than they[5] ». This, while it begs many questions, also has the corresponding virtue of leaving many of those important for us open, and of admitting a large variety of practices under the heading of ' magic '.

The practice of magic was ubiquitous in Antiquity ; theorising about it was rare. The only sophisticated attempt at a theory I know of is Augustine's ; but to place it in some sort of intellectual context, we must start with teasing out some scraps of theory from other Late Antique writers. It is a meagre harvest ; but, broadly, in so far as any ' theory ' can be identified, we can discern two main directions of thought. They correspond roughly to two ways many modern interpretations of magic have attempted to explain magical rites. These explanations are open to many objections, but, for all that, these are the lines followed, by and large, by ancient theory.

The first sees magic as dependent on a cosmology of world-harmony, or universal sympathy : you do something here, and as a consequence something happens there. To quote from the biginning of Plotinus's exposition of the subject :

---

4. For a survey of approaches by anthropologists, see M. & R. WAX, « The notion of magic », *Current anthropology* 4 (1963) 495-518, with the comments and reply in the ' CA treatment ', 503-17. For their application to ancient magic, see D.E. AUNE, « Magic in early Christianity », *ANRW* II.23.2 (1980) 1507-1557. For more general discussions see : S.J. TAMBIAH, « Form and meaning of magical acts : a point of view », in R. HORTON, & R. FINNEGAN, edd., *Modes of thought* (London 1973), 199-229 ; 199 : « ...magical acts are ritual acts, and ritual acts are in turn performative acts whose positive and creative meaning is missed and whose persuasive validity is misjudged if they are subjected to that kind of empirical verification associated with scientific activity », and p. 218-227 on their non-scientific, ritual, character. *Id.*, *Magic science, religion and the scope of morality* (The Lewis Henry Morgan Lectures, 1984. Cambridge, 1989) contains a wide-ranging discussion of the concepts and their history in anthropological thought. On their application in the study of Antiquity, see G.E.R. LLOYD, *Magic, reason, experience* (Cambridge, 1979).

5. V.I.J. FLINT, *The rise of magic in early medieval Europe* (Oxford, 1991), 3. Cf my review of the book in *EHR* (1992) 378-80.

But how does magic (*goeteia*) work ? By sympathy and by the fact that there is a natural concord of things that are alike and opposition of things that are different...[6]

To leave it at this is, no doubt, to oversimplify the thought of one of the greatest thinkers of Late Antiquity ; but it will do for our present purpose, which is to point to a general direction, not to give an account of his subtle and complex cosmology. The efficacy of magical rituals depends, on such a view, on natural forces. The laws governing these connections may be unknown to most of us, may be hidden even from the magician ; but it is in virtue of organic, natural, relationships, the rational harmony built into the cosmos − the *carmen uniuersitatis* as Augustine would call it[7] − that magic works. Ancients were no less ready than we are to discriminate between genuine and charlatan claims to the expertise which enables the nexus of things to be exploited by various techniques. Magic is in effect a branch of physics. In our modern terms such a theory would translate into a theory of magic as false science[8].

The second view considered magic as dependent on collaboration with demons : forming a community with them, so that whatever happens is a consequence of demonic power brought to the aid of the magician. Religion and magic belong together as against « scientific » manipulations of phenomena. They are distinguished on other grounds : most fundamentally according to whether they are generally approved (for whatever reasons) or disapproved. We might, for convenience, designate this distinction a « sociological » one. Just how magic is related to religion in this view is a question that will receive different answers according to what the religion concerned is. Generally we can perceive a strong tendency to treat magic as a parody or perversion of true religion. This second notion seems to have been more commonly held, though it is often found in combination with the first.

These two ways of thinking of magical activity did not generally have to be distinguished in Antiquity, and it was easy to hold them side by side. There was no pressure on non-Christians to distinguish the exercise of a scientific *techne* from recourse to the help of higher powers ; both were quite legitimate activities. But in a Christian perspective this ambiguity had to be banished ; for if a magical rite was not a case of exercising the art of medicine, or some other natural *techne*, then it must be a religious, though false, and therefore blasphemous, ritual. If magic is demonic and the demonic is wicked, idolatrous or godless, then there is a new and urgent need to distinguish between scientific activity and religious ritual. (Origen may stand for Christian thinkers in general in drawing so sharp a contrast between magic and true religion, leaving a separate, neutral, area to be occupied by human techniques based on the natural sciences[9].) The sharp distinction

6. Plotinus, *Enn.* IV.4.40 (trans. A.H. Armstrong). The discussion extends to 4.44.

7. *De musica* VI.11.29.

8. For a widely known example of treating magic among medical (and pseudo-medical) ' remedies ', see Pliny *HN* XXXVIII and XXX.1.

9. In *C. Cels.* VIII.61 Origen commends the medical arts and prayer to God for healing bodily infirmity as better than the ministrations of demons. Christian thinkers were not always equally clear on this subject.

between magic and science is a result of Christian pressure on a range of activities which could often remain undifferentiated. In a Christian perspective, if a rite was neither the exercise of a human *ars*, nor the performance of an approved rite of Christian worship, then it was necessarily demonic magic. Augustine's views on astrology (closely related to those on magic and divination) provide a good example of this manner of driving a wedge between what we might describe as ' scientific ' and as ' superstitious ' predictions[10]. As *artes*, that of the *mathematicus* and that of *diuinatio*, are now radically distinguished, even though the terminology remained fluid.

Christians shared with almost all their contemporaries in Antiquity a sense of living in a world surrounded by invisible powers[11]. These powers could be benevolent or malevolent ; the important point for us is that they were *there*. For Plato they were intermediaries between men and the gods (e.g. *Sympos.* 202E-203A ; for comment, see Augustine *De ciuitate Dei* VIII. 18). In Christian eyes the gods, and any power that allowed men to communicate with them, were sinister powers of evil. The *daimon* and the gods were subsumed within the class of demons ; and they became « demonic ». It is in this perspective they saw all pagan magical, divinatory, and similar rites. Thus Firmicus Maternus, for instance, caricatured the non-Christian rites of the fourth century as counterfeits of the true Christian rites[12]. Conversely, the pagan Celsus was very ready to believe that Christians got their powers from the demons[13]. Origen, in his reply to Celsus, consistently attributes the power of magical rites to demons, and contrasts their wickedness with the goodness of God[14].

II. — AUGUSTINE'S ' THEORY ' OF MAGIC

Augustine's theory of magic is cast, as one would expect, within the context of the cosmology he shared with Late Antique people at large. The structure of his spiritual universe was, in effect, not very different from, to take a particularly fine example, Porphyry's[15]. Porphyry's world contains good and bad demons within

---

10. Cf. the fine study by B. BRUNING, « De l'astrologie à la grâce » in *Collectanea Augustiniana : Mélanges T. J. Van Bavel*, t. 2 (Roma, 1991) 575-643. Augustine's fullest discussion of the distinction is in *De doctr. chr.* II.20.30-21.32. Cf. also *De diu. daem.* 1.2, 6.10 ; *De ciu. Dei* V.9.

11. N. BROX, ' Magie und Aberglaube an den Anfängen des Christentums ', *Trierer theol. Zeits.* 83 (1974) 157-180 contains a useful survey ; 172-9 on Augustine.

12. Cf. *De errore prof. rel.* 18-27.

13. *Apud* Origen, *C. Cels.* I.6.

14. See especially *C. Cels.* I.60 ; II.51 ; VII.69 ; VIII.36 (on angels and demons) ; 59-60. Cf. Lactantius, *Div. Inst.* II.15-17.

15. Porphyre, *De l'abstinence*, ed. & trad. J. BOUFFARTIGUE & M. PATILLON. (Paris, Les Belles Lettres, 1977-79). References in this paragraph (in brackets) are given to this edition,

a monotheistic universe (II.37 ; 103-4) ; the good demons rule over both natural processes and human souls and their activities when engaged in their proper *technai*, notably the liberal arts, education, music, gymnastics, medicine (II.38.2 ; 104). The bad demons delude, master and collude with wicked, turbulent and rebellious human beings (II.40 ; 106-7). They hate and seek to harm the human race. Good demons communicate with the human race through significant action (*semaino-mena*) such as dreams, inspired words or other means ; bad ones through sorcery (*goeteia*) (II.41 ; 108). This cosmology and its attendant concept of magic has very close affinities with Augustine's.

Some of the fundamental ideas that came to dominate Augustine's views on magic appear in his earliest formal discussion of this subject in the context of a question about the efficacy of magical rites performed by Pharaoh's magicians and the way they differ from the wonders performed by ' God's servants '. A somewhat muddled discussion begins with a distinction which seems oddly remote, but is in fact crucial to all his reflection on this theme : the ' private ' and the ' public ' laws which govern individual action. The spirits which govern every agent in the visible world do so in accordance with both private and public law ; piety subjects the private to the public, obeying the latter willingly, for ' the universal law is divine wisdom '. The more any agent turns aside from God to his private good, the more he is turned in upon himself and subjected to ' those powers which desire their own private good, to be honoured by men like gods. ' To these powers divine law often concedes, through a private law (*priuato illo iure*), the ability to assist those who are subjected to them with a certain power akin to the miraculous (*miraculorum aliquid*) ; but where divine law rules as a public law, it overcomes private licence. Magicians, thus, work private quasi-miracles for selfish ends ; whereas visible ' miracles ' are wrought by God's servants when it is deemed — by God, presumably — useful for them to have this power ; and it is wielded in accordance with that ' public and imperial law ' which governs the universe, « that is to say, they command the lower powers according to God's supreme power... In them God Himself commands, for they are His temples, and they burn with love of Him, despising their own private power[16]. » The opposition between ' public ' and ' private ', a doublet which was to remain fundamental in much of Augustine's thought[17], is the key to the distinction between magicians' wonders and miracles

---

Book II, chapter and page number in vol. 2. I wish to thank Hilary Armstrong for drawing my attention to this text.

16. *De diu. quaest. LXXXIII* 79.1. The work consists of notes taken on discussions held by Augustine with his *fratres* prior to his episcopal ordination, collected into a book — *Retract.* I.26. I see no good grounds for denying the authenticity of this question. For a later treatment of this theme, see *De Trin.* III.7.12.

17. On the fundamental opposition in Augustine's mind between *commune* and *priuatum*, the key text is *Enarr. in Ps.* 103.ii.11. Lying here emerges as the archetypal ' private ' utterance. See also : *De Trin.* X.5.7 ; XII.9.14 ; *De Gen. c. Man.* II.16.24 ; *Ep.* 140.26.63 ; *De cons. euang.* I.19.27. The relevance of the concept to Augustine's views on astrology has been noted by Bruning (*art. cit.*, above, 10), 620. The centrality of the notion of the ' private ' to much of Augustine's thought still needs a thorough study. See, however, my remarks in *Saeculum.*

of the saints : the former mobilise the powers they control (through secret pacts, Augustine suspects) for their own, selfish and partial ends ; the latter mobilise powers subject to God for disinterested, ' public ', ends, in line with God's universal purposes.

So the things done by magicians and by saints are often alike ; but in fact they are done ' for different ends and by different rights ' (*diuerso fine et diuerso iure*) : « for the magicians do them seeking their own glory, the saints seeking God's glory ; the former carry them out... as private transactions or sorceries (*quasi priuata commercia uel ueneficia*) ; the latter as public ministry (*publica administratione*) in obedience to Him to whom all creatures are subject... Hence it is one thing when magicians perform wonders, another when good Christians... perform them : magicians do it through private contracts [with the evil powers], good Christians through public righteousness...[18] » This « sociological » way of contrasting magic and religion in terms of their ' private ' or ' public ' character, with reference to a moral community, has distinctly Durkheimian overtones[19]. It is, moreover, very much in line with the criteria invoked by Late Roman writers and legislators to distinguish magic from religion[20].

The essential ground for the distinction between miracles worked by saints and those worked by magicians seems to be the end for which they are respectively performed, God's glory and the public good, *versus* their own, selfish and private ends. There appears to be a subordinate distinction between the powers respectively invoked by magicians and saints : the former's accomplices obey them in virtue of a prior pact of association ; the latter invoke divine power or its agencies. Though of crucial importance to Christian preachers[21], for our purpose this

---

History and society in the theology of Saint Augustine, 2nd ed. (Cambridge, 1988), pp. xvii-xviii and 60 ; and in *The end of ancient Christianity*, (Cambridge, 1990), pp. 77-79. See also my « *De ciuitate dei* : Pride and the common good », *Proceedings of the PMR Conference*, 12-13 (1989) 1-16 ; also in : *Collectanea Augustiniana : Augustine : « Second Founder of the Faith »*, ed. J.C. SCHNABELT & F. VAN FLETEREN (New York & c., 1990) 245-59.

18. *De div. quaest. LXXXIII*, 79.4 (reading *ueneficia*, not with some MSS, *beneficia*).

19. See E. DURKHEIM, *Elementary forms of the religious life* (N.Y., 1965) 57-63, who refers (n. 62) to Robertson Smith in this connection ; and on Durkheim, see AUNE, « Magic in early Christianity », (above, n. 4), at 1514-1515. Aune here suggests that « The sociological description of the nature and function of magic in relation to religion... appears to be the most satisfying theoretical perspective from which to analyze magic in Graeco-Roman religions », and gives references (n. 27) to « some significant studies of social deviance ». J. GOODY, « Religion and ritual : the definitional problem », *Br. J. of Sociol.* 12 (1961) 142-64, who criticises (145) Durkheim's « sacred/profane » dichotomy as not universally applicable. Cf. M. DOUGLAS, *Purity and danger* (London 1966), 22, 58-72.

20. See NOCK, *op. cit.* (above, n. 2), 315-318. « What gets the name of magic is a varied complex of things, mainly *qua* professional or *qua* criminal in intent or *qua* alien » (317-18). Nock refers (p. 316) as an important ilustration to Constantine's law, *C.Th.* IX.16.3.

21. For instance to John Chrysostom : see A.A. BARB, « The survival of the magic arts », in *The Conflict between paganism and Christianity in the fourth century*, ed. A. MOMIGLIANO (Oxford, 1963), 100-125, at 106.

difference may be ignored, for both give magic a semiotic explanation : it is the result of communication and shared meanings. In neither case is the efficacy of the act direct, mobilising a natural force, like manipulating a mechanism, pulling a lever ; rather, it is mediated by spiritual beings, involving wills and intelligence. Augustine's explanation of magical (including miraculous) efficacy follows in the track of the second of the ancient traditions distinguished above (see p. 2f.) — the explanation in terms of mobilising demonic powers rather than in terms of cosmic « sympathy ». Religion, in the words of a recent study, is ' magic made respectable '[22] ; magic belongs, phenomenologically, to the same realm of action as sacraments[23]. Both, for Augustine, were systems of communication : for ' human beings cannot share a religion, whether true or false, without being associated within it by means of some shared system of symbols or visible rituals [*nisi aliquo signaculorum vel sacramentorum visibilium consortio colligentur*][24]. His account of magic would allow us easily to understand the more or less permanent state of competition between what in any particular society is recognised as ' religion ' and as ' magic'.

His fullest discussion, in the *De doctrina christiana*, is entirely in line with this. The work was the outcome of Augustine's preoccupation with the problems of learning, teaching, and, at the most fundamental level, of communication. This preoccupation set the context for his fullest and richest account of magic. Here the germs of the explanation given in the early work are filled out within the framework of a fully fledged theory of signs[25]. Augustine devotes several chapters (II.20.30-24.37) to idolatrous, magical, divinatory, or astrological practices which he groups together under the heading of ' superstitions '. The class comprises practices (*quicquid institutum est ab hominibus*) that pertain to the making and worshipping of idols, or to the worship of creatures, or parts of creatures, as divine ; also ' consultations and pacts about certain meanings agreed with demons by contract, such as the undertakings (*molimina*) of the magical arts'. Haruspication, augury, amulets and charms ' also condemned by medical science ', ligatures and ' thousands of vacuous observances ', Augustine tells us, all belong here (II.20.30-31).

Book II of this work explores the question of how communities are constituted by the way they understand and use the symbolic systems (i.e. all that Augustine includes under his category of *signa data*) established within them. Any human group is defined by the boundaries of the system of signs in use among its members. On Augustine's theory signs mean something to somebody ; the somebodies who agree on their meaning constitute a (linguistic) community. In

---

22. FLINT (see above, n. 5), 32.

23. See the remarks of Mary DOUGLAS, *Natural symbols* (London, 1970), 8, and below, Section 3.

24. See below, n. 27.

25. On this see my paper « Signs, communication and communities in Augustine's *De doctrina chritiana* », forthcoming in Proceedings of Notre Dame symposium on the *De doctrina christiana*, where, however, I did not consider magic.

the *De doctrina christiana* Augustine makes use of his general semiological theory to explore the relationships of groups sharing a culture, or of sub-cultures within a society.

Superstitious practices link demons and human beings into an association created by a ' pact ' or an ' agreement '. Magical and other ' superstitious ' practices rest on ' pacts about certain meanings agreed with demons by contract ' (*pacta quaedam significationum cum daemonibus placita atque foederata* — II.20.30). The idea of such agreements is at first sight puzzling : magicians and soothsayers do not obviously make agreements with demons and then go on to use the conventions agreed on. But Augustine insists on this ' pact ' repeatedly, in language of almost legal precision[26]. He leaves us in no doubt that he thought of the agreed symbolic system as the bond of association : ' these arts of idle and noxious superstition [are] constituted by a certain association through faithless and deceitful friendship' (*pacta infidelis et dolosae amicitiae* — II.23.36) ; ' they [omens, auguries etc.] are valid only to the extent that they have been established by presumptuous minds as a common language agreed with demons' (*tantum ualent, quantum praesumptione animorum quasi communi quadam lingua cum daemonibus foederata sunt* — II.24.37). Like words,

all these meanings are understood according to the conventions of the society, and, as these conventions differ, are understood differently ; nor are they agreed upon among men because they already had a meaning, but they receive their meaning from the agreement' (*hae omnes significationes pro suae cuiusque societatis consensione animos mouent et, quia diuersa consensio est, diuerse mouent, nec ideo consenserunt in eas homines, quia iam ualebant ad significationem, sed ideo ualent quia consenserunt in eas* — II.24.37).

Leaving aside, for the moment, the puzzle about the status and origin of this pact of association between men and demons, what Augustine's account makes wholly clear is that magic and the like are symbolic systems, a language of words, signs and rituals, which, in the first place, secure the association of men and demons ; and, in doing so, establish the cohesion of the group on which the magical efficacy of its rites rests. ' Men cannot be brought together ', Augustine wrote soon after working out his views on symbolic communities in the *De doctrina christiana,* ' in the name of any religion, whether true or false, without being associated by means of some shared visible symbols or rituals '[27].

Turning, now, to the puzzling ' pact ' by which wicked men associate with demons, it is not immediately clear how Augustine wishes us to construe this. It was clear to Augustine that if the meanings of expressions are ' conventional ' in the sense that their links with their referents are not fixed by nature, they are,

---

26. *De doctrina christiana* II.20 30 ; 22.34 ; 23.36 ; 24.37 ; 25.38 ; 39.58. The same notion is adumbrated in *De diu. quaest. LXXXIII* 79.1 (cf. above, n. 16), and used regularly by Augustine.

27. *In nullum autem nomen religionis, se uerum seu falsum, coagulari homines possunt, nisi aliquo signaculorum uel sacramentorum uisibilium consortio colligentur.* (*C. Faust.* XIX.11).

nevertheless, not freely chosen by the language-user, but imposed by the conventions of the existing linguistic community, its habits and traditions[28]. You do not *choose* to use the language of demons, thereby entering a community with them ; rather, you belong to their community, so you speak their language. The primary fact is the belonging ; by belonging, one comes to share the language that constitutes this community of human and demonic beings. A clue to how he is thinking of the establishment of such conventions can be found in his earlier discussion of magic (see above, n. 16) in *De diu. quaest. LXXXIII* 79.1. There Augustine envisages a community brought into being through evil men, seeking their own, selfish and ' private ' ends, being assisted by demonic powers similarly intent or their own, ' private ', glorification. The community sharing a symbolic system is brought into being by the identity of intentions. It must be the intention to enter such an association that lies at the roots of the conventions which hold it together. It is as if a person entered the ' contract ' with the demons in the very movement of his will towards the demons with whom he associates himself.

There is much in the *De doctrina christiana* to confirm this crucial role assigned to intention. Intention, for instance, is decisive in determining the meaning to be given to certain polysemic symbols. Augustine notes that there are practices which can be ambiguous : hanging certain objects on one's body, for instance, or taking certain foods or drinks, might be either sinister acts of superstition, or sensible medication (II.20.30 ; cf. 29.45). Augustine seems to treat such signs as capable of belonging to two different sign systems : either to a language resting on demonic convention, or to something different, resting, harmlessly, on human contrivance. Which of the two symbol systems the particular rite belongs to is determined by the agent's intention. Augustine's explanation differs from, for instance Porphyry's, (see above, n. 15) mainly by assigning the initiative in magical transactions to the human rather than the demonic partners.

Crucial for Augustine's view of magic is this anchorage of sign systems in intentionality. Meaning is bound up with will. This colours all he has to say about them in the *De doctrina christiana*[29]. From the start of the work the will is central : ' We are on a road, one which is a road not from place to place, but a road of the affections ' (I.17.16 ; cf. I.36.41). So communication between sentient beings

---

28. Cf. Augustine, *Conf.* I.18.29 : *Vide, domine Deus, et patienter, ut vides, vide quomodo diligenter observent filli hominum pacta litterarum et syllabarum accepta a prioribus locutoribus...* ; Cf. F. DE SAUSSURE, *Cours de linguistique générale*, publiée par C. BALLY, A. SCHEHAYE & A. RIEDLINGER, 3rd. ed. (Paris, 1967) : « Si par rapport à l'idée qu'il représente, le signifiant apparaît comme librement choisi, en revanche, par rapport à la communauté linguistique qui l'emploie, il n'est pas libre, il est imposé » (p. 104).

29. See on this the contributions to the Notre Dame symposium (forthcoming ; see above, n. 25) by W.S. BABCOK, ' *Caritas* and signification in *De doctrina christiana* 1-3 ', and by D. DAWSON, « Sign theory, allegory and the notions of the soul in the *De doctrina christiana* », to both of which I owe much. See also M. D. JORDAN, « Words and word : Incarnation and signification in Augustine's *De doctrina christiana* », *Augustinian Studies* 11 (1980) 177-96 : « ...an intentional sign is the kind of thing which starts a motion towards what it signifies and, mediately, towards whomever employs it as a sign » (186).

---

involves more than the manipulation of disembodied signs : hearing a voice ' we attend to the motion of the mind ' (*affectionem animi* - II.1.1) ; speech requires us to respond to the speaker's inner disposition, and, similarly, communicating with others by signs we seek to ' make another a participant of our will ' (*uoluntatis nostrae participem* — II.3.4). The speech-act performed overtly in any act of communication ' brings forth ', or ' expresses ', an inner movement of the mind (*quod animo gerimus*; ...*gerit*; ...*quod corde gestamus*; I.13.12 ; II.2.3 ; I.13.12)[30]. It seems that it is this affective element, the presence of will within acts of communication, that Augustine's ' pact ' with demonic powers ultimately rests on. Some speech-acts, he seems to be saying, are demonic from their inception in virtue of the direction of the speaker's ' affections '. Their significance unfolds within a community created by the selfish, ' private ', purposes. The superstitious rites of magic and similar ' demonic ' observances thus pertain « to a [system of signs] not divinely instituted for the sake of the love of God and the neighbour, as it were publicly, but they dissipate the hearts of the wretched through the private desire of temporal things » (II.23.36). This society of men and demons being « constituted, as it were, by a pact of faithless and deceitful friendship » (see above, n. 26) is self-stultifying in that the pattern of signification is constantly subverted within it by the ' spirits who wish to deceive ' manipulating the signs « so that they affect different people in different ways, according to their own thoughts and presumptions » (*ideo diuersis diuerse proueniunt secundum cogitationes et prae-sumptiones suas* — *ibid.*) « Far from joining person to person in genuine sociality, then, such a world-view actually caters to their private desires, reinforces their separate presumptions, and thus tacitly undermines the very social order that it appears to secure[31] ». Magic is the language of a group which parodies and undermines a true social order.

On the lines of Augustine's exposition we should not, then, interpret magic as failed science, or pseudo-science ; it belongs, rather, to the realm of illocutionary or performative acts such as we have in ritual ; « ...magical acts are ritual acts, and ritual acts are in turn performative acts whose positive and creative meaning is missed and whose persuasive validity is misjudged if they are subjected to that kind of empirical verification associated with scientific activity[32] ». It might be pressing anachronism too far to suggest that the illocutionary force of a magical rite is entry into a demonic society, its perlocutionary aim the peformance or occurrence of certain acts, events, or states of affairs ; that, to use J.L. Austin's language, *in* performing a magical rite or uttering an incantation one is entering into such a relationship, and that *by* doing so one intends to bring about something[33]. But something like this would be in line with Augustine's view.

---

30. This has been well brought out by Dawson, (see above, n. 29).

31. Babcock, (n. 29, above).

32. S.J. TAMBIAH, ' Form and meaning of magical acts : a point of view ', in R. HORTON & R. FINNEGAN, edd., *Modes of thought* (London, 1973), 199-229, at 199.

33. Cf. M. HANCHER, « Performative utterance, the Word of God, and the death of the author », *Semeia* 41 (1988) (*Speech act theory and biblical criticism*, ed. H.C. White), 27-40. I owe knowledge of this to the kindness of John Gager.

III. — MAGIC AND COGNATE RITES

In a study[34] of the efficacy of a Jewish ritual Jacob Milgrom concludes that for Judaism « it was inconceivable that any rite was inherently efficacious. In the absence of rational explanation there was, solely and sufficiently, the inscrutable will of God ». The efficacy of the rite rests simply on God's communication with man and man's with God. God can listen to the prayer of his faithful, and He can promise to come to their aid ; but He cannot be coerced by human words or acts. His sovereign freedom and monopoly of power is what distinguishes the miracles wrought by Moses and Aaron from the wonders worked by pagan magicians. Milgrom has traced with great elegance the emergence of Jewish monotheism from its pagan milieu, and characterised in a wonderfully persuasive manner that which distinguishes the one from the other. This can help us to understand Augustine's way of making sense of magic, for it is cast in a similar mould : like Milgrom's monotheistic Jew, Augustine refuses to credit any human ritual act with intrinsic power.

Augustine's theory of magic (if we may, as we surely may, call it a ' theory ') remained remarkably constant throughout his career. From the early discussions with his *fratres* (see above, n. 16) to the polemic in the *City of God* VIII-X his view remains, in substance, unchanged. The only major development it seems to have undergone in the course of his career is its incorporation in a wider theory of signs, communication, and community in the *De doctrina christiana*[35]. This was not devised to provide a framework within which an explanation of magic could be articulated ; but once formulated, it was a powerful theory with wide bearings in a number of disparate areas, and it lurks in the background of Augustine's treatment of a number of themes, including magic[36]. Prayer, sacraments, exorcism, the cult of relics, as well as magical rites, are among the practices on which Augustine's notion of signs might be expected to shed light. He accounts for magic and sacramental ritual in what are essentially the same, semiotic, terms. Both are systems of signs, in use in rival speech communities. One set of signs has validity

---

34. « The paradox of the Red Cow », in *Studies in cultic theology and terminology* (Studies in Judaism in Late Antiquity, 36. Leiden, 1983), 85-93. Quotation from p. 93. See also his « Magic, monotheism and the sin of Moses », in *The Quest for the Kingdom of God : Studies in honor of E. Mendenhall*, ed. H.B. HUFFMON, F.A. SPINA & A.R.W. GREEN (Winona Lake, Indiana, 1983) 251-265. I wish to thank Mary Douglas for bringing these marvellous studies to my attention, as well as for much other generous advice.

35. Also hinted at in the roughly contemporary *De fide et symbolo*, preached at the Council of Carthage, 393.

36. See the studies of C.P. MAYER, especially *Die Zeichen in der geistigen Entwicklung und in der Theologie des jungen Augustinus* (Cassiciacum, 24,1. Würzburg, 1969) ; and *Die Zeichen in der geistigen Entwicklung und in der Theologie Augustinus* : II. Teil : *Die antimanichäische Epoche* (Cassiciacum, 24/2. Würzburg, 1974). For a bibliography, see my paper referred to above, n. 25. The theory clearly underlies the *De diuinatione daemonum*.

in a perverse community of individuals working for their own selfish ends and deceiving each other, the other in a community united in their service of God and the common good.

Augustine's theology of the *ex opere operato* efficacy of sacraments, especially of baptism, even if administered by schismatic or unworthy ministers, has often been held to have encouraged a magical view of sacramental efficacy[37]. It is important, however, to be clear that such *ex opere operato* efficacy did not involve, for Augustine, the direct efficacy of word or rite at the cost of the elision of spiritual (in this case divine) agency. Writing of the eucharist, in one of his most summary passages Augustine observed that « so far as the action of human hands is concerned... it is not consecrated to be so great a sacrament (*sacramentum* : ' mystery ' ?) except by the invisible working of God's Spirit... » (*De Trin.* III.4.10). The alleged ' magicisation ' of the rite is usually held to appear in the fact that the communal dimension of the rite and the element of intentionality in it were by-passed, and its efficacy construed as a direct mechanical transaction, without the mediation of any spiritual agency. The spell came to take the place of prayer and invocation[38]. Meaning has ceased to be, so it is said, something to be understood within a speech-community.

Moreover, this model of magical efficacy is thought to have encouraged wider ripples of imagined or expected control over events : baptism, for instance, came to be expected to bring political (and other) success, bodily as well as spiritual health, and so forth[39]. It was, so it is generally held, only a short step from an *ex opere operato* theology of the sacraments to a wider magical interpretation of ritual action ; and the Reformation, on such a view, will tend to appear as a deliverance from a mechanical ritualism, even from ' magic '[40]. This is too vast a theme to discuss here ; moreover, Augustine's theology of baptism cuts confusingly across the grain of some of his reflection on ritual action. I therefore consider another, and less well known theme as an example.

---

37. For instance, A. ANGENENDT, « Taufe und Politik im frühen Mittelalter », *Frühmittelalterliche Studien* 7 (1973) 143-168, at 147 observes that Augustine's views on the efficacy of baptism « scheint nie vergessen ». For a remarkable study of baptismal theology in terms of the kinds of social context which encourage — or discourage — certain conceptions of ritual efficacy, see J. Patout BURNS, « On Rebaptism : Social Organization in the Third Century », *Journal of early Christian studies* 1 (1993) 367-403. For a somewhat unsatisfactory attempt to exonerate Augustine, see E.G. WELTIN, « The concept of *ex opere operato* efficacy in the Fathers as an evidence of magic in early Christianity', *GRBS* 3 (1960) 74-100.

38. The two often overlap, as S.J. Tambiah observes in « The magical power of words », *Man* n.s. 3 (1968) 175-208.

39. See ANGENENDT, n. 37, above.

40. Cf. DOUGLAS, in *Natural symbols* (see above, n. 23), 10, 47ff. Also, for some of the debate over K. THOMAS, *Religion and the decline of magic* (London, 1971), see H. GEERTZ, « An anthropology of religion and magic, I », *J. of Interdisciplinary history*, 6 (1975) 71-89 and K. THOMAS, « An anthropology of religion and magic, II », *J. of Interdisciplinary history*, 6 (1975) 91-109 (reply to Geertz). On Reformation views, see B. VOGLER, ' La Réforme et le concept de miracle au XVIe siècle ', *Revue d'histoire de la spiritualité* 48 (1972) 145-50.

A revealing case is furnished by the cult of the dead at the tomb, and especially the custom of burial near the tomb of a saint (« *ad sanctos* »), a question Augustine considered with particular care, in his response to that devoted promoter of the cult, Paulinus of Nola. We have been given a careful study of Augustine's view and of contemporary practice as revealed in funerary inscriptions by Mme Yvette Duval[41]. Her conclusions will save us the task of surveying the evidence and analysing Augustine's text. Augustine's answer to Paulinus is stark and simple : the dead cannot expect any benefit from the *place* of their burial, only from the prayers of the living who may visit the place. Place by itself has no efficacy : « what may benefit the spirit of the dead is not the place of its dead body but the affection of a mother kindled by the memory attached to the place » (*ex loci memoria uiuus matris affectus — De cura pro mort. ger.* 6). This belief is frequently attested by funerary inscriptions (and, incidentally, by Gregory the Great, *Dial.* IV.52) which express the hope that the dead might be received among the elect thanks to the prayers of his friends and relatives (as well as his merits). Such an understanding of these burial practices accords well with the thought of Augustine, Gregory, and reflective thinkers and churchmen. But, as Mme Duval has shown, there is also another current of thought to be found among these inscriptions : that the dead body keeps a trace of the spirit it had lived by, which operates through the bodily remains on those in contact with or proximity to it[42]. There is a wide gap between popular belief in the direct magical efficacy of the buried saint's remains and Augustine's determination not to short-circuit prayer and God's providence.

What are we to make of this difference in views, on the one hand as represented by Augustine, on the other, by the many epitaphs, hagiographical stories and images which attest another, and perhaps more widespread notion ?

We are apt, as I have said, to think this way of short-circuiting the symbolic element of ritual action as turning the action into a pseudo-scientific act, and then to interpret such an act — presumably because there is a widely diffused notion among us of magic as ' pseudo-scientific ' — as ' magical ', in contradistinction to ' religious '. Augustine would certainly not have interpreted it in this way. He would have not have seen ' magic ' at work, because the essential element of communication with the demonic world was absent. On the other hand, he might well have admitted that it fell short of the properly ' religious ', for it by-passed the element of communication with the divine. He seems, rather, to have taken it upon himself, in his treatise on *The Care for the dead*, to supply this suppressed element. He appears to have thought that what was lacking in popular piety was the explicit articulation of something which was, nevertheless, present.

The short-circuiting of prayer in the rite could perhaps be understood in terms of Mary Douglas's discussion of ' ritualism '. This attitude she defines as « sensitivity to condensed symbols[43] » ; a sensitivity which will be operative in both sacramental and magical behaviour :

---

41. *Auprès des saints corps et âme. L'inhumation « ad sanctos » dans la chrétienté d'Orient et d'Occident du III* au VII* siècle* (Paris, 1988).

42. DUVAL, *op. cit.*, 211.

43. *Natural symbols* (above, n. 23), 8.

The Bog Irishman in his faithfulness to the rule of Friday abstinence is undeniably like the primitive ritualist. Magical rules have always an expressive function. Whatever other functions they perform, disciplinary, anxiety-reducing, or sanctioning of moral codes, they have first and foremost a symbolic function. The official symbolism of Friday abstinence was originally personal mortification, a small weekly celebration of Good Friday. Thus it pointed directly to Calvary and Redemption[44].

Could we say that burying our dead near the holy burials is a similar piece of ritualism ? Acting as a condensed symbol of the communion of saints enacted whenever one of the living prays at the graveside, and tenaciously adhered to even when the original symbolism is forgotten – just as Friday abstinence continued to be ? If we accept this, then the modern (and discredited) idea that ' magic ' tends to be ' manipulative ' whereas ' religion ' is ' supplicative ' is beside the mark. Popular piety has condensed prayer and ritual into a single act, not fully explicated. Augustine has simply supplied the missing explication.

To sum up : Augustine distinguishes two semiotic structures. One is authentically public, shared by the whole language-using community, and is used by its members to communicate with one another as well as with God ; the other is a ' private ' code, restricted to some members of this community and used only by them, to communicate with demons. Magic is part of this second semiotic system[45].

Robert A. MARKUS
100 Park Road Chilwell, Beeston
G.B. – NOTTINGHAM NG9 4DE

ABSTRACT : The article seeks to study Augustine's theory of magic in the context of ancient magical theory. In the scraps of ancient theory devoted to this theme magic was interpreted either as the result of action within a nexus of occult interrelated causes, or as the result of communication with invisible powers. Augustine's view falls in the second class. He was the only Christian or non-Christian thinker of Antiquity to develop a full theory of magical action ; and he does this in terms of his carefully worked out theory of signs. Magical and sacramental rituals are both acts of communication : the one with demonic, the other with divine powers.

---

44. *Ibid.*, 37. For parallel « learned » interpretations of the healing action of relics, see ROUSSELLE, A., *Croire et guérir : La foi en Gaule dans l'Antiquité tardive* (Paris, 1990) 231-250.

45. Cf. BRUNING (see above, n. 10), 614 : « On pourrait dire qu'[Augustin] aborde la *superstitio* comme un phénomène linguistique ».

Early Christian Martyrdom and Civil Disobedience

EVERETT FERGUSON

The success of non-violent resistance as employed by Gandhi and Martin Luther King for political ends prompts an inquiry concerning possible parallels with early Christian martyrdom. The martyr literature of the early church, in addition to theological motifs, does occasionally take note of practical aspects, such as "church-state" relations. The two elements of civil disobedience identified by David Daube—non-violence and unselfish motivation for the conduct—are present in early Christian martyrdom, but not in an unmixed way. Some early Christians did aim to convert the Roman Empire, and some noted martyrdom as contributing to this, but there is no indication that martyrdom was a conscious strategy to attain this goal.

The tactics of Gandhi in securing independence for India and of Martin Luther King, Jr. in the American civil rights movement have directed attention in the twentieth century to non-violent resistance as an instrument of political policy. An objection to these tactics has been raised on the grounds that the methods of Gandhi in India or of Martin Luther King in the United States would be ineffective against a Nazi Germany or a Communist China. According to this reasoning the moral power of Gandhi and King was in part due to their dealing with governing authorities which were at least nominally Christian and informed by a Christian conscience. This consideration prompts an examination of the experience of the early Christians with the pagan Roman Empire. Although there are differences between early Christian martyrdom (and the whole tradition of "evangelical pacifism") and modern strategies of non-violent confrontation, the query

1992 NAPS Presidential Address. Research for this paper was supported in part by the Research Council of Abilene Christian University through the generosity of the Cullen Foundation.

Journal of Early Christian Studies 1:1, 73–83 © 1993 The Johns Hopkins University Press

whether elements of the modern practice or an awareness of them is found among the early martyrs may cast light on the theme of non-violent resistance to persecution and its effectiveness in attaining toleration or other political goals. George Williams discussed "four modalities of violence" in Christian history: dying for the heavenly homeland, holy violence actualized, sublimation of violence in spiritual warfare, and the conversion of alienation into reconciliation.[1] Early Christian martyrdom falls in the first category: dying for the heavenly homeland.

Early Christian martyrdom has been studied from many standpoints: the meaning of the word,[2] the persecutions by Rome,[3] the concept of martyrdom,[4] its relation to suicide,[5] the theology of martyrdom,[6] as an example of social control,[7] and according to the ethical problems raised.[8] It is proposed here to consider what mutual understanding is gained by examining early Christian martyrdom in relation to modern concerns about civil disobedience. David Daube has defined civil disobedience as involving non-violence and the motivation that the conduct is right and not selfish.[9] He sets a context for our theme but does not himself include the Christian martyrs in his survey.[10] The examination here is limited, with few

1. George Huntston Williams, "Four Modalities of Violence, With Special Reference to the Writings of George Sorel, Parts Two and Three," *JChSt* 16 (1974):252–254.

2. Norbert Brox, *Zeuge und Märtyrer: Untersuchungen zur frühchristlichen Zeugnis-Terminologie* (Munich: Kösel, 1961); B. Dehandschutter, "Martyr-Martyrium: Quelques observations à propos d'un christianisme sémantique," *Eulogia: Mélanges offerts à Antoon A. R. Bastiaensen*, ed. G. J. M. Bartelink et al. (Steenbrugis: Abbatia S. Petri, 1991), 33–39.

3. W. H. C. Frend, *Martyrdom and Persecution in the Early Church* (Oxford: Basil Blackwell, 1965).

4. Hans von Campenhausen, *Die Idee des Martyriums in der alten Kirche* (Göttingen: Vandenhoeck and Ruprecht, 1964).

5. Arthur J. Droge and James D. Tabor, *A Noble Death: Suicide and Martyrdom Among Christians and Jews in Antiquity* (San Francisco: Harper, 1991).

6. Theofrid Baumeister, *Die Anfänge der Theologie des Martyriums* (Münster: Aschendorf, 1980).

7. Donald W. Riddle, *The Martyrs: A Study in Social Control* (Chicago: University of Chicago, 1931); Maureen A. Tilley, "Scripture as an Element of Social Control: Two Martyr Stories of Christian North Africa," *HTR* 83 (1990): 383–397.

8. D. Wendebourg, "Das Martyrium in der Alten Kirche als ethische Problem," *ZKG* 98 (1987): 295–320.

9. David Daube, *Civil Disobedience in Antiquity* (Edinburgh: University Press, 1972), 1–4, 43.

10. Cf. Wendebourg, "Martyrium," pp. 297–303 on the philosophical idea of a "beautiful death." Tertullian, *apol.* 50 and Clement of Alexandria, *str.* 4.8 list pagan examples of endurance of suffering, but Origen claims that although others may have a heroic death, only the "elect race" dies for religion—*mart.* 5.

exceptions, to statements in the early Christian literature of martyrdom— the acts and passions of the martyrs and exhortations to martyrdom. The importance of martyrdom for the early Christians is demonstrated by the way it was interpreted in terms of major theological motifs. Martyrdom was a baptism of blood, which brought forgiveness of sins to the martyr.[11] It was a eucharist, in which one drank the cup of sufferings of Christ.[12] It was an anticipation of the eschaton, an orthodox version of radically realized eschatology, in which the martyr brought the events of the last days to immediate fruition for himself.[13] It was a defeat of Satan and the demons through identification with the victory of Christ on the cross.[14] The martyr was filled with the Holy Spirit, who gave words to say to the authorities, visions of the other world, and supernatural strength to endure sufferings.[15] Martyrdom was an imitation of Christ, in which one shared in the sufferings of Christ and was brought into direct contact with the Lord,[16] and the glory of Christ himself was manifested in the martyr.[17]

The importance of martyrdom was further emphasized by relating it to divine election and providence. Martyrdom was not for everyone. God chose the worthy for martyrdom. Or, as one author put it, he assigned it to some on account of their worth, and to others he gave it on account of his mercy.[18] According to the mainstream teaching, one was not to volunteer for martyrdom. The church had some unfortunate experiences with those who rushed forward to confess their faith and then did not stand up under

11. E. Dassmann, *Sundenvergebung durch Taufe, Busse, und Martyrerfürbitte in den Zeugnissen frühchristlichen Frömmigkeit und Kunst* (Münster: Aschendorf, 1973), 153–171.

12. Joachim Kettel, "Martyrium und Eucharistie," *GeiLeb* 30 (1957): 34–46.

13. Robert Wayne Willis, "A Study of Some Eschatological Motifs in the Martyr Literature of the Early Church" (Thesis, Abilene Christian University, 1966); W. Rordorf, "L'espérance des martyrs chrétiens," *Forma Futuri: Studi in onore del Card. Michele Pellegrino* (Turin, 1975), 445–461.

14. Eusebius, *h.e.* 5.1.23 and 27; *M. Apoll.* 47; *M. Fruct.* 7.2; *M. Agap.* 1. 2. 4; Hermas, *sim.* 8.3.6; Origen, *Mart.* 42; *Cels.* 8.44.

15. M. Viller, "Les Martyrs et l'Esprit," *RSR* 14 (1924): 544–551; William C. Weinrich, *Spirit and Martyrdom: A Study of the Work of the Holy Spirit in Contexts of Persecution and Martyrdom in the New Testament and Early Christian Literature* (Washington: University Press of America, 1981).

16. M. Pellegrino, "L'Imitation du Christ dans les Acts des martyrs," *VS* 98 (1958): 38–54.

17. Denis Farkasfalvy, "Christological Content and its Biblical Basis in the Letter of the Martyrs of Gaul," *SecCent* 9 (1992): 7–12.

18. Ps-Cyprian, *laud. mart.* 23. Note also *M. Polyc.* 14; 20; *M. Carp.* 41; 42; *M. Perp.* 21.11; *M. Cyp.* 2.1; *M. Mar.* 2.3; 3.4; *M. Iren.* 5.2; Clement of Alexandria, *str.* 4.12; Hippolytus, *Dan.* III.26; Cyprian, *mort.* 17.

the pressure.[19] The doctrine that God chose his martyrs tempered enthusiasm for self-chosen martyrdom; it also highlights the self-consciousness of the church about the significance of martyrdom. The emphasis on the will of God is pertinent to some of the less theological aspects of martyrdom to which this paper addresses itself.

Although more attention seems to be given in the early Christian literature about martyrdom to the theological significance of martyrdom, Christians were not unaware of the practical significance of the act. For instance, the missionary motif was noted. Tertullian's declaration that the blood of the martyrs is seed and by their deeds the martyrs make other disciples[20] has become proverbial. Less well known is the claim of Apollonius, "The more they kill those who believe in God, so much the more will their numbers grow by God's aid."[21] Justin Martyr, for one, testified to the influence of the martyrs on his own conversion.[22] The martyrs thus truly lived up to their title as "witnesses." Even when they were not able to speak directly to pagan onlookers, as the sources occasionally note occurring,[23] their deed was a public testimony to unbelievers to the gospel.[24] In a world without television spectaculars and Billy Graham campaigns a place on the program at the month's spectacles in the amphitheater was the best advertising available.[25]

Ignatius may have dwelled on the personal aspects of martyrdom, but others were aware of the community dimensions of the deed.[26] A faithful wideness confirmed others in the faith and prepared them to resist under

---

19. *M. Polyc.* 4. The emphasis on martyrdom "according to the will of God" is directed against a Gnostic denial of martyrdom and not Montanist enthusiasm according to B. Dehandschutter, "Le Martyre de Polycarpe et le développment de la conception du martyre au deuxième siècle," *SP* 17.2 (Oxford: Pergamon, 1982), 659–668. That the early Montanists did not differ from their orthodox opponents on voluntary martyrdom is argued by William Tabbernee, "Early Montanism and Voluntary Martyrdom," *Colloq.* 17 (1985): 33–43.

20. *Apol.* 50; compare Justin, *dial.* 110; Hippolytus, *Dan.* 2.38.

21. *M. Apoll.* 24. References and quotations are taken from Herbert Musurillo, *The Acts of the Christian Martyrs* (Oxford: Clarendon Press, 1972).

22. Justin, *2 apol.* 12.

23. *M. Carp.* 40; Eusebius, *h.e.* 5.2.4 and 5. The author of the *M. Mar.* makes a direct address to pagans at 6.1.

24. *M. Fruct.* 6.3 for death confirming life and teaching. Reactions by pagan onlookers are noted in *M. Polyc.* 2; 16; *M. Carp.* 45; Eusebius, *h.e.* 5.1.56; *M. Perp.* 17.3.

25. A. D. Nock, *Conversion* (Oxford: Clarendon Press, 1933), 193–202; Adolf von Harnack, *The Mission and Expansion of Christianity* (New York: Harper, 1962 reprint), 492–493; Hans von Campenhausen, "Das Martyrium in der Mission," *Kirchengeschichte als Missionsgeschichte*, Vol. 1, ed. H. Frohnes and U. W. Knorr (Munich: Chr. Kaiser, 1974), 71–85.

26. M. Pellegrino, "Le Sense ecclésial du martyre," *RevScRel* 35 (1961): 152–175.

similar pressure.[27] Indeed the annual commemoration of the martyr's "birthday to immortality" served expressly to strengthen and train those who would come after.[28] The compiler of the *Martyrdom of Perpetua and Felicitas* in stating the purpose in writing explains that "God always achieves what he promises, as a witness to the non-believer and a blessing to the faithful."[29]

The doctrine that martyrdom was within God's providence highlights further that martyrdom was a witness to the State of its subordination to the God of heaven. The Acts of the Martyrs delighted in contrasts often formulated in sharp antitheses. These Acts feature the demand made of Christians to sacrifice to the pagan gods, so the contest is seen principally in religious terms.[30] This demand lent itself to a contrast between the worship of the one God and the worship of the many gods. When Pionius, presbyter of Smyrna, during the Decian persecution was ordered, "Offer sacrifice," he replied, "My prayers mut be offered to God." The proconsul insisted, "We reverence all the gods."[31] But for Christians belief in God was reason not to sacrifice.[32] In contrast to the requirement to sacrifice to the gods, the Christian martyrs could interpret their death as a sacrifice to God.[33] Dasius, martyr under Diocletian, said to the soldiers, "Seeing that you force me to such a despicable act, better is it for me to become a sacrifice to the Lord Christ by my own choice rather than immolate myself to your idol Saturn."[34] Or, the confession of faith itself could be understood as a sacrifice to God.[35]

Quite prominent in the martyr and apologetic literature is the identification of the gods to whom sacrifice was required with demons[36] and the

27. M. *Polyc.* 1; 19; Eusebius, *h.e.* 5.1.23, 41–42; M. *Apoll.* 47; M. *Pion.* 22.4; Eusebius, *h.e.* 8.10.11; M. *Mar.* 3.5; 9.2–4; 12.8; Origen, *Cels.* 8.8.

28. M. *Polyc.* 18.

29. M. *Perp.* 1.5. Compare Clement of Alexandria, *str.* 4.9 for the church confirmed and heathen led to faith by the martyr's confession. Other references for strengthening Christians as the purpose of preserving accounts of martyrdom include M. *Mar.* 1.3 and M. *Pion.* 1.

30. M. *Polyc.* 12; *Mart. Scill.* 3–4; Tertullian, *apol.* 10 says that the chief charge against Christians was religious, that is the refusal to sacrifice.

31. M. *Pion.* 19.

32. M. *Agap.* 3.4.

33. R. Jacob, "Le Martyre, épanouissement du sacerdoce des Chrétiens, dans la littérature patristique jusqu' en 258," *MScRel* 24 (1967): 57–83, 153–172, 177–209; E. Ferguson, "Spiritual Sacrifice in Early Christianity and its Environment," *ANRW*, II.23.1 (Berlin: DeGruyter, 1980), 1169–70, 1180, 1186.

34. M. *Das.* 5.2; see also M. *Polyc.* 14; M. *Con.* 6.7; M. *Fel.* 30.

35. M. *Iren.* 2.4.

36. M. *Carp.* 6; M. *Crisp.* 1.7; Justin, *1 apol.* 5; Tertullian, *spect.* 13; Origen, *Cels.* 7.69.

assertion that the demons or the devil were responsible for the persecutions.[37] Hence, to sacrifice to demons was to deny God.[38] It was impossible for Christians "to sacrifice to these demons with their deceptive appearances, for those who sacrifice to them are like them." The gods are dead, and "The living do not offer sacrifice to the dead."[39]

The threat of torture for failure to sacrifice and the promise of rewards for sacrifice set up a quite natural antithesis between temporal and eternal punishments and between present and future rewards. Those who worship God are said to take on his image and become immortal with him, but those who worship the gods take on the image of demons and perish along with them in Gehenna.[40] The *Martyrdom of Polycarp* 2 speaks of those who despised the tortures of this world "buying themselves an exemption from the eternal fire." Christians "despise death because of the faith they have in God."[41] On the other hand, eternal punishment was for the persecutors. "You have condemned us, but God will condemn you."[42] Although reference to punishment of persecutors is more frequent, as might be expected, there is also much said about the reward of perseverance.[43] Perhaps in response to criticism of the readiness for martyrdom, it was said that the martyrs were not "rushing toward death but toward life."[44] It was easy for the keen, rhetorical mind of Tertullian to contrast judgment before the proconsul with judgment before God,[45] but the more pedestrian Carpus of Pergamum too looked to the "judgment seat of truth."[46] Eschatological sanctions are a constant feature of the literature about martyrdom. Of the "four modalities of violence" in Christian history identified by George Williams, the martyrs' threats of eschatological punishments are

37. *M. Carp.* 17; Eusebius, *h.E.* 5.1.5 and 25; *M.Mar.* 2.2 and 5; Justin, *1 apol.* 57; *2 apol.* 1; Tertullian, *fuga* 2; Origen, *Cels.* 8.43. E. Ferguson, *Demonology of the Early Christian World* (New York: Edwin Mellen, 1984), 121–122.
38. *M. Iren.* 2.2.
39. *M. Carp.* 6 and 12.
40. Ibid., 7.
41. *M. Iren.* 4.12; compare *M. Con.* 5.
42. *M. Perp.* 18.8.
43. For threats of punishment: *M. Polyc.* 11; Eusebius, *h.e.* 5.1.26; *M. Pion.* 4.24; 7.4; *M. Iul.* 2.4; *M. Agap.* 5.2; *M. Crisp.* 2.2; Ps-Cyprian, *laud. mart.* 19–20. For rewards of perseverance: *M. Just.* (A) 5; *M. Apollon.* 42; *M. Pion.* 7.5; *M. Fruct.* 3.3; 4.3; 7.2; *M. Mont.* 22.2; Ps-Cyprian, *laud. mart.* 7; 9; 11; 21.
44. *M. Pion.* 20.5 and 21.4; for eternal life as the martyr's reward see also *M. Polyc.* 14; *M. Iul.* 3.4; *M. Das.* 4; Hippolytus, *Dan.* 3.24.
45. *Mart.* 2.
46. *M. Carp.* 40.

expressions of the category of dying for the heavenly homeland, in which violence is eschatologically postponed.[47]

Although the contest was viewed by Christians as between God and idolatry[48] and not between church and state, there were political implications and these are sometime explicitly noted. The sacrifices were "for the welfare of the emperors"[49] or were directed to the gods and the image of the emperor,[50] and the decrees to offer sacrifice came from the emperor.[51] The refusal to "obey the gods and submit to the orders of the emperors"[52] was "to blaspheme the gods and the august emperors."[53] The Christian position, however, was, "A divine decree cannot be quelled by a decree of man."[54] The emperor's command to sacrifice to the gods could not replace God's command to worship him alone.[55] Christians would obey only the edict of Christ.[56] Although the words of Acts 5:29, "We must obey God rather than man," are quoted only once in the Acts of the Martyrs, the description of God in Acts 4:24 as the one "who made heaven and earth and the sea and all that is in them" is frequent and carries the same force in indicating the one who must be obeyed.[57] He is the "Father and king of heaven," to whom the martyr goes at death.[58] God or Christ are often asserted to be king or emperor; in the Acts of the Martyrs this terminology must be in conscious contrast to the earthly ruler.[59] God dispenses kingdoms and sets up kings.[60] Christians claimed for themselves a higher

47. George Huntston Williams, "Four Modalities of Violence, With Special Reference to the Writings of George Sorel: Part One," *JChSt* 16 (1974): 11–30, esp. 15–18.

48. This is clear in Origen, *mart.* and Cyprian, *Dem.* Tertullian, *apol.* 28 considers the political charge secondary to the religious charge (see note 26). Robert M. Grant, "Sacrifices and Oaths as Required of Early Christians," *Kyriakon: Festschrift Johannes Quasten*, ed. P. Granfield and J. A. Jungmann, Vol. 1 (Münster: Aschendorff, 1970), 12–17 points out that the requirement of sacrifices and oaths was secondary to the charge of being a Christian.

49. *M. Perp.* 6.3; *M. Crisp.* 1.

50. *M. Apoll.* 7; *M. Fruct.* 2.6.

51. *M. Carp.* 4; *M. Agap.* 3.4.

52. *M. Just.* (B) 2.1.

53. *M. Carp.* 21.

54. *M. Apoll.* 24.

55. *M. Pion.* 3.2–3; *M. Iul.* 3.3; Origen, *mart.* 34–35; *Cels.* 8.26; 55.

56. *M. Crisp.* 1.6.

57. Musurillo, *Acts*, p. 378. The quotation of Acts 5:29 occurs in *M. Fel.* 15–17. For the use of Acts 4:19 in such a context, see Hippolytus, *Dan.* 3.23.

58. Justin, *2 apol.* 2.

59. *M. Polyc.* 9; 17; Eusebius, *h.e.* 5.1.55; *Mart. Scill.* 6; *M. Con.* 3–4.

60. Tertullian, *apol.* 26; Hippolytus, *Dan.* 3.4; Origen, *Cels.* 8.68.

citizenship.[61] After the author of the *Martyrdom of Polycarp* appended to his formula dating the death of Polycarp the phrase, "while Jesus Christ was reigning eternally,"[62] it became a regular feature of this literature to supplement dates with a reference to the reign or kingship of Christ.[63]

This defiance of imperial decrees made Christians guilty of civil disobedience, or even of treason.[64] Nevertheless, the authorities were not desirous of making martyrs, so the accounts of martyrdom are full of the efforts to dissuade Christians from their defiance.[65] In view of modern ethical discussions, note may be taken that the prefect Maximus made the argument to Julius the Veteran that since a higher authority was forcing him to sacrifice he was not responsible for the act, but Julius rejected the argument.[66] Christians, for their part, insisted that they were taught to respect the authorities.[67] They honored the emperor[68] and prayed for him.[69] As diverse personalities as Tertullian and Origen could argue that the Christians respected the emperor and empire and that Christian prayers were more help than soldiers to the welfare of the empire.[70] By putting the emperor in his proper place, under God and over the gods, Christians commended him to divine favor.[71] Christian teaching trained good citizens.[72]

The Christians' obedience to the emperor was limited by their understanding of the divine law. Thus their refusal to obey the decrees concerning sacrifice corresponds to Daube's requirement that civil disobedience be motivated by a higher conviction of what is right. The absence of selfishness, as it pertains to this world, is also evident. The appeal to conscience is sometimes made explicit. The martyr Agape declared, "I refuse to destroy my conscience."[73] Phileas insisted, "Our conscience with respect to God is prior to all."[74] Religion, therefore, is not a matter of compulsion. In re-

---

61. *M. Just.* (C) 1. The sense of contest is heightened in recension C.
62. *M. Polyc.* 21.
63. *M. Pion.* 23; *M. Marcell.* (N) 5.2; *M. Iren.* 6.
64. *M. Agap.* 5.3.
65. For example, *M. Polyc.* 9–12; *M. Carp.* passim; *M. Perp.* 6; *M. Pion.* 4–5; 12; 20; *M. Con.* 3–4; *M. Agap.* 5.2.
66. *M. Iul.* 2.5–6.
67. *M. Polyc.* 10; compare Origen, *Cels.* 8.65.
68. *M. Apollon.* 6; 9.
69. *M. Cypr.* 1.2.
70. Tertullian, *apol.* 30–33; Origen, *Cels.* 7.73; compare Cyprian, *Dem.* 20 and Hippolytus, *Dan.* 3.24.
71. Tertullian, *apol.* 30; 33–34.
72. Origen, *Cels.* 8.74.
73. *M. Agap.* 3.3.
74. *M. Phil.* col. 9, as restored.

sponse to a proconsul's threat to force respect for the gods, Crispina affirmed, "That piety is worthless which forces persons to be crushed against their will."[75] Thus the Christians claimed "freedom of religion."[76] The theme of freedom of religion was reiterated by the apologists.[77]

The other feature of civil disobedience noted by Daube is its nonviolence. Martyrdom was certainly a violent act by those who caused it, but the disobedience which provoked it was non-violent. It is true that Christians sometimes were guilty of deliberate provocation.[78] But the model which was commended as normative Christian conduct showed a more submissive demeanor in its resistance.[79] Tertullian insisted that Christians had not and would not revolt.[80] A fairly frequent theme in the exhortations to martyrdom and in the apologies is that Christians do not take revenge. This insistence is balanced by the assurance that although Christians do not offer resistance, God will avenge.[81] Christians injure nobody, Tertullian affirms. He countered the charge that Christians hated the human race[82] by saying that they were enemies not of the human race but of human error.[83] In fact, he goes so far as to renounce any form of resistance, even nonviolent.[84] This insistence for some authors took the form of complete pacifism—non-participation in military service and avoidance of political office.[85] In the Acts of the military martyrs the refusal of governmental demands takes the form of a choice between the military and the church.[86] The soldier Marinus was confronted by bishop Theotecnus of Caesarea with a choice of the Gospels or the sword, and he chose the Gospels.[87] The

75. M. Crisp. 2.1.
76. Cyprian, Dem. 14.
77. E. Ferguson, "Voices of Religious Liberty in the Early Church," RestQ 19 (1976): 13–22.
78. As in M. Eupl. 1. See Bernhard Kötting, "Martyrium und Provokation," Kerygma und Logos, ed. A. M. Ritter (Göttingen: Vandenhoeck and Ruprecht, 1979), 329–336.
79. See Clement of Alexandria, str. 4.10 on not provoking martyrdom or persecution.
80. Tertullian, apol. 37.
81. Cyprian, Dem. 17; Tertullian, apol. 37; 41; Origen, Cels. 3.7–8.
82. Tacitus, Ann. 15.44.2–8.
83. Tertullian, apol. 39; 41; 37.
84. Ibid., 37.
85. Michel Spanneut, "La non-violence chez les Pères africains avant Constantin," Kyriakon I:36–39.
86. Texts in translations in J. Helgeland, R. J. Daly, and J. P. Burns, Christians and the Military: The Early Experience (Philadelphia: Fortress, 1985), 56–66; pacifist interpretation by J.-M. Hornus, It Is Not Lawful for Me to Fight: Early Christian Attitudes Toward War, Violence, and the State (Scottdale: Herald, 1980).
87. Eusebius, h.e. 7.15.4.

recruit Maximilian refused military service because he was a Christian: "I will not serve this world, but only my God."[88] The centurion Marcellus renounced military service seemingly because of the pagan religious practices involved, but then he also refused to fight.[89] The soldier Dasius said, "I do not fight for any earthly king but for the king of heaven,"[90] but it is not clear what kind of fighting he meant. The veteran Julius was a Christian for the twenty-seven years of his military service, but he became a martyr under Diocletian on the grounds that a Christian could not obey the laws to sacrifice.[91] By the time of the persecution under Diocletian there were many Christians in the army and in high positions in the government. Some were already there nearly a century earlier when Origen was justifying Christians not taking civil offices because those who were qualified chose to rule the church under the great King and because Christians by their moral influence preserved the order of society.[92] Tertullian had gone further in this direction by affirming that affairs of state were foreign to Christians and they did not aspire to public office.[93] Christians could not be emperors, he indicates, but perhaps because of the idolatrous nature of the office.[94] Such views were a concrete expression of the hatred of the world and separation from the world voiced in the exhortations to martyrdom.[95] Capable of a more positive development was Tertullian's implicit separation of religion and government, anticipating Augustine's *City of God*.[96]

The Acts of the Martyrs and related literature belong to the history of civil disobedience, and perhaps few exercises of non-violent resistance for the sake of higher law have accomplished as much. Daube states that civil disobedience may be in order to put the government on the right path or to bring it down.[97] In spite of the occasional extreme language against Roman authorities, the implicit purpose of the Christian martyrs seems to have been to set the government on the right path. What is missing from the literature of martyrdom is the conviction that massive civil disobedience would in fact change the laws. The apologists did say that they aimed to achieve this by their arguments. There is not voiced expressly, however, the

88. *M. Maximil.* 2.1 and 8.
89. *M. Marcell.* (M) 1.1; 4.3.
90. *M. Das.* 7.2.
91. *M. Iul.* 1.3–4; 2.1.
92. Origen, *Cels.* 8.75; 70; 73.
93. Tertullian, *apol.* 38; 41.
94. Ibid. 21.
95. Tertullian, *mart.* 2; Ps-Cyprian, *laud. mart.* passim.
96. Tertullian, *apol.* 25.
97. Daube, *Civil Disobedience*, 64.

view that passive resistance was an instrument for political ends. Yet I have no reason to doubt that the steadfastness of the martyrs contributed to the recognition of Christianity and the profound change in political policy effected by Constantine. And the church was clearly not totally innocent of the social and political implications of martyrdom. Polycarp, called upon to curse Christ replied, "For eighty-six years I have been his servant and he has done me no wrong. How can I blaspheme against my king and savior?"[98] He and the host of faithful witnesses before and after him gave a testimony to the supreme claims of God and the limitations of the State. The fruition of the implications of their testimony was long time in coming, but the early Christian witness was an important step in desacralizing the State, elevating the individual conscience, and asserting the value of principles on which religious toleration rests.

Everett Ferguson is Professor of Religion at Abilene Christian University

98. *M. Polyc.* 9.

Christological Content and Its Biblical Basis in the Letter of the Martyrs of Gaul

DENIS FARKASFALVY

Eusebius of Caesarea, to whom we owe the preservation of substantial excerpts from the Letter of the Martyrs of Gaul (LMG),[1] considers this document "not only a historical but also a doctrinal presentation."[2] Indeed, besides describing the sequence of events that led to the martyrdom in 177 of about fifty Christians of Lyons and Vienne in Gaul,[3] it provides us with a spirituality of martyrdom permeated with Christological reflections.

Both the dating and the authenticity of the document rest on the judgment of Eusebius. Neither has gone unchallenged,[4] but the vast majority of both historians and patristic experts still recognize the validity of the data found in the *Historia ecclesiastica*. The letter was written shortly

---

DENIS FARKASFALVY is Abbot of the Cistercian Monastery, Irving, TX 75039-4501.

[1] I have used two editions: H. Musurillo, *The Acts of the Christian Martyrs*, Oxford Early Christian Texts (Oxford: Clarendon, 1972) 62–85; G. Bardy, ed. *Eusèbe de Césarée, Histoire ecclésiastique, Libres V–VII*, Sources chrétiennes 41 (Paris, 1955) 6–26. The latter translation is generaly more literal. LMG was preserved by Eusebius in the first two chapters of Book V of his *Ecclesiastical History*. Quotations will indicate chapter and verse only. Musurillo's edition has left out from Eusebius's text, as edited by Bardy, the introduction, the first couple of verses from chapter 1 (1.1–2) and all of chapter 3 (the dream of the martyr Attalus). For these I follow Bardy's text. I use, for quoting the text, Musurillo's English translation but with corrections based on Bardy's French translation.

[2] οὐχ ἱστορικὴν αὐτὸ μόνον, ἀλλὰ καὶ διδασκαλὴν διήγησιν (*H.E.* V. Introd.).

[3] The list of the martyrs of Gaul has been preserved in a manuscript of Rufinus's translation of our text, in the martyrology of St. Jerome, and in a text by St. Gregory of Tours. They seem to add up to 48 persons, yet this number is, because of uncertainties about the identification of each person's name (some persons' full names are given in two or three words) is uncertain. Nor is the list guaranteed to be complete. Cf. Bardy's note in *Sources chrétiennes* Vol. 41, p. 21.

[4] For this subject see Musurillo's introduction to our text (op. cit. xx–xxii).

after the events. Allegations of interpolation are all based on assumptions about the rate and mode of doctrinal developments, or to put it bluntly, the assumptions are built on doctrinal bias.[5] Our own analysis below confirms the authenticity of the document from another point of view, that of an exegetical approach. While exhibiting the strong contours of an emerging New Testament canon, it reflects a particular kind of "actualizing" exegesis of the New Testament with a somewhat loose handling of the actual wording of the scriptural text. This approach receded in the church as the advancement of the Gnostic crisis and confrontations with Montanism called for more attention to the original wording and the context of the biblical texts. Thus, we can assume the authenticity of the document as it stands in its critical edition as well as its dating from about 178. Only occasionally shall we make remarks about one phrase or another raising doubts about one or the other of these suppositions.

Should we search for a brief summary of the doctrinal content of the letter, we might best quote the following statement: "All who suffer for Chirst's glory (δόξα) will have everlasting fellowship with the living God (κοινωνία μετὰ τοῦ ζῶντος Θεοῦ)" (I.41). This sentence is inserted into one of the most dramatic scenes described by the document. Blandina, a frail slave girl, after having undergone unbelievable tortures with heroic patience, is finally presented in the arena hanging on a post and exposed as bait for wild animals. She hangs in the form of a cross while uttering fervent prayers. For her Christian companions this gruesome spectacle has the value of revealing Christ's on-going presence in their midst: "They saw in the person of their sister him who was crucified for them, so that he [i.e. Christ] might convince those who believe in him (πιστεύοντας εἰς αὐτὸν) that all who suffer for Christ's glory (πᾶς ὁ ὑπὲρ τῆς Χριστοῦ δόξης παθὼν) will have everlasting fellowship with the living God." The

---

[5]Musurillo decides for the "substantial authenticity" of the letter but leaves open the possibility that an editor may have "reworked a primitive document some time in the third century, lending the earlier account a vividness and excitement of his own" (op. cit. xxi). His arguments are, however, rather vague. That "the treatment of the Christian dead (I.59–60) seems gratuitously cruel and (therefore) may have been invented" supposes that a mob and the authority trying to please it may not be "gratuitously cruel." The mentioning of the "virgin Mother" as image of the church in I.45 will be dealt with below in note 11. Parallels with the *Symposium* of Methodius of Olympus (III.8) are best explained by supposing that Methodius is elaborating and systematizing imagery well known in the second century. That the entire persecution is conceived as "the work of the Beast" is a view that permeates the letter and is due to the influence of Revelation together with 2 Thess. and John. For a Christian community living in the second half of the second century and having roots in Asia Minor such influences should not appear surprising.

structure of the sentence exhibits a stylistic anomaly. Two references are made to Christ, first by means of a participle (τὸν αὐτῶν ἐσταυρωμένον), then by a personal pronoun (εἰς αὐτὸν); yet the final generalizaton introduces Christ again by name: "all who suffer for Christ's glory. . . ." Here we should expect αὐτοῦ instead of Χριστοῦ. This irregularity of style is best explained, if we see in the final sentence a quotation (introduced by "convince those who believe in him that") or at least a maxim known to both writer and reader about the meaning and purpose of martyrdom. As we shall see, most of the theological content of the letter is, indeed, easily grouped about the two central concepts of this phrase: (1) the glory of Christ and (2) the life of God shared through suffering.

I
SUFFERING FOR THE SAKE OF CHRIST'S GLORY

The moving image of Blandina, hanging from a pole and representing the crucified Lord, makes modern students of this text speak about the theology of martyrdom in the early Church as a way of "seeking to attain the closest possible imitation of Christ's Passion and death." These are W. H. C. Frend's words introducing the theological evaluation of the LMG, which he highly appreciates for both its historical and theological content.[6] Nevertheless, the image of Christ, present on every page of the document, is not that of the suffering but of the glorious Christ. Even in the case of Blandina, while the Christians looking at her see with their physical eyes the image of the crucified Lord, Christ's glory and their own everlasting share in it is made manifest to their faith.

In fact, the expression "suffering for Christ's glory" carries an unprecedented emphasis. We can find the expressions "suffering for God's kingdom" in 2 Thessalonians 1:5 and "suffering for his (Christ's) name" in Polycarp, *Philippians* (8.2) or simply as "suffering for him (Christ)" already in Paul (Phil. 1:29), but ὑπὲρ τῆς Χριστοῦ δόξης παθὼν expresses this document's special concentration on the glorious Christ. What the wording "for the sake of Christ's glory" might exactly mean for the author of the LGM is to be collected from the document's numerous other references to the glorious Christ.

There are two major aspects to be considered. On the one hand, the whole story of multiple martyrdoms is conceived by the author as a chain of instances at which (and through which) the glory of Christ is made manifest. On the other hand, the martyrs themselves appropriate and share the glory of Christ as this becomes manifested in their sufferings. This

[6]*Martyrdom and Persecution in the Early Church* (Garden City, N.Y.: Doubleday, 1967) 14.

second aspect, participation in Christ's glory through suffering, is intimately connected with a very special theme. For the author of LMG receiving a share in the glory coincides with *partaking of* or *birth into God's life*, a topic that surfaces time and again in the document.

The manifestation of God's glory taking place in the suffering martyrs is linked to two literary *topoi* of early Christian martyrdom, present in the Pastoral Epistles and *The Martyrdom of Polycarp*. In the first, Christian life is compared to an athletic contest, in the second to a military battle. The first is especially well suited to describe events taking place in an arena before a crowd of passionate spectators. For our author, however, both the real athletic match as well as the real battle take place on a spiritual level. For he emphasizes the contrast that, while in the eyes of the bloodthirsty crowd the martyrs are defeated as miserable and pathetic victims, in reality—a reality that only faith can perceive—they are victorious athletes performing acts of heroism.

In the case of the little maidservant, Blandina, there is a great difference between what meets the eye and what is truly taking place: through her "Christ proved that the things which men regard as cheap, ugly, and contemptuous, are deemed worthy of glory before God" (I.17). With a body broken and torn "this blessed woman as a true athlete became renewed in her confession (of faith)" (I.19). In a similar way, all martyrs are called noble athletes, sustaining a brilliant contest and achieving a glorious victory (I.36); their renewed tortures are called "repeated fights" leading to the victor's crown (I.38; cf. also I.42). The author points out that, while their martyrdom has been used "to replace the varied entertainment of the gladiatorial combats," the true meaning of their performance goes beyond a mere spectacle. Probably with an allusion to 1 Corinthians 4:9, the martyrs are said to have become "a spectacle [θέαμα, Paul uses θέατρον) to the world" (I.40), obviously not only in a theatrical but also and foremost in a theological sense. After Blandina had represented the crucified Lord before the physical eyes of the onlookers, she remained untouched by the animals and was taken down to be brought back later for "another fight" (εἰς ἄλλον ἀγῶνα) so that "by her victory in further contests she would make irreversible the condemnation of the crooked serpent" (I.42). Her fight is against Satan (here evoked by a reference to Is. 27:1),[7] and she can win it only "because she had put on Christ"—a Pauline image known from Romans 13:14 and Galatians 3:24— "that mighty and invincible athlete who had overcome the Adversary [ἀντικείμενος; cf. 2 Thess. 2:4] in many contests" (ibid.).

---

[7] Satan is called ὄφις four times in the New Testament: once by Paul (2 Cor. 11:3) and three times in Relevation (12:9, 15; 20:2).

The subsequent description of Attalus's fight parallels the text about Blandina: "He entered the arena as a warrior well prepared for the contest" (I.43). This means practically the same kind of "fitness" that comes from "putting on Christ." By reason of his "good conscience," by his being "trained in the Christian discipline," by having been "a witness among us to the truth," he is ready to go through martyrdom. In fact, the document abundantly testifies to the virtues of the martyrs as "a manifestation of the power of martyrdom by deed," describing "their open profession of faith [παρρησία], their nobility, perseverance, fearlessness and courage" (II.4). Yet neither their contest nor their victory is conceived of as a result of their own personal attributes. The martyrs themselves see Christ as the only martyr: "the true and faithful witness" (Rev. 3:14).

The martyrs are declared at the end "all-victorious" (κατὰ πάντα νικηφόροι) (II.7). It is clear that their victory is perceived only by those who share their faith. The letter candidly describes how a sizable number of Christians denied their faith and depicts the gloating persecutors, who declare that by burning the bodies of the martyrs and throwing their ashes into the river Rhône they have frustrated the Christian belief in the resurrection of those bodies (I.60–61). It seems that, in the eyes of the author, the apparent success of the persecutors belongs to the crude reality of martyrdom. From the very beginning of his narrative he is aware that understanding the real issue underlying the events is a matter of faith. Nevertheless, the data furnished by the letter also reveal a great deal about the social and political background of the events. The pagans were motivated by their hatred toward a culturally alien immigrant minority from Asia Minor, a resurgence of "Roman patriotism" taking place among the newly Latinized inhabitants of southern Gaul. There was probably also some manipulation of these sentiments by local leaders who needed suitable vicitms for the gladiatorial games or, possibly, also substitutes for the ritual-sacrificial volunteers to be immolated at the annual festival of the three Gauls.[8] But in the eyes of our author the real battle was not fought on mere earthly terrain. We witness the ongoing cosmic fight between Christ and the Devil (I.28), his Adversary. The expression "Adversary" (ἀντικείμενος) is used with preference (I.5, 23, 42). The most plausible source for this term is 2 Thessalonians 2:4, where "the Adversary's" appearance is put into the context of apostasy, forced idolatry, and the apparent victory of falsehood which is then overcome by the Christians' fidelity to truth, achieving the final glory of Jesus Christ (2:3–

---

[8]About his general reconstruction of the historical background see W. H. C. Frend (op. cit. 3–18).

14). The immediate source may, of course, be *The Martyrdom of Polycarp,* in which also the Devil is called ἀντικείμενος (17.1). The expression "sons of perdition" applied to some of the arrested Christians at their final failure (I.48) seems to be derived from 2 Thessalonians 2:3 rather than John 17:12 (the usual reference in the editions), since the author understands their apostasy as the manifestation of the fact that "they never had even a trace of the faith" (I.48). In other words, their apostasy is conceived of as part of the general manifestation of "the Adversary" at which every υἱὸς τῆς ἀπωλείας will also be made manifest.

In such a cosmic context, the manifestation of Christ's glory through the sufferings of the martyrs is thought of as the continuation of God's great deeds with an eschatological perspective. Christ himself performs through the martyrs "great glories" (μέγαλας δόξας)—i.e. great miracles[9]—evidencing in this way not only his continued presence among the believers but also his glorious state and our actual share in it. It is remarkable how the quotation of Romans 8:18 is introduced (I.6). By regarding all suffering and torments as insignificant, the martyrs went in haste to Christ by thus "demonstrating (ἐνδεικνύμενοι) that the sufferings of the present times are not comparable to the future glory which is to be revealed in us." What Paul introduces in his letter by "it seems to me" is quoted in the LMG as demonstrated through events. The suffering of the martyrs thus brings both the expected glory and the truth of scripture into evidence, almost within reach, although without suppressing its eschatological dimension.

The glory of Christ becomes apparent also through the inner experience of the suffering martyrs: they radiate their experience of spiritual union with Christ. To show this, the LMG describes in detail the contrast between those who persisted in their faith and those who denied it. The first group is radiant with χάρις and δόξα, while the others are embarrassed and humiliated over their defection. It seems that the triplet εἰρήνη, χάρις καὶ δόξα in the letter's address is not just a routine formula. Δόξα is not found in the address of any epistle in the New Testament, nor in the letter of Clement of Rome, nor in the letters of Ignatius or Polycarp. Its presence in this letter is another proof that for its author the concept of "glory"

---

[9]The plural of δόξα I.23 is rare in early Christian literature. In the New Testament it appears with the meaning of "(angelic?) powers" or "(human?) authorities" (Jd. 8; 2 Pet. 2:10), but neither of these applies here. In 1 Pet. 1:11 we might find a more fitting parallel (καὶ τὰς μετὰ ταῦτα [i.e. παθήματα] δόξας). In any case, Bardy's translation ("Le Christ . . . accomplissait de grand prodiges") is to be preferred to Musurillo's ("Christ . . . achieved great glory"). The text obviously speaks of the "miraculous" events that follow, and, in particular, the fact that Blandina's love for her fellow Christians resulted in fortifying the weak and gaining them back for martyrdom.

is central. Similarly, the other two nouns connected with δόξα in the address also receive some special emphasis in the body of the letter (χάρις in I.35 and εἰρήνη in II.7) as the spiritual goods obtained by the martyrs for both themselves and the Christian community.

Related to the theme of the divine δόξα shared by the martyrs is that of "their crown" or "the crown of incorruptibility," appearing three times in the document (I.36, 38, 42). As it has been shown by A. J. Brekemans' dissertation,[10] this image has a double background. It has ancient Jewish roots and, at the same time, is a broadly used symbol in the Hellenistic world. In our text the latter background is unmistakable: the text speaks of a crown made of flowers of all kinds and all colors corresponding to the varied forms of combat by which the martyrs reach their victory (I.36). The martyrs sustain "many contests for the victor's crown," just like athletes do (I.38); Blandina wins her fight over the crooked serpent in order to "be crowned by a crown of incorruptibility" (I.42). This last passage evokes *The Martyrdom of Polycarp,* where we read:

> He was not only a noble teacher but a distinguished martyr whose martyrdom all desire to imitate as one according to the gospel of Christ. By his patient endurance he overcame the wicked magistrate [ἄδικον ἄρχοντα] and so received the crown of incorruptibility; and he rejoices with the apostles and all the righteous to glorify God the Father Almighty and to bless our Lord Jesus Christ. (19.2)

Several elements are common with LMG I.42. The "wicked archon" might be a reference to Satan (cf. ὁ ἄρχων τοῦ κόσμου: Jn. 12:31; 14:30; 16:11), rather than to the magistrate, or, at least, it could have been interpreted as such by ancient readers, familiar with the Johannine vocabulary. However, in Polycarp's case "the crown of incorruptibility" is more directly and narrowly identified with his glorious state obtained through suffering, while in the LMG it retains its thematic connection with the fight and victory, and appears as a crown due to the athlete at the successful completion of his fight. Grammatically, in both texts the genitive (τῆς ἀφθαρσίας) could be explained either as a genitive of identification or explanation (crown that is immortality) or as a genitive of quality (an unfading crown, opposed to a crown of physical flowers that withers). A hint to the latter interpretation might be seen in the LMG with its explicit mentioning of flowers (I.36).

But the real background to this imagery is to be sought in the New Testament. Both the text of Polycarp's martyrdom and the LMG rely on a Christian usage that goes back to 1 Corinthians 9:25 ("those to win a

---

[10]A. J. Brekemans, *Martyrerkranz. Eine symbolgeschichtliche Untersuchung im frühchristlichen Schrifttum* (Rome: Gregoriana, 1965).

crown that withers [φθαρτὸν στέφανον], but we a crown that is imparishable [ἄφθαρτον]"). For our text 1 Peter 5:4 might be even more important: "so that when the Chief Shepherd appears you will win for yourselves an unfading crown of glory [ἀμαράντινον τῆς δόξης στέφανον]." While the Pauline text is more explicit about the athletic combat, the verse from First Peter establishes a closer parallel for the meaning of the image in its context of martyrdom: the crown of glory is an eschatological gift to be received from Christ; its unfading character is explained in terms of his immortal, risen life. A further link can be established with 2 Timothy 4:6–8, where the connection is made between the eschatological crown and martyrdom, described as a combat (ἀγῶνα ἠγώνισμαι: v. 6). Paul's own "libation" is presented here as leading to "the crown of righteousness" (v. 8).

One might be tempted to say that the LMG adds very little to a well established Christian imagery. Yet, at a closer look, our document shows two features in which the theme is carried somewhat further. Unlike any New Testament text or even *The Martyrdom of Polycarp*, our letter presents Christ himself as "a mighty and invincible athlete" (I. 42). Thus not only the fight and the crown but also the athlete have been lifted up into the transcendental realm. Briefly, here "martyrology" goes over into "Christology." The martyr's description as an athlete has finally resulted in the application of *the title to Christ himself, as he is united with his martyr in agony*. There is little doubt that such a title applied to Christ successfully appropriates a popular Hellenistic concept with its cultural and emotional context in order to present Christianity's ideal in a language most understandable for the Greco-Roman world. A second peculiarity of our text is its conscious emphasis on the obtainment of glory as new life, showing a very explicit connection between the glory of martyrdom and the new life being born in the martyrs as they die. Ultimately, it is in this way that the image of "the crown of immortality" is fully explained: while their share seems to be death and defeat, they obtain glory and life.[11]

II
LIFE THROUGH DEATH AND REBIRTH

One of the most original features of our text is its way of treating the dialectic of death and life implied in Christian martyrdom. As a text destined for Christian use, the LMG does not treat apologetic questions about Christian faith in the resurrection of the body. It shows, however, keen

---

[11]The "crown of life" in James 1:12 and in Rev. 2:10 also seems to point in the same direction.

awareness that it was mainly because of their belief in the resurrection of the body (both Christ's and their own) that the Christians encountered rejection and were accused of having introduced an absurd and irrational religion. The burning of the bodies of the martyrs of Gaul and the dispersal of the ashes into the Rhône was staged by the authorities for the sake of constituting evidence against such a belief: "that they might have no hope in the resurrection in which they put their trust when they introduce this strange new cult among us" (I.63). The document expresses only grief over the refusal of the right of burial but otherwise does not show any theological concern about the loss of the martyrs' remains. It rather expresses spontaneously the conviction that the martyrs obtained life at their death (II.7), triumphantly joined "the bridal banquet" (I.55), obtained "eternal fellowship with the living God" (I.41).

The preoccupation of the author does not lie in dialoguing with pagans and defending these fundamental Christian convictions but rather in evaluating the case of those who, under the influence of intimidation and torture, denied their faith. It might be even asserted that the main thrust of the letter—a principal reason for its composition—was to document the martyrs' attitude toward their weak brethren. When handling this theme, our letter expresses a particular theology of the life of God shared by the Christian, describing the conception, development and eventual miscarriage of this life, the possibility of a "return to the womb," and the moment of final birth at the completion of martyrdom.

This theology receives unusual expression in the case of Alexander, a physician from Phrygia, as he is pictured "standing in front of the tribunal" and encouraging the tortured Christians by sign language. He has obviously not yet been identified, accused, or arrested as a Christian and can therefore be present in the arena as a mere spectator. What he does amounts to some sort of pantomime: he imitates the behavior of a woman giving birth. As the context indicates, the significance of his behavior for a while makes sense only for the Christians until the audience realizes that it prompts several of the fallen-away Christians to change their minds: "those who had previously denied the faith were now confessing it once more" (I.49). The spectators shout in anger against him till he is himself arrested and put among the martyrs. The narrative clearly supposes that we are dealing with symbolism known to the Christians of Lyons as well as to those in Asia Minor to whom the letter was addressed.

In fact, we can find several scattered references to this theme in the letter: the Christians denying their faith are called "aborted" (I.11); their return to confessing their faith gives joy to "the Virgin Mother," who now "recovers alive those whom she had cast forth stillborn" (I.45); "they were conceived and brought again to life in the womb" (I.46). The "Virgin

Mother" must be identified with the church. Our text is usually considered to be the first clearly attested reference to the church as virgin and mother.[12] Musurillo insinuates that it may be an interpolation because of its resemblance to a passage by Methodius of Olympus.[13] However, right at the end of the second century there is a rather wide stream of tradition about the motherhood of the church witnessed to by Irenaeus, Tertullian, and Hippolytus.[14] But we have also earlier texts. In the third *Vision* of the *Shepherd* of Hermas, the church is personified as a mother giving instruction to her children. Here no mention is made of a virginal motherhood, yet, of course, *spiritual* maternity is meant.[15] *The Letter to Diognetus* presents the figure of a virgin contrasted with Eve, which can-

---

[12]H. de Lubac, *The Motherhood of the Church* (San Francisco: Ignatius, 1982); French original: *Les églises particulières dans l'Église universelle, suivi de La maternité de l'église et d'une interview recueillie par G. Jarczyk* (Paris: Aubier, 1971) 55.

[13]Musurillo has edited the *Symposium* of St. Methodius both in the *Sources Chrétiennes*, Vol. 95 and the *Ancient Christian Writers*, Vol. 27. In *The Acts of the Christian Martyrs*, pp. xxif. and lxv, note 17, he points out that our text (I.45 and II.7) "parallels the expressions used by Methodius of Olympus in his *Symposium* (iii.18)" and thus there is the "possibility" of a third-century "editor" for our text. He provides no further proof for this claim in any of his three works quoted. A closer look at these texts reveals the improbability of Musurillo's suggestion. The expression νηδύς instead of κοιλία is missing from the text of Methodius. Similarly, the imagery of "maternity" and "virginity" applied to the martyrs individually and to the church collectively is not restricted to the two passages which Musurillo quotes but is spread across the whole document: cf. I.10 (quoting Rev. 14:4, which is about virgins); I.11 ("ten were stillborn"); I.22 (Christ's heavenly "womb"); I.35 (the martyrs wear their chain as a bride wears her golden embroidered tassels: reference to Ps. 45:12–15); I.45 (the virgin Mother to whom the stillborn return); I.46 ("conceived and quickened again"); I.48 ("wedding garment"); I.49 (Alexander "as if in birth pangs"); I.55 (Blandina "like a noble mother" and "as though she had been invited to a bridal banquet"); II.6 (reference to Rev. 12:6; "maternal love" of the martyrs); II.7 (no pain for "their mother," i.e., the church). These are *twelve* informal and fragmentary references to a theme which then in Methodius's work is presented in a rather elaborate system with rich imagery. It is therefore clear that Methodius is the one who depends on a less elaborate tradition surfacing already in the LMG.

[14]Texts assembled by de Lubac, pp. 47–84, starting in the second century and continuing into more recent times. For Irenaeus: "those who do not share in the Spirit are not drawing sustenance of life from the breasts of their mother" (*Adversus haereses* III.24.1); Tertullian: "the Church . . . this true mother of the living" (*De anima* 43); Hippolytus: "The mouth of the Father has begotten a pure Word; this word appears a second time, born of the saints. Constantly producing saints, it is also itself reproduced by its saints" (*In Danielem* I.10). The maternity of the church is explicit in Gal. 4:26, but the patristic development of the comparison is elaborated within the wider context of the threefold parallel "Eve—Mary—Church" using Johannine theology and the symbolism expressed in John 19:25–27 and in Rev. 12.

[15]The "elderly lady," identified as the church in *Vision* II.4 (8.1), starts speaking to her "children" (τέκνα) in *Vision* III.9 (17.1).

not be simply identified with Mary; the passage speaks of a virginity "which the serpent cannot touch or defile" by seduction as opposed to the defiled (=seduced) virginity of Eve.[16] More impressively, the 19th *Ode of Solomon* speaks of a "Virgin and Mother" whose features go beyond the individuality of Jesus' mother and seem to take general features that aptly describe the church:

> And the Virgin became a Mother
> with many mercies:
> and she travailed and brought forth a son
> without incurring pain . . . ,
> She brought forth,
> as if she were a man,
> of her own will,
> and she brought him forth openly,
> and acquired him in great power,
> and loved him in salvation,
> and guarded him in kindness,
> and showed him in majesty.[17]

Therefore, it is not anachronistic to suppose that at the end of the second century a rather short mentioning of the image of the "Virgin Mother" was understood by the readers of the text as a symbol for the church.

In the background of these fragments we must assume a soteriology which compares the process of salvation to the process of birth with its pains, dangers, and final joyful result. Such a background is constituted by John 16:21, which, however, the LMG (more precisely, its portion preserved by Eusebius) does not quote. But another famous text about the "messianic birth," Revelation 12:1–5, is certainly in the author's mind as he writes about the martyrs who, when leading the apostates back to confessing their faith, "forced the throttled Beast to disgorge alive all those whom he at first thought he had devoured" (II.6). Since these same

---

[16]12.8. Interpretations vary. According to Richardson "it is fairly clear that the author intends to state the common Patristic contrast between Eve, the disobedient mother of death, and Mary the obedient mother of life, in which case the πάρθενος of the text will be the blessed Virgin Mary." *Early Christian Fathers* (New York: Macmillan, 1979) 224. Kleist has the following note: "The writer is not here speaking of the church as a paradise of delight, but of every Christian individual soul endowed with knowledge of life. It is important to bear this in mind in interpreting 12:8 where such a soul is referred to as 'Eve' and 'a virgin.'" *Ancient Christian Writers* (Westminster: Newman, 1948) 221. These two interpretations can be reconciled only if we do not separate the traditional "Eve/Mary" theme from a wider context, the triplet "Church—Mary—Eve." The latter alone can explain the mixture of collective and individual aspects.

[17]This text, usually dated to the middle of the second century, is reproduced in J. Quasten, *Patrology* I (Westminster: Newman, 1951) 163–164. An exclusively Marian interpretation would not adequately explain the last five lines.

people were said to be "miscarried" and then "returned to the womb" of the Virgin Mother, it is quite plausible that we are dealing with somewhat fragmentary references to the scene in Revelation 12 about the Woman clothed in the sun with twelve stars around her head giving birth in pain to a child whom then the Beast is trying to swallow alive without prevailing.

According to the text the result of the apostates' "returning to the womb" was obtained by the fellow martyrs and their charity (I.46). In this, however, we should not see just the manifestation of some personal virtue or strength on their side but rather the exercise of an "apostolic charisma," mentioned explicitly in connection with Alexander's "pantomime" (I.49). The fact that Alexander, a man, "looked like as if he were in birth pangs" should not be read as an odd or miscast image. For we find the same word ὠδίνων in Galatians 4:19, where Paul says: "my children for whom I again experience birth pangs." Thus, the "apostolic charism" mentioned in the text might in fact refer to what Paul speaks of in Galatians 4:19: Alexander managed to give birth *again* to these Christians by returning them from apostasy.

The "redemptive" role—an ecclesial function—ascribed to the martyrs is ultimately attributed to Christ himself; the martyrs are only instrumental: "through their perseverance the infinite mercy of Christ was revealed. Through the living the dead were restored to life" (I.45). It is made clear that the martyrs were μιμηταὶ Χριστοῦ. They express their awareness of this fact in their humble refusal to be called martyrs because Christ is the only martyr (II.2–3). Similarly, Christ, constituted in his heavenly glory, is the ultimate fountain of life for the martyrs: it is from him, more exactly "from his belly" or, probably with more precision, "from his womb," that they draw "the water of life" (I.22).

This text deserves a closer look. It refers to the deacon Sanctus, seated on red-hot bronze plates which burn the "tenderest parts of his body" (I.21). He remains firm in his profession of faith, "cooled and strengthened by the heavenly fountain of the water of life that flows from the side [=womb, belly, interior parts] of Christ [ὑπὸ τῆς οὐρανίου πηγῆς τοῦ ὕδατος τῆς ζωῆς τοῦ ἐξιόντος ἐκ τῆς νηδύος τοῦ Χριστοῦ]." The Greek phrase is concise and compact, but the underlying Johannine images and ideas are unmistakable. The clearest reference is John 7:37–38: "He who thirsts let him come to me and let him drink, the one who believes in me. As scripture says, 'rivers of living water will spring forth from his side.'" For the punctuation of the gospel text there exist two traditions, but our author certainly read it in the way in which we present it here: it is from Christ's side (and not from the side of the believer) that the "living water" is said to flow.[18] John's text uses κοιλία, which in both the LXX and the New Testament might stand for either "the heart" (cf. e.g. Acts 2:30 and Rev. 10:9) or "the uterus" (more frequently in the New Testament: Lk. 1:41, 44; 2:21; 11:27; 23:29; Gal. 1:15). In the LMG the noun used is νήδυς, a word not found in the New Testament, but synonymous with κοιλία in its meaning of "belly, womb." In the phrase, "Christ's womb" is conceived as a "heavenly well of living water" with possible reference to John 4:10. The image as a whole is a new construction built from Johannine elements: the glorified Christ is pictured as the "well of living water," cooling and refreshing the martyr. But the whole scene makes sense fully only if one knows that Christ's side was pierced, and that what flowed from it, "the water and the blood" (John 19:34), was accompanied by the Spirit, so that the three produced one single witness (1 John 5:6). Of course, the Johannine gospel also calls our attention to the fact that the wounded side remained recognizable on the risen body of the Lord and that the doubting disciple arrived at his act of faith only after he had been invited to put his hand into it (John 20:25, 27). The latter two facts about the body of Christ, killed and risen, must be presupposed if it is to be represented as a well of living waters which is both heavenly and bodily in nature. What appears unique is the fact that the maternal function of the church, shared and carried out by the martyrs, is thus ultimately reduced to its source, the glorious passion of Christ, or even more simply the glorified body of the crucified Lord from which the "maternal love" (μητρικὰ σπλάγχνα ἔχοντες) of the martyrs (II.6) emanates.[19]

The two Christological titles, "first-born from the dead" (cf. Col. 1:18 and Rev. 1:15) and "author of life" (ἀρχηγὸς τῆς ζωῆς = initiator or prince of life; cf. Acts 3:15),[20] in fact, very appropriately accompany the title "faithful and true witness/martyr" (cf. Rev. 3:14) because, as our document explains, the martyrs did not accept any glory for themselves

[18]Cf. H. Rahner, "Flumina de ventre Christi. Die patristische Auslegung von Joh 7:37–38," *Biblica* 22 (1941): 269–302; 367–403. This "Christological" interpretation shared by the LMG is found also in Irenaeus, Hippolytus, Tertullian, Cyprian, and early Syriac patristic texts (Aphraates, Ephraem). The alternative punctuation resulting in a text that states the same thing about the believer appears in Origen and the later Greek Fathers.

[19]Quite close to our text is Irenaeus' passage about "the breasts of the mother," the church juxtaposed with the glorious body of Christ as a "well of life" from which the gift of the spirit flows (*Adversus haereses* III.24.1: SC 211, 475).

[20]The expression πρωτότοκος τῶν νεκρῶν καὶ ἀρχηγὸς τῆς ζωῆς Θέου is found in Irenaeus with exactly the same wording (*Adversus haereses* III.24.1: SC 100, 699). It is built from Col. 1:18 (or Rev 1:15) and Act 3:14 with the last word, *Theou*, being added. Such a long phrase cannot be coincidental; we might be dealing here with a Christological (liturgical?) title used in Lyons.

but saw the work and person of Christ become manifest and active in all their accomplishments (II.3). It is clearly the connection between Christ's glorifying and vivifying activity that sets the center stage for the letter's Christological message. The on-going presence of Christ in the church is experienced under these two aspects: he manifests his glory by achieving his martyrs' victory, and he assures the communication of heavenly life by being for them (and through them for others) an actual source of strength, vitality, and virtue. To be a Christian means for the author to bear "the all-honorable, *glorious and life-giving* name" (τὴν πάντιμον καὶ ἔνδοξον καὶ ζωοποιὸν προσηγορίαν) (I.35), a phrase which well demonstrates the author's conscious focusing on these two aspects of Christ's action in the church.

III
THE BIBLICAL BASIS OF THE LETTER'S CHRISTOLOGY

It goes without saying that our document is not intended to cover all aspects of its author's Christological thought. Furthermore, the selected passages that survived in Eusebius's *Ecclesiatical History* are not guaranteed to preserve all of its major themes. (This latter reason, of course, justifies us in attributing special importance to those topics that surface repeatedly even if in a fleeting and fragmentary way.) We might still attempt to see how the Christological thought, summarized above, relates to biblical sources. We will, therefore, enumerate the biblical passages that played a role in expressing and thematizing the experiences of persecution and martyrdom.

From the Old Testament, we find that a rather small number of passages have been taken. None is an explicit quotation.

Is. 53:2.5 (lack of resemblance to "human form") in I.23;

Is. 27:1 (about the devil as the "crooked serpent"; possibly combined with Rev. 12:9 and 20:2, which, in turn, refer to Gen. 3:15) in I.42.

Ez. 33:11 ("God does not want the death of the sinner") in I.46;

Ps. 20:5 (the martyrs "asked life and you gave it to them") in II.7;

2 Macc. 7:21–29 (Blandina is compared to the martyred mother of seven sons) in I.55.

The New Testament texts are more numerous; several are introduced by a formula of quotation:

Mt. 16:19 (or 18:18) (the martyrs "absolve all, do not hold fast anyone," a peculiar exegesis of the power of absolving or holding fast sins) in II.5;

Mt. 22:11 (the "nuptial garment") in I.48;

*Lk. 1:6 (reference to Zachariah, to whom Attalus was comparable by "walking blamelessly in all the commandments and precepts of the Lord") in I.10;

Lk. 11:51 (par. Mt. 23:38; "the blood of Zachariah" must have been understood by our author as referring to the father of John the Baptist, otherwise he would not talk about his *martyria* and compare Attalus to him) in I.10;[21]

Jn. 7:38 (living water flowing from the "side" of Christ) in I.22;

*Jn. 16:2 (word for word and explicit quotation introduced as "the Lord's saying" which "was fulfilled") in I.15;

Jn. 17:12 ("the sons of perdition" are the apostates who do not repent; but the reference may not be to this Johannine verse speaking in the singular about Judas but rather to 2 Thess. 2:3, which can be understood about the eschatalogical manifestation of everyone who is a "son of perdition") in I.48;

Jn. 19:34 and 20:38 are indirectly referred to in that the "side" (womb) of Christ is said to be a "well of living water") in I.22;

Acts 3:15 (Christ as the "ruler of life") in II.3;

Acts 7:54 (the "gnashing of teeth" of those stoning Stephen; one of the verse's two verbs is quoted at each place) in I.15 and I.60;

*Acts 7:60 (explicit quotation of Stephen's prayer for his persecutors; used here to exalt the martyrs' prayer for their fellow Christians) in II.5;

Acts 15:29 (from the apostolic decree: Christians are not permitted to consume blood) in I.26;

Acts 18:25 (a phrase about Apollos applied to the martyr Vettius Epagathus) in I.9;

*Rom. 8:18 (introduced as a quotation: the martyrs have demonstrated its truth) in I.6;

Rom. 13:14 (possibly referred to: "putting on Christ") in I.42;

Gal. 3:27 (other possible source for the same Pauline phrase) in I.42;

Gal. 4:19 (Alexander experiencing "the pangs of birth") in I.49;

Gal. 6:4 and 5:22 are rather doubtful (weak verbal similarities) in II.6 resp. II.7;

1 Cor. 4:9 (the martyrs became "a spectacle to the world") in I.40;

1 Cor. 9:25 (incorruptible crown) in I.42;

2 Cor. 2:14 (so that Christ might triumph through the martyr; the Pauline phrase has God triumphing in Christ) in I.29;

2 Cor. 2:15 (the martyrs become "Christ's good odor" in a physical, miraculous way; this is a sure quotation and makes the allusion to v. 14, signaled above, probable) in I.35;

2 Thess. 2:3 (sons of perdition) in I.48;

2 Thess. 2:4 ("the Adversary") in I.5, 23, and 42;

Phil. 2:6 (applied to the humility of the martyrs not accepting the glorious title) in II.2;

Col. 1:18 (Christ as the firstborn from the dead) in II.3;

1 Tim. 3:15 (the martyrs as "solid pillars") in I.8 and 17.

1 Tim. 6:14 ("good witness/martyrdom") in I.30;

[21]The identification of the Zachariah mentioned in Mt. 23:34 (par. Lk. 11:51) with the father of John the Baptist is quite ancient. Cf. Origen, *Comm. in Mt.* 25 (GS 38: 42–45); the fragment n. 457 of the "catena" from the *Comm. on Mt.* (ibid. p. 190). Most interesting is the so called *Protevangelium Jacobi* in which we read: "And Zacharias said: I am a martyr of God. Take my blood in the forecourt of the temple of the Lord" (23.3).

2 Tim. 4:6–8 (contest leading to the crown) I.42;

Heb. 10:33 (the wrath of the Evil One; possible allusion) in I.6; another verbal similarity in I.40 (spectacle to the world);

1 Pet. 5:6 (humbled themselves under God's mighty hand) in II.5;

2 Pet. 1:18 (neither futile nor fruitless) in I.45;

2 Pet. 2:2 (by whom the way of truth is blasphemed) in I.48;

1 Jn. 3:16 ("to lay down his life"—a frequent Johannine expression: cf. Jn. 10:11,15,17; 13:37,38; 15:13; etc.) in I.10;

Rev. 1:5 (possible quotation: Christ the "firstborn from the dead") in II.3;

Rev. 3:14 (Christ as the faithful and true martyr) in II.3;

Rev. 14:4 in I.10;

Rev. 12:4b (the Beast swallowing the child born of the Woman) in II.6;

Rev. 21:6 (the well of the water of life) in I.22;

*Rev. 22:11 (explicit quotation: "that the scriptures may be fulfilled; let the lawless be lawless," etc.) in I.58.

This list contains five references to the Old Testament and about forty allusions or quotations pertaining to the New. The passages marked by an asterisk (*) refer to the explicit quotations, for each of which some introductory formula is used or (in the case of Lk. 1:6) a biblical name proves that a conscious reference is made to some particular passage.

The list has special significance from at least three points of view:

(1) While the Old Testament passages are rather few in number, almost the whole New Testament is attested in some way. The only books not clearly quoted are: Mark, Ephesians, 1 Thessalonians, Titus, Philemon, James, Jude, 2 and 3 John. One might argue that the reference to Colossians 1:18 could be dropped since the phrase in question (πρωτότοκος ἐκ τῶν νεκρῶν) is found also in Rev 1:5 in almost the same form (πρωτότοκος τῶν νεκρῶν), a book which is used five more times by LMG. Nevertheless, close parallels in Irenaeus, where this phrase is certainly taken from Colossians, indicate that also in LMG the quotation refers to the same Pauline letter.[22] Of course, since we do not possess the whole text of the letter, only selections made by Eusebius, we cannot be quite sure that our author has not used other books from the New Testament. Nor can it be said with certainty that the document did not use apocryphal writings because, quite probably, Eusebius would have left out the passages with quotations from apocryphal writings. In spite of these cautions, one is entitled to conjecture that the canon of the Martyrs of Gaul—a community of Christians with roots in Asia Minor and writing to fellow Chris-

---

[22]*Adversus haereses* III.16.3 (SC 21,299) πρωτότοκος τῶν νεκρῶν is immediately followed by a quotation from Col. 1:15. It is, therefore, quite clear that in Irenaeus's mind this verse belongs to Colossians. The occurrence of the combined phrase in Irenaeus and the LMG seems to indicate that our letter's quotation stems from Colossians.

tians of Asia Minor—closely resembles the one we find in Irenaeus who, according to Eusebius, carried their letter to bishop Eleutherius of Rome. From the writings of Irenaeus, Philemon, Hebrews, James, Jude and 3 John are missing. The difference between his canon and the canon of the LMG is only four books: Mark, Ephesians, Titus, and 2 John.

Considering the fact that excerpts of our document are printed on less than twelve pages in Musurillo's edition, we must conclude that our text is rather saturated with NT references, and the variety of the quotations and allusions is larger than would be expected. Polycarp's *Philippians* may be the only second-century document more densely filled with New Testament references. The accumulation of biblical passages is often clearly purposeful, but the purpose can only be guessed. It might be that the writer is concerned to refer to the common basis that connects the faith of the community of Lyons with the faith of those in Asia Minor. But it is equally possible that many of the scriptural themes alluded to are essential for him if he is to express and authenticate the faith experience produced under the hardships of persecution and shared in the letter. The way in which our author reached out to so many books to compose a letter about martyrdom shows in some real sense that the canon of the late second century was a "canon of martyrs."[23]

(2) Few of the biblical references are of only stylistic nature. In three cases (the mother from 2 Maccabees, Stephen in Acts, Zachariah in Lk. 1:6) examples of martyrdom are quoted; yet also in these cases a definite doctrinal intent appears. Surprisingly, we find no reference to the history of the passion—only once is the crucified Lord mentioned—while the rest of the biblical quotations are of directly doctrinal nature.

(3) In general, the use of the synoptic gospels is scarce (they appear altogether three times), while Johannine theology is more abundantly present than the four references from John would indicate. For although the references to Christ's δόξα often take place in terms of Pauline texts, the concept of δόξα resembles more its use in Johannine sources. Typical, for example, is the use of Romans 8:18, introduced against a Johannine theological background. According to the letter, the suffering of the martyrs *manifests* the truth of the saying that the future glory is incomparable

---

[23]The scriptural identifications made by the Lawlor-Oulton edition of Eusebius' *Ecclesiastical History* and quoted by W. R. Farmer in his essay, "A Study of the Development of the New Testament Canon," *The Formation of the New Testament Canon* (New York: Paulist, 1983) 39–40, are probably inflated. Yet I agree with Farmer's conclusion that the LMG contributes to the evidence that our NT canon is "a martyrs' canon of scripture." However, concerning the way in which the Lord's passion and Stephen's example are handled by this document, the issue appears to me in a different light. See further below, the conclusion of this essay.

to our present suffering. This *manifestation*, of course, displays an anticipated glory amidst actual suffering, glory perceivable only to the eye of faith. This concept permeates the Fourth Gospel and is characteristic of the Johannine Passion Narrative with its actualized eschatology. Similarly, the use of a Pauline phrase about "the birth pangs" of the martyrs (Gal. 4:19) does not diminish the dependence of the letter's theology of divine life on the Johannine themes of the "messianic birth" (Jn. 16:21), the return to the womb (Jn. 3:4–5), the symbolic character of the "Woman" under the cross (Jn. 19:26–27), and the living water flowing from the glorified Christ's interior (Jn. 7:38). While on the literary level the expression "sons of perdition" in I.48 as well as the repeated use of the name "Adversary" for the Devil probably evoke 2 Thessalonians, the theology which they express is Johannine. The Adversary appears as the Johannine "Prince of this world" (Jn. 12:31; 14:30; 16:11) in a strongly dualistic perspective. Furthermore, the fallen-away Christians who do not repent are said to "have never known even a vestige of the faith," another typically Johannine thought which considers defection as the manifestation of those who never belonged to Christ (cf. esp. 1 Jn. 2:19).

Our document shows an advanced stage of cross-fertilization between Johannine and Pauline thought, yet in such a way that the Pauline texts are molded according to guidelines of Johannine thought. This is in no way accidental. Persecution and martyrdom created for the Christians antagonistic relationships with the world that are more in accord with basic Johannine views than with Paul's optimistic outlook on Roman society and state. Nevertheless, the Pauline texts about suffering and glory are equally part of the "martyrs' canon," with their demand for endurance, faithfulness, and sharing in Christ's suffering for the sake of sharing his glory.

IV

CONCLUSION

The LMG is not a typical document that would receive high priority in the investigation of any main doctrinal issue, such as Christology in the second century. In fact, it contains little or no reflection on Christ's divine and human nature as such. It offers no speculations that would reflect Gnostic influence, nor does it refer to disputes that would reveal anti-Gnostic tendencies. It carries some statements with elements pointing in the direction of Montanism, but as far as doctrine is concerned one finds no indication that "the new prophecy" had penetrated the churches of Gaul. The sections preserved by Eusebius convey exactly the opposite tendency: the martyrs of Lyons have manifested an attitude of mercy, forgiveness, and maternal concern about the fallen-away Christians and offered them a second chance to reverse their apostasy. Of course, one might point out that, while the document reflects the martyrs' charity toward those fallen brethren who were ready to change their minds and join them in martyrdom, it says very little about what the survivors did about those set free at the price of apostasy. Was the possibility of conversion offered to them? In any case, there is no trace of the rigorism, self-righteous prophetic zeal, or claim of new revelations which, for example, fill the Montanist works of Tertullian.

In spite of such "doctrinally neutral" features, the letter gives rich testimony to the convictions and attitudes connected with persecution. We might speak here of a "spirituality" of martyrdom being formulated at the end of the second century. This spirituality is centered upon the glorious Christ, represented as actively present in the life of the Church and the individual Christian. Christ is thought of as a heavenly source of life, strength, dynamism, and consolation. His earthly passion is properly relegated to the past, but *his glorious presence in the suffering martyrs* makes it evident that the martyrs of every era extend in time and space the "glorious passion" of the Lord presented with such glowing features in the Fourth Gospel. Although Christ's glorious life belongs to a realm other than this earth, the martyrs truly participate in it while undergoing their suffering. Through their agony they become sharers of both his life and glory. The figure of Christ that this document projects is, therefore, both crucified and glorious, both present in history and still to come, "a noble and victorious athlete" who continues to be involved in bloody fighting, repeated trials, and unceasing tribulations. The abundance of love and mercy in the martyrs is the greatest gift they receive from the glorious Lord and thus achieve by their witness a public manifestation of God's glory and advance the last phase of the eschatological process already in course: the final condemnation of "the Adversary." There is little evidence that either the μίμησις of Christ by the martyrs or their παρρησία (free access for intercession), obtained at the price of their sufferings, would compromise the uniqueness of Christ's role as Savior and intercessor, as von Campenhausen has claimed.[24] All achievements, virtues, and excellence that our author finds in the martyrs are systematically re-

---

[24]H. von Campenhausen builds the LMG into a reconstructed evolutionary scheme of the cult of the martyrs. He sees in this document the first signs that the martyrs "step beside Christ as mediators of redemption (*Heilsvermittler*)." He also thinks that in this letter, just as in the *Martyrdom of Polycarp*, the idea of Christ's "imitation" (*Nachahmung*) replaces the idea of "following" him (*Nachfolge*) with the consequence that the martyrdom now obtains a technical sense and the martyr is exalted over the common Christian. *Die Idee des Martyriums in der alten Kirche* (Göttingen: Vandenhoeck & Ruprecht, 1964) 86–89.

duced to their font and origin, Christ himself. The concept of κοινωνία (sharing, participation) is explicitly used to explain the martyr's relationship of dependence on "the living God" (I.41). Nothing can the martyrs achieve by themselves.

But from another point of view my analysis does raise some concerns and can lead to dissatisfaction with the spirituality of martyrdom found in this document. At first sight, it appears that the drama of the martyrs' "abortions" and "returns to the womb" offers a real possibility for personal tragedies within the ranks of the Christians, a matter of true concern and compassion for the Christian community. Yet our author does not seem to envisage the possibility of what one can call a real failure or loss. According to him, whoever finally succumbs to the power of the Devil has never belonged to Christ. At this point, in the letter's theology, there appears a certain uncompromising harshness which leads to statements of condemnation and rejection, and excludes both the perception of true human freedom and genuine human tragedy. Nor does this outlook allow sympathy or prayer for the spiritual victims of persecution.

We detect here, in my opinion, the consequences of a preponderantly Johannine Christology with one-sided emphasis on present-day manifestation of glory and on judgment already actualized. In this perspective one can hardly avoid the pretension that Christ is "all-victorious" in such a radical sense that only the sons of perdition who have never truly belonged to the flock and no one else (none of the true Christians) can fall away from the faith. Of course, the letter contains some potentially "counterbalancing" elements. Most importantly, by quoting Matthew 18:18, it says that the martyrs "loosed (=absolved) all, and bound (=condemned, blamed, declared guilty) none" (II.5), and so, when departing, they left no pain for their Mother, the church, but "joy, peace, harmony and love" (II.7). In other words, we are reassured that the martyrdom of the saints had a healing effect on the whole membership of the church. At first, we would think the example of Stephen, quoted in this context, left a deep impression on the persecuted Christians of Gaul so that they prayed not only for those who had failed but also for their persecutors. Yet this assumption is nowhere substantiated in the account. The document quotes Stephen's example but then applies it with a disappointing twist: "If he (Stephen) prayed for those who were stoning him, how much more would he have done so for his fellow Christians?" (II.7). This translation by Musurillo is quite correct; it seems to be unjustified to change the subject and paraphrase as we have it in the Lawlor-Oulton edition: "how much more should *we* pray for the *brethren who lapsed.*" The sentence, in fact, rather than showing that the martyrs of Gaul followed the example of Stephen, "the perfect martyr," turns this logic upside down and proves the contrary: Stephen is quoted as corresponding to the norms set by the martyrs of Gaul. *Their concern*, throughout their passion story, remains restricted to the lapsed so that they manage to return back "into the womb." The question of salvation for those remaining outside of "the womb" deserves no further concern: they are (have always been!) "sons of perdition." Even less do we hear about prayers offered for the persecutors. It seems therefore legitimate to remark that the love for the enemy or for the lapsed brother remaining in sin are left totally outside the horizon of LMG, although its author was clearly aware of such teachings through his familiarity with both the gospels of Matthew and of Luke and with Acts.[25] We are dealing here with an ecclesial community dangerously close to a rigoristic condemnation of all those who are "outside" its ranks. This church appears to be quite closed upon itself and thus preoccupied only with "brotherly love" in a narrowly ecclesial sense.[26]

Obviously, therefore, the synoptic tradition plays a relatively small role in offering biblical foundations to the LMG when it deals with these questions. We might even go as far as to say that our author's appropriation and appreciation of the four-gospel canon is deficient: the exaggerated primacy of John makes him somewhat (at least selectively) blind and deaf to the other gospels. The consequences are far reaching: attitudes of closure and isolation were allowed to persist, a result understandable for an ostracized ecclesial community, yet extremely dangerous for its future. For a short while, such attitudes can produce feats of heroism but on the long run they cannot be sustained. Do we not catch here a serious weakness which signals the approach of crises: first, the crisis of Montanism to be followed by that of the prolonged disputes over penance and forgiveness available for the lapsed, leading finally to battles with the Donatists, crises which have indeed cost so much pain and loss of peace for "the Virgin Mother" throughout the third century?

[25]Bardy's French text tries to remain as ambiguous as possible but suggests the meaning of Musurillo's translation: "Si celui-ci a prié pour ceux qui le lapidaient, combien plus pour les frères." There is no reason to suppose that the original text contained an exhortation addressed to the Christians in Asia Minor to pray for the lapsed (and thus freed) ex-Christians. They have been written off already as "sons of perdition"!

[26]The question which I touch on here can be formulated also in the following way: why is the precept of loving one's enemy absent from John? This question, obviously too broad for further treatment here, might be somewhat tempered by taking note that the Fourth Gospel contains Jn. 3:16–17 about *God's love for the world*, motivating him to give over to death his only Son.

WOMEN AMONG THE EARLY MARTYRS

by STUART G. HALL

T HE Pentecostal sermon attributed to Peter in Acts announces Joel's prophecy fulfilled:

It shall happen in the last days, says God, that I will pour some of my Spirit upon all flesh, and your sons and your daughters shall prophesy, your youths shall see visions and your elders shall dream dreams; yes, even on my slaves and slavegirls in those days I will pour some of my Spirit, and they shall prophesy.[1]

The gift thus overrides sex, rank, and social status; it is often overlooked that the company on whom the Spirit falls in Acts 2 includes, beside the restored Twelve, 'women and Mary the mother of Jesus and his brothers',[2] and Acts in this respect agrees with Paul that in Christ 'there is no Jew nor Greek, there is no slave nor free man, there is no male and female; you are all one person in Christ Jesus.'[3]

This gift of the Spirit is primarily baptismal; it is a baptism of the Spirit which washing in the name of Jesus Christ represents. Manifestations of the Spirit include prophecy and divination, which soon in the Church are seen as a special gift. Among those to whom that spiritual gift is accorded are those who face public trial for the Name of Jesus, and who attest their faith under that testing:

When they turn you in, do not be anxious about how you are to speak or what to say; it will be given you at that time what you are to say. It is not you that speak, but the Spirit of your Father that speaks in you.[4]

There is no restriction to males in this process. The Spirit falls on women in baptism, giving words of prophecy and visions, and so does martyrdom, and with it the opportunity to witness and speak with the voice of the Spirit.

Dead martyrs no longer speak. But while they still live, they have become vessels of that special gift, and must be listened to with appropriate care. Dionysius the Great, Bishop of Alexandria during the Decian

---

[1] Acts 2.17–18, adapting Joel 2.28–9.
[2] Acts 1.14.
[3] Galatians 3.28.
[4] Matthew 10.19–20, and parallels.

persecution of 249 to 251, deploys the authority of the martyrs to justify a moderate position in disciplining the lapsed. He stated his case to Fabius of Antioch, who favoured a rigorous policy, first listing the heroic acts of those who faced trial and died, and concluding:

> The divine martyrs themselves among us, who now are assessors of Christ, and share the fellowship of his kingdom, and take part in his decisions and judge along with him,[5] have espoused the cause of certain of the fallen brethren who became answerable for the charge of sacrificing; and seeing their conversion and repentance, they judged it had the power to prove acceptable to him who hath no pleasure in the death of the sinner, but rather his repentance; and so they received and admitted them to the worship of the Church as 'consistentes', and gave them fellowship in their prayers and feasts.[6]

Those concerned had probably been 'perfected' as martyrs by death before Dionysius wrote, though it is not certain. But clearly they are still alive when they make the judgement, and the possibility is open that they might somehow survive the persecution, and the special status of their words has to be recognized in the churches.

A clarification of terms is needed, commonplace in itself.[7] A martyr, μάρτυς, is simply a 'witness'. So living martyrs are quite possible. They have given their testimony, μαρτυρία. If they ratify it, confirming their testimony by dying, it becomes stronger, a present proof of Christ's Resurrection and the truth of the faith.[8] But essentially it is no different from 'confession', ὁμολογία, which can be 'unto death'. Confessors and martyrs are one and the same. We find living martyrs not only among the Montanists,[9] but at Rome, and even among the bishops around AD 200,

---

[5] Alluding to Matthew 19.28; I Corinthians 6.2–3; Revelation 20.4.

[6] Quoted by Eusebius, *Ecclesiastical History*, 6,42,5. I use *Eusebius Bishop of Caesarea. The Ecclesiastical History and The Martyrs of Palestine*, tr. with intro. and notes Hugh Jackson Lawlor and John Ernest Leonard Oulton (London, 1954, repr. 1927). The generally excellent Penguin Classics edition (*Eusebius, The History of the Church from Christ to Constantine* tr. G. A. Williams, rev. edn and intro. Andrew Louth, 2nd edn (Harmondsworth, 1989)), lacks complete marginal numeration, making its scholarly use very difficult.

[7] See, for instance, Michael Slusser, 'Martyrium III', *Theologische Realenzyklopädie*, 22 (1992), pp. 207–11, and bibliography; *A Patristic Greek Lexicon*, ed. G. W. H. Lampe (Oxford, 1961), under μάρτυς, ὁμολογέω and cognates. J. Ruyschart, 'Les "martyrs" et les "confesseurs" de la lettre des églises de Lyon et de Vienne', in *Les Martyrs de Lyon*, 177 = *Colloques Internationaux du Centre National de la Recherche Scientifique*, no. 575 (Paris, 1978), pp. 233–47, emphasizes the fluidity of the terms, and uses 'témoin' in preference to 'martyr' throughout.

[8] So Athanasius, *De Incarnatione*, 28–9 = *SC*, 199, pp. 362–70.

[9] Eusebius, *Ecclesiastical History*, 5,18,5–6.

Natalius[10] and Kallistos (= Calixtus I) as well as those imprisoned with Kallistos.[11] These confessors are an interesting reflection on the ecclesiastical status which their witness conveyed. They belong to the period when the formal orders of the Church are encroaching upon the traditional charismatic functions: apostles have been replaced in the succession of 'bishops and deacons',[12] and the duties and gifts of teachers and prophets are now associated with bishops and presbyters. Traditionally teachers ran their schools alongside, and sometimes in competition with, the episcopal congregations. Justin Martyr, Clement of Alexandria, and Perpetua's instructor Saturus are typical examples. Most of them end up labelled as heretics, like Valentinus and Ptolomaeus. Origen began independently, with a female patron, but in his time ordination to the presbyterate was coming to be needed.[13]

The Church at the end of the second century is in process of bringing order into its leadership and organization. It is no accident that the reconstructed *Apostolic Tradition* of Hippolytus of Rome gives us the classic account of the ecclesiastical status of the confessor. After describing the procedures for ordaining bishops, presbyters, and deacons he writes:

> But if a confessor has been in chains for the Name, hands are not laid on him for the diaconate or the presbyter's office. For he has the honour ($\tau \iota \mu \acute{\eta}$) of the presbyterate by his confession. But if he be appointed bishop, hands shall be laid on him. And if he be a confessor who was not brought before a public authority nor punished with chains nor condemned to any penalty, but was only by chance derided for the name of our Lord and [perhaps = 'or'] was punished domestically, even though he confessed, hands shall be laid upon him for every order of which he is worthy.[14]

Thus the Church acknowledges the privilege granted to the confessor who has borne witness, seating him with the elders and awarding him

[10] Eusebius, *Ecclesiastical History*, 5,28,10.
[11] Hippolytus, *Refutation* 9,11,4, and 9,12,10–11, ed. Miroslav Marcovich, *Patristische Texte und Studien*, 25 (Berlin, 1986), 350, lines 25–30, and 352, lines 46–55.
[12] So first *I Clement*, 42–4, and *Didache*, 15 [conveniently in *The Apostolic Fathers*, I, Eng. tr. Kirsopp Lake = *LCL* (1912)].
[13] Full discussion in Ulrich Neymeyr, *Die christlichen Lehrer im zweiten Jahrhundert. Ihre Lehrtätigkeit, ihr Selbsverständnis und ihre Geschichte* = *Supplements to Vigiliae Christianae*, IV (Leiden, 1989).
[14] *Apostolic Tradition*, 10, 1–2, *The Treatise on the Apostolic Tradition of St Hippolytus of Rome*, ed. Gregory Dix (London, 1937), rev. edn Henry Chadwick (London, 1968), pp. 18–19; also in *Hippolyte de Rome, La Tradition apostolique*, intro. etc., Bernard Botte, 2nd edn (Paris, 1968) = *SC*, 11,2, ch. 9, p. 64, from which some of the wording above is derived.

allocation of the gifts by which the clergy lived (if τιμή, 'honour', be taken in the sense of clerical remuneration, as apparently in I Timothy 5. 17). But it protects itself from presumption to episcopal status, as in the case of Natalius at Rome,[15] and against aspiring confessors who had suffered only informal harassment, such as slaves, wives, and children beaten at home for their Christianity.

Hippolytus in the passage quoted refers to domestic violence. I need hardly say this was commonplace, and Roman society offered little protection against it. Even the Bible recommends it as a method of education (Proverbs 12. 7–11). Its extent and acceptability can perhaps be judged by canon 5 of the Council of Elvira, about 305.

> If any woman, impelled by furious anger, beat her maidservant with a lash so that she gives up the ghost within three days, and it be uncertain whether her death was intentional or accidental, she shall be admitted to communion after seven years if intentional, five years if accidental, after the performance of due penance.[16]

If a Christian lady can get away so lightly with murder, there were probably many slaves of both sexes who suffered or died for their faith almost unnoticed, unsung as martyrs and unrecognized as confessors. It also throws light on Hippolytus' insistence that slaves might not be baptized without the consent of a Christian owner, and not at all if their owner is pagan (ἐθνικός).[17] Wives and children are also subject to domestic violence, of which we know little.

Whatever the situation over domestic violence, subordination is a powerful theme in respectable Christian circles, and is indeed a leitmotiv of the so-called *First Letter of Clement*. The Corinthians are there congratulated on their former godliness, honouring elders, moderating the young, and

> to the women you gave instruction that they should do all things with a blameless and seemly and pure conscience, yielding dutiful affection to their husbands. And you taught them to abide by the rule of subordination and to manage their households with seemliness, quite soberly.[18]

---

15 See above, n. 10.
16 Quoted from J. Stevenson, *A New Eusebius. Documents Illustrating the History of the Church to AD 337*, rev. edn W. H. C. Frend (London, 1987), p. 290, where further notes on cruelty to slaves are added.
17 Hippolytus, *Apostolic Tradition*, 16, 4–5, Dix edn, pp. 23–4: 15 Botte edn, pp. 69–70.
18 *I Clement*, 1,3 (tr. adapted from Lake's LCL edn).

Women among the Early Martyrs

The disorders current in Corinth are, says the author, due to envious ambition, and he lists its victims: first the biblical heroes, then the great Apostles Peter and Paul, and with them, in words echoed by Tacitus in his independent account of the persecution of Christians in Rome under Nero, 'a great multitude of the elect', who 'offered among us the fairest example in their endurance under many indignities and tortures'.[19] Finally, the women: 'Through jealous envy women were persecuted, Danaids and Dirkai, suffering terrible and unholy indignities: they steadfastly finished the course of faith and received a noble reward, weak in the body though they were.'[20] The terms 'Danaids' and 'Dirkai', which are certain in the oldest forms of the text, refer to classical myths. The fifty daughters of Danaus had suitors imported from Egypt, whom they slew in their marriage beds. Dirke, as a punishment for her atrocious cruelty to the helpless Antiope, was tied by her hair to the tail of a bull and dragged to death. Exegesis defeated commentators until a brilliant article by Hanns Christof Brennecke,[21] who took up a suggestion of A. W. Ziegler to show that the whole account of the apostolic and other martyrs in *I Clement*, 5–6, is expressed in athletic terms, and thus the point of comparison is that the women joined the men in the race, and won the same victory, crowned with martyrdom. In some forms of the myth[22] the Danaids were made prizes to be competed for by the suitors, which adds colour to the comparison: the women were not prizes, but prize-winners. The other comparison with Dirke similarly has only one point: her violent and horrible death. We thus find the author praising women among the martyrs. Their subordination is maintained, for they appear last; but their achievement is as noble as that of the male elect, despite their bodily infirmity.

Some of the later martyrological accounts find women in such a subordinate yet heroic role. In the various versions of *The Martyrdom of Justin and his Companions*,[23] Justin himself, the head of the school, is first questioned in some detail. Then the six members of the school are questioned more briefly. One is a woman named Charito, who in all

---

[19] *I Clement*, 6,1.
[20] Ibid., 6,2.
[21] Hanns Christof Brennecke, 'Danaiden und Dirken. Zu 1 Cl 6,2', *Zeitschrift für Kirchengeschichte*, 2 (1977), pp. 302–8. Brennecke gives full *Forschungsgeschichte* and documentation.
[22] Ibid., p. 305, n. 21.
[23] *Mart. Just.*, conveniently ed. in three Greek recensions and tr. Herbert Musurillo, *The Acts of the Christian Martyrs* (Oxford, 1972) = *Oxford Early Christian Texts*, pp. 42–61 [hereafter Musurillo]. Musurillo's translations, though useful, are at times sadly inaccurate.

recensions is the third to be questioned, following Justin and Chariton. In the earlier recensions the interrogation runs:

> To Chariton the prefect Rusticus said, 'Chariton, are you a Christian too?' 'I am a Christian,' said Chariton, 'by God's command.' Turning to Charito Rusticus the prefect said, 'And what do you say, Charito?' Charito said, 'I am a Christian by God's gift.'[24]

After the others are questioned, and Justin addressed again, all are led to flogging and execution with the phrase, 'They perfected their martyrdom in the confession of our Saviour.'[25] They are apparently free citizens, being beheaded for their crime.[26] In the group of pupils Chariton comes first, by chance or design. Charito is apparently dependent upon him, the similarity of names suggesting that she is not his wife, but his sister or daughter. She is the only female in the class, and is perhaps there as his dependant: a free-standing woman would be more remarkable. Her answer imitates Chariton's, only substituting 'gift' for 'command'. The expansive recension C piously suggests she is a dedicated virgin:

> 'I am not deceived,' said Charito to the magistrate. 'Rather I have become God's servant and a Christian, and by his power I keep myself pure and unstained by the taints of the flesh.'[27]

But this is not to be relied upon.

The proportions are different in two African martyrologies. Of the Scillitan Martyrs one, the spokesman and apparently teacher (he takes copies of 'books and letters of Paul, a just man' to court with him),[28] is accompanied by six other men and five women.[29] Since the women are listed separately, and the interrogations are not complete, we cannot detect whether there are married or otherwise related couples. In the case of *The Martyrdom of Saints Perpetua and Felicitas*,[30] the compiler lists the men first, beginning with the slaves 'Revocatus and his fellow-slave (*conserua*) Felicitas', where *conserua* plainly means that she is his matrimonial partner

---

[24] *Mart. Just.*, A,4,1–2; B,4,1–2. The longer question and Charito's answer in C,3,2–3, revealing an attitude of contempt for female judgement, are clearly secondary.

[25] Ibid., A,6; B,6; ἐτελείωσαν τὸ μαρτύριον ἐν τῇ τοῦ σωτῆρος ἡμῶν ὁμολογίᾳ, unhelpfully misrendered by Musurillo, 'fulfilled their testimony by their act of faith in our Saviour'.

[26] Ibid., A,5,1.6; B,5,1.8.

[27] Ibid., C,3,3.

[28] *Passio Sanctorum Scillitanorum*, Musurillo, 86–9, p. 12.

[29] Ibid., see especially the list at p. 15, where the name Speratus is misprinted as Sperata in the English.

[30] *Mart. Perp.*, Musurillo, pp. 106–31. See 2,1 and 4,5.

in so far as slaves may be such. After Saturninus and Secundulus, 'with them Vibia Perpetua'. The five are later joined by their instructor, Saturus. Here we have three men and two women in the class. Felicity is named after her partner; Perpetua as a single woman is named last, even though she is the leading figure.

In another martyrology the subordinate heroism of the woman is distinct. *The Martyrdom of Saints Carpus, Papylos and Agathonice*[31] records a trial at Pergamum, which Eusebius mentions in connection with the persecutions under Marcus Aurelius, but the Latin recension and some moderns prefer to place under Decius.[32] Carpus is apparently the leader, and is called 'Bishop of Gordos' in the opening of the Latin recension; he argues theologically in his own defence.[33] Papylos is in the Latin called Pamfilus and given the ecclesiastical rank of 'a deacon of Thyatira'. In fact, the joke he makes, asserting that he has 'many children', by which he means, 'children in the Lord in every province and city',[34] suggests that he is a travelling teacher; Carpus' apologetic argument might suggest he also is a teacher. The ecclesiastical ranks may well be secondary.

In the Greek recension, Agathonice is a spectator, and not on trial. Nailed to the stake for burning, Carpus declares that he has seen the glory of the Lord.[35] After the account of his death, the Greek continues:

> There was a woman named Agathonice standing there who had seen the glory of the Lord, which Carpus said he had seen; recognizing that this was a call from heaven, she raised her voice at once: 'Here is a meal that has been prepared for me. I must partake and eat of this glorious repast.' The mob shouted out: 'Have pity on your son.' And the blessed Agathonice said: 'He has God who can take pity on him; for he has providence over all. Let me do what I have come for.' And taking off her cloak, she threw herself joyfully upon the stake.[36]

Clearly she is a mother with a male child. In that she resembles Perpetua and Felicitas. Perpetua is finally relieved of her child by her father, and presumably by her Christian relatives, as we shall see. Felicitas' new-born daughter is entrusted to one of the sisters to bring up as her own.[37]

---

[31] *Mart. Carp.*; Musurillo, pp. 22–37, prints both recensions.
[32] Eusebius, *Ecclesiastical History*, 4,15,48; see Musurillo, p. xv and n. 8.
[33] *Mart. Carp.* A,5–20; B,2,1–4,6.
[34] Ibid., A.28–32; B,3,2–3.
[35] Ibid., A,38–9; εἶδον should be understood as, 'I have just seen.' This episode is attributed to Pamfilus in B,4,3, and is not related to Agathonice.
[36] Ibid., A,42–4.
[37] *Mart. Perp.*, 6,7–8; 15,7.

Whatever may be said of Agathonice's attitude to her son, it is not utterly improvident in committing him solely to God: the fellowship of the Church would do God's work for him. In the Roman Church about the year 250 there were 'above fifteen hundred widows and persons in distress, all of whom are supported by the grace and lovingkindness of the Master', that is, by the gifts of the faithful.[38]

Most striking is the voluntary suicidal martyrdom, resembling a death by suttee. In this she is not alone. During the local Egyptian persecution which anticipated the formal decrees of Decius in 248–9, one victim was an elderly virgin called Apollonia. They

> broke out all her teeth with blows on her jaws, and piling up a pyre before the city threatened to burn her alive, if she refused to recite along with them their blasphemous sayings. But she asked for a brief space, and, being released, without flinching she leaped into the fire and was consumed.[39]

This comes nearer the case of Agathonice than some other examples, such as the unnamed Roman matron who stabbed herself to death rather than be procured by Maxentius.[40] That matron is commended as a moral lesson, but not called a confessor or martyr. Valentina, who protested against the torture of another Christian woman, and was herself duly tried and killed, is similarly distant.[41] Much more germane is the case of Quintus:

> A certain Quintus, a Phrygian recently arrived from Phrygia, saw the beasts and turned coward. He it was who had made himself and some others come forward voluntarily. The governor used many persuasions on him, and got him to swear and to offer sacrifice. For this reason, brothers, we do not approve of those who come forward by themselves, since the Gospel does not so teach.[42]

This is probably an interpolation in the *Martyrdom of Polycarp*. The following chapter begins, 'At first the most admirable Polycarp when he heard this was not disturbed. . . .' That plainly refers not to the incident of Quintus, but to the cries of the mob at the Smyrna games for Polycarp to be sought for, which precedes the account of Quintus. I therefore suppose

---

[38] Eusebius, *Ecclesiastical History*, 6,43,11.
[39] Ibid., 6,41,7.
[40] Ibid., 8,14,17.
[41] Eusebius, *Martyrs of Palestine*, 8,6–8.
[42] *Martyrdom of Polycarp*, 4, Musurillo, pp. 4–5.

the latter to be a polemical interpolation. Interpolated or not, it is distinctly polemical, and attacks the voluntary self-offering which it studiously attributes to the Phrygians. The incident takes place in Smyrna, another of the cities of Asia, like Pergamum, where Agathonice dies, and like Thyatira, from which her companion Papylos comes. We are thus in the prime area for the heresy we usually call 'Montanism', which the Greeks simply call the 'Phrygian heresy'. It is perhaps best to call it by its own members' name, the 'New Prophecy'.[43] Enemies of the New Prophecy certainly associate it with voluntary martyrdom, and perhaps rightly. Tertullian, the only disciple of the New Prophecy from whom we have any substantial writings, plainly adopts a rigorous and uncompromising view of persecution and martyrdom. Whereas in his earlier days he was prepared to permit the reconciliation of the lapsed and the avoidance of persecution, when he comes to write *On flight — De fuga* —any such evasion of God's good gift is apostasy, and there is no second penance. So significant is this that Frederick C. Klawiter has recently argued that voluntary martyrdom is the chief distinguishing point of the New Prophecy.[44]

I do not agree wholly with Klawiter. But the point remains that the New Prophecy boasts living martyrs, encourages voluntarism, and takes a hard line against the lapsed. This throws light on the two recensions of *The Martyrdom of Saints Carpus, Papylos and Agathonice*. The Latin is much tidier. Carpus has become a bishop, Pamfilus a deacon. Agathonice also is improved: she has more than one son (*miserere tibi et filiis tuis*),[45] her beauty when she removes her clothing is commented on by the crowd.[46] More importantly the lady is brought forward in regular order by the command of the proconsul, who demands that she sacrifice; and a formal sentence and execution by burning follow her refusal. One might too readily conclude that an account which gives no ecclesiastical rank to the men and which leaves the woman a voluntary martyr is original, and that it has been improved in an orthodox direction in the Latin version. But there are

---

[43] Recent accounts and documentation in W. H. C. Frend, 'Montanism. A movement of prophecy and regional identity in the early church', *BJRL*, 70 (1988), pp. 25–34; 'Montanismus': *Theologische Realenzyklopädie* (forthcoming); Ronald E. Heine, *The Montanist Oracles and Testimonia = North American Patristic Society, Patristic Monograph Series 14* (Macon, GA, 1989), which supersedes earlier collections of documents.

[44] 'The role of martyrdom and persecution in developing the priestly authority of women in early Christianity. A case study of Montanism', *ChH*, 49 (1980), pp. 251–61.

[45] *Mart. Carp.* B, 6,2.

[46] Ibid., B, 6,4–5.

indications that the Latin is in some respects older than the Greek, and specifically in the proconsul's interrogation:

'What do you say? Offer sacrifice. Or would you follow the thinking of your teachers (*doctorum tuorum*)?' She replied, 'I am a Christian and have never sacrificed to the demons, but only to God. I desire gladly, if I am worthy, to follow the steps of the saints and of my teachers (*sanctorum doctorumque meorum*).'[47]

Both proconsul and martyr refer to Carpus and Papylos as Agathonice's teachers, *doctorum tuorum*, *doctorum meorum*. This tallies with the evidence of their own interrogations, as we have seen, in which Carpus discourses like an apologist, and Papylos confesses to having spiritual children in various places. We then have, as in other cases, the martyrdom of teachers and pupil together. Since this fits the position of teachers in the second century, and not so well with the ecclesiastical ranks of bishop and deacon, we may therefore be faced with two secondary versions of the martyrology: a Greek recension which has, by accident or design, been improved in a Phrygian direction, heightening the voluntary character of her death, and with a Latin one which has improved the status of her teachers with ecclesiastical office, but has preserved an original interrogation.

We turn to the martyrs of Lyons, probably to be dated to 177.[48] They include a large group of women, most of whose names are preserved in an ancient list. This list, divided into those beheaded, those given to the beasts, and those who died in prison, was already known to Eusebius,[49] and is presented by later sources, such as Gregory of Tours.[50] In the later sources it is stated that they numbered forty-eight in all; Gregory himself then gives the names of twenty-four men and twenty-one women. They were therefore in nearly equal numbers. There are three groups, the second and third explicitly naming those who were thrown to the beasts and those who died in prison. In each group the men are listed first, save for the final name of the bishop Photinus.

---

[47] Ibid., B, 6,1.
[48] Eusebius, *Ecclesiastical History*, 5, preface and 1–4, cites the martyrology at length (also in Musurillo, pp. 62–85).
[49] Eusebius, *Ecclesiastical History*, 5,4,3.
[50] *Glory of the martyrs*, 48; conveniently accessible in English in Raymond van Dam, ed. and tr. with intro., *Gregory of Tours. Glory of the Martyrs = Translated Texts for Historians. Latin Series* 3 (Liverpool, 1988), which has a useful note on p. 73.

We do not know the precise history of the martyrs of Lyons,[51] but some things are clear. One is that the allegations of monstrous practices of incest and (particularly) cannibalism are prominent. Christians prepared to deny their faith were not, as in other cases since Pliny, released, but continued to be held on a charge of murder, and suffered more in prison than those held as Christians.[52] The allegation of cannibalism was confirmed by non-Christian slaves belonging to the martyrs, who were terrified by the tortures; this turned formerly sympathetic members of the community against the Christians.[53] The ruling of the Emperor was finally sought, and at the second hearing the surviving apostates were given the opportunity to confirm their denial and go free.[54] The official position thus continued to sustain the line originally adopted by Pliny and confirmed by Trajan about 112, ignoring the alleged secret crimes, and punishing for mere Christianity.[55]

This provides a context for Biblis. Since her name appears in the first section of Gregory's list, she was apparently decapitated, and therefore a Roman citizen,[56] like half the total group. Confession of cannibalism by one who had been a Christian was anxiously sought.

> Biblis too, one of those who had denied, the devil supposed that he had already devoured; but wishing to use her slander as a further ground of condemnation, he brought her to punishment, that he might compel an already fragile and craven woman to state impieties against us. She however regained her senses under the torture and awoke, so to speak, from a deep sleep, when the passing retribution recalled to her mind the eternal punishment in hell; and she directly

[51] The celebration volume, *Les Martyrs de Lyon* (see above, n. 7), is essential reading but somewhat disappointing. For a judicious discussion of the problems generally, see W. H. C. Frend, *Martyrdom and Persecution in the Early Church* (Oxford, 1965), pp. 1–30, and for a comprehensive recent analysis, Winrich A. Löhr, 'Der Brief der Gemeinden von Lyon und Vienne (Eusebius, h.e. V,1–2[4])', *Oecumenica et Patristica. Festschrift für Wilhelm Schneemelcher* (Chambésy and Stuttgart, 1989), pp. 135–49. Some connection with the *senatusconsultum* of 175 seems probable (see J. H. Oliver and R. E. A. Palmer, 'Minutes of an Act of the Roman Senate', *Hesperia*, 24 (1955), pp. 320–49), though the Christian sources show no knowledge of the legal niceties or the price of gladiators, and most of the martyrs did not perform in the ring. For the polemical orientation against the New Prophecy, though not for the date, Pierre Nautin, *Lettres et écrivains chrétiens des iième et iiième siècles* (Paris, 1961), ch. 2, deserves more attention than it has received.
[52] Eusebius, *Ecclesiastical History*, 5,1,33.
[53] Ibid., 5,1,14–16.
[54] Ibid., 5,1,47–8.
[55] Pliny, *Epistulae*, 10,96,5–6, and esp. 97,2 (cited from Eng. version in Stevenson, *New Eusebius*, pp. 18–21).
[56] Eusebius, *Ecclesiastical History*, 5,1, 47 for the sentences.

contradicted the slanderers, saying: 'How could they eat their children, when they may not eat the blood even of irrational beasts?' And henceforth she confessed herself a Christian, and joined the inheritance of the martyrs.[57]

We must not delay on the identifying of the persecutors with the Devil, the motive of terror in Christian obedience, or the adherence to kosher food. First, we note that she is not the only one tortured for the same purpose of getting evidence of the atrocities: Sanctus, Maturus, Attalus, and Blandina are also singled out.[58] Biblis shares the experience of the two female deacons (*ministrae*) whom Pliny had tortured for the same information.[59] It was precisely their failure to confirm the horror stories which precipitated Pliny's enquiry to the Emperor as to whether it was the name of Christian, or the secret crimes connected with the name, that was punished; and it is plain that he is interested in what Christians ate.[60] The second thing about Biblis is that the martyrologist records the remembered words of confession, even though they are obscurely put in a rhetorical question: 'How could they eat their children, when they may not eat the blood even of irrational beasts?' This is her Spirit-given word, lovingly recorded. The third and most important is that she is a penitent apostate, and is added to the martyrs.

The letter in which the account survives is a polemical document. It is addressed to the churches of Asia and Phrygia, which are precisely those torn by the New Prophecy dispute. A copy is apparently directed to Rome in the name of the martyrs themselves, if not actually written by them as Eusebius says.[61] The vital point is that the martyrs in prison won back most of the ten who denied at the first hearing, and reconciled them to the faith. Some presumably died in prison, where about eighteen perished altogether, and the conditions were worse for those held as murderers than for those held as Christians. At the second hearing, after the Emperor's ruling had been obtained, these penitents made a good confession and were executed with the rest.[62] The process of restoration is introduced thus: 'A mighty dispensation of God came to pass, and the measureless compassion of Jesus was displayed, in a manner rarely vouch-

---

[57] Ibid., 5,1,25–6.
[58] Ibid., 5,1,17–24.
[59] Pliny, *Epistulae*, 10,96,8.
[60] Ibid., 10,96,2 and 7.
[61] Eusebius, *Ecclesiastical History*, 5,4.
[62] Ibid., 5,1,11.32–5.45–8.

safed among the brethren, but not beyond the skill of Christ.'[63] This shows that it was not the rights of the confessor-martyrs that was in question, but the way they used it. So in the polemical passage of which extracts survive, the martyrs

> who also were such emulators and imitators of Christ ... neither proclaimed themselves martyrs nor indeed did they permit us to address them by this name . . .. They loosed all and bound none . . ... They did not indulge in boasting against the fallen, but with a mother's compassion supplied the more needy with that wherein they themselves abounded; and pouring forth many tears on their behalf to the Father, they asked life, and he gave it them.[64]

Eusebius immediately emphasizes the relevance of this to the harsh treatment of the lapsed, and goes on to introduce his first account of the New Prophecy in Phrygia, before describing the letter in the name of the martyrs to Rome. It is not the authenticity of what is revealed to confessors that the document argues: their privileged judgement is presupposed. What is argued on the basis of their judgement is the rightness of reconciling the lapsed. Not only was it the judgement of the confessors: it was a special providence of Christ's mercy to keep the fallen Christians in prison where they could be brought to repentance and reconciled; and there is implicit appeal to the judgement of God in ratifying the reconciliation, when Biblis and the others made their confession good at the end.

Here a sharper line is needed than is sometimes drawn. W. H. C. Frend suggests that

> Montanism itself, and the *Acta Martyrum* from Lyon and Carthage [that is, of Perpetua and Felicity] all point to a movement within Christianity in the last quarter of the second century based on a profound conviction of the approaching end of the existing age and the glorification of the role of the confessor and martyr as vehicles of the Holy Spirit in bringing that about.[65]

Learnedly though this is argued, it misses the crucial point. The New Prophecy was not objectionable because it claimed rights for prophets and confessors, nor because it held to the imminence of the end of the world; these were widely-held views. It was objectionable because of the new

[63] Ibid., 5,1,32.
[64] Ibid., 5,2,2–6.
[65] *Les Martyrs de Lyon*, p. 174.

strictness which its prophets commended, tightening discipline over marriage, fasting, veiling, flight in persecution, and, above all, over the treatment of moral and religious lapse. This can be verified by simply comparing the early works of Tertullian with those he wrote after he accepted the New Prophecy. The martyrs of Lyons are thus champions of peace for the penitent lapsed, and their martyrology lies before us to argue that case against the New Prophets of Phrygia. Frederick C. Klawiter also misconstrues the position, when he argues that 'priestly power' was exercised by confessors like Perpetua among the Montanists, because unlike the Catholics they allowed confessors clerical authority even though they had not consummated their confession by martyrdom. This misplaces the issue, and obliges him incidentally to postulate that the founding women of the New Prophecy (Priscilla and Maximilla) were confessors, for which there is no evidence.[66]

At the head of the confessor-martyrs of Lyons stands another woman: Blandina. She is one of those singled out for pressure to confirm the allegations of monstrous behaviour. She is a slave, whose mistress, herself among the martyrs, fears that Blandina's physical weakness (or illness) will lead her to yield under torture. But she does not, and astonishes people by her vitality and endurance, repeatedly giving her testimony: 'I am a Christian, and with us no evil has any place.'[67] During this first phase of the interrogations, while Attalus, Maturus, and Sanctus suffer, Blandina is hung cruciform in the middle of the arena, exposed to the beasts, though they did not touch her.

> Even to look on her, as she hung cross-wise in earnest prayer, wrought great eagerness in those who were contending, for in their conflict they beheld with their outward eyes in the form of their sister him who was crucified for them, that he might persuade those who believe in him that all who suffer for the glory of Christ have unbroken fellowship with the living God. . . . she was taken down and reserved for another conflict . . . she the small, the weak, the despised, who had put on Christ the great and invincible Champion, and who in many rounds vanquished the adversary and through conflict was crowned with the crown of incorruptibility.[68]

---

[66] 'The role of martyrdom and persecution in developing the priestly authority of women in early Christianity. A case study of Montanism', ChH, 49 (1980), pp. 251–61.
[67] Eusebius, Ecclesiastical History, 5,1,17–19.
[68] Ibid., 5,1,41–2.

The slave-girl among the confessors thus embodies the merciful Christ, and her judgement must be among those who reconciled the lapsed. It is difficult to see her as other than the leader, by divine appointment. Her final conflicts at the summer games are described in terms which confirm this. She encouraged especially the fifteen-year-old Ponticus, who is described as 'her brother', whether in the flesh her brother or not. Then,

> last of all, having like a highborn mother exhorted her children and sent them forth victorious to the King, travelled herself along the same path of conflicts as they did, and hastened to them . . . And after the scourging, after the wild beasts, after the frying-pan, she was at last put in a basket and presented to a wild bull. For a time the animal tossed her, though by now she was unconscious . . . Then she too was sacrificed [presumably her throat was cut], and even the heathen themselves acknowledged that never in their experience had a woman endured so many and terrible sufferings.[69]

The parallel with the Maccabean mother of martyrs[70] is obvious and has often been noticed. Less frequently, if ever, noticed is the paradoxical eminence of a woman and slave among the confessors. Dionysius of Alexandria included women in his tale of the Decian persecution, which concludes with the judgement of 'the divine martyrs among us' in favour of remitting sins to the lapsed.[71] But I know no discussion of the status of women as confessors, which is so pointed up by Blandina: she is the chosen embodiment of Christ's own death, the mother of all the martyrs. Their glory, and the judgement they give, must be hers. Suppose she had survived and turned up in Hippolytus' congregation in Rome as a confessor, would she have been seated with the presbyters? Presumably not, since the sexes were normally sharply separated. She could be given the same portion of the offerings, the same τιμή. She might have sat with the official Widows. Clearly the charisma she is endowed with does not match the rising codes of ecclesial order, of which Hippolytus' is the best early example.

We turn finally to Vibia Perpetua and Felicitas.[72] Their martyrology is edited (by general consent) in the interest of the New Prophecy. The

---

[69] Ibid., 5,1,53–6.
[70] II Maccabees 7, esp. 20–41.
[71] Eusebius, *Ecclesiastical History*, 6,41,1–42,6.
[72] *Passio sanctarum Perpetuae et Felicitatis* [hereafter *Passio*]; Latin and English in Musurillo, pp. 106–31. See also W. H. C. Frend, 'Blandina and Perpetua. Two early Christian heroines'. *Les Martyrs de Lyon*, pp. 167–77.

editor from the start challenges those who would restrict 'the one power of the one Holy Spirit to particular periods, since the more recent are to be considered greater' in view of the promise for the last times; that promise is the prophecy of Joel with which this lecture began, quoted in rather disorderly form from memory. He or she concludes, 'So we too recognize and honour not only prophecies but visions equally promised, and reckon the other powers of the Holy Spirit as for the service of the Church . . .'.[73] Is the editor right in using the story in this way? I believe so. Almost half the narrative (chapters 3–10) is written by Perpetua herself, a little less by the editor (1–2 and 14–21), and the remainder (11–13) by another martyr, Saturus. We should ask, why did Perpetua record her experiences? The answer is not far to seek. She recognizes herself as a competent confessor, and records her own sayings, visions, and spiritual experiences because they are of value to the Church. After her first arrest, imprisonment, and baptism, her brother urges her:

> 'Dear sister, you are now greatly privileged [*iam in magna dignatione es*; Musurillo fails to render the crucial *iam*], so that you might ask for a vision and it be shown you whether it is to be suffering or deferment (*an passio sit an commeatus*).' For my part, whatever I knew myself to speak about with the Lord, whose benefits I had experienced, I promised faithfully to report to him, and said, 'Tomorrow I will tell you.' And I asked, and this is what was shown me . . .[74]

This incident may be what determined Perpetua to write down all her experiences, since the vision she received showed her passion to be imminent. She recognized that she had a claim upon God, and exercised it. She does the same in the matter of prayer. She wakes suddenly with the name of her brother Dinocrates on her lips, and 'I knew at once that I was worthy and ought to pray for him. I began to make earnest prayer for him and to plead with the Lord.' Her first vision of Dinocrates, who had died as a child of a facial cancer, shows him unable to reach a pool of water to drink. He was presumably unbaptized, as were Perpetua and her other brother or brothers when the story begins.[75] But she persists in prayer until they are moved to the military prison ready for the games. Then another vision is granted, in which Dinocrates can reach the water and is playing happily. Thus her martyr-prayers can reach even the unbaptized dead.

---

[73] *Passio*, 1,3–5.
[74] Ibid., unfortunately Musurillo's English is very faulty.
[75] Against Augustine, *De origine animae* 1,12, *CSEL*, 60, p. 312, see Musurillo, n. 11.

Consideration of the other material confirms this. There is a clear message in the vision of Saturus, in which he visits heaven with Perpetua, interviews earlier martyrs, and returns with a strong moral message for 'the bishops Optatus and Aspasius the presbyter-teacher (*presbyterum doctorem*)' that they should settle their quarrel.[76] The other narrative material, which has apparently come to the editor by oral tradition, is similarly determined by the desire to record the confession. Poor Felicitas, eight months pregnant, fears she may have her execution deferred and not be allowed to suffer with the others. The others pray for her, and their prayer brings her an early delivery, with great pain. The climax comes in these words:

> One of the assistants to the prison guards said to her: 'You suffer much now—what will you do when you are tossed to the beasts? Little did you think of them when you refused to sacrifice.' 'Now what I suffer I suffer myself,' she replied. 'There, another will be in me to suffer for me, because I too will be suffering for him.'[77]

Even the gestures of the men going into the arena are interpreted as prophetic words of judgement upon the magistrates.[78] We should therefore see Perpetua's notes and the other material as a record of the words, graces, and visions accorded to the privileged confessors, written for the good of the Church. The confessors share the hopes and faith of their editor.

What else shall we say of Perpetua? She comes from a largely Christian home, despite her father's pleas to her to yield. After recording his most earnest plea to her not to bring disgrace on himself, her brothers, her mother, her aunt, and her child, she says, 'I was sorry for my father's plight, because he alone of all my kin was not going to rejoice at my passion.'[79] We know nothing of her husband, which is strange. No one in the story refers to him, though Perpetua is described as 'respectably married' (*matronaliter nupta*) by the editor. He might have been hostile. Justin's account of the martyrdom of Ptolomaeus and Lucius[80] includes an interesting female non-martyr. A well-connected Roman woman accepted the teachings of Christ, which alienated her from her husband's licentious ways. While he was away in Alexandria, he got involved in

---

[76] *Passio*, 11–13.
[77] Ibid., 15.
[78] Ibid., 18,7–8.
[79] Ibid., 5,1–5.
[80] Justin, *2 Apologia* 2, repr. with Eng. tr., Musurillo, pp. 38–41.

some other criminal practices, and she finally decided to divorce him. He then filed a suit against her and accused her of Christianity, but she obtained a ruling that her action for divorce be taken first. Frustrated in his prosecution of her, presumably because she had influential relatives and property, he took her teacher ($\delta\iota\delta\acute{a}\sigma\kappa\alpha\lambda o\nu$) to court. The weight of Justin's argument falls on the fact that the teacher, Ptolomaeus, was convicted and executed solely on the confession of being a Christian, and without any reference to any crime. Lucius was there, and protested against this injustice, and was himself arrested and executed too, on similar grounds, and a third with them. But the woman appears to have escaped unpunished. Presumably the same could have happened for Perpetua, being of a propertied family, and her father's repeated persuasions were directed to modifying her attitude. Perhaps she also had a hostile husband. I incline to the view that he was actually dead, and that there was no cause to mention him in her notes of events; the editor had no information, and so wrote nothing about it. The editor is not too scrupulous about the family: his own summary fails to mention that her family were mostly Christian, noting only that one brother was a catechumen.[81] One reason for preferring this view is that the male child is finally left with Perpetua's father and family; another is that she is treated as a 'lady' (*dominam*) by her father,[82] as though she were of independent standing. Ignorance of her widowhood on the part of her editor is certainly possible. But none of this is compelling.

Secondly, there is Perpetua's teacher. She belonged to a class, a group which was arrested together: a slave couple, two men, and Perpetua. Of Saturus, Perpetua writes, when describing how she saw him in her dream about the ladder guarded by weapons and a fierce dragon, 'Saturus was the first to go up, he who had afterwards given himself up voluntarily on our account, because he had himself been our instructor (*ipse nos aedificauerat*), and when we were arrested he had not been present.'[83] Saturus would later fulfil the dream by leading the way to the scaffold. His position is comparable to that of Origen in Alexandria, who at the same period claims to have accompanied martyrs to their trial and execution, without being arrested himself. They included his own pupils, and some catechumens, including one named woman, Herais.[84] That Origen escaped arrest must

---

[81] *Passio*, 2,2.
[82] Ibid., 5,5.
[83] Ibid., 4,5.
[84] Eusebius, *Ecclesiastical History*, 6,3–4. That Origen's own apologetic letter is the source is apparent from his remark about Herais, quoted in 6,4,3.

be due to the influence of some of his admirers, or to the fact that he had been brought up a Christian and was not himself a convert: the Alexandrian martyrs of the period, like Perpetua's companions, were newly baptized or candidates for baptism. So, for what it is worth, was Alban, the British protomartyr, who perished at this period, if the oldest version of the martyrology is to be trusted, against Bede.[85] Frend tellingly argues that Severus did in 202 issue some edict against conversions to Judaism and Christianity, and is right to argue that the preponderance of converts among the martyrs of the period reflects it.[86]

Saturus, then, is a trainer of catechumens, who are baptized after their first arrest,[87] and he gives himself up in order to lead them through their trials. This is not regarded as improper or unusual, but reminds us of Quintus at Smyrna (who was perhaps the teacher of a group) and Agathonike at Pergamum. He is also a visionary, whose visions acknowledge Perpetua as his chief companion, as hers acknowledge him.

Perpetua herself, though said to be well educated (*liberaliter instituta*)[88] uses only conversational Latin, and could not have spoken or written as Tertullian or Cyprian do. She could never have become a teacher as the Early Church boasted teachers, sharing the difficulty of women generally. One or two teaching women can be named. Hermas was directed to give copies of his prophecy to Clement for the churches outside Rome, and to read one copy in the city in the presence of the presbyters who govern it, and to give one copy to Grapte—'and Grapte shall instruct the widows and orphans.'[89] The five women mentioned as teachers among Christian sects by Celsus (Helena, Marcellina, Salome, Mariamne, and Martha) are all doubtful starters except Marcellina, who appears to have promoted Carpocratianism in Rome.[90] The group of seven women who are tried in *The Martyrdom of Saints Agape, Irene and Chione*[91] appear to live a monastic life in flight from the persecution under Diocletian. Irene is accused of possessing 'so many tablets, books, parchments, codices and pages of writings of former Christians'. Being asked about their recent use, she

---

[85] So John Morris,'The date of St Alban', *Hertfordshire Archaeology*, I (1968), pp. 1–8.

[86] Frend, *Martyrdom and Persecution*, pp. 319–21. He underestimates the degree of Christianity in Perpetua's family.

[87] *Passio*, 3,5.

[88] Ibid., 2,2.

[89] Hermas, *The Shepherd*, Vis. II,4 = 8,3, ed. Molly Whittaker, *Die griechische christlichen Schriftsteller der ersten Jahrhunderte*, 48, 2 (Berlin, 1967). p. 7, 14–18.

[90] Origen, *Contra Celsum* 5,62; Irenaeus, *Adversus haereses* 1,25,6. Notes and further references in *Origène, Contre Celse III*, ed. with intro. Marcel Borret = SC, 147, pp. 168–9; *Origen, Contra Celsum*, ed. and tr., 2nd edn Henry Chadwick (Cambridge and New York, 1979), p. 312.

[91] Musurillo, pp. 280–93.

says, 'They were in our house and we did not dare to bring them out. In fact, it caused us much distress that we could not devote ourselves to them night and day as we had done from the beginning until that day last year when we hid them.'[92] These ladies were clearly students, and probably had a female leader. But such cases are rarely reported.

Among the followers of the New Prophecy, however, Perpetua, had she survived, could have taken the place of honour without difficulty. The early Tertullian could attack the disorderly and changeable ministries of the 'heretics', and he includes in sound subordinationist fashion: 'The very women ... how pert they are! They are bold enough to teach, to dispute, to enact exorcisms, to undertake cures—it may be even to baptize.'[93] Once he becomes a disciple of the New Prophecy, things are different. The movement itself is led by women. He calls it 'The Prophecies of Montanus and Prisca and Maximilla'.[94] When he attacks the decree encouraging moral laxity issued by the bishop of Carthage (or, as some suppose, Rome), he will not allow remission of adultery and fornication by bishops; even martyrs atone only for their own sin, and cannot acquit others. He can quote an oracle from the new prophecy, 'The Church has power to remit sin, but I will not do it, so that they may not commit other sins.'[95] One may suppose he was willing to allow prophets to determine individual cases. On one occasion he actually quotes the judgement of a prophet to clinch a metaphysical argument, a prophet who receives visions during the conduct of divine worship, and converses with angels and the Lord himself, discerning hearts and healing diseases. It is a woman he quotes.[96] In a church where the judgement of bishops is subordinate to the prophecies of assembled prophets of either sex, we may suppose that, if Perpetua had survived, she might have been found a place of honour.

But the New Prophecy was not to prevail, and neither could the rights of confessors. The show-down was to come when Cyprian, Bishop of Carthage, would clamp down on the leniency of confessors in Carthage, and oppose the rigour of Novatianist confessors in Rome, in the name of the exclusive judicial rights of bishops. But that is another story.[97]

[92] *Martyrdom*, 5.
[93] Tertullian, *De praescriptione*, 41; English from Stevenson, *New Eusebius*, p. 170.
[94] Tertullian, *Adversus Praxean*, 1.
[95] Tertullian, *De pudicitia*, 21,7.
[96] Tertullian, *De anima*, 9; conveniently in Stevenson, *New Eusebius*, pp. 175–6.
[97] E. R. Hardy, 'The decline and fall of the Confessor-Presbyter', *Studia Patristica* 15 (Berlin, 1984) = *Texte und Untersuchungen*, 128, pp. 221–5, provides a useful discussion, but the only woman he mentions is Julian of Norwich.

SOME CONCLUSIONS

In observing the women martyrs of the early period I have sailed into unexpected waters. It is not an area well worked. The views on women of the New Testament writers and the Gnostics have been well worked over. So have those of the classic monastic writers.[98] We find matters of order and authority prominent. Teachers play an unexpectedly large role, as against presbyters and bishops. So do the privileges of confessors and martyrs. While the customary second place of women may be expressed in their position in martyr-lists, their achievement is seen as bringing them level with their male counterparts, and by a remarkable inversion bringing the slave-girl Blandina to the very head. The social position of women may sometimes inhibit martyrdom, though in the case of Perpetua it makes her a natural leader, and she is literate enough to record her own martyr-confession for the use of the Church. Like male confessors, prophets, and teachers, the women were not to prevail. With the assimilation of bishops and presbyters to the cultic role of pagan and Israelite priesthoods, the primary functions of teaching, prophecy, and critical discernment were discontinued, or else engrossed by the same cultic officials. It is no accident that in recent times it is by putting all the weight on the purely cultic, irrational, and artificial factors, and rating as distinct, and ultimately subordinate, the doctrinal, diaconal, medical, and judicial work which women are patently competent to manage, that the strongest case can be made for excluding them from the Church's leading offices.[99] In the last resort I would rather be with the martyrs than with the priests.

King's College London

---

[98] For example, *Die Frau im Urchristentum*, ed. Gerhard Dautzenberger et al. (Freiburg, Basle, and Vienna, 1983); Elaine Pagels, *The Gnostic Gospels* (London and New York, 1979); Rosemary Radford Ruether, 'Misogyny and virginal feminism in the Fathers of the Church', in R. R. Ruether, ed., *Religion and Sexism. Images of Women in the Jewish and Christian Traditions* (New York, 1974), pp. 150–63; and on the Cappadocians, Graham Gould, 'Women in the writings of the Fathers. Language, belief and reality', in W. J. Sheils and Diana Wood, eds, *Women in the Church*, SCH, 27, pp. 1–13.

[99] Louis Bouyer, *Women in the Church* (San Francisco, 1984) [tr. from *Mystère et ministères de la femme dans l'église* (Paris, 1976)]; note esp. p. 88.

Religion and Politics in the Writings of Eusebius: Reassessing the First "Court Theologian"

MICHAEL J. HOLLERICH

Ever since Jacob Burckhardt dismissed him as "the first thoroughly dishonest historian of antiquity," Eusebius has been an inviting target for students of the Constantinian era.[1] At one time or another they have characterized him as a political propagandist, a good courtier, the shrewd and worldly adviser of the Emperor Constantine, the great publicist of the first Christian emperor, the first in a long succession of ecclesiastical politicians, the herald of Byzantinism, a political theologian, a political metaphysician, and a caesaropapist.[2] It is obvious that these are not, in the main, neutral descriptions. Much traditional scholarship, sometimes with barely suppressed disdain, has regarded Eusebius as one who risked his orthodoxy and perhaps his character because of his zeal for the Constantinian establishment. Scholars have often observed, for example, that his literary works in defense

1. "Er [Eusebius] ist aber der erste durch and durch unredliche Geschichtsschreiber des Altertums. Seine Taktik . . . bestand darin, den ersten Beschützer der Kirche um jeden Preis zu einem Ideal für künftige Fürsten zu machen"; Jacob Burckhardt, *Die Zeit Constantins des Grosen*, 2d ed. (Leipzig, 1880), pp. 334–335, cited in G. Ruhbach, "Die politische Theologie Eusebs von Caesarea," in *Die Kirche angesichts der Konstantinischen Wende*, ed. G. Ruhbach (Darmstadt, 1976), p. 238. The spirit of Burckhardt's picture of Constantine and Eusebius still lives in the recent book by liberation theologian Alistair Kee, *Constantine Versus Christ: The Triumph of Ideology* (London, 1982).
2. Respectively, these are citations from Erik Peterson, *Der Monotheismus als politisches Problem* (Munich, 1951), p. 91; Henri Grégoire, "L'authenticité et l'historicité de la *Vita Constantini* attribuée à Eusèbe de Césarée," *Bulletin de l'Académie Royale de Belgique, Classe des Lettres*, 39 (1953): 462–479, quoted in T. D. Barnes, *Constantine and Eusebius* (Cambridge, Mass., 1981), p. 401; Arnaldo Momigliano, "Pagan and Christian Historiography in the Fourth Century," in *The Conflict between Paganism and Christianity in the Fourth Century*, ed. A. Momigliano (Oxford, 1963), p. 85; Robert Markus, "The Roman Empire in Early Christian Historiography," *The Downside Review* 81 (1963): 343; Charles N. Cochrane, *Christianity and Classical Culture* (1940; reprint, Oxford, 1966), p. 183; Hendrik Berkhof, *Die Theologie des Eusebius von Caesarea* (Amsterdam, 1939), pp. 21–22; Hans Eger, "Kaiser und Kirche in der Geschichtstheologie Eusebs von Cäsarea," *Zeitschrift für die neutestamentliche Wissenschaft* 38 (1939): 115; Per Beskow, *Rex Gloriae. The Kingship of Christ in the Early Church* (Uppsala, 1962), p. 318; J. M. Sansterre, "Eusèbe de Césarée et la naissance de la théorie 'césaropapiste,' " *Byzantion* 42 (1972): 593.

Mr. Hollerich is assistant professor of religious studies in Santa Clara University, Santa Clara, California.

of the new order depict Constantine and his reign in eschatological terms that rival and even supplant the Incarnation and *Parousia* in salvation history.[3]

To be sure, this assessment relies on abundant documentation: in the *Life of Constantine* and in the *Tricennial Oration*, delivered on the thirtieth anniversary of Constantine's reign, as well as in other books, Eusebius gave an enthusiastic Christian endorsement both to Constantine and to the Roman Empire.[4] Nevertheless, this paper argues that the standard assessment has exaggerated the importance of political themes and political motives in Eusebius's life and writings and has failed to do justice to him as a churchman and a scholar. Its purpose is to supplement traditional treatments of the political dimension in Eusebius, by paying attention to his interpretation of the Bible. The first part of the paper points out shortcomings of the older scholarship and introduces some recent reevaluations. The second part examines Eusebius's comparisons of Moses with Jesus and with Constantine, as illustrations of one of his central apologetic themes—the biblical notion of

3. This is a summary judgment, but I think it fairly describes a theme that runs throughout much of the literature, for example, R. Farina, *L'impero e l'imperatore cristiano in Eusebio di Cesarea: La prima teologia politica del cristianesimo* (Zürich, 1966), pp. 161–163 (the *pax Romano-christiana* a messianic epoch); Jean Sirinelli, *Les vues historiques d'Eusèbe de Césarée durant la période prénicéenne* (Dakar, 1961), p. 482 (the *Parousia* a dysfunctional relic of his view of history); H. G. Opitz, "Euseb von Caesarea als Theologe," *Zeitschrift für die neutestamentliche Wissenschaft* 34 (1935): 1–19, esp. p. 14 (eschatological fulfillment of history in the reign of Constantine); Eger, "Kaiser und Kirche," p. 114 (Constantine's assumption of the royal dominion of Christ.) Glenn Chesnut has tried to balance such overly immanentist interpretations of Eusebius's eschatology by drawing attention to elements of apocalyptic eschatology embedded in his picture of Constantine: see his *The First Christian Histories* (Paris, 1977), pp. 156–166. The result is only partly convincing. I see no evidence that Eusebius expected the Roman Empire to convert to Satan's side, in conformity with the apocalyptic scenario of Revelation 20:8, contrary to Chesnut (ibid., pp. 160–161), who misreads Eusebius in *Demonstratio Evangelica* [hereafter cited as *DE*] (I. Heikel, ed., *Die Demonstratio Evangelica*, vol. 6 of *Eusebius' Werke*, Die griechischen christlichen Schriftsteller der ersten Jahrhunderte [hereafter cited as GCS] 23 [Leipzig, 1913]) 9.3.5–6 (miscited as Book 8 on p. 162 n. 118): Eusebius did identify "Gog" as the Roman Empire, on the basis of Jewish exegesis, but only to establish a synchronism between the growth of the Roman Empire and the birth of Christ, not with any apocalyptic scenario in mind. Chesnut's analysis is skewed by his frequent reference to the Book of Revelation, which Eusebius preferred to ignore. The *Demonstratio* only cites Revelation once, in discussing the sealed prophecy of Daniel 9:24; despite Chesnut (p. 165), Eusebius sees the Seven Seals of Revelation 5:5 as a reference to the sealed prophecies of the Old Testament, which Christ has opened, and not to the wrath of God at the end of time (*DE* 8.2.30–34).

4. A central theme of the *Life*, as recently emphasized by Averil Cameron, "Eusebius of Caesarea and the Re-Thinking of History," in *Tria Corda. Scritti in onore di Arnaldo Momigliano*, ed. E. Gabba (Como, 1983), pp. 82–88; among many passages, see the preface of *De Vita Constantini* 1.1–12 (hereafter cited as *VC*), ed. F. Winkelmann, *Über das Leben des Kaiser Konstantins*, vol. 1 of *Eusebius' Werke*, GCS, 2d ed. (Berlin, 1975). See also Eusebius, *De Laudibus Constantini* 2.1–3.6, 16.1–7 (hereafter cited as *LC*), ed. I. Heikel, *Die Tricennatsrede an Constantin*, vol. 1 of *Eusebius' Werke*, GCS 7 (Leipzig, 1902); *Historia Ecclesiastica* 10.8.6–9 (hereafter cited as *HE*), ed. E. Schwartz, *Die Kirchengeschichte*, vol. 2, pts. 1–3 of *Eusebius' Werke*, GCS 9, pts. 1–3 (Leipzig, 1903–1909).

God's sovereignty of history—which shaped the way he regarded political events and realities.

1.

The conventional image of Eusebius has overestimated the priority of politics in his life and writings. One obvious reason for this is his central importance as a chronicler of the Constantinian era. Within little more than a generation Christianity lurched from de facto tolerance to persecution to de jure tolerance and finally to public patronage by the emperor. Eusebius's scholarly training and employment in Pamphilus's research institute in Caesarea and his later emergence as a leading churchman in the East qualified him to record this drastic transition, which he did especially in Books 8 through 10 of the *Church History* and in the eulogistic and biographical works on Constantine. These are the works which have traditionally drawn scholars' attention, to the relative neglect of his apologetic treatises and of his biblical exegesis.[5] Not surprisingly, the consequence has been to think of him as permanently absorbed with the subject of the church's relation to the empire. His literary output, from the first editions of the *Chronicle* and the *Church History* (Books 1 through 7) before the outbreak of the Great Persecution in 303 to the *Life of Constantine*, apparently left incomplete at his death in 339, embraces the whole period.[6] This proximity to events has fed discussion about the extent to which his political views developed in response to changing circumstances.[7]

Theological commitments sometimes played a role in the shaping of the conventional view. H. Berkhof, author of the only comprehensive monograph on Eusebius's theology, wrote as a Neo-orthodox Reformed theologian with little sympathy for post-Constantinian church-state relations, whether of the Latin or Byzantine variety.[8] The Roman Catholic convert Erik Peterson saw a logical connection between Eusebius's subordinationist theology and his poltiical views. In *Der Monotheismus als politisches Problem*, a classic study of ancient political theology which has exerted a steady influence since its first appearance more than fifty years ago, Peterson gave Eusebius a prominent

---

5. Selective bibliography in J. Quasten, *Patrology*, vol. 3 (Westminster, Md., 1983), pp. 309–345, and F. Young, *From Nicaea to Chalcedon* (Philadelphia, 1983), pp. 335–337, 355–358.
6. See Barnes, *Constantine and Eusebius*, pp. 128–129, 148–150, for the dating of the *Church History*, and pp. 265–268. For the *Life of Constantine*, see G. Chesnut, *The First Christian Histories*, rev. ed. (Macon, Ga., 1986), pp. 113–125 (hereafter cited as *FCH*).
7. For example, Eger, "Kaiser und Kirche," pp. 97–115; Sansterre, "Eusèbe de Césarée," pp. 131–195, 532–594; Chesnut, *FCH*, pp. 111–140, and see n. 33 below.
8. Compare Berkhof, *Die Theologie des Eusebius von Caesarea*, pp. 53–59, and idem, *Kirche und Kaiser. Eine Untersuchung der byzantinischen und theokratischen Staatsauffassung im vierten Jahrhundert* (Zürich, 1947), pp. 100–104.

role in the Christian appropriation of Graeco-Roman monarchical theory.[9] His interpretation was introduced to an American readership through its influence on the work of G. H. Williams.[10] From yet another theological perspective, H.-G. Opitz interpreted Eusebius as a kind of precocious rationalist who, rather in the fashion of the cultural Protestantism of nineteenth-century Germany, sought to ally the church with the civilizing institutions of the Roman Empire.[11] Such theologically based analyses have been quick to focus on the political implications of theology and doctrine, sometimes obscuring for us the degree to which theology, doctrine, and church life might have been perceived, by Eusebius and his contemporaries, as autonomous enterprises. One often reads in the literature that the ancients did not distinguish the spheres of the political and the religious with the clarity born of modern secularization.[12] Even if this generalization holds true for classical culture, we should be wary of reading it into Christian sources, even of authors so apparently preoccupied with political subjects as Eusebius.

The older scholarship seems in retrospect to have been written with one eye focused on the later history of church-state relations, leading to anachronistic portrayals of Eusebius as a kind of court theologian or minister for ecclesiastical affairs—a fourth-century predecessor of someone like Alcuin in the court of Charlemagne. Recent scholarship on Eusebius is correcting this unhistorical perspective. In 1980 Robert M. Grant's *Eusebius as Church Historian* recommended that we should look upon Eusebius simply "as a human being, neither a saint nor intentionally a scoundrel."[13] Grant's analysis of the composition and themes of the *Church History* paid careful attention to the themes that Eusebius actually chose to write about, showing how he changed his mind on several subjects during the course of the book's composition. A year later T. D. Barnes published *Constantine and Eusebius*, which sought a fairer and more comprehensive picture of Eusebius by a fresh reading of all his works, not just the ones scholars normally studied.[14] Barnes defended Eusebius's integrity as a scholar. He reminded us that Eusebius was perhaps fifty years old when the Battle of the Mulvian Bridge was fought, already solidly established as a scholar and an apologist, and soon to become a bishop. Scholarship and the church were the governing preoccupations of his life. Eusebius's positive attitude toward the empire and human history thus

---

9. See Peterson, *Der Monotheismus als politisches Problem*, pp. 45–157 (pp. 86–94 on Eusebius). Peterson's monograph has been reviewed in the exhaustive but rather unsympathetic study of Alfred Schindler, ed., *Monotheismus als politisches Problem? Erik Peterson und die Kritik der politischen Theologie* (Gütersloh, 1978).

10. G. H. Williams, "Christology and Church-State Relations in the Fourth Century," *Church History* 20, 3 (1951): 1–33, 20, 4 (1951):1–26.

11. Opitz, "Eusebius von Caesarea als Theologe," pp. 1–19.

12. Ibid., p. 1.

13. R. M. Grant, *Eusebius as Church Historian* (Oxford, 1980), p. 164.

14. Barnes, *Constantine and Eusebius*, pp. v–vi.

took shape long before Constantine entered the scene and reflected a wide-spread optimism in the Greek East in the half century before the Great Persecution.[15]

Barnes also argued that Eusebius's direct personal contact with Constantine was much more restricted—perhaps amounting to only four meetings—than has often been assumed.[16] His minimalist interpretation received support at the 1987 Oxford Patristics Conference in a paper by classical historian B. H. Warmington, who questioned whether Constantine ever had churchmen in his presence who could properly be called "ecclesiastical advisors."[17] A similar tendency to detach Eusebius from too tight a connection with Constantine's imperial agenda can be found in publications of the German scholar Gerhard Ruhbach. In his research on Eusebius's apologetic works and on the Constantinian literature Ruhbach denied that Eusebius was a "political theologian" in any meaningful sense of the word and argued that Eusebius had no interest in politics for its own sake; his orientation to political developments was exclusively theological and ecclesiastical.[18] Ruhbach found that Eusebius's attitude toward God's involvement in history was fundamentally shaped by the Bible, in particular, the Old Testament.[19]

This is the same conclusion I have reached through research on Eusebius's exegesis in his Commentary on Isaiah, a work which had never been closely studied, having only become available to scholars in a form close to its original condition in 1975.[20] The commentary gives only marginal attention to the empire and to Constantine, who is never mentioned by name. It is the church, boldly called "the godly polity" (theosebes politeuma) and "the city of God" (polis tou theou), which Eusebius sees as the primary fulfillment of Isaiah's

---

15. Ibid., p. 186.
16. Ibid., p. 266. H. A. Drake, "What Eusebius Knew: The Genesis of the Vita Constantini," Classical Philology 83 (1988): 20–38, argues that Eusebius made a fifth visit to Constantinople around Easter of 337, in order to begin work on the VC (contrary to the usual judgment that it was only begun after the emperor's death), and that he had broached the idea for the book as early as November 335. Even if Drake's hypothesis on the composition of the VC is correct, it does not alter the general fact that most of Eusebius's work as a churchman and scholar was conducted at considerable remove from the emperor and his court.
17. B. H. Warmington, "Did Constantine Have 'Religious Advisers?' " in Studia Patristica, ed. Elizabeth A. Livingstone, vol. 19 (Louvain, 1990).
18. See Ruhbach, "Die politische Theologie des Eusebs von Caesarea," pp. 236–258, based on his "Apologetik und Geschichte. Untersuchungen zur Theologie Eusebs von Caesarea" (Dissertation, Heidelberg University, 1962).
19. Ruhbach, "Die politische Theologie des Eusebs," p. 254.
20. Michael J. Hollerich, "The Godly Polity in the Light of Prophecy: A Study of Eusebius of Caesarea's Commentary on Isaiah" (Ph.D. diss., University of Chicago, 1986). The commentary was long known only on the basis of incomplete medieval catenae edited in the eighteenth century by Montfaucon. In the twentieth century a nearly complete version was discovered and has now been edited by J. Ziegler, Der Jesajakommentar [hereafter cited as CI], vol. 9 of Eusebius' Werke, GCS (Berlin, 1975).

prophecies.[21] The godly polity is firmly episcopal in its authority structure: according to Eusebius, numerous passages in Isaiah anticipated the Christian bishop's monopoly of authority.[22] This ecclesiastical orientation reflects Eusebius's long career in the service of the church. It only seems noteworthy if our picture of Eusebius is shaped mainly by the Constantinian orations and the biography, in which the emperor is presented as a divinely favored representative of God on earth.[23] But the sacralized imperialism in these works owes much to rhetorical convention and is an insufficient basis for a comprehensive statement of Eusebius's views on church and empire.[24] A balanced interpretation needs to take into account the high view of the bishop's authority found in the *Commentary on Isaiah*.[25]

The commentary repeats apologetic themes familiar to Eusebius's other works, such as the synchronization of the birth of Christ with the reign of Augustus and the disappearance of autonomous national kingdoms, and the role of the Pax Romana in aiding the evangelizing of the empire.[26] In one passage Eusebius appears to apply the peace prophecy of Isaiah 2:1-4 to the reign of Constantine.[27] But there is no mention at all of the emperor's imitation of the *Logos*, a motif which would have contradicted the strong emphasis on the bishops as the leaders of the godly polity, and which perhaps had no place in the genre of a biblical commentary. The emperor is unable to usurp the eschatological glory of Christ because that role has already been co-opted by the bishops. The emperor and his entourage appear only in passing allusions and vignettes which stress their service to the church: attending sacred services, offering gifts to the church and succoring the poor, and confiscating and melting down pagan idols.[28] The subordinate status of the imperial government in the church is illustrated in Eusebius's exegesis of

21. See, for example, *CI* 12.22-28, 121.13-28, 304.26-29, 342.15-16, 375.14-17, and so on.
22. For example, Isaiah 16:5 (LXX)—"Then a throne will be established in mercy and there will take his seat on it with truth in the tent of David and one who judges and seeks justice and is swift to do righteousness"—which in the *Prophetic Eclogues* (4.9) he had applied to Christ's return to glory, is ascribed in the *Commentary on Isaiah* to the Christian bishop. (*CI* 109.4-110.11). See also 83.33-84.17 (on Isa. 11:6-9), 148.6-20 (on Isa. 22:21-24), 377.5-19 (on Isa. 60:17-18), 381.22-29 (on Isa. 61:6-7; given a christological interpretation in *DE* 4.16), 408.14-410.17 (on Isa. 66:18-23).
23. Most conspicuously in *LC* 2-3. Still an excellent guide to the ideological background of this text in Graeco-Roman monarchical theory is N. H. Baynes, "Eusebius and the Christian Empire," in his *Byzantine Studies and Other Essays* (London, 1955), pp. 168-172.
24. On the influence of rhetoric on Eusebius's political writings, see Gerald S. Vigna, "The Influence of Epideictic Rhetoric on Eusebius of Caesarea's Political Theology" (Ph.D. diss., Northwestern University, 1980).
25. A doctrine not limited to the commentary. See the speech delivered at the dedication of the basilica of Tyre, which describes the bishop as the one "in whom the entire Christ has taken his seat" (*HE* 10.4.67).
26. On these motifs, compare *CI* 91.21-92.5, 114.7-115.16, 126.28-127.16, 14.32-15.14.
27. Ibid., 14.32-15.14
28. Ibid., 316.17-25, 316.10-16, 20.29-21.5.

the messianic prophecy of Isaiah 11:6, in which the domesticated wild animals are allegorized as imperial officials, and the little child who leads them symbolizes the Christian clergy.[29]

The pagan Roman Empire plays a more important role in the commentary than its Christian successor. Most references to the empire are to its role as the divinely appointed scourge of the Jews in A.D. 70 and 135.[30] This strongly biblical notion that the kings of the earth are God's instruments for executing God's will treated the Romans as fundamentally no different from other nations which had served as rods of God's anger. Had Eusebius wished, Isaiah offered him rich material for a favorable and flattering portrait of Constantine, most obviously in the person of Cyrus, the Lord's anointed. But the Cyrus passages are given a scrupulously historical interpretation.[31]

The episcopal foundations of the godly polity in the *Commentary on Isaiah* are especially significant in view of its late date of composition, probably soon after the Council of Nicaea, when we might expect much greater attention to the Roman Empire and to the person of Constantine.[32] The ecclesiastical emphasis suggests that Eusebius was not so overwhelmed with the prospect of a Christianized empire that he ceased to be, first and foremost, a devoted churchman. The commentary puts us in a better position to evaluate the *Life of Constantine*, the *Tricennial Oration*, and the *Speech on the Holy Sepulchre*. The importance of these works, written near the end of both Constantine's and Eusebius's lives, has perhaps been swollen out of proportion. Aside from the doctrine of the emperor's imitation of the *Logos*, adopted from Hellenistic monarchical theory, it is not clear that the biography and the speeches significantly change the laudatory picture of the Roman Empire and of Constantine as an actively Christian emperor, which we find already in Books 9 and 10 of the *Church History*. Eusebius endorsed Constantine from the time the emperor's rising star moved into his line of vision, but only because he was already disposed to see the empire as having an essential role to play in God's plan. A Christian emperor rounded out the picture but did not appreciably change it. Constantine's conversion was the natural and

---

29. Ibid., 84.8–17.
30. Ibid., 10.12–20, 14.13–25, 18.23–28, 25.29–36, 31.4–5, and passim.
31. Compare Eusebius's commentary on Isaiah 44:8–45:13, which is given a literal interpretation except at the very end of the section, where 45:13 is applied to Christ (*CI* 293.12–294.2).
32. Constantinian policies are mentioned which could not have been implemented in the east until after the defeat of Licinius, such as the granting of a grain ration for the poor of the church (*CI* 316.9–22 and 376.36–377.3, also mentioned in *VC* 4.28 and alluded to in Theodoret, *Church History* 1.11, but unfortunately not datable), and Constantine's confiscation of temple treasures and cult objects (*CI* 20.29–21.5, also *LC* 8.1–4 and *VC* 3.54), which Barnes dates sometimes soon after 324 (*Constantine and Eusebius*, p. 247). A more precise dating to shortly after Nicaea is suggested by the commentary's avoidance of such subordinationist terms as *deuteros theos*, which are common in Eusebius's pre-Nicene works (for example, *DE* 4.5.3, 4.7.2, 5.Pref.20, 23, 5.6.7; *HE* 1.2.3, 5, 9; *PE* 11.14–19), and by the absence of any mention of Constantine's building program in the Holy Land.

appropriate culmination of a view of the empire which Eusebius always held.[33]

2.

This historiographical sketch suggests that a defect of older scholarship is its insufficient attention to Eusebius's interpretation of the Bible. Let us now take a closer look at one aspect of Eusebius's exegesis in order to illustrate the centrality of historical demonstration in Eusebius's apologetics and its dependence on the biblical doctrine of divine sovereignty. As long ago as 1935 Erik Peterson had made soundings in Eusebius's exegesis with this purpose in mind. In *Monotheismus als politisches Problem* he observed that Eusebius applied Old Testament messianic and eschatological peace prophecies like Micah 5:3–4 and 4:1–9, Psalms 71:7 (LXX), and Isaiah 2:4 to the Pax Romana. Such a "striking lack of exegetical tact" led, in Peterson's judgment, to the secularizing and politicizing of biblical eschatology.[34] Peterson's thesis was widely accepted and became an important element in the conventional interpretation of Eusebius's political views. But as we have noted, the *Commentary on Isaiah* reveals a significantly different dimension of Eusebius's biblical interpretation in its application of eschatological prophecy to the

---

33. Glenn Chesnut argues for a fundamental change in Eusebius's attitude to the empire on the question of religious toleration. Chesnut argues that the trauma of the Great Persecution moved Eusebius away from an original commitment to religious liberty toward a later endorsement of stern measures against paganism, and that this change helps explain his eventual support for an alliance of church and empire (*FCH*, pp. 114–140).

   This interpretation reads too much development into a point of view which remained substantially the same. It requires Chesnut to ignore or deemphasize important evidence that Eusebius was not as "strongly antimilitarist" as he claims, and that he was ready and willing, at all points in his career, to embrace an alliance of church and empire. In the first edition of the *Church History* Eusebius proudly reported the widespread tradition of the Christian legion whose prayers had saved Marcus Aurelius while on campaign against the Sarmatians and Germans (*HE* 4.5.1–7). Similarly, the first edition reported approvingly the emperor Aurelian's "extremely just decision" to evict Paul of Samosata from the church of Antioch after his condemnation by the eastern bishops (ibid., 7.30.19). In the third edition of the *Church History* (*HE* 9.9.1–8) Eusebius's enthusiastic description of the Battle of the Mulvian Bridge as a reprise of the escape through the Red Sea, with Christians singing the Song of Miriam, leaves no doubt that as early as 315 he was wholly convinced that Constantine was an instrument of God's purposes. Finally, Chesnut's attempt to see a development in Eusebius's use of the "good emperor, bad emperor" scheme is unconvincing. Eusebius didn't need the letters of Dionysius to give him the idea that God supported just kings and subverted wicked ones (*FCH*, p. 126). The scheme is already expressed in Melito of Sardis, quoted by Eusebius in *HE* 4.26.7, as Chesnut acknowledges, and derives from Christian attitudes deeply rooted in Scripture.

34. Peterson, *Monotheismus als politisches Problem*, pp. 89–90, 134–135. Compare *DE* 7.2.20–24 for Micah 5:3–4, and Psalms 71:7; *DE* 8.3.13–15 for Micah 4:1–4; and *Praeparatio Evangelica* [hereafter cited as *PE*] 1.4.4–5, ed. K. Mras, *Die Praeparatio Evangelica*, vol. 8, pts. 1–2 of *Eusebius' Werke*, GCS 43, pts. 1–2 (Berlin, 1954–1956), for Isaiah 2:4 and Psalms 71:7.

institutional church, which serves to offset the importance of his occasional political interpretations.

Eusebius's eschatology is a complex subject which cannot be understood without a careful contextual reading of the many passages in which he uses eschatological language and symbolism.[35] Rather than focus on the eschatological fulfillment of prophecy, I propose instead to look at Eusebius's use of biblical typology in his comparison of Moses first with Jesus, then with Constantine. In both cases we will identify a distinctive conception of God's presence in history which also underlies Eusebius's reconciliation of Christianity with the Roman Empire.

Moses is a central figure in Eusebius's interpretation of the relationship of Christianity to Judaism. In his historical reconstruction of that relationship Christianity is not a departure from Judaism but a restitution of the pure religion of the pre-Mosaic patriarchs. These "friends of God," whom Eusebius calls "Hebrews," in contrast to Jews in the strict sense (this term referring to followers of the Mosaic sacrificial cult and ceremonial law), practiced an elevated ethical monotheism.[36] The degeneration of the descendants of Jacob in Egypt under the malign influence of Egyptian customs showed the inability of large numbers of people to sustain this rational and spiritual religion. Therefore, Moses instituted a polity (*politeia*) appropriate to their weakened souls, which was at once political and religious in character, being both a national legal code and a system of external ritual and cultic observances.[37] Thus Judaism is only a secondary grade (*bathmos*) of piety compared to the Hebrew predecessors of the Jews.[38] It is secondary in

35. C. Odahl, "The Use of Apocalyptic Imagery in Constantine's Christian Propaganda," *Centerpoint* 4 (1981): 9–20, argues that Constantine consciously used apocalyptic biblical symbols such as the defeat of the dragon-serpent in his imperial iconography as a signal to Christian subjects alienated by the persecution that his victories over Maxentius, and then over Licinius, were the beginning of a new era of earthly bliss; this, rather than the return of Christ in judgment, was the meaning of apocalyptic texts such as Isaiah 27:1 (compare Ps. 74:12–13, Ezek. 29:3) and Revelation 12–13 (compare Luke 10:17–19). On the basis of Eusebius's interpretation of the portrait of a pierced dragon which Constantine hung over the palace portico (*VC* 3.3), Odahl argues that Eusebius was privy to this hermeneutical defusing of apocalyptic hopes and supported it. But *VC* 3.3 merely shows Eusebius's exploitation of biblical sanctions to dignify Constantine's achievements, as with his handling of the biblical symbol of the new Jerusalem in *VC* 3.33. It says nothing whatever about his actual end-expectations. Eusebius rejected apocalypticism in the millennialist scenario of Revelation. But he had no disagreement with eschatological themes such as the return of Christ in glory and the last judgment, with a final separation of the good and the wicked. Compare *Commentary on Isaiah* 172.5–174.19, which interprets Isaiah 27:1 in ways typical of conventional eschatology. The more conventional side of Eusebius's eschatological views is correctly stressed by F. Thielman, "Another Look at the Eschatology of Eusebius of Caesarea," *Vigiliae Christianae* 41 (1987): 226–237.
36. Compare *DE* 1.2.1, and Book 1 passim. The distinction between "Hebrews" and "Jews" was already proposed in *HE* 1.4.5 and *PE* 7.6–8.
37. *PE* 7.8.37–39; 7.9.1.
38. Ibid., 8.Pref.2.

two respects. The Judaism established by Moses preserved the Hebrews' high spiritual ideals but in a symbolic and enigmatic form. Second, in keeping with its newly national and cultic expression, it had Jerusalem as its physical locus; hence it was bound by spatial and geographical limitations that were unknown in the ethical monotheism of the Hebrew patriarchs.[39]

In the opening of the *Proof of the Gospel* Eusebius defines the relation of Christianity to Judaism and to paganism: "Christianity would therefore be not a form of Hellenism nor of Judaism, but something between the two, the most ancient institution [*politeuma*] for holiness and the most venerable philosophy, only lately codified as the law for all mankind in the whole world."[40] Christianity therefore lays claim to the antiquity of the Hebrew patriarchs and to the philosophical and universalist character of their religion, thus freeing it from the geographical restriction of Mosaic Judaism. But Christianity since the Incarnation has also taken on features of Mosaic Judaism. It too has been incorporated as a legally defined community or polity by its founding lawgiver, Jesus Christ. Like Judaism, this polity is able to assimilate masses of people, most of whom are not expected to live up to the rigorous philosophical and perfectionist demands of patriarchal religion. In the Christian church there is room for a majority who will live as responsible members of secular society, making the necessary accommodations to family life, economic activity, and political and military responsibilities.[41] Only an elite minority live "above nature" by eschewing marriage and property. This concession to human weakness is necessary for a church poised for a great expansion. Christianity's bipartite constitution thus has a structural or formal continuity with the "secondary degree of piety" which Moses designed to accommodate masses of believers, although Eusebius insists that the Christian "polity for holiness" is superior even as a legal codification to its Jewish predecessor, because it depends not on a sacrificial cult or ceremonial law but on worship in spirit and truth.[42]

Moses and Jesus thus share a common historical distinction as founders of religious polities. The similarity of their accomplishments as founders is developed in great detail in a lengthy comparison in *The Proof of the Gospel*.[43] The context is an attempt by Eusebius to show that Jesus is the Mosaic prophet predicted by Deuteronomy 18:15–18:

> Moses was the first leader of the Jewish race. He found them attached to the deceitful polytheism of Eygpt, and was the first to turn them from it, by enacting

---

39. Argued in detail in *DE* 1.3.
40. Ibid., 1.2.10.
41. Ibid., 1.8; also, briefly, 6.18.30. The *Commentary on Isaiah* (382.12–35) also reflects the existence of two classes of members of the church.
42. *DE*, 1.6.1, 42.
43. *DE* 3.2.1–30. See J. E. Bruns, "The 'Agreement of Moses and Jesus' in the *Demonstratio Evangelica of Eusebius*," *Vigiliae Christianae* 31 (1977): 117–125.

the severest punishment for idolatry. He was the first also to publish the theology of the one God, bidding them worship only the Creator and Maker of all things. He was the first to draw up for the same hearers a scheme of godly life, and is acknowledged to have been the first and only lawgiver of their religious polity. But Jesus Christ too, like Moses, on a grander stage, was the first to introduce the instruction about true religion for the other nations, and the first to accomplish the rout of the idolatry that embraced the whole world. He was the first to introduce to all men the knowledge and religion of the one Almighty God. And he is proved to be the first author and lawgiver of a new life and of a polity [*politeia*] fit for the godly.[44]

The parallelism is quite close, except that Jesus worked on a worldwide scale by spreading the gospel of monotheism and the godly polity to the gentiles. Jesus and Moses, Eusebius continues, agreed substantially in their teaching on the origin of the world, the immortality of the soul, and "other doctrines of philosophy."[45] Furthermore, they both authenticated their proclamations with miraculous works. Moses liberated the people from slavery in Egypt; Jesus Christ summoned the whole human race to freedom from their "Egyptian" bondage to idolatry. Moses promised a holy land and a blessed life for those who kept his laws; so did Jesus when he promised the meek that they would inherit the earth, meaning a heavenly country. Besides these, Eusebius notes, Jesus performed other works which were greater than those of Moses and yet resembled his, such as fasting forty days, feeding a hungry people with miraculous bread, leading the people safely through the sea (matched, "only more divinely," by Peter's walking on water), calming the waters, being transfigured before their followers, cleansing a leper, commandeering the finger of God (Moses for the writing of the tablets of the Law, Jesus for exorcism), and lastly the ignorance of Moses' death or burial, said to resemble the lack of witnesses to Jesus' resurrection into the divine. Throughout this litany of sixteen distinct parallels, while routinely saying that Jesus' deeds were grander in scope and power, Eusebius is at pains to demonstrate their essential resemblance, even to the point of equating the anonymity of Moses' death with the absence of witnesses to the Resurrection.

The originality of this typological construction is its stress on the parallelism of type and antitype. Conventional typology, on the contrary, proposed a relationship of promise and fulfillment, of shadow and reality, in which primary stress was on the innate superiority of antitype to type. John Chrysostom's interpretation of the Exodus in relation to Christian baptism is a classic expression of this traditional and widespread way of reading the Bible:

In both cases we are dealing with water—in one case water in a bath, in the other it is the sea, and in both cases you go down into the water. You would like to know

ACT

44. *DE* 3.2.6, trans. W. J. Ferrar (adapted).
45. Ibid., 3.2.7.

now what the truth is which the coloring brings out. Once they were delivered by the sea from Egypt; now it is from idolatry; once Pharoh was drowned, now it is the devil; once it was the Egyptians who were suffocated, now the ancient enemy is stifled beneath our sins. You see now the relationship of the type with the anti-type, and of the superiority of the latter over the former. If the type had nothing in common with the anti-type, then there would be nothing typical. Nor on the other has one to be identical with the other, or it would be the reality itself. There must be that proportion, so that it neither possesses all that the reality has, nor is it entirely lacking . . . for surely it is of the nature of the reality to excel its type, though without any opposition or contention.[46]

Conventional typology thus assumed the historicity of the Old Testament record and saw Old Testament events, persons, and institutions as foreshadowings of realities yet to come, which shared typical features with their predecessors but essentially transcended them.

Eusebius's comparison of Moses and Jesus in *Demonstratio Evangelica* 3.2 illustrates what has been called "similar situation" typology, in which the fulfillment to come is virtually a recurrence of past history.[47] Examples of it have been found in sources emanating from circles where ties between Christians and Jews were still close, such as the Gospel of Matthew and the Syriac *Demonstrations* of the Persian Christian Aphrahat, a contemporary of Eusebius.[48] In general, however, interest simply in the external narrative similarities in the careers of Moses and Jesus was not common in the patristic period; *Demonstratio Evangelica* 3.2 stands apart in this respect.[49]

The comparison of Moses and Constantine in the *Church History* and the *Life of Constantine* functions very much like the comparison of Moses and Jesus: here too we see a typological construction in which the present is a virtual repetititon of the past. The earlier version of the comparison in the *Church History*, written around 315, describes Constantine's defeat of Maxentius at the Mulvian Bridge as a repetititon of the death of Pharaoh and his soldiers during the Israelites' miraculous escape through the parted waters of the Red Sea:

> The emperor [Constantine], closely relying on the help that comes from God, attacked the first, second and third of the tyrant's [Maxentius's] armies, and capturing them all with ease advanced over a large part of Italy, actually coming very near to Rome itself . . . [then] those things which were inscribed long ago in the sacred books against wicked men—to which as a myth very many gave no

46. John Chrysostom, *In I Cor 10:1ff.* (*PG* 51.248), cited in Jean Daniélou, *From Shadow to Reality: Studies in the Biblical Typology of the Fathers* (Westminster, Md., 1960), p. 192. For patristic typology of the Exodus, see ibid., pp. 167–226, and Daniélou, "Exodus," *Reallexikon für Antike und Christentum* [hereafter cited as *RAC*] 7:32–39.
47. R. P. C. Hanson, *Allegory and Event* (London, 1959), p. 14, cited in Bruns, " 'Agreement of Moses and Jesus,' " p. 117.
48. On Matthew, see Daniélou, *Shadow to Reality*, pp. 157–160; on Aphrahat, see Bruns, " 'Agreement of Moses and Jesus,' " p. 119.
49. Daniélou, *Shadow to Reality*, p. 197.

faith, yet were they worthy of faith to the faithful—now by their very clearness found faith, to put it simply, with all, believers and unbelievers alike, who perceived the miracle with their eyes. As, for example, in the days of Moses himself and the ancient and godly race of the Hebrews, "Pharaoh's chariots and his host hath he cast into the sea, his chosen horesmen, even captains, they were sunk in the Red Sea, the deep covered them"; in the same way also Maxentius and the armed soldiers and guards around him "went down into the depths like a stone," when he turned his back before the God-sent power that was with Constantine. . . . Thus verily, through the breaking of the bridge over the river, the passage collapsed, and down went the boats all at once, men and all, into the deep; and first of all he himself [Maxentius], that most wicked of men, and then also the shield-bearers around him, as the divine oracles foretell [hêi ta theia proanaphônei logia], sank as lead in the mighty waters. So that suitably, if not in words, at least in deeds, like the followers of the great servant Moses, those who had won the victory by the help of God might in some sort hymn the very same words which were uttered against the wicked tyrant of old, and say: "Let us sing unto the Lord, for gloriously hath he been glorified in saints, marvelous in praises, doing wonders."[50]

The Song of Miriam, sung of old to celebrate the God who sent Pharaoh and his troops to the bottom like lead, is now to be sung by Christians for the divine victory of the first Christian emperor. Unlike Chrysostom's typology of the Exodus, which treated spiritual liberation as superior in substance to Moses' historical liberation, type and fulfillment are here based on the same kind of event, the defeat and drowning of an opposing army. For Eusebius the parallel between past and present is very close, except that the present is a more persuasive demonstration of theodicy because it is verifiable.

A quarter of a century later Eusebius returned to Moses as a model for presenting Constantine in the preface to his *Life of Constantine*, a partly panegyrical, partly biographical work written right after the emperor's death.[51]

> An ancient story relates that a cruel race of tyrants oppressed the Hebrew nation; and that God, who is favorably disposed to the oppressed, provided that the prophet Moses, who was then an infant, should be brought up in the very palaces and bosoms of the oppressors, and instructed in all the wisdom they possessed. And when in the course of time he had arrived at manhood, and justice, which is the avenger of those who have been wronged, fell upon the wrong-doers, then the prophet of God, in obedience to the will of a more powerful Lord, forsook the royal household, and estranging himself in word and deed from the tyrants by whom he had been brought up, showed that he knew who in reality his true brothers and kinsmen were. And then God raised him up as the leader of the whole people, and he liberated the Hebrews from slavery to their enemies, but the master race he subjected to divinely-ordained punishments.

This ancient story, passed on to the many in the form of a myth, had earlier

---

50. *HE* 9.9.3–5, 7–8, trans. J. E. L. Oulton.
51. *VC* 1.12. The *Life of Constantine*'s account of the Battle of the Mulvanian Bridge is borrowed verbatim from the *Church History*: *VC* 1.37.2–40.2 = *HE* 9.9.3–11.

reached the ears of all. But now the same God has given us to be eye-witnesses of marvels greater than myths, and, from their recent appearance, more authentic than any report. For the tyrants of our day have ventured to war against the supreme God, and have sorely oppressed his church. And in the midst of these, Constantine, who was shortly to become the tyrants' destroyer, but at that time of tender age, and blooming with the down of early youth, dwelt, as that other servant of God had done, in the very home of the tyrants, but young as he was did not share the life of the ungodly; for from that early period his noble nature, under the leading of the divine spirit, inclined him to piety and a life acceptable to God.[52]

In the terminology of classical rhetoric this version of the comparison is a *synkrisis* as well as a typology.[53] A long tradition of Jewish apologetic literature had made Moses better known to educated pagans than any other figure in Scripture.[54] In this literature Moses was presented not just as a religious founder but as a secular hero with rich cultural accomplishments to his credit.[55] Eusebius was quite familiar with this apologetic effort on behalf of Moses, which provided his hero with a thoroughly biblical exemplar who was yet well known to pagans. For his Christian readers Eusebius chose Moses because the new dispensation under Constantine did not match well with New Testament notions of history and the state. The political liberation which Constantine brought to a persecuted Christian church could be interpreted more easily in terms of the intramundane eschatology of Exodus than within the apocalyptic horizon of the New Testament. The *Life of Constantine* thus describes Moses and Constantine as divinely commissioned liberators of God's oppressed people. Both these servants and friends of God, as Eusebius calls them, were raised in the households of the oppressors before turning against them and rescuing the people of God. Elsewhere in the *Life* we learn that when Constantine went to war against Licinius he erected a tabernacle for the cross outside his military encampment, where he could retire for prayer and divine enlightenment, just as Moses had done (Exodus 33:7-11).[56]

---

52. *VC* 1.12, rev. trans. by E. C. Richardson, in *A Select Library of Nicene and Post-Nicene Fathers*, 2d ser., vol. 1, p. 485 (translation considerably altered).

53. For the role of the comparison (*synkrisis*) in the genre of epideictic rhetoric known as the *basilikos logos*, to which the *Life of Constantine* partially conforms, see the instructional treatise *Peri epideiktikôn* attributed to Menander of Laodicea, roughly contemporary with Eusebius: *Menander Rhetor*, ed. D. A. Russell and N. G. Wilson (Oxford, 1981), 372.14-25, 376.31-377.10.

54. See J. Gager, *Moses in Greco-Roman Paganism* (Nashville, 1972), pp. 25-79.

55. Military: Josephus, *Jewish Antiquities* 2.243-253; Artapanus, *Concerning the Jews*, in Eusebius *PE* 9.27. Legislative: Josephus, *Against Apion* 2.145-289, esp. 154, 161. Cultural: Eupolemus, *On the Kings of Judaea* (Moses the inventor of writing), in Eusebius *PE* 9.26; Artapanus, *Concerning the Jews* (Moses as teacher of Orpheus, the inventor of ships and of engineering devices), in Eusebius *PE* 9.27. Philosophical: Philo, *Life of Moses* 2.1-2 (Moses as a philosopher-king).

56. *VC* 2.12.

The Moses-Constantine comparison is a secular application of biblical typology without precedent in Christian literature before Eusebius.[57] It blends religious and political symbols and concerns in a way that can seem to justify the critical interpretations of Eusebius which were surveyed in the first part of this paper. I suggest that a more helpful approach is to focus on what the comparison tells us about Eusebius's sense of God's action in history. The Moses-Jesus comparison is instructive here. Both of the Moses typologies reveal the same assumption of how God deals with humanity. Eusebius believed that in the narrated lives of all three individuals—Moses, Jesus, and Constantine—God's sovereign will was manifested *historically*, that is, publicly and in time. This does not mean, however, that he believed each of the three played an equally important role in God's saving plan, which would represent an extraordinary levelling of the difference between Jesus and other men. Eusebius was a subordinationist in his trinitarian theology, but he showed no patience for low views of the Incarnation.[58]

The value of history as a public and verifiable demonstration of God's solicitude for his people was a core notion of Eusebius's exegesis and apologetics.[59] It is a prominent feature, for example, of the *Commentary on Isaiah*, which regularly notes prohecy's vindication in the course of historical events *(ekbasis tôn pragmatôn)*.[60] The prophetic interpretation of history which he found in the Book of Isaiah conceived of history as the earthly journey of the godly polity, first in its Mosaic constitution as biblical Israel and, since the Incarnation and the calling of the gentiles, as the Christian church. Eusebius saw Constantine in terms of this grand historical scheme. In the *Commentary on Isaiah* he made room for Cyrus, Augustus, Vespasian, and Hadrian, all of whom he treated as God's agents executing his purpose.[61] Constantine is merely the latest of such agents, though the first to favor the church. The *Commentary on Isaiah* lacks the patina of pagan royal theology which overlies Constantine's image in the panegyrical literature. The scat-

---

57. Dionysius of Alexandria's reference of Isaiah 42:9 to the Emperor Gallienus (in Eusebius *HE* 7.23) does not seem to be "Messianic language," as in R. L. Fox, *Pagans and Christians* (New York, 1987), p. 554, but the sort of biblical flourish common in Dionysius's correspondence, as in his appeal to the Exodus, Eden, and the flood of Noah—all in the same letter—to illuminate conditions in wartorn Alexandria (compare *HE* 7.21).
58. Compare his denunciations of the Ebionites and Paul of Samosata for their low appreciations of Christ's divinity (*HE* 3.27, 7.30). On Eusebius's Christology, see A. Grillmeier, *Christ in Christian Tradition* (New York, 1965), pp. 180–182.
59. Opitz, "Eusebius von Caesarea als Theologe," pp. 5–9; Barnes, *Constantine and Eusebius*, chap. 10; Sirinelli, *Les vues historiques d'Eusèbe de Césarée*, passim.
60. For example, *CI* 46.14–15 (on Isa. 7:5–9), 68.21 (Isa. 9:7), 126.31 (Isa. 19:4), and 304.3–5 (Isa. 48:3–4).
61. References to Augustus, Vespasian, and Hadrian: *CI* 10.12–20; 14.13–25; 18.23–28; 25.29–36; 31.4–5 and passim. Cyrus is discussed in the commentary wherever the text of Isaiah mentions him by name, for example, Isaiah 44:28 and 45:1.

tered Constantinian allusions which we noted above could never claim an eschatological dignity. They are no threat to displace, either rhetorically or substantively, the supreme importance of the first and the second coming of the *Logos* in Jesus Christ.

Constantine's conversion and patronage of the church are rather to be seen as evidence of God's continuing intervention in history. The real novelty in Eusebius's thought, and the key to his approach to politics, is this apologetic conception of history, which encouraged him to incorporate the present into an ongoing, biblically grounded *demonstratio evangelica*. From this religious perspective, naive though it might be, he judged the epochal events of his time. History, and therefore politics, was assessed from a religious standpoint, and not the other way around. The difference is important, but scholars have not always respected it.[62]

3.

Such is how we might proceed more adequately to evaluate the political dimension in Eusebius's thought. This brief presentation has tried to ground Eusebius's attitude to political developments in categories and concerns that are demonstrably fundamental to his exegetical and apologetical works rather than considering only the Constantinian literature.

At the risk of repeating the anachronism we have just criticized, it is worth noting that Eusebius's reliance on Old Testament motifs to interpret Christianity's new situation is not without its disquieting side. Fifty years ago Charles Cochrane derided Eusebius's Christiantiy as a "success philosophy," because he saw Eusebius as the very model of those who put their religion's resources at the service of the Constantinian *renovatio*.[63] There is a sense in which the criticism is justified. The surface meaning of the Exodus story is that God reveals his partiality for his people by defeating their human enemies—such at least seems to be the gist of the song of Miriam—which should make us ask how felicitous was Eusebius's secular use of his biblical paradigm. His approach to the Old Testament tends to flatten out the distinction between the covenants and to see history as a continuous chain of divine deliverances linking the biblical past to contemporary history. This approach reflects a sanguine optimism about identifying God's will in history

---

62. See, for example, Erik Peterson's discussion of Eusebius's interpretation of the prophecy of the messianic peace in Micah 4:4 in *DE* 8.3.13-15. According to Peterson, *Der Monotheismus als politisches Problem*, p. 90, Eusebius's invocation of the Pax Romana is a political reading of biblical prophecy. But Eusebius's main interest is christological polemic against the Jews, not political propaganda: he wants to prove that the prophecy was fulfilled with the birth of Jesus. He is using secular history for religious purposes, not subordinating religious texts to secular ends.

63. Cochrane, *Christianity and Classical Culture*, pp. 183-187.

which Augustine in *The City of God* was to reject as fallacious.[64] Modern
secular appropriations of the Exodus story suggest that Augustine was wiser
on this score than Eusebius. Michael Walzer's recent book *Exodus and
Revolution* opens with a rich litany of examples.[65] Some of these are
attractive, such as the appeal of the civil rights movement to the Exodus story.
But others are disturbing, such as muckraking journalist Lincoln Steffens's
depiction of Lenin as "Moses in red," in his book of that title, or Benjamin
Franklin's suggestion that the Great Seal of the United States display the
escape through the Red Sea, replete with drowning Egyptian soldiers.

On the contemporary theological scene, the popularity of the Exodus story
as a paradigm of divine deliverance in liberation theology prompts the
question whether Eusebius and liberation theology have an unsuspected
affinity. *Prima facie*, it seems unlikely that a man excoriated as the theological
architect of the Constantinian establishment should have any connection to a
consciously "post-Constantinian" Christianity. And yet Eusebius insisted
that the God of the Exodus revealed himself as "favorably disposed to the
oppressed" precisely when God raised up Constantine as their liberator.[66] In
his readiness to read the signs of the times, and to see God taking sides in
historical and social conflict, there may be less separating Eusebius from some
of his most vigorous critics than they think.[67]

---

64. This is the convincing argument in R. A. Markus's *Saeculum: History and Society in the
   Theology of St. Augustine* (Cambridge, 1970), esp. pp. 51–71. Augustine's agnosticism about
   reading the divine will in history is a major theme of *The City of God*; see for example,
   18.52–53.
65. Michael Walzer, *Exodus and Revolution* (New York, 1985), pp. 3–6.
66. *Theon de tois kataponoumenois eumenê* (*VC* 1.12.1).
67. On the same basis, Richard Neuhaus, *The Catholic Moment* (New York, 1987), pp.
   214–231, has found a similar affinity between Emmanuel Hirsch's call to German Christians in the 1930s to stand alongside Hitler's program of national renewal and the insistence
   of certain expressions of liberation theology that we are bound in conscience to support social
   movements upon which God's favor rests unambiguously.

Richard Krautheimer

THE ECCLESIASTICAL BUILDING POLICY
OF CONSTANTINE

Constantine's building policies stand within the framework of his religious commitment and the ensuing policy as it gradually moved from favouring Christianity and benign neglect of paganism towards a new vision : to create here a Christian Empire on earth which would integrate Church and State and mirror Christ's reign in Heaven. Inevitably likewise his ecclesiastical building policy was linked to the general building policy imposed on him by his and his time's concept of the position and the obligations of a Roman emperor. The implementation of such ideologies and of the policies sprung therefrom were confronted by and had to seek accommodation within the framework of Roman building custom, building legislation and financing as prevailing by the early fourth century.

* * *

Church foundations and church buildings necessarily posed new problems in the face of that framework. Building laws long evolved by Roman jurists distinguished between constructions in the public and those in the private sphere [1]. Those in the public sphere, *opera publica*, comprised everything as long as it belonged to the State,

---

[1] *RE* I, 1, 444, *aedes* (Habel); *ibid.*, IV, 2, 1787 ff., *curatores* (Kornemann) ; *ibid.*, X, 1, 1212 ff., *ius divinum* (Berger) ; *ibid.*, XVIII, 1, 826 ff., *opus publicum* (Lenzle) ; *ibid.*, IA, 1656 ff., *sacra* (Geiger) ; *ibid.*, VAI, 480 f., *templum* (Weinstock).

rose on public ground and served the needs of the community – from sewers, highways and city walls to *thermae*, basilicas, State buildings and temples. Temples, however, in the legal context of *opera publica* were only those dedicated to a god recognized by the religious authorities of the State, the *pontifices* : a Roman god or one officially introduced by a *senatus consultum*, as was the *Magna Mater* as early as 205 BC. Ever since Augustus administration of the *opera publica*, new construction and maintenance were in Rome in the hands of a college of *curatores*, each responsible for a category of constructions — one for the temples, another for highways and so forth down to the *curator alvei Tiberis* and the *curator riparum*. In the provinces the *opera publica* by the second century, if not before, were subordinate to the provincial governors and their magistrates.

Into the private sphere, on the other hand, fell everything built by and for the use of individuals : houses, tenements, mansions. Imperial palaces, too, belonged to the private sphere, if built by Emperors over the centuries for their private use ; that is all palaces save those on the Palatine which were considered to be public. Important in our context is the provision that the private sphere of building also comprised religious structures : temples, that is, built on private ground by individuals or families and dedicated to a god *suae religionis causa*, for the sake of their own beliefs : a divinity that is, not recognized by the Roman State through the *pontifices*, Mithras, for instance. Such temples, therefore, were not *sacra* according to religious law.

Financing likewise fell into a public and a private sphere. Public finance was handled by the *fiscus*, which collected, administered and disposed of the government revenues. These were drawn mostly from taxes levied on individuals and corporations such as provinces and cities. Additional revenues were produced by mints and mines, and by State–owned industries, such as armament factories and weaving mills and, originally anyway, by public lands. All were managed by the vast bureaucracy of the *fiscus*, which in turn took care of all government expenses, at least in theory.

In the private sphere was obviously an individual's or a family's property, their *patrimonium*. In the case of the emperor, that *patrimonium*, his private property comprised what he had inherited from his family or acquired by marriage : palaces, gardens, villas, domains ; also mines, ships, herds and slaves. Furthermore, ever since Augustus, the emperor's *patrimonium* was constantly enlarged by war booty, confiscation, donations and legacies willed to the ruling emperor by his friends, whatever that meant – lapses were most unhealthy. Conversely, since Augustus' days the vast income from the emperor's *patrimonium* paid for a goodly part of public expenses beside the costs of the court : for the building of the Imperial Fora in Rome, for instance, and of their temples and for the circus games [2].

Whereas after the emperor's death the *patrimonium* in theory anyhow, stayed with the familiy, its place ever since Septimus Severus was increasingly taken by the *res privata* : crown property, at the emperor's free disposal *qua* holder of the throne [3].

Accumulated over the centuries, the *res privata* was continously swelled : by purchases, legacies, war booty, and by confiscations which by unwritten law fell to the emperor : the estate of an usurper or a co–emperor or a predecessor defeated; of anyone condemned for a capital crime ; or, for that matter, of any rich individual, considered disloyal or arbitrarily proscribed. In practice by the late third century the *patrimonium* appears to have been merged into the *res privata*. The bulk of the *res privata* seems to have consisted of real estate, agricultural or urban. By the fourth century, according to A. H. M. Jones, the *res privata* handled all landed property not in individual hands, regardless of its original ownership, the *fiscus*, the emperor's *patrimonium*, the *res privata*. Administration of the *res privata* was in the hands of a huge managerial staff, somewhat parallel to that of the *fiscus* and headed, by Constantine's time, first by a *magister rei privatae*, later called *comes rerum privatarum* or *comes sacrarum largitionum*. Subordinate to him were *rationales rei privatae*, each responsible for the crown property located

---

[2] *Res gestae Divini Augusti* IV, 19 ff., (ed. F. Shipley, *LCL*, 1961), 374 ff. ; *RE* IA1, 631 ff., *res privata* (Liebenam) ; X, 493 ff., *patrimonium* (Kränzlein).

[3] R. His, *Die Domänen der römischen Kaiserzeit*, Leipzig 1896 ; A. H. M. Jones, *The Later Roman Empire*, II, Oxford 1964, 411 ff. and *passim* (henceforth *LRE*) ; *RE* IV, 238 ff. (Kornemann) ; A. Masi, *Ricerche sulla 'res privata' del 'princeps'*, Milano 1971.

Kränzlein, as in previous note, doubts that crown property as separate from the emperor's *patrimonium* ever existed ; *res privata* in his view only designates the special administration of the Imperial domains which had swallowed up the former fiscal and temple lands as well.

in one of the provinces or part thereof and supported by a vast clerical staff.

Present–day scholarship assumes perhaps all too readily that the emperor by the fourth century, if not before, drew at his will for projects of his own on the resources of any of the three departments – *fiscus, patrimonium, res privata*. No doubt the borderlines were fluid and an Imperial nod would bend law and precedent. Nonetheless, the lawyers at work in Constantine's chancellery and all the administration of the empire tended, it seems, to maintain orderly procedure both in language and in practice. Thus his ecclesiastical building policy, too, and its implementation should be seen, if not within the established framework of legal, administrative and financial organisation, then with that framework in mind.

* * *

Evidence for Constantine's ecclesiastical building policy and its legal and administrative context is provided by a handful of documents and by a wealth of archaeological finds. From that material the guidelines of his policy can perhaps be extrapolated. An Imperial circular addressed to the bishops in the Eastern provinces, one would like to think right after the victory over Licinius, hence perhaps still late in 324, points to the neglect under the past «tyranny» of « the buildings of all the congregations, ...πασῶν τῶν ἐκκλησίων ἔργα »; ἔργα being the equivalent of the technical term *opera*. Therefore the heads presiding over the congregations, laymen or clerics (*scil.* in the bishop's diocese) are urged to restore or to enlarge them or, where need be, to build new ones. Going through the bishop the heads of the congregations moreover are to request « what is needed » from the governors and the office of the *praefectus praetorio*, these being the Latin equivalents of « τῶν ἡγεμονευόντων καὶ τῆς ἐπαρχικῆς τάξεως ». These, the highest civilian authorities locally responsible, have been commanded to be at the service of the bishop's words. Financing for the building operation was provided through them by the fiscus « τῶν βασιλικῶν θησαύρων τὰς ἐπισκευὰς ποιεῖσθαι » [4].

---

[4] Eus., *VC* II, 46 : «σπουδάζειν περὶ τὰ ἔργα τῶν ἐκκλησίων, ἢ ἐπανορθοῦσθα τὰ ὄντα ἢ εἰς μείζονα αὔξειν ἢ ἔνθα ἂν χρεία ἀπαιτῇ καινὰ ποιεῖν : αἰτήσεις δὲ καὶ

Ecclesiastical and civilian authorities thus are ordered to cooperate in building for the needs of Christian congregations. The rescript does not go into details. It does not explain the meaning of « what is needed », nor the terms of cooperation between civil service and Church authorities, nor the underlying political aims. The implementation of that policy, however, is outlined unmistakably in a few more letters issued by Constantine's chancellery and preserved by Eusebius.

In 325/26 Constantine addressed a letter to bishop Makarios of Jerusalem regarding the constructions to be erected near the Holy Sepulchre [5]. The letter, preserved in the *Vita Constantini (VC* III, 30–32) is introduced by Eusebius' account of the tomb's rediscovery a short while back. The tomb, so he reports, had been hidden below an earth platform cast up and paved to carry a shrine of Aphrodite, presumably Astaroth [6]. Platform and shrine were

---

αὐτὸς καὶ διὰ σοῦ οἱ λοιποὶ τὰ ἀναγκαῖα, παρά τε τῶν ἡγεμονευόντων καὶ τῆς ἐπαρχικῆς τάξεως. τούτοις γὰρ ἐπεστάλη πάσῃ προθυμίᾳ ἐξυπηρετήσασθαι τοῖς ὑπὸ τῆς σῆς ὁσιότητος λεγομένοις ».
The letter while adressed to Eusebius is presumably a circular mailed to all bishops in the eastern provinces. See also the summary provided *VC* II, 45 : « ... ὁ δὲ τῶν εὐκτηρίων οἴκων τὰς οἰκοδομὰς ὑψοῦν αὔξειν τε εἰς πλάτος καὶ μῆκος τὰς ἐκκλησίας τοῦ θεοῦ διαγορεύων, ὡσανεὶ μελλόντων τῷ θεῷ σχεδὸν εἰπεῖν ἁπάντων ἀνθρώπων... τοιαῦτα γὰρ φρονεῖν τε καὶ γράφειν τοῖς κατὰ τόπον ἄρχουσι βασιλέα ἡ αὐτοῦ περὶ τὸν θεὸν ἐνῆγεν ὁσία, χρημάτων δὲ μὴ φείδεσθαι δόσεως, ἀλλ'ἐξ αὐτῶν τῶν βασιλικῶν θησαυρῶν τὰς ἐπισκευὰς περιεῖχεν ὁ νόμος ».
I doubt that νόμος refers to a regular law ; rather, Eusebius means an Imperial rescript.
See also F. W. DEICHMANN, *Review of A. Arbeiter, Alt–Skt.–Peter...*, « BZ » 83 (1990), 296 ff.
[5] The earliest and most reliable sources regarding foundation, plan, elevation and fittings of the structure at the Holy Sepulchre are : EUS., *VC* III, 26 ff. ; Etheria (Silvia), *Peregrinatio...* ; and Arculfus (Adamnanus), *De locis sanctis*, the latter two conveniently in *Itineraria Hierosolymitana*, ed. P. Geyer, Vienna 1895 (*CSEL* 38), 34 f. and 219 ff. resp. The latest stand of the archaeological evidence is found in V. CORBO, *Il Santo Sepolcro*, Jerusalem 1981/82.
[6] No trace of the platform has come to light so far. A few walls traced inside the Anastasis rotunda, to the East of the Sepulchre have been interpreted as : the foundations of the three–cell capitolium of Roman Jerusalem — the shrine of Aphrodite being but a tabernacle on Golgatha (CORBO, as note 5, 33 ff.) ; those of a peristlyle temple of Aphrodite (J. E. PHILIPS, *The Site of the Holy Sepulchre*, Ph. D. thesis, University of Texas, 1977) ;

demolished on the emperor's orders thus bringing the tomb to light (*VC* III, 26–28). The tale poses four questions. Two are irrelevant in our context and insoluble – what did the shrine look like and how was the tomb's hide–away known. The other two are relevant: how was Constantine informed of its existence and what was the administrative procedure employed in its rediscovery ? One can but surmise that Makarios, possibly through Eusebius, his fellow–bishop in nearby Phoenicia, brought the matter to the emperor's attention. The council of Nicaea in the early summer of 325 would have been a good opportunity for such an approach.

Constantine's letter to Makarios hints at a key element of his building policy, and it clearly outlines administrative procedure and financing. A few introductory sentences set forth his intention « to make shine with the beauty of buildings » the site of Christ's Tomb previously hidden below the idol's shrine [7].

Coming down to specifics the emperor commands Makarios to devise, « διατάξαι » everything so that the basilica to be built should be more beautiful than any other or for that matter outshine anything built in any city [8]. (The term 'basilica' is used generically so as to refer to places of assembly, meeting halls of any kind, secular, pagan, Christian : just so the pilgrim from Bordeaux in 333 has to specify the basilica's being a church — *basilica id est dominicum* [9]). The bishop is thus appointed as the emperor's executive arm, his local agent in planning the church : a rational device — no one else could determine better the lay–out with an eye to conditions locally prevailing : the site of the Sepulchre, the placing of the ba-

---

of a fourth century courtyard preceding planning and construction of the Rotunda (CHS. COÜASNON, *The Holy Sepulchre in Jerusalem* (*Schweich Lectures British Academy*), London 1974, 21 ff.).

The meagre evidence, archaeological and documentary, so far available allows for no conclusions. In particular, I know of no evidence for the existence on the site of either the *Capitolium* or a large temple.

[7] EUS., *VC* III, 30 : « ...ὅπως τὸν ἱερὸν ἐκεῖνον τόπον,... οἰκοδομημάτων κάλλει κοσμήσωμεν ».

[8] EUS. *VC* III, 31. 1 : « Προσήκει τοίνυν τὴν σὴν ἀγχίνοιαν οὕτω διατάξαι τε καὶ ἑκάστου τῶν ἀναγκαίων ποιήσασθαι πρόνοιαν, ὡς οὐ μόνον βασιλικὴν τῶν ἀπανταχοῦ βελτίονα ἀλλὰ καὶ τὰ λοιπὰ τοιαῦτα γίνεσθαι, ὡς πάντα τὰ ἐφ' ἑκάστης καλλιστεύοντα πόλεως ὑπὸ τοῦ κτίσματος τούτου νικᾶσθαι ».

[9] *Itinerarium burdigaleuse*, in *Itinera Hierosolomytana*, as note 5 ; also *ThLL*, V. 2, 1892.

silica and access to both; the size of clergy and congregation, resident and pilgrims to be expected ; the requirements of the liturgy locally prevailing and their impact on the church plan. Moreover, it had been customary since at least the second century to appoint a local representative to supervise planning and execution of a building donated by the emperor [10]. Constantine's rescript to Makarios separates the tasks. Building operations — construction of the walls and architectural decoration — «τῆς τῶν τοίχων ἐγερσεώς καὶ καλλιεργίας...», so it goes on, have been entrusted to Drakilianos, the acting *praefectus praetorio per Orientem* and to the governor of the province, presumably the *consularis Palaestinae* [11]. They are in descending order the two highest ranking officials locally responsible. It is on them that the *opera publica* depend through which they have to act on site. But, as Constanine's letter says, it is not they, but the bishop who will have to determine strength and kind of the work force, skilled and unskilled, « καὶ τεχνίτας καὶ ἐργάτας », and amounts and type of building materials and request from the civil authorities these and « what else is needed ». Given the place of the *opera publica* in the administrative Table of Organisation, all expenses, wages and so forth would have been charged to the *fiscus*.

As to columns and marbles — these latter presumably for pavement and wall revetment, and to « what you judge more costly and useful .... as it results from your estimate », σύνοψις, the bishop is told to report to the emperor quantity and quality « so it can be provided from anywhere» [12]. Further Makarios is to inform the emperor, whether he wants the ceiling of the new church coffered and gilded — an Imperial command and an offer to bear the expense ; just as the hint was unmistakable to ask for costly fit-

---

[10] R. MacMullen, *Roman Imperial building in the provinces*, Harvard Studies in Classical Philology 64 (1959), 207 ff.

[11] The Greek translation has « ...Δρακιλλιανῷ τῷ ἡμετέρῳ φίλῳ, τῷ διέποντι τὰ τῶν λαμπροτάτων ⌐ἐπάρχων⌐ μέρη, καὶ τῷ τῆς ἐπαρχίας ἄρχοντι... ».

Drakilianos was *vicarius Orientis*, acting for the two *praefecti praetorio*, young Constantius (May 325 – June 327) and Evagrius (August 325 – August 326) ; see *CTh* II. 33. 1 (adressed : *Ad Dracilianum agentem vices p⟨raefectorum⟩ p⟨raetorio⟩*).

[12] Eus., *VC* III, 31. 3 : « ...περὶ δὲ τῶν κιόνων εἴτ' οὖν μαρμάρων, ἃ δ' ἂν νομίσειας εἶναι τιμιώτερά τε καὶ χρησιμώτερα, αὐτὸς συνόψεως γενομένης πρὸς ἡμᾶς γράψαι σπούδασον, ἵν' ὅσων δ' ἂν καὶ ὁποίων χρείαν εἶναι διὰ τοῦ σοῦ γράμματος ἐπιγνῶμεν, ταῦτα πανταχόθεν μετενεχθῆναι δυνηθῆ' ».

tings — one thinks of the « tasteful gifts and the profusion of votive offerings in gold and silver and precious stones », praised by Eusebius when in 336 the church was consecrated and of the mosaics and textile hangings described as Constantine's gift by Etheria fifty years later [13]. Clearly in Constantine's letter to Makarios, all precious extras, starting with columns and marble are set apart from the building expenses proper. They are to be provided and funded, rather than by the *fiscus*, by the emperor himself, that is by the *res privata*.

Needless to say, the bishop would depend on expert advice to live up to the tasks thrust upon him. Only an architect could devise the plan of the church, draw up lists of the labour force and the materials needed and estimate the time required for construction ; all information the *opera publica* would require. It appears that the *martyrion* at the Holy Sepulchre was built by the presbyter Eustathios from Constantinople and by one Zenobius [14]. To judge by his Syrian name the latter would seem to have been a local builder or one from neighbouring Syria. Eustathios was presumably a trained architect turned priest and sent down possibly with a plan to Jerusalem, where his kind was not readily available.

The procedure outlined in the Makarios letter provides an insight into the details of the procedure followed in founding and building churches under Constantine in these years. The emperor takes the initiative in founding a church if and when approached with a specific proposal. Cooperation between ecclesiastical and civilian authorities is basic to implementing the task in hand ; the former are responsible for devising the plan and listing materials and labour needed, the latter for the execution. But it is not always easy to tell whether or how far funding was provided by the *fiscus* or by the *res privata* or whether both interacted. Early in 330 or before, the Catholic bishop at Constantina – Cirte, a small town in

---

[13] Eus., *VC* IV, 46 : « ...Οἷος δ' ὁ τοῦ σωτῆρος νεώς, οἷον τὸ σωτήριον ἄντρον, οἷαί τε αἱ βασιλέως φιλοκαλίαι ἀναθημάτων τε πλήθη ἐν χρυσῷ τε καὶ ἀργύρῳ καὶ λίθοις τιμίοις πεποιημένων... » ; also, Etheria, *Peregrinatio*, in *Itinera Hierosolymitana*, as above note 5, 76 ; and Theodoret, *HE* I, 29 (*PG* 82, 988).

[14] Theophanes, *Chronographia*, ed. C. de Boer, Leipzig 1883, 33, « ad an. 5848 (328 a.D.) » ; Prosper of Aquitaine, *Chronicum integrum* I, Nepotiano et Facundo (336 A.D.) (*PL* 51, 567).

Numidia, had turned to the emperor with a letter of complaint: the Donatists had occupied and refused to return to the rightful owners the church built by Constantine for the Catholics [15]. Therefore, the bishop asks the emperor for a site to build a new church, *locum fiscalem*, a site belonging to the *fiscus*. In response the emperor, that is of course the chancellery, informs the bishop that he has commanded the *rationalis* to transfer with all legal rights to the ownership of the Catholic congregation, rather than a terrain of fiscal property, a house from our estates « ...*ad rationalem competentes litteras dedi ut domum bonorum nostrorum transgredi faciat cum omni iure suo ad dominium ecclesiae catholicae* ». *Bonorum nostrorum* means from our *res privata* ; indeed, « ἡμετέρων κτημάτων » (the Latin original would have had *bonorum nostrorum*), is the term used as early as 312 by the jurists in the Imperial chancellery for the emperor's *res privata* in a rescript concerning financial subventions for the anti–Donatist clergy in Africa [16]. Likewise, the « ἐπίτροπος» referred to in that passage of 312 is the *rationalis* of the *res privata*, the business manager of crown property in the province. The switch made by the chancellery in providing the bishop of Cirte with a house of crown property, this rather than a lot belonging to the *fiscus* as requested, is worth noting. However it has to be discussed in a broader context.

Planning and building the presumably small church at Cirte follows the same procedures as those outlined in Constantine's letter to Makarios regarding the structures at the Holy Sepulchre, the most prestigious enterprise in his ecclesiastical building program. The orders for undertaking construction go to the *consularis Numidiae*, the provincial governor responsible for Cirte. Through him they reach the *opera publica* to be carried out presumably through a local contractor. Also it is specifically stated that the *fiscus* is to bear the expense « ...*sumptu fiscali basilicam erigi praecepi...* ». The charge to the local bishop to prepare plan and building survey while not specified is implied in the phrase that the *consularis* should assist

---

[15] *Optati Milevitani Libri VII*, ed. C. Ziwsa (*CSEL* 38), Vienna 1893, 213 ff.

[16] The rescript survives only in Greek translation in EUS., *HE* X, 6, 1 ff. (*LCL* II, ed. F. E. L. Oulton and H. F. Lawlor, London and New York 1932, 460 f.).

the bishop throughout in building the new church « *ut ipse in eiusdem ecclesiae fabricatione in omnibus sanctimoniam vestram iuvaret* ».

Similarily Constantine acts upon an outsider's, albeit a family member's, suggestion in founding the church at Mamre, at the Terebinth of Abraham. Such action upon an outsider's request is good old Roman Imperial custom [17]. And again, planning the building and financing construction rests on the interaction between the ecclesiastic authorities, the civil service, the *opera publica*, the *fiscus* and the *res privata*. A rescript addressed by Constantine to Makarios of Jerusalem, presumably qua primate, and the other bishops of Palestine [18] sets forth that his mother–in–law, Eutropia — a Syrian and a Christian from way back [19] — had informed him of a deplorable situation. Pagan services were held at the tree of Abraham where God had revealed himself to the patriarch ; wooden idols were displayed nearby and there was an altar for « unclean », that is bloody sacrifices ; and how come, pray — so the letter — that the bishops had failed to take note of such scandalous goings–on ? Anyway, the emperor had ordered the *comes* Akakios to have these horrors removed, the idols burnt and the site thoroughly cleansed. This done, the bishops were to devise « διατυπώσητε » and jointly with those of neighbouring Phoenicia — the emperor willing to bear the expense of the meeting — to draw up « διαγράψαι » the plan or project of a basilica « worthy of our generosity ». Their cooperation was essential also in view of the local situation : since

---

[17] MacMullen, as above note 10.

[18] Eus., *VC* III, 52 f. While undated, the rescript was issued obviously after 324, possibly in 328 when the *comes* Akakios, entrusted with building operations, was active in other affairs in nearby Antioch (Eusebius, *VC* III, 63). The church was completed by 333 when visited by the pilgrim of Bordeaux « *...basilica facta est iussu Constantini mirae pulchritudinis* » (as above note 9), 25.

[19] The relationship between Constantine and Eutropia is somewhat involved. From her first marriage she had a daughter Theodora who around 289 was given in marriage to Constantius I and thus became Constantine's step–mother (*RE, Suppl.*, VA, 1773 f. ; Ensslin). From a third marriage to Maxentius around 298 Eutropia had another daughter, Fausta who in her early childhood was betrothed to and in 307 was married to Constantine (*RE* VI, 2, 2048). Hence Eutropia was both his mother–in–law and his step–grandmother. Theodora's given name suggests her mother's having been Christian already by the time of Theodora's birth, presumably around 275 (*RE* VI, 1, 1519 ; Seeck).

time immemorial a fair had been held bi–annually at the site, attended by people from all over Palestine, Phoenicia and elsewhere. Hence a large enclosure was needed to hold traders and buyers, non–Christian and Christian ; a small church inside that enclosure would suffice to shelter a tiny congregation, faithful and clergy [20].

Construction, so Constantine's letter says, was to be taken care of by the *comes* Akakios. The emperor's intimate and personal representative, a *comes* acts as a kind of roving inspector [21]. Therefore, in theory, he stands outside the hierarchy of the civil service. To fulfill the task thrust upon him, he would nonetheless have to turn to the civil service locally responsible, and through them to the *opera publica* : they would, through local contractors, take care of clearing the site, demolishing altar and idols, and building the church, providing materials and manpower. The *fiscus* would have borne the expense.

We thus dispose of a good deal of information on the distribution of responsibilities and on the procedures followed in founding, planning and building churches — during the later half of Constantine's reign, that is. All the evidence quoted so far follows, after all, the decisive victory on September 28, 324 which gave him the rule over the eastern part of the Empire as well. Also, there is no reason to suspect that in these years proceedings in church building under his aegis elsewhere differed from those followed at Jerusalem, Mamre and Cirte — at Antioch for instance or at Bethlehem or Constantinople, or in the far West, at Trier.

* * *

For the first half of Constantine's reign on the other hand, from Ponte Milvio to Chrysopolis, information available on his policy and practice in founding and building churches is very different in nature. It is plentiful. However, rather than being widespread, it is limited topographically. The bulk concerns one locale, Rome and its *suburbium* ; a few items refer to church foundations near

---

[20] The scarse remains uncovered hardly suffice to support a reconstruction as proposed by the excavator (E. MADER, *Mambre...*, Freiburg 1957).

[21] On history and functions of *comites*, see *RE* IV, 1, 622 ff. (Seeck).

Rome and in Campania, at Ostia, Albano, Capua and Naples. More-over, the evidence available tells us nothing about the procedures and the distribution of tasks followed in planning, building and outfitting churches. One is tempted to assume they were the same as those applied in later years. But caution is called for. Planning, it seems reasonable, may well have been thrust upon the clergy also at Rome, as documented for Jerusalem and Mamre. The Ro-man bishop's staff, with the help of an architect would presumably have prepared the plans and estimates of materials and work force required for building the Lateran cathedral and probably the co-vered cemeteries in the *suburbium*. The local bishops at Ostia and Albano and in Campania would have acted correspondingly. On the other hand a court architect may well have redesigned a hall inside her residence, the Sessorian Palace, to serve as a church for the empress dowager Helena.

Construction, on the other hand, in Rome could hardly have been entrusted to the civilian authorities. The *opera publica* in Rome were under the jurisdiction of the Senate. Given the preponde-rance of pagans in that body and their susceptibilities, Constantine would have been careful not to approach them with a request to undertake the construction of Christian churches through the *cu-ratores operum publicorum*. Rather he would have commanded the *res privata* to provide through contracting firms workmen and materials and have had them carry out the work. The cost would have been charged to the emperor's private purse, that is to the crown. At Naples, Capua, Albano and Ostia or for that matter, anywhere in the West, the emperor might well have entrusted to the *opera publica* construction of churches founded or subventioned by him. However, all this remains to be proven.

On the other hand, the evidence both archaeological and do-cumentary furnishes precise complementary information on the initiative in founding, on the sources drawn upon for providing the building site, and on the funding of maintenance and servicing of the church once completed.

That information rests primarily on the lists of Constantine's donations made to churches founded by him or by members of his family in Rome and its surroundings, and on the archaeological evidence provided by the remains surviving. Incorporated by the sixth century compiler into the *Liber Pontificalis* these lists are apparently copied either *verbatim* or excerpted from the original deeds as presumably preserved then in the church archives [22]. Their reliability is attested to by topographical and administrative particulars contained in the lists; only rarely has the compiler inserted an anachronistic gloss [23]. Starting possibly as early as the late fall of 312, the emperor's donations to churches of his foundation are documented to at least 326 when he broke for good with Rome, never to return to the West; from the Lateran cathedral and its baptistery and S. Croce in Gerusalemme, the two churches of his *intra moenia*, to the burial and martyrs' basilicas on the Imperial estates *extra moenia* — St. Peter's, S. Agnese, S. Lorenzo, SS. Marcellino e Pietro — as well as the churches founded near Rome and as far south as Naples [24].

---

[22] H. GEERTMAN, *Nota sul 'Liber Pontificalis' come fonte archeologica*, in *Quaeritur inventus colitur*, Miscellanea Umberto Fasola, ed. Ph. Pergola and F. Bisconti, I (Studi di antichità Christiana 40), Vatican City 1989, 347 ff.

[23] The only major insert made by the compiler of the *Liber Pontificalis* or by an earlier redactor regards the entry for S. Paolo f.l.m. The original donation made to the first small church erected over the grave on the Via Ostiensis, whether by Constantine or one of his sons, but in any case after 324, was the island Gordianum, off Tarsus producing an income of six hundred *solidi*. That entry the redactor left standing. However, he felt uneasy by the modest size of the donation in view of Saint Paul's re-emergence late in the fourth century; a pre-eminence confirmed in his eyes by the grandeur of the new church, built by the Three Emperors starting in 385 or a year earlier, as large, monumental and splendid as St. Peter's at the Vatinac. Thus he inserted in the text an awkward general phrase as to Constantine's having donated to S. Paolo f.l.m. gifts in gold and silver to the same value as those made to St. Peter's. Also he added a 'Constantinian' donation list of landed estates, producing an income higher than that assigned to St. Peter's; all located in the East and all fictitious, as witness the topographical and grammatical mistakes – « sub civitate Tyria », « sub civitate Aegyptia ». See R. KRAUTHEIMER, *Intorno alla fondazione di S. Paolo fuori le mura*, APARAR 53–54 (1980/82), 207 ff.

[24] While archaeological evidence is plentiful for all of Constantine's church foundations documented in Rome, both *intra* and *extra moenia*, no such evidence has come to light so far for those listed by the *Liber Pontificalis* as founded or subventioned by him elsewhere in Italy; nor have the sites ever been established. However, the donation lists seem to be reliable : type and weight of the gifts in silver (none in gold) and annual income rank somewhat below those of minor Roman churches, except the donations given to the church at Ostia. A Constantinian date for the church at Albano is supported by an outside *terminus ante quem non* (*LP* I, CL).

To be sure, one wants to remember that the compiler of the *Liber Pontificalis* has severely contracted the particulars of the deeds of foundation of the individual churches. These were no doubt contained in the original document as required by Roman Law [25]. The consular date of year and day has given way to a « *huius temporibus* » or « *eodem tempore* », 'the « *huius* » referring to Pope Sylvester into whose biography the donations are inserted. Name and full title of donor and the solemn dedication formula « *do et dedico* » or « *dedico consacroque...* » complemented by the name of the divinity have been abbreviated to « *Constantinus Augustus fecit basilicam...* » The contractions deprive us of the exact date of the individual donations made to the emperor's church foundations in Rome. Except those given to St. Peter's, obviously after September 324 and all scattered *per diocesem Orientis*, the bulk of the landed properties enumerated in the donation lists were located in Latium and nearby Campania and southern Umbria. Only the Lateran basilica, its baptistery and the coemeterium–basilica of SS. Marcellino e Pietro jointly with Constantine's and Helena's mausoleum were endowed with estates situated further away, in Sicily, Sardinia, and North Africa, on Malta and Kephalonia; mostly *latifundia* of enormous size, bearing incomes of up to and over 1000 *solidi* [26]. Moreover, the urban real estate, part of the endowment donated to the Lateran Baptistery and yielding 2000 *solidi* a year, made the Roman bishop one of the major landholders in the city. However, such donations must be seen as costly extras, as it were, to refer to Constantine's letter to Makarios.

The location in the West of all these landed possessions except those given to St. Peter's has led to the conclusion that their donation and foundation invariably dates prior to 324 while Constantine ruled only the West. That may well hold for the majority. However, one must not generalize; the location of the properties close to Rome and often close to the churches endowed, such as S. Croce in Gerusalemme, S. Agnese, S. Lorenzo, may as well be due to their easy accessibility to managers and working crews.

---

[25] L. VOELKL, *Die Kirchenstiftungen des Kaisers Konstantin im Lichte des römischen Sakralrechts* (Arbeitsgemeinschaft des Landes Nordrhein-Westfalen, Heft 117), Köln–Opladen 1964, esp. 23 ff.

[26] *LP* I, CLXV ff. ; CHS. PIÉTRI, *Rome Chrétienne*, 79 ff., has calculated the size of the landed donations based on the income quoted.

The brevity of the formula « *Constantinus Augustus fecit* » also intimates that the initiative for the foundation throughout came from the emperor himself. This is unlikely. Constantine was never at home in Rome ; his visits were rare, brief and far between — in 312/313, in 315 and in 326, and never more than three months at a time. He never felt comfortable there and never got used to the Roman climate, political and religious, whether pagan or Christian. The Church had, it seems, won over a fair minority among the poor and the middle classes, some well–to–do. Among the great families, the men almost as a body clung to the old ways as a national duty. The enlightened might lean towards a vague monotheistic deism ; their wives might even join the new faith. But it was the men, seated in the Senate, that counted as a political and as an economic force. Any move of Constantine's might trigger unrest : on entering conquered Rome, his refusal to pay hommage to Capitoline Jove had caused a good deal of grumbling [27] ; so had apparently his placing a challenging inscription on the base and a Chi–Rho in the hand of a statue of himself, set up in the Forum near the *Curia Senatus* [28]. The ground was equally slippery on the Christian side of the fence. The individual congregations which composed the Roman community, led by their presbyters, for a century and more had resisted the bishop's moves to establish firmly his and his staff's authority: theologically, politically and presumably financially [29]. Constantine needed guidance.

To be sure, the foundation of the Lateran cathedral in all likelihood on November 11, 312, not quite a fortnight after the battle at Ponte Milvio and its dedication to the Saviour are best understood as Constantine's personal thanksgiving to Christ, giver of victory [30]. Quite possibly, before the battle Constantine had made

---

[27] J. STRAUB, *Konstantins Verzicht auf den Gang zum Kapitol*, Historia 4 (1963), 297 ff. ; ID., *Regeneratio Imperii*, Darmstadt 1972, 100 ff.

[28] EUS., *VC* I, 40 ; also *Three Capitals*, 37.

[29] G. LA PIANA, *The Roman Church at the end of the second century*, HThR 18 (1925), 201 ff. The struggle between bishop and deacons on one side, congregations and presbyters on the other continued through the fourth century. As late as 412 the Romain bishop still refused presbyters the right to consecrate the species (R. CABIÈ, *La lettre du Pape Innocent Ier à Decentius de Gubbio*, Louvain 1973).

[30] *Three Capitals*, 15 ff.

a formal *votum* promising Christ the building of a temple dedicated
to Him in the city to be conquered, as Roman generals had long been
wont to do for their gods [31]. But someone would have advised him ;
presumably an ecclesiastic, familiar in particular with the sensitive
situation within the Christian community in Rome, with its bishop's
difficult standing and with the claims for a relative independence
on the part of the insubordinate congregations. He may have been
the bishop of Rome himself, Miltiades. More likely though, he was
one of Constantine's Christian intimates at headquarters, such as
bishop Hosius of Cordova, who for some time had been in his confidence. Whoever he was, that advisor was intent on strengthening
the bishop's hand by seeing him set up in a cathedral, grand and
splendidly appointed, as were the emperor's public buildings, whatever their function; and thus set apart from the emphatically private
structures where the individual congregations assembled. A cathedral, moreover, whose endowment made the bishop one of the big
holders of landed properties through the richest provinces of Italy
and of urban real estate in the capital. Likewise the covered cemeteries on the Imperial estates were richly endowed – they, too,
it appears were under the bishop's administration [32]. On the other
hand, it is worth noting that no funding goes to the congregations
in support of possible building activities.

Just as later, also in his earlier years, the initiative in church
founding may have frequently been suggested to Constantine from
outside. The transformation into a church of a large hall in the
Sessorian Palace (S. Croce in Gerusalemme), would have been proposed to him by Helena or by her staff once the empress dowager
had moved her permanent residence there, whenever that was.
Occasionally, in fact, an entry in the *Liber Pontificalis* appears to
record the incentives for a foundation having come from outside.
The Cononian excerptor of the *Liber Pontificalis* reports that St.
Peter's was built by Constantine *ex rogatu Sylvestri*, at the behest
of bishop Sylvester of Rome [33]. That may have been the case indeed.

---

[31] R. ROHDE, *Die Bedeutung der Tempelgründungen im Staatsleben der
Römer*, in ID., *Studien und Interpretationen*, Berlin 1963, 183 ff.

[32] After the mid–fifth century, the bishop's office assigns the administration of the cemeteries to the clergy of the various regions intra moenia
LP I, 249.

[33] *LP* I, 78.

When work started on the basilica on the Vatican Hill around 320, give or take a couple of years, a discrete word from the bishop or the *praefectus urbi* would have reminded the Majesty of the key position in both ecclesiastical and secular politics held by the Apostle, founder of the Church in the capital of the Roman World and of the increasing attraction his grave was gaining among Christians, West and East. Likewise, Sylvester may have approached the emperor as to founding the *coemeterium* by the grave of Saint Lawrence, archmartyr of Rome and much beloved by the Romans, and outfitting his tomb chamber with precious gifts. But, then, the *ex rogatu* formula remains somewhat suspect when it appears in the *Liber Pontificalis* and its derivatives (and that happens only twice). The *coemeterium Agnetis*, so the entry, was built by Constantine at the behest of his daughter Constantina–Constantia. The compiler, to be sure, may have drawn his information from the fourth century deed whence he excerpted the accompanying authentic donation list. However, the princess' dedicatory inscription, once in the church, stated *expressis verbis* that she had the structure erected at her own expense : « *...omnibus impensis devota mente paratis...* » [34]. Possibly then, young Constantina, upon her request, had been delegated by her father to found the *coemeterium* with the understanding that the cost of construction would be charged to her own *patrimonium* — an *ex voto* of the teenage princess to the teenage martyr. Obviously « (Constantinus)... *fecit basilicam ex rogatu* » might as well be the compiler's insert — great names attract attribution.

Foundation of a church *ex rogatu* by Constantine or under his name at times was linked to participation by the petitioner. At Ostia a church richly endowed by the emperor with silver fittings and income from lands received additional donations from one Gallicanus : a smallish number of liturgical vessels and one chandelier ; but estates almost equal in income to those given by Constantine [35]. Gallicanus, presumably a local *potens*, would have approached the emperor for a subvention in support of the church built, one suspects, by the petitioner, this rather than by Constantine. Cooperation on

---

[34] F. W. Deichmann, *Die Lage der konstantinischen Basilika der Heiligen Agnes*, (RivAC) 22 (1946) 213 ff. ; Voelkl, as above note 25, p. 26 ; see also R. Krautheimer, *The Building Inscriptions...*, RJbBH 25 (1989), note 132.

[35] *LP* I, 183 f.

a far larger and closer scale obtained, one surmises, as Constantine and his mother, the empress–dowajer Helena, were engaged in founding, erecting and endowing the structures at Tor Pignattara on the Via Labicana : the coemeterium–basilica over the catacomb housing the remains of the deacon Marcellinus and the exorcist Petrus, martyrs of the Diocletian persecution ; and, it seems, the mausoleum attached to it, whether or not planned from the outset [36]. Catacomb and church were located on the grounds of an Imperial villa, property of the *res privata* as far back as the late second century and hence fallen to Constantine in 312 [37]. Helena seems to have used it as her suburban residence, under whatever legal form — cession or usufruct — when she transferred her residence to Rome ; and she was deeply involved in the endowment and presumably the foundation of the buildings on the site. Part of the landed endowment was a huge fundus owned by the empress dowager, *possessio Helenae Augustae,* so the donation list. Enclosing and adjoining the original villa that fundus was a wedge of land extending from Porta Maggiore next to her palace *intra moenia,* for a length of five kilometers and more between the Via Latina and the

---

[36] *LP* I, 182 f. ; F. W. DEICHMANN – A. v. TSCHIRA, *Das Mausoleum der Kaiserin Helena...,* JDAI 72 (1957), 44 ff. (Deichmann–Tschira) ; J. GUYON, *Le Cimitière aux deux lauriers,* Vatican City, 1987 (GUYON, *Cimetière*). For the genesis, around 260, and the expansion of the catacomb through the late third and the fourth centuries see GUYON, *Cimetière, passim.* The remains of the two martyrs, originally perhaps buried in the open air graveyard above the catacomb were installed around 320 within, in a *cubiculum–mausoleum* (GUYON, *Cimetière,* 234 ff.). Their names missing from the *depositio martyrum* has been explained convincingly by that list's being incomplete, when compiled (DEICHMANN–TSCHIRA, 72) – in the 320's in my opinion (KRAUTHEIMER, *The Building Inscriptions* [note 34], esp. 18 ff.).

[38] For the history of the villa and the cemetery of the *equites singulares* thereon, Deichmann–Tschira, 68 ff. and GUYON, *Cimitière,* 7 ff. A few hints, albeit scarce, suggest that successive emperors from the early third to the fifth century, Constantine among them, established at the villa their *comitatus,* Imperial headquarters. I appreciate the scepticism of Deichmann–Tschira and Guyon; but I have a hard time getting around the entry in the *depositio martyrum,* hence in the 320's, which locates *in comitatum* the commemoration of the Quattro Coronati, martyrs under Diocletian, whose resting place in the catacomb on the Labicana is recorded by a graffito (GUYON, *Cimetière,* 131 f. ; ID., *Les Quattre Couronnés...,* MEFRA 87 (1975), 505 ff.).

Praenestina. It would have been her contribution to the foundation made by her son and in his name. Likewise, the donation list for the church records among liturgical vessels a gift of hers, a heavy *scyphus* of the purest gold « *ubi nomen Auguste designatur* » [38]. Intended as the coemeterium–basilica presumably was for the Christian slaves and employees working on the estate, and Helena being in occupancy or indeed the landowner, Constantine would have built it presumably *ex rogatu* of his mother. But clearly she participated from the outset in the enterprise.

It remains open, when work was started on the coemeterium–basilica. A date still in the second decade of the century but obviously after October 312 has been proposed [39]. Myself, I incline towards

---

[38] *LP* I, 18. For the expanse of the *fundus*, see Deichmann–Tschira, 74 and fig. 1 ; Guyon, *Cimetière*, 234 ff. I see no reason for dating the donation of the fundus to the church (and to the mausoleum ?) after Helena's death (A. Piganiol, *L'empereur Constantin*, Paris 1937, 113 ; Deichmann–Tschira, 75). To be sure, the compiler of the *LP* lists it as a donation of Constantine « *...donum dedit...* ». Under the same heading, however, he places the *scyphus* « *ubi nomen augustae designatur* » ; and it seems highly implausible to view as a posthumous legacy a vessel thus inscribed. As I see it, *fundus* and *sycphus* were both part of a donation made jointly by Constantine and Helena during her lifetime, that is before the winter 327/28 or possibly the following winter (Krautheimer, *The Building Inscriptions* [note 34], 3 f.).

[39] Deichmann–Tschira, 74 ; Guyon, *Cimetière*, 238 f., prefers a date not too long before 324–326, the presumable *terminus ad* or *post* for the completion of the mausoleum (below, note 41). His arguments for so late a date, however, are not cogent. In the light of the speed of construction of Imperial buildings customary from Diocletian to Constantine twelve years or more, 312–324/26 were plenty of time for Constantine's builders to complete both basilica and mausoleum.

The date of Helena's involvement in the foundation and endowment of the structures at Tor Pignattara is obviously linked to that of her residence in Rome and her occupancy of the Sessorian Palace. The latter, while documented only by indirection, can be taken for granted ; it is supported by the neighborhood of the Sessorium to the *Thermae Helenianae* (A. M. Colini, *Horti Spei Veteris*, APARAM VIII (1955), 137 ff). ; by a few inscriptions in her honor from that site ; and by her close connection with the church S. Croce in Gerusalemme, installed in one of the palace halls (Colini, *ibid.* ; *CBCR* I, 165 ff.). Of the inscriptions two carry dates, both approximate and from the last decade of her life. *CIL* 6, 1134, in recording her having restored the *thermae* after a fire, refers to her as *avia Caesarum nostrorum* and thus dates after 317 when two of the half–brothers of Crispus were born, Constantius and Constantine. There is, however, no

a date around 315 for the start of work. Obviously though, the donation was made when construction was well underway or in fact completed — on both the basilica and the mausoleum [40]. For, as work on the basilica was terminated a huge mausoleum was built against its eastward end, preceded by the link of a wide vestibule : a domed rotunda, it was articulated on ground level by eight niches cutting deeply into the thickness of the wall ; the clerestory wall, set inward, was pierced by eight huge windows ; and the interior, well lit, was revetted top to bottom in *opus sectile*. A colossal golden chandelier carrying 120 lamps, listed among the donations made to the mausoleum — specifically set apart from those to the basilica — would have hung from the dome. By 324–326 or slightly later work was underway on the revetment. In the eastward niche facing the entrance, a huge porphyry battle sarcophagus was installed. Before it, a silver altar was set up provided with liturgical vessels all of gold. Helena's remains were laid to rest in the sarcophagus when transferred right after her death to Rome, presumably from Nicomedia [41].

---

terminus ante, except her death. The other inscription, *CIL* 6, 31243, mentions by name the *caesares* Constans and Constantinus and therefore dates after 323, the former's year of birth. But again no *terminus ante* during her lifetime can be established; for, missing is not only the name of Crispus – *damnatio memoriae* 326 – but also that of Constantius. Hence the omissions are meaningless.

No source known to me, documents or intimates Helena's occupancy of the palace « shortly after 312 » (*RAC* XI, 355 ff. ; R. Klein). Nothing, however, contradicts an early date, coincident for instance with Constantine's visit to Rome, in 315.

[40] If the inscription on the *scyphus* designated her as *Augusta* as seems likely, the gift of the *scyphus* must date after she was raised to that rank, either November 8, 324 or possibly July 25, 325. In ither case that particular gift or perhaps the entire donation would coincide with work on the *opus sectile* revetment of the mausoleum ; see the following note.

[41] The mausoleum, preceded by a deep vestibule, was built against the foundations of the (inner) narthex of the basilica ; hence its construction follows that of the former (Deichmann–Tschira, 56). However, the interval may have been of the shortest ; and the addition of the mausoleum may have been planned while work on the basilica was underway or indeed from the outset (GUYON, *Cimetière,* 238).

A coin issued between 324 and 326, found embedded reportedly in the mortarbed of the *opus sectile* revetment, furnishes a *terminus post* or possibly *ad* for the interior decoration (DEICHMANN–TSCHIRA, 64).

Ever since, sarcophagus and rotunda have carried the name of Helena. However, it has long been suggested that originally both were intended for Constantine [42]. The bellicose theme of the sarcophagus and its Imperial porphyry material loudly proclaim its having been designed for a victorious emperor. Its place in the dominating niche of the mausoleum, an altar standing before it, proclaim equally loudly that that emperor was Constantine. Just so he joined the site for the celebration of Mass to his own resting place in the Holy Apostles in Constantinople, scandalizing a later generation [43]. Obviously too, the mausoleum was planned before, and one would like to think long before the alienation between Constantine and Rome had come near the breaking point ; possibly it was planned quite early, even before 320. Only after he had definitely made up his mind to abandon Rome and move East and perhaps only after he had decided on founding Constantinople did he give up the idea of using the mausoleum at Tor Pignattara for himself.

However, I strongly question that the mausoleum when planned and under construction was meant for Constantine alone. In my view Helena's burial, in one of the other niches was foreseen from the start ; possibly also, the burial of other family members in the remaining niches was envisaged. Eusebius when recording the transfer

---

For the sarcophagus and its history, W. HELBIG, *Führer durch die öffentlichen Sammlungen klassischer Altertümer in Rom*, ed. H. Speier, I, Tübingen 1964, 25 ; for the gold chandelier, the altar, the liturgical vessels and its siting « *...ante sepulchrum... Helenae Augustae qui sepulchrum est ex metallus porphyriticus exsculptus sigillis* », *LP* I, 180.

For the transfer of Helena's body to Rome, the « Imperial City » and her burial « in the Imperial tombs », EUS., *VC* III, 47, 1: « ...Καὶ τὸ σκῆνος δὲ τῆς μακαρίας οὐ τῆς τυχούσης ἠξιοῦτο σπουδῆς... ἐπὶ τὴν βασιλεύουσαν πόλιν ἀνεκομίζετο, ἐνταυθοῖ τε ἡρίοις βασιλικοῖς ἀπετίθετο... ».

[42] For the intended use by Constantine of mausoleum and sarcophagus, DEICHMANN–TSCHIRA, 74.

[43] EUS., *VC* IV, 71, 2, brings out the analogous proximity of Constantine's sarcophagus and the celebration of Mass in the Holy Apostles where « even now the body of the thrice blessed soul (is)... worthy of Divine Services and the celebration of Mass... » : εἰσέτι καὶ νῦν τὸ μὲν τῆς τρισμακαρίας ψυχῆς σκῆνος τῷ λαῷ τοῦ θεοῦ συναγελαζόμενον, θεσμῶν τε θείων καὶ μυστικῆς λειτουργίας ἀξιούμενον... » ; also R. KRAUTHEIMER, *Zu Konstantins Apostelkirche*, in *Mullus, Festschrift für Theodor Klauser* (JbAC, Suppl. 1), 1964, 224 ff. ; ID., *Three Capitals*, 60.

to Rome and burial of Helena's body, speaks of the Imperial tombs, in the plural [44]. Possibly at the time Eusebius' source learned of the transfer, Constantine's decision about his own resting place was still in the balance. It was made only or anticipated by the local authorities in Rome when it was resolved to use the battle sarcophagus for the empress dowager.

* * *

The building sites provided by Constantine for his church foundations, in Rome anyway, and nearby, during the first twelve years of his reign, all seem to have come from the *res privata*. The Lateran cathedral occupies a large part of the grounds of the *castra equitum singularium* [45]. The regiment, having fought for Maxentius, was cashiered. Its bǎrracks were confiscated and thus become crown property, the buildings were razed, and the foundations of the church were sunk into the basement level. Likewise a house sacrificed to build the apse of the basilica and a thermal building located below the baptistery would have belonged to the crown [46]. The *res privata* indeed, as early as the third century seems to have owned all property in the *area Lateranorum* [47]. Certainly the *domus Faustae in Lateranis* was crown property, the residence, presumably already before her marriage, of Fausta, Constantine's wife and half–sister of Maxentius [48]. The palace was lent, this rather than donated, by Constantine to the Roman bishop for assembling and probably housing the Church council of 313. S. Croce in Gerusalemme, *ipso facto* was property of the *res privata*, installed as it was inside an Imperial palace, Helena's residence, the *palatium Sessorianun*. Both

---

[44] See above note 42.

[45] COLINI, *Celio*. APARAM VII (1944), 353 ff. ; *CBCR·*V, 1 ff.

[46] COLINI, *op. cit.*, 350 ff. G. PELLICONI, *Le nuove scoperte... Battistero Lateranense*, APARAM XII (1973), *passim*.

[47] V. SANTA MARIA SCRINARI, *Contributi all'urbanistica tardo–antica sul Campo laterano*, *CAC Lyon 1987*, Roma 1989, 2201 ff. The author locates the head office of the *res privata*, presumably for Rome and the *suburbium*, below the north wing of the (old) Ospedale di S. Giovanni.

[48] *Ibid.*, 2207. It is still under dispute whether or not the remains of a palace with impressive murals located below the palazzone of the INPS downhill on Via Amba Aradam are those of the *domus Faustae*.

churches founded by Constantine within the walls thus rose on ground at his own free disposal. Moreover, the sites were on the south eastern rim of the city, in the vast greenbelt formed by the parks and *domus* of the rich encircling the busy center. They were far from the show area where the public buildings rose, all under the jurisdiction of the Senate : the theatres and circusses, the *ther*‑ *mae*, the temples on the Forum Romanum, on the Imperial Fora and elsewhere, the *curia senatus*, the palaces on the Palatine. To keep clear of such sensitive monuments and to avoid friction with the senatorial class, overwhelmingly pagan, and their prerogatives, was apparently a major preoccupation on Constantine's mind.

Likewise, the cemetery churches outside the city walls occupied crown property. All rose on Imperial estates. SS. Marcellino e Pietro was built on the *territorium inter duas lauros* ; S. Agnese rose on or near the *ager Agnetis* on the grounds of the villa where the princess Constantina resided, and where later she built her mausoleum attached to the *coemeterium*, Sta Costanza. The Gardens on the Vatican hill where St. Peter's was laid out had been property of the *res privata* ever since Nero's days. (The crown, to be sure, had apparently leased, this rather than sold, part as a burial ground to private individuals and families ; by the second century the area was densely occupied by luxurious *mausolea*, except a small plot where a Christian congregation set up the *tropaion* of the apostle [49]. To allow demolition of the pagan *mausolea*, Constantine, presumably *qua pontifex maximus*, temporarily seems to have lifted the laws prosecuting *violationes sepulchrorum* [50]). Likewise, Constantine could freely dispose of the ground where rose the coemeterium–basilica of S. Lorenzo f.l.m. and of the hill which sheltered the martyr's grave [51].

---

[49] *Esplorazioni sotto la Confessione di San Pietro in Vaticano*, Vatican City 1951, 107 ff.

[50] KRAUTHEIMER, *The Building Inscriptions* [note 33], 20 ff. ; W. SE‑ STON, *Hypothèse sur la date de... Saint Pierre de Rome*, Cahiers Archéologiques 2 (1947), 153 ff.

[51] The ownership situation is involved. The *fundus* (*ager*) *Veranus* (*LP* I, 181, resp. 182) became Imperial property apparently with Lucius Verus, 151–169. Part of it, presumably the hill which housed the catacomb where Laurence was buried in or after 258, was presumably purchased from the *res privata* by Cyriaca. During the Diocletian persecution it was con‑ fiscated, thus returning to the *res privata*. The ground at the south foot of

The donation lists incorporated into the *Liber Pontificalis* bring to light further elements of Constantine's building policy. Each foundation is endowed with income–producing real estate and on each are heaped altar vessels, lighting fixtures and liturgical furniture in silver and gold. The total weight and value of the individual gifts of these fittings, is significantly graded [52] ; the rationale underlying that pecking order seems to be the individual church's importance to Constantine, in terms of either his general or his ecclesiastical policy — but the two policies are inseparable. The donation to the Lateran basilica and its baptistery is the richest — the weight of the silverware, liturgical vessels and lighting fixtures, is over 10,000 lbs., of those in gold close to 1200 lbs.; not counting the value of gems and of vessels made of other costly materials such as coral. The gift includes a *fastigium* with 18 figures, covered with hammered silver — but does not this date later in the century ? ; seven silver altars, likewise silver veneered ; a colossal golden chanlier ; seven gold patens, each weighing 30 lbs., and seven gold chalices ; and a gilded apse vault.

No other foundation of Constantine's in Rome reaches that amount in precious fittings. But two come close to it. The coemeterium–basilica of SS. Marcellinus and Peter and the attached mausoleum were shimmering like the Lateran basilica and its baptistery in gold, silver and gems. The mausoleum was by far the richer : a gold chandelier bearing 120 lamps ; three gold patens weighing 35 lbs. and two mass jugs, *amae*, weighing 40 or 60 lbs., quite a weight to lift in either case ; finally a silver altar placed in front of the sarcophagus prepared for Constantine. The donations to the basilica rank lower, but they still are abundant and include the heavy golden *scyphus* given by Helena and a huge annual gift of rare oil, aromas and incense. An amount of gold and silver fittings, roughly equal to that donated jointly to mausoleum and basilica, went to St. Peter's after Constantine's conquest of the East, possibly when

---

the hill where the *coemeterium–basilica* was built had possibly remained throughout in the hands of the *res privata*.

[52] GUYON, *Cimetière*, 249, has tabulated the total figures for each donation. We exclude those given for S. Paolo f.l.m. (above note 23). He has also pointed out that the figures given by the *Liber Pontificalis* are frequently unreliable. Suffice it to look at the variants given in Duchesne's edition.

he last visited Rome in the summer of 326 : an afterthought, construction had started six years before and by then was quite advanced [53]. The gift included a gold cross, jointly donated by the emperor and his mother and set on the shrine of the apostle, a golden chandelier in front of the shrine, and a large silver altar, studded with 400 precious stones. The apse vault over the shrine was gilded and the walls of the transept nearby shimmered with mosaic [54]. Outside, too, the gilded bronze tiles of the roof shone far above the olive grove surrounding the church [55]. Building churches impressive by showy grandeur and shimmering splendour remained an integral element of Constantine's policy from beginning to end. Like St. Peter's in Rome, the cathedral in Antioch built in these same years, the Golden Octagon, drew its name from its gilded roofing. Also in the Lateran basilica, probably Constantine's earliest church foundation, the apse was gilded and the arcades separating the aisles rested on a set of forty-two columns of precious green speckled marble. In the Baptistery, the font, made of porphyry, was sheathed with hammered silver. Bishop Makarios of Jerusalem was told in so many words to have the ceiling of the church of the Holy Sepulchre coffered and gilded and to ask for whatever expensive extras he could think of. Constantine himself, it seems, shouldered the cost for a hexagonal canopy all of silver resting on twelve columns to enclose Christ's tomb behind the basilica [56]. When in 336 the church was completed, Eusebius praised the emperor's φιλοκαλίαι, his beautiful gifts in gold, in silver and precious stones. Even at the end of the century, the Lady Etheria marvelled at the gold, the mosaic, and the precious marbles donated by Constantine. Yet another source, apparently well informed, records as his gift textile hangings around the chancel part and liturgical vessels of gold set with precious stones [57].

The endowment in income-producing real estate donated by Constantine and his family members to each of his church foundations in Rome was graded roughly in the same order as his gifts

---

[53] KRAUTHEIMER, The Building Inscriptions [note 33].

[54] See the inscription on the gold cross as recorded by the LP I, 176 : « ...simili fulgore corruscans aula... ».

[55] PRUDENT., Peristephanon XII, 31.

[56] Eus., VC III, 38 ; A. GRABAR, Ampoules de Terre Sainte, Paris 1958.

[57] Eus., VC IV, 45 ; ETHERIA, Peregrinatio, Itinera Hierosolymitana, 76 ; THEOD., HE, I, 31 (PG 82, 988).

in precious fitting. The properties are landed and, rarely, urban, No donations of real estate are documented for Constantine's church foundations in the Holy Land or elsewhere in the East. However, that they were given can be taken for granted. Land, whether agricultural or urban, was the basic source of income throughout antiquity [58].

The available evidence suggests that the estates donated, in large part or all, came from the *patrimonium* or the *res privata*. Indeed, to establish clear title, the lawyers in the offices of the *res privata* marked a number of properties expressly as having been given to Constantine or otherwise acquired by him and passed on to one of his foundations [59]. There are the « *possessio Herculi quod donavit Augusto et Augustus obtulit ecclesiae Hierusalem* », that is S. Croce in Gerusalemme ; among the endowment of S. Lorenzo f.l.m. the « *possessio Augusti... praest. nomini Christianorum sol. CXX* », and the « *possessio cuiusdam Cyriacae... quod fiscus occupaverat tempore persecutionis* » — it would have gone automatically to the *res privata* ; the « *massa Festi praepositi sacri cubiculi quem donavit Constantino Augusto* » that went to the Lateran cathedral. Finally, there are in this group four among the estates donated to St. Peter's, all located in the Eastern provinces : near Antioch the « *possessio Sybilles donata Augusto* » ; in Egypt, the « *possessio Agapi quod donavit Augusto* », and another « *possessio quod donavit Constantino Aug. Hybromius...* » ; and near Alexandria the « *possessio Timialaca donata Augusto ab Ambrosio...* ». All or some may well have been intended to make Constantine forgive the former owners' past links to his enemies.

The revenues from real estate were annual, and being comparatively small, they could not be used to cover construction. That latter, a major one-time expense, was apparently borne, in Constantine's later years anyhow, by the *fiscus* : as witness his rescripts addressed to Makarios of Jerusalem and to the bishop of Cirte. In the first half of his reign the cost for the churches built in Rome may have been carried by the Imperial founder, that is, by the *res*

---

[58] P. VEYNE, *Geschichte des privaten Lebens*, ed. PH. ARIÈS and G. DUBY, vol. I, Frankfurt 1989, 156 f.

[59] VOELKL, as above note 25, p. 25, believed these properties, erroneously in my view, to be participatory gifts by the owners to the endowment provided by the emperor.

privata. The annual income minutely recorded in the donation lists‍ for the Roman foundations, whether in specie only or in both specie and *naturalibus* was specified for use *in servitio luminum* [60] or *in redditum* [61].

That latter term in fifth and sith century legal parlance in Rome as well as in the East of the Empire, meant income for repair and maintenance. To that end, a Church decree, first cited in the last third of the fifth century, but obviously older « *...sicit dudum est decretum* », set aside one quarter of the Roman Church's total income [62]. Of the other three quarters, one went to the bishop, one to the clergy, another to the poor and to pilgrims. A *novella* of Justinian's dated 538 apportions part of a church's endowment for maintenance of the structure ; another portion is earmarked for lighting, another part still for servicing and upkeep of the clergy [63]. Lighting, then, is bracketed with maintenance of construction as an essential item to be provided for. It seems probable that in Constantine's deeds of donation the two items likewise were bracketed ; the compiler of the *Liber Pontificalis* would have abbreviated the original text by listing for each donation only one of the two — either *in redditum* or *in servitio luminum.* Lighting in any event was very costly. In the Lateran basilica a thousand or so lighting fixtures, whether huge wax candles or oil lamps, were burning presumably day and night [64]. Of the latter over one thousand were fed with expensive aromatic oil, *oleus nardicus pisticus.* The sum of 4390

---

[60] *LP* I, 173, 177.

[61] *LP* I, 177, 180.

[62] SIMPLICIUS (468–483), *ep.* 2, « in ecclesiarum fabricatione » (*PL* 58, 37); GELASIUS (492–496), *ep.* 9, *cap.* 27, « *Quatuor... tam de reditu quam de oblatione fidelium... sicut dudum est decretum, convenit fieri portiones... quarum... quarta fabricis applicanda... Ea vero quae ecclesiasticis aedificiis attributa... locorum doceat instauratio manifesta sanctorum...* » (*PL* 59, 56).

[63] Nov. LXVII, Intr.: « πολλοὶ γὰρ ὀνόματος ἕνεκεν πρὸς ποίησιν· ἁγιωτάτων ἐκκλησιῶν ὁρμῶσιν εἶτα ταύτας οἰκοδομησάμενοι οὐκέτι φροντίδα τίθενται τοῦ καὶ δαπάνην αὐταῖς ἀφορίσαι πρέπουσαν εἴς τε λυχνοκαΐαν εἴς τε τὴν τῶν προσεδευόντων ἀποτροφὴν καὶ τὴν ἱερὰν λειτουργίαν ».

See also the Council of Braga, 572 where, canon 2, one third of church revenue is apportioned « *pro luminariis ecclesiae vel recuperatione...* » (G. D. MANSI, *Sacrorum Conciliorum noua et amplissima Collectio*, 9, repr. Graz 1960, 389). All passages are cited *LRE* 1376, note 68.

[64] *LP* I, 173.

---

solidi set aside *in servitio luminum* for the Roman cathedral is perhaps not exaggerated ; if it seems so, that is only in keeping with Constantine's understanding of his own much–vaunted generosity.

Constantine, then, would have anticipated the funding of maintenance and lighting for the churches of his foundation as later codified by ecclesiastical and civil Law. In this, however, he seems to have only followed a practice traditional through antiquity and stipulated in Roman Sacred Law — income from the *fundi iuris templorum* [65].

* * *

The written evidence then brings forth with reasonable clarity the implementation of Costantine's ecclesiastical building policy : whence the initiative ; whence the funding for construction, fitting, splendour, servicing and maintenance ; whose the responsibility for planning and whose for building operations. That documentation is supported and complemented by archaeological finds all over the Empire. Jointly archaeological and written evidence provide the basis for extrapolating the major conceits and aims guiding that policy, its development and changes.

The sources in conformity attribute the initiative for Constantine's church foundations with but few exceptions to himself alone. This is what the concept of the emperor in the Roman world and

---

[65] F. HILLER VON GÄRTRINGEN, *Inschriften in Priene*, Berlin 1906, no. 174 ; JONES, *LRE, passim*.

Correspondence and differences between Constantine's practice of funding and its later codifications are obvious. Justinian's Novella, along with maintenance of construction and cost of lighting sets aside amounts for servicing, « τὴν ἱερὰν λειτουργίαν » and for upkeep of the clergy. Servicing may possibly have come under the heading of *in redditum* in Constantine's original deeds as well as in the ecclesiastical decrees obtaining in fifth–century Rome. These decrees, one recalls, also apportion one quarter of a local Church's income to the upkeep of the clergy. No such provision appears to have been made by Constantine during the first half of his reign.

Throughout, Constantine's ways of funding are tightened up in the later legislation. In Justianian's novella endowment had to coincide with the act of foundation. Constantine in at least one case disregards that practice : construction of St. Peter's, begun probably by 320, was well underway when late in 324 or a year after, he made his grand donation *in redditum* of estates, all *per diocesem Orientis*.

Imperial ritual demanded ; the emperor, whoever and wherever he was, was omniscient and omnipresent. Constantine's own rescripts sustain that pretense. The procedures of implementation as well as the major guidelines of his building policy continue with slight modifications those long prevailing in antecedent Imperial building policy and building practice. In reality he wanted guidance to acquaint him with and advise him on the local situation, its needs and pitfalls. Occasionally the nature of such guidance is patent, at other times it is adumbrated. The local bishop — of Jerusalem or of Cirte — requests the building of a church, or the emperor lends his ear to the behest of a person close to him : his mother, a daughter, his mother–in–law. They in turn were guided presumably by an ecclesiastic, whether in their suite or local.

The *res privata* or, as far as it still led a separate existence, the emperor's *patrimonium*, provided the building sites certainly during the first half of Constantine's reign. The documentation for his church foundations in Rome and the archaeological evidence leave no doubt. The same holds true of some major churches built by the emperor after 324, where they rise on the grounds of or near Imperial palaces : at Trier, at Constantinople, Antioch. We are less sure regarding the structures around the Holy Sepulchre. Indications are that the area may have been occupied by public buildings, hence fiscal ground. To be sure, by a simple act of confiscation that ground could have been turned into crown property ; and if indeed the terrain originally was owned by the *fiscus*, such legalistic fiction would perhaps been desirable in the eyes of the Imperial chancellery.

The lawyers in that office, in fact, appear to have been wary about placing churches of the emperor's foundation on ground other than the crown's. To the bishop of Cirte, in 330 one recalls, a house owned by the *res privata* was assigned for the building of a new church instead of a lot belonging to the *fiscus*, as he had re-quested. The switch is noteworthy. A house is hardly the equivalent of a building lot. To build in its place a church, it has to be torn down, a detour creating needless expense and delay. Possibly no empty lot in the gift of the crown was available ; equally possi-bly, it was a piece of bureaucratic chicanery by an anti–Christian official. However, the shift made by the chancellery from fiscal to crown property is of relevance in our context. The jurists composing the emperor's response to the small–town Numidian bishop may have had honest legal scruples about occupying fiscal ground for church buildings. They may well have remembered the distinction made in Roman Law between temples of Roman gods and therefore public and erected on public ground ; and other temples built by individuals or families on private ground, *suae religionis causa*. Constantine, to be sure, was the emperor. He confessed himself a Christian and by all means in his power favoured Christianiy. Still, Christianity was his personal belief, *sua religio* ; its temples could not occupy public ground, — so a good lawyer, possibly hostile to Christianity or just a pedant, might argue around 330.

* * *

Planning, we saw, was thrust as a rule on the shoulders of the resident ecclesiastical authorities. Working through a local representative was long–standing Imperial custom [66]. Being familiar with local conditions and requirements and supported by expert advice at hand or, exceptionally, supplied by the court, they were best suited to prepare plans and estimates of materials and work force needed. Archaeological evidence throughout confirms the written documentation on this point. A dozen or so churches founded by Constantine from Rome to Trier, Constantinople, Syria and the Holy Land can be reliably visualized from surviving remains or contemporary descriptions [67]. Every single one differs from the others in plan, elevation, materials and execution. Nearly all, to be sure, are variants on the *genus* basilica, assembly hall, which in the Roman world in many variations had served for centuries meetings of many kinds, secular and religious. Sprung within that *genus* as one more variant, Christian basilicas shared but one standard feature : a lengthwise plan, as required by the congregation's facing the altar and the presiding clergy and as incidentally anticipated by judiciary basilicas and audience halls. For the rest, lay–out and shape of any church, whether or not founded by Constantine, was determined by its specific function and by local conditions : the size of the structure ; the presence or lack of an atrium or of a precinct, of twin aisles or galleries ; the plan of the chancel part, an apse,

---

[66] MacMullen, *Roman Imperial building* [note 10].

[67] *Pelican, passim* ; and for Rome, *CBCR, passim* ; also older bibliography supplied therein.

whether semi–circular or square, flanked or not by side chambers; the presence of a *memoria* to serve as a focus for the plan, whether enshrined in a transept at St. Peter's, in an octagon attached to a basilical nave at Bethlehem [68], in the center of a cross plan at the Holy Apostles in Constantinople. In the cemetery basilicas in the Roman *suburbium*, and only there, the nave rested on piers or was colonnaded and an inner ambulatory enveloped the apse; at Trier two huge basilicas, parallel to another and joined by a baptistery and other halls, formed a twin cathedral; the functions of the type and of its components is far from clear. All these variations depend on the interplay of a number of factors : the topography of the site ; size and kind of attendance envisaged — clergy, re-sidents, pilgrims, the plainly curious to be eventually won over ; the particulars of the liturgy locally prevailing, role and visibility of the clergy, ratio of faithful in full standing to catechumens, postulants, outsiders; the preparation of the eucharist in or out of sight of the faithful ; the depository of the species and of the church treasure; the specific function of the church, whether cathe-dral, pilgrimage goal, roofed–in cemetery, in–house chapel or two or more of these jointly.

Only rarely did Constantinian builders depart from what appears to have been a standard plan — the basilica, lengthwise extended and composed of nave and aisles, variations notwithstanding. At S. Croce in Gerusalemme the single nave was divided transversally by two triple arcades; but that solution was conditioned by the use of an old hall in the palace. For the church of the Holy Apostles in Constantinople, where Constantine in the end wanted to be and was buried, his architects apparently devised a cross plan placing in the center his sarcophagus and the altar [69]. The cathedral of Antioch was laid out along more unusual lines. An eight–sided central space surmounted by a vault, perhaps in wood, was enveloped, it seems, by a double–tiered ambulatory ; into that ambulatory eight niches

---

[68] For plan and reconstruction based on Harvey's soundings in the 1930's, *Pelican*, 50 and note 44. The construction *iussu Constantini* and completion before 333 are attested by the Pilgrim of Bordeaux (*Itinera Hierosolymitana*, 25) and EUSEB., *VC* III, 41. It is possible, though un-documented, that Helena acted as her son's delegate.

[69] EUS., *VC* IV ; KRAUTHEIMER, *Zu Konstantis Apostelkirche* [note 43] ; ID., *Three Capitals*, 56 ff.

billowed out from the center space. The church thus would have looked much like S. Vitale in Ravenna two centuries later [70].

Adapting a design evolved in the context of villa and palace planning for ecclesiastical use may well be credited, one surmises, to the emperor's representative in charge, either the *archon* Plutarchos or more likely his successor the *comes* and chamberlain Gorgonios. He did, indeed, in an inscription claim to have devised (ὕφανε) the church [71].

Construction, so the written evidence, was entrusted to the civilian authorities. The Imperial rescripts were addressed to the highest officials responsible. The gist went down the chain of command to the *opera publica*. That office in turn placed the execution into the hands of local contractors and building crews. To this the archaeological evidence attests. Techniques of construction in Constantine's churches vary regionally as they had for centuries : *opus lateritium*, the bricks in Rome mostly re–used, newly made in the Rhineland; *opus listatum* in the Roman *suburbium*; at Constantinople alternate bands of brickwork and rubble faced with small blocks of stone [72]; ashlar, *opus quadratum*, in the Holy Land. The cost of construction would be charged to the *fiscus*. However, the written documentation on that point happens to be limited to the years after 324. Prior to that the *res privata* may have borne the expense; certainly in Rome where the *opera publica* were under the Senate's jurdiction. Costly extras of construction and fittings were provided anyway by the *res privata* both before and after 324 : marble columns ; a gilded ceiling ; tapestries ; lighting fixtures and liturgical vessels ; wall revetment in *opus sectile* or mosaics.

Likewise, the *res privata* or possibly the emperor's *patrimonium* was the source for the landed donations whence came the annual

---

[70] ELTESTER, *Die Kirchen Antiochiens im IV. Jahrhundert*, ZNTW 36 (1937), 251 ; J. W. DYNES, *The first Christian Palace Church Type*, Marsyas 11 (1964), 1 ff. The term palace church, erroneously used, unfortunately stems from me. However, Mr. Dynes' reconstruction of the plan is convincing in my view. The sources for the reconstruction of the church and the older bibliography are given, *Pelican*, 465, n. 19 and 20.

[71] G. DOWNEY, *A History of Antioch*, Princeton 1961, 358, 362 : completed by Constantius 341.

[72] *The Great Palace of the Byzantine Emperors, Second Report*, ed. D.T. Rice, Edinburgh 1958, 64 (J. B. Ward Perkins).

income of the churches for maintenance of the structure, for lighting and possibly for general servicing. Documentation admittedly survives only for Rome and for Constantine's few church foundations or participatory donations elsewhere in Italy, and thus dates prior to 324 or possibly 326. However, there would hardly have been any change after that year in such funding and its sources : this in view of the antecedents and the survival and legislative reception of such donations customarily made and indeed required of founders of temples and churches.

Later legislation also extended such funding to the support of the clergy [73]. There is no evidence for Constantine's having in his early years provided the clergy's salaries on a permanent basis ; the monies, paid in 312 from the *res privata* to a select number of anti–Donatist ecclesiastics in North Africa, would seem to have been a one–time subvention, perhaps in compensation for losses caused them by their opponents. The situation changes after 324, in the East anyhow. After Nicaea, the emperor makes arrangements to have clerical stipends secured on a permanent basis. Nor are these funds provided by the *res privata* ; instead a share of the taxes due from each city to the *fiscus* was set aside, and a law promulgated to that end [74].

* * *

A few guidelines of Constantine's building policy can be extra-polated from the evidence accumulated. No concept of a common style underlies Constantinian church planning or design, and no orders to that effect ever went forth from the emperor and his chancellery. Inevitably, having to plan a structure designed to house a sizeable assembly would evoke among patrons and ar-chitects the concept of the infinitely adaptable *genus* basilica adjusted to the requirements of Christian divine service. Suffice it to recall the cathedral at Tyre, a basilica whatever the details. Consecrated around 315 and thus contemporary with Constantine's earliest churches in Rome, it was obviously planned on its own by the local bishop and his architect [75].

---

[73] See above note 65.

[74] THEODORET, *HE* I, 29 (*PG* 82, 988).

[75] EUS., *HE* X IV. 34 ff. ; also M. H. SHEPHERD, *The earliest Christian basilica*, Yearbook of Liturgical Studies (1965), 73 ff.

Within Constantine's building program churches of basilical type offered a further advantage. The lay–out was straightforward and construction simple. Raising the foundation walls was made easy where they were sunk into the void of pre–existing structures — the graveyard under St. Peter's, the barracks under the Lateran cathedral. Setting up nave and aisles was helped by using spoils — the columns being ready–made and at hand [76], nor was timber roofing time–consuming. The time factor entered with the size of the struc-ture. But that was a question of providing man–power and or-ganizing logistics. In both respects Roman builders had been su-perb forever. Also, man–power meant no more than assembling, feeding and housing hordes of slaves, of unemployed, if need be, of soldiers. The funds would be forthcoming.

Speed was essential to Constantine. Every church built won him new favour with the Godhead ; and it would raise the number of converts to the new faith. Moreover, linked to speed was low cost of the bare construction ; if it was unloaded on the *fiscus*, so much the better. The funds of the *res privata* were employed to greater advantage in providing splendidly for revetments in *opus sectile*, mosaics, gilded ceilings and roofs, chandeliers and altar vessels in precious metals. The sheen of gold and silver would make a deeper impression on the masses — and not only them — than the sophisti-cated interplay of spaces or daring vaulting. The Golden Octagon is unique among an exception in Constantinian churches.

What Constantine expected to see in any church and mostly in churches founded by himself was that they stood out in every way. In all towns in the East, presumably large or small, so the emperor's circular in 325, extant churches, presumably meeting houses, should be enlarged and heightened. [77]. Constantine's new churches rose high above such buldings and altogether above the urban environment. Size, height and splendour are the features he foremost demanded in his church building: the Lateran basilica, over

---

[76] A. ESCH, *Spolien*, in « Archiv. für Kulturgeschichte » 51, 1969, 1 ff. ; F. W. DEICHMANN, *Säule und Ordnung in der frühchristlichen Architektur*, in RM 55, 1946, 114 ff. [repr. IDEM, *Rom, Ravenna, Konstantinopel und Naher Osten*, Wiersbaden 1975, 159 ff.] ; IDEM, *Die Spolien in der spätantiken Ar-chitektur*, Bayerische Akademie der Wissenschaften, Phil.–hist. Klasse, Sitzungsberichte, 1975, Heft 6.

[77] Above, note 4.

330 feet long, 100 wide and the nave roughly 60 tall; St. Peter's almost 400 feet long, 210 wide and rising to a height of 110 feet. H. Sophia in Costantinople and the church at the Holy Sepulchre, while smaller, reached a length of roughly 240 and 180 feet respectively, and both, like St. Peter's, were approached over a high and wide flight of steps. The donation lists for the foundations in Rome, the gilded roofs of St. Peter's and Antioch speak for themselves; so do the rare green speckled columns, the marble revetment on the arcades between the aisles and the coloured marble pavement of the nave in the Lateran basilica. The walls or the ceiling of St. Peter's « shine with the same glimmer » as the gold cross on the shrine, Constantine's and Helena's gift [78]. Inside and outside, Constantine's churches were to glitter in gold, silver, precious marbles, costly textiles. Ostentatiousness is an ultimate aim. Makarios, one recalls, is told to make sure his basilica would outshine in beauty all buildings in any city. Beauty, one is afraid, to Constantine (and to Eusebius) meant showiness, flaunting the wealth the emperor was heaping on the Church out of his riches. To glorify Christ and overwhelm the faithful come to pray as well as the casual visitor with sheer magnitude and the radiance of precious materials and flickering lights – these seem to be the foremost aims of Constantine's policy in building churches – and not only those.

The driving forces underlying this policy indeed lie deeper. Undeniably Constantine felt and had imbued those closest to him, his mother foremost, with a sincere devotion to Christ. That devotion was inseparable from his gratitude to the Godhead on Whose help he had relied since Ponte Milvio. On that day and ever after, Christ had granted him victory and he meant to insure His continued support. Obviously, too, Constantine being a Roman emperor would clad his thanks and his reliance on unvaried divine favour in the forms customary for presenting to the world the Imperial image; an image traditional if modified by the ruler's personal belief: powerful in war and peace, benefactor of his people, favourite of the heavenly powers and visibly expressing this gratitude; and conscious of the need to signal to the world his political aims and his perception of his own Imperial role and changes therein [79].

---

[78] *LP* I, 176.
[79] F. W. DEICHMANN, *Die Architektur des konstantinischen Zeitalters.*

Inherent in the Roman emperor and expected of him were the ruler's virtues : greatness and might ; riches and splendour ; and not least munificence, φιλοτιμία, *liberalitas* – the willingness and obligation to spend freely for his subjects and coincidentally manifesting his own inexhaustible wealth [80]. Public building had served that end ever since Augustus : temples and triumphal arches, *thermae*, theaters, circusses, palaces. Constantine did his share : in Rome, Trier, Constantinople and in Gaul. When, after 312, he extended to the Church as well his building program, he thought within the accustomed frame of Imperial *liberalitas*, best met by erecting impressive and lavish public structures. The basilica to be built at the Holy Sepulchre must overshadow all public buildings anywhere, and even a church as insignificant as the one planned at Mamre must be « worthy of my φιλοτιμία ». Hence the large scale and the riches ostentatiously showered on his buildings, secular and ecclesiastic. These riches were manifest evidence of his being favoured by the Godhead, τῷ δεῷ φίλος, dear to the Lord ; and not so different from his predecessors, favourites of Hercules, of Jupiter, of Sol Invictus, as was Constantine's father, and for that matter Constantine himself before Ponte Milvio, and as he went on styling himself as late as 317 [81].

Concomitantly, Constantine's ecclesiastical building program signaled to all, Christians and non–Christians, that he was taking the new faith under his wing. How close he felt to it in those first years had best remain open. However, from the very start he seems to have viewed church building as a tool to manifest and further his political aims. By setting up the Roman bishop in a cathedral as grand and as richly appointed and endowed as the Lateran and thus strengthening his hand against the congregations, Constantine takes his stand in favour of authority, the monarchical principle,

---

Rom, Ravenna, Konstantinopel und Naher Osten, Wiesbaden 1975, 112 ff. : « primarily a grand imperial architecture of representation and power ».

[80] *RE* XIII, 1, 82 ff. ; R. MacMullen, *Constantine*, London, 1969, 49 ff. F. Millar, *The Emperor in the Roman World*, London 1977, 133 ff. and *passim*.

[81] N. H. Baynes, *Constantine the Great and the Christian Church* (Raleigh Lecture, British Academy), London 1929, 97 ff. ; A. Alfoeldi, *The Conversion of Costantine*, Oxford 1948, 54 ff.

unity enforced [82] ; just so he supports at the same time Caecilian, bishop of Carthage, the provincial capital, against the Donatists of the hinterland [83]. By the same token, he established from the outset the claim of the temporal power's interfering in Church matters.

Analogously, I submit, his mausoleum at Tor Pignattara should be viewed as a political statement. When planning the building and presumably for quite some time afterwards, Constantine viewed himself not only as emperor of the West as indeed he was, but he saw in Rome the capital whence he meant to rule and where ultimately he meant to be laid to rest. A Roman emperor was expected to have his mausoleum built during his lifetime in his capital, as did Galerius in Thessalonike ; in Rome, given the taboo against burial *intra moenia*, it had to be outside the walls, as was Hadrian's or that of Maxentius' son, Romulus. That Constantine's was attached to the *coemeterium subteglatum* of Saints Marcellinus and Petrus, was concomitantly a statement of his considering himself a member of the Church. He was a Christian and he was emperor ; but no more than that.

There is in fact inherent in the churches built by Constantine in Rome, that is prior to 324, a notable dilemma. By virtue of being founded by the emperor and by being built on a large scale, shining from afar, gorgeously appointed and filled with what was most costly, they claimed ideologically and visually to rank with the grandest public buildings and to draw the same admiring attention from those entering or casually passing by. However, all rose far from the public area of Rome around the Fora and the Campus Martius, where temples and state buildings crowded another and where Constantine himself set up his own public buildings : the Thermae on the Quirinal ; the Janus Quadrifrons on the Forum Boarium ; not to forget his colossal statue in the Basilica Nova appropriated from Maxentius by the victor. Moreover, unlike such *opera publica*, his churches rose on ground not public, but of the *res privata*. Constantine at that point obviously meant to avoid

---

[82] E. PETERSON, *Der Monotheismus als politisches Problem*, Leipzig 1935.

[83] Eus., *HE* X, 6 ; W. H. C. FREND, *The Donatist Church*, Oxford 1952, 155 ff.

causing annoyance to his non–Christian subjects, foremost the Roman aristocracy.

Constantine's Roman churches then, evinced his having taken Christianity under his wing and spending richly on furthering it. They also manifested his intention of placing Christian ecclesiastical building on the level of public architecture. By their siting, however, these churches would draw the attention primarily of Christians, or of members of the court and workers on the Imperial estates, whether Christians or not. The fiction that the churches were private foundations, built by an individual, albeit the emperor, « *suae religionis causa* » was maintained.

* *

The radical change in Constantine's policies after his conquest of the East in 324, reinforced after the Council of Nicaea the following summer, has often been remarked upon. It rests on the new vision Constantine now held of himself. No longer is he a Roman emperor and a Christian; he is a Christian emperor charged with a sacred duty. That image is reflected in the inscription placed on the triumphal arch of Old St. Peter's in or shortly after 326, I submit.

QUOD DUCE TE MUNDUS SURREXIT IN ASTRA TRIUMPHANS
HANC CONSTANTINUS VICTOR TIBI CONDIDIT AULAM.

Constantine's victory interlocks with Christ's, and it is his, the emperor's, mission to secure and advance the triumphal ascent to Heaven of the world led by Christ.

The conquest of the East and the Council of Nicaea also mark a turnabout in Constantine's building policies. He freely draws on the *fiscus* for providing the clergy's salaries and occasionally perhaps building sites, quickly turned legalistically by confiscation into property of the *res privata*. At Jerusalem, right after Nicaea, the structures at the Holy Sepulchre were placed in the very center of Aelia Capitolina as laid out by Hadrian. Off the colonnaded main street, they rose right in the show area of the Roman city taking the place and incorporating parts of public buildings — a Roman arch, whether or not a gate of the Forum [84]. On the mosaic map of Madaba the basilica and the dome of the Anastasis are shown approached by a wide flight of steps looming high over Jerusalem and as its very fulcrum [85] ; a sixth century re–interpretation of the situation no doubt. But this is how Christians ever since Makarios wanted to see the structures at the Tomb of Christ. Pagan opposition no longer mattered. On the contrary the bishop, Makarios meant to challenge it aggressively.

Constantine must have approved. In the years to follow he caused with equal aggressiveness in three of his capitals cathedrals to be laid out, loudly claiming public status through their grandeur and their siting among public buildings. All three were closely linked to Imperial palaces. At Antioch the new cathedral, the Octagon, with its gilded roof shining afar, begun in 327, has been plausibly located on the Orontes island [86]. Set apart from the rest of town, the island was long dominated by the palaces of the Seleucid kings and the Roman emperors ; there Constantine too resided when visiting as did the Caesar Constantius as his resident representative in his absence. Two colonnaded streets appear to have crossed the island, perpendicular to another, the intersection surmounted by a *tetrapylon*. The church took the place of a *thermae* building, a royal foundation, but then out of use. A vast square spread before the church ; beyond, the visitor would pass a monumental city gate, the hippodrome and the palaces nearby. At Trier, in the far West at roughly the same time as the Golden Octagon, Constantine built a huge cathedral closely linked to the Imperial palace where one of his sons resided in his stead. Some time after 326 a large section of the palace was sacrificed and on the vacant site were erected the two basilicas and the baptistery of the twin cathedral. Rising high, they faced westward the *cardo* of the Toman town across their forecourts. To the left and east of the churches extended the palace buildings ; two blocks south stood Constantine's audience

---

[84] L. H. VINCENT and F. M. ABEL, *Jerusalem Nouvelle*, II, 1, Paris 1914, 000 ff.

[85] M. AVI-YONAH, *The Madaba Mosaic Map*, Jerusalem 1954.

[86] ELTESTER, *Die Kirchen Antiochiens* [note 70] ; A. GRABAR, *Martyrium* I, Paris 1946, 214 ; G. DOWNEY, *A History* [note 71]. The older cathedral somewhere in the city off the island, continued to function jointly with the new one; its dates of construction remain in suspense.

hall, the *sedes iustitiae*, built in or shortly before 310 [87]. Further southeast was the hippodrome, an integral element of any Imperial residence. Constantine thus meant the cathedral to be seen as part and parcel of the Imperial, the representational quarter of Trier. In Constantinople, Constantine's Own City, his cathedral, the first H. Sophia, stood on the site where Justinian's church now rises [88]:

---

[87] The excavations, begun in 1946, but long dormant, are to be soon to be resumed. A summary of the *status quaestionis* and the bibliographical sources has been provided by W. WEBER, *Die Anfänge des Trierer Doms*, in « Trierer Theologische Zeitschrift » 98, 1989, 147 ff.

[88] The date of foundation of the first H. Sophia and its attribution, whether to Constantine or Constantius, are under discussion. The start of construction is given by Socrates (*HE* II, 16, *PG* 67, 217) as roughly at the time Makedonios became bishop of Constantinople and the Arians took over, hence 342–343 and is attributed to Constantius, ἐκτίσε. On the other hand, the *Chronicon Paschale* (*PG* 92, 737) when recording the consecration on February 15, 360, assigns the foundation and start of construction to Constantine : « Κωνσταντίνος νικητής σεβάστος », who laid the foundations, « θεμελίους κατεβάλετο » approximately thirty–four years before, ἐτῶν λδ' μικρῷπρόσω ». The use of the emperor's full title, *Constantinus Victor Augustus*, strongly suggests to me that the author of the *Chronicon Paschale* drew on a good Constantinian source, possibly an inscription or a copy of one. Moreover 326 or roughly so, is when planning of the city and of the palace with the adjoining state buildings was underway. More than half a century ago, A. M. Schneider (*Die vorjustinianische Sophienkirche*, BZ 36, 1936, 78) has called attention to the axial correspondence of church, hippodrome, palace, *regia* and *mese* and tentatively suggested the existence of an overall plan of Constantinian date. Notwithstanding the doubts of Dagron (*Naissance d'une capitale*, Paris 1976, 397 ff.), I therefore remain steadfast in my « imprudent » conclusion that the first H. Sophia was planned and possibly work begun under Constantine.

I also remain steadfast in viewing the second H. Sophia, consecrated in 415 (*Chronicon Paschale* (*PG* 92, 788), as essentially a rebuilding of Constantine's church, this rather than a new construction from scratch. Only the *propylaion* was built entirely anew. The fire of 408 would have destroyed the roof and gutted the interior. Zosimus', (*Nouvelle Histoire*, ed. F. PASCHOUD, Paris 1971, V, 24) summary « κατεφλέγετο πάσα », it burnt all down » sounds less reliable than the « ἐκάη », it burnt, it caught fire, of the *Chronicon Paschale* (*PG* 92, 782, under the year 404). Likewise, Palladius' eye witness description conveys the impression of a fire, bad but less than all–consuming (*Dialogue sur la vie de Jean Chrysostome*, SC, 341, ed. A. H. MALONGREY, Paris 1988, 210). Moreover, as early as 406 the sanctuary was in a state good enough for deposing a relic (JANIN, *Eglises*, 472). The outer walls would have remained in place in large part ; in any

a basilica and one would like to envisage it much as its fifth century successor: the nave flanked by twin aisles right and left surmounted by galleries, nearly as wide and not much shorter than Justinian's church. Also like the fifth century church, Constantine's would have been preceded by an atrium and possibly by a flight of steps ascending from street level.

Thus the Constantinian H. Sophia, when completed in 360, would have risen to the left and forward of a visitor approaching Constantine's palace along the *regia*, the double tiered and comparatively short colonnaded street that led to Constantine's palace starting from a marble tetrapylon, the *milion*. That nodal point was linked by the *mese*, the main street of Constantinople, to the anchor point of Constantine's urban plan, the forum where his statue in the guise of Helios rose on a porphyry column. Coming from there and turning into the *regia*, the visitor saw ahead the tall main gate of the palace, the *Chalke* ; the palace itself, a complex of mostly low buildings, of courtyards and gardens was hidden from the visitor by two monumental structures he passed to the right, the hippodrome and the *thermae* of Zeuxippos. Both adjoined, but were outside of the sacred precinct of the palace proper. Yet they were integral to a Roman emperor's palace in contemporary eyes, hence also in Constantine's. Both signalled the emperor's

---

event the foundations would have been re-used and caused a rebuilding on the old plan (*Pelican*, 460, n. 27 ; so already SCHNEIDER, as above note 84, 1936). One wants to recall also John B. Ward Perkins' suggestion that the surviving masonry of the atrium wall – the rear wall of the *propylaion* – might be part of the original first church (*The Great Palace of the Byzantine Emperors*, II, ed. D. T. RICE, Edinburgh 1958, 64). A convincing, descriptive reconstruction of the first church, based on Palladius (*PG* 47, 35 f.) has been proposed by TH. F. MATHEWS, *The early Churches of Constantinople*, University Park and London, 1971, 12 ff.

[89] DEICHMANN, *Das Oktogon von Antiocheia...*, « BZ » 65 (1972), 40 ff. In countering a mistaken hypothesis of mine proffered at the time (*Pelican*[1], 1965, 53) has emphasized that the H. Sophia as well as the Golden Octagon at Antioch were the local cathedrals, this rather than palace churches. In this context he pointed out that the palace and the H. Sophia are listed in different *regiones* of Constantinople. Granted this administrative split-up, he seems to me to have overshot the mark when denying any link between church and palace. A visual tie-up of the first H. Sophia, the Augusteon, the Senate House, the palace and its gate and the *regia* did exist, after all.

freehandedness and his approachability. The Bath restored, richly appointed with colourful marble, filled with ancient statuary and liberally endowed, was opened to the people on May 11, 330. That same day the hippodrome, enlarged by Constantine, was re-opened for the inaugural ceremonies of his new capital: the site — in Rome the Circus Maximus — where traditionally the emperor enthroned in his box manifested himself to his subjects assembled *en masse* to receive their adulation, or at times to listen unwillingly to the *vox populi*. Readying these two structures for the great day, Constantine considered a foremost task, Roman emperor that he was.

Ahead of the visitor coming along the *regia*, Constantine's planners foresaw a group of structures, outside yet equally integral to the emperor's, that is this emperor's palace: straight on the *Chalke*, the palace gate ; left forward the cathedral, the first H. Sophia ; joining the two, this rather than separating [89], a monumental square, the *Augusteon* ; and, rising at its far end, the Senate House. In any event, the *Augusteon*, the Senate House and the church were envisaged, it seems to me, as a closely knit and highly visible complex of outstanding structures. Like the hippodrome and the thermae, they are placed outside the palace ; yet they are intimately linked to it and integral to the emperor's public image, certainly in Constantine's eyes at that time in his life. They are state buildings where the emperor personifying the state reveals himself in different functions and facets to different layers of the people. In the hippodrome he faced the crowds, pagan and Christian, low and high. In the Senate House he appeared before a picked assembly of notables to listen to panegyrics addressed to himself. In the cathedral he would have shown himself to his Christian subjects on nearly all the great holidays of the year to attend services, thus manifesting the interaction of the ruler, personification of the State and the Godhead [90].

With the H. Sophia, as planned by Constantine, his new building policy reaches its apogee.

---

[90] JANIN, *Eglises* [note 85], 483 regarding the emperor's attendance at the great feast days in the H. Sophia.

LIST OF FREQUENTLY QUOTED TITLES:

APARAM	Atti della Pontificia Accademia Romana di Archeologia. Memorie
APARAR	Atti della Pontificia Accademia Romana di Archeologia. Rendiconti
BZ	Byzantinische Zeitschrift
CAC	Congresso Internazionale di Archeologia Cristiana
CBCR	R. KRAUTHEIMER and others, *Corpus Basilicarum Christianarum Romae* I–V, Vatican City/New York 1937–77
CSEL	Corpus Scriptorum Ecclesiasticorum Latinorum
CIL	Corpus Inscriptionum Latinarum
CTh	Theodosiani Libri XVI, ed. Th. Mommsen, repr. Berlin 1961
HE	Historia Ecclesiastica
JbAC	Jahrbuch für Antike und Christentum
JDAI	Jahrbuch des Deutschen Archäologischen Instituts
LCL	Loeb Classical Library
LRE	A. H. M. JONES, *The Later Roman Empire*, Oxford 1973
LP	L. DUCHESNE, *Le Liber Pontificalis*, Paris ¹1886–92 ; repr. 2nd ed., Paris 1955
MEFRA	Melanges d'Archéologie et d'Histoire. Ecole Française de Rome, Antiquité
Pelican	R. KRAUTHEIMER, *Early Christian and Byzantine Architecture, The Pelican History of Art*, Harmondsworth 1965
PG	Patrologiae Cursus Completus, Series Graeca
PL	Patrologiae Cursus Completus, Series Latina
RAC	Reallexikon für Antike und Christentum
RE	Paulys Realencyclopaedie der classischen Altertumswissenschaft
RJbBH	Römisches Jahrbuch für Kunstgeschichte (Kunstgeschichtliches Jahrbuch der Bibliotheca Hertziana)
RivAC	Rivista di Archeologia Cristiana
RM	Mitteilungen des Deutschen Archäologischen Instituts, Römische Abteilung
SC	Sources Chrétiennes

ThLL   Thesaurus Linguae Latinae

Three   R. KRAUTHEIMER, *Three Christian Capitals : Rome, Constan-*
Capitals,   *tinople, Milan,* Berkeley 1983

VC   Eusebius Werke, I. 1, *Über das Leben des Kaisers Konstantin,*
              Ed. F. Winkelmann, Berlin 1975

ZNTW   Zeitschrift für neutestamentliche Wissenschaft

Constantine and Consensus

H. A. DRAKE

The church historian Socrates Scholasticus tells a story about an encounter during the Council of Nicaea between the emperor Constantine and the schismatic bishop Acesius. On learning that Acesius's dispute had nothing to do with the Creed or the date of Easter—the two major issues under debate at that Council—Constantine asked, "For what reason then do you separate yourself from communion with the rest of the Church?" Acesius replied that his sect objected to the relative leniency with which other Christians had treated those who had cracked under the empire-wide persecutions of the third century. He then "referred to the rigidness of that austere canon which declares, that it is not right that persons who after baptism have committed a sin, which the sacred Scriptures denominate 'a sin unto death' be considered worthy of participation in the sacraments." Whereupon, Socrates continues, the emperor said to him, "Place a ladder, Acesius, and climb alone into heaven."[1]

Although it appears in no contemporary source, there is every reason to believe that Socrates's story, recorded a century after the Council, is accurate. Socrates was a careful scholar, and he claims to have heard it from an elderly man who as a youth had accompanied Acesius to the Council, and who "simply stated what had taken place in the course of a narrative about the Council" (*hōs historēsas ta kata tēn sunodon elegen*). This last comment is revealing, for it suggests that Socrates knew that Constantine had already become a model of a sort—the exemplary Christian emperor, the subject of stories told more for their hortatory than their historical value. It was, therefore, significant to Socrates that his source was telling the story simply as a story, and not to make a point. Even more revealing is the way Constantine behaves in this story. The model Constantine was a pious son of the church who very predictably bowed to bishops and quaked before saints. But this Constantine is a self-confident ruler with a clear sense of what kind of Christian did and did not belong in his program. Acesius did not belong.

The author wishes to thank Naphtali Lewis and Jeffrey Burton Russell for their many helpful suggestions.
1. *Historia Ecclesiastica* [*HE*] 10, tr. A. Zenos in P. Schaff and H. Wace, eds., A Select Library of Nicene and Post-Nicene Fathers of the Christian Church, 2nd ser. (New York, 1890) 2:17, with slight emendation. Acesius's scriptural reference is to John 5:15.

Mr. Drake is professor of history at the University of California in Santa Barbara, California.

Socrates's story provides an opportunity to reconsider Constantine's goals with regard to the Christian church. Much has been written about this topic, too much of it governed by questions framed in an atmosphere of religious polemic. One gauntlet was thrown down more than a century and a half ago when Jacob Burckhardt characterized Constantine in *The Age of Constantine the Great* as an "essentially unreligious" statesman who grasped the strength of Christian organization and turned it to his own political ends: "Attempts have often been made to penetrate into the religious consciousness of Constantine and to construct a hypothetical picture of changes in his religious convictions. Such efforts are futile. In a genius driven without surcease by ambition and lust for power there can be no question of Christianity and paganism, of conscious religiosity or irreligiosity; such a man is essentially unreligious, even if he pictures himself standing in the midst of a churchly community."[2]

Critical reaction against Burckhardt's anachronistic reading has been decisive, and his work continues to be cited as proof that modern political analysis cannot be applied to the age of Constantine. The judgment is misleading on two counts: first, because many of Burckhardt's assumptions have gone unchallenged despite rejection of his conclusion; second, because for all the talk of power and organization, his attack on the traditional account of Constantine's piety can in no realistic sense be called a political analysis. In using political motives to question the sincerity of Constantine's conversion, Burckhardt pursued a line of inquiry that is rooted in the Reformation, not in political methodology. "Political" is not merely a pejorative term, the antithesis of "spiritual." Politics is a dimension of every organized activity; study of its procedures, and the skill of the individuals who use them, has as much to offer to our understanding of organized religious experience as it does to any other realm of human activity. Although central to later debates about the purity of the church that he empowered, the sincerity of Constantine's faith has little if anything to do with a real political analysis. This article, then, is not an attempt to revive Burckhardt's argument. Rather, it is my aim briefly to indicate some hidden traps in his analysis that have tainted subsequent studies, and then to suggest a few of the ways in which a genuinely political approach might resolve many of the problems that continue to divide Constantine scholars.

Although every student new to late antiquity immediately learns the flaw in Burckhardt's refusal to recognize the sincerity of Constantine's religious motivation, rarely is similar consideration given to his grounds for that conclusion. Burckhardt found Constantine's sincerity questionable in part

---

2. Tr. Moses Hadas (New York, 1949; repr. Berkeley, 1983), p. 292. The first German edition appeared in 1853 as *Die Zeit Constantin's des Grossen*. The second edition (from which the English translation was made) was published in 1880.

because of evidence that the emperor continued to tolerate and even to support traditional religion. Implicit in this approach is the assumption that Christian belief necessarily entails intolerance—one of the more questionable legacies of Enlightenment scholarship. In faulting his reasoning, Burckhardt's detractors did not question this premise. Instead, they merely turned the argument on its head, insisting that it is the sincerity of Constantine's compromises and acts favoring traditional religion that must be questioned, not the sincerity of his conversion. Saddled with a pagan Senate in Rome and a non-Christian colleague in the east, Constantine, according to this argument, made a virtue of necessity by tempering his zeal for his new faith and sharing largesse with traditional cults. But after defeating his eastern colleague Licinius in 324 and moving operations to his new eponymous capital, Constantine finally was able to implement the repressive measures that heretofore he had only been able to recommend.[3]

For Burckhardt's critics as much as for Burckhardt, being Christian meant being intent on suppressing variant belief. Few would deny that such coercion has been all too prevalent a part of Christian history. But is this the only option that would have been open to Constantine? To think so is to assume a uniformity in attitude that the record belies. Certainly there were Christians who yearned to pay back their pagan oppressors in kind, to coerce their opponents into submission—Christians who, in the well-known words of one scholar, lived "in a mood of resentment and vengeance," their voices "shrill with implacable hatred."[4] But just as there was a spectrum of theological positions in the Christian movement, so also was there a spectrum of opinion with regard to the proper relationship of Christianity to Rome. For every Donatus demanding to know "What has the emperor to do with the church?" there was a Eusebius or Lactantius trying to reconcile Christianity with Rome.[5] Given this spectrum, it begs a very large question to speak of

---

3. This was the position taken by Norman Baynes in his monumental Raleigh Lecture of 1929, *Constantine the Great and the Christian Church*, ed. Henry Chadwick (London, 1972), p. 19: "As the years passed, toleration of paganism gave place to active repression; the emperor felt that he was strong enough to advance to a frontal attack upon paganism. The important fact to realize, however, is that this alteration in policy entailed no change of spirit, only a change of method. What Constantine would have recommended in 323 he later felt free to proclaim as the imperial will." In *The Conversion of Constantine and Pagan Rome*, tr. H. Mattingly (Oxford, 1948), A. Alföldi built on this position by dividing Constantine's policy into three stages to correspond roughly with his political situation.

4. A. Momigliano, "Pagan and Christian Historiography in the Fourth Century A.D.," in *The Conflict Between Paganism and Christianity in the Fourth Century* (Oxford, 1963), p. 79.

5. On the variety of Christian attitudes toward Rome see Alan Wardman, *Religion and Statecraft Among the Romans* (London, 1982), p. 136. As the "Father of Church History," Eusebius of Caesarea decisively influenced the subsequent study of early Christianity by distinguishing a single orthodox tradition from heretical variations. See R. A. Markus, "Church History and Early Church Historians," in D. Baker, ed., *The Materials, Sources and Methods of Ecclesiastical History*, Studies in Church History 11

Constantine's commitment to "the triumph of the church" without first asking "which Church?" and "what kind of triumph?"[6]

The significance of Socrates's anecdote of the encounter between Constantine and Acesius now becomes clear: it shows that Constantine did not convert to a church that would be limited to a small body of the pristine elect. The same conclusion may be drawn from his first recorded reaction to the Arian heresy, which is notorious for its indifference to the issues that generated half a century of turmoil throughout the empire. Writing to the chief adversaries, the presbyter Arius and Bishop Alexander of Alexandria, Constantine dismissed their dispute over the relationship of Father and Son as "intrinsically trifling and of little moment." His reason for finding so little value in a matter of such great theological significance was his recognition of the need to accomodate diversity. "For we are not all of us like-minded on every subject," he wrote, "nor is there such a thing as one disposition and judgment common to all alike." Accordingly, he then put foward his own criteria: "As far, then, as regards the Divine Providence, let there be one faith, and one understanding among you, one united judgment in reference to God. But as to your subtle disputations of questions of little or no significance, though you may be unable to harmonize in sentiment, such differences should be consigned to the secret custody of your own minds and thoughts."[7] This emphasis on diversity and a broad, vaguely defined standard of orthodoxy indicates very clearly the type of organization Constantine envisioned. He thought of Christianity as an "umbrella" organization, able to hold a number of different wings or factions together under a "big tent" of overarching mutual interest. The chief distinguishing element of such an organization is sufficient ambiguity and flexibility with regard to the basic

---

(Cambridge, 1975), pp. 1–17. On the importance of local traditions in early Christianity, see W. Bauer, *Rechtgläubigkeit und Ketzerei im ältesten Christentum*, 2nd ed. (Tübingen, 1964); Eng. tr. *Orthodoxy and Heresy in Earliest Christianity* (Philadelphia, 1971). On the Christian tradition that true belief could not be coerced, see P. Garnsey, "Religious Toleration in Classical Antiquity," in W. J. Shiels, ed., *Persecution and Toleration*, Studies in Church History 21 (Oxford, 1984), pp. 1–27. E. Digeser, "Lactantius and Constantine's Letter to Arles: Dating the Divine Institutes," *Journal of Early Christian Studies* 2 (1994): 33–52, offers a fresh appreciation of this tradition on Constantine. For Donatus's question, asked in reply to an offer of subsidies from Constantine's son Constans, see Optatus, ed. C. Ziwsa, CSEL 26 (Vienna, 1893), 3.3: "qui cum ad Donatum, patrem tuum [frater Parmeniane], venirent [Paulus et Macarius] et, quare venerant, indicarent. ille solito furore succensus in haec uerba prorupit: 'quid est imperatori cum ecclesia?' et de fonte leuitatis suae multa maledicta effudit. . . ."

6. The phrase is Norman Baynes's: "the emperor's consistent aim was the triumph of Christianity and the union of the Roman state with the Christian Church." See *Constantine the Great*, n. 57.

7. *De Vita constantini* [VC] 2.61, rev. tr. by E. C. Richardson in Schaff and Wace, eds., *Nicene and Post-Nicene Fathers*, 2nd. ser. 1:517–518.

criteria for membership as to prevent the movement from splintering into small, isolated, and competing groups.[8]

Effective leadership of such an organization requires skill at finding common ground—building consensus and smoothing over differences. These, and not theological standards, are the criteria by which Constantine's methods and goals need to be interpreted. There is abundant evidence that Constantine appreciated this need. Socrates uses the incident with Acesius as an example of how much Constantine "desired peace" and "ecclesiastical harmony." Constantine's contemporary biographer, Eusebius of Caesarea, tells us that whenever given a choice among the various types of Christians, the emperor always sided with those who favored consensus.[9] He preferred, in other words, pragmatists over ideologues. It is possible to be even more specific about the type of harmony he sought, for Constantine's reaction to the pious mouthings of Acesius is consistent with the position he took during a string of clashes with Donatist rigorists, unyielding Arian theologians, and purist Nicene fathers. In all of these situations, Constantine favored not only peace and harmony, but also inclusiveness and flexibility.

Such a conclusion is not likely to generate much argument, Constantine's commitment to unity in the church being one policy on which virtually all parties agree. Conflict arises when the topic shifts to treatment of non-Christians: how far did Constantine's concern for harmony and consensus extend? Here is where apparent inconsistencies—continued use of pagan symbols and endowment of traditional priesthoods on the one hand, confiscation of temple treasures and refusal to participate in sacrificial rites on the other—have led to the most widespread disagreement. His biographer, Eusebius of Caesarea, claims that Constantine ordered the temples closed, but the specific examples that he gives are easy to explain as police actions, and Eusebius's statement of a more general ban therefore is usually taken as a bit of rhetorical exaggeration.[10] Another claim is more problematic. In his

---

8. A standard study remains that of David B. Truman, *The Governmental Process: Political Interests and Public Opinion*, 2nd ed. (New York, 1971); see esp. ch. 6: "Internal Politics: The Problem of Cohesion."

9. "However many he saw responsive to a superior sentiment and endowed with a sound and like-minded character he received eagerly, showing that he himself rejoiced in the mutual agreement of all. But those who stayed unyielding he turned away from." *VC* 1.44. Eusebius may be speaking specifically of the Council of Arles in this passage, but the statement holds true for every period of Constantine's career. For instance, Eusebius's summary of Constantine's remarks to the bishops following the Council of Nicaea at *VC* 3.21, has the emperor exhorting them "above all else to honor mutual harmony" (*pantōn peri pollou timōmenōn tēn symphōnon harmonian*). A decade later, Eusebius says at *VC* 4.41, Constantine urged the bishops at the Council of Tyre "to conduct themselves with concord and harmony" (*sun homonoia kai sumphōnia tē pasē ekhesthai*).

10. The chapter heading for *VC* 3.54 proclaims "The destruction of idol temples and images everywhere" (*Eidōleiōn kai xoanōn pantakhou katalusis*), but the text of the chapter only describes the collection of temple treasures. Immediately subsequent chapters

Life of Constantine, Eusebius says Constantine ordered the traditional rites of animal sacrifice suppressed. It is clear that Constantine personally abhorred animal sacrifice, and that he removed the requirement from the duties of imperial officials. But indications of a more sweeping ban can only be teased out of tenuous readings and marginal comments, which then must be reconciled with abundant evidence for the continued performance of sacrifice on a fairly wide scale. Is this another case of exaggeration? If so, a law of Constantine's sons in 341 abolishing "the madness of sacrifices" demands explanation, because in it the emperors refer to their father's previous ban.[11]

But more than specific actions, it is Constantine's proclamations and public utterances that account for differing interpretations of his policy toward non-Christians. As early as 313, in the document commonly known as the "Edict of Milan," Constantine expresses a desire to allow freedom of worship to all inhabitants of the empire. After seizing the eastern half of the empire from his co-emperor (and the Edict's co-author) Licinius, Constantine restated this principle in the "Edict to the Provincials," where he extolls "the advantages of peace and quiet" for "those who delight in error alike with those who believe," and exhorted his subjects to "Let no one disturb another, let each man hold fast to that which his soul wishes, and make full use of this."[12] Such statements at one time led to characterizations of his age as one of toleration and religious liberty, and even a suggestion that his aim was not to insure the success of Christianity at all, but rather to create a new,

---

name three temples that were destroyed—two of Aphrodite (at Aphaca, 3.55, and Heliopolis, 3.58) and the Asclepius temple at Aegai (3.56), to which may be added a third Aphrodite temple on the site of the Holy Sepulchre in Jerusalem (3.26) and pagan idols at the oak of Mambre (3.52). H. Dorries, *Constantine and Religious Liberty,* tr. Roland Bainton (New Haven, 1960), p. 45, found only the Asclepius temple could not be explained by non-religious reasons. More recently, Robin Lane Fox, *Pagans and Christians: Religion and the Religious Life from the Second to the Fourth Century A.D.* (New York, 1986), p. 671, suggests it was due to association with the pagan holy man Apollonius of Tyana, who had been held up as a rival to Christ during the Great Persecution.

11. *Codex Theodosianus* 16.10.2. In "The Constantinian Reformation," *The Crake Lectures, 1984* (Sackville, Can., 1986), p. 50, T. D. Barnes has made a general ban on sacrifice "the lynch-pin of the thesis that Constantine carried through a religious Reformation." He finds support for such a ban in Constantine's failure specifically to refer to sacrifices in an edict "To the Provincials" permitting continued use of the temples (*VC* 2.23–42): "Constantine's Prohibition of Pagan Sacrifice," *American Journal of Philology* 105 (1984): 70. More recently, S. Bradbury has cited the orator Libanius's reference in his *Autobiography* (*Or.* 1.27) to a man who continued to perform sacrifice "despite the law which banned it" as evidence that such a ban existed (to be so, the remark must be read as a specific reference to the year in question—339 or 340—rather than as a general assessment of the man's character, in which case it refers to a year when the ban, if it existed, is generally conceded to have become a dead letter): "Constantine and the Problem of Anti-Pagan Legislation in the Fourth Century," *Classical Philology* 89 (1994): 129.

12. See *VC* 2.48–60 for the letter, and for this passage *VC* 2.56.1: "mēdeis ton heteron parenokhleitō; hekastos hoper hē psukhē bouletai katekhetō, toutō katakekhrēsthō."

syncretist faith of Christians and monotheistic pagans.[13] But these interpretations have rightly been criticized for failing to take into account the bitterness with which Constantine assails pagan "temples of falsehood" in the latter document, which also includes denunciations of idolatry and superstition lacking in the earlier one. Such language, combined with the evidence of a general ban on sacrifice, supports the argument that Constantine's tolerance was minimal and grudging.[14]

One recent effort interprets the general ban on sacrifice as a "moral proclamation" that "placated certain pressure groups" but had "no practical effect on society."[15] The reminder that even late Roman emperors did not have the luxury of indulging their own preferences without concern for the wishes of constituencies is a salutary one. I will argue here that this concern proves that Constantine's goal was to create a neutral public space in which Christians and pagans could both function, and that he was far more successful in creating a stable coalition of both Christians and non-Christians in support of this program of "peaceful co-existence" than has generally been recognized. If correct, this argument would mean that Constantine's preference for Christians who chose peace and unity over doctrinal rigor and theological clarity extended beyond the confines of the church itself, and that he would not have favored coercion as a means of promoting Christian belief.

Constantine stakes out precisely this goal in his letter to Arius and Alexander. Although the bulk of this letter deals with the immediate problem of the Arian dispute, its introductory sentences lay out a more general program:

> I make that god my witness who is the helpmate of my endeavors and savior of all, that there were two reasons for those duties which I undertook to perform. The first was to unite the inclination of all peoples regarding divine matters into a single sustaining habit; second, I was eager to restore and rejoin the body of our common empire which had been stricken as if with a terrible wound. The former I planned to provide for through the hidden eye of the mind; the latter I attempted to correct by the power of military arms, knowing that if I were to establish through my prayers a common agreement among all the servants of god, the conduct of public affairs would enjoy a change concurrent with the pious sentiments of all.[16]

---

13. H. Dorries, *Constantine and Religious Liberty*. The argument for syncretism is made most persuasively by L. Salvatorelli, "La politica religiosa e la religiosità di Costantino," *Richerche Religiose* 4 (1928): 289–328.
14. T. D. Barnes, *Constantine and Eusebius* (Cambridge, Mass., 1981), p. 210.
15. Bradbury, "Anti-Pagan Legislation," pp. 137–138.
16. *VC* 2.65 (ed. Winkelmann): "Prôton men gar tēn hapantôn tôn ethnôn peri to theion prothesin eis mian hexeōs sustasin henōsai, deuteron de to tēs koinēs oikoumenēs sōma kathaper khalepô tini traumati peponēkos anaktēsasthai kai sunarmosai prouthumēthēn. ha dē proskopôn heteron men aporrētō tēs dianoias ophthalmō sunelogizomēn, heteron de tē tēs stratiōtikēs kheiros exousia katorthoun epeirōmēn, eidōs hōs ei koinēn hapasi tois tou theou therapousin ep' eukhais tais emais homonoian katastēsaimi, kai hē tôn dēmosiōn pragmatôn khreia sundromon tais hapantôn eusebesi gnōmais tēn metabolēn karpōsetai."

By the "duties which I undertook to perform" Constantine undoubtedly meant the recently concluded campaign against his former colleague, the eastern emperor Licinius, whose removal had accomplished the second of his two purposes. There remained his foremost goal, religious unity. Does he refer here just to Christian unity? The remainder of the letter could lead one to think so. In the next sentence, Constantine writes of the Donatist schism and his hope that the Christians of the east might help him repair it, then urges Arius and Alexander to resolve their differences for the good of the greater Christian body. But the phrase "of all peoples" (*hapantōn tōn ethnōn*) in the opening passage indicates a more diverse community. For an empire expressly based on divine support, as Rome had been at least since Diocletian established the Jovian dynasty, the lack of a consensus on religious matters was no small thing. Achieving it was undoubtedly at least one goal of Diocletian's Great Persecution, and his failure to do so had if anything made the problem even more urgent. The unspoken link between this introductory statement and the rest of the letter, then, was Constantine's anticipation of a united Christian church to help him achieve this broader goal.

Do these words then mean that Constantine meant to "unite the inclination of all peoples regarding divine matters into a single sustaining habit" by making everyone in the empire Christian? The maddeningly elliptical style of late imperial prose makes it impossible to rule out such a possibility, though the passage as a whole more likely suggests that the search for a common denominator was still in progress than that one had been found and only awaited implementation. In any case, more germane to the problem at hand is Constantine's intention to use "the hidden eye of the mind" (*tous tēs dianoias parapempontas ophthalmous*) to accomplish this goal. This phrase, which probably refers to spiritual exhortation or prayer, does not spell out an exact program, but it is clear that Constantine considers this method to be different from the use of military force.[17]

This passage from Constantine's letter thus carries the same message as the "Edict to the Provincials," issued during the same period, in which Constantine argued that "it is one thing to undertake the contest for immortality voluntarily, another to compel it with punishment."[18] Another document now thought also to date from this period contains a similar message. This is an oration of Constantine, intriguingly entitled "To the Assembly of the Saints" that comes down as an appendix to Eusebius of Caesarea's *Life of*

---

17. At *VC* 4.19, Eusebius records that Constantine ordered a Sunday prayer for non-Christians in the army in which they were to seek God with "their mind's eyes" (*tous tēs dianoias . . . ophthalmous*), and in his speech "On the Holy Sepulchre," 16.8, Eusebius calls on his hearers to "open the eyes of your mind" (*dianoixon tēs sautou dianoias tous ophthalmous*) to consider God's power.

18. "Allo gar esti ton huper athanasias athlon hekousiōs epanaireisthai, allo to meta timōrias epanagkazein" (*VC* 2.60.1–2). See also at n. 13 above.

Constantine. The oration is a clumsy document—Eusebius says it is a Greek translation of a Latin original—and for the better part of a century it was held at arm's length by most scholars. Textual problems now appear soluble, however, and the oration finally is receiving serious attention as a source for Constantine's thought and policy.[19] At one point in this speech, Constantine speaks in favor of diversity, despite the fact that it works to the detriment of "confirming the faith in each individual" (*pros to bebaiousthai tēn kath' hekastou pistin*). Constantine ridicules those who criticize God for allowing human beings to be of different character. Such critics, he tells his audience, might just as well complain about the difference between day and night or land and sea; "wanting all men to be the same character" (*to de tous anthrōpous pantas homoiotropous einai*) is as laughable as "not realizing that the order of the universe is not identical with this world, nor physics consubstantial with ethics, nor the experiences of the flesh the same as those of the spirit."[20] There is even an echo of the attitude Constantine shows in Socrates's story of his encounter with Acesius. He mocks "those who stir hatred against the differences in our natures, who want all mankind to be one and the same worth," and he chides those who resent that "the human race" has "a share in the divine goodness." Constantine's target in this passage appears to be atheists and materialists—near its end, he mocks "those who are vexed by the distinction of beings, who want all things to have one and the same value," and chides those who resent that "the human race is not excluded from the divine goodness."[21] But it is not difficult to see how the same reasoning could lead to reject a rigorist like Acesius as well.

Taken together, these documents indicate that Constantine's religious policy was not limited to creating consensus within the church, but also aimed to include the church in a broader coalition built around the same criteria that he proposed in his letter to Arius and Alexander: agreement in public on the existence of a "Divine Providence"—no doubt the same Divine Providence that Constantine elsewhere described as his own helpmate and

---

19. Eusebius promises at *VC* 4.32 to append a speech Constantine gave "To the Assembly of the Saints" to his account of the emperor's life. In the manuscripts, a speech entitled *Oratio Constantini ad Coetum Sanctorum* (*Basileōs Kōnstantinou logos hon egrapse tō tōn hagiōn sullogō*) follows Book 4, preceding Eusebius's own *Tricennial Oration* to Constantine, which he also promises to append (at *VC* 4.46). In some manuscripts, Constantine's Oration is labelled as Book 5 of the *VC*. I cite it in the following notes as *OC* (*Oratio Constantini*), using the text of Ivar A. Heikel, ed., *Eusebius Werke* (Leipzig, 1902) 1:154–192. On the troubled history of this oration, see David Ison, "The Constantinian Oration to the Saints—Authorship and Background," (Ph.D. diss., University of London, 1985).
20. *OC* 13.1 (Heikel, 1:171–172).
21. *OC* 13.1 (Heikel, 1:173.5–11): "asebes de kai to enthumēma tōn pros tēn diaphoran tōn ontōn apekhthanomenōn, mian te kai tēn autēn axian pantōn khrēmatōn einai thelontōn. . . . kai tēs theias agathotētos ouk amoiron to tōn anthrōpoōn genos. . ." I am grateful to Robert Renehan for his advice on this passage.

source of his right to rule—generally defined, with more specific attributes or definition confined to private assemblies. This is not to say that he aimed to create a syncretistic religion that merged Christianity with other beliefs, that he did not himself distinguish between Christianity and other forms of monotheism, or that he did not personally desire and work for the conversion of the largest possible number to Christian truth. It is a statement about policy, not belief.

Was such a policy feasible, or even conceivable, if Constantine had been truly converted? According to the traditional view, no. In this view, although there were points of contact and overlap between Christian and pagan monotheism, the distinctions between the two were clear, and irreconcilable. Such connections, according to this view, could only have served as a bridge, facilitating movement over a chasm that was narrow but exceedingly deep. What is emerging from more recent scholarship, however, is a sense that even a century later the division between Christian and pagan—at least on the level of educated lay individuals—was far less distinct than it has been portrayed.[22] Such findings make a broadly inclusive program such as posited here more practical than it once seemed.

The conventional view of a "life and death struggle" also requires us to see pagans as uniformly hostile to Christianity, even though Christian sources themselves tell us of pagans who were revolted by the excesses of the Great Persecution, and who provided shelter to Christian neighbors.[23] Indeed, it

22. In a review of a collection of essays on the relationship of Neoplatonism to Christianity, Felice Lifshitz points out "how very much we have been oversimplifying by looking only through neat little spectacles, spectacles with one lens called 'Hellenistic Philosophies' and another called 'Christianity.'" *Bryn Mawr Classics Review* 4 (September 1993): 22. Mark D. Smith, "Eusebius of Caesarea: Scholar and Apologist. A Study of His Religious Terminology and Its Application to the Emperor Constantine" (Ph.D. diss., University of California at Santa Barbara, 1989), p. 121, reaches a similar conclusion through analysis of Eusebius's religious terminology. On common sentiments regarding monotheism in late antiquity, see G. Fowden, *Empire to Commonwealth. Consequences of Monotheism in Late Antiquity*, (Princeton, 1993). A case in point is that of Synesius of Cyrene—a Christian bishop whose philosophical leanings still lead scholars to describe him as a late and incomplete convert to Christianity. As Frances Young has observed, "To state whether one thinks Synesius was really a Christian or not, says more about one's own understanding of Christianity than about Synesius himself." See Young, *From Nicaea to Chalcedon: A Guide to the Literature and Its Background* (Philadelphia, 1983), p. 177. See also A. Cameron and J. Long, *Barbarians and Politics at the Court of Arcadius* (Berkeley, 1992); M. Salzman, *On Roman Time: The Codex-Calendar of 354 and the Rhythms of Urban Life in Late Antiquity* (Berkeley, 1990); and D. Hunt, "Christianising the Roman Empire: The Evidence of the Code," in J. Harries and I. Wood, eds., *The Theodosian Code: Studies in the Imperial Law of Late Antiquity* (London, 1993), pp. 143–158.

23. On the general lack of enthusiasm for the persecution, see A. H. M. Jones, *The Later Roman Empire: A Social, Economic and Administrative Survey* (Norman, Okla., 1964), 1:73. Eusebius wrote that with the apparent end to persecution after Galerius's edict in 311, "even they who had formerly thirsted for our blood, when they saw the unexpected wonder, congratulated us on what had taken place." *HE* 9.1.11. In the *Divine Institutes* (5.13.11), Lactantius claimed that many pagans abandoned worship of their gods in

may well be that Constantine's success in creating the coalition is due in no small part to the fact that the turmoil, and ultimate failure, of the Great Persecution had thoroughly discredited the cause of those extremists on the pagan side who appear to have lobbied for, and perhaps even engineered, such a policy. In the aftermath of such a catastrophe, a commitment to renounce coercion and rebuild public life around a religiously neutral framework that could include Christians as well as pagans not only made good sense, it also made good politics. As in so many other ways in the late empire, the army was the model. On Sundays, Eusebius tells us, Constantine sent his Christian soldiers to church, while requiring all others to recite a monotheistic prayer in which they acknowledged a generic "God of All" (*ton d' epi pantōn . . . theon*) as the author of victory and preserver of the Constantinian house.[24]

The program entailed risks. It meant alienating not only rigorists like Acesius, but also those Christian militants who did live up to modern expectations and "thirst for revenge." Constantine had already reined in this latter group by making clear in the Edict to the Provincials that he would not permit attacks on pagan temples.[25] But Constantine had the politician's gift of knowing how to court those whom he opposed.[26] The "Oration to the Saints" shows how he mollified militants.

Scholars have looked at the Oration primarily for what it can tell us about Constantine's own views. Read in this way, as a pure expression of Constantine's personal thought framed without regard to any external considerations, it amounts to a disappointing amalgam of muddled theology and pious platitudes, whose rambling point seems to be that Divine Providence rewards virtue and punishes vice. But in the context of public policy, even

---

revulsion of the cruelties of the persecution, and elsewhere (5.11.13) conceded in a backhanded way that some officials did not enforce the death penalty so as to keep their "virtue" intact. Athanasius, *History of the Arians* 64, reported that pagans sheltered Christians even though they "frequently suffered the loss of their own substance, and had trial of imprisonment, solely that they might not betray the fugitives. They protected those who fled to them for refuge, as they would have done their own persons, and were determined to run all risks on their behalf." Tr. Newman , rev. and ed. A. Robertson in Schaff and Wace, *Nicene and Post-Nicene Fathers*, 2d ser., 4:293–294.

24. *VC* 4.18–20.

25. Constantine ends his edict with a clear distinction between persuasion and coercion: "For it is one thing to undertake the contest for immortality voluntarily, another to compel it with punishment." Immediately following this sentiment, he writes, "I have said these things and gone through them at greater length than my customary concern requires, since I did not wish my belief in the truth to be hidden, and *especially because I hear some people are saying the customs of the temples and the power of darkness have been taken away.*" These final words, which I have emphasized, suggest that Constantine was writing either in response to, or to preempt, attacks against pagan temples, and for such an offense Christian zealots are the most reasonable suspects.

26. Eusebius puts it somewhat differently. At *VC* 4.4, he says that Constantine never let a litigant leave his presence empty-handed, awarding him something even if he lost his suit. But the skill is recognizable enough.

platitudes can be revealing, especially when it is the emperor who speaks them. This is especially the case when the organization is an umbrella, because then the stock of common symbols and core texts from which these platitudes are drawn is likely to contain a number of ambiguous and even contradictory meanings that can be manipulated according to the speaker's purposes. Regarding coercion, for instance, it is possible to cite Jesus's injunctions to "turn the other cheek" and "love your enemies" in order to advocate a policy of non-intervention, or to remind hearers of the need to resist Satan and use the example of Jesus driving out the moneylenders to justify a more aggressive program.[27] It is precisely such ambiguities that make the role of discourse so important in the Christian community, because adherents rely on these interpretive messages to explain how they must react to any given situation.

For this reason, it is less important to try to fix an exact date for the Oration, as scholars lately have tried to do, and more important to remember that Eusebius appended it to the *Life of Constantine* as an example of the type of speech that, he says, Constantine was accustomed to giving.[28] Its message is one that Constantine frequently repeated, suggesting that it should be read for signs of a more immediate, more political, conflict—over the control of the Christian message. Reading the oration in this way, not as an expression of personal belief but as the work of someone who was attempting to set the course of a large and diverse movement, is another means of ascertaining Constantine's goals and the means he chose to implement them.

In this context, the Oration has a two-fold relevance. First, it shows where Constantine placed himself among the variety of positions Christians took in defining themselves in relation to outsiders; second, it reveals an underrated skill for expressing his position in a way that was likely to gain the broadest possible approbation. As an example of both, Constantine at one point defines God as the Being "properly worshipped by the wisest and most sensible peoples and states," and in another ridicules those who complain that God did not make all humans of one character and one faith.[29] The former statement opens the door to a broader spectrum of beliefs than Christian rigorists likely would have accepted, while at the same time putting those who would refute it in the uncomfortable position of seeming to deny that the Christian position was the "wisest and most sensible." The latter, in

27. On the "contradictory element" in ideological movements see G. Rudé, *Ideology and Popular Protest* (New York, 1980), p. 23. Regarding the ambiguities in Christian core texts, see G. Stroumsa, "Early Christianity as Radical Religion," in *Israel Oriental Studies* 14 (1994): 173–193. I am grateful to the author for an opportunity to read an advance copy of this article.

28. *VC* 4.29, 32. Robin Lane Fox observes of the Oration: "if genuine, it is our longest surviving statement from an Emperor between Marcus's *Meditations* and Julian's letters." *Pagans and Christians* (New York, 1986), p. 627.

29. *OC* 11.7, 13.1 (*pros to bebaiousthai tēn kath' hekastou pistin*, 171.32–33).

attacking critics of God, served to isolate Christians like Acesius as readily as pagan unbelievers.

One passage from the Oration demonstrates how Constantine used core Christian texts both to provide moral cover for his policy of toleration and to discredit the case for coercion, while at the same time making the case for an umbrella Christianity that would cover much classical belief as well. Here he uses the moment of Jesus's arrest to remind his audience of the way Jesus rebuked the disciple who tried to defend him with the words "all they that take the sword shall perish by the sword." In Constantine's version, however, this "heavenly wisdom" is restated as a decision "to choose rather to endure than to inflict injury, and to be ready, should necessity so require, to suffer, but not to do, wrong"—words reminiscent as much of Plato's *Apology of Socrates* as of the Gospel.[30] In another passage he singles out as God's greatest attributes both his capacity to forgive the "foolish notions" of humankind and the firmness with which he refuses at any time to lessen "his innate benevolence." To do otherwise, Constantine says, is "witless and impious."[31] In the context of public policy, such comments amount to more than mere moral platitudes. They indicate a clear preference for a movement capable of being both tolerant and diversified. Constantine's argument in the Oration, combined with the minimal theological standard that he set in the letter to Arius and Alexander, indicates that he aligned himself with a type of Christianity whose self-definition would allow for a broad range of contrary and even conflicting views—precisely the type of group now defined by the title as an umbrella organization.

The martyr is in many ways the quintessential Christian symbol. As imitators of Christ's suffering, martyrs can symbolize the need to endure evil, to suffer for others, to pay back hatred with love. But because they would not yield to injustice at any cost, martyrs are also heroes of resistance, the front line in the war against Satan. Constantine's use of the martyrs in the Oration, therefore, is particularly instructive. Before an audience that was likely to include many who had lived through Diocletian's persecution, Constantine predictably showers the martyrs with praise. He speaks of "the fearlessness even before death that comes from pure faith and undiluted dedication to God," and in another line that may well have been inserted specifically for the applause it would provoke, he even praises the "faith that does not shrink before the powers of the royal chambers."[32] Such lines demonstrate Constantine's solidarity with Christian militants. But when it comes to drawing lessons from the example of the martyrs, Constantine has a different message. He points out that "the martyr's life is chaste and obedient," and claims

30. *OC* 15.4. The scriptural quotation is from Matt. 26:52.
31. *OC* 11.7.
32. *OC* 12.3, 20.2.

that the significance of a martyr's death is that it "shows him full of magnanimity and gentility."[33] This was Constantine's constant message. Writing to the Catholic bishops of North Africa around the year 321 to tell them he will not use force against their Donatist opponents, he defuses any potential disappointment by arguing that "our faith ought to trust that whatever shall be suffered from the madness of men of this ilk will avail before God for the grace of martyrdom. For what else in this world is it to conquer in God's name than to endure with steadfast heart the rude onslaughts of persons who harass the people of the law of peace?"[34]

With such language, Constantine turns the martyrs from symbols of resistance into exemplars of endurance and fortitude. He did even more. By appropriating the powerful symbol of the martyrs and turning it to his own purposes, Constantine managed at one and the same time to play to the militants and to turn their own rhetoric against them. The importance of such "internal propaganda" for molding and unifying group opinion cannot be overestimated.[35] By stressing the irenic side of the Christian message, Constantine was able to create moral cover for moderates who shared his view of an umbrella faith, and at the same time create a rhetorical environment in which Christians who favored coercive measures looked like extremists.

Situating Constantine as the leader of a large and potentially volatile movement resolves the discrepancies between fierce language and relatively mild action that have led to such differing depictions of Constantine's character and intentions. This behavior pattern is not limited to his actions regarding pagans; it extends to his treatment of Jews, and even dissident Christians.[36] The answer lies not in theology, but in the nature of Christianity

---

33. *OC* 12.4: "eiper ho te bios sōphrōn tou marturos kai tōn panaggelmatōn mnēmōn, hē te teleutē plērēs heurisketai megalopsukhas te kai eugeneias."

34. "...maxime cum debeat fides nostra confidere quicquid ab huiusmodi hominum furore patietur martyrii gratia apud deum esse valiturum. Quid est enim aliud in hoc saeculo in nomine dei uincere quam inconditos hominum impetus quietae legis populum lacessentes constanti pectore sustinere?" *Le dossier du Donatisme*, vol. 1: *Des origenes à la mort de Constance II (303–361)*, ed. J.-L. Maier (Berlin, 1987), p. 242, 2.37–45.

35. Truman, *Governmental Process*, pp. 195–196.

36. On Constantine and the Jews, two recent works reach diametrically opposite conclusions. In "Eusebius as a Polemical Interpreter of Scripture," in H. Attridge and G. Hata, eds., *Eusebius, Christianity, and Judaism* (Detroit, 1992), p. 594, Michael Hollerich chides scholars for underestimating "the hostile language with which his [Constantine's] legislation refers to the Jews, who are styled as 'a deadly, nefarious sect.'" Conversely, Garth Fowden, looking at Constantine's actions, concludes that he was "relatively tolerant" of Jews: *Empire to Commonwealth: Consequences of Monotheism in Late Antiquity* (Princeton, 1993), p. 87. A similar observation might be made about Constantine's oft-cited complaint against the Donatists in his letter to the bishops at Arles in 314: "They demand my judgment, but I myself await Christ's judgment!" (*Meum iudicium postulant, qui ipse iudicium Christi exspecto!*) Maier, ed., *Le Dossier*, p. 169, 2:69–70. Despite this outburst, Constantine in fact proceeded to hear their appeal. J. H. W. G.

as a mass movement with a militant wing. Constantine kept the loyalty of this wing by throwing them rhetorical tidbits, while at the same time exploiting the irenic side of the Gospel message to lead the movement onto the broader ground of a faith that would be tolerant, broadly based, and inclusive. In modern parlance, he seized control of the discourse, using the ambiguities in the Christian message to isolate Christians who advocated coercive measures, making them appear to be at variance from the faith's core teachings, and thereby vulnerable to a charge of extremism. Doing so, he neutralized the potential liability that his policies entailed. Even the most hardline rigorist would have difficulty opposing a policy that seemed to flow directly from Jesus's own teaching.

The Oration thus opens a new door to understanding the great transformation that took place during the age of Constantine and its aftermath. The key to the Constantinian period is an emperor who was Christian, but who resisted pressure from any quarter to use coercion to enforce belief. His aim was to restore the coexistence that prevailed for half a century prior to the Great Persecution, and the success he enjoyed is perhaps the greatest casualty of the traditional paradigm of pagan-Christian "conflict," which has so conditioned us to hear only the voices of extremists that the endurance of this coalition for most of the fourth century goes largely unnoticed. The traditional model is unsatisfactory not just because it takes Christian coercion for granted, but also because in doing so it completely misinterprets the changes that took place under Constantine, obscuring that age's most important development. That development, I would argue, was the creation of a consensus in favor of a broadly inclusive monotheism under which both Christians and most pagans could live in harmony.[37] Hindsight lets us speak of a Constantinian "Revolution" or "Reformation," but it would be truer to the age to speak of a Constantinian "consensus" as that emperor's principal goal and contribution.

Liebeschuetz, *Continuity and Change in Roman Religion* (Oxford, 1979), p. 298, refers to such conditions as "a paradox" and "evidence of internal conflict."

37. In his classic study of modern revolutions, Crane Brinton observed that moderates dominate in early stages of a revolution, extremists in the crisis stage. *The Anatomy of Revolution*, rev. ed. (New York, 1965), p. 95. In this sense, the Age of Constantine might still be said to conform to a revolutionary pattern.

Acknowledgments

Blowers, Paul M. "Origen, the Rabbis, and the Bible: Toward a Picture of Judaism and Christianity in Third-Century Caesarea." In *Origen of Alexandria: His World and His Legacy,* edited by Charles Kannengiesser and William L. Petersen (Notre Dame: University of Notre Dame Press, 1988): 96–116. Reprinted with the permission of the University of Notre Dame Press.

McGuckin, John A. "Origen on the Jews." *Studies in Church History* 29 (1992): 1–13. Reprinted with the permission of the Ecclesiastical History Society.

Fredriksen, Paula. "*Excaecati Occulta Justitia Dei*: Augustine on Jews and Judaism." *Journal of Early Christian Studies* 3 (1995): 299–324. Reprinted with the permission of Johns Hopkins University Press.

Miles, Margaret R. "Santa Maria Maggiore's Fifth-Century Mosaics: Triumphal Christianity and the Jews." *Harvard Theological Review* 86 (1993): 155–75. Copyright 1993 by the President and Fellows of Harvard College. Reprinted by permission.

Edwards, M.J. "Justin's Logos and the Word of God." *Journal of Early Christian Studies* 3 (1995): 261–80. Reprinted with the permission of Johns Hopkins University Press.

Osborn, Eric. "Arguments for Faith in Clement of Alexandria." *Vigiliae Christianae* 48 (1994): 1–24. Reprinted with the permission of E.J. Brill Academic Publishers.

Heine, Ronald E. "Stoic Logic as Handmaid to Exegesis and Theology in Origen's Commentary on the Gospel of John." *Journal of Theological Studies,* n.s. 44 (1993): 90–117. Reprinted with the permission of Oxford University Press.

Wiles, Maurice. "The Philosophy in Christianity: Arius and Athanasius." In *The Philosophy in Christianity,* edited by Godfrey Vesey (New York: Cambridge University Press, 1989): 41–52. Reprinted with the permission of the Royal Institute of Philosophy.

Mosshammer, Alden A. "Non-Being and Evil in Gregory of Nyssa." *Vigiliae Christianae* 44 (1990): 136–67. Reprinted with the permission of E.J. Brill Academic Publishers.

Teske, Roland. "St. Augustine as Philosopher: The Birth of Christian Metaphysics." *Augustinian Studies* 23 (1992): 7–32. Reprinted with the permission of *Augustinian Studies.*

Cavadini, John. "The Structure and Intention of Augustine's *De Trinitate*." *Augustinian Studies* 23 (1992): 103–23. Reprinted with the permission of *Augustinian Studies*.

Markus, Robert A. "Augustine on Magic: A Neglected Semiotic Theory." *Revue des Études Augustiniennes* 40 (1994): 375–88. Reprinted with the permission of Institut d'Études Augustiniennes.

Ferguson, Everett. "Early Christian Martyrdom and Civil Disobedience." *Journal of Early Christian Studies* 1 (1993): 73–83. Reprinted with the permission of Johns Hopkins University Press.

Farkasfalvy, Denis. "Christological Content and Its Biblical Basis in the Letter of the Martyrs of Gaul." *The Second Century* 9 (1992): 5–25. Reprinted with the permission of Johns Hopkins University Press.

Hall, Stuart G. "Women Among the Early Martyrs." *Studies in Church History* 30 (1993): 1–21. Reprinted with the permission of the Ecclesiastical History Society.

Hollerich, Michael J. "Religion and Politics in the Writings of Eusebius: Reassessing the First 'Court Theologian.'" *Church History* 59 (1990): 309–25. Reprinted with permission from *Church History*.

Krautheimer, Richard. "The Ecclesiastical Building Policy of Constantine." In *Costantino il Grande dall'antichità all 'umanesimo: Colloquio sul Christianesimo nel mondo antico, Macerata, 18-20 Dicembre 1990,* vol. 2 (Macerata: Università degli studi di Macerata, 1993): 509–52. Reprinted with the permission of Università degli studi di Macerata.

Drake, H.A. "Constantine and Consensus." *Church History* 64 (1995): 1–15. Reprinted with permission from *Church History*.